Dalmatia

HISTORY OF THE PROVINCES OF THE ROMAN EMPIRE

Edited by
Glen Bowersock
Professor of Greek and Latin, Harvard University

Donald Dudley
Professor of Latin, University of Birmingham

Sheppard Frere
Professor of the Archaeology of the Roman Empire
in the University of Oxford

John Ward Perkins
Director, British School at Rome

Graham Webster
Lecturer in Archaeology, University of Birmingham

FRONTISPIECE

Early fourth-century relief depicting Spirit of Salona, a woman holding
in her right hand banner with letters M(*artia*) I(*ulia*) V(*aleria*) S(*alona*)
F(*elix*) and with her left arm resting on a wine-barrel and sheaves of
barley (p. 221). Keystone from arch found in southern part of *urbs nova*,
M. Abramic, VAHD 52 (1935–49) 279 ff.

Dalmatia

by J. J. Wilkes

Lecturer in Roman History,
University of Birmingham

ROUTLEDGE & KEGAN PAUL   LONDON

© J. J. Wilkes 1969

First published 1969
by Routledge & Kegan Paul Limited
Broadway House, 68–74 Carter Lane
London, E.C.4

Printed in Great Britain
by Richard Clay (The Chaucer Press) Ltd
Bungay, Suffolk

SBN 7100 6285 0

PARENTĬBVS OPTIMIS

Contents

Contents

List of plates

List of plates

List of text-figures

Preface

This is the second volume to be published in a series on the History of the Roman Provinces. In his study of Britannia Professor Frere brought to the fore the narrative history, based equally on literary and archaeological evidence, the latter deriving from the labours of many scholars, amateur and professional.

In this study the two sections of historical narrative take up less than one quarter of the main text, describing first the events leading to the creation of Roman Dalmatia and, second, its gradual extinction during the Late Empire until the Slavs reached the Adriatic about 614. The main body of the work presents an anatomy of Dalmatia under the Principate, based primarily on the evidence of inscriptions. Here the purpose is to examine in detail the different facets of provincial development; the impact of the Roman army and administration as a political and social force; the progress of urbanization and enfranchisement of the native population; the composition of the upper classes, beginning with Italian settlement in the coastal cities and leading on to the rise of native grandees in the second and third centuries. Next there follows a survey of the meagre archaeological evidence for the individual cities and rural settlements, together with the evidence for trade. Little is offered on the art or religious life of Roman Dalmatia, except for a brief section on Christianity in the last chapter.

In the historical experience of the area east of the Adriatic from the seventh century B.C. to the present day Roman Dalmatia was an anomaly. To link the Bosnian valleys with military and political centres on or near the Adriatic (and this was done even in a physical sense by the construction of major roads radiating from Salona under Tiberius) was an unparalleled concept. Greek colonists had remained anchored to the Dalmatian coast and islands. In the Middle Ages the coast remained divided from even the most immediate hinterland, the boundary between Byzantine and Slav, and later between Ottomans and the great Dalmatian cities Zara, Spalato and Ragusa. Today the thin strip of Dalmatia adheres to the Republic of Croatia, screening Bosnia and Hercegovina from virtually the entire Adriatic seaboard.

The major source is epigraphy. Dalmatian inscriptions were first collated by Theodor Mommsen in the third volume of the *Corpus Inscriptionum Latinarum* published in 1873, and supplemented up to 1902 by additional volumes in the series. In this century the impetus of that great project has been lost (although for Dalmatia the recent compilation by J. Šašel has filled the gap for the years 1940–60) and one must seek the evidence for different areas in various local periodicals. Archaeology, especially excavations, occupies a smaller place among the source material than is perhaps the case for any other European province of the Empire. Before the First World War Patsch and his colleagues, working from Sarajevo, made numerous surveys of sites in Bosnia and Hercegovina, and later their work was continued alone on a reduced scale by Dimitri Sergejevski. Elsewhere little has been done. At Salona the labours of Fr. Bulić and M. Abramić of Split, R. Egger and W. Gerber of the Austrian Archaeological Institute, and E. Dyggve and his colleagues from Copenhagen, have yielded much evidence, especially from the Christian monuments: in the Southeast Doclea stands out alone, its remains admirably described and planned by P. Sticotti more than fifty years ago. In recent years much has been added to our knowledge of the native population in the pre-Roman and Roman periods by the publications of colloquia organized by A. Benac at Sarajevo, while special mention must be made of the investigations now being carried on at Liburnian and Roman sites in the Ravni kotari around Zadar. It must be emphasized, however, that great benefit has been derived from the numerous historical and epigraphic studies published by modern scholars in the area. These are acknowledged at appropriate places in the footnotes.

This study incorporates material which was submitted in a thesis to the University of Durham in 1962. During my three years there as a research student I had the privilege of supervision by Eric Birley as well as constant advice and encouragement from J. C. Mann. In Birmingham I have received encouragement and much practical help from my head of department D. R. Dudley and numerous other colleagues. My former teacher John Morris, of University College London, and Anthony Birley, of the University of Leeds, have read and commented upon various parts of the manuscript. At a later stage Professor

S. S. Frere read through the whole text, correcting errors and adding many improvements.

During my visits to Yugoslavia I received much help and many kindnesses from Yugoslav scholars. In particular I should like to thank Professor Grga Novak, President of the Yugoslav Academy of Arts and Sciences in Zagreb; Professor D. Rendić-Miočević and Dr. Marin Zaninović of Zagreb University; the late Esad Pašalić of Sarajevo University; the late Dimitri Sergejevski and Dr. Irma Čremošnik of the Bosnia–Hercegovina Museum in Sarajevo; Dr. B. Gabričević of the Archaeological Museum in Split; Dr. M. Suić, formerly of the Archaeological Institute and Museum in Zadar, now of Zagreb University. Dr. Jaro Šašel of the Slovenian Academy in Ljubljana has extended generous hospitality and has regularly guided me to many local Yugoslav publications which are not readily available in English libraries. My greatest debt is to Dr. Géza Alföldy, now of Bonn University. His penetrating study of the society and population of Roman Dalmatia, together with many papers on historical and epigraphic problems, have assisted me on almost all the topics with which this book is concerned. In addition he has been kind enough to make available two major studies as yet unpublished, concerning the personal names and senatorial families; both have been utilized on many points.

During the later stages of preparation I have received generous assistance from Messrs. J. Hogan and R. Swift of the Geography Department here in Birmingham in connection with the maps and illustrations. In Split Mr. Harold Sheff of Minnesota University patiently photographed many stones in the museum. Finally, during the passage of this book through the press, my friends Heather Openshaw and Ian DuQuesnay have given most generously of their time, especially in the preparation of the indexes. To these, and many others, I am most grateful.

1 April 1969   J.J.W.

Geographical Outline

The area occupied by Roman Dalmatia included not only the eastern shore of the Adriatic which bears that name today but a large tract of territory extending northeastwards into the Danube Basin. It occupied the triangle of territory between Istria, Belgrade, and the Albanian Drin, bounded on the north by the valley of the Save and extending eastwards to the edge of the Serbian plain and the Kosmet region around Mitrovica. Apart from a small area of Albania around Scodra (Skhöder) the whole of Roman Dalmatia is contained within the frontiers of the modern Republic of Yugoslavia.

In the south few stretches of Mediterranean seaboard are so rocky or deeply indented with rock-bound harbours as the Dalmatian coast. Much of it is screened by ranges of islands, some of which support communities of several thousand people. In the north the islands of the Quarnerno, Cres, Lošinj, Krk, and Rab, contain areas of arable land and have harbours which are sheltered from the worst of the winter storms. Further south few of the numerous small islands in the archipelago support large communities, but in the central sector the larger islands of Hvar, Korčula, Brač, and Vis enjoy an excellent climate and contain large areas of good land.

Much of the coastline is mountainous and quite bare of vegetation and for long stretches reveals little sign of inhabitation. In the north the Velebit mountains run south to the hinterland of Zadar, rising in places to a height of more than 5,500 feet. In antiquity there was no coast road and only a few settlements clung to the precipitous shore around small harbours. The only crossing places over the Velebit were from Senia (Senj), where in antiquity a route led to the Iapodes in the Lika and on to Siscia in the Save valley, and at the south end of the Velebit

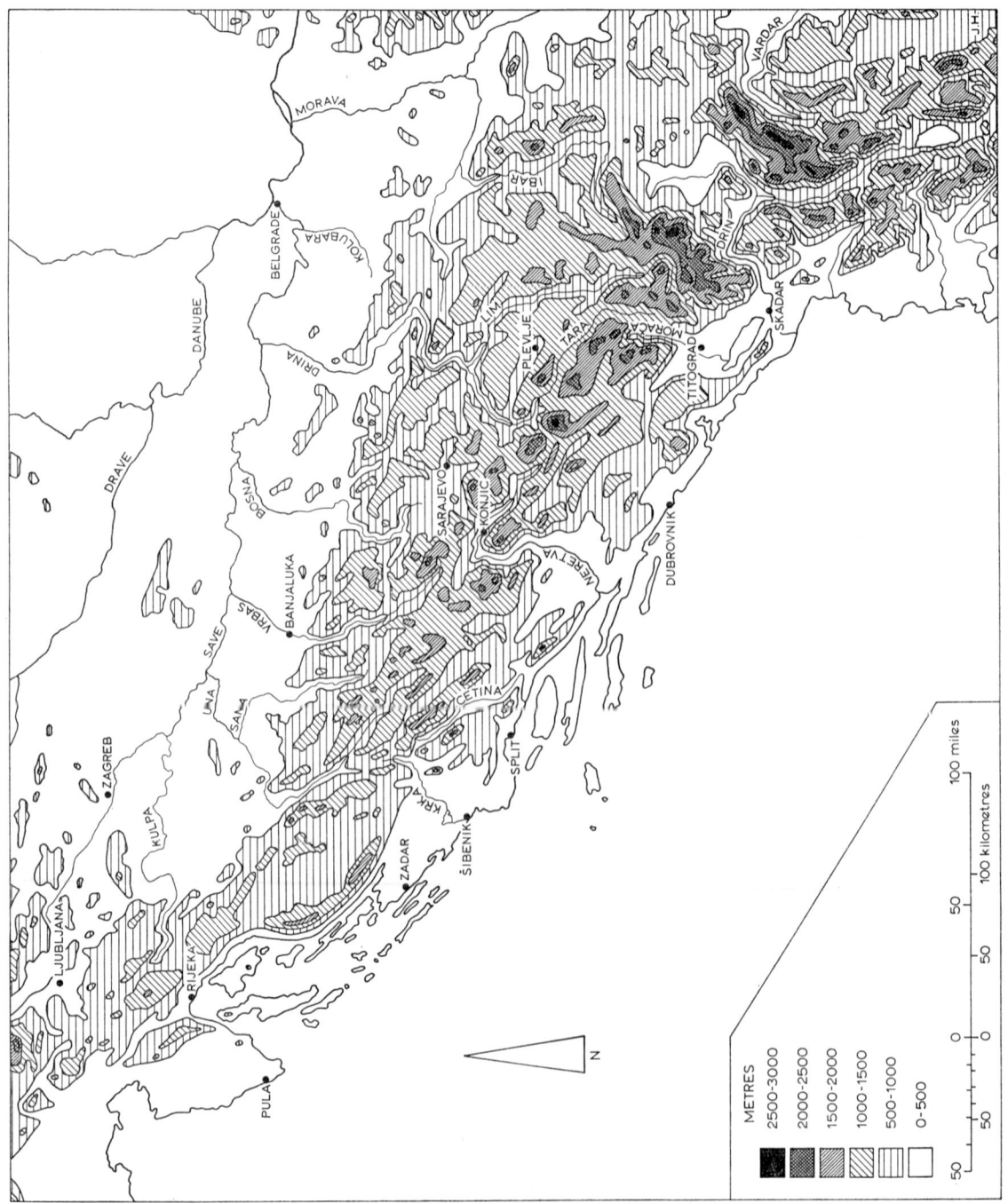

Figure 1 Physical Map

xxii

where another pass linked the Lika with the Ravni kotari (level corner) plain around Zadar; but otherwise the barrier was complete.

South of the river Krka and the Lake by Šibenik the coast is rocky with numerous sheltered inlets, until the natural harbour of ancient Salona behind the island Čiovo and the Marijan peninsula near Split. Around the bay is a narrow plain of fertile land shut off from the interior by the mountain ranges of Kosjak and Mosor which tower over the area to a height of more than 5,000 feet. The main route to the interior crossed between these heights by a pass at Klis towards Sinjskopolje and the hinterland. South of Split the coastline is mountainous without a break until the marshy delta of the river Neretva below Metković, screened from the open Adriatic by the long northward-facing peninsula Pelješac. South of Dubrovnik (Ragusa) and its ancient predecessor Epidaurum (Cavtat) the islands cease and the coast becomes more mountainous until the Gulf of Kotor (Boka Kotorska), a large inlet with a number of branches. Screened by mountains on all sides, it is similar in appearance to a Norwegian fiord. Further south around Ulcinj the coast becomes less rocky and in Northern Albania it is mainly flat and marshy around the Drin and its associated rivers.

Between the coast and the series of mountain ranges which form a backbone for the province parallel to the coast from Istria to Montenegro, the hinterland enjoys few of the natural advantages of the coast. Here the land might be compared to a petrified sponge, with mile after mile of bare limestone hills honeycombed with caverns and watercourses. Rivers emerge in full spate and disappear just as suddenly underground to emerge on the other side of a mountain ridge. The Trebišnjica of Popovopolje behind Dubrovnik flows into the sea from the foot of a mountain and also as a fresh water spring on the bed of the sea. In this hinterland, named the Dalmatian karst, occasional depressions between the hills (poljes) contain fertile soil but are unhealthy places to live. Seasonal rains bring extensive flooding but most of the water disappears almost immediately into the ground. Life for the population of such areas as Popovopolje, Gačkopolje, and Imotskipolje is hard, especially with a chronic shortage of water for much of the year. Further south the coastal hinterland in Montenegro is one of the most desolate and forbidding areas of Europe, with an almost unbroken area of mountains from the coast as far as the great peaks around Durmitor (nearly 8,000 feet) at the head of the Piva and Tara valleys. Around the Lake of Scodra the plain is not very fertile and the region is made more unattractive by the fierce summer heat and the unhealthy areas of marshes around the fringes of the Lake.

The largest river in this part of the province is the Neretva which rises at the foot of the Lebršnik Mountains. It flows westward around the north side of the high mountains of Hercegovina south of Konjic and reaches the hinterland by turning southwards to flow through a deep gorge between the highest of the mountains, Prenj (6,800 feet) and Cvršnica (7,200 feet). Otherwise in Dalmatia only three rivers reach the Adriatic after a course of more than twenty-five miles. In the north the Žrmanja and the Krka enclose the Ravni kotari plain on the north and south. The former rises from the southern end of the Velebit and reaches the sea through the large natural harbour at Novigrad, while the latter flows through the Strmica pass above Knin, passing by the Promina hills to reach the sea through Lake Proklijan and the natural harbour at Šibenik. Above Skradin a series of spectacular waterfalls makes the Krka of little use for navigation. Its major tributary the river Čikola flows westwards from the hills south of Sinj and its valley carries the main route linking the Krka valley with the hinterland behind Split. The river Cetina emerges in full spate from the foot of Mount Dinara (6,007 feet) and flows southwards past Sinj into Sinjskopolje to reach the coast at Omiš through the mountains behind Split.

The climate of the coast and hinterland south of the main watershed is mild, and snow is rarely seen in the winter, apart from on the highest peaks. In particular the islands and the coastal settlements enjoy all the advantages of a sub-tropical Mediterreanean climate. The sea abounds with fish and provides a livelihood for many small communities. The small areas of agricultural land are very fertile and in some areas bear crops all the year round. Away from the coast, especially in Hercegovina around the Neretva valley, the land is barely able to support the peasants who live in the poljes. The summer heat can be unbearable and communications are difficult in many areas. In the winter the fierce Bora wind blows from the north and can make navigation along the coast very dangerous, although the many sheltered inlets protect most of the local shipping.

Between the watershed and the Save valley, Northern Dalmatia is totally different in character from the coast and its hinterland. Nothing illustrates the contrast more strikingly than the few hours' train journey between Sarajevo, the capital of Bosnia, and Mostar, capital of Hercegovina. At first one travels through the wooded valleys of Bosnia with large and smooth flowing rivers. After crossing the Ivan pass between the Bosnia and Neretva watersheds, the upper Neretva valley around Konjic is fertile but the snow-covered peaks of the Prenj mountains mark the end of this green landscape. Quite suddenly the vegetation becomes sparse and the temperature rises. After the twelve-mile gorge of the Neretva the valley opens out around Mostar and the bleached rock of Hercegovina stretches away into the haze in all directions.

Among the central mountains of the watershed are the high mountain poljes of Livno, Glamoč, and Kupres, most of which are at a height of about 3,000 feet,

xxiv

beyond which rise some of the large rivers of Bosnia. The main rivers of Northern Dalmatia from the Kulpa in the west to the Drina in the east belong the watershed of the Save. Only the Western Morava and its tributaries around Čačak flow eastwards into Serbia and the Danube below Belgrade. The longest river in the province is the Drina, which is formed at the Montenegrin border by the Tara, and the Piva, and then flows for 150 miles through the evergreen forests of eastern Bosnia to reach the Save at Rača in Serbia, a short distance west of Sirmium. Further west the Bosna emerges in a number of springs around the northern fringe of the Bjelašnica mountain and, after crossing the plain near Sarajevo, passes into a series of wooded glens until below Zenica it takes up a winding course through dense woodland to flow into the Save valley at Doboj, the northern boundary of Dalmatia. With a length of 107 miles it is the most direct route to the centre of Bosnia, to Travnik in the Lašva valley, and to Sarajevo further south. It was a route used by many invading armies, especially by the Hungarians in the later Middle Ages.

The Vrbas rises from the Vranjica mountains north of Konjic and between Bugojno and Jajce flows through a deep defile, eventually to reach the Save after a distance of 94 miles. Much of Western Bosnia belongs to the watershed of the rivers Una and Sana which unite at Bosnian Novi, the northern boundary of Roman Dalmatia. The Una, and its longer tributary the Unac, rise from the northern slopes of the Dinara and flow for many miles through dense areas of forest where few roads have ever passed until they widen to form a plain around Bihać, the chief centre of western Bosnia. Two rivers in southern Croatia flow from the ridges of the Mala and Velika Kapela, which shut off the Lika polje on the north and east, the Kulpa and the Glina, the latter flowing into the Kulpa shortly before its confluence with the Save at Siscia (Sisak).

The rich vegetation of Bosnia and adjacent areas presents a complete contrast to the bleached rock of Dalmatia, Hercegovina, and Montenegro. Most of Bosnia, especially in the east, is still covered with forest, dense deciduous oak in the valleys with birch on the upper slopes and coniferous forest on the areas above 4,000 feet. Timber is an abundant asset and even today it is only beginning to be exploited. There is also great mineral wealth, especially in silver, gold, and iron ore, while the precious commodity of salt is available at Tuzla north of Sarajevo and near Konjic. The climate is totally different from the south. The summers are mild, if rather wet, but the winters are bitterly cold with snow lying for several months in many regions.

Around the coast and among the islands all communications were by water, and only along a few sectors of the coastline was there a major road. The mountainous character of the coast has always had the effect of isolating even the larger communities from adjacent areas of the hinterland. Places along the coast have always been linked closely together, as well as to the major Italian centres across the Adriatic. Away from the coast the movement of people and goods over long distances, apart from the seasonal migrations of men and flocks from summer to winter pastures, has never been very great. In the north only two routes cross the Velebit, both by difficult passes, the road from Senia to Siscia across the Northern Lika, and that from the Ravni kotari into the Southern Lika. In the former area communications have always been good and the inland cities closely associated with the main ports. The only route to the interior crosses the watershed by the Strmica pass into the Una and Sana valleys; in the Roman period this way was opened up under Claudius, probably by the Roman army. In the hinterland an important route built and garrisoned by the provincial army led from Burnum to Narona, through Andetrium (Muć) along the Čikola valley, through Sinjskopolje and Imotskipolje into the Trebižat valley around Ljubuški and Narona. A group of routes to the interior radiated from the provincial capital Salona across the watershed and along the Bosnian valley towards the Save. The three principal routes were planned and built by the Roman legions under Tiberius. To the north a route led from Salona to Sinj (Aequum) and crossed the main ridge of the Dinaric Alps by the Prolog pass (*in Alperio* on the Peutinger Map) into the poljes of Livno and Glamoč. Thence it reached Servitium along the western fringe of the Vrbas valley. To the northeast another route crossed the Cetina at Tilurium (Gardun) and then the low pass by Aržano into Duvjanskopolje. From there it crossed by the pass over the northern slopes of Ljubuša (*Mons Bulsinius*) into the Rama valley and then passed along the Neretva valley as far as Konjic. Turning northwards it crossed the Ivan pass and reached the Bosna valley. No route existed along the Neretva gorge in antiquity, and the road which linked the area of Mostar with the interior may have passed around the east side of the Prenj mountains. Another route branched off from the Salona road through Duvjanskopolje north to Kupres and into the upper Vrbas valley around Bugojno and then into the Lašva valley around Travnik. The principal mediaeval trade route between Ragusa and the interior passed though Gačkopolje and across the mountains into the Drina valley around Foča, but there is no evidence that it was ever used as a road in the Roman period beyond Gačko.

Fom Narona a route led through Popovopolje to Trebinje but then made a detour (the same line followed by the railway) to the north to avoid the mountains around the Boka Kotorska, reaching Nikšić at the head of the Zeta valley. From there it followed the Zeta to Scodra and then crossed the provincial boundary on the river Drin at Lissus.

There are few routes across Northern Dalmatia from east to west. It was normally convenient for most long-distance traffic to pass northward along the main valleys and use the Save valley for lateral communications. The main route between Salona and Sirmium took the shortest route across the interior to Servitium and then followed the Save for a longer distance by the road eastward through Cibalae (Vinkovci) to Sirmium. The route eastwards from the Sarajevo areas was important in the Roman period. The main branch was to the northeast to the mining settlements on the Drina and then along the river through Zvornik to Sirmium. East of Sarajevo it had to cross the steep-sided Romanja plateau (5,000 feet), but numerous milestones of the third century show that it was a major route kept in good repair. Another branch from the same route may have crossed the Drina at Goražde and then reached the Drina valley mines around Domavia through Višegrad, while another branch led through Užice to Čačak in the western Morava valley and on into Moesia Superior. Further south a road led from the Drina at Foča along the Čehotina valley to Plevlje and then across the Bijelopolje in the Lim valley. Further east it passed through Novipazar to Mitrovica, while a branch to the north probably reached the Čačak area along the Moravice valley through Ivanjica.

Although there is epigraphic evidence for individual contacts between the Adriatic coast and the northern part of Dalmatia these were never close, and the two areas remained physically isolated from one another. Many areas in the province were devoid of communications even with adjacent areas. They remained unaffected by outside influences and economically backward, except where special factors such as mineral wealth made their development attractive to the government.

Chapter 1
The Greeks in Dalmatia

1 *Exploration, Trade, and Settlement to the Fourth Century B.C.*

The foundation of the Greek colonies Epidamnus on the promontory of Dyrrhachium and Apollonia on the Bay of Valona in the late seventh century B.C. brought the peoples of the Dalmatian Islands and Coast into regular trading contact with the Greek World. The clearest sign of this is the Corinthian pottery which began to be sold along the coast during the sixth century.[1] The Phocaeans were probably first of the Greeks to make voyages of exploration in the Adriatic. Herodotus records that: 'The Phocaeans were the first of the Greeks who performed long voyages and it was they who made the Greeks acquainted with the Adriatic and Tyrrhenia, with Iberia and the city of Tartessus.' How much the Phocaeans derived from their knowledge of the Adriatic is not known. Most probably they were seeking the route for the tin trade, and once they had found it in Spain they concentrated their energies upon that region.[2]

The most striking feature about Greek knowledge of the Illyrian peoples and their lands is a persistence of the misconception about the position of the Adriatic in relation to their own world and the Mediterranean as a whole. As late as the fourth century it was still widely believed that the northern extremity of the Adriatic was very close to the Black Sea and the mouth of the Danube, and that only a narrow isthmus separated them. This belief probably arose from the coincidence between the names of the people in Istria and the Greek name for the Danube (Ister). Theopompus recorded the idea and many later writers copied

[1] R. L. Beaumont, *JHS*, 56 (1936), 166 ff.
[2] Hdt., i, 163. On the tin trade see M. Cary, *JHS*, 44 (1924), 166 ff.

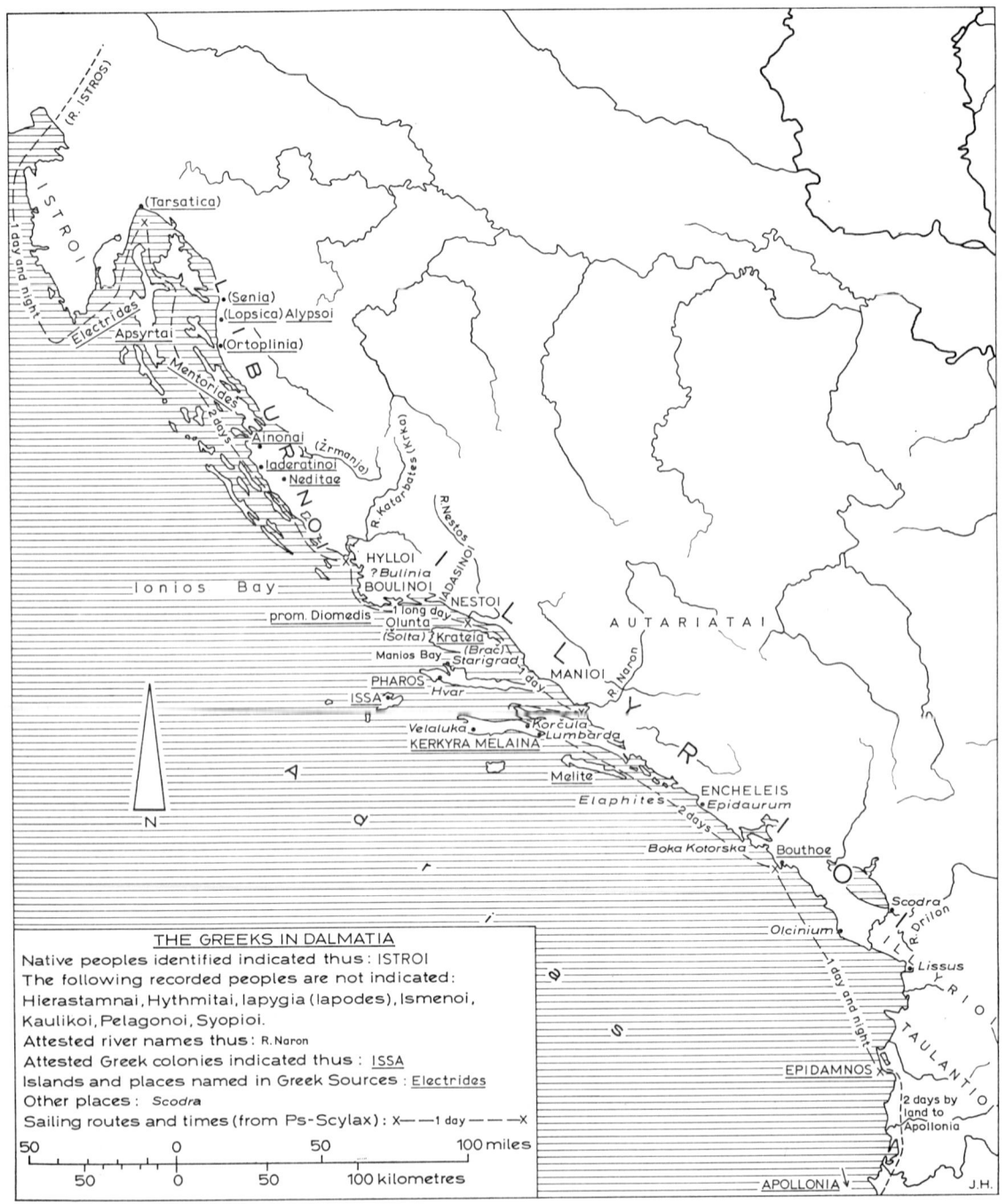

The map contains the following labels:

(R. ISTROS)

ISTROI

(Tarsatica)

Electrides

(Senia)
(Lopsica) Alypsoi
Apsyrtai
(Ortoplinia)

Mentorides
2 days

LIBURNOI

Ainonai
(Žrmanja)
Iaderatinoi
Neditae

R. Katarbates (Krka)

R. Nestos

ADASINOI

HYLLOI
?Bulinia
BOULINOI
NESTOI

Ionios Bay

prom. Diomedis
1 long day
Olunta
(Šolta) Krateia
(Brač)
Manios Bay Starigrad
1 day
MANIOI

AUTARIATAI

PHAROS
ISSA Hvar
R. Naron

Velaluka
Korčula
Lumbarda
KERKYRA MELAINA

ILLYR

Melite

Elaphites
2 days

ENCHELEIS
Epidaurum

Boka Kotorska Bouthoe

N

Olcinium
Scodra
R. Drilon

ILLYRIOI

Lissus

TAULANTIO

EPIDAMNOS

2 days by
land to
Apollonia

APOLLONIA

J.H.

THE GREEKS IN DALMATIA
Native peoples identified indicated thus : ISTROI
The following recorded peoples are not indicated:
Hierastamnai, Hythmitai, Iapygia (Iapodes), Ismenoi,
Kaulikoi, Pelagonoi, Syopioi.
Attested river names thus : R.Naron
Attested Greek colonies indicated thus : ISSA
Islands and places named in Greek Sources : Electrides
Other places : Scodra
Sailing routes and times (from Ps-Scylax) : x——1 day ——x

50   0   50   100 miles
50   0   50   100 kilometres

Figure 2 The Greeks in Dalmatia

2

it from him, including Pseudo-Scymnus.[1] The *Periplus* of Pseudo-Scylax has a
different version of the story: he speaks of an arm of the Danube flowing through
the territory of the Istria into the Adriatic.[2] Possibly some Greeks discovered
that by crossing the low barrier of the Julian Alps into the upper valley of the
Save around Ljubljana, it was possible to sail from there to the Black Sea by
river. The existence and repetition of these stories about an isthmus and branches
of the Danube flowing into the Adriatic suggests that few Greeks can have made
journeys in this area before the colonies on both sides of the Adriatic were established. It also suggests that Greek merchants did not venture far inland from the
coast until much later, and that the possibility of an overland trade route from
the head of the Adriatic to the Aegean is slight.

The earliest known written record of peoples who dwelt along the Dalmatian
coast appears in the *Europe* of Hecataeus of Miletus, a writer of the sixth century
B.C., fragments of which are preserved in the reference work of Stephanus
Byzantius. Here are listed in their alphabetical places the *Kaulikoi*, *Liburnoi*,
Mentores, *Syopioi*, and *Hythmitai*, while the Iapodes are recorded by *Iapygia*, the
name of a place (*polis*) in Italy and in Illyria.[3] The first coherent account of the
areas which has survived is in the *Periplus* of Pseudo-Scylax from Caryanda composed about 330 B.C. The work used the results of more recent voyages, although it incorporated much earlier material. It names the *Liburnoi*, *Illyrioi* (a
general designation of all the peoples between Liburnia and Chaonia), the
Hierastamnai (otherwise unknown), *Boulinoi*, *Hylloi*, *Nestoi*, *Manioi*, *Autariatai*,
Enchelleis (located around the Gulf of Kotor), and lastly the *Taulantioi* in the
hinterland of Epidamnus.[4] A much later compilation, but utilizing earlier sources
including Theopompus, is the *Periegesis* of Pseudo-Scymnus (*c.* 110 B.C.). He
lists in his long description of the coast the *Ismenoi*, *Mentores*, *Pelagonoi*, *Liburnoi*,
Boulinoi, and the *Illyrioi*. As with Pseudo-Scylax, this last name is a general term
for a group of individual peoples.[5] On the basis of these three dated sources, together with fragments from other writers which appear in the Roman sources
(Pliny, Strabo, etc.), it is possible to reconstruct the political and ethnic geography of the Eastern Adriatic from Istria to the Albanian Drilo (Drin) in the
fourth century, before the picture altered considerably with the great upheavals
associated with the movements of the Celtic peoples in the late fourth and early

[1] Pseudo-Scymnus, lines 369–71 (*GGM*, 1, p. 211).
[2] Pseudo-Scylax, c. 20 (*GGM*, 1, p. 26).
[3] *FGrHist*, 1, 93–7. The *Kaulikoi* are mentioned by Apoll. Rhod., iv, 324, and also by Pliny,
HN, iii, 130 (*Culici*). The *Syopioi* and the *Hythmitai* are otherwise unknown.
[4] Pseudo-Scylax, c, 21–26. On the date of composition see Fr. Gisinger, *RE* 3A (1929), 635 f.
[5] Pseudo-Scymnus, ll. 369–438. On the date of composition and the sources used see Fr.
Gisinger, *RE* 3A (1939), 661 ff.

third centuries B.C. It is only after this that there is any record of the well-known peoples in the coastal area, such as the Delmatae, Ardiaei, Daorsii, and others. Only in the north of Dalmatia, with the Liburnians and the Iapodes, is there a suggestion of a continuity from the earliest phase of Greek exploration into the Roman period.

There is a tradition that the Liburnians once occupied a large part of the Eastern Adriatic coastline. In the eighth century they were expelled from the island Corcyra (Corfu) by the Corinthian colonists under the leadership of Chersicrates, while the poem of Apollonius the Rhodian records that they were once in possession of the islands in Central Dalmatia.[1] In the fourth century they are located on the northern sector of coast which is named after them. Pseudo-Scylax locates them south of the Istrians and north of the river *Katarbates*. This could be the Roman Tedanius (Žrmanja), as Müller suggested, but it is more likely that it is the Titius (Krka), established as the southern boundary of the Liburnians in the first century B.C. The same author lists a number of Liburnian places (*poleis*) along the coast. The traditional reading of the text has been interpreted to list cities which are known to have existed in the Roman period on the northern coast of Liburnia between Istria and the river Žrmanja, Tarsatica (Trsat near Rijeka), Lopsica (Sv. Juraj), Senia (Senj), and the Ortoplini (Stinica). However, a new reading of the manuscripts by M. Suić has revealed the names of peoples not only in the north, but also in the Ravni Kotari (the plain of Liburnia between the Tedanius and the Titius) south of the Žrmanja. If this reading is correct then Pseudo-Scylax lists the *Apsyrtai* (Apsyrtides), *Alypsoi* (Lopsica), *Olsoi*, *Nedetai* (Nedinum), *Ainonoi* (Aenona), and the *Iaderatinoi* (Iader), while the *Katarbates* must be the river Titius.[2] Islands in the Quarnerno are listed: the *Elektrides* (Amber Islands) include the large islands Krk, Cres, and Lošinj, the *Mentores* or *Mentorides* are probably Rab (Arba), Pag (Cissa), and the smaller islands in the Archipelago. An island *Istris* recorded by Pseudo-Scylax measuring 310 by 120 stades (40 by 15 miles), is hardly the Istrian peninsula, but more probably Cres or a similar island.[3]

---

[1] Apol. Rhod., iv, 564.   [2] M. Suić, *Rad*, 306 (1955), 121 ff.

[3] The *Elektrides* derived their name from the ancient trade in amber (*elektron*) which ran from the Baltic through Central Europe to Northeast Italy and the head of the Adriatic and thence to the eastern Mediterranean. The name is recorded by Pseudo-Scylax, c. 21; Pseudo-Scymnus, l. 347; Pseudo-Arist., *mir. ausc.*, 81; Apoll. Rhod., iv, 505 f.; Strabo, v, 1, 2; Plin., *HN*, iii, 152, xxxvii, 32; Pomp. Mela, ii, 114. *Mentores*: Hecataeus (*FGrHist*, 1, 94); Pseudo-Scymnus, l. 394; Apoll. Rhod., iv, 551; Plin. *HN*, iii, 139. *Mentorike*: Pseudo-Arist. *mir. ausc.*, 104. *Mentorides* Islands: Pseudo-Scyl., c. 21. The *Ismenoi* named by Pseudo-Scymnus along with the *Mentores* are not listed in the other Greek sources but are probably the *Himani* of Plin., *HN*, iii, 139, see below, p. 484.

After the Liburnians are the *Illyrioi,* who reach from the Liburnians down the coast as far as Corcyra (Corfu).[1] Generally it is a name for all the peoples along this stretch of coastline, although Pseudo-Scylax uses it for a group of small peoples between the Liburnians and the river *Nestos,* the Roman Hippius (Cetina). The *Hierastamnai* are not listed by any other source, while the *Hylloi,* descended from Hyllus the mythical son of Heracles, gave their name to Cape Planka on the coast south of Šibenik, the *peninsula Hyllica,* which was also associated with the hero Diomede (*promuntorium Diomedis*). Some trace of the *Bulinoi* is found in *Bulinia,* a place on the Peutinger Map between Tragurium (Trogir) and Oneum/Almissa (Omiš). The precise location of these peoples between the rivers Krka and the Cetina is uncertain. Pseudo-Scymnus lists them in a different order from Pseudo-Scylax, placing the *Bulinoi* between the Liburnians and the *Hylloi.*[2] Next are the *Nestoi* who dwelt around the river *Nestos* (Cetina).[3] The indentation of the coast between Cape Planka and the long northward arm of the peninsula Pelješac was called *Manios kolpos* (Bay), a name which survives on the Greek decree of 56 B.C. in Salona.[4] Apart from the two islands Issa and Pharos (Pharia), Pseudo-Scylax records two islands in the bay, *Krateia* and *Olunta,* probably Brattia (Brač), and Solentia (Šolta).[5]

The *Manioi* dwelt around the river *Naron,* the Roman Narenta (Neretva).[6] The section of Pseudo-Scylax listing the rivers *Naron* and *Arion* (presumably the Roman Drilo, the Albanian Drin) is corrupt beyond restoration. The statement that the *Naron* flows from a lake has caused difficulties for many scholars, and some have tried to identify it with the waterlogged Hutovo blato, but this is incorrect since the Narenta does not flow through it nor, in fact, anywhere near it. It seems most reasonable to follow Suić's suggestion that the author or his

[1] Pseudo-Scylax, c. 22. The people called *Illyrioi* were a small people around the area of Scodra and Lissus (Plin., *HN,* iii, 144: *Illyrii proprii dicti* see p. 166), although the name was already used by the Greeks to describe the peoples between the Liburnians and Epirus. The concept of *Illyricum,* extending from the Adriatic to the Danube belongs to the Roman period only.

[2] 'The promontory of Diomede or, according to others, the Hyllis peninsula', Plin., *HN,* iii, 141. The *Boulinoi* survive in the later accounts of Pliny and Ptolemy; see p. 486. The name *Bulinia* is not on a Peutinger road route, but written in larger letters over the road between Andetrium and Magnum (from Muć to Balijina Glavica), and may refer to the name of the district.

[3] Pseudo-Scylax, c. 23–4; Apoll. Rhod., iv, 337, 1213, calling them *Nestaioi.* Also Steph. Byz. s.v. *Nestos,* a *polis* and river of Illyria.

[4] Pseudo-Scylax, 23. On the Salona decree, *VAHD,* 48 (1925–6), 5 ff. and below, p. 39: '. . . within the] Manios [Bay . . .'

[5] Pseudo-Scylax, c. 23; cf. Suić, op. cit., 129, 172–3.

[6] Pseudo-Scylax, c. 24: 'after the Nestoi comes the river Naron . . . and the people here are the Illyrian Manioi.'

source has confused the Narenta and the Drilo, and that the lake referred to is the large Lake of Scodra (Skhöder), through which the waters of the Drilo have flowed at various times in its history.[1] The only well-known people named in this region by Pseudo-Scylax are the *Autariatai*, a powerful people who once disputed with the *Ardiaei* the possession of some salt pans near their common border. They probably lived in the upper Narenta around Konjic.[2] Next come the *Enchelei* around the Gulf of Kotor (Boka Kotorska, the Roman *sinus Rhizonicus*). Legend had it that it was to this people that Cadmus the Phoenician came from Greece by the overland route, and settled among them to become their king. He was honoured with a temple near the Gulf and the legend, which is as old as the fifth century B.C., also told that he gave Bouthoe, the Roman Butua (Budva), its name. The Enchelei are located in different areas at different periods. Hecataeus places them in Northern Epirus, also near Apollonia and near the river Drilo.[3]

Apart from the names of the Illyrian peoples recorded in the earlier Greek writers, the spread of Greek cults along the Dalmatian coast (in most instances probably the hellenizing of existing native cults), attests the spread of the Greeks into the Adriatic during the fifth and fourth centuries and their close contact with particular areas.[4] The most widespread around the Adriatic as a whole was the worship of Diomede; it is particularly common on the Italian coast, especially in northern Apulia. From this area it probably spread across the Adriatic to Cape Planka.[5] In the south the legend of Cadmus among the Enchelei is as old as the fifth century, while in the far north the names of the Apsyrtides islands in the Quarnerno reflects the exploits of the Argonauts who travelled along the mythical branch of the Danube which flowed into the head of the Adriatic. Perhaps some element in the tradition may have spread from the south, where, according to Pliny, the small town of Olcinium (Ulcinj) took its name from the Colchians.[6] The link between the Italic (V)eneti around the north Adriatic with

---

[1] Pseudo-Scylax, c. 24; cf. Suić, op. cit., 127, 174–5, and *GZMS*, 8 (1953), 111–29.

[2] Pseudo-Scylax, c. 24; cf. Strabo, vii, 5, 11. Once a powerful people in the late fourth century they moved away eastwards and a large number of them finally ended up around the headwaters of the river Strymon. There is no trace in the later sources of any who may have remained in their own homeland near the Adriatic; cf. Zippel, 34 ff.

[3] Pseudo-Scylax, c. 25 locates them around the Gulf of Kotor, but later they were at Damastion near Apollonia, Strabo, vii, 7, 8. On Bouthoe, the Cadmus legend is recorded by *Etymologicum Magnum*, 207, 13. For the spread of the Adriatic legend see Beaumont, 196 f.

[4] Beaumont, Appendix I, 194 ff.   [5] See n. 2 on p. 5.

[6] The Apsyrtides legend appeared in Theopompus, quoted by Pseudo-Scymnus, l. 307; on Olcinium, Pliny, *HN*, iii, 144: 'Olcinium, earlier called Colchinium, was founded by the Colchi.' For the date of the Argonaut legend in the Adriatic see Beaumont, 197.

a Paphlagonian people of the same name is probably the reason for introducing the hero Antenor. He is supposed to have travelled to the Adriatic after the fall of Troy, where he is associated with Corcyra Nigra.[1]

The archaeological evidence for Greek trade suggests that peoples of the Dalmatian coast were of much less interest to traders than those in other areas of the Adriatic. Strabo records a story of Theopompus that Chian and Thiasian pottery could be found in the bed of the river Narenta.[2] The Pseudo-Aristotelian tract *On Marvellous Things Heard* records that 'when the Mentores who live near the Adriatic climb this peak (*Delphium* between *Mentorice* and *Istrianon*) they can apparently see ships sailing in the Pontos (Black Sea). There is a place in the gap, in the middle of which, when a common market is held, Lesbian, Chian, and Thiasian goods are bought from the merchants who come up from Pontos, and Corcyraean *amphorae* from those who come from the Adriatic' (*c.* 104). It is clear that the stories of an overland trade route between the Black Sea and the Adriatic were bound up with the notions of an isthmus between these two seas, and the story about a branch of the Danube flowing into the Adriatic, and underground rivers linking the Adriatic and the Aegean. The last story was probably derived from the strange behaviour of rivers in the karst hinterland of Dalmatia, which often disappear underground to appear in full flow on the other side of a range of mountains. Similarly the link between the Danube and the Adriatic may have been suggested by the behaviour of the Timavus (Timao) in the Istrian karst, which is also connected with the voyage of the Argo. What archaeological evidence suggests is that Greek imports to Dalmatia reached their destination through the Adriatic.[3]

For trade to exist on any scale there must have existed some real basis of commercial exchange, and it is difficult to imagine what this can have been. Apart from silver in the mountains of Northern Albania, which were exploited by the Corinthians, the Dalmatian coast had nothing to offer traders from the Greek cities far to the south[4] Only when permanent settlements were established on the Dalmatian islands was a regular exchange begun, but this was on a purely local scale. The Illyrians could offer salt, corn, and cattle, with which the islands were ill-provided. On their side the Greeks could offer wine and manufactured goods from Greece.[5] The lack of any locally produced coinage until the colonization of the fourth century indicates the absence of a developed commerce between

[1] He is attested on Corcyra Nigra, Dictys Cretensis, v, 17. For the connection with the *Enetoi*: Strabo, xiii, 1, 53; Pomp. Mela, ii, 60; Liv. i, 1.
[2] vii, 5, 9.   [3] Beaumont, 199 f.
[4] O. Davies, *RME*, 239.
[5] Salt and cattle are mentioned by the *Etymologicum Magnum*, 138; cf. Strabo, vii, 5, 11.

settlers and the native population. Although there is no evidence for a long-distance trade route between the East and the Adriatic, some Greek imports probably reached Dalmatia through Macedonia and Paeonia and then along the Drin valley to the region of Lissus and Scodra. Fifth-century Attic pottery has been discovered at the crossing of the Drin near Scodra, a good place for a market, and a sixth-century Corinthian bronze figure comes from Gourizi east of Scodra.[1]

Greek trade with the Narenta valley probably began at the end of the sixth century. Pseudo-Scylax records the river as suitable for the passage of triremes and merchant ships, which used to sail as much as 10 miles inland to a trading centre.[2] There is Corinthian pottery known on the islands and the adjacent mainland, but there is no suggestion that Greeks were responsible for carrying trade any distance inland.[3] The Greek imports which reached the interior probably travelled over the same route used centuries later by Ragusa merchants into the Turkish Empire, while a few objects reached the hinterland of Hercegovina.[4] The factors limiting the trade are obvious. Mass-produced goods travelled only short distances, while the traffic to the interior was based on the sale of expensive articles to the few rich families in the area. Hostility from the native population is never advanced as a reason for lack of interest by the Greeks. To the fourth-century travellers the peoples on the Dalmatian coast were worthy and hospitable, enjoying the pleasures of a peaceful society,[5] but barely a century later the Illyrian Ardiaci were execrated as barbarous plunderers of the cities in Western Greece.

The first Greek settlement recorded in Dalmatia was the Cnidian colony on the island Corcyra Nigra (Korčula), so called because of its thick sub-tropical vegetation to distinguish it from its more famous namesake (Corfu) further south. Early in the sixth century the Cnidians placed the Corcyraeans in their debt by rescuing three hundred boys from the cruel vengeance of Periander, tyrant of Corinth,[6] and the resulting friendship between the two cities was confirmed soon

---

[1] Beaumont, 184 f., n. 181, and 201.

[2] Pseudo-Scylax, c. 24: 'After the Nestoi is the river Naron. The mouth is broad, and both triremes and merchant ships sail upstream to a trading station (*emporion*) which is situated eighty stades from the sea.'

[3] Beaumont, 186, n. 185–6.

[4] For the few imports found in the interior see below, p. 410

[5] Pseudo-Scymnus, ll. 422–5 and below, p. 177. The absence of evidence for Illyrian piracy before the rule of Agron (d. 230 B.C.) is emphasized by Harry J. Dell, *Historia*, 16 (1967), 344 ff., and it was most probably the Etruscans who were responsible for plundering shipping in the Adriatic.

[6] Hdt., iii, 49; Plut., *On the Spite of Herodotus* (*De Herodoti Malignitate*), 860B.

afterwards by a colonizing venture in the Adriatic.[1] The name Corcyra was adopted by the Cnidians as a mark of respect to their friends, but it is also possible that part of the settlers came from Corcyra. The site of the colony is unknown but as most of the island is rocky and infertile there are only three likely sites for such a settlement. In the northeast corner the modern town Korčula commands the strait between the island and the mainland. It would have been an excellent site for a colony, a small peninsula with good harbours. As yet, however, there is no evidence for a Greek settlement there. Another possible site is Lumbarda, in the southeast of the island with an excellent harbour. In the fourth century it was chosen by Issa (Vis) for a colonizing venture of its own, and this may have been an addition to the existing settlement. The third site is Velaluka in the west of the island, where a Corinthian pot has been discovered.[2] There is more fertile land than in the other places, and the fourth-century coins with the legend ΚΟΡΚΥΡΑΙΩΝ may belong to the Cnidian, rather than to the Issaean settlement, for whose autonomy there is no evidence.[3] The ear of corn upon the coins points to a settlement at Velaluka, where much of the land is good for growing crops.[4] Nothing is known of the later history of the Cnidian colony.

II *Colonization in the Fourth Century B.C.*

Diodorus the Sicilian records that in 385 B.C. the tyrant Dionysius of Syracuse decided to settle cities in the Adriatic. His intention was to control the Ionian Sea, safeguarding the route to Epirus and providing harbours for his ships, while as part of this policy he sent weapons and armour to the Illyrians at war with the Epirote Molossians. At the same time the Parians, acting on the instructions of an oracle, dispatched a colony to the Adriatic, which they settled on Pharos with the co-operation of Dionysius. In the following year the natives on the island, who had been permitted by the settlers to remain in their stronghold, attacked the colony and called for reinforcements from the mainland. Not many years before Dionysius had founded his own settlement at Lissus, and when the Illyrians crossed to Pharos in their fast small boats (*lembi*) and killed many of the colonists his governor sailed from Lissus with his triremes and defeated them, taking many prisoner.[5] Some scholars have emended the text of Diodorus to

[1] Pseudo-Scymnus, l. 421; cf. Strabo vii, 5, 5 and Plin., *HN*, iii, 152.
[2] *AEM*, 9 (1886), 33, n. 5.
[3] Brunšmid, 69, n. 1. On the Issaean settlement see p. 10.
[4] While they were willing to journey to isolated trading stations the Greeks never settled a colony where there was not sufficient land to grow their own food.
[5] Diod., xv, 13, 1; 14, 2.

make Dionysius' colony Issa instead of Lissus.[1] The former was a Syracusan colony and was in existence by the fourth century, when it was sending its own colony to Corcyra Nigra.[2] It is also more likely that there would be time to mount a rescue operation from Issa than from Lissus, but this does not rule out Lissus since Diodorus does not say how long help for Pharos took to arrive. There is nothing Greek in the history of Lissus, however, and when it next emerges into history it is an Illyrian stronghold.[3]

Little is known about the history of Greek cities in Dalmatia. Both Issa and Pharos minted their own coins. There are a few inscriptions, mostly family tombstones.[4] One stone from Pharos dates to the city's earliest struggles, mentioning 'arms captured from the *Iadasinoi* and their allies', an Illyrian people who dwelt in the hinterland of Salona,[5] while the fragment of a decree recording an embassy to Delphi may concern the same events.[6] The site of the city is not identified; almost certainly it was at Starigrad in the northwest corner. At Lumbarda on Corcyra Nigra a decree records the settlement of a colony by Issa, some time during the fourth century.[7] It may have been the result of civil strife (*stasis*) or overpopulation in the metropolis. It details the agreement arranged between the settlers and the local landowners Pullus and Dazos, both Illyrians. Most of the text concerns the amount of land awarded to each settler family inside and outside the walls of the new settlement; it also makes provision for the assignment of unoccupied land. The names of the colonists are listed under the three Dorian tribes (proper to a Syracusan colony), *Dymanes*, *Hylleis*, and *Pamphyloi*.

The earliest coins issued by the two Greek cities are modelled on the heavier types of Syracuse. In Pharos the earliest group bears the head of Zeus, which was replaced at the end of the fourth century by a new series with Persephone and Artemis. The first series of Issaean coins bears the legend ιονιο(ς), possibly an older name for the island. These were replaced at the end of the fourth century

---

[1] In the text the colony is called Λίσσον (13, 4) and ἐν τῇ Λίσσῳ (14, 2). Beaumont preferred Lissus, on the ground that a garrison there was much more logical for operations around Epirus and the Ionian Sea (202 ff.), while G. Novak, *SH* 111 ff., prefers Issa, on the grounds that Issa was a Syracusan colony and must have figured in the enterprise of Dionysius, whereas nothing Greek is known from Lissus.

[2] See n. 7 below. [3] G. Novak, *SH,* 111 ff.

[4] Brunšmid, 1 ff. (inscriptions), 35 ff. (coins).

[5] Brunšmid, 16, n. 3: Φάριοι ἀπὸ ᾿Ιαδασίνων καὶ τῶν συμμάχων τὰ ὅπλα. The people dwelt on the mainland around the river Iadro, D. Rendić-Miočević, *VAHD,* 52 (1950), 19 ff. (summary 317).

[6] Brunšmid, n. 4, found at Starigrad. On the topography of the city, M. Nikolanci, *VAHD.* 56-59/2 (1954-7), pt. 2, 52 ff.

[7] Brunšmid, p. 2 ff. (*SIG³,* 141). On the names of the landowners see Mayer, 114, 281.

by a new series with Nymph portraits, similar to the contemporary Artemis and Persephone series at Pharos.[1] Two other groups of fourth-century coins which circulated in the areas cannot be associated with any known settlement in the areas. A series known at Pharos with the legend HERAKL indicates the existence of a city Heraclea, possibly another settlement on the islands.[2] The second group is not a separate series but consists of fourth-century issues of Issa and Pharos overstruck with the letters DI, in one case DIM. A connection with the known place Dimale is out of the question as this is far to the south, and it may be the result of a local tyrant utilizing the earlier coins for his own advertisement.[3] Like Issa, the citizens of Pharos founded their own new settlement, a place called Anchiale which has not been identified.[4]

The Elder Pliny's remark about the 'fading memory of a number of Greek cities' in the southern sector of the Dalmatian coast has led some scholars to suggest that many of the small coves and headlands were occupied by Greek settlements.[5] Bouthoe was known to the Greek World for its connection with the legend of Cadmus and the Enchelei.[6] The site is not ideal, although there is a good stretch of fertile land in the nearby plain of Grbalj. The climate is much wetter than further north, and the small harbour is dominated by the mountainous coastline. Some rich jewellery of the third century B.C. found there may be the result of piracy.[7] There is no evidence for a Greek settlement at Epidaurum, although the name is Greek, and the first record of it is as a settlement of Italian settlers in the time of Caesar.[8] Some of the smaller islands may have been occupied by Greeks, for instance Melite (Mljet) and the small Elaphites (Šipan, Locrum, etc.).[9] In 35 B.C. Melite was attacked by the fleet of Caesar Octavianus as a pirate stronghold.[10]

---

[1] Brunšmid, 40 ff. (Pharos), 58 ff. (Issa).

[2] Brunšmid, 54–8. Novak, *SB*, 655–8, connects these coins with a *Herakleia* mentioned in the Dalmatian section of Pseudo-Scylax (c. 22), but this is much further south in the area of Corcyra (Corfu).

[3] Brunšmid, 52 f., who dates it to the middle or later fourth century. Novak, *SB*, 655 f., identified the coins with a city *Dimos*. A later date is suggested by D. Rendić-Miočević, *First Int. Cong. of Numismatics* (Paris, 1953), 2, 83–7.

[4] Steph. Byz. s.v., *Anchiale*.

[5] Plin., *HN*, iii, 144: 'multorum Graeciae oppidorum deficiens memoria nec non et civitatium validarum.'

[6] Pseudo-Scylax, c. 25, and p. 6 above.   [7] D. Rendić-Miočević, *Opusc. Arch.* (Zagreb), 4.

[8] *Bell. Alex.*, 44 and below, p. 42. For the Greek settlement Beaumont (188) and Patsch (*RE*, 6, 61) cite only the evidence of Evans, *Archaeologia*, 48 (1884), 6. This consists of third- and second-century B.C. coins from Dyrrhachium and Apollonia, which are widespread in the southern part of the province (p. 395), and some isolated small finds.

[9] *Melite* is named by Pseudo-Scylax, c. 23. *Elaphites*: Plin., *HN*, iii, 152.   [10] Appian, *Ill.*, 16.

The Greeks in Dalmatia

Apart from the larger islands of the central coast, Dalmatia offered little inducement to Greek traders and settlers. In the south the coast, if not the people, was inhospitable, while off the Liburnian coast the prevailing winds hinder the growth of vegetation on many of the islands. The coastal peoples offered little to the Greeks for exploitation or exchange, nor could the wealthier societies in the interior be reached without a difficult journey. By the middle of the third century B.C. all the Greek settlements of Dalmatia, with the exception of Issa, were subject to the Illyrian kingdom, and it was Issa's appeal for aid that was partly responsible for the first Roman army crossing the Adriatic in 229 B.C.[1]

[1] The version of Cassius Dio, xii, frg. 49, 1.

Chapter 2
The Kingdom of Illyria (230–167 B.C.)

The beginnings of the Roman advance into the area which later became the province of Dalmatia were bound up with the prolonged struggle against the kingdom of Macedon, for long the most powerful opponent of Roman expansion in the East. After the death of Alexander the Great in 323 B.C. Macedon was one of the prizes fought for by the surviving generals, the Successors (*Diadochoi*). By 270 B.C. three main political powers had emerged, Macedon ruled by the descendants of Antigonus 'the one-eyed' (*Monophthalmos*), Syria under the descendants of Seleucus, and Egypt under the Ptolemies. These powers dominated the Eastern Mediterreanean until they were eventually engulfed by the expansion of Roman power. Although the first Roman actions in Illyria were the result of Illyrian piracy against Adriatic shipping, it was not long before Macedon was involved, and the final overthrow of the Illyrian kingdom in 168 B.C. was part of the larger war which brought to an end the monarchy in Macedon. Throughout most of the period between 229 and 168 B.C. it is not possible to give a history of Illyria and its relations with Rome without constant reference to Macedon, whose most northwesterly territories in the region of Lychnidus (Lake Ohrid) bordered on Illyrian territory. The history of Roman expansion to world empire, especially in the Eastern Mediterranean, has fascinated historians for many generations. In the nineteenth century the diplomatic manoeuvrings of the European powers appeared so similar to events in the history of Roman expansion, that they suggested the study and comparison of the latter in the same context. Therefore it is not surprising that Roman policy in Illyria, as in many other regions, was seen as part of a planned programme of conquest and territorial annexation, and that Roman policy in the last decades of the third century

B.C. anticipated the later conflicts and the eventual conquest of Macedon.[1] Since then new currents in historiography have encouraged scholars in different fields to emphasize how important events occurred through quite accidental combinations of circumstances, with the result that more recently the Roman expansion into the Mediterranean has been explained as a series of reactions to particular situations in a fairly predictable manner, rather than as the result of consistent long-term policies.

The principal narrative source for these years is the work of the Greek historian Polybius, son of a leading statesman in the Achaean League, who was brought as a hostage to Rome after the defeat of Macedon in 168 B.C.; there he spent the remainder of his life under the patronage of Scipio Aemilianus writing a history of the Roman advance to world empire. Born with all the prejudices of an Achaean, he disliked the Illyrians intensely, and generally dismisses them as little better than savages. For his account of the earliest contacts between Rome and the Illyrians he relied greatly on the patriotic Roman historian Q. Fabius Pictor, a senator who wrote in Greek at the end of the Second Punic War, mainly to enlighten the Greek World about the qualities of the Roman State and the virtues of its rulers. His account can be demonstrated as inaccurate and incomplete on some points, but it remains a substantially trustworthy and near-contemporary source. The later accounts in the *Illyrike* of Appian and the History of Cassius Dio are based on the compilations by Roman annalists in the second and first centuries B.C., and they contain some modified versions of particular episodes. The Augustan historian Livy gives much useful information about the last years and the overthrow of the Illyrian kingdom, mainly because much of his account is copied directly from those books of Polybius which have not survived.

During the middle years of the third century B.C. the kingdom of Epirus went into a swift and fatal decline. In its great days it had been an expanding power of Western Greece. Under Alexander, the uncle of Alexander the Great, who ruled at the end of the fourth century, it had risen to the peak of its power, when he sought to emulate the Eastern exploits of his nephew by creating an empire in the West. A generation later its ruler was Pyrrhus, one of the ablest of all the Hellenistic rulers, who invaded Italy and demonstrated to the Romans a standard of warfare far superior to anything they had yet experienced. After fruitless years in Sicily, however, he turned his attention back to Greece and suffered ignominious death in the streets of Argos in 272 B.C. With the death of his less able son Alexander II about 240 B.C. Epirus virtually ceased to exist as a political entity. It was the weakness in this area which gave new opportunities to a rising power

[1] M. Holleaux, *CAH*, 7, 822 ff.

in the north based on the fortresses around the Lake of Scodra and the river Drilo, the Illyrian kingdom ruled by Agron, son of Pleuratus from the royal house of the Ardiaei.[1]

Only Cassius Dio records that the new power arose from the Ardiaei, a new people since the Greek descriptions of the Dalmatian coast in the fourth century B.C., although known to Theopompus.[2] They were noted for their skill with ships among the harbours and inlets of the coast, as Greek and Italian traders apparently soon found to their cost. Their ships were the *lembi*, small galleys with a single bank of oars and a low freeboard, but sufficiently roomy to hold fifty fighting men in addition to the crew. For greater speed they had dispensed with the ram, which was the usual fashion of the period, and replaced it with a prow tapered to a point.[3] Although such vessels could not match up to a well-managed fleet of triremes in battle, for quick raids on merchant shipping and attacks on coastal cities they had no equal. The expansion of Illyrian power was rapid, and is described by Appian: 'Agron was king of that part of Illyria which borders the Adriatic sea, over which sea Pyrrhus, the king of Epirus, and his successors held sway. In turn Agron captured part of Epirus and also Corcyra, Epidamnus, and Pharos in succession, and established garrisons in them' (*Illyrike* 7). The northern limit of their power along the coast is uncertain, but in the early second century B.C. they had established control over at least part of the Delmatae.[4]

The danger from the Illyrians became apparent to the Greeks when they were employed by Demetrius II of Macedon against the Greek Leagues. Because of the weakness of Epirus, Acarnania had managed to assert her independence but was soon threatened by the Aetolians, and to counter the latter Demetrius used the raiding ability of the Illyrian fleet. In return for a subsidy Agron sailed south with 100 *lembi* and 5,000 fighting men to attack the Aetolians who were blockading the Acarnanians in Medion. To universal astonishment the Aetolians were defeated and the Illyrians fleet returned home with large quantities of booty. In the following winter Agron died (231–230 B.C.) and the command of Illyrian forces was assumed by his widow Teuta. After successful raids on Elis and Messenia, she attacked the Epirote capital Phoenice and captured it with the help of its Gallic mercenary garrison, putting to flight another force sent to relieve the place. Desperate appeals had been sent for aid to the Aetolian and

[1] N. G. L. Hammond, *ABSA*, 61 (1966), 239–53.
[2] Theopompus, frg. 39 (*FGrHist*, II. B, p. 543; Athenaeus, x, 60, p. 443 *AB*).
[3] R. Grosse, *RE*, 12 (1925), 1895. They were used later by Philip V, Pol., v, 109 and below, p. 21.
[4] Pol., xxxii, 18.

Achaean Leagues, but before these forces arrived the Illyrians had returned home to deal with a rebellion in their own territory. The object of these raids was to gain booty and there is no evidence that they were seeking territory. However, the efficiency and ruthlessness of the Illyrians horrified the Greeks, and they made no secret of their revulsion against Demetrius for encouraging them in the first instance.[1]

Teuta's activities in 230 B.C. had interfered seriously with the trade routes across the Ionian Sea, which were used by Roman allies in Italy and Sicily. They had suffered from the Illyrians on earlier occasions but never before on this scale. Moreover, a few of the Illyrian raiders, while searching for booty during their blockade of Phoenice, had killed some Italian traders and held others to ransom. With a show of indignation the Roman Senate sent the brothers L. and Cn. Coruncanius to protest to Teuta about these attacks on Roman allies.[2] The reasons for this embassy, coupled with the unusually large forces sent later against the Illyrians, have been explained by some scholars as a Roman fear of Macedon, but there is no need, nor any evidence, to regard it as caused by anything more than Roman annoyance towards the Illyrians, who were becoming a dangerous power in their own right.[3] Such attacks on Italians could not be left unanswered, or the Illyrians would soon cross the Adriatic and raid the Italian cities, as the traders were probably not slow to point out when demanding action from the senate.[4] Teuta was unmoved by this embassy, nor was she concerned when one of the Roman envoys was killed by some of her subjects. Instead she resumed her raids against Western Greece. After failing to overwhelm Epidamnus, she proceeded to blockade Corcyra, and both of these cities immediately asked for aid from the Leagues. This time the Illyrians were brought to battle, but they triumphed over the Greeks with help from their Acarnanian allies in a great naval battle off Paxos. Corcyra was taken and placed under the Illyrian commander Demetrius, the dynast of Pharos and possibly a descendant of Greek settlers, along with a large garrison.[5]

The Romans decided to send a force across the Adriatic for the first time, and command in the First Illyrian War was entrusted to the consuls of the year (229 B.C.), Cn. Fulvius Centumalus in command of the fleet, and L. Postumius Albinus commanding the land forces.[6] They did not attack the strongholds at

---

[1] Pol., ii, 9–10. For Epirus the most serious loss was Atintania, commanding the Aous-Drynon route to Northwest Greece, cf. M. Holleaux, 110, n.1.

[2] Pol., ii, 8.   [3] M. Holleaux, 78.

[4] E. Badian, *PBSR*, 20 (1952), 76 f. (SGRH 4 ff.).   [5] Pol., ii, 9–10.

[6] Apart from Pol., ii, 11–12, the sources for the war are: Dio, xii, frg. 49 (Zon. viii 9); Appian, *Ill.*, 8; Liv., *Per.*, xx; Eutrop., iii, 4; Florus, i, 21. The triumph of Fulvius is attested in the Fasti

the centre of the Illyrian kingdom but moved against Teuta's conquests further to the south. Demetrius immediately handed over Corcyra to the consuls and acted as an adviser to the Romans for the remainder of the campaign. There was still no advance against Illyria itself: instead, the consuls made a progress along the coast visiting the victims of the recent Illyrian raids, and made alliances with Corcyra, Apollonia, and Epidamnus as they moved northwards. Alliances were made with peoples who had not been involved in these events, the native Parthini and Atintanes in the hinterland behind the coastal cities.[1] On the northern frontier of the Illyrians, Greek Issa had been struggling to preserve her independence from the Illyrians. Like Pharos she expected to be conquered soon, and it was during an Illyrian attack on Issa that the Roman embassy obtained their interviews with Teuta. Consequently the Roman intervention across the Adriatic was most opportune. Issa eagerly sought an alliance, which was granted by the consuls along with a guarantee of her freedom. The piecemeal detaching of her recent conquests by the Romans, together with the defection of Demetrius and the loss of her garrison on Corcyra, had its effect on Teuta, and at the end of the season she withdrew into her most sheltered naval base at Rhizon in the inner recesses of the Gulf of Kotor. In the spring of 228 B.C. she capitulated to the Romans and surrendered most of her kingdom. The sources are not clear, and on some details differ, about what happened to Illyria afterwards. Certainly Teuta disappears from the scene and her power was taken over by Demetrius, now with the status of a Roman client (*cliens*). In the version of Cassius Dio, Teuta abdicated her regency over Agron's infant heir Pinnes (he is not mentioned in the account of Polybius) who, according to Appian, retained all his possessions except for those 'surrendered to the Romans'.[2] The situation at the end of the war appears to have been that the Illyrian kingdom was left substantially intact, but with recent conquests detached and under the umbrella of Roman protection, while in Illyria itself Demetrius ruled with Roman approval.

The precise nature of the ties made after the war with the Greek communities

---

[1] The Roman alliance with these peoples was purely fortuitous and does not conceal hidden motives of conquest. The Romans were passing along the coast and pleasantries were exchanged with peoples neutral to the war, Badian, *PBSR*, 20, (1952), 77 ff. (*SGRH*, 23 ff.).
[2] Dio, xii, frg. 49, 7 (Zon., viii, 19); Appian *Ill.*, 7.

Triumphales, *Inscr. It.*, XIII, 1, 78–9; cf. 549–50. Dio records that one of the causes of the war was the surrender (*deditio*) made to Rome by Issa, in return for Roman protection against Teuta. On the other hand, the narrative of Polybius leaves no doubt that the alliance with Issa was made after the defeat of Teuta.

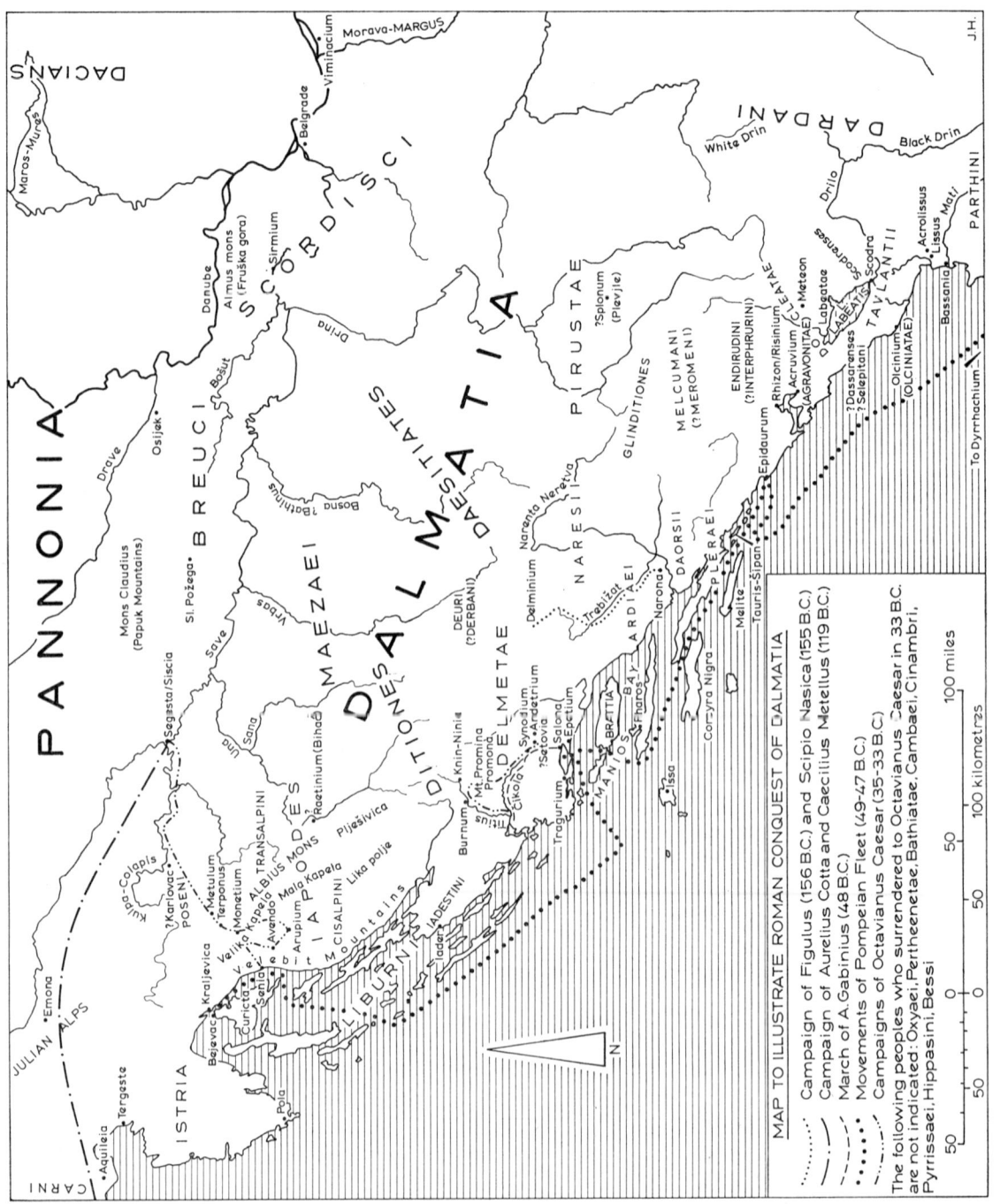

Figure 3 The Roman Conquest

released from the Illyrian danger was clear to the Roman Senate, even if it was not to the states themselves. As with most of the Greek cities in Sicily, those in Illyria were free from garrison or tribute and enjoyed complete internal autonomy, but Rome expected all her allies in the region to provide military support when it was required. While wintering across the Adriatic after the campaign of 229 B.C. the consul Postumius had augmented his land forces with contingents from his new allies in the region, including possibly the Parthini and the Atintanes. On the other hand the needs of Rome's allies were reflected in the settlement after the war which laid down that not more than two Illyrian ships should sail along the coast south of Lissus at the same time.[1] This is the only requirement known to have been made by the Romans and was designed to end the raiding and plundering of the coastal cities by large fleets of *lembi* such as had occurred in the last three years. The protection of Northwestern Greece from Illyrian raids was a great propaganda achievement for the Romans made at a trifling cost, and it would be interesting to know what was the reaction, if any, of the Macedonians when they heard news of the victory from the herald sent by the consuls to inform all the Greeks.[2]

During the decade after 229 B.C. Rome did not intervene in affairs across the Adriatic. The settlement which she arranged appears to have proved satisfactory. Demetrius was a capable ruler, and provided he behaved well in Illyria, his activities in Greek politics were ignored.[3] This is striking, since Demetrius' main preoccupation was now his alliance with Macedon. After a difficult beginning the regent Antigonos Doson (229–219 B.C.) had restored Macedonian fortunes in Greece. He welcomed Demetrius as a valuable ally, and the latter played a major part in Doson's victory over the Spartans at Sellasia in 222 B.C.[4] Although this action brought no reprimand from Rome, and there is no reason why it should have, Demetrius was willing to risk Roman hostility while trusting in his good position with Doson.[5] In 221 B.C. Doson died and control in Macedon fell to the young king Philip V, an able but unpredictable ruler. In the version of Polybius, Demetrius chose this moment of Macedonian weakness to sail south

[1] Pol., ii, 12, 3.   [2] Pol., ii, 12, 8.
[3] Appian's comment (*Ill.*, 8) that Demetrius was allowed to retain only a small number of possessions because of his untrustworthiness appears to be an annalist's invention in the light of later events. It appears in no other source, and Polybius expressly states that Demetrius was left to rule 'most of the Illyrians', ii, 11, 17.
[4] Pol., ii, 65, 4 ff.
[5] M. Holleaux, 131 f., note 5, argues that Demetrius' alliance with Doson may have been struck as early as 225 B.C., since Polybius specifically mentions Rome's problems with the Gauls as a factor which influenced Demetrius. Appian states no reasons, but implies that he was openly hostile to Rome after 225.

beyond Lissus and attack cities which were in alliance with Rome. Not only was Demetrius expecting Macedonian support in any future war, but Polybius adds that he chose this time for attack quite carefully since the Romans were pre-occupied with the Gauls in Northern Italy and the Carthaginians in Spain. Yet in 220 B.C. neither of these conditions existed: Rome had defeated the Gauls, and there was no indication yet of the crisis with Hannibal in Spain. There must be some reason why Demetrius felt he could make raids in this way, and it is not reasonable merely to dismiss such conduct as barbarian rashness in a man of his ability.[1] This is the version of Demetrius' actions which Polybius gives in his section on Roman affairs and which was taken from a Roman source. Quite a different version of the same raid in 220 B.C. appears under Polybius' section on Greek affairs. The leader of the raid was not Demetrius but another dynast Scerdilaidas, who had commanded the Illyrian land forces under Agron in 230 B.C. In company with Demetrius he sailed south of Lissus with a fleet of ninety *lembi* and, after touching first at Pylos, pillaged the Cyclades. In this section Polybius does not mention any attacks on Roman allies, although Appian's version records that Demetrius attempted to detach the Parthini and the Atintanes from their alliance with Rome.[2] The war which Rome waged in Illyria in 219 B.C. was against the personal power of Demetrius, who in the judgement of the Senate had proved an unsatisfactory client by joining in the enterprise of Scerdilaidas.[3] There is no evidence of any wider motives for the Roman campaign, and they did not prevent Scerdilaidas from assuming the power of Demetrius, even though he had become an ally of Philip V. Once again the campaign in Illyria was conducted by the two consuls of the year, L. Aemilius Paullus and M. Livius Salinator, suggesting that the forces may have been as large as those sent against Teuta ten years before.[4] The Romans chose to attack two strongholds, Dimale in the territory of the Parthini near Apollonia, and Demetrius' own stronghold on Pharos (Hvar) in the north.[5] Both were taken,

[1] Pol., iii, 16, 2–5; cf. S. I. Oost, 22. F. W. Walbank, *Comm. Pol.*, 324 observes: 'a member of a semi-barbarous people, and so likely to act with what would have been irresponsibility in a Greek or Roman.'

[2] Pol., iv, 16, 6 f., where the role of Scerdilaidas is made clear; Appian, *Ill.*, 8.

[3] Sources for the war: Pol., iii, 18–19; Appian, *Ill.*, 8; Dio, xii, frg. 53 (Zon. viii, 20).

[4] Livius is not mentioned by Polybius, possibly because his source was biased in favour of the Aemilii. It could be Fabius Pictor, no friend of the Livii, or possibly a Greek source, de Sanctis, *Storia di Roma*, III, 3, 169–70.

[5] Dimale is the Dimallum of Liv., xxix, 12, 3, besieged by the Parthini in 205 B.C. It has now been located at Krotine near Apollonia, N. G. L. Hammond, *JRS*, 58 (1968), 13 ff. Pharos may have been destroyed in 219 B.C., although Beaumont, 188, n. 200, argues that there were two cities on the island, the Parian colony and the stronghold of Demetrius. In spite of his

and Demetrius made his escape to Macedon. While the power of Scerdilaidas was permitted,[1] Pinnes was confirmed as ruler and, apart from the payment of a war indemnity, forfeited none of his possessions.[2]

The alliance of Scerdilaidas with Philip V proved far from profitable, however, and he soon began to raid Macedonian territory in the hope of recouping some of his campaign expenses.[3] In 217 B.C. Philip at last listened to advice from Demetrius about the new danger from Rome, and made peace with the Leagues to give himself a free hand for affairs in the West. By this time Hannibal was already in Italy and defeating one Roman army after another, and Philip began to see new fields for conquest across the Adriatic. Initially his object was to secure a bridgehead on the Adriatic but to achieve this he had to defeat the fleet of Scerdilaidas in its own waters. Early in 216 B.C. he sailed to Illyria with a fleet of new ships, one hundred *lembi* built for him by Illyrians, and Scerdilaidas, realizing that his position was desperate, appealed to Rome for help. A Macedonian fleet based in the Adriatic was a dangerous threat, and accordingly the Senate immediately dispatched a flotilla of ten warships to investigate. At the sight of them Philip, imagining he was about to face the full Roman war fleet, abandoned the venture.[4] The lesson was not lost on the Romans, however, and from now on a small naval force was stationed in the Adriatic to observe Macedonian movements.[5]

After a year of inaction an alliance with Hannibal restored Philip's confidence and he ventured once more into the Adriatic. With 120 *lembi* he captured Oricus and in 214 B.C. blockaded Apollonia. The Roman admiral Valerius Laevinus moved against him and once more his nerve failed: he abandoned the attack, burnt his fleet, and retreated overland to Macedon.[6] Once there he marched

---

[1] J. V. A. Fine, *JRS*, 26 (1936), 24 ff., suggests that Demetrius had no encouragement from Philip in 220 B.C. and that his alliance was with Scerdilaidas, by which he was expected to attack the coasts of Aetolia, but there is no evidence for such a pact. Demetrius was the trusted ally.

[2] Liv., xxii, 33, 5, where envoys were sent in 217 B.C. to demand arrears of tribute.

[3] He assisted Philip V in Greece in 218 B.C., Pol., v, 4, 5. He was soon attacking Macedon, Pol., v, 95, 1 f.; 101, 1 f.; 108, 1 f., although there is no evidence for Roman contact with Scerdilaidas at this time.

[4] Pol., v, 109–110; cf. F. W. Walbank, *Philip V*, 64 f.

[5] Liv., xxiii, 32, 17; 38, 7 f. 'not only to protect the coast of Italy, but to keep watch on the Macedonian War'.

[6] Liv., xxiv, 40.

---

arguments that the site of Starigrad could not be reconciled with Polybius' account of the Roman attack (iii, 18), there is enough evidence for the city at Starigrad from archaeological discoveries, while the topography can be matched to Polybius, M. Nikolanci, *VAHD*, 56–59/2 (1954–7), pt. 2, 52 ff. with sketch map, p. 57.

boldly back into Illyria and captured Lissus near the mouth of the Drilo, cutting off Scerdilaidas from his Roman allies.[1] The threat which was appearing in Illyria never materialized, however, since the Roman alliance with Aetolia in 211 B.C. forced Philip to concentrate his energies once more on Greece. He may have retained his Illyrian conquests for a couple of years, but hardly for any time after 208 B.C. when the possibility of co-operation with the Carthaginian fleet had disappeared; Philip could never have contemplated an invasion of Italy from his own resources.[2] At Phoenice in 205 B.C. the Romans made peace with Philip on the basis of the *status quo*, a policy which meant the surrender of some Roman allies in the area, notably the Atintanes. During these years nothing is known about affairs in Illyria. Not long before 205 B.C. Scerdilaidas had been succeeded by his son Pleuratus, who proved to be one of the most acceptable rulers in Illyria to Roman eyes.[3] With the disappearance of any independent power, Illyrian fortunes awaited the outcome of dealings between the major powers. In the conference before the battle of Cynoscephalae in 197 B.C. the Roman proconsul T. Quinctius Flamininus demanded that Philip should return lands which he had obtained since the peace at Phoenice.[4] It is not certain whether this refers to gains he had obtained in contravention of, or as a result of the Phoenice settlement. Whatever was the case, the earlier treaty had done much damage to Roman prestige among the Greeks, although her neglect of allies in Greece was due to an eagerness to finish the war with Carthage. The second war with Macedon gave Rome an opportunity to retrieve her position on a number of counts, and the affairs of Illyria were just one of the items in the negotiations between Rome and Philip V.

The remaining history of the kingdom of Illyria is the story of two kings, Pleuratus and Gentius. As rulers of a Roman client state their fortunes differed greatly: Pleuratus was hailed an ally as loyal as the Numidian Masinissa, while Gentius was led in a Roman triumph as the humiliated ally of Perseus of Mace-

---

[1] Conquests of Philip: Pol., viii, 13–14b (Lissus, Dassaretae, Hyscana (Uscana) north of Lychnidus); Liv., xxix, 12, 3 (Dimale, Parthini, and the Atintanes) which he controlled in 205 B.C. Lissus was the limit of his advance. There is no evidence that he subdued the entire kingdom because Livy lists the Ardiaei (Liv., xxvii, 30, 17). He sought a naval base and Lissus was ideal for the purpose.

[2] J. M. F. May, *JRS*, 36 (1946), 49.

[3] T. Lenschau, *RE*, 21 (1951), 237 f.

[4] According to Polybius, xviii, 1, 14, Philip is required to τοὺς κατὰ τὴν Ἰλλυρίδα τόπους παραδοῦναι Ῥωμαίοις, ὧν γέγονε κύριος μετὰ τὰς ἐν Ἠπείρῳ διαλύσεις, which is translated by Livy, xxxii, 33, 3, 'restituenda . . . loca quae post pacem in Epiro (Phoenice) factam occupasset'. The sense must surely refer to illegal acquisitions, as argued by J. P. V. D. Balsdon, *CQ*, 47 (1953), 162 f.; *JRS*, 44 (1954), 35 ff.

don.[1] At the beginning of the Second Macedonian War Pleuratus offered his services to the Roman commander Ser. Sulpicius Galba, but they were politely refused, a prudent decision when the results of the Macedonian alliance with Illyria would still be well remembered in Greece.[2] After the defeat of Philip in 197 B.C., however, Pleuratus was recognized as an ally of the Romans and was rewarded with the Lychnidus territory around Lake Ohrid.[3] This was hardly a gain for Pleuratus as it was too far inland. Rome simply wished to take it away from Philip, and Pleuratus was the most convenient ally to whom it could be transferred. The real gain was Rome's, as Illyrian possession of Lychnidus on Philip's northwestern frontier would enable her to observe any Macedonian activity in that quarter. In 189 B.C. Pleuratus' offer of help against the Aetolian League was accepted by M. Fulvius Nobilior and he plundered enemy territory with a fleet of 60 *lembi*; however, he was awarded no new territories at the end of the war.[4]

In 181 B.C. Pleuratus was dead and his son Gentius ruled in Illyria. From events which took place later in his reign it is possible to estimate the territory he controlled, or which at least acknowledged his sovereignty. The centre of his realm was the fortresses of Scodra, Lissus, and Rhizon. Further south beyond Lissus there were cities and peoples in alliance with Rome, but now there appears to have been no objection to Gentius sailing south with his war fleet beyond Lissus. Inland he may have still controlled the lands transferred to him after the defeat of Philip, by which he could control the Drilo valley which cut through the mountains to the northern frontier of Illyria. In the north, Greek Issa was still independent although Gentius controlled Pharos, and his rule was acknowledged by at least some of the Delmatae and Daorsii, mainland peoples north and south of the river Narenta; nevertheless the Delmatae were able to throw off this allegiance after the accession of Gentius.[5] His relations with Rome were considerably less happy than those of his predecessor, and twice he was accused of piracy before the Roman Senate. In 180 B.C. the praetor L. Duronius, who had been responsible in the previous year for coastal protection of Italy from Istria to Apulia, returned to Brundisium with some ships of Gentius which he claimed had been captured in the act of piracy. An embassy was sent to Illyria to demand an explanation, but it failed to meet Gentius. He sent envoys to Rome to explain that when the Roman envoys were in Illyria he was lying ill in a remote part of his kingdom, and he requested the Senate not to pay any heed to the charges made against him. Duronius then stated that some Roman citizens and

[1] His loyalty is mentioned on two separate occasions, Pol., xxi, 11, 7; 21, 3.
[2] Liv., xxxi, 28.   [3] Pol., xvii, 47; cf. Liv., xxxiii, 34.
[4] Liv., xxxviii, 7.   [5] Pol., xxxii, 18.

Latin allies had been injured in his kingdom, and that other Roman citizens were being held to ransom in Corcyra (presumably Corcyra Nigra (Korčula), which lay well within his kingdom). The Senate decided that these prisoners should be brought to Rome and the praetor *peregrinus* should interrogate them, and until then no decision would be made about Gentius. Judging from the fact that nothing more is heard about these matters, it is possible that the charges against him were proved false, as his envoys claimed.[1] The next incident occurs ten years later when Issa accused him of plotting war against Rome in concert with Perseus of Macedon.[2]

The last years of Philip V of Macedon were a fit subject for a Greek tragedy. His long reign had seen Macedon deprived of her power in Greece and encircled by Roman alliances. During the last decade of his reign every enterprise of his, no matter in what quarter, would sooner or later end by being discussed in the Senate, to be condoned or censured as the *patres* thought fit.[3] When Philip died in 179 B.C. he was succeeded by Perseus, and a further clash with Rome was imminent. In 172 B.C. when the crisis was at its height, a delegation from Issa appeared before the Senate, accused Gentius of plotting war in concert with Perseus, and claimed that all the Illyrians envoys who came to Rome were really spying for Macedon. This time the Senate was less interested in ascertaining the facts, and when Gentius' envoys arrived in Rome to speak his case, they were prevented from addressing the Senate on the technicality that they had not reported their arrival in Rome to the appropriate magistrate.[4] To the Senate Gentius was now an enemy, and fifty-four of his *lembi* were seized by the Romans in the harbour at Epidamnus, hardly an anchorage for a fleet planning war on Rome.[5] Finally, in the year before the war with Macedon broke out L. Decimius was sent to Illyria to remind Gentius formally of his friendship (*amicitia*) with Rome.[6] Gentius' close association with Perseus can be seen in the coinage he produced during the last years of his reign.

Eighty years ago Sir Arthur Evans published an interesting hoard of coins from Selcë in the Klementi mountains northeast of Scodra.[7] They are Illyrian coins and he dated their deposition to the Roman conquest in 168 B.C. Most interesting are twelve small bronze pieces of Scodra which bear a Macedonian

[1] Liv., xl, 42. At this time relations between Rome and Macedon were deteriorating rapidly— Philip's son Demetrius was put to death at about this time.

[2] It appears that during this period the Romans were unable to judge the worth of Gentius apart from the problems with Philip and Perseus. Like Demetrius two generations before, all the actions of Gentius are ascribed to his native recklessness and irresponsibility.

[3] E. Badian, *FC*, 94 ff. [4] Liv., xlii, 26, 2–7. [5] Liv., xlii, 48, 6–8.

[6] Liv., xlii, 37, 2, and return to Rome, xlii, 45, 8.

[7] *NC*, 20 (1880), 269 ff.

shield motif, and two similar coins, where the name of Gentius replaces that of Scodra. Their execution is slightly cruder than the rest.[1] Evans suggested that the coins of Scodra could be dated to the late third century when it was subject to strong Macedonian influence, if not actual control, while the pieces with the name of Gentius were minted by him after the end of Macedonian control. This interpretation does not fit with the literary evidence (Macedonian control in the late third century was very short-lived), and these coins must be dated later anyway, since the chronology of the Macedonian prototypes upon which they are based has since been revised. The coinage of Scodra and Gentius cannot be earlier than 186 B.C., when the Macedonian shield motif was first introduced.[2] The chronology of the Illyrian coins has recently been established by J. M. F. May: first, there are Macedonian types struck on behalf of Scodra only, secondly, a short-lived issue with the legend of both the city and of Gentius (only one example is attested) and, thirdly, Macedonian types with Gentius' name alone.[3] For a coinage commencing after 186 B.C. this typology reflects very well Gentius gradually being drawn, or rather driven, into a Macedonian alliance. There is no doubt that coinage of this type could not have been issued in Illyria after the removal of Gentius in 168 B.C., when some of the coins circulating in the area then are known and show marked Roman influence. All the coins discussed above were minted at the Illyrian capital Scodra. There is a second series of his coins, simpler in design and cruder in execution than the Macedonian issues from Scodra, which was produced at his other stronghold Lissus.[4] In place of the Macedonian shield the reverse of the coins carries a *lembus*. The existence of this coinage does not necessarily suggest that Gentius was in league with Perseus against Rome, although it does indicate that the principal cultural and economic influence came from Macedon, while the need for coinage suggests possibly a more settled pattern of life with an increase in trade and property in the area of the kingdom.

Perseus made the first gesture towards an alliance with Illyria. He sent two envoys, including an Illyrian exile Pleuratus, who met Gentius at Lissus. He agreed to an alliance in principle but refused to commit himself until he had received a subsidy. This was agreed at three hundred talents, and three Illyrians were sent to collect it from the Macedonian capital Pella.[5] Rather unwisely,

---

[1] Evans, op. cit., 270, n. 1 (12 ex. Scodra), n. 3 (2 ex. Gentius).

[2] May, op. cit., 50, n. 11.   [3] May, op. cit., 53; cf. pl. VIII, fig. 3.

[4] Evans, op. cit., 271, n. 4 and pl. XIII, 6; cf. May, 53 and pl. VIII, 7, 8.

[5] Pol., xxxviii, 8; Liv., xliv, 23. The Illyrian envoys were allowed to mark the silver with their own stamp. None of this appears to have been minted by Gentius, since all the known Illyrian coinage is bronze.

Gentius waited only until he had secured the advance payment of ten talents before he threw some Roman ambassadors into prison. Hearing that Gentius had committed himself against the Romans, Perseus withdrew the remainder of the subsidy.[1] In the ensuing war thirty days sufficed to destroy Gentius.[2] He assembled a force of 15,000 men at Lissus, where also what remained of his fleet after the seizure at Epidamnus was presumably stationed. After detaching 1,000 infantry and 50 horsemen under his brother Caravantius to subdue the Cavi, a neighbouring people who appeared likely to support Rome but are otherwise unknown, he advanced southwards for 5 miles and attacked Bassania, a city in alliance with Rome. The war against Gentius was the province of L. Anicius Gallus, a praetor in 168 B.C. He was based at Apollonia with a force of Roman and allied infantry, including 2,000 infantry and 200 cavalry under the command of Epicadus and Algalsus, chieftains of the Illyrian Parthini. At this point there is a break in the account of Livy, and the early stages are lost from the text. It appears that Gentius sent his fleet southward along the coast in an attempt to cut the Roman supply lines but it was defeated by Anicius.[3] The fate of any land expedition he might have made is unknown. With the collapse of his forces Gentius abandoned Lissus and retreated to Scodra, where he hoped to hold out until his brother Caravantius could come to his aid, but after failing to drive off a Roman attack Gentius surrendered to the praetor. The Roman army then advanced northwards to Meteon (Medun), the stronghold at the north end of the Scodra Lake, and captured Caravantius, Gentius' queen Etleva, his two sons Scerdilaidas and Pleuratus, and released the imprisoned Roman ambassadors. Illyria was now 'under the jurisdiction of the Roman People' (*sub dicione populi Romani*)[4].

The settlement imposed on the Illyrians followed the same policy by which the Senate had dealt leniently with Macedon after the death of Perseus which occurred about the same time. Rome was prepared to be generous to harmless ex-enemies.[5] The details of the settlement are recorded by Livy in a form that is close to the original document.[6] When the five envoys arrived from Rome Anicius returned to Scodra and, after calling together all the chiefs (*principes*) of the area, read aloud from a tribunal the decisions of the Roman Senate and People about their future. They were all to be free and all the occupying garri-

[1] Liv., xliv, 23; Pol., xxix, 2; cf. Appian, *Mac.*, 16.

[2] Sources for the war against Gentius: Liv., xliv, 30–32; cf. Eutrop., iv, 6; Dio, xxxi, 8, 10; Plut., *Aem. Paull.*, 13, 2; Florus, i, 29; Appian, *Ill.*, 9.

[3] Appian, *Ill.*, 9.

[4] Liv., xlv, 8. Triumph of Anicius, *Inscr. It.*, XIII, 1, 81; cf. 556.

[5] Badian, *FC*, 97.   [6] Liv., xlv, 26.

sons would be withdrawn. Almost all of the peoples were to be free from tribute, because most of the people had deserted Gentius while he was still undefeated. The freedom of Issa was reaffirmed, but there is no mention of Pharos, presumably now regarded as merely an Illyrian stronghold. Freedom and immunity from tribute were granted to some Illyrian peoples who, although they acknowledged Gentius' rule, appear to have taken no part in the war. These included the Taulantii,[1] not the main people but probably a northern part of them, the Pirustae of Dassaretia[2] who dwelt across the mountains, and the Daorsii near the river Narenta, because they had refused to help Caravantius.[3] Next came the conditions for the peoples who dwelt in the immediate vicinity of Gentius' fortresses: 'The Scodrenses, Dassarenses, and Selepitani, and the rest of the Illyrians shall pay a tribute, half of what they were paying to the king. Then Anicius divided the kingdom into three parts: the one mentioned above (around Scodra), the second of the Labeatae (around Meteon), and the third the Agravonitae (Acruvium), Rhizonitae (Risinium), Olciniatae (Olcinium), and others in the area'. The division of the kingdom into three recalls the conditions imposed on Macedon at the same time, divided into four areas and paying the same scale of tribute. The small communities actually involved in the settlement were all around Scodra and the Lake, and will have been the basis of Gentius' personal power from which he exercised control over the rest of his kingdom with varying success.[4] After the settlement Anicius withdrew all his forces from the strongholds and moved to winter-quarters in Epirus. Roman policy towards the kingdom of Illyria was never directed towards achieving any particular goal.

[1] M. Fluss, *RE* 4A (1932), 252, 6 ff. Although once a great people, they had suffered greatly from the Celtic invasions and lost much of their territory.

[2] On the Pirustae see below, p. 173. Mayer, 264, suggests that *Daesitiatium* should be read instead of *Dassaretiorum*. Impossible: the Daesiatiates lived 150 miles away in Central Bosnia, p. 170.

[3] They dwelt near the coast south of the river Narenta mouth, see below, p. 164. Later in the second century B.C. they minted their own coins with the legend DAORSON, Brunšmid, 74 f.; Schlosser, 42.

[4] The text of Livy (xlv, 26) is corrupt on one point: 'inde in tres partes Illyricum divisit. unam eam fecit quod †supra dictam est†, alteram Labeatas omnis, tertiam Agravonitas', etc. Here the meaning has been taken to make the first region of Illyria the Scodrenses, Dassarenses, and Selepitani, who are not included in the other two, while these three areas form a compact block of territory around the Scodra Lake. To emend and read Issa, as Madvig, 606, is geographically unreasonable, as that was a free Greek city and not part of the kingdom, nor is the suggestion of C. Müller, 308, ad ii, 16, 3, that it refers to *Pistam*, a place on the Peutinger Map south of Lissus, convincing. All the other communities involved are known, while the Agravonitae and the others on the coast had already been under the control of Roman *praefecti*, Liv., xliv, 31.

The Senate dealt with each situation as it arose and once Roman interests were secure matters were allowed to drift.[1] With the horizons of Roman foreign policy increasing rapidly in the early second century B.C. Illyria became merely one of many smaller powers whose independence was threatened by clashes between the major powers. The final struggle with Macedon placed Illyria on the knife-edge: Gentius chose the wrong side and defeat for Macedon brought his ruin.

[1] 'The history of the Illyrian wars does not, it must be admitted, give us occasion to observe in the Roman authorities either that agressive ambition or that clearsightedness and consistency in the conduct of foreign affairs, or that love for and skill in political intrigue which has often been attributed to them', M. Holleaux, *CAH*, 7, 856.

Chapter 3
Rome and Illyria (167–59 B.C.)

Coins furnish some evidence for the internal affairs of Illyria after the settlement of 167 B.C. They record the names of at least one, and perhaps two, rulers in the area. Nearly a century ago Evans studied a group of coins, mostly from Pharos and Rhizon (Risinium), which were issued by a dynast or king named Ballaios.[1] They are well executed, and were modelled on Greek types; they are matched by another series of coins with the name of Rhizon only, as well as barbarous copies of the Ballaios coins. There are also coins of a possible successor with the legend MUN.[2] These show clear traces of Roman influence in their production. There is no precise indication of the dates of any of these series, although Evans believed (and he was followed by Brunšmid) that they were minted in the middle and later second century B.C.[3] Two coins with the legend RIZANOTAN are typologically earlier than the Ballaios series, and may have been issued in the years immediately after the defeat of Gentius.[4] The Ballaios coins were minted at both Pharos and Rhizon; the products of the two mints can easily be distinguished, but they were probably made at the same time. On the Rhizon types the legend is commonly BASILEOS BALLAIOS, but the regal title is very rare on the Pharos issues. It is possible that after the removal of Gentius the Roman authorities did not object to a reliable Illyrian dynast establishing himself along the coast. He may have been responsible for the disturbance which caused the Roman attacks on the Ardiaei and the Pleraei in 135 B.C., who were accused of plundering their neighbours (p. 32).

The defeat of Gentius and the settlement of Illyria did not result in the establishment of a regular Roman province across the Adriatic, as happened with

---

[1] Evans, NC, 20 (1880), 292 f., pl. I. [2] Evans, op. cit., 294, pl. IV, 1–5.
[3] Brunšmid, 76. [4] Evans, op. cit., 292, 1–2, pl. I, 9–10.

Macedon after 148 B.C. It secured Roman interests by imposing a settlement over a territory much greater than that which had been involved in the recent war, enabling Rome to intervene in almost any matters affecting Illyria whenever she chose. The role which Rome assumed after 167 B.C. in Illyria encouraged merchants from Italy to operate in the area under the umbrella of Roman prestige, and it is possible that some of the later attested settlements of Roman citizens (*conventus civium Romanorum*) were beginning already as Roman and Italian trading posts in the second century B.C. With a Roman alliance now of more than sixty years standing Issa enjoyed a privileged position. In the past the threats to her independence came from the Illyrian kingdom, but after this was ended clashes began with the native Delmatae, who now controlled the coast and the hinterland between the river Titius (Krka) and the Narenta. The first of many Roman wars against the Delmatae arose through complaints made against them by Issa.

In 158 B.C. Issa protested that her recently established mainland possessions at Epetion (Stobreč) and Tragurion (Trogir) on either side of the Bay of Salona were being attacked by the Delmatae.[1] Under Roman protection Issa was apparently seeking to dominate the commerce with the mainland peoples, and it is not surprising that the Delmatae opposed the establishment of Issaean colonies in their territory. The Roman reaction was to send a commission of investigation under the consular senator C. Fannius Strabo 'to enquire into the state of Illyria, with particular reference to the conduct of the Delmatae'.[2] Possibly the senators believed that the appearance of an ex-consul would be sufficient to overawe them, but the answer given by the Delmatae to his enquiries left little doubt about their attitude. When he returned from Illyria Fannius told the Senate that not only had the Delmatae refused to listen to him, but they had not even observed the elementary diplomatic courtesies. They had told him bluntly that affairs across the Adriatic 'were no concern of the Romans'. As Polybius remarks it was Roman indignation at their attitude that was as much responsible for the ensuing campaigns, as any willingness on the part of the Romans to support Issa's mainland ambitions. Another reason for the campaign advanced by Polybius is hardly credible. According to him the Senate felt that the 'long years of peace since the defeat of Perseus' were having a detrimental effect on the fighting efficiency of the army, and they judged that a brief but vigorous campaign in Illyria was exactly what was required to put matters right. It is true that Illyria

---

[1] Pol., xxxii, 9. Apparently the Delmatae were once subject to Pleuratus but later broke away from this allegiance and attacked neighbouring peoples, forcing them to pay tribute in cattle and corn (see p. 23). This is the earliest record of the Delmatae.

[2] Pol., xxxii, 9. C. Fannius Strabo was consul in 161 B.C., and apparently a *novus homo*, MRR, 1, 446.

was thought later as an army proving ground, by Cinna and Octavianus, but for the Senate to think in these terms in the middle of the second century B.C. is surprising, especially when so much effort at this time was being put into the Spanish campaigns.[1]

The campaign against the Delmatae was carried out efficiently and, if the interpretation of its topography is correct, even brilliantly.[2] Command was entrusted to a consul of the year (156 B.C.), C. Marcius Figulus. At first things did not go too well: while pitching their camp the Romans were attacked and forced to retreat to the river Narenta. They resumed the offensive, however, and eventually laid siege to the capital Delminium. Starting from the mouth of the Narenta, Figulus probably advanced northward up the valley of the tributary river Trebižat, and then across a low pass over the Dinaric Alps into Duvjans-kopolje, in which the site of Delminium has been located on the Lib planina near Županac.[3] The attack was made late in the campaigning season in the hope that it would take the Delmatae by surprise, but they were still in the field awaiting the Romans. Although he managed to establish a blockade on the fortress Figulus' attempts to capture it by storm made little impression, and he had to be content with reducing many of the minor hill-settlements in the vicinity, Before he returned to Rome at the end of 156 B.C. he had managed to set part of the fortress on fire, but the final capture was left to his successor in the following season, the consul P. Cornelius Scipio Nasica. The winter blockade instituted by Figulus had achieved its purpose, and when Scipio arrived in his province the capture of Delminium did not take long. The fortifications were destroyed and the plain around it was turned into a sheep pasture.[4] After a victory which had been achieved largely by his predecessor, Scipio returned to Rome and celebrated a triumph over the Delmatae: the Senate would hardly refuse such an honour to a Scipio. Appian says nothing about the campaign of Scipio and the capture of Delminium, but this is more likely to be the result of poor research on his part than any source he used being unfavourable to the family of the Cornelii Scipiones.[5] In extent and achievement, although perhaps not in motive, the war against the Delmatae in 156–155 B.C. was an exception to the normal Roman

[1] Pol., xxxii, 13.

[2] Appian, *Ill.*, 11; cf. Liv., *Per.*, 47; Florus, i, 25. On Marcius Figulus, *MRR*, I, 447.

[3] Patsch, *WMBH*, 9 (1904), 171 ff., and p. 271. [4] Strabo, vii, 5, 5.

[5] The success of Scipio is well attested, Front., *Strat.*, iii, 6, 2; Zon., ix, 25; Ampelius, xix, 11, *Auct. de vir ill.*, xliv, 4; Liv., *Per.*, xlvii; Iul. Obseq., 16; Strabo, vii, 5, 5. His triumph appears in the Fasti, *Inscr. It.*, XIII, 1, 82 f.; cf. 557 under 155 B.C. This disproves a later tradition that Scipio refused his triumph (Ampelius, *Auct. de vir. ill.*). The above sources also make it quite impossible that the tradition has produced a duplication of a single year's campaign, as argued by J. Salanki, *Arch. Ért*, 1940, 258–60.

policy in Illyria. Apart from the ill-reported campaigns of C. Cosconius (78–76), Roman arms were not employed seriously against the Delmatae until the years before Actium (34–33 B.C.), though as allies of the Pompeians in the Civil War between Pompey and Caesar they inflicted serious defeats on Roman armies. In the context the achievements of Figulus and Scipio were creditable feats of arms, particularly when compared with the activities of L. Caecilius Metellus in 118–117 B.C.

From the military standpoint the next episode of Roman warfare in Illyria was on a smaller scale, but the diplomatic activity which preceded it exhibits the same pattern as occurred before the war against the Delmatae. According to the version of Appian, in 135 B.C. the Ardiaeoi and Palarioi (Pleraei) attacked 'Roman Illyria', and when they failed to make any amends for this behaviour the Senate dispatched a force of 10,000 infantry and 600 cavalry under the consul Ser. Fulvius Flaccus. The Illyrians tried to open negotiations at the last minute but as they could not meet the terms laid down by the Senate, the consul was ordered to proceed with his attack. Appian calls the expedition 'merely a raid', and adds that he could find no record of the outcome.[1] On the other hand, Livy's statement that Flaccus 'subdued the (V)ardaei' leaves no doubt that the consul accomplished his task.[2]

Beyond the northeast of the Adriatic the Iapodes were the equal of the Delmatae in military power. Rome had been in contact with the western fringe of this people since 171 B.C. Then apologies were made to them and other peoples in the area for the aggressive activities of the consul L. Cassius Longinus, who had seriously planned to attack Perseus of Macedon overland from Northeast Italy.[3] The next episode involving the Iapodes occurs forty years later, when a Roman consul campaigned against them and was awarded a triumph. In the middle of the crisis over the Gracchan Land Commission in 129 B.C. the consul C. Sempronius Tuditanus suddenly left Rome on the pretext that he had to fight the Iapodes and he was only saved from disaster by D. Iunius Brutus, hero of the Lusitanian War.[4] The consul's only motive for the campaign appears to have been his desire to escape from the political situation at Rome. The role of Iunius Brutus against the Iapodes is recorded by Livy, but not by Appian. He records that Sempronius was assisted by Ti. (Latinius) Pandusa.[5] Following an earlier suggestion of Gaebler, Münzer assumed that Pandusa was propraetor in Macedon at the time, but this is unlikely since it implies that Roman forces had established overland contact between Italy and Macedonia, a link which was not

[1] Appian, *Ill.*, 10.   [2] Liv., *Per.*, lvi.
[3] Liv., xli, 1–5; 6, 1–3; 7, 4–10; xliii, 1, 4–12; 5, 7–10; cf. *MRR*, 1, 416.
[4] Liv., *Per.*, lix; cf. H. Last, *CAH*, 9, 42 f.   [5] Appian, *Ill.*, 10; cf. *BC*, i, 19.

achieved until the reign of Augustus.[1] Perhaps Pandusa was commanding some troops in Northern Italy, and when the sudden campaign of Sempronius was planned he was required to assist.[2] Sempronius held his triumph over the Iapodes on the 1 October 129 B.C. while he was still consul, but his operation were not confined to this people.[3] The Elder Pliny records that Sempronius Tuditanus conquered the Histri and inscribed on his statue: 'from Aquileia to the river Titius, 2,000 stades';[4] while fragments of his *elogium* set up at Aquileia have been discovered,[5] part of which may read: 'he forced the Taurisci, Carni, and the Liburni to leave the mountains'. It is remarkable that not only did Sempronius as consul have enough time to win a triumph from the Iapodes by October, but also to defeat the Taurisci further north, and explore the coast of Liburnia as far as the Delmatae. Some of these campaigns may have been undertaken by Pandusa acting independently but on the consul's behalf.

The next series of operations in Illyria were against the Delmatae and may have followed from campaigns in Northeast Italy. Appian records: 'The Segestani seem to have been subdued by L. (Aurelius) Cotta and L. (Caecilius) Metellus', presumably when the two men were colleagues in the consulship of 119 B.C.[6] The Segestani occupied part of the Save valley around their city Segesta, the later Roman Siscia (Sisak). For a Roman force to reach the middle Save valley at this date, even with a large force under the two consuls, was a remarkable advance. Appian's statement cannot be rejected in detail, since he mentions Segesta later in his *Illyrike* in connection with the well documented campaigns of Octavianus in 35 B.C. In the following year Metellus campaigned alone against the Delmatae, and celebrated his triumph over them in 117 B.C., taking at the same time the honorific title *Delmaticus*.[7] Appian explains the background: 'At a later period . . . war was declared against the Dalmatians, although they had been guilty of no offence, because he (Metellus) desired a

---

[1] F. Münzer, *RE*, 12 (1925), 927, n. 6; cf. H. Gaebler, *ZfN*, 23, 162 f.

[2] Thus Zippel, 136. Otherwise nothing is known of Pandusa. A descendant was probably Ti. Latinius Pandusa, the legate in Moesia who was succeeded by C. Poppaeus Sabinus under Tiberius, Tac., *ann.*, ii, 26. The cognomen Pandusa points to Lucania or Bruttium, *RE*, 12 (1925), 927, n. 6.

[3] *Inscr. It.*, XIII, 1, 82 f., cf. 559.

[4] Plin., *HN*, iii, 129. The MSS read 'M stadia', but MM (app. 250 miles) must be read. Tuditanus put the words on his own statue set up at Aquileia.

[5] *Inscr. It.*, XIII, 3, 73 ff., n. 90, also another dedication, possibly a statue base, from Duino in Venetia, *Fast. Arch.*, 5 (1950), 332, n. 3972 (*AE*, 1953, 95) with his name only.

[6] Appian, *Ill.*, 10.

[7] Appian, *Ill.*, 11. Triumph of Metellus, *Inscr. It.*, XIII, 1, 83; cf. 560, also Liv., *Per.*, lxii; Eutrop., iv, 23, 2.

triumph. They received him as a friend, and he wintered among them at the town of Salona, after which he returned to Rome and was awarded a triumph'. Even a Metellus at this period could not acquire a triumph for doing nothing, and Livy records that he did win some victories. It is most unlikely that Metellus moved against the Delmatae overland by a southward route from Segesta, as some scholars have assumed.[1] It is strange that no reward or recognition appears to have been made for the capture of Segesta in 119 B.C., which could honestly be claimed as a major advance for one season's operations. The tone of Appian's account suggests that his source for these events was biased against the Metelli, and is not due to the carelessness which is apparent in the account he gives of the earlier operation against the Delmatae.[2]

For nearly thirty years after 117 B.C. no campaigns were undertaken in Illyria by the Romans. The Jugurthine War and the Cimbric invasions, followed soon by the Italian and the Civil Wars, afforded Roman commanders few opportunities to seek military glory in obscure regions. An incident in the years 84 B.C. suggests that the leaders of the *populares* faction L. (Cornelius) Cinna and Cn. (Papirius) Carbo were planning a campaign across the Adriatic which, if it had taken place, would have anticipated those of Octavianus in 35–33 B.C. According to Appian, when all hope of a reconciliation with the outlaw Cornelius Sulla had gone, the two *populares* 'traversed Italy, collecting soldiers whom they carried across on shipboard to Liburnia, which was to act as their base against Sulla. The first detachment crossed in safety; the next encountered a storm, and those who reached land escaped home immediately, as they did not relish the prospect of fighting their fellow-citizens. When the rest learned this they too refused to

---

[1] Thus Zippel, 137.

[2] The principal source for affairs in Illyria in the second half of the second century B.C. is the *Illyrike* of Appian, a civil servant under Antoninus Pius. His work is fairly complete up to 167 B.C., if unreliable in details; after this the material is meagre and the omissions are serious. Thus there is no record of Scipio in 155 B.C. after a good account of Figulus in the previous year. The campaign of 135 B.C. is dismissed as a raid, but Livy (p. 32) shows that there was more to it. Tuditanus in 129 B.C. is recorded, together with the interesting detail of Pandusa, while the dismissal of Metellus in 118–117 B.C. as triumph-hunting is clearly the bias of his source. No other campaign is recorded between then and the proconsulship of Caesar. There is no obvious explanation for this unevenness, except that he was hard put to it to find material for this particular book; an inordinate amount of space (c, 16–30) is given to the detailed account of the campaigns in 35–33 B.C. This he took from Augustus' own memoirs, although he revised the scheme to present the material chronologically. Otherwise the arrangement of the book is more topographical, with Flaccus against the Ardiaei in 135 B.C. preceding Figulus against the Delmatae in 156 B.C. The individual monographs on the regional wars were apparently written to about the same length, and once Appian found so much in Augustus he bothered little about earlier events.

cross to Liburnia'.¹ Soon afterwards Cinna was killed in a riot, and Carbo was forced to recall those troops which were already in Liburnia. It is most unlikely that their intention was to prepare to meet Sulla in Liburnia or even oppose his crossing to Italy from there. If this was their intention then it was to bases in Southern Italy (Brundisium) or across the Adriatic (Epidamnus, Apollonia) that the troops should have been sent. The only reasonable explanation for these landings is that Cinna and Carbo hoped to train their raw and unwilling levies to battle worthiness by some rigorous campaigning in Illyria before they had to face Sulla's veterans.²

In the early seventies B.C. there was more fighting against the Delmatae. In the brief account given by Eutropius, C. Cosconius went to Illyria as proconsul and subdued most of the Delmatae in a two-year campaign, ending with the capture of their chief port Salona.³ This fighting probably took place in 78–76 B.C., although there is no definite evidence, but it would fit well with the revival of Roman power after the weakening internal strife of the previous decade, and the war was definitely over before 74 B.C.⁴ Cosconius' final achievement in taking Salona reveals how little the Roman power in the area had advanced since the wars in the second century.⁵ Salona (near modern Split) now became a permanent Roman possession, and within twenty years a settlement of Roman citizens, many of them traders, was established there and at other places along the coast, although Narona may have been occupied by such a community already for many years.⁶

---

¹ Appian, *BC*, i, 77–8.

² E. Badian, *JRS*, 52 (1962), 58 (*SGRH*, 227 f.). The objections of J. P. V. D. Balsdon are not convincing, *JRS*, 55 (1965), 232. A passage in Eutropius, v, 7, which connects the proconsul Sulla with campaigns against the Delmatae before his return to Italy, is certainly mistaken. Possibly the Denseletae (or Dentheletae) are to be understood: they were defeated by Sulla at this time along with the Dardanians for attacking Macedonia, Granus Licinianus, xxxv (ed. Flemisch, p. 28); cf. Zippel, 161 f.

³ Eutrop., vi, 4; Orosius, *Hist.*, v, 23, 23.

⁴ *MRR*, 2, 88, n. 4. F. Münzer, *RE*, 4 (1901), 1667, n. 3, identifies the proconsul with a praetorian commander operating in Apulia in 89 B.C.

⁵ Figulus probably operated from the Narenta valley and did not need control over the Manios Bay area, but Metellus in 118–17 B.C. was clearly in control of the Salona area.

⁶ This is the total of known Roman enterprises across the Adriatic in Illyria before the proconsulship of Caesar, apart from two ill-reported episodes of uncertain date. A fragment of the Historiae of Sallust (ed. Maurenbrecher, p. 73, frg. 40) reads 'primam modo in Iapydiam ingresus', probably referring to somebody campaigning in the seventies B.C., but not to Cosconius who was concerned with the Delmatae around Salona. He could be the otherwise unknown P. Licinius (?Crassus), a Roman commander against the Iapodes at some period, who was deceived by the ruse of a feigned retreat, Front., *Strat.*, ii, 5, 28; cf. F. Münzer, *RE*, 13 (1926), 221, n. 27.

Rome and Illyria (167–59 B.C.)

The record of the Romans in Illyria during these years shows that they never held the region to be important. Only when Gentius had joined Perseus as an active ally was a praetor sent to remove him and impose a general political settlement on the area, which left Rome free to intervene at any time she chose but which did not involve any administrative or military commitments. The rapid withdrawal of troops and universal grants of freedom suggest that once the ally of Perseus had been removed, they were content to let the Illyrians go their own way. The causes and motives of the different ventures by Roman commanders into the area are instructive in their variety, combining one basic element: events within Illyria had usually nothing to do with the projects undertaken. Polybius tells that the motive behind the war against the Delmatae in 156–165 B.C. was the need, imagined or real, to keep up the standards of the Roman forces in general, while a similar intention, that of training an army, lay behind the activities of Cinna and Carbo in 84 B.C. and the more grandiose, but nevertheless carefully limited, ventures of Octavianus in 35–33 B.C. The attacks on the Ardiaei and Pleraei in 135 B.C. appear actually to have been caused by the behaviour of these peoples; Sempronius Tuditanus the consul found in the Iapodes a convenient escape from Roman politics in 129 B.C., and yet no historian hints at the reason for the campaign. Metellus in 118–117 B.C. may have achieved something more than Appian credits to him, but the motive of triumph-hunting is probably true. Not surprisingly in terms of territorial possessions and effective political control the sum total of these expeditions was negligible; in fact until the first century the Romans were losing their control rather than extending it. Under the Republic Dalmatia was never constituted as a regular province, with regular Roman governors: it was a place where Rome had some ancient alliances with one or two Greek communities, and where fighting would break out from time to time. Usually a consul in office was sent to the area, and the only known proconsul (apart possibly from Metellus) in the area was C. Cosconius whose achievement was to capture Salona. None of this is surprising. Illyria lay on no major route and, apart from a potential nuisance of piracy, had no importance for communications with the eastern Mediterranean. While the obvious route to this area was still the short sea crossing from Brundisium, it was not necessary to go to the enormous expense of opening up the land route between Northern Italy and the east. At this time a Roman army would have been unwise to attempt the route along the Illyrian coast or across the interior, if it was to have any hope of reaching its destination intact. When Roman armies went to Illyria they went to fight: either to train an army for a civil war, or to gain a reputation and glory for a commander.

Chapter 4
Illyria in the Civil Wars (59-39 B.C.)

In 60 B.C. the Roman Republic passed under the control of three men, Cn. Pompeius, M. Licinius Crassus, and C. Iulius Caesar. They had formed a secret compact, known later as the First Triumvirate, to achieve their own different aims, which each had had thwarted by the small minority of traditionalists in the Senate. The weapon was to be Caesar's consulship in the following year, supported by the money and patronage of Crassus, and the greedy veterans of Pompeius. Among their different measures in 59 B.C. the 'Vatinian Law concerning the province of Caesar' set aside the Senate's allocation of consular provinces for the following year, and conferred upon Caesar command (*imperium*) for five years in Cisalpine Gaul with an army of three legions to which, on the death of Q. Metellus Celer, Transalpine Gaul was added with its one legion. Coupled with Cisalpine Gaul was Illyricum, the new Roman name for land east of the Adriatic between Istria and Epirus; there is, however, no mention of any Roman troops being stationed there.[1] By this period it may have been the normal practice for the proconsul who was sent annually to Cisalpine Gaul to attend to Roman interests across the Adriatic, or possibly it may have been included at Caesar's own request. If the latter was the case he may have visualized his prin-

---

[1] *MRR*, 2, 190. There is some variation in the terms of the law as reported in different sources: 'Gallia Cisalpina with Illyricum and four legions for five years', Plut., *Caes.*, 14; *Pomp.*, 48, 3; *Crassus*, 14, 3; 'Illyricum and Gallia Cisalpina with three legions for five years and Transalpina added with another legion', Dio, xxxviii, 85; 'Cisalpine Gaul with Illyricum added (*adiectum*) and Gallia Comata added later', Suet., *Caes.*, 22; 'Galliae for five years', Vell., Pat., ii, 44, 5; 'the three provinces Gallia Transalpina, Cisalpina, and Illyricum with Gallia Comata added later', Orosius, *Hist.*, vi, 7, 1. Q. Metellus Celer (*cos.* 60 B.C.) had died before April 59 B.C. without leaving Rome, *MRR*, 2, 183.

cipal military project as an advance northeast from Italy into the Danube basin, the area where Italy has always been most vulnerable to attacks from the north. If he had advanced into the Save valley and across Northern Bosnia, then command in Illyricum also would not only be useful from a military point of view, but it would also rule out any possibility of his being attacked by the Senate for moving outside the limits of his *imperium*. On the other hand there is no evidence that Caesar had any such plans, while his later activities in Illyricum suggest that the attachment of Illyricum to Cisalpine Gaul was merely routine. If Caesar did have plans to attack the Danube area the province he should have taken was Macedonia, where Roman proconsuls had been gradually advancing the frontiers of Roman control up the Vardar (Axios)–Morava corridor to the plain of Serbia and the river Danube around Belgrade.

The first episode in Caesar's proconsulship involving Illyricum occurred in the winter 57–56 B.C. After the summer's successes against the Germans and the Belgae, Caesar deployed his legions in their winter quarters and set out for Illyricum 'to acquaint himself with the country and the peoples who inhabited it'.[1] Before he reached his destination, however, he was forced to return to Gaul to deal with the rebellion of the Veneti and rescue the younger Crassus and his trapped legion.[2] There is no evidence where Caesar was planning to go in Illyricum, but he probably intended to sail to Central Dalmatia and visit the Roman settlements at Salona and Narona. From the area two inscriptions, both dated to 56 B.C., reflected Caesar's interest in the province. From Salona three fragments from a Greek inscription record an embassy which appeared before Caesar at Aquileia on 3 March 56 B.C. It is dated by the Roman consuls and calendar, as well as the priests and Dorian Calendar of Issa, the state which initiated the embassy. Next are listed the names of the delegates from Issa who spoke before Caesar on behalf of their city, and then the Roman G. Gavenius G. f. Fab(ia tribu), probably a representative of the Roman settlers, who spoke about the free status of the Issaeans and their friendship with the Roman people. The stone is broken at this point and only two fragments survive from the text of Caesar's reply to the Issaeans which was reproduced on the stone. The proconsul seems to have confirmed the status of Issa as a free allied community, along with a specific mention of her rights of free access to the Manios Bay and some guarantee for the Issaean mainland settlements at Epetium and Tragurium; these were the places attacked more than a century before by the Delmatae. The situation which caused the embassy is not clear. There may have been more trouble with the Delmatae, but it is possible that there was some trouble between

---

[1] *BG*, ii, 35, at the beginning of winter 57 B.C.
[2] *BG*, iii, 7.

the Greeks and the Roman settlers, foreshadowing the political alignments which can be recognized during the Civil War in the next decade. Apart from this the decree reflects the pattern of Roman administration, with much of the government being carried on from Aquileia, now the leading city of the Northern Adriatic.[1] Another result of the Issaean embassy may have been Caesar's decision to establish one of his legates in Illyricum as a permanent administrator. Q. Numerius Rufus, who is attested at Issa, was a tribune of the plebs at Rome 57 B.C., and as an agent of Caesar opposed the recall of Cicero from exile in that year. With the triumphant return of Cicero to the Roman scene and the end of Numerius' tribunate (9 December), it was prudent to avoid the orator's vengeance by accepting an appointment on Caesar's staff. A Latin inscription at Issa records that he financed the rebuilding of a portico, doubtless on behalf of his patron, and suggests that the Roman administration in the area was now based at Issa.[2]

It is two years before anything further is heard of Illyricum. After completing some tours of administration in Gaul early in 54 B.C., Caesar travelled to Illyricum where he had heard that some Roman allies 'in remote parts' were suffering from raids by the Pirustae. Caesar gave orders in advance for the Roman allies to assemble their forces, and this on its own was sufficient to make the Pirustae offer reparations to the injured parties. After demanding hostages for their conduct and assigning arbitrators to assess the damages, Caesar held a judicial circuit (*conventus*) and returned to Gaul.[3] The account of Caesar's last visit to the area is found not in his own Commentaries but in Appian's *Illyrike*. He records that when the Delmatae were 'prospering' they and other Illyrians captured the fortress Promona (on the Promina mountains) from the Liburnians. The latter sought help from the Romans, in particular from Caesar who was in the vicinity at the time. He ordered them to restore Promona to the Liburnians, and when they refused sent a force against them which was defeated with great loss. However, Caesar could do nothing further about the matter owing to the mounting tension with Pompeius and the Senate; this indicates that the episode took place

---

[1] The best publication is now D. Rendić-Miočević, *Studi Aquileiesi etc.* 67–81: ἐν 'Ἀκολήία ἐπὶ Γαίου Ἰουλί[ου] Καί[σαρος] αὐτοκράτορος, Γαῖος Γαουένιο[ς Γαίου ? υἱ]ὸς Φαβία, λόγους ἐποιήσα[το περὶ τῆς τε] ἐλευ[θε]ρίας τῶν Ἰσσαίω[ν καὶ τῆς φιλίας] τ[ῶν Ῥωμαίω]ν καὶ Ἰσσαί[ων. . . .
On the larger upper fragment lines 6–7 were read πρεσβε[υ]σάντων ΠΑΓΙΑ but this can be read ΤΡΑΓΥΡΙ[ΝΩΝ] from Rendić-Miočević, op. cit., 73. Elsewhere the [ΤΡΑΓΟ]ΥΡΙΝΟΙ appear on a small fragment of the stone published by M. Abramić, *VAHD*, 47–8 (1924–7), 3 ff.
[2] III, 3078, from the city wall at Issa. Numerius Rufus was quaestor in Africa in 60 B.C., *ILS*, 9482; as tribune in 57 he opposed Cicero's recall alone with Atilius Serranus, *MRR*, 2, 202, 219. On his connections with Caesar, F. Münzer, *RE*, 17 (1937), 1326 f., n. 5.
[3] *BG*, v, 1–2.

39

towards the end of his proconsulship.[1] The two occasions when Caesar is known to have been in Cisalpine Gaul were the winter 53–52 B.C. and early in 50 B.C., and Appian's reference to the tension with Pompeius makes the latter date more likely.[2] The force which the Delmatae defeated was probably a collection of allied contingents from Illyricum under the command of a Roman officer, and no legion appears to have been involved. Caesar's neglect of this situation was to cause him serious problems during the coming war. The Delmatae were expanding their power, and were willing allies of the Pompeians against the Roman settlers.

In 49 B.C. the world was engulfed by the war between Caesar and Pompeius. Most areas of the Roman Empire witnessed bitter struggles between the two factions. In the main campaigns, in Africa, Spain, and Asia Minor, the Pompeians after initial successes against Caesar's legates were eventually defeated by Caesar in person. In Illyricum the outcome of the struggle was decided without the presence of either protagonist. This was not because of the insignificance of Illyricum, but because Caesar's legates, aided by the settler communities along the coast, struggled through to victory over the Pompeian fleet and the Delmatae.

The first round in the struggle was diasastrous to the Caesarians. Early in 49 B.C. C. Antonius, the brother of M. Antonius, was placed in charge of Illyricum supported by P. Cornelius Dolabella (*cos.* 44 B.C.) who commanded a small fleet. The Pompeian forces consisted of a strong fleet under M. Octavius and L. Scribonius Libo (*cos.* 34 B.C.), which makes Antonius' decision to establish his forces on the island Curicta quite illogical. The few ships under Dolabella were brushed aside and the Caesarian forces were trapped on the island. In spite of some determined resistance by Gallic auxiliaries sent by Caesar, Antonius was forced to surrender his forces, and fifteen cohorts were transferred to strengthen Pompeius' army in Greece. The capitulation was witnessed by another Caesarian force encamped on the Liburnian mainland opposite Curicta under L. Minucius Basilus and the historian C. Sallustius Crispus, who were powerless to intervene without ships. The camp of Antonius was probably on the east side of the island, where the peninsula Bejevac extends towards the mainland, while the other army was probably on one of the coastal inlets, Kraljevica or Sv. Jakov.[3]

---

[1] Appian, *Ill.*, 12. On the Promona fortifications see p. 54.

[2] *BG*, vii, 7, 1 (53/2 B.C.); viii, 50 (51 B.C.).

[3] Appian, *BC*, ii, 41; Dio, xli, 40, and xlii 11, 1; Florus, ii, 30–3; Orosius, *Hist.*, vi, 15, 8–9; Liv., *Per.*, cx; Lucan, *Phars.*, iv, 402–581. Caesar's own account is lost from the text, but he refers back to the disaster, *BC*, iii, 4, 2, iii, 10, 5 (where the MSS 'Corcyra' must be emended to Curicta), iii, 67, 5. Zippel, 203, suggests that the account came at *BC*, ii, 22, where the opening

This victory gave the Pompeians a mastery over the Adriatic which Octavius began to exploit by attacks on the Italian settlements loyal to Caesar. He moved first against Salona. Greek Issa was already in his possession and served, probably willingly, as the headquarters of the Pompeians until they were defeated by Vatinius in 47 B.C. The attack of Octavius was resisted valiantly by the settlers: slaves were set free to fight and women fought alongside the men with such success that eventually they were able to make a sortie and break the blockade. Octavius' first attempt to follow up the success at Curicta was a failure, and he retreated to Dyrrhachium after failing to take any of the coastal settlements.[1]

After Caesar's victory over Pompeius at Pharsalus in June 48 B.C. Illyricum was one of the areas where the Pompeians tried to revive their cause.[2] To counter this and to deal with the troublesome Delmatae, Caesar sent Q. Cornificius there as *quaestor pro praetore* with two legions,[3] but apart from a minor naval success achieved with some ships borrowed from the Liburnian Iadertini,[4] Caesar records nothing of his operations. It was soon clear, however, that more forces were required in the area and Caesar ordered to Illyricum A. Gabinius (*cos.* 58 B.C.), who had been an active partisan of Pompeius many years before. Late in the summer of 48 B.C. Gabinius marched overland to Illyricum around the Adriatic with fifteen cohorts and three thousand cavalry, the first occasion a Roman army is known to have attempted this difficult journey.[5] After entering the territory of the Delmatae he was ambushed in a deep river gorge (probably the Čikola) near Synodion, and lost five of his cohorts with their standards.[6] He persevered in his advance and eventually reached Salona, probably in midwinter 48–47 B.C. Supplies were short and he was forced to continue campaigning

---

[1] Caes., *BC*, iii, 9; Dio, xlii, 11; Orosius, *Hist.*, vi, 15, 8–9.

[2] The Bellum Octavianum is described in *Bell. Alex.*, 42–7.

[3] On his career, F. Münzer, *RE*, 4 (1901), 1624, n. 8.

[4] The inhabitants of the later colony Iader, see p. 206 ff.

[5] *Bell. Alex.*, 43; Appian, *Ill.*, 12, cf. 25, 27; *BC*, ii, 58–9, Dio, xlii, 11; Plut., *Ant.*, 7; Cic., *Epp. ad Att.*, xi, 16, 1 (2 June 47). The last part of Gabinius' route to Salona was known later as the *via Gabiniana*, below, p. 453.

[6] Synodion or Sinotion (Strabo, vii, 5, 5) was captured by Octavianus in 34 B.C., p. 54, and was probably at Balijina Glavica near the later city Magnum. The standards taken from Gabinius were also recovered.

'iisdem temporibus' appears to link the defeat of Curio in mid-August with the capture of Massilia after the victory over Afranius and Petreius, which was mid-September at the earliest. The coincidence between the defeats of Antonius and Curio is suggested by Lucan's dating of the former to the summer solstice (iv, 526 f.), which would have occurred in August on the calendar then in use. For the topography of the campaign see G. Veith, *SB*, 267 ff.

against the Delmatae around Salona, suffering many casualties. His losses are given by Caesar as four tribunes, thirty-eight centurions, and more than 2,000 infantry, figures which probably include the Synodion disaster recorded by Appian. Early in 47 B.C. Gabinius died after a long illness, and the Pompeians prepared to renew the attack on the other commander Q. Cornificius, now isolated further south. The latter was too far from the Caesarian armies in Cisalpine Gaul and sent a desperate appeal for assistance to P. Vatinius at Brundisium, who was in charge of the wounded troops Caesar had left behind after crossing to Epirus. With great energy Vatinius created a makeshift fleet and crossed the Adriatic with the veterans in spring 47 B.C. At the time M. Octavius, who had returned to the area with his fleet, was besieging Caesar's stronghold (*praesidium*) at Epidaurum. This was probably the main base of Cornificius, who does not appear to have ever made any contact with Gabinius' force at Salona further north.[1] With more ships from Achaea Vatinius defeated the Pompeian fleet in a narrow channel near the island Tauris, probably Šipan north of Dubrovnik.[2] Octavius then withdrew 'to the harbour from which he had set out before the battle', where he remained for three days. He then collected his supporters from Issa and abandoned the Adriatic to continue the struggle in other areas of the Mediterreanean. His task of rescue completed, Vatinius returned to Italy and held his consulship late in 47 B.C.[3]

Q. Cornificius did not remain long in his command, and in the next year he is found serving Caesar in Cilicia.[4] His successor was P. Sulpicius Rufus who was hailed *imperator* and awarded a thanksgiving (*supplicatio*).[5] During his command in Illyricum he received a letter from Cicero asking if he could help in tracing Dionysius, one of his slaves who had run away (probably when Cicero was in the Pompeian camp two years before) and was last seen by a friend, probably a trader, called M. Bolanus in the settlement at Narona. Sulpicius failed to find Dionysius, and Cicero was still seeking him in the following year when Vatinius was proconsul. There was clearly some fighting in Illyricum during Sulpicius' term, probably against the Delmatae: not long afterwards seven cohorts of legionary infantry are found fighting in Africa after 'fighting in the fleet with

[1] *Bell. Alex.*, 44. This is the earliest reference to Epidaurum. On the career of P. Vatinius, Gundel, *RE* 8A (1955), 495 ff., n. 3.

[2] Suggested by N. Štuk, *SB*, 275 f., although Veith, op. cit., proposes Šćedre (Italian Torčula), but this is too far north of Epidaurum. Tauris appears on the Peutinger Map between Pharos and Corcyra Nigra.

[3] Elected with Q. Fufius Calenus after Caesar's return from the east in September, *MRR*, 2, 286.

[4] Cic., *Epp. ad fam.*, xii, 17–19.

[5] Cic., *Epp. ad fam.*, xiii, 77, written in August 46 B.C. Sulpicius had been praetor in 48 B.C.

Vatinius and Sulpicius'.[1] Sulpicius remained only one year in Illyricum and in 45 B.C. he was succeeded by P. Vatinius, now sent as proconsul by Caesar against the Delmatae with three legions and a strong force of cavalry. He was instructed to claim the hostages and to exact the light tribute which they had offered to pay after the Pompeian defeat. According to Appian, the Illyrians were now disposed to seek Caesar's friendship, since they feared that some of the dictator's future expeditions, especially that rumoured against the Dacians and Getae, might involve them. When they heard about his murder, however, their reaction was to attack Vatinius and destroy five of his cohorts, killing one of his senatorial legates Baebius. After this the proconsul retreated with his army to Dyrrhachium which lay outside his province, and the Senate promptly transferred the troops to the forces of the assassin Brutus.[2] Clearly Appian's version is incomplete and quite a different light is thrown on his proconsulship by his correspondence with Cicero, with whom he appears to have enjoyed cordial relations, in spite of what the orator had once said about his character. Three letters from Vatinius and one from Cicero were written between 11 July 45 and January 44 B.C.[3] In the first Vatinius speaks of dispatches about his campaigns which he had sent already to the Senate, and he requests Cicero's support in his application for a thanksgiving when the discussion took place. In the same letter he tells Cicero that his runaway slave appears to have taken refuge among the (V)ardaei, and promised to find and return him if he was still in the province.[4] Vatinius wrote the letter from his base camp at Narona, which at this time was probably the most flourishing of the coastal settlements, probably already a *colonia*.[5]

The Senate granted Vatinius the thanksgiving. In the next letter, which is dated 5 December 45 B.C., he writes that as soon as he heard about the decision he moved out on campaign and captured six strongholds (*oppida*), one of which had to be captured no less than four times. He goes on to complain how frustrating it was to be forced to abandon all his conquests because the approach of winter, ended any hope of final victory that season.[6] The reference to winter conditions suggests that Vatinius was probably operating against the northern Delmatae beyond the main Dinaric ridge, where the climate is much worse than the coastal hinterland in the south. The last letter, which was addressed to Cicero early in 44 B.C., reveals an embittered Vatinius complaining about Caesar's refusal to grant him the triumph which he believes he has earned. He blames the refusal on the gross underestimation of the power of the Delmatae generally current at Rome: they have sixty strongholds (*oppida*), not twenty as

---

[1] *Bell. Afr.*, 10.   [2] Appian, *Ill.*, 13.
[3] Cic., *Epp. ad fam.*, v, 9, 10a, 10b. Cicero's reply, v, 11.
[4] v, 9 (dated 11 July 45 B.C.).   [5] Below, p. 245 ff.   [6] v, 10b.

was commonly supposed.[1] This correspondence with Cicero corrects the impression given by Appian, who suggests that Vatinius' difficulties began only after the death of Caesar was known abroad.

After the Ides of March Vatinius found himself isolated with an army which, according to Dio,[2] did not have a good opinion of its commander, an attitude which is understandable after winter campaigns against the Delmatae under a general desperately seeking a triumph. He remained in his province until late in 44 or early in 43 B.C., when he left for Dyrrhachium and held it against the forces of M. Brutus, but his troops were glad to take their leave of him and joined the other side.[3] Vatinius eventually enjoyed his triumph, but not before an interval of eighteen months (31 July 42 B.C.).[4] There seems good reason to believe the claims of Vatinius, and that he had broken the power of the Delmatae. Certainly Octavianus was able to operate in their territory a decade later with no great risk, although he wisely remained south of the Dinara. In the long run, however, any campaigns mounted solely from the Adriatic would make little headway into the interior. Pacification of the interior depended upon a much wider appreciation of geography than was current in the later decades of the Republic.

The division of the Roman World made at Brundisium in 40 B.C. gave to Octavianus the western provinces, apart from Africa, and to M. Antonius the East. The line of demarcation between their commands was fixed at the old Illyrian capital Scodra, emphasizing how great a physical and psychological barrier the mountains of Montenegro and Northern Albania still remained.[5] Command in Macedonia, Antonius' only major European province, was given to C. Asinius Pollio, the consul of 40 B.C., through whose efforts of mediation the quarrelling Triumvirs had been induced to come together at Brundisium. As proconsul in Macedonia he began operations against the Parthini, who still lived in the hinterland of Dyrrhachium.[6] The object was to keep the legions usefully, and if possible gainfully, employed by winter manoeuvres instead of dangerous idleness in winter quarters. The Parthini were chosen for this attention because they had recently shown a strong attachment to the cause of M. Brutus. Pollio defeated them in a few battles and celebrated a triumph over them

[1] v, 10a (written early 44 B.C.).
[2] Dio, xlvii, 21, 6.
[3] Appian, *Ill.*, 13; cf Liv., *Per.*, cviii; Appian, *BC*, iv, 75; Cic., *Philip.*, x, 13; Plut., *Brutus*, 25; Vell. Pat., ii, 69, 3–4.
[4] *Inscr. It.*, XIII, 1, 86, 342 f., 567 f.
[5] Dio, xlviii, 28, 4; cf. 1, 6, 4–5, and Appian, *BC*, v, 65, mentioning Scodra.
[6] There is no doubt about the location of the Parthini, Strabo, vii, 7, 8; Plin., *HN*, iii, 145, etc. For the inscriptions referring to the Partheni in the Morava valley on the Dalmatian–Moesian border, see below, p. 165.

on 25 October of 39 or 38 B.C.[1] Other writers connect Pollio with a war against the Delmatae: Florus records that he confiscated their flocks, weapons, and lands, while Horace addresses him in an Ode as *Delmaticus*.[2] Florus is a notoriously unreliable and confused source, and Horace was employing a well known triumphal title, in preference to the technically correct but hardly flattering *Parthinicus*. Pollio cannot have operated against the Delmatae as Antonius' proconsul in Macedonia, since the people were far to the north and well within the territories of Octavianus. Finally scholiasts on Virgil's Fourth Eclogue explain the name of Pollio's son Saloninus by making the former capture Salona and name his newborn son after the event. This is an invention: at this time Saloninus does not derive from the city, for which the adjective is Salonitanus. There is no evidence to connect Pollio with Salona or to suggest that he ever fought against the Delmatae.[3]

[1] Dio, xlviii, 41, 7; Appian, *BC*, v, 75; *Inscr. It.*, XIII, 1, 86, 342. The triumph was probably held in the earlier year since Dio, loc. cit., implies that the campaign was brief. With the booty he obtained Pollio rebuilt the Hall of Liberty (*Atrium Libertatis*) at Rome, MRR, 2, 387–9.
[2] Florus, ii, 25; Hor., *Carm.*, ii, 1, 16.
[3] Thus R. Syme, *CQ*, 31 (1937), 39 ff. For the ethnic of Salona, cf. *L. Valerius Acutus Salonit-(anus)*, a diploma witness in 70, XVI, 11; cf. III, 2108, 8804, Steph. Byz. s.v. For the scholiast references, *PIR*², A 1241. Later Saloninus may be linked with Salona; see below p. 334 n- 1.

Chapter 5
The Augustan Conquest (35 B.C.–A.D. 9)

Three series of campaigns established Roman control over the Western Balkans, with a frontier line along the river Danube. These were Octavianus' operations against the Iapodes, Pannonians, and the Delmatae in 35–33 B.C., the Bellum Pannonicum of 13–9 B.C., and the suppression of the great rebellion in A.D. 6–9. As a result Rome secured control of the strategic route which linked Northern Italy with the principal Roman centres along the Middle and Lower Danube, as well as with Asia Minor and the eastern frontier. This route, which passed through Siscia, Sirmium (Mitrovica), and Serdica (Sofia), formed the vital overland bridge between the eastern and western halves of the Roman world, and when it was severed by barbarian invasion at the end of the fourth century A.D. East and West soon went their separate ways. A more immediate result of the campaigns was the transformation of the Roman position in the area from the two quite unconnected proconsular commands in Illyricum and Macedonia into a vast area reaching to the Danube and governed by consular legates of the emperor, controlling a combined army of more than seven legions. From it were formed the three great Danubian provinces of Moesia (between Thrace and the Lower Danube), Lower Illyricum (between the Save and the Middle Danube), and Upper Illyricum (between the Save and the Adriatic). Moesia first appears shortly before A.D. 6; the others resulted from the subdivision of the great Augustan province of Illyricum soon after A.D. 9, and were soon to be known by their permanent names Pannonia and Dalmatia. The conquest and organization of the province Dalmatia, the triangle of territory enclosing Dalmatian karst, Bosnian forest, and Montenegrin mountains, was merely a part of the greatest military achievement of Augustus' long Principate, and can be fully appreciated only in the context of the grand strategy employed by Augustus and his military advisers. It was an achievement largely ignored by the poets of the age, yet unlike Germany or the East it was not an undertaking that could be pursued or neglected as the local conditions changed. If the Danubian area and the lands to the south were to be made safe and linked firmly to the rest of the Empire the conquest of Illyricum was a necessity.[1]

The principal source for the operations of Octavianus in 35–33 B.C. is the commander-in-chief himself. Much of the *Illyrike* of Appian was devoted to a narrative of these wars, for which he drew extensively on the Memoirs of Augustus.[2] Part of this consisted of a transcript of the official summary (*relatio*) which Octavianus presented to the Senate at the end of the war, to which he added a detailed account of his own experiences in the field as the army commander. After his brief digression on the Pannonian peoples Appian remarks: 'This much I have been able to discover about the early history of the Illyrians and the Pannonians, and not even in the commentaries of the second Caesar, called Augustus, could I find anything earlier concerning the Pannonians. Nevertheless I think that other peoples besides those mentioned had previously come under Roman control. In what manner I do not know, for Augustus did not write about the doings of others so much as his own, telling how he brought back those who had revolted, making them resume the payment of tribute, how he conquered all the tribes that inhabit the summits of the Alps, barbarous and warlike peoples, who often plundered neighbouring Italy'.[3] These Alpine peoples included the Salassi of the Dora Baltea around Aosta, notorious for their raids on Italy and their obstruction of the routes across the mountains to Gaul. In the parts of his Memoirs used by Appian, Augustus included accounts of operations conducted against them at this time on his behalf by M. Valerius Messalla Corvinus (*cos. suff.* 31 B.C.) in 34 B.C. and by C. Antistius Vetus (*cos.* 30 B.C.) in 35 B.C.[4] In his records of the operations to the north and east of Italy, Appian's reliance on Augustus is complete, unlike Dio's, whose account

---

[1] Apart from the recent detailed studies of individual campaigns by Schmitthenner, Koestermann, and Pašalić (see below), the last general discussion of these wars is by R. Syme, *CAH*, 10, 340 ff.; cf. J. Wilkes, *UBHJ*, 10 (1965), 1 ff.

[2] Appian, *Ill.*, 14–28; Dio, xlix, 34–8, 43, 8; Strabo, iv, 6, 10, vii 5, 2–4; Liv., *Per.*, cxxxi–ii; Vell. Pat., ii, 78, 2; Florus, ii, 23; Suet., *Aug.*, 20; Orosius, *Hist.*, vi, 19, 3.

[3] Appian, *Ill.*, 14–15 and n. 2 above, p. 34.

[4] Antistius: Appian, *Ill.*, 17; cf. Strabo, iv, 6, 7, probably as legate in Transalpine Gaul, *MRR*, 2, 407. Dio, xlix, 38, 3, places the operations of Corvinus between Octavianus' operations against the Pannonians (35 B.C.) and the Delmatae (34 B.C.). In 35 B.C. he was in Illyricum fighting against the Iapodes in the Lika, *Pan. Mess.*, 106–17 mentioning the Arupini; cf. Schmitthenner, 234 ff.

differs on a number of significant points, especially with regard to the reasons for the campaigns and the planning of further exploits. After experiencing considerable difficulty in composing a coherent narrative of the Roman wars in Illyria (see the passage quoted above) it was with some relief that Appian turned to the Memoirs of Augustus and filled his pages with accounts of the Emperor's exploits.

The motives behind Octavianus' military exploits are clear, and place them firmly in the Republican tradition of operations undertaken for reasons which had little to do with the area involved. His personal performance as a field commander fell far below the standard that was expected from the adopted son of the great Julius, particularly in the recent war against Sex. Pompeius in Sicily, and he possessed little of the magnetism of the dictator fostered by daring exploits on campaign. Octavianus realized that his legions required some realistic training and some harsh discipline under campaigning conditions to remove the smouldering dissatisfaction which could well escalate into a serious mutiny at any time. Velleius is specific on this point and treats all the operations in 35–33 B.C. as manoeuvres for the benefit of army and general alike, with an eye to the coming struggle against M. Antonius. On more than one occasion Octavianus felt it necessary to expose his person in the thick of the battle, and even to suffer wounds which endeared him to the mass of the troops, especially when they heard that he was not dead as was once feared. Such were the distasteful devices to which Octavianus found himself driven in order to cultivate a personality that came naturally to a Julius or an Antonius. Over a wide arc extending from the Western Alps, across the northeast of Italy to the Dalmatian coast to the limit of his territory at Scodra, some military operations were necessary, especially against the Salassi and the Iapodes, who in the previous twenty years had twice overrun Aquileia and plundered the colony at Tergeste (Trieste). Across the Adriatic some of the old Roman settlements in the territory of the Delmatae had by now been raised to the status of colonies, a reward for their support of the Caesarian cause in the Civil War. Naturally they looked to Caesar's heir for support and protection against the Delmatae, who had not laid down their arms for more than a decade and still held the standards captured from A. Gabinius in 48 B.C. Most urgent was the need for some action to protect Italy from the northeast, the easiest entry for an invader. Since the death of king Burebista about ten years before the threat from the expanding Dacians had receded, but many remembered the anxious months during the Civil War when an invasion seemed possible. The knowledge that Caesar was planning some operations against them before his death passed the task to Octavianus as an inheritance. In the period before Actium both of the surviving Triumvirs courted the

Dacians with diplomatic promises, with the object of preventing the other side from obtaining their help as a diversionary raiding force in the coming struggle. There was indeed no shortage of military tasks for the young revolutionary.[1]

In the summary of his campaigns delivered to the Senate, Octavianus began with a claim aimed directly at his rival in the East: 'He informed the Senate, by way of contrast with Antonius' slothfulness, that he had freed Italy from the savage tribes that had so often raided it'.[2] Then he listed the names of the peoples conquered, or who had submitted to him, under three headings according to the amount of resistance they had offered to him. Those in the first list were overcome 'with one stroke', the second group demanded 'a greater effort', and finally those who 'caused him most difficulty'. Limited to his own exploits, the narrative in Augustus' Memoirs concerns only the peoples listed under the third heading, and it is possible to trace his journeys on the map with reasonable accuracy. Many of the other peoples listed, most of those in the first group, and some of those in the second, are names not attested elsewhere and were probably communities of the better known larger peoples, while others were far removed from the war and their conquest probably consisted of formal submission through envoys sent to Octavianus' camp.[3]

The people overcome 'with one blow' were the Oxyaei, Pertheenetae, Bathiatae, Taulantii, Cambaei, Cinambri, Meromeni, and Pyrissaei. Most of these can be matched with a group of small peoples placed by Pliny in the southeast of Dalmatia near to the coast between the Narenta and the Drilo.[4] The second group, those conquered 'with a greater effort', were the Docleatae, Carni, Interphrurini, Naresii, Glintidiones, Taurisci, Hippasini, Bessi, Meliteni, Corcyreni, Liburni, and the Cisalpine Iapodes. All except three of these are well-

---

[1] Vell. Pat., ii, 78, 2: 'Caesar per haec tempora, ne res disciplinae inimicissimum otium corrumperet militem, crebris in Illyrico Delmatiaque expeditionibus patentia periculorum bellique exercitus experentia durabat exercitum'; cf. Dio, xlix, 36, 1 in the same vein, and adding the economic motive of supporting his army at the expense of an alien people. After the war in Sicily Octavianus had faced a serious mutiny of troops claiming discharges and their rewards, Appian, *BC*, v, 128–9; Dio, xlix, 34, 3–5. There is no evidence that Octavianus envisaged his advance to the northeast as a military precaution against M. Antonius. It is interesting to note that one of the consuls nominated by Octavianus to replace the departed Antonian consuls of 32 B.C. was L. Cornelius Cinna, grandson of Sulla's enemy who had planned similar training campaigns across the Adriatic, R. Syme, *RR*, 279, n. 3.

[2] Appian, *Ill.*, 16.

[3] For the locations and identifications of the peoples listed see p. 154 ff.

[4] Appian, *Ill.*, 16: Ὀξαίους μὲν δὴ καὶ Περθεηνάτας καὶ βαθιάτας καὶ Ταυλαντίους καὶ Καμβάίους καὶ Κινάμβρους καὶ Μερομέννους καὶ Πυρισσαίους εἷλε δι' ὅλης πείρας; cf. Plin., *HN*, iii, 143.

known peoples who can be located precisely. In the extreme north the Carni, centred on Iulium Carnicum (Zuglio) and Carnium (Kranj), dwelt astride the modern frontier between Italy and Slovenia; the powerful Celtic Taurisci, mentioned also by Dio, were their neighbours on the north and northeast. Their submission probably took place during the advance against the Iapodes and the Pannonians in 35 B.C.[1] According to Appian, after the submission of the Taurisci two neighbouring peoples, the Hippasini and the Bessi, followed their example. The first name is completely unknown, while the latter are only known as a powerful people of Thrace far away to the east in the Hebrus (Marica) valley.[2] The remainder of the list presents few problems: the Docleatae inhabited the later city Doclea in the southeast; the Naresii (in the Narenta valley) and the Glintidiones (further north) were neighbours of the Delmatae whose submission took place in 33 B.C. The island communities of the Corcyreni (Corcyra Nigra) and the Meliteni (Melite) were attacked by the fleet and their people enslaved 'because they practised piracy', as also were some of the Liburnians. These attacks were made when the fleet was sailing northwards along the Dalmatian coast on its voyage from Sicily. Apart from this the peoples fall clearly into two geographic groups, one in the northeast and the other in Central Dalmatia, which bordered on the main centres of opposition. These are named in the third group, those 'who caused him most difficulty', where are included the major peoples which figure in the operations directed by Octavianus in person, and which he described in considerable detail for his later Memoirs. Examination reveals nothing misleading about Augustus' record of his own campaigns, regarding either their scope or achievements.[3]

Octavianus probably began his advance in 35 B.C. against the Iapodes from the Liburnian port Senia (Senj) and crossed the Velebit to enter the Lika polje which was inhabited by the Cisalpine Iapodes.[4] The Moentini of Monetium (Brinje) and the Avendeatae of Avendo (Crkvinje near Otočač) surrendered at

---

[1] Appian, *Ill.*, 16: ἔργῳ δὲ μείζονι ἐλήφθησαν, καὶ φόρους ὅσους ἐξέλιπον ἠναγκάσθησαν ἀποδοῦναι, Δοκλεᾶταί τε καὶ Κάρνοι καὶ Ἰντερφρουρῖνοι καὶ Ναρήσιοι καὶ Γλιντιδίωνες καὶ Ταυρίσκοι. On the Carni, *RE*, 3 (1899), 1598 f., and the Taurisci, G. Alföldy, *Historia*, 15 (1966), 224 ff.

[2] Appian clearly implies that both bordered the Taurisci, and therefore the Hippasini cannot be the Hemasini of Plin., *HN*, iii, 143, near the Adriatic.

[3] Appian, *Ill.*, 17: μάλιστα δ' ἠνώχλησαν αὐτὸν Σαλασσοί τε καὶ Ἰάποδες οἱ πέραν Ἄλπεων καὶ Σεγεστανοὶ καὶ Δαλματαὶ καὶ Δαισιοί (*var.* τε Δέσιοί τε) καὶ Παίονες .... The *Dasioi* are not known, and Schweighäuser (ed. 1785) proposed to emend Δαισιτᾶται, the people around Sarajevo (below, p. 170), but these are nowhere recorded in the detailed record of the operations, and are far removed from the areas involved.

[4] For the movements of Octavianus and the sites involved in 35–33 B.C. see G. Veith, *Feldzüge*, etc., *passim*.

his approach, but the more numerous Arupini of Arupium (Prozor) at first held out in their fortress on the Vital hill but later retreated into the forest. Octavianus did not destroy their stronghold, but allowed them to reoccupy it after they had made submission.[1] From there he moved eastwards across the Alps (Velika and Mala Kapela, Plješevica) to reach the Transalpine Iapodes. To avoid the danger of ambush in the densely wooded countryside Octavianus marched his force in separate columns, advancing simultaneously along the valleys and the heights. From the Lika polje his route followed the line of the modern road from Senj to Karlovac on the river Kulpa, the Roman Colapis; along this line were the two principal strongholds of the Transalpine Iapodes, Terponus (Gornje Modruš) and Metulum (Vinčica Hill near Ogulin)[2] The first of these was taken with little difficulty and, as earlier with the Arupini, he did not destroy the fortifications but allowed the inhabitants to remain there after they had made submission. If he could obtain some satisfactory 'submission' Octavianus was clearly happy to move on and avoid time-wasting sieges of such places. The political centre of the Transalpine Iapodes was Metulum which lay in the more open country near Josipdol, and here Octavianus came up against organized resistance. The first Roman assault was brushed aside and both sides prepared for a full-scale siege, for which the Iapodes had managed to capture some Roman siege equipment from the disintegrating army of D. Brutus after Mutina in 43 B.C., and used it to harass the enemy lines. Octavianus decided on another mass assault, but this also failed and the commander was slightly wounded. The fall of Metulum was due not to the Roman efforts but to dissensions among the Iapodes, and even when the main part of the fortress had been handed over some preferred to fight on in the citadel. Eventually it was completely destroyed by fire and not a trace of the defences remained, 'although it had been the greatest settlement (*polis*) in those parts'. The ensuing surrender of the Iapodes marked the first occasion on which the Transalpine communities had been brought under Roman control. After the main force had moved on towards the Pannonians in the Save valley, the Poseni, one of the Iapodian communities, rebelled but they were crushed by the garrison left by Octavianus in their country under M. Helvius, who killed the leaders and enslaved the rest.[3]

Next Octavianus devastated the territory of the Pannonians in the Colapis

---

[1] On their locations and later cities see p. 264 ff.

[2] Appian, *Ill.*, 18 ff.; Dio, xlix, 35; Florus, ii, 23; cf. Veith, 29 ff. During the twenties a fierce controversy raged over the site of Metulum; cf. T. Rice Holmes, *Architect, etc.*, 1, 226 f. The point is settled by III, 10060; cf. p. 266.

[3] Some of the retreating army of D. Brutus reached the Iapodes after Mutina, Dio, xlvi, 53, 2. When Octavianus was wounded at Metulum the army believed that he had been trapped by the

valley for eight days until he reached Segesta, which lay at the confluence with the Save. According to Augustus' Memoirs, 'the Romans twice attacked the country of the Segestani, but obtained no hostages nor anything else, for which reason the Segestani became very arrogant'. One of these attacks is probably the successful expedition by the consuls of 119 B.C., Aurelius Cotta and Metellus, already recorded by Appian.[1] The place is described as 'strongly protected by the river (Save) and with a very large ditch encircling it'. Dio records that this encircling ditch was constructed much later: 'for while they (Segestani) possessed strong walls also, they placed their trust wholly in two navigable rivers. The one named the Colops (Colapis) flows past the very line of the wall and empties into the Save not very far distant. It has now encircled the entire city, for Tiberius gave it this shape by constructing a great canal through which it returns to its original course. But at that time between the Colops, on the one hand, which flowed past the very walls, and the Save on the other, which flowed at a little distance, the gap which had been left had been fortified by palisades and ditches.' Appian's description does not include the ditch dug by Tiberius, probably during one of his early campaigns in the region in 12 B.C.[2]

Apart from the description of Segesta, the accounts of Appian and Dio differ markedly about the motive for Octavianus' attack and the role that was planned for the ships involved in the campaign. According to the former Octavianus ordered ships to be constructed for him on the Save, not for the attack on Segesta, but to transport his supply columns to the Danube for his next operations against the Dacians and the Bastarnae.[3] The capture of Segesta is seen merely as a preliminary to the major advance against the Dacians, for which it was vital as a base. At first he even asked the people if they were willing to let him use their city for this purpose. The ruling group had actually agreed to this, when the common people shut the gates against him and he was compelled to take it by force.[4] On the other hand, the version of Dio is totally different: 'he [Octavianus]

---

[1] Cotta and Metellus: Appian, *Ill.*, 11, and p. 33. The Pannonians involved were the Colapiani, Plin., *HN*, iii, 147 f.

[2] Appian, *Ill.*, 22; Dio, xlix, 37, 3–4; cf. G. Veith, p. 47, for plan of the city.

[3] Appian, *Ill.*, 23.

[4] One cannot rule out, however, some political contact with the Dacians at this time. Antonian propaganda may be responsible for the story about Octavianus offering a marriage alliance with Cotiso, Suet., *Aug.*, 63; cf. M. P. Charlesworth, *CQ*, 27 (1933), 173 ff.

Iapodes. Augustus' description of the incident, as preserved in Appian, matches in many details the heroic episode involving Alexander the Great at the attack against the city of the Mallians in the Indus valley, when he also was trapped in the fortress with a handful of friends, Arrian, *Anab.*, vi, 9 ff. Nothing is known about M. Helvius, although R. Syme, *RR*, 251, n. 3, speculates on a possible connection with the poet M. Helvius Cinna.

had no complaint to bring against them, not having been wronged in any way, but he wanted to give his soldiers practice at the expense of an alien people, for he regarded every demonstration against a weaker people as just, when it was acceptable to one with superior force'. In Dio's version the ships he used were obtained from 'allies in the vicinity'.[1] They had been towed along the Danube (Ister), up the Save and then into the Colapis where he attacked the Pannonians. The assault was a failure and was repulsed with heavy losses among the troops and sailors, including the admiral Menodorus (Menas) once a freedman of Sex. Pompeius.[2] Only when the Segestani realized that they were cut off from any relief did they surrender their city after a blockade lasting thirty days. The allied ships mentioned by Dio may have come from the Taurisci, and other Norican allies, and were probably taken down the Drave into the Danube for short stretch between Osijek and Belgrade, and then westward back up the Save to Segesta. After the capture of the city some Roman troops may have accompanied the ships on their return journey, thus justifying Octavianus' claim in his speech to his troops before Actium that they 'had subdued the Pannonians and advanced as far as the Ister'.[3] After the surrender Octavianus walled off a part of the city and left a garrison of twenty-five cohorts under Fufius Geminus and returned to Rome. Some time later a counter attack by the Segestani caused Octavianus to return hurriedly, but when he reached the scene he found that his garrison had retrieved the position.[4]

In the following season Octavianus switched his area of operations to Dalmatia. The Dacians and Bastarnae were no longer in his mind. In Appian's account the change is hardly noted. Since the Segestani were no longer causing trouble, 'therefore Augustus turned his forces against the Delmatae'.[5] They had not faced Roman arms since the campaigns of P. Vatinius ten years before, and they still held the five cohort standards taken from A. Gabinius in 48 B.C. at Synodion: 'since then they had not laid down their arms for ten years'.[6] To face the attack by Octavianus the Delmatae combined their forces under the general Verzo, who gathered an army of more than twelve thousand men. Dio records that the operations were begun by M. Agrippa; this was probably early in 34 B.C.

[1] Dio, xlix, 36, 1. He mentions neither Bastarnae nor Dacians, but notes that Octavianus planned a visit to Britain, and had only reached Gaul when recalled by the rebellion of the Segestani, xlix, 38, 2.

[2] *MRR*, 2, 410.

[3] Dio, l, 26, 3–4.

[4] Appian, *Ill.*, 24. Geminus was probably father of C. Fufius Geminus, suffect consul in 2 B.C.

[5] Appian, *Ill.*, 24, following directly after the suppression of the Segestani.

[6] Appian, *Ill.*, 25.

F

since he was present at the attack on Metulum in the previous year.[1] The first objective was Promona, once a Liburnian stronghold but captured by the Delmatae more than twenty years before.[2] Verzo established himself there and placed the main part of his force in the central stronghold,[3] while the remainder were sent to hold the surrounding hills which overlooked the Roman positions. Octavianus began to organize a blockade of the site, and sent an assault to test the main stronghold on the principal hill. A simultaneous attack on some of the smaller garrisons caused panic, and the outlying garrisons retreated within the main defences to avoid being cut off from their comrades. Only this and two of the smaller posts were held when a relieving force of the Delmatae appeared under Testimus, but Octavianus was able to drive this off and almost immediately captured Promona because of the rashness of the defenders, even before his own lines of circumvallation were complete. In the ensuing fighting a third of the population was slain. Some attempted a stand in the citadel but this was soon taken, although not before a Roman cohort had suffered the field punishment of decimation by lot (*decimatio*) after it had been caught off guard. Verzo perished in the fighting and Testimus ordered the rest of the Delmatae to scatter into the country.[4]

Next Octavianus captured Synodion at the edge of the forest in which Gabinius was ambushed.[5] After setting it on fire he advanced along a deep gorge, probably following the same route as Gabinius along the Čikola valley, avoiding an ambush by marching his forces in parallel columns along the valley and on the heights, as in the previous year in the country of the Iapodes. During the attack on Setovia (in the Sutina gorge)[6] Octavianus was struck a painful blow on the knee by a stone during a skirmish against a relieving force; after this he returned to Rome to hold the consulship for 33 B.C., leaving Statilius Taurus (*cos.* 37 B.C.) to take charge of the siege.[7] Strabo adds that he also captured Ninia (perhaps Knin on the river Titius), but this was probably achieved by a column sent away from the main force about the time he was operating around Promona.[8]

---

[1] Dio, xlix, 38, 3. Agrippa at Metulum, Appian, *Ill.*, 20.   [2] Appian, *Ill.*, 12.

[3] On the topography, G. Veith, 63 ff., also W. Büttler, 21 *BerRGK* (1931), 196 ff., nos. 33–6.

[4] Appian, *Ill.*, 26; Dio, xlix, 38, 4; Strabo, vii, 5, 5.

[5] Appian, *Ill.*, 27; Strabo, vii, 5, 5, refers to his capture of 'Old and New Sinotion'.

[6] Appian, *Ill.*, 27; cf. Rav., iv, 19: *Situa* (*Citua*). A *dec(urio) Set(oviae ?)* is attested at Rider, below, p. 244.

[7] He must have joined Octavianus in Illyricum after his African triumph on 30 June 34 B.C., *Inscr. It.*, XIII, 1, p. 569, and remained there until the end of the following year.

[8] Strabo, vii, 5, 5. He does not say that Octavianus captured all the strongholds listed but only the two Sinotion strongholds to which the phrase ἃς ἐνέπρησεν ὁ Σεβαστός refers, G. Alföldy, *Bevölkerung*, 123, n. 44.

Octavianus resigned the consular fasces on the same day he took them up and, after appointing L. Autronius Paetus as his replacement (*suffectus*), returned to Illyricum where he received the surrender of the Delmatae, now suffering the effects of the winter blockade organized by Statilius Taurus.[1] They handed over seven hundred hostages, and returned the standards taken from Gabinius. These were placed in the Portico of Octavius in Rome which was rebuilt with booty taken in the campaign.[2] The Delmatae also promised 'to pay the tribute which had been owing since the time of Caesar, and henceforward they were obedient'. Formal submissions were also collected from other peoples in the area. When he moved against the Derbani, neighbours of the Delmatae on the northeast, they asked forgiveness, promised to hand over hostages, and to pay the arrears of tribute. Others he could not reach, however, because of his injury, and no submissions or hostages were received from them.[3] The modest achievements in these years were used by Octavianus in his propaganda against Antonius before Actium, but he did not celebrate his triumph until 29 B.C. along with those over Egypt and Antonius (Actium).[4]

With the detailed narrative lifted by Appian from the Memoirs of Augustus it is surprising that the scope and achievements of these campaigns have been the subject of controversy. The movements of the commander are clearly described, and the topographical study of G. Veith has made it possible to trace his route on the map with accuracy.[5] In 35 B.C. he marched through the Iapodes and captured Segesta (Siscia): in the next year he fought and conquered the Delmatae on the central Dalmatian coast and received submissions from some of their smaller neighbours, but nowhere did he cross the Dinaric Alps. In addition he, or his legates, received the formal surrender of some peoples bordering on Northeast Italy and another group of smaller peoples in Southeast Dalmatia near the coast. In 1932 E. Swoboda, following upon the earlier studies of N. Vulić, argued that

---

[1] Appian, *Ill.*, 28.

[2] Appian, *Ill.*, 28; cf. Dio, xlix, 43, 8. The portico was built by Cn. Octavius (cos. 165 B.C.) who commanded the navy of Aemilius Paullus in 167 B.C. against Perseus, *MRR*, 1, 434, rather than the later Augustan Portico of Octavia, dedicated to the sister of Augustus. The recovery of the standards (*signa*) is recorded, along with others from Spain and Gaul, in *Res Gestae*, 29.

[3] Appian, *Ill.*, 28. They are probably the Deuri, a small people in the Salona *conventus*, below p. 170.

[4] The war is recorded by the Fasti of Venusia under 34 B.C., *Inscr. It.*, XIII, 1, 254 (*bellum Hiluricum*). The triumph in 29 B.C. is generally called Illyrian (Appian, *Ill.*, 28) or *Delmaticum* (*Fasti Barb.*, 'de Dalmatis' on 13 August 29 B.C., *Inscr. It.*, XIII, 1 344; cf. Suet., *Aug.*, 20: 'per se gessit (bellum) Delmaticum adhuc adulescens', 22: 'Delmaticum triumphum egit.'). Dio speaks of his triumph over Pannonians, Delmatae, and Iapodes, li, 21, 5.

[5] J. Kromayer, *Hermes*, 33 (1898), 1 ff., G. Veith, *Feldzüge, etc.*; cf. Schmitthenner, 189, n. 1.

these campaigns conquered an area equivalent to the later province Dalmatia.[1] The views were based on vague statements of Appian summing up the operations: 'Thus Augustus subdued the whole of Illyris, not only those parts that had revolted from the Romans, but those that had never before been under their rule'.[2] To the third-century historian Dio, who had governed both Pannonia and Dalmatia at various times in his career, the terms Pannonia and Dalmatia (which he uses throughout the narrative) were synonymous with the later provinces. Before these concepts were planted firmly in the minds of historians, some more correct descriptions of the area and its peoples, at least from the ethnic point of view, can be recognized. For instance Appian locates the Pannonians in wooded country between the Iapodes and the Dardanians, that is the interior of the later province Dalmatia, while Illyris was a term still restricted to the Iapodes and other peoples near the coast extending south to Epirus, including the Delmatae, Liburnians, Derbani, and all the other small peoples carefully listed in the dispatches of Octavianus. This limited concept of Illyris can only have been altered after the major conquests in 13–9 B.C., where there first emerges the Roman concept of Illyricum, extending from the Adriatic to the Middle Danube. The names of none of the great Pannonian peoples who inhabited the Bosnian valley and later were mostly included in Dalmatia (Maezaei, Ditiones, Daesitiates, etc.) appear in the narrative of Augustus' Memoirs. Their conquest did not even begin until the Bellum Pannonicum (13–9 B.C.) and they were still fighting in A.D. 9.[3]

For Caesar Octavianus the campaigns of 35–33 B.C. in Illyricum served their purpose. As with the exploits of his adoptive father in Gaul and Britian, the city of Rome was kept well informed about the attacks on enemies and marauders of Italy, and also about Octavianus' valiant wounds suffered in the thick of battle. As Dio attests, the successes of the first season were soon exploited. Late in 35 B.C. Octavianus deferred the triumph over the Iapodes and the Pannonians that had been offered to him, but he used the occasion to elevate the status of women in his family. Statues were decreed for Livia and Octavia and both ladies were awarded the tribunician sacrosanctity, which the Triumvir had already taken for himself after the victory over Sex. Pompeius in the previous year.[4] Yet his position at Rome was still far from assured. In the competition with Antonius in the matter of triumphs, those celebrated by his supporters T. Statilius Taurus over

---

[1] N. Vulić, *RSA*, 7 (1903), 489 ff.; *JRS*, 24 (1934), 163 ff.; E. Swoboda, *Octavian und Illyricum* (1932); cf. R. Syme, *JRS*, 23 (1933), 63 ff.   [2] Appian, *Ill.*, 28.
[3] Appian, *Ill.*, 22. On the Pannonian peoples, Strabo, vii, 5, 3, and below, p. 167 ff.
[4] Dio, xlix, 38, 1. Legally the honour was conferred on Octavia as the wife of Antonius, but there is no doubt that it was to the benefit of Octavianus, Schmitthenner, 218, n. 4.

Africa (30 June 34 B.C.) and C. Norbanus Flaccus (*cos.* 38 B.C.) over Spain (12 October 34 B.C.) were completely outshone by the brilliance of Antonius' great general C. Sosius (*cos.* 32 B.C.) over Judaea (3 September 34 B.C.).[1] The turning point for Octavianus came in the following year. Entering the consulship on the 1 January 33 B.C. Octavianus had full opportunity to tell the Senate and People about his campaigns over the last two years, contrasting his energy with the lethargy of Antonius. He emphasized the claim by leaving Rome immediately to return to Illyricum after resigning the consulship on the first day. In that year only his men held triumphs, while Octavianus himself was parading the recovered standards, contrasting them with the much more famous standards lost with Crassus at Carrhae in 53 B.C. and still in the hands of the Parthians. On 31 December 33 B.C. the Triumvirate legally expired and both consuls designated for the next year were Antonius' men, C. Sosius and Cn. Domitius Ahenobarbus. Using his prestige (*auctoritas*) and, more to the point, his veterans, Octavianus confronted the consuls in the Senate, and they fled to the East taking with them more than a third of the senators.[2]

In Illyricum the achievement of Octavianus was modest and solid rather than spectacular. The Iapodes and part of the Pannonians remained firmly under Roman control: moreover, the dangerous hostility of the Delmatae appears to have ceased for many years. On the other hand, little progress was made towards the annexation of the area which later formed the greater part of the province Dalmatia, nor are any of the later military dispositions in the karst hinterland between Burnum and Narona known to have been instituted in the years immediately following. On the coast colonies were established at Pola in Istria and Iader in Liburnia, and the older Caesarian colonies, Salona, Narona, and Epidaurum, were strengthened by new settlements.[3]

Once he had gained the initiative over Antonius the Illyricum campaigns were dropped from the propaganda of Octavianus. Had he chosen to continue extracting glory from his achievements, they could easily have acquired the same notoriety later attached to Claudius' exploits in Britain. Even the applauding poets of the next decade ignored the campaigns. The Panegyric of Messalla mentions only the operations of Messalla Corvinus against the Pannonians and the Iapodes (specifically the Arupini), nor does Virgil mention the campaigns

---

[1] *Inscr. It.*, XIII, 1, 342; cf. 569 (*Fasti Barberini*).

[2] Octavianus' triumphs in 33 B.C. were L. Marcius Philippus (*cos.* 38 B.C.), Ap. Claudius Pulcher (*cos.* 38 B.C.) both over Spain, L. Cornificius (*cos.* 35 B.C.) over Africa, *Inscr. It.*, XIII, loc. cit. Flight of senators: Dio, 1, 2, 3–7. Out of a total of one thousand, seven hundred senators fought for Octavianus at Actium, *Res Gestae*, 25.

[3] On *colonia Iulia Pietas Pola*, see A. Degrassi, *Confine*, 60 ff.

despite his numerous references to Actium and the Cantabrian War. In a poem published soon after Actium Propertius mentions Mutina, Philippi, the Sicilian campaign, and Actium, but nothing about Illyricum.[1] With the notable exception of Appian's *Illyrike,* none of the writers in later generations records the operations in the roll of great Roman conquests.[2]

Such were the last Republican campaigns across the Adriatic. True to those traditions they were conducted for many reasons, but virtually none of these concerned affairs in Illyricum, With the final victory over Antonius at Actium in 31 B.C. and the seizure of sole power on behalf of 'Tota Italia', Octavianus is transformed into Augustus (27 B.C.), a change involving far more than just a name. The disturbing memory of the great Caesar, so zealously cultivated in the last fifteen years, is relegated to the background for the good of the new order. As the ruthless and bloodthirsty young revolutionary is transformed into the father-figure honoured by all parties, so the partisan campaigner and privateer seen recently in Illyricum emerges as a far-seeing strategist evolving vast programmes of expansion and consolidation for the Empire. It mattered little now if the achievements appeared unspectacular: no longer was it necessary to dazzle the Roman populace with eastern conquests such as those of Cn. Pompeius, or thrilling accounts of dangerous campaigns beyond the ocean in Britain like those of Caesar. Augustus' message for the Roman World was Pax, symbolized by the closing of Janus' temple in 25 B.C. Until 19 B.C. Augustus was still distracted by successive political crises at Rome, but soon he could leave Rome safely for years and reside in cities within his territories such as Tarraco in Spain or Lugdunum in Gaul, organizing administration and planning campaigns to be conducted by his legates.

After Actium there was an urgent need to pacify the Alpine tribes whose raids were still causing disturbance to the cities of the Cisalpine plain. A beginning

---

[1] *Pan. Mess.*, 11. 106–17; Propert., ii, 1:

> 'Bella resque . . . memoravem Caesaris
>
> . . .
>
> Nam quotiens Mutinam aut, civilia busta, Philippos
> Aut canerem Siculae classica bella fugae
> Eversosque foros antiquae gentis Etruscae
> Et Ptolemaei litora capta Phari.'

[2] Liv., *Per.*, cxxxi (35/4 B.C.): 'Caesar conquered the Iapodes, Dalmatians, and Pannonians', and cxxxii (33 B.C.): 'he conquered the Dalmatians'; cf. Orosius, *Hist.*, vi, 19, 3: 'In wars Caesar conquered and pacified Illyricum, Pannonia, and part of Italy'; Suetonius, *Aug.*, 20, mentions the war (p. 55 above) but in his list of territory conquered 'Pannonia, Dalmatia with all Illyricum' follows after the Cantabrian War (27–5 B.C.). Velleius, ii, 90, 1, regarded 9 B.C. as the end of Dalmatian independence.

was made in the years before Actium by C. Antistius Vetus (*cos.* 30 B.C.) and Valerius Messalla Corvinus (*cos.* 31 B.C.). against the Salassi.[1] This tribe was finally dealt with in 25 B.C. by A. Terentius Varro Murena (*cos.* 23 B.C.) who devastated their settlements and sold 44,000 of them into slavery at Eporedia.[2] At the same time other commanders, including the later commander in Illyricum M. Vinicius (*cos.* 19 B.C.), were operating from the Gallic side, as Antistius Vetus had done when legate in Transalpine Gaul.[3] Next followed operations against peoples further east. In 17 or 16 B.C. P. Silius Nerva (*cos.* 20 B.C.) now proconsul in Illyricum attacked and subdued the Cammunes of the Val Camonica and the Venni (Vennones or Venostes) of the Upper Adige (Val Venosta, Vintschgau). During the absence of Silius in the west some Norican and Pannonian peoples invaded Istria but were defeated by his legates, and this was probably the pretext for the annexation of Noricum which took place soon afterwards.[4] The operations of 15 B.C. were more ambitious, when Augustus' younger stepson Drusus led the army of Illyricum northwards through the Central Alps, probably along the Val Venosta and into the Inn Valley across the Brenner Pass, where he joined his elder brother Tiberius who had been advancing eastwards from Gaul against the Vindelici of Bavaria and the Raetians.[5] The long-delayed pacification of the Alps was the first achievement of Augustus' own house, and it was commemorated by a triumphal monument at La Turbie on the hills behind Monaco. Here were recorded 'all the Alpine peoples who dwell between the upper and lower sea brought under the rule of the Roman people' in a list of forty-nine names.[6] By these operations Cisalpine Gaul was secured to Italy and would no longer require proconsuls with the legions from Illyricum to ward off invasions from the north; at the same time, the Alpine peoples were brought into closer contact with Cisalpine Gaul by attribution to the cities in the plain;[7] nevertheless a garrison was still needed north of the Alps among the Raetians.[8]

On the Lower Danube little progress was made during the last decades of the Republic. The army remained after Actium controlled by the proconsul in Macedonia, whose main task for more than a century had been to keep out the Thracian and Illyrian peoples (Scordisci, Dardanians, Bessi, Dentheletae, etc.) from Macedonia and Greece. Triumphs were frequently awarded but with little permanent gain.[9] In the extreme northeast Roman arms had reached the Greek

[1] P. 47 n. 4.   [2] Dio, liii, 25, 3–5; Strabo, iv, 6, 7.
[3] Dio, liii, 26, 4, mentioning operations against Germans.
[4] Dio, liv, 20, 1–2. Silius is attested as proconsul and patron at Aenona, III, 2973 and below, p. 205.
[5] One of the most famous of Augustan campaigns; for references see *PIR*[2], *C*, 941.
[6] Plin., *HN*, iii, 136–7, who gives the text. Fragments of the original are known, V, 7817.
[7] Chilver, *CG*, 23 ff.   [8] *ILS*, 847; cf. Ritterling, *legio* 1226 f.
[9] Ten triumphs were awarded between 146 and 30 B.C.

colonies on the Black Sea (Apollonia, Callatis, Tomi, Istros) in 72–71 B.C. under the proconsul M. Terentius Varro Lucullus (*cos.* 73 B.C.).[1] The expansion of the Dacian kingdom from Transylvania under Burebista was a dangerous development for Rome, threatening not only attacks against Macedonia but also the more dangerous prospect of invasions into Italy from the northeast. Rumours about such invasions were circulating at Rome during the dictatorship of Caesar, who was said to have been planning operations against them in the months before his death.[2]

In the critical years before Actium a valuable recruit to the party of Octavianus was M. Licinius Crassus, grandson of the Triumvir, compensating for the lack of noble names among his supporters. The promised reward for Crassus was the consulship in 30 B.C. and a proconsular command in Macedonia.[3] Here the migrations of the Bastarnae were causing trouble south of the Danube. They had defeated a Roman army sent against them some thirty years previously and captured some eagles, but as long as they did not pass south of the Haemus (Balkan) range they were little danger to Roman Macedonia.[4] Not long before 29 B.C., however, they raided the Strymon valley and attacked some Roman allies. In 29 B.C. Crassus drove them back across the Haemus and massacred their force near the river Cebrus (Cibrica), which later formed the boundary between Upper and Lower Moesia.[5] After attacks on some Moesian peoples, Crassus returned to his province for the winter. Next year the Bastarnae, apparently undaunted by the recent massacre, attacked again and were defeated by Crassus for a second time, who this time penetrated into the Dobrudja where he recovered the lost eagles after taking the stronghold Genucla from the Getae.[6] Crassus was awarded a triumph 'over Thrace and the Getae', but his claim for the supreme honour of the *spolia opima*, for killing the enemy leader with his own hand, was vetoed. Augustus could not allow such prestige to a rival and the request was refused on a technicality: Crassus' triumph was postponed for eighteen months.[7] Roman control was now established on the Lower Danube and along the Black Sea coast, while further to the west Getic chieftains enjoyed the status of Roman clients.[8]

[1] *MRR*, 2, 118, 124.

[2] F. E. Adcock, *CAH*, 9, 714 f.

[3] Sources for Crassus: Dio, li, 23, 2–27, 3; Liv., *Per.*, cxxxiv–v; Florus, ii, 26, On the topography, Patsch, *Beiträge*, V/1, 69 ff.

[4] Once there was a real fear that Perseus of Macedon would send them into Northern Italy.

[5] Dio, li, 23, 2 ff.   [6] On the location of Genucla, Patsch, *Beiträge*, V/1, 70 f.

[7] 'Over Thrace and the Getae' on 4 July 27 B.C., *Inscr. It.*, XIII, 1, p. 86, 344, 571. On the *spolia opima* affair, R. Syme, *RR*, 308.

[8] Roles of the Getae was thus recognized, Dio, li, 24, 7; 26, 1.

In the years after 27 B.C. a few isolated raids are recorded; the Thracian tribes were not given to inactivity and on more than one occasion Roman intervention was necessary in the affairs of the Odrysian kingdom, for instance by M. Lollius (*cos.* 21 B.C.) in 19–18 B.C.[1] About two years later the Sarmatians crossed the Danube; Macedonia too began to suffer raids from the Celtic–Illyrian Scordisci and the Dentheletae.[2] In reply to the Scordisci some advance was made by the army in Macedonia into their territory around Sirmium between the Lower Drave and Save. It may have been the work of Tiberius in 14–13 B.C., since the Scordisci are next recorded as Roman allies helping Tiberius in the conquest of the Pannonian Breuci on the middle Save in 12 B.C.[3] The absence of the army from Macedonia in 14–13 B.C. may be the reason why L. Cornelius Piso (*cos.* 15 B.C.) was brought with an army from Pamphylia in Asia Minor to put down a Thracian rebellion which began in 13 B.C. or soon afterwards.[4]

During the decade or so after the campaigns of Crassus the Roman advance towards control of the Danube basin stagnated. The Princeps could not risk long campaigns in Illyricum, and one season in Spain had proved too much for his frail health, nor could M. Agrippa be spared for the task. At Rome the political situation remained tense until after 19 B.C. After the diplomatic success against Parthia in 20 B.C., when the lost standards were recovered, and the ordering of affairs in Rome, the situation improved for Augustus. His stepsons Tiberius, who had already held his first independent command during the crisis of 20 B.C., and Drusus were both showing signs of military competence at an early age.[5] A succession of able men, from both new and ancient families, was passing through the consulship, providing Augustus with suitable army commanders.[6] Not the least important new factor was a complete change in the character of the army. The unhealthy traditions kept alive by the Civil War veterans disappeared with the discharges after Actium, and in their place a much younger and more highly trained army had been recruited. Between 15 B.C. and

---

[1] Dio, liv, 20, 3; cf. *BCH*, 56 (1932), 207 ff., a dedication at Philippi.

[2] Dio, liv, 20, 3, under 16 B.C.

[3] There is no definite evidence for what Tiberius was doing between the Alpine campaigns and the Bellum Pannonicum in 12 B.C. Velleius, ii, 39, 3, claims that he added the Scordisci to the Empire, as also does the Eusebius Chronicle (ed. Helm, p. 166): 'Tiberius made provinces of the Vindelici and those who live on the borders of Thrace'; cf. *Consol. ad Liviam*, 367 f.

[4] Dio, liv, 34, 5–6, places the war in 11 B.C., but this may be the last year, since Velleius, ii, 98, says that it lasted three years.

[5] Tiberius had served as tribune in the Cantabrian War, and in 20 B.C. at the age of 22 led a major army from the Danube to the East and restored Tigranes in Armenia, *PIR*², C, 941.

[6] R. Syme, *RR*, 387 ff.

the years 7–2 B.C. when it was discharged the New Army was at its peak and equal to any campaign.[1]

During the decade after Actium Augustus and his military advisers must have become increasingly aware of the inadequacy of the Roman position in the Danubian area. Communications with the East were still difficult, and even Macedonia and Greece were made to seem remote by the mountains of Bosnia, Montenegro, and Albania. It was perhaps during this period also that really accurate information about the physical and ethnic geography of the Danube lands began to be collected, in particular about the strategic importance of the overland route through the Save valley linking Italy and the east.[2] The strategy exhibited by the Bellum Pannonicum of 13–9 B.C. certainly presupposes a full appreciation of the importance of Siscia and Sirmium in the Save valley for the securing of Illyricum. One of the greatest benefits to the Roman state arising from Augustus' unified control of virtually all the army was the possibility of strategic co-ordination between the different provincial army groups. It can be recognized for the first time in Spain against the peoples of the Cantabrian hills and a decade later in the brilliant marches of Drusus and Tiberius which secured the Alps in 15 B.C. Illyricum demanded such strategy at every stage, with forces operating from centres as remote from one another as the upper Save valley, the central Dalmatian coast, and the plain of Serbia. The plan was for armies to advance simultaneously into enemy territory and meet in the middle to consolidate the gains. Such concerted campaigns between armies of five legions would have been impossible under the Republic. Most proconsuls, even the Triumvirs, were obsessed with their personal prestige (*dignitas*) and any form of co-operation with another commander, which might be interpreted as subordination, was anathema to such men. This is one of the reasons why so little progress was made in the area by Republican proconsuls, either from the Italian or from the Macedonian side. In spite of this the achievement never seems to have been fully appreciated by contemporaries, and, apart from the hero-worship of Velleius Paterculus, Tiberius' feats of generalship are rarely given their due. Often it is difficult to discover the precise character of the different stages of the advance, especially those against the Pannonians south of the Save.[3]

---

[1] R. Syme, *JRS*, 23 (1933), 20.

[2] As late as 43 B.C. D. Brutus could attempt a march from North Italy to Macedonia after his defeat at Mutina (p. 51 n. 3). Pliny the Elder's information on Pannonia is very meagre (iii, 147–8) when compared with that for Dalmatia (iii, 139 ff.), while the Map of Agrippa, published a little before 7 B.C., records information only about the Save and Drave valleys.

[3] On the evolution of this strategy, J. Wilkes, *UBHR*, 10 (1965), 1 ff.

The first problem of the conquest of Illyricum is the year in which the campaigns began. Under 14 B.C. Dio records that 'the Pannonians revolted again and were subdued', but he adds no further detail.[1] The passage refers back to the events of 16 B.C. when they were expelled from Istria by the legates of the proconsul P. Silius Nerva, but it may indicate that operations had already been commenced by M. Vinicius, who is not named by Dio but is mentioned by Velleius as having commanded the forces along with M. Agrippa in 13 B.C.[2] Further south near the Adriatic, some progress may be concealed in Dio's remark under 16 B.C. about 'uprisings in Spain and Dalmatia which were put down in a short time'.[3] It was planned that Agrippa should carry through the conquest of Illyricum. After receiving a new grant of *maius imperium* he advanced in 13 B.C. against the Pannonians, even though winter was approaching, because they were 'eager for war'; but when he arrived with the army they gave up any plans for 'rebellion'. The severe Pannonian winter proved too much for Agrippa, however, and he returned to Italy to die the next spring.[4] Velleius records the beginning of the war in 13 B.C. by Agrippa and M. Vinicius, but for him these operations were merely a prelude to the triumphs of his hero Tiberius.[5] From Florus, who also mentions the role of Vinicius, it emerges that the operations in this year were against the peoples between the Drave and the Save, probably the Breuci. It is probably at this time that the legionary base was established at Poetovio (Ptuj) on the Drave, complementing that at Siscia on the Save.[6]

After the death of Agrippa command in Illyricum was entrusted to Tiberius, fresh from his consulship and already a general of proved ability at the age of 28. Nothing is known of the legates who served Tiberius in the campaigns of the next four years; M. Vinicius the new man (*novus homo*) and probably not a confidant of the new general disappears from the scene.[7] The nature of the campaign in 12 B.C. is revealed by Dio: 'Tiberius overcame the Pannonians with the aid of

---

[1] Dio, liv, 28, 1.

[2] Sources for the war: Dio, liv, 31, 2 f.; 34, 3 f; 36, 3 f; lv, 2, 4; Vell. Pat., ii, 96, 2; Suet., *Tib.*, 9; Florus, ii, 24, 8 ff.; Liv., *Per.*, cxli; *Res Gestae*, 30; Front., *strat.*, ii, 1, 15, an incident from Tiberius' campaigns under the heading: 'On how to choose the time for battle.'

[3] Dio, liv, 20, 3, in the same context as the operations of P. Silius.   [4] Dio, liv, 28, 1–3.

[5] Vell. Pat., ii, 96, 2: 'Then came the Bellum Pannonicum, begun by M. Agrippa and M. Vinicius, your own grandfather, dear consul (referring to M. Vinicius *cos.* 30 to whom Velleius dedicated his work), a great and savage war, which even threatened the neighbouring part of Italy, waged by (Tiberius) Nero.'

[6] Florus, ii, 24, 8 f. There is no definite date for when the legionary fortress at Poetovio, attested later under Augustus, was first established.

[7] Before he left for Illyricum Tiberius had married Julia, the daughter of Augustus and widow of Agrippa, Dio, liv, 31, 2.

the Scordisci, whom he used as much as possible'.[1] Suetonius identifies the Pannonians as the Breuci, who occupied the Papuk mountains around Sl. Požega between the Save and the Drave.[2] The link between Italy and Macedonia was finally established, but it was as yet far from secure. It was necessary to obtain submission from those Pannonians who inhabited the valleys of Bosnia to the south. Although they were now completely encircled by Roman territory they were still dangerous and difficult to approach; and only when the Save valley had been secured could any advances be made against them. Tiberius returned to Rome and received triumphal insignia, Augustus having vetoed the full triumph offered to him by the Senate.[3] Tiberius' work in Illyricum was as yet far from completed.

For the second campaign in 11 B.C. Dio once again reveals the scope of the operations and the strategy which lay behind them: 'Tiberius subdued the Dalmatians, who began a rebellion, and later the Pannonians, who likewise revolted, taking advantage of the absence of himself and the larger part of his army. He made war on both of them at the same time, moving now to one sector and now to the other'.[4] Here it is possible that the Dalmatians mentioned were the Delmatae around Salona. Tiberius began operations from the Adriatic against the interior peoples, but was forced to return to the Save because of disturbances. After dealing with these he may have instituted an advance south from the Save valley into Bosnia, complementing the operations with another from the direction of the Adriatic. The movement from one area to another reveals that he was concerting attacks on the interior from both north and south at the same time, and in order to keep in regular touch with the different columns he had to travel by a roundabout route, probably through the Iapodes and the Liburnians.[5] The discovery that the subjugation of the interior of Illyricum required simultaneous operations from north and south was probably the main reason why in that year the new conquests in the north and the old proconsular area near the coast were combined to form the new imperial command of Illyricum, administered by Augustus' legates. The change is reported by Dio: 'after this [the campaign of 11 B.C.] Dalmatia was handed over to the care of Augustus, because it was felt that it would always require forces because of its own nature and because of the nearness of the Pannonians'.[6] In 10 B.C. Tiberius left the province to join

[1] Dio, liv, 31, 3.
[2] Suet., *Tib.*, 9: 'In the Bellum Pannonicum he subdued the Breuci and the Dalmatians.'
[3] Dio, liv, 31, 4; Suet., *Tib.*, 9, 2.
[4] Dio, liv, 34, 3. The 11 B.C. campaign was planned in advance, although that in the following year was not, since it prevented the planned closing of the Janus Temple, Dio, liv, 36, 2, nor was that in 9 B.C. when he had to return to Illyricum from Gaul (see below).
[5] J. Wilkes, *AAnt. Hung.*, 13 (1965), 118 f.   [6] Dio, liv, 34, 4.

Augustus in Gaul, but soon had to return because of Dacian attacks on the Pannonians and rebellion among the Dalmatians against payment of tribute. These matters were soon dealt with and Tiberius returned to Rome at the end of the year, in company with Augustus and Drusus.[1] In the fourth campaign of 9 B.C. Tiberius 'overcame the Pannonians and Dalmatians', but he still had time to reach Germany before the death of his brother Drusus late in the summer.[2] Dio supplies no detail on either of these campaigns, but most probably by this time the Save valley was firmly secured and the forces were engaged in the long task of subjugating the Pannonian peoples south of the Save. This was the first occasion when Roman forces entered the area which later became the northern part of the province Dalmatia. Significantly Velleius regards the campaign of 9 B.C. as the end of the independence of the Dalmatians, their 'rebellion' having lasted since 229 B.C.[3]

For his achievements in Illyricum Tiberius celebrated an ovation, probably the most hard-earned second category triumph in Roman history, and feasted the populace of Rome on the Capitol.[4] Later tradition does credit Tiberius with the conquest of the Pannonians at this time, and his achievements are proudly recorded by Augustus in his *Res Gestae*: 'Through Ti(berius) Nero, then my stepson and legate, I have brought under Roman authority the peoples of the Pannonians which no Roman army had approached before my Principate and I have pushed forward the boundaries of Illyricum to the bank of the river Danube'.[5] The advance to the Danube was that along the Save and Drave valleys towards the area of Belgrade in alliance with the Scordisci: the Pannonians never approached before were those between the river Save and the Dinaric Alps, all later included in the province Dalmatia.[6] It is doubtful whether any effective Roman control was exercised over these peoples until after the suppression of the great rebellion in A.D. 9. All the peoples probably made submissions eventually to Tiberius, and in A.D. 6 they were expecting to contribute troops to the Roman forces for the march against Maroboduus. Yet both Illyricum and Thrace were now judged secure by the Roman high command, and it was possible to contemplate major advances into Europe beyond the limits of Roman control along the rivers Rhine and Danube. Illyricum was now an organized imperial command with an army probably numbering five legions, while on the lower Danube a new imperial command of Moesia (first attested in

[1] Dio, liv, 36, 2–4.   [2] Dio, lv, 2, 1, 4.   [3] Vell. Pat., ii, 90, 1.

[4] In 12 B.C. he received triumphal insignia, after the proffered triumph was vetoed by Augustus. In 11 B.C. the salutation as *imperator* made by the troops was forbidden by Augustus, Dio, liv, 33, 5. For his *ovatio*, Dio, lv, 2, 4; Suet., *Tib.*, 9, 2; Euseb., *Chron.* (ed. Helm, p. 167), under 10 B.C.

[5] *Res Gestae*, 30.

[6] R. Syme, *RIÉB*, 3 (1937), 33–46. On the peoples involved see below, p. 167 ff.

A.D. 6) had probably been established after the three-year war of Piso against the Dacians.[1] By now Augustus and his advisers were considering the possibilities of further advances into Europe. In the west Drusus had overrun the lands between the Rhine and the Elbe in a series of rapid sweeps with a small army that could not have been bettered even by the great Caesar. If such a gain could be made on the west, then other advances from the middle and upper Danube would push the line of Roman territory northwards to occupy Bohemia, and all the territory to the east on the south of the Carpathians, including the Dacians in Transylvania. All these enterprises followed on from the securing of Illyricum and the immense advantages gained from reliable communications between Italy and the main armies in the north. On the other hand, it was rebellion in this area, behind the Danube and close to Italy, that was to bring the ambitious schemes of Augustus' middle years crashing to the ground.[2]

The final subjugation of the Pannonians was probably completed in 8 B.C. by the elderly Sex. Appuleius, consul more than twenty years before (29 B.C.) and a survivor from an earlier generation.[3] He may have supervised the final annexation of the thinly populated plain between the Drave and the Danube, where the peoples were probably only too glad to receive some form of protection from the pitiless raiding of the Dacians from the east.[4] Soon after the advance to the Elbe and the conquest of Illyricum, which were both judged completed in 9 B.C., the general advance of the legions to a shorter line of defence was contemplated. There was much to attract Augustus in this scheme, despite the death of Drusus in 9 B.C. and the departure of Tiberius to Rhodes a few years later in self-imposed exile.[5] In contrast with the journey of almost 2,000 miles from the mouth of the Rhine to that of the Danube, there was a clear geographic frontier not far to the north about half this length, running along the Elbe to Prague, and thence along the Carpathians to the mouth of the Danube. Within this area there were two centres of power which would have to be attacked and destroyed, Maroboduus with the German Marcomanni in Bohemia, and the kingdom of Dacia in Transylvania; this latter was then weakened by civil war. In the years

[1] A. Caecina Severus is the first definitely attested legate in Moesia (below, p. 70), although L. Piso who crushed the Thracians may have been the first legate: he is called *legatus* by Velleius, ii, 98.

[2] It seems logical that Augustus must have planned the conquest of Dacia to follow immediately on the elimination of Maroboduus, J. Wilkes, *UBHR*, 10 (1965), 1 ff.

[3] Cassiodorus, *chron.*, (*MGH, Chron. min.*, 1, p. 135).

[4] Patsch, *Beiträge*, V/1, 109.

[5] In a matter of a few years Augustus' grandsons, L. and G. Caesar, might be ready for high command, while more experienced men were still active enough for army commands, M. Lollius (*cos.* 21 B.C.), and M. Vinicius (*cos.* 19 B.C.).

between 8 B.C. and A.D. 6 considerable progress was made towards achieving this advance: Maroboduus was on the point of being eliminated, while the Dacians had been pushed back from the Danube. At this moment the whole project was halted by the major rebellion of the Pannonians between the river Drave and the Dinaric Alps, followed soon after by the loss of the three legions in Germany under P. Quinctilius Varus in A.D. 9.

Unfortunately the operations in the years between the end of the Bellum Pannonicum and the Pannonian rebellion are poorly reported in the sources, though for quite different reasons. The surviving text of Dio, which provides the main narrative for the earlier campaigns, is incomplete although one fragment furnishes valuable testimony for the operations of L. Domitius Ahenobarbus.[1] The account in the history of Velleius is also seriously deficient, but in his case it was deliberate. For him the absence of Tiberius from the command of Roman armies in Europe between 6 B.C. and A.D. 6 was a disaster, to emphasize which he records none of the exploits of the commanders who took over the roles of Drusus and Tiberius, save for a passing reference (and that unflattering) to the activities of M. Vinicius (*cos.* 19 B.C.) in Germany, grandfather of the man to whom his history was dedicated.[2] There is some valuable testimony in the accounts of Florus, particularly for the operations of Cn. Cornelius Lentulus, and of Strabo. Otherwise there is only the *elogium* of an unknown senator at Tibur which records operations far beyond the Danube at this period.[3]

About the time that Tiberius left Rome for Rhodes a new menace appeared on the northern frontier, in the person of Maroboduus, king of the German Marcomanni. This ruler had migrated with his people eastward soon after 9 B.C. from the river Main to the mountain fortress of Bohemia which brooded dangerously over the long Roman defensive line on the middle and upper Danube.[4] In face of the real danger that he might combine forces with other German peoples to the west, as well as the Dacians to the east, operations were begun by the Romans to isolate him from these areas. Although the first move was made to the west of his territory, it originated with an advance from Illyricum. The legate L. Domitius Ahenobarbus (*cos.* 16 B.C.) crossed the Danube somewhere along its upper course and met with the German Hermunduri, then migrating in search of a new home. Domitius settled them on the western

---

[1] Dio, lv, 10a, 2; cf. R. Syme, *JRS*, 24 (1934), 121.

[2] Three chapters (ii, 100–2) cover the years of Tiberius' absence in Rhodes, and these are devoted largely to the misdeeds of Julia and her circle.

[3] Florus, ii, 28–9, 18–20; Strabo, vii, 3, 11, 13; *ILS*, 8965; cf. *Inscr. It.*, XIII, 3, p. 76, n. 91.

[4] Drusus had dealings with them in 9 B.C., Florus, ii, 30, 23; Orosius, *Hist.*, vi, 21, 5; Dio, lv, 2, 1 (Suebi).

fringes of the Marcomanni (in Franconia and Thuringia), where they remained for many years staunch allies of the Romans. From there he reached the river Elbe. Meeting with no opposition, he erected an altar to Augustus and moved westwards into the Rhineland where he had assumed command by 1 B.C.[1] The next operations were directed to achieving the same results on Maroboduus' eastern borders. The senator recorded at Tibur was Augustus' legate in Illyricum during these years; he crossed the Danube to defeat the Bastarnae and then entered into some form of treaty arrangements with certain small peoples dwelling roughly between Maroboduus and the Dacians, the Cotini and the Anartii, thus interposing a group of Roman allies between the Germans and the Dacians.[2] The sequel to these operation was apparently a direct assault on the Dacians, not for conquest but merely to ensure that they would not intervene when the armies moved against Maroboduus. The next commander in Illyricum was Cn. Cornelius Lentulus who moved up the river Theiss and then eastwards along its tributary the Mureş (or Marosch) towards the Iron Gates of Transylvania (Tapae), the scene of later battles under Domitian and Trajan. As Florus clearly explains, this was not intended as a conquest of the Dacians, but a 'pushing back', as the consuls' lictors pushed back the crowds in Rome during state occasions.[3] Lentulus was also engaged on the Lower Danube, and he received triumphal insignia (now the highest reward for an imperial legate not of Augustus' family) for victories over the Getae.[4]

M. Vinicius may have been the legate who conducted the operations on the east flank of Maroboduus, and when he was succeeded there by Lentulus about A.D. 1 he moved to replace Ahenobarbus in Germany, where he remained in command until the return of Tiberius to the scene in A.D. 4. Velleius is pleased to record how Vinicius began to get into difficulties, until at length he was replaced by Tiberius to the great delight of the Rhine legions.[5] Thereupon the momentum was revived and in A.D. 4 the Bructeri and Cherusci submitted. In the following year the Langobardi were overcome, and the army once more reached the

---

[1] Dio, lv, 10a, 2–3. He built the famous causeway (*pontes longi*) across the marshy ground between the Rhine and the Ems, Tac., *Ann.*, i, 63, and was awarded with triumphal insignia, Suet., *Nero*, 4; Tac., *Ann.*, iv, 44.

[2] *ILS*, 8965. Only the letters . . .] CIVS [. . . survive from the *gentilicium*. He could be P. Sulpicius Quirinius (*cos.* 12 B.C.), as E. Groag, *RE*, 4 A (1931), 827 f., although all his known career was in the eastern provinces and most have preferred M. Vinicius (*cos.* 19 B.C.), R. Syme, *CQ*, 27 (1933), 142 ff.; A. v. Premerstein, *JÖAI*, 28 (1933), 140–63, 29 (1935), 60–81; C. Patsch, *Beiträge*, V-1, 96–110.

[3] Florus, ii, 28–9; *Res Gestae*, 30–1; Strabo, vii, 3, 11, 13; cf. R. Syme, *JRS*, 24 (1934), 113 ff.

[4] Tac., *Ann.*, iv, 44.

[5] Vell. Pat., ii, 105–8.

Elbe, where it was met by the fleet which had explored the coast as far as Jutland. Here two of the ancient foes of the Romans, the Sennones (conquerors of Rome in 390 B.C.) and the Cimbri (invaders of Italy in 101 B.C.) made atonement for past misdeeds by seeking the friendship of Augustus.[1] All was now prepared for the great advance against Maroboduus in A.D. 6. C. Sentius Saturninus (*cos.* 19 B.C.) was to advance eastward with the army of Upper Germany and Raetia, while Tiberius would cross the Danube at Carnuntum leading the army of Illyricum.[2] The strategy was to join near the centre of Maroboduus' realm and eliminate him. The advance was well forward and the submission of Maroboduus imminent, when news arrived that nearly all Illyricum was in rebellion. Terms were hastily made with the Germans and Tiberius rushed back to his province.[3]

According to Velleius, who served for a time in Pannonia as a legate of Tiberius, it was the Pannonians who began the rebellion, bringing in the Dalmatians later.[4] Dio is more explicit and explains that the person responsible for the uprising was Bato, the chief of the Daesitiates around Sarajevo in Central Bosnia.[5] He chose the moment when all the peoples of the region had assembled their forces in response to a Roman demand for contingents to serve in the war against Maroboduus. Pointing to their great strength Bato at first succeeded in persuading only a minority to join him, but when a slight success had been obtained over a Roman force the rebellion spread throughout the land. The immediate cause appears to have been the behaviour of Roman officials and their manner of demanding tribute.[6] In Illyricum fifteen years had passed since the conquest by Tiberius and a new generation had grown up eager to recover the freedom lost by their fathers. After the successes of the peoples in Bosnia the Pannonian Breuci joined the revolt under their leaders Bato and Pinnes, causing the loss to the Romans of all Illyricum between the Drave and the Dinaric Alps. Velleius estimates the total strength of the insurgents as 200,000 infantry and 9,000 cavalry.[7] They were led by men who, like Maroboduus and Arminius, had served in the Roman army as junior officers and knew much about the methods and discipline of their adversaries. Because of this, remarks Velleius, no

---

[1] Vell. Pat., ii, 105–8, 122, 2; Dio, lv, 28, 5–7, 29, 1, 30, 1; Tac., *Ann.*, ii, 46.

[2] Vell. Pat., ii, 109, 5. Cn. Sentius Saturninus was among the senior generals of the age. After 9 B.C. he governed Syria and Gaul, while both his sons held the consulship in A.D. 4, one as *ordinarius*, RE, 2 A (1923), 1511 ff., n. 9.

[3] Vell. Pat., ii, 110, 3: 'Then more urgent matters were placed above glorious achievements', but Dio reveals no trace of the impact which the rebellion had on Augustus' schemes in Europe.

[4] Vell. Pat., ii, 110, 2.   [5] Dio, lv, 29, 2–3.

[6] Dio, lv, 29, 1. Nothing of this aspect appears in Velleius. He refers to 'Pannonia insolens longae pacis bonis'.

[7] Vell. Pat., ii, 110, 3.

G

nation ever followed through so quickly the planning of the campaigns with the actual campaigns themselves.[1]

The first victims of the Pannonians were found in their own territories. Roman citizens were overwhelmed, traders massacred, and a large force of legionary veterans still serving with the colours (*magnus vexillariorum numerus*) stationed in a remote part of the country was exterminated.[2] In spite of their background of Roman training, however, the leaders of the rebellion failed to follow up these successes by capturing the two key Roman strongpoints at Siscia and Sirmium before the main Roman forces returned from the north. Bato of the Breuci did attack Sirmium but failed to take it because the delay had enabled the legate in Moesia, A. Caecina Severus (*cos.* 1 B.C.), to move rapidly westwards as soon as the news of the rebellion reached him. He halted the Pannonians at the river Drave, though not without heavy losses to the Roman forces.[3] Unfortunately Bato of the Daesitiates, instead of joining his allies in the attack on Sirmium or making his own attempt at Siscia, then still virtually undefended, turned his troops southwards across the Dinaric Alps to attack Salona and other coastal cities. In a foray against Salona Bato was wounded by a missile and after failing to capture the colony, he sent bands to raid the coast and hinterland as far south as Apollonia.[4] By the time he turned northward against Siscia his chance of taking the place had passed. When news of the rebellion reached Tiberius he immediately ordered M. Valerius Messalla (*cos.* 3 B.C.), the son of Corvinus, to secure Siscia by advancing rapidly ahead of the main army with part of the XXth legion. At first he suffered defeat in an open battle but later trapped Bato, still suffering from the effects of his wound, and routed his army. Siscia was thus secured, and with the other fortress Sirmium still held the fate of the rebellion was sealed. Valerius received the triumphal insignia for his exploits in this year: perhaps Legion XX received the honorary titles *Valeria victrix*. With the northwest and Italy closed to him Bato moved down the Save Valley and joined his Breucian namesake in the assault on Sirmium, where the outcome was still in the balance. The united forces of the insurgents established themselves on the Mons Almus (Fruška Gora), which extends along the south bank of the Danube and overlooks Sirmium from the north. Here they suffered a defeat from the Roman ally king Rhoemetalces, with his Thracian cavalry, acting under the

[1] Vell. Pat., ii, 110, 5.

[2] Vell. Pat., ii, 110, 6. There is no evidence for where the slain veterans were stationed, although the area 'most remote' from Tiberius at the time was the coastal hinterland of Dalmatia.

[3] Vell. Pat., ii, 110, 4; Dio, lv, 29, 3. The initial strategy of the rebels was a triple division of their forces, one to attack Italy through Nauportus and Tergeste, another to move towards Macedonia (Save–Morava valley), and the third to remain behind as a garrison for their territory.   [4] Dio, lv, 29, 4.

command of Caecina Severus. His own attack against them, however, was a failure and he was soon forced to return to Moesia to deal with raids by the Dacians and Sarmatians, while Rhoemetalces too returned to his kingdom to seek reinforcements.[1] Evidently Caecina judged that Sirmium was safe for the following winter (6–7). Tiberius had reached Siscia and kept his army there for the remainder of the campaigning season, making minor raids on the territory of the rebels, especially on that of the Daesitiates and their allies, now unable to leave to Mons Almus to defend them.[2]

In Rome the initial panic, which had for a time affected even Augustus himself fearing an invasion of Italy, was soon replaced by a determination to see that adequate forces were available for Tiberius' coming campaigns. In an atmosphere reminiscent of the heroic days after Cannae new forces were assembled. All available veterans were recalled to service and ex-slaves were requisitioned from their patrons.[3] The first body of these reinforcements was taken to Tiberius at Siscia late in 6 by the young senator C. Velleius Paterculus, who had been nominated for a quaestorship.[4] Another similar force was brought a little later by the young Germanicus Caesar, nephew of Tiberius, which caused malicious and unfounded rumours that Augustus was dissatisfied with Tiberius' conduct of the war.[5] The ageing Princeps even summoned up the energy to move from

---

[1] Vell. Pat., ii, 112, 1–2; cf. Dio, lv, 30, 1–5. The Legion XX is not attested with these titles until the later first century, and it is possible that they were received for exploits in the British rebellion in 60, although the *gentilicium* Valeria points to A.D. 6. A *signifer* decorated by Tiberius in this war does not attest the titles on his tombstone, V 4365 Brixia. Another possibility, suggested by A. R. Birley, is that they came from its role in the Claudian invasion of Britain in 43 and were chosen after his first empress Valeria Messallina, in the same way that he named his son Britannicus, while a later colony in Germany was named after his second empress Agrippina, *colonia Agrippinensis* (Köln).

[2] Dio, lv, 30, 6. The passage is very confused and is probably corrupt, but the interpretation proposed here does not conflict with the text.

[3] Vell. Pat., ii, 111, 1–4; Dio, lv, 31, 1–2; cf. Macrob., *Sat.*, i, 11, 32; Suet., *Aug.*, 25. The new formations were not the later well-known permanent citizen auxiliary units (*cohortes voluntariorum c.R.*) as is generally assumed, cf. K. Kraft, *Rekrutierung* 87 ff. Suetonius describes them as 'a defence for colonies bordering Illyricum', suggesting that they were stationed in Northeast Italy and on the Dalmatian coast.

[4] Vell. Pat., ii, 111, 4. Born in Capua the son of an equestrian (i, 7) he was military tribune in Thrace, Macedonia, Achaea, and Asia, and in A.D. 3 commander of cavalry in Germany. In A.D. 5 he was designated quaestor, then appointed legate to Tiberius in 7–8 and took part in the triumph of Tiberius in 12. For a comparison between the accounts of the war in Dio and Velleius, see *A Ant. Hung.*, 13 (1965), 112 ff.

[5] Dio, lv, 31, 1, naturally ignored by Velleius. Throughout the war Germanicus was a subordinate of Tiberius, except for the short, and unsuccessful, period of independent command early in 9, see p. 74.

Rome to Ariminum, where he was reasonably close at hand for consultations with Tiberius.[1]

In the summer of 7 Tiberius began his advance eastwards from Siscia, and managed to trap some of the rebels on the Mons Claudius (Papuk hills), the centre of Breucian territory between the Save and the Drave.[2] Further east the rebels were dominant in the field. Late in the year two legions arrived from Asia under M. Plautius Silvanus (*cos.* 2 B.C.), bringing the Moesian army to equality with the five legions of the army of Illyricum under Tiberius.[3] The two commanders, accompanied by Rhoemetalces and his reinforced Thracian cavalry, then moved their forces westwards to effect a meeting with Tiberius. Leaving Sirmium they advanced along the river Bošut towards the area of the later Cibalae (Vinkovci). Half-way between there is a place where the firm ground between the Mons Almus and the Volcaean Marshes is very narrow. The two Batos were still based on the Mons Almus and they were able to wait until the Roman forces were extended and then attack the army trapped between them and the marshes to the south; these were very similar tactics to Hannibal's in the battle of Trasimene (217 B.C.). To make the Roman position worse the two commanders appear to have been guilty of negligence, and the rebel attack came as a complete surprise while the army was in its camp. The Thracian cavalry was brushed aside, and the auxiliaries, both infantry and cavalry, fled from the field at the first onslaught. Panic spread even among the legions, and many officers perished, but eventually with great discipline they formed ranks in the shelter of their camp defences and drove off the attackers. Once again a near disaster brought on by the negligence of a commander, was turned into victory by the steadiness of the legionaries.[4] The way to Siscia was now open and the two commanders continued their journey towards the army of Tiberius which by now was probably well on its way along the Save valley. The forces met and moved to Siscia where a united camp was established, witnessed, and marvelled at by Velleius.[5] Under Tiberius there was gathered at Siscia an army of ten legions, more than seventy auxiliary cohorts, fourteen cavalry *alae*, ten thousand serving

[1] Dio, lv, 34, 3 under A.D. 8, but referring back to one or two years before.
[2] Vell. Pat., ii, 112, 3. Dio is brief for A.D. 7, recording summarily only the Volcaean Marshes battle and the raid of Germanicus against the Maezaei. It is not certain which of the rebel forces was on the Mons Claudius. Pliny, *HN*, iii, 148, places it between the Taurisci and the Scordisci. For the topography, E. Koerstermann, 360 f.
[3] Vell. Pat., ii, 112, 4. The surviving account of Dio does not mention Silvanus until A.D. 8, lv, 34, 6; previously he had been imperial legate in Galatia-Pamphylia, R. Syme, *Klio*, 27 (1934), 122.
[4] Vell. Pat., ii, 112, 4–6. Only Dio mentions the marshes, south of the Moravić, lv, 32, 3.
[5] Vell., Pat., ii, 113, 1–2. On the identity of the legions involved see p. 92 ff.

veterans, the large forces of volunteers raised the year before in Italy, and the cavalry of Rhoemetalces, It was the largest concentration of forces seen since the end of the civil wars.

It was not the intention of Tiberius to keep such an army together for long. Once the consultations among the army commanders had been completed and plans for the coming campaigns against the rebels had been settled, the augmented army of Moesia was escorted back to Moesia, after which Tiberius dispersed his troops into winter quarters around Siscia.[1] Caecina returned to his own province Moesia, leaving Plautius Silvanus in command at Sirmium. In the latter part of the season Tiberius had allowed Germanicus to make forays against the Maezaei in the Vrbas and Una valleys of Northwest Bosnia to destroy the harvests before the winter closed in.[2] The severity of the winter favoured the Romans, and Tiberius could return to Rome confident that the coming of spring would find the rebels still cut off from their homelands and in a much weaker condition. The crisis was now passed.[3] When the army of Siscia moved eastwards early in 8 the Breuci eventually left their hills and came down to the river Bathinus (probably the Bosna) and surrendered to Tiberius on 3 August. Their leader Bato had made his colleague Pinnes a prisoner and surrendered himself and the latter to the Romans in return for which he was allowed to remain ruler, of the Breuci.[4] The war in the Save valley was now over and the army returned to Siscia to winter quarters under its commander M. Aemilius Lepidus (*cos.* 6). Before the winter, however, Bato the Breucian was captured and killed by his rebel namesake, and many of the Pannonians were induced to join the rebellion once more. The situation, however, was retrieved by Plautius Silvanus with the army at Sirmium; he managed to drive Bato south out of the Save valley and bring back the Breuci to their allegiance, after which he remained in the field until the end of the year putting down the remnants of the rebellion in Pannonia.[5] Tiberius did not return to Rome until the end of winter early in 9, where

[1] Caecina is no longer involved in the war, being back in Moesia fighting off the raiding Dacians and Sarmatians. Plautius' position at Sirmium is attested by Dio's record that he conquered the Breuci in 8, lv, 34, 6–7.

[2] Dio, lv, 32, 4.

[3] In the winter A.D. 7-8 Scenobarbus (otherwise unknown) attempted to make contact with the garrison commander M' Ennius at Siscia, but the text of Dio breaks off at this point, lv, 33, 22.

[4] Vell. Pat., ii, 114, 4; Dio, lv, 34, 4 (referring only to the betrayal of Pinnes). The victory is recorded in the Antium Calendar, 1², 248; cf. 324; cf. O. Hirschfeld, *Kl. Schr.* 394 ff. On the Bathinus, B. Saria, *Klio*, 23 (1930), 92–7, argues for the Bosna, while E. Koestermann, 365 f., n. 4, prefers the Bošut further east, but see Alföldy, *AArch. Hung.*, 16 (1964), 251 f.

[5] Vell. Pat., ii, 114, 5; Dio, lv, 34, 4–7.

he was met by Augustus in the suburbs of the city. During the winter he had been ensuring that the blockade of Bato was secure and capturing some of the more accessible strongholds.[1]

The destruction of Bato and his allies in 9 and the end of the war was intended to be a task for the legates left behind in Illyricum, M. Aemilius Lepidus at Siscia, M. Plautius Silvanus at Sirmium, and Germanicus now operating as an independent commander south of the Dinaric Alps.[2] Like P. Vatinius half a century before, Germanicus was far from successful when faced with the task of capturing well defended strongholds in the interior; in spite of considerable personal courage his inexperienced attacks made little impression. At Splonum (Plevlje) he was successful because of a fortunate collapse of part of the defences, but at Raetinium a rash assault ended in heavy Roman casualties, although he succeeded in taking another stronghold Seretium, attacked on a former occasion without success by Tiberius.[3] Augustus now felt that the war was dragging on for too long, and the delay was hampering his attempts to relieve the severe famine then raging in Italy: therefore he sent Tiberius back to Illyricum. He found that the morale of the Roman forces was low and, according to Dio, this was one of the reasons why he divided the army into three separate divisions, two in the north under Lepidus and Silvanus, with the third under his own command operating from the south. This division had already existed when Tiberius was in Illyricum before. What happened was that Augustus decided that Tiberius had to return and take over command from the inexperienced Germanicus, for whom the task in Dalmatia was proving too difficult. Such an explanation could hardly have been admitted by Dio who repeats all the distortion of the tradition which later favours the young nephew of Tiberius.[4] Nothing is known of Silvanus' operations, except that they were successful, but Velleius gives a vivid picture of the march by Lepidus from Siscia through the middle of Illyricum to join Tiberius, an exploit for which he received triumphal insignia.[5]

[1] Dio, lvi, 1, 1. The evidence is crucial for understanding the strategy planned for A.D. 9, a triple advance from Siscia, Sirmium, and the Adriatic, *AAnt. Hung.*, 13 (1965), 115 f.

[2] Dio, lvi, 11–17. The role of Germanicus is grossly exaggerated, but even Dio cannot disguise the failure of the commanders to capture Bato.

[3] For the location of Splonum, *AAnt. Hung.*, 13 (1965), 112 ff. and p. 282. Another possibility, Šipovo in the Pliva valley, which was suggested by G. Alföldy, *AAnt. Hung.*, 10 (1962), 3–12, does not fit the strategy and army movements of 9. Germanicus' force was in the south not in the northwest.

[4] Dio, lvi, 12, 1 ff. The seriousness of the crisis is indicated by the Elder Pliny, *HN*, vii, 149; 'then coincided so many misfortunes: shortage of finance, rebellion of Illyricum, the levying of slaves, scarcity of young men, plague in the city, and famine in Italy.'

[5] Vell. Pat., ii, 115, 2–3.

Now Velleius was no longer serving Tiberius, but his source was his brother Magius Celer Velleianus who was serving as legate to Tiberius when he witnessed the meeting of the two armies.[1] The line of Lepidus' march was probably along the Una or Vrbas valley, across the Strmica pass (Mons Ditionum) above Knin to the final destination at Burnum (Šuplja Crkva), where the camp of Legion XX was established.[2]

Meanwhile Tiberius trapped Bato at Andetrium (Gornje Muć) not twenty miles inland from Salona, but his army was ill-equipped to sustain a siege and the troops soon suffered conditions more appropriate to the besieged. There was a real danger of mutiny breaking out as the blockade of the fortress dragged on and on, while for his part Bato was unable to come to terms with Tiberius as he wished, owing to the large numbers of deserters from the Roman side in the stronghold who feared the consequences of surrender. Eventually Bato escaped from Andetrium, but those left behind fought on until Tiberius captured it by discovering a secret path which led up the hill to a place where he could attack the fortifications. Most of the garrison fled to the surrounding forests where they were hunted and slain like wild beasts. Tiberius now turned to the task of arranging the terms of settlement for the peoples in the area, and the affairs of those who had already surrendered. Once more Germanicus was dispatched on his own to deal with the few strongholds where resistance was still maintained, mostly by deserters from the Roman side forcing the local population to continue the struggle against their will. At Arduba the deserters were expelled by the local population, in spite of the fanatical support they enjoyed from the latter's womenfolk, and the place was handed over to Germanicus.[3] After this success he rejoined Tiberius, leaving the remnants of the rebellion among the Daesitiates and the Pirustae to be crushed by C. Vibius Postumus (*cos.* 5) who later received triumphal insignia for his achievements.[4] Bato sent his son Scenas to Tiberius to request a safe-conduct for his father, and when this was granted he came in person.[5] His speech of defiance, defending not his own actions but those of his supporters, was probably comparable to those spoken by many later enemies of Rome which appear in the pages of Tacitus. All that Dio records is

---

[1] Vell. Pat., ii, 115, 1. He obtained the praetorship in 15 as a nominee (*candidatus*) of Tiberius, ii, 124.

[2] See p. 98 f. Lepidus is probably attested at Gradac near Posušje, III, 13885; cf. Patsch, *Hercegovina*, 62, fig. 17: [M. Aemi]lio [P. f. L]epido.

[3] Dio, lvi, 12, 3–15, 3. In his account of A.D. 9 Velleius mentions only the march of Lepidus and the crushing of the Daesitiates and Pirustae.

[4] Vell. Pat., ii, 115, 4. On Vibius, see p. 81.

[5] The MSS of Dio give *Sceuas*, but the Illyrian Scenas is a common personal name, Mayer, *Sprache*, 81.

the no doubt justifiable claim that it was the Romans who were to blame for the rebellion: 'you send as guardians of your flocks, not dogs or shepherds but wolves'.[1] The life of the leader of the Daesitiates was spared and he was treated with great generosity by Tiberius, who sent him to Italy; there he spent the rest of his life in comfortable internment at Ravenna.[2]

The terrible four years war was at an end. The Roman losses had been heavy not only in man power but also in resources: 'for ever so many legions were maintained for these campaigns and but very little booty taken'.[3] Tiberius left Illyricum late in 9 and entered Rome wearing the victor's laurels on 16 January 10.[4] Both Augustus and Tiberius received salutations as *imperator* (conquering general), the latter probably for the fifth time.[5] They accepted the triumphs offered to them and permitted the construction of two triumphal arches somewhere in Illyricum to commemorate their victory.[6] Like the other legates in the war, Germanicus was awarded the triumphal insignia and also the senatorial status of praetor which gave him the privilege of speaking in the Senate after the consulars. He was also promised the prospect of reaching the consulship at an earlier age than the rules of office normally allowed. Even Tiberius' young son Drusus was enrolled into the Senate to hold the rank of a praetorian after his quaestorship.[7]

The elation at such a hard-won victory was quickly shattered when, only five days after the war was declared officially at an end, news arrived from Germany of the disaster to three legions under P. Quinctilius Varus in the ambush of Arminius.[8] Tiberius was forced to postpone his triumph and hasten yet again to the scene of a Roman disaster. Eventually he returned to the capital and in 12 celebrated his triumph over the Dalmatians and the Pannonians on 23 October, the fifty-fourth anniversary of the victory over Caesar's assassins at Philippi.[9] 'Even though he achieved enough for seven triumphs he was content with three',

[1] Dio, lvi, 16, 3.
[2] Suet., *Tib.*, 20. Ironically he may have lived to meet Maroboduus, saved by the rebellion of A.D. 6, but who was later eliminated by diplomacy and interned at Ravenna in 18, *PIR*[1], M 250.
[3] Dio, lvi, 16, 4; cf. Suet., *Tib.*, 16: 'The most serious of all foreign wars since the Punic.'
[4] Praeneste Fasti, *Inscr. It.*, XIII, 2, p. 114, and other references, *PIR*[2], C, 941, p. 223.
[5] Dio, lvi, 17, 1. The fifth salutation of Tiberius appears on coins of A.D. 10/11, *RIC*, 1, 82, 220.
[6] Dio, lvi, 17, 1.
[7] Dio, lvi, 17, 2–4.
[8] Vell. Pat., ii, 117, 1; cf. Dio, lvi, 18, recording the arrival of the news immediately after these decrees had been passed.
[9] Vell. Pat., ii, 121, 2–3; cf. Suet., *Tib.*, 20; *Inscr. It.*, XIII, 2, p. 134 (*Fasti Praenestini*). The forthcoming triumph is mentioned by Ovid, *Ex pont.*, ii, 1, dedicated to Germanicus.

marvels his admirer Velleius.[1] More tasks remained for Tiberius in Illyricum, however, and in the summer of 14 he set out once more but had barely arrived when news reached him of the final illness of Augustus.[2] With his accession to the Principate in September, Tiberius' years of active campaigning were at an end. The large task of pacification and administration to be completed in Illyricum would have to be continued by others.

[1] Vell. Pat., ii, 122, 1.
[2] Suet., *Aug.*, 97, 3; Vell. Pat., ii, 123, 1; Dio, lvi, 31, 1; Tac., *Ann.*, i, 5: 'He had scarcely entered Illyricum when he was recalled by the letters from his mother.'

Chapter 6
The Roman Province and its Governors

1 The Boundaries of Dalmatia under the Principate

Roman Dalmatia as constituted at the end of Augustus' reign included not only the Adriatic coastline which still bears that name today, but also all the modern Yugoslav Republics of Bosnia–Hercegovina and Montenegro, most of Southern Croatia, together with a large slice of Western Serbia. On the Adriatic it began in the north at the river Arsia (Raša) in Western Istria and extended as far south as Lissus (Lješ) at the mouth of the Albanian Drin (Drilo), also included were the islands of the Quarnerno (Gulf of Rijeka) as well as those which lie off the Dalmatian coast.[1] Inland there is some doubt about the precise line followed by the boundaries with Pannonia and Moesia Superior, but there is little question now which areas fell within the province.

In the northwest the boundary with Italy followed the Arsia as far as its source and then continued to the region of Jelšane near the Julian Alps, where Pannonia began. The line then continued eastwards in the general direction of Belgrade along the northern fringes of the Bosnian hills south of the Save valley.[2] In detail the line can be traced south of the Colapis valley (Kulpa) and crossed the river Glina at Velika Kladuša, where a frontier station was maintained and staffed by men detached from the Legion XIIII Gemina Martia victrix, whose permanent base was the Danubian fortress at Carnuntum the capital of Pannonia Superior.[3] This place can be identified with the *ad fines* recorded in the Antonine

---

[1] Plin., *HN*, iii, 129, 145; cf. Ptol., ii, 16, 1. For modern discussions see G. Alföldy, *Bevölkerung* 27 f.
[2] Ptol, ii, 16, 1.
[3] Plin., *HN*, iii, 147. Tiles of the legion are known: III 14023 (13339³).

Itinerary on the route through Liburnia between Aquileia and Siscia.[1] Further east the boundary crossed the river Vrbas valley at Laktaši north of Banjaluka, the *ad fines* station on the route between Servitium (Bos. Gradiška on the Save) and Salona.[2] Ptolemy speaks of the southern boundary of Pannonia as extending from the Albius Mons to the Baebii or Biblii Montes.[3] Looked at from the Dalmatian side these were hills along the northern boundary west of the river Vrbas, since to the east of this Dalmatia adjoins Pannonia Inferior. The Albius Mons is probably the northern range of the Velika Kapela, while the Baebii were the Kozara hills between Velika Kladuša and Laktaši.[4] The next valley east of the Vrbas is the Bosna and here the boundary crossed at Doboj, where for some time was stationed the auxiliary unit Cohort I Flavia Hispanorum.[5] A short distance to the east of Doboj the frontier line impinged on the Save and then turned southwards in the direction of the Scardus Mons (Šar planina), west of the Meosian city Scupi (Skopje). This is the general description given by Ptolemy of the western boundary of Moesia Superior.[6] Dalmatia met the Save at the point where it flows in a tortuous course between Sirmium and Belgrade, and probably left it along its southern tributary the river Kolubara in the direction of Čačak. Included in Dalmatia was the lead-mining area around Mount Šturac, where pigs have been discovered with the provincial mines stamp. At Čačak in the Morava valley there was a frontier station, manned after the second century by auxiliaries from the army of Dalmatia. South from Čačak the frontier ran west of Ivanjica, the centre of the Celegeri in Moesia Superior, and then followed the watershed between the Lim and the Ibar, the former river in Dalmatia, the latter in Moesia Superior.[7] Excluded from the province was the area of Kossovo polje (Kosmet), where lay the city Ulpiana (Lipljan), and Mitrovica where the tombstones of upper class families from Scupi and Ulpiana have been found.[8] Further south, Peč was also probably within Moesia because of the Ulpii attested there with Trajanic citizenship, doubtless belonging to the Moesian Ulpiana.[9] At the

---

[1] *It. Ant.*, 274, 6.

[2] Pašalić, *Naselja*, 18. On the *beneficiarii* at Laktaši see p. 125.

[3] Ptol. ii, 14, 1.

[4] A. Mocsy, *RE* supp. 9 (1962), 523 f., A. Graf, *Geographie*, etc., 12 f.

[5] III, 14619 (12759) and p. 143.

[6] Ptol., ii, 15, 1; 16, 1; iii, 9, 1. For the boundary line see Alföldy, *Bevölkerung*, 27 f.

[7] The stamps from the Kosmaj and Rudnik regions may belong to the Dalmatian-Pannonian mines, although some have contended that the area was part of Moesia Superior, M. Veličković, *ZRNM*, 1 (1958), 955, or of Pannonia, F. Papazoglu, *ŽA*, 7 (1957), 122. For the military post at Čačak see p. 473.

[8] E. Čerškov—Lj. Popović, *GMKM*, 1 (1956), 316 ff.; E. Čerškov, *GMKM*, 2 (1957), 65 ff.

[9] III, 8177; *JÖAI*, 6 (1903), Bb. 33 f.; Sp. 98, 49; 71, 112–13.

Scardus Mons the frontier turned southwestwards and followed the river Drin to Lissus and the Adriatic.

11 *The Provincial Governors from Augustus to Gallienus* (See Appendix II)

For more than two hundred and fifty years the area outlined above was controlled by a Roman senator acting as the legate of the emperor, with the title *legatus Augusti pro praetore provinciae Dalmatiae*. He was responsible for all military and civil administration within the province and from his decisions there was no appeal, except in the case of Roman citizens condemned to death. The only means by which a province could protest against an unjust governor was to wait until the governor had finished his tour of duty. Then the representative provincial council drawn from the cities could refuse the customary testimonial to his stewardship; in some provinces it was possible to instigate a prosecution before the Senate, where they could expect support from other senators who looked after the interests of the province at Rome. Usually proceedings of this kind arose only from the wealthier senatorial provinces, for instance Asia or Bithynia, and no legate of Dalmatia is known to have incurred the hostility of the provincials. This situation was due more to the difficulty of organizing and sustaining such an expression of opinion among backward and scattered communities, than to the blameless character of the administration. By the middle of the third century a large part of the Senatorial Order had contracted out of the tasks of administering and defending the Empire, and under Gallienus they were formally replaced in provincial governorships by members of the Equestrian Order whose title in Dalmatia was *praeses provinciae Dalmatiae*. Literary evidence tells us virtually nothing about the standard of administration of individual governors; normally the only occasion when they are mentioned is when one of them rebelled or when the provincial army was involved in a civil war.

The existence of over fifty *legati* and *praesides* is attested by literary and epigraphic evidence: the names of forty are known in full, four only by their *cognomina* and another eight are unidentified. Such lists of provincial governors can be studied as material for the composition of the ruling class of the Empire and the changes that took place within it, while the changing character of the Dalmatian governorship and the attitude of the government towards it can be revealed by studying the place it held over the years in the hierarchy of provincial commands. Dalmatia is unusual in that it starts out as a major military command with two legions, each with their own praetorian senatorial commanders, and a large force of auxiliaries; but with the shift of military activity towards the Danube it became an unarmed province (*provincia inermis*) with a police force of three auxiliary regiments long before the end of the first century. One might have expected that the status of the province would be reduced and the consular replaced by praetorian legates. Dalmatia remained a consular province, however, although within that category it was one of the most junior, being normally held immediately after the consulate. The size and nature of the province still demanded the greater experience of a consular senator, because of its closeness and strategic importance to such key military commands as Pannonia Superior and Inferior, and Moesia Superior; many of its attested governors soon proceeded to command the large frontier armies along the Rhine and Danube and in Syria. It was an appointment quite different from the other non-military consular province, Hispania Tarraconensis, which was often reserved for an older senator close to retirement. As a group of people the Dalmatian governors are a mixed collection: they include a would-be emperor, the father of an emperor and one who actually achieved the Purple, not to mention the great senatorial historian of Rome Cassius Dio Cocceianus, and in an earlier generation his father M. Cassius Apronianus. Chronologically they fall into two distinct groups, those who governed the province when it held its legions and those who governed it after the army (apart from the small auxiliary garrison) had been withdrawn.

When Dalmatia became a regular independent command at the end of Augustus' reign, there must have been two main considerations which weighed with the emperor and his advisers in choosing their man. In the first place he would have to be a competent general. Even after control over the population of the interior had finally been established in the most costly war of Augustus' reign, it could hardly be regarded as any more pacified than was Germany when Varus advanced across the Rhine towards disaster in 9. No fighting is recorded after the capture of Bato of the Daesitiates in 9, but the opening of the road routes through the interior between the Adriatic and the Save valley was a task which must have required constant vigilance against ambush and sudden revolt. In second place, but hardly less important, came the political considerations. A province so close to Italy containing an army smouldering with dissatisfaction (if we may judge by the mutiny of the nearby Pannonian legions in 14) with their meagre rewards following on the recent victories was a command which could be entrusted only to those of proved loyalty.

The task of C. Vibius Postumus was merely a prolongation of that which he had carried out in 9 as legate under Tiberius. Both he and his brother, A. Vibius Habitus, were 'new men' from Samnite Larinum and emerge (Postumus was consul in 5, his brother three years later) with the ascendancy of Tiberius after his return from Rhodes. After his triumphal insignia in the victory celebrations of 9 Postumus began the attempt to recover from Dalmatia some of the money which had been poured out for its conquest by organizing the working of its gold deposits in the interior. If L. Aelius Lamia (*cos. 3*) commanded the army in Dalmatia in the years 12–14 (Pannonia is equally possible: Velleius calls his province Illyricum) the reason for his choice was similar to that of Vibius Postumus. His selection also was due to Tiberius, under whom he had served in Germany during the campaigns after Varus' disaster (10–12). Although the first consul from his family he enjoyed considerable social distinction, and a reputation for liveliness in his old age. The last year of his life was spent as prefect of the City (32–33). Tiberius is famous as an emperor who kept his legates in office for unusually long tours of duty, and the Dalmatian governorship was no exception. Apart from a possible interval of a few years in the twenties only two legates served for the entire reign, P. Cornelius Dolabella (14–20) and L. Volusius Saturninus (before 29 to about 40). Dolabella belonged to an ancient patrician family which had suffered eclipse after the triumviral wars. His father missed the consulship under Augustus, but the son revived the family honours after the return of Tiberius from Rhodes by obtaining the ordinary consulship (10) which his lineage demanded. As legate already of Upper Illyricum (Dalmatia) before the death of Augustus in August 14 he may have been host to Tiberius when the urgent summons reached him from Livia to hasten back to Italy where Augustus was dying, if not already dead. As legate of the province he was active in completing the pacification of the interior and all the major military roads from the coast were finished during his administration. At the provincial capital Salona he held an honorary position as magistrate (*IIIIvir quinquennalis*); this was probably in A.D. 15, since the honour was next accepted by Tiberius' son Drusus Germanicus Caesar during his visit to Dalmatia in 20. Dolabella was also honoured at Epidaurum with a statue by the provincial cities of Upper Illyricum (*civitates superioris provinciae Hillyrici*), where he is described as legate of both Augustus and Tiberius. The active life of the next attested governor, L. Volusius Saturninus (*cos. 3*), extended throughout the entire Julio–Claudian dynasty. When he died in 56 at the age of 93 he had served five emperors as a close adviser with consistent loyalty. When he was appointed to Dalmatia he was nearly 70, but was no less active a governor than Dolabella. The programme of road building through the interior was now completed, and much of his time was taken up with organizing the settlement of numerous boundary disputes among provincial communities, especially in Liburnia. While he was in Dalmatia and during the years afterwards he was honoured as patron at Aenona with more than one statue.

When the unbalanced emperor Gaius (Caligula) was murdered on 24 January 41 the Senate met, proclaimed the Republic, and passed decrees condemning the memory of the whole house of Caesar, unaware that the praetorians had already hailed the scholarly Claudius as their emperor. During that meeting of the Senate many spoke in a way they were later to regret. The armies accepted the proclamation of the new emperor, in spite of his being hardly known to them, because he was an heir to the Julio–Claudian House. The behaviour of the Senate in 41 must have made Claudius suspicious of that body, and with good reason, because when his reign was barely a year old he faced rebellion in the name of Senate and People from his legate in Dalmatia. The son of M. Furius Camillus (*cos.* 8) adopted by L. Arruntius (*cos.* 6), L. Arruntius Camillus Scribonianus (*cos.* 32) possessed an ancestry that few could match, including a link with the family of Pompeius. In Dalmatia his army (Legions VII and XI) soon deserted him, however, and he fled to Issa, where he perished. His followers at Rome were tried and condemned: some were allowed suicide, including his chief supporter L. Annius Vinicianus who had himself aspired to become emperor in the previous year. For their loyalty the two legions were awarded the titles *Claudia pia fidelis* which they were to carry for the reminder of their existence. There are two records of Arruntius' governorship in the province, a boundary settlement from Vaganj near the head of the Vrbas valley and the gravestone of Felicius, a member of his household who died at Salona during his administration. Arruntius' successor was L. Salvius Otho (*cos.* 33) who was unusually zealous in seeking out supporters of the rebellion, in spite of some disapproval from Claudius. After he had uncovered a later conspiracy, however, Claudius raised him to the rank of Patrician, still an inner circle of power and influence within the oligarchy of the Senate. His son was emperor for a brief period early in 69. His tenure of the province was short (42–3), since he was soon back in the capital protecting Claudius from more conspiracies. During the early years of his reign Claudius sought to win over the most influential families in the Senate, among whom were still the Calpurnii Pisones. The Piso recorded on a boundary settlement near Salona may be the consul of 27, son of the Piso who was popularly believed to have poisoned the emperor's brother Germanicus in Syria. The next attested legate is P. Anteius Rufus (50– *c.* 54). His name appears on three inscriptions recording some building in the headquarters of the legionary fortress of Legion XI Claudia at Burnum during the years 50–2. Later Anteius perished during the conspiracy of Piso against Nero because, it was said, of his wealth and an unhealthy interest in horoscopes. His name was erased from two of the Burnum texts after his death in 66, but was soon restored after the condemnation of Nero's memory. Only two facts are recorded about C. Calpetanus Rantius Sedatus, who was in Dalmatia early under Nero; he was of Etruscan origin and earlier in his career held the post of Superintendent of Public Records (*curator tabulariorum publicorum*). A. Ducenius Geminus (63–7) is attested on three boundary settlements, and was honoured as patron at Narona with a statue. In his own right he may have set up a dedication to Aesculapius, but the interpretation of the stone in uncertain. After leaving Dalmatia Ducenius Geminus became Prefect of the City, and in that capacity was present at the imperial council when Galba decided to adopt Piso Frugi as his successor.

In the struggle between Vitellius and Vespasian during the latter half of 69 the allegiance of the consular governors in Dalmatia and Pannonia was crucial. The former was held by M. Pompeius Silvanus (*cos.* 45), the latter by L. Tampius Flavianus, both timid and wealthy old men. The driving force which brought the Danubian armies to the Flavian cause came from the younger and ambitious legionary commanders, Antonius Primus of VII Gemina and Annius Bassus of XI Claudia, supported by the energetic procurator of the two provinces Cornelius Fuscus. In Dalmatia the administration of Pompeius Silvanus (67–70) is attested by a boundary settlement in Liburnia. In spite of their inactive support to the Flavians the two governors received their reward in the conjoint distinction of a second consulship a few years later. From 70 until about 83 Dalmatia remained a military province, but with an army reduced to one legion (IIII Flavia felix). An early legate under Vespasian was the jurist Pegasus. Before the end of the reign he was appointed Prefect of the City, a choice commented on unfavourably by Juvenal. In Dalmatia he is attested on a boundary settlement from Southern Liburnia, arranged by C. Petillius Firmus, tribune of the new Legion IIII Flavia felix then stationed at Burnum. Another Flavian governor was L. Funisulanus Vettonianus (*cos.* ?78). As a legionary commander nearly twenty years before his career had been shattered by involvement in Caesennius Paetus' disgraceful capitulation to the Parthians. His appointment to Dalmatia was probably due more to internal politics and a recent rehabilitation, than to his competence as a military commander. In the province he also is attested on a boundary settlement between the lands of the Vesii family and another party not far north of Trebinje in Popovopolje. With the mounting crisis on the Danube under Domitian the province lost its legion about 86, and accordingly dropped in status as a provincial command, although still under a consular.

It is unfortunate that few names of legionary commanders in Dalmatia are recorded. In the civil war of 69 Annius Bassus of Legion XI Claudia was an eager partisan of the Flavians, and, like many other legionary commanders in the Danubian and eastern armies, he was rewarded with rapid promotion to the consulate. It would be revealing to know the names of the men who controlled the Dalmatian legions when Arruntius rebelled in 42 against Claudius: they may well have saved the dynasty. One of the last legionary commanders in the province was the eminent Flavian lawyer C. Octavius Tidius Tossianus L. Iavolenus Priscus (*cos.* 86). As the legate of Legion IIII Flavia felix at Burnum around 81 he had some connection with the Octavii family of nearby Nedinum, where he was honoured some years later with a statue by his friend P. Mutilius Crispinus.

Until the outbreak of the Marcomannic Wars, when half a dozen army commanders and governors are recorded within a period of about ten years, the names of only six or seven governors are attested, and in most cases little else is known about them. The governorship of Q. Pomponius Rufus is unusual because he held the post as praetorian senator (*c.* 92–4) and held his consulship immediately afterwards (*suff.* 95). The appointment was probably due not so much to the tidy mind of Domitian realizing that usually non-military imperial provinces should be governed by praetorian senators as to a tense political situation at Rome and a shortage of suitable consulars. The experiment was discontinued, however, and Rufus' successor C. Cilnius Proculus (*cos.* 87), a member of the ancient royal house of Etruscan Arretium, held the governorship as a consular. Proculus' successor in Dalmatia may have been the upright Macer to whom Martial addressed a poem in 98. Dalmatia was little affected by Trajan's expeditions into Dacia, and in the middle years of that reign the province was under C. Minicius Fundanus (*cos.* 107), a cultivated friend and correspondent of the Younger Pliny, mentioned also in one of Plutarch's Dialogues.

No governor is definitely attested in the reign of Hadrian (117–38). One may be the senator with high social connections whose fragmentary career inscription was discovered in the debris of the Salona Amphitheatre. A near contemporary of this man was P. Coelius Balbinus Vibullius Pius (*cos.* 137). A number of gravestones recording slaves and freedman members of his household at Salona could point to a governorship held by him under Antonius Pius but, more likely perhaps, he could have been a native of the province or owned property there. Only two governors are attested for the reign of Pius. M. Aemilius Papus from Salpensa in Baetica is recorded on two career inscriptions set up in his native city, while the otherwise unknown Sex. Aemilius Equester appears on a building record from the camp of the Cohort VIII Voluntariorum at Tilurium. Neither's tenure can be dated precisely: Aemilius Papus was there in 147, preceding Aemilius Equester who was there in the latter half of Pius' reign. Under Marcus Aurelius (161–180) Dalmatia re-emerges as an area of military importance, both on account of the Marcomannic invasions during the second half of the reign and because of possible disturbances in remoter areas of the interior (see p. 117 f). In the period 170–80 at least five, and possibly six, governors are known, an unusually rapid turn-round due to the continuous

H

warfare of the period which had resulted in some serious losses in the Roman high command. Among the governors at this time was M. Didius Iulianus the future emperor, chosen as a competent commander to deal with disturbances in the province. There were some disturbances in the interior of the Danubian area at this time, although there the problem never became so serious as the rebellion of Maternus in Gaul and Spain under Commodus. A similar task may have been alloted to L. Vitrasius Flamininus, member of an old Campanian family, who perhaps commanded an army operating in Northern Dalmatia at the same time that he was governing Moesia Superior; there is some doubt, however, whether his unusual command does belong to the reign of Marcus Aurelius, for he could have belonged to an earlier generation and be identical with the L. Vitrasius Flamininus who was consul in 122. A governor who certainly held office in this period was C. Vettius Sabinianus Iulius Hospes who had been promoted into the senatorial order under Pius before his long military career under Marcus Aurelius.

Under Commodus (180–92) M. Cassius Apronianus, from a leading family of Nicaea in Bithynia, governed the province about 185, a post in which his son Cassius Dio Cocceianus the historian was to follow him forty years later. Under Caracalla (211–7) C. Iulius Avitus Alexianus was related to the Syrian family of Iulia Domna, Septimius Severus' empress, and thus to the emperors Elagabalus and Severus Alexander. The fragmentary record of his career from Salona records that he rose from equestrian to senatorial rank, doubtless through his connection with the imperial family.

There is very little evidence to indicate the relative popularity or competence of the men who governed most of the Empire's provinces. In some cases the occasional prosecutions of proconsuls for extortion before the Senate at Rome reveal an alarmingly low standard of conduct, especially from the period under Trajan recorded by the Younger Pliny, when the governors no longer had to fear the severe scrutiny applied to their conduct by the 'tyrant' Domitian. The expensive business of sustaining a prosecution was possible only for provinces with the wealth of many large cities, and which had connections with Rome through local senators. Such a province was Baetica in Southern Spain, while in the East Bithynia accused more than one of its proconsuls at this period. The major military commands, where civilian life was overshadowed by the army, offer no such picture. In Dalmatia the peoples in the interior still preferred to express their discontent with open rebellion rather than make representations to the emperor at Rome. From the historian Cassius Dio we have his own admission that the troops in Pannonia complained to the praetorian prefect Ulpian about his excessive severity, and his general unpopularity in Rome was such that he found it prudent to retire to his native Bithynia. Judging from his re-marks about the indiscipline of provincial armies in general, one may suspect that that he was equally unpopular during his term of office in Dalmatia (*c.* 224–6) a few years earlier. After the governorship of Cassius Dio only four senatorial legates are recorded, none of whom is more than a name.

A catalogue of the governors of Dalmatia during the Principate tells us little about the history of the province or its population. Individual records of their activities can furnish details on such matters as road building or the status of communities in various parts of the province, but from this one can learn very little about the character of the administration and how it developed over nearly three centuries. For a clearer picture one must look to other provinces where the evidence is more abundant. On the other hand such a list is useful for indicating the status which the governorship of Dalmatia held in the hierarchy of imperial commands. Here the most significant feature is the contrast between the ex-perienced men appointed under the Julio–Claudians and the relatively insignifi-cant names attested for the second century when the province no longer required military specialists, except in the temporary emergency of the Marcomannic Wars. In another direction a catalogue of governors can be relevant to the in-vestigation of the composition of the ruling oligarchy in the Empire and how it changed from century to century, sometimes from reign to reign. In this respect the Dalmatian list can give a misleading impression: in the matter of origins of legates, only three governors can be demonstrated to have come from provincial families, four if one includes P. Coelius Balbinus Vibullius Pius. This suggests a massive predominance of Roman and Italian families. Yet other provinces reveal quite a different picture: in Britian, where military ability was always necessary, a preponderance of new provincial families is revealed long before the end of the first century.

Chapter 7
The Roman Army in Dalmatia

1 Before A.D. 9

Leaving aside the sporadic warfare between Macedon and the Illyrians on her northwestern borders, the earliest military action that is recorded in Illyria was undertaken not by a Roman but by a Greek force.[1] When the Parian colonists who had settled on Pharos (Hvar) in 385 B.C. were attacked in the following year by Illyrians, Dionysius' forces came to their assistance (p. 9 f). A prefect established at Lissus (Lješ) sailed northward with a fleet of triremes and defeated the Illyrians in their *lembi*, taking many prisoners. It is unlikely that the force at Lissus was maintained after the death of Dionysius in 367 B.C.[2]

Both the Roman expeditions in 229 B.C. and 219 B.C. were under the command of the two consuls of the year (p. 16 ff). In the earlier war the forces totalled twenty thousand infantry and two hundred ships, a full consular army – as presumably was that sent in 219 B.C. against Demetrius of Pharos.[3]

Apart from embassies in force to complain about piracy, no Roman army landed in Illyria until 168 B.C., when Gentius was removed from his kingdom by the praetor L. Anicius Gallus (p. 26). Gentius managed to gather a force of 15,000 at Lissus,[4] but the size of the Roman force is not known. It is not likely to have been large since it was thought desirable to supplement it with Illyrian

[1] On these episodes see Fanoula Papazoglu, *Historia*, 14 (1965), 150 ff., and N. G. L. Hammond, *ABSA*, 61 (1966), 239–53.
[2] Diod., xv, 13, 14, 2.
[3] Pol., ii, 11, 1 (two hundred ships), ii, 11, 7 (twenty thousand infantry and two hundred cavalry).
[4] Gentius' forces, Liv., xliv, 30.

88

allies, 200 cavalry and 2,000 infantry under Epicadus and Algalsus, nobles of the Parthini. The army which fought the Delmatae in 156–155 B.C. was probably larger (p. 31), since it was able to defeat the Delmatae after maintaining a winter blockade of their capital Delminium (Županac). This was the first occasion when a campaign in Illyria was undertaken for reasons largely unconnected with affairs across the Adriatic, the aim being to keep the army in fighting condition by some hard campaigning far away from the luxury of large cities.[1] The punitive measure against the Ardiaei and Pleraei in 135 B.C. may (p. 32), as Appian suggests, have been no more than a raid, but it was carried out by 10,000 infantry and 600 cavalry.[2] No details are recorded of the armies which attacked the Iapodes in 129 B.C., although it is known that more than one force was involved.[3] The activities of Metellus Delmaticus in 118–117 B.C. were designed to provide another triumphal honour for the Caecilii Metelli (p. 33). The next known landing across the Adriatic was another training expedition. In 84 B.C. Cinna and Carbo landed some of their raw levies in Liburnia (p. 34 f) not, as has usually been assumed, to prevent Sulla landing in Italy, but to obtain some battle experience before they faced Sulla's veterans.[4]

In 59 B.C. the Lex Vatinia conferred on Caesar command in Cisalpine Gaul. Transalpine Gaul, and Illyricum, but there is no evidence that any of his legions ever operated in Illyricum. He may have taken some forces with him when he set out for Illyricum in the winter 57–56 B.C., but he was forced to turn back to deal with rebellion among the Veneti.[5] By this time Roman settlements on the Illyrian coast were thriving, and a Roman commander could look to them for troops to deal with local troubles. When the Pirustae caused trouble in 54 B.C. Caesar ordered Roman allies to assemble their forces.[6] These forces would be under the command of *praefecti* who may have been nominated from the Roman settlements. Caesar hoped to deal with the Delmatae in a similar manner when they attacked the Liburni at Promona without having to send his own troops, but the war with Pompeius intervened.[7]

With the outbreak of civil war in 49 B.C. the weakness of the Roman position was fully exposed. At first there were two Caesarian forces in the northern Adriatic, one commanded by C. Antonius on Curicta, consisting of at least fifteen legionary cohorts and some Gallic *auxilia*, another under Minucius Basilus and the historian Sallustius Crispus on the mainland nearby (p. 40 f). For the size of the latter force there is no evidence, nor is it known what happened to it after

---

[1] Pol., xxxii, 13, 5–6.   [2] Appian, *Ill.*, 10.
[3] One was commanded by Ti. Latinius Pandusa, Appian, *Ill.*, 10.
[4] Appian, *BC*, i, 77–8.   [5] Caes., *BG*, ii, 35.
[6] Caes., *BG*, v, 1–2.   [7] Appian, *Ill.*, 12.

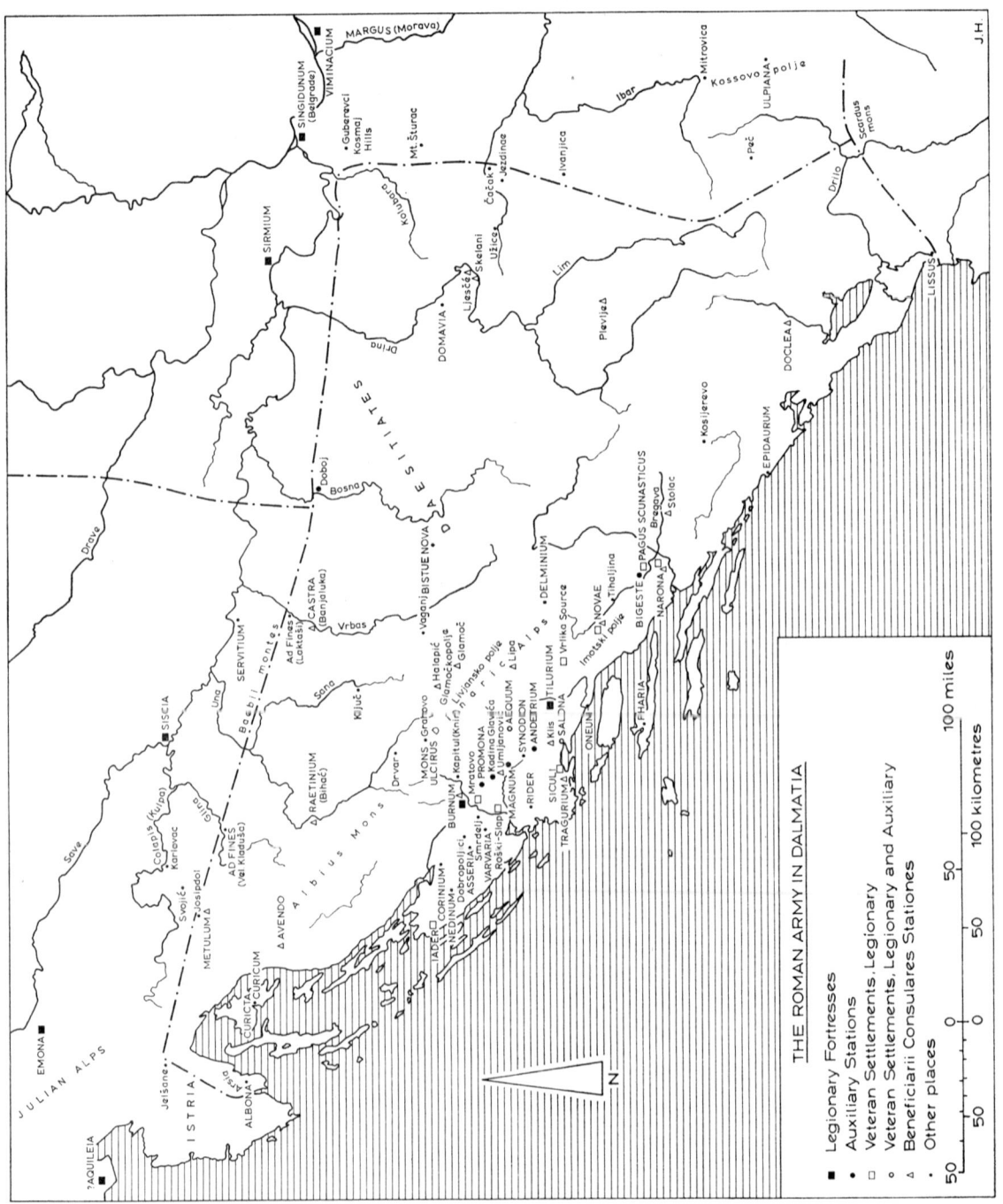

Figure 4 The Roman Army in Dalmatia

Antonius surrendered his force to the Pompeians.[1] After Pharsalus Q. Cornificius was sent to Illyricum with two legions, where he established himself somewhere in the south, probably at Epidaurum. At the same time another force under A. Gabinius, consisting of fifteen cohorts and 3,000 cavalry, was dispatched to Illyricum by the land route around the head of the Adriatic. Appian records that Gabinius lost ten of his cohorts at Synodion in an ambush, but this seems an exaggeration since Caesar lists Gabinius' total losses as four tribunes, thirty-eight centurions, and more than 2,000 infantry, which must include later casualties in the campaigns based on Salona.[2] After he had defeated the Pompeian navy with legionary reserves from Brundisium P. Vatinius was sent to Illyricum with three legions and a strong force of cavalry (p. 43 ff). From his base at Narona he made headway against the Delmatae, but when the murder of Caesar was known his army forced him to retire southward to Dyrrhachium, where it was absorbed into the forces of Brutus and Cassius.[3] Once again there were no Roman forces in Illyricum.

The operations of Octavianus in 35–33 B.C. (p. 47 ff) were designed rather to improve the reputation of the commander and the efficiency of his army than to reassert Roman authority among the Illyrians. It is a matter for speculation what contribution they made towards the creation of the network of forts and other stations in Illyricum which were to prove vital during the reconquest of the area in A.D. 6–9. Siscia was held, perhaps permanently, and the road across the Julian Alps to the Save valley opened up.[4] Yet that must have been the limit. South of Siscia, the Iapodes between the Pannonians and Liburnia were chastised, and are not known to have caused any further disturbance. From the Adriatic side Octavianus scattered the forces of the Delmatae, or rather that part of them which dwelt between the Dinaric Alps and the Adriatic. It has been suggested that these operations resulted in the creation of the line of military strong-points from Burnum, through Promona, Magnum, Andetrium, Tilurium, and then through Imotskipolje to Bigeste near Narona.[5] Burnum and Tilurium are known later as legionary fortresses, while the others were all auxiliary stations. There is, however, no epigraphic evidence to support the view that this scheme dates from as early as 33 B.C. Furthermore, Octavianus was not yet Augustus and during these years his preoccupation was not primarily with the Delmatae. He did not fight these wars merely to create a defensive line of forts

---

[1] It is unlikely that it moved southwards towards the Salona region.

[2] *Bell. Alex.*, 42–7.   [3] Cic., *Epp. ad fam.*, v, 9, 10b.

[4] There is no record of what happened to the garrison of twenty-five cohorts under Fufius Geminus left there by Octavianus.

[5] For instance by G. Alföldy, *A Arch. Hung.*, 14 (1962), 284.

through the karst hinterland of the Adriatic, even if he ever contemplated leaving any forces in Illyricum at all, but to obtain an army suitable to lead on campaigns elsewhere. Thirdly, the defensive line Burnum–Bigeste is not the whole system: on its own such a scheme would have made very little headway against the real danger, the Delmatae and other peoples across the Dinaric Alps. It must be part of a wider system based on the Save and Drave valley in the north, where centres such as Poetovio, probably occupied about 13 B.C., Siscia, and Sirmium, held the peoples of Illyricum within their mountains and enabled Roman armies to begin penetration from the north and south. The deployment of legionaries and *auxilia* on the Burnum–Bigeste line belongs to a later age, when strategy on the grand scale was being employed, not to the partisan operations in years before Actium.[1]

Between the end of Octavianus' campaigns and the outbreak of war in 6–9 there is only a little more evidence for the numbers and deployment of the army in Illyricum than is available for the later years of the Republic. Illyricum was constituted as an imperial province in 11 B.C. and formed a large command extending from the mountains of Albania and Macedonia in the south to the Middle Danube in the north. The subjugation of this area was the most arduous and the most enduring military achievement of Augustus' principate. In comparison with their importance these wars are poorly reported in the ancient writers: there was no Elder Drusus or Germanicus to attract writers, while in later years few people were interested in learning of Tiberius' achievement as a general during the reign of Augustus. The only means of approaching the problems of the army in Illyricum before A.D. 9 is to begin with the evidence at that date and work backwards.[2]

After A.D. 9 the army in Illyricum numbered five legions: three were in Pannonia, VIII Augusta, IX Hispana, and XV Apollinaris, and two in Dalmatia, VII and XI.[3] During the war of 6–9 other legions served in Illyricum, and their identity and movements can be traced with reasonable accuracy. At the outbreak of the war in 6 the five in Illyricum were probably IX Hispana, XIII Gemina, XIV Gemina, XV Apollinaris, and XX. In the second year of the war Tiberius was joined at Siscia by another five, brought from Moesia and the East under A. Caecina and M. Plautius Silvanus, making a total of ten legions in all.[4] Almost

[1] Plin., *HN*, iii, 142: 'in hoc tractu sunt Burnum, Andetrium, Tribulium (for Tilurium) nobilitate proeliis castella', referring to the later wars under Augustus: earlier wars are ignored by Pliny.
[2] For the overall pattern of legionary movements under Augustus see R. Syme, *JRS*, 23 (1933), 14–33.
[3] Pannonia: Tac., *Ann.*, i, 23, 30; Dalmatia: *Ann.*, iv, 5, without naming the legions.
[4] Vell. Pat., ii, 112, 4 (five legions under Plautius Silvanus and A. Caecina at the Volcaean Marshes, see p. 72); ii, 113, 1 (ten legions at Siscia in 7).

immediately Tiberius ordered this force to return along the route by which it had reached Siscia, and escorted it part of the way with his own army.[1] Caecina, who had been legate in Moesia on the outbreak of the war, was needed in his own province, and he apparently returned there taking with him the two legions brought from the East by Silvanus, IV Scythica and V Macedonia, which then formed the garrison force of Moesia.[2] At the same time Plautius Silvanus remained at Sirmium during the winter 7–8, commanding the three legions which had previously formed the army of Moesia under Caecina, VII, VIII Augusta, and XI, and assisted Tiberius in overcoming the Pannonians in 8 and the Dalmatians in 9.[3]

Turning to the evidence for the individual legions, XX is well attested and occupied Burnum until it left Illyricum for Germany, where reinforcements were required after the disaster of Varus in 9.[4] It was replaced at Burnum by XI. Very little is known of the movements of XIII Gemina and XIV Gemina during this period, but what there is points to their having been part of the army of Illyricum.[5] A *miles* of XIII originating from Ariminum and buried at Narona received decorations from Tiberius before he was appointed centurion in the citizen Cohort I Campana, which was stationed in Dalmatia at this time. Similar decorations, presumably from Tiberius in Illyricum, were received by a *primuspilus* of the same legion buried at Aquileia, a popular centre at that time for men serving in the army of Illyricum.[6] The only evidence for XIV, attested at Mogontiacum (Mainz) in A.D. 9, is a *miles* buried at Aquileia.[7] Three legions were moved from somewhere to make up the losses on the Rhine after the disaster of Varus, and it seems reasonable to assume that they were drawn from Illyricum, and that they were XIII Gemina, XIV Gemina, and XX.

The seven other legions which had been in Illyricum during the war remained to form the garrisons of the later provinces Pannonia, Dalmatia, and Moesia:

[1] Vell. Pat., ii, 113, 2–3.

[2] Cass. Dio, lv, 29, 3 (A. Caecina in Moesia in 6).

[3] Cass. Dio, lv, 34, 6–7 (in 8); lvi, 12, 2–3 (in 9).

[4] The legion was originally based at or near Aquileia, where tombstones of early serving soldiers are known, V 939, 948. At Burnum there is a *hastatus prior*, III, 2836; and there are veterans at Salona, III, 2030; and Iader, III, 2911. Another early serving soldier comes from Reselec on the river Oescus in Moesia, and presumably dates to the period of the war of 6–9, III, 7452 (*ILS*, 2270); cf. Ritterling, 1770. By 14 it was stationed at Ara Ubiorum (Cologne), Tac., *Ann.*, i, 39.

[5] R. Syme, *JRS*, 23 (1933), 28–9.

[6] III, 8438: *miles* at Narona; Pais, supp. V, 1163 (*ILS*, 2638): *primuspilus* at Aquileia.

[7] V 8272 (Aquileia). It could have been stationed in either Transpadana or Illyricum, Ritterling, 1728, but certainly served under Tiberius in Illyricum during the war of 6–9.

VIII Augusta, IX Hispana, and XV Apollinaris in Pannonia, VII and XI in Dalmatia, IV Scythica and V Macedonica in Moesia.[1] Included in this number must be the two which Plautius Silvanus brought from the East. IX and XV appear to have been in Illyricum for many years: IX may have been at Tilurium, later occupied by VII,[2] while XV was at Emona until it moved to Carnuntum in A.D. 14.[3] Nothing is known of the whereabouts of XI before it replaced XX at Burnum in 9: the earliest record of the legion is an elderly veteran invalided from service (*veteranus missicius*) at Poetovio, later occupied by VIII Augusta, but this is not definite evidence that it was ever stationed there.[4] Both VIII and V are known to have had veterans settled at Berytus in Syria in 14 B.C., and they could well have formed part of the eastern army for some period under Augustus.[5] VII has many veterans of eastern origin settled in Dalmatia, outnumbering those from Italy or the western provinces, and these are not likely to have been recruited while the legion was in Dalmatia; but recruiting from the East could have been the practice when the legion was part of the proconsular army in Macedonia (its earliest record gives the title *Macedonica,* and comes from the Thracian Chersonese) and later in Moesia.[6] It might have taken part in the Thracian campaign under L. Piso about 13–11 B.C. either as part of the Macedonian army, or, if that was busy in the far northwest helping Tiberius in Illyricum, as a special draft from the East brought by L. Piso especially for service against the Thracians.[7] Wherever it was, the presence of eastern recruits in VII make it most unlikely that it had reached Illyricum before 6. Some years ago O. Cuntz pointed to the fact that many of the legionaries of eastern origin serving in VII bore *nomina* of M. Antonius' legates in the years before Actium. From this he suggested that these men were Antonian legionaries, recruited originally as *peregrini* and granted the *civitas* by the various commanders, and that they were later taken over by Augustus after Actium. On this theory VII must have reached Dalmatia much earlier under Augustus, in fact not later than 15 B.C. to agree with the lowest years of service (*stipendia*) on the tombstones. None of the veterans in Dalmatia can be dated as early as this, while some can be dated to the very last years of Augustus. Moreover, as we have seen, there is sufficient evi-

[1] The earliest records of Legions IV and V in Moesia are the two inscriptions carved on the south side of the Danubian Iron Gates (Djerdap) dating to 33/4, *ILS*, 2281; cf. Šašel, 57, 60 with full bibliography. There appear to be only two Tiberian inscriptions and not three, as was believed earlier.

[2] III, 13977; cf. Ritterling, 1665.   [3] *CQ*, 56 (1963), 268 ff.

[4] *AE*, 1920, 63; cf. Ritterling, 1691.   [5] R. Syme, *JRS*, 23 (1933), 30, n. 116.

[6] III, 7386. Other records of VII Macedonica: X, 4723, 8241. Ritterling, 1616, suggests that the legion remained in Macedonia until 6.

[7] See p. 61 above.

dence for the earlier movements of VII in areas where it could be reasonably expected to have acquired recruits of eastern origin.[1]

Perhaps the two legions which are most likely to have been brought from the east were the two stationed later in Moesia, IV Scythica and V Macedonica.[2] In this case they will have been left there by Plautius Silvanus to serve in Moesia under A. Caecina, while he took over Plautius' army, which was more accustomed to the rigours and techniques of Danubian warfare, in order to cooperate with Tiberius from a base at Sirmium. Accordingly, the three drawn from Moesia will have been VII, VIII Augusta, and XI. As Syme has observed, the pattern of reinforcement during these critical years appears to have been consistently in an east–west direction: Germany draws from Illyricum and Raetia, Illyricum from Moesia, and Moesia from the eastern provinces.[3]

II *The Role of the Legionary Garrison in the First Century A.D.*

In A.D. 9 or not long afterwards the province of Dalmatia (earlier Illyricum Superius) was established, with a provincial garrison consisting of two of the legions (VII and XI) which had taken part in the reconquest of Illyricum in the years 6–9. How much pacification was required after 9 is not known: one cannot assume that all was peaceful in Dalmatia during the first century (or for that matter at any other time under the Empire) merely because there is no mention of any disturbance in any of the sources which survive. The government will not have risked any repetition of the events of 6. None will have known better than the emperor Tiberius how delicately the work of twenty years hung then in the balance. The loss of three legions by Quinctilius Varus in Germany in 9 could be made good only by the transfer of legions from Illyricum where, by good fortune, most of the fighting was over. However, the Empire was now less able to stand such strains: recruits were desperately short and no new legions had been created to replace those lost in Germany. Consequently one expects an overcautious policy from the government, as was the case in Spain where a large army was maintained long after the conquest had appeared effective.[4] The garri-

---

[1] See, on the date of these veterans, below, p. 112 f.

[2] The earliest record of Legion IV Scythica is provided by the Iron Gates inscriptions of 33/4 (n. 1 on p. 94). Before it reached Moesia it may have been in Macedonia, and Ritterling, 1556–7, suggests that it obtained its title as part of the Macedonian proconsular army under M. Licinius Crassus in the Dobrudja in 29–28 B.C. The *V Scytica* (*sic*) *in Ar*[*menia*] on a fragmentary elogium at Peltuinum (IX, 3427; cf. Ritterling, 1586) is Trajanic and can be connected with the career of Larcius Priscus *cos.* 110.

[3] *JRS*, 23 (1933), 31.

[4] In 23 Spain still held three legions (IV Macedonica, VI Victrix, and X Gemina), Tac., *Ann.*, iv, 5, reduced to one (VI Victrix) by the death of Nero, Parker, *RL*, 140.

son of Dalmatia remained at two legions throughout the reigns of Tiberius and Gaius: when a legion was detached from Illyricum for service in Africa against Tacfarinas, the unit chosen (IX Hispana) was taken from the three-legion army in Pannonia. The departure of Legion VII C.p.f. under Claudius to Viminacium (Kostolac) in Moesia Superior was part of redeployment of legions associated with the build-up of forces in the East as relations with Parthia deteriorated rapidly in the last years of the reign.[1] On the other hand it is possible that the revolt of L. Arruntius Scribonianus may have suggested that two legions in Dalmatia were dangerously close to Italy, and as a result a transfer was arranged at the earliest convenient moment. Although both legions were awarded the titles *Claudia pia fidelis* in 42, some of the troops had at first listened favourably to the pretensions of Arruntius Scribonianus. VII at Tilurium (Gardun on the Cetina) was much closer to the provincial capital Salona where presumably the rebellion began. After Arruntius Scribonianus' death on Issa there must have been many people in Dalmatia whose conduct during the uprising gave rise to suspicion, and among them may have been tribunes and senior centurions of VII at Tilurium. It is worth noting that, according to Suetonius, Scribonianus' successor in Dalmatia L. Salvius Otho, father of the emperor, even put to death some soldiers because they had murdered their own officers who had taken part in the rebellion, despite the fact that Claudius had already rewarded these men for their loyalty.[2] XI C.p.f. remained at Burnum until the civil war of 68–9. In the latter year it left for Italy to fight on the side of Otho against Vitellius; however, it failed to reach Bedriacum in time for the battle and was ordered back to its station by Vitellius. Later it marched with the Flavian forces, fought at Cremona, and continued on to Rome. In 70 it was moved to the Rhine to join in

[1] There is no precise evidence for the date when Legion VII was moved from Dalmatia to Moesia. It was still in the former when L. Arruntius Scribonianus rebelled in 42 (Dio, lx, 14, 5) when it received its titles for loyalty from the emperor Claudius, but it had left by 66 when Josephus lists only one legion in Dalmatia (*Bell. Iud.*, xi, 16, 4), which can only be Legion XI. Ritterling, 1619, suggests that the most likely occasion for its transfer was the winter of 56/7, the time when Legion IV Scythica was moved to the east. H. Nesselhauf, LA 2, 42, argued that it left Dalmatia much earlier, perhaps in 45 when Thrace was annexed, because of the very small number of records of Legion VII in Dalmatia which are dated after 42 (p. 99 f). The presence of tiles at Aequum and possibly Tilurium stamped LEG VII C P F suggests that it remained for more than three years after the rebellion of Arruntius. Furthermore if the veteran of legion VII from Salona who was settled at Scupi under Domitian was a local recruit, he can hardly have joined much before 56, *Sp.*, 71 (1931), p. 243, n. 650.

[2] Suet., *Otho*, 1: 'Ausus etiam est in Illyrico milites quosdam, quod motu Camilli ex paenitentia praepositos suos quasi defectionis adversus Claudius auctores occiderant, capite punire, et quidem ante se principia se coram, quamvis ob id ipsum promotos in ampliorem gradum a Claudio sciret.'

suppressing the rebellion of the Batavian leader Civilis.[1] In Dalmatia it was replaced almost immediately at Burnum by the reorganized Flavian Legion IIII Flavia felix, which remained in the province until about 86 when the crisis on the Danube brought it to Singidunum (Belgrade) in Moesia Superior.[2] Apart from temporary detachments during the Marcomannic Wars under Marcus Aurelius and in the early third century, no legions were stationed in Dalmatia after this date.

Both permanent legionary fortresses were established at strategic points, commanding important routes into the interior, yet they were close enough for rapid communication with the coastal cities. No other legionary fortresses are known in Dalmatia, and it seems that both Burnum and Tilurium were occupied on the arrival of the legions in the province. Burnum was the destination of Legion XX in its great march through Illyricum under M. Aemilius Lepidus in 9, but before the end of the year it was probably moved to Germany because of the disaster of Varus.[3] The station of VII was at Tilurium (Gardun), situated on the edge of the Sinjsko polje at its southernmost point, where the river Hippius (Cetina) enters the hills behind Salona on its wandering course to the sea at Oneum (Omiš) a few miles to the south.[4] The site is rich in inscriptions, mostly tombstones of serving legionaries, many of which are built into a small church nearby. Traces of part of the fortress defences (probably the northwest corner) still survive built into farm buildings. The main part of the site lies under arable fields where tiles and other objects are constantly turning up under the plough. The site commands the crossing of the Cetina (*pons Tiluri*) on the route between Salona and the capital of the Delmatae at Delminium (Županac) in Duvno polje. Both Burnum and Tilurium lie on a road that was employed as a *limes* by the army in their attacks on the peoples beyond the Dinaric Alps. From Burnum it links a chain of auxiliary stations and at Tilurium it passes across the Hippius to Imotskipolje, then into the Trebižat valley to its southern base at Bigeste (Humac) close to Narona.

[1] Legion XI was still in Dalmatia at the death of Nero, Tac., *Hist.*, ii, 11; ordered back there by Vitellius, ii, 67; joined the Flavians, iii, 50; taken to Gaul by Licinius Mucianus, ibid., iv, 68. It was stationed for a period at Vindonissa on the upper Rhine, Ritterling, 1694.

[2] Legion IV Flavia felix was created by Vespasian, probably early in 70, Cass. Dio, lv, 24, 3, and was among the newly recruited troops taken to Gaul by Mucianus in 70, Tac., *Hist.*, iv, 68. It probably had some connection with the Legion IV Macedonica, which was disbanded by Vespasian at this time, E. Birley, *JRS*, 18 (1928), 56 ff. There is no evidence when it was moved to Dalmatia, nor is there any record of the date when it was transferred to Moesia. About 86, the year of crisis on the Lower Danube, seems the obvious time, Ritterling, 1542.

[3] Note 4 on p. 93.

[4] There has been no study of the site of the legionary fortress at Tilurium (Gardun): the following notes are based on observations during a brief visit in 1960.

As has already been suggested this route may have been employed by P. Vatinius and Octavianus during their campaigns against the Delmatae (p. 43), but there is no evidence that this system of forts was in use before the great wars of conquest in Illyricum which began in 14 B.C.[1] Much more is known of the fortress at Burnum. Arches from the façade of the headquarters (*principia*) *basilica* are still standing today, although since the time when Fortis made his drawing in the eighteenth century, the major central arch then standing has collapsed. Before the First World War excavations in the *principia* were carried out for the Austrian Archaeological Institute. Two superimposed structures were uncovered, both orientated towards the south. Of the smaller and earlier *principia* only the *sacellum* and some of the rooms in the rear range survive. It was believed, though virtually no dating evidence has been examined, that this earlier *principia* belongs to the period of occupation by XI C.p.f. At some subsequent period a new *principia* was constructed, on an alignment slightly further to the north, due probably to the erosion of the south defences of the fortress by the swift-flowing river Krka in the area of the *porta praetoria*.[2] The new and larger *principia* was probably built in the last years of Claudius, and is the building work recorded by two fine building plaques mentioning the legate P. Anteius Rufus and the Legion XI C.p.f. in 50.[3] Apart from a doubtful record from Burnum of the legate P. Cornelius Dolabella (14–20), neither Burnum nor Tilurium have produced other building inscriptions from the period of legionary occupation.[4]

Burnum was the centre of the Liburnian Burnistae, while Tilurium lay within the territory of the Delmatae. Neither place developed into an important civil centre after the legions departed. The creation of the colony Claudia Aequum (at Čitluk near Sinj) attracted most of the settlers in that area, while an auxiliary cohort remained to garrison Tilurium (Cohort VIII Voluntariorum c. R.).[5] Burnum, on the other hand, did attract settlers of both native and Italian origin, and it acquired the status of a *municipium*, probably in the first year of Hadrian's

---

[1] On this line of military stations see Patsch, *Hercegovina*, 56 f.

[2] E. Reisch, *JÖAI*, 16 (1913), Bb. 112 f.

[3] Two apparently identical inscriptions are known from the Burnum headquarters building: *Ti. Claudius Drusi f. Caesar Aug. German. pontifex maximus tr. p. [XII] imp. XXI p.p. censor p. P. Anteio Rufo leg. Aug. pro pr. le[g. XI C.p.f.]*. The text is based on the fragments of the two copies, III, 14987/1 (14321/16) and Abramić, *SB*, 222, fig. 2. The date is early 51: Claudius was *cos.* V in 51, while his twenty-first imperial salutation belongs to 50, the next to 51, *PIR*², C 942.

[4] III, 14321/18: *P.] Corn[elius Dolabella*?, proposed by Patsch. The fragments of a monumental inscription set up under Trajan, III, 14988: [*Imp. Caesar Nerva Traianus Ge]rmanic. Dacic.* [. . . , may be connected with the later city at Burnum, first attested in 118, III, 9890, add. n. 2828.

[5] Appendix IX.

reign.[1] but large areas of neighbouring land which had originally been earmarked to support the legionary garrison (*prata legionis*), were retained by the government and administered by the procurator of the province.[2]

Conquest and policing of the more backward areas of the province was only part of the role of the legionary garrison. As the interior gradually became more settled, so the amount of purely military duties decreased, while building and administration took up a greater share of the legionaries' time. In Dalmatia there is a quantity of evidence showing the legions at work in a number of spheres, including road-building and the settlement of boundary disputes between provincial communities (by tribunes and senior centurions whom the governor had appointed as *iudices dati*).[3] In spite of this, however, the majority of legionary manpower still had military duties to perform. The task of controlling the area between the Save Valley and the Adriatic was no less exacting than that of defending an external frontier of the empire. The first, and by far the largest, category of evidence for the legions concerns the deployment of legionaries throughout the province, and is based on the tombstones of serving legionaries who in most cases can be assumed to have been buried at the place where they were stationed. From this category one must exclude the records of veterans, who were theoretically free agents and entitled to settle where they chose, and also those legionaries attached to special duties in the *officium* of the governor (for instance *beneficiarii consulares*), mostly in the provincial capital Salona. One point on the dating of tombstones must be noted. In this and other sections it is assumed that when the legions lack the titles *C.p.f.* (later generally *Claudia*) then the record in question was set up before the legions received these titles after the rebellion in 42: conversely the presence of these titles must date the stone after that year.[4] This chronological division of the evidence at a point about midway in the period of the legionary occupation also gives an approximate division between the earlier and the later Julio–Claudian period.

Of the nineteen legionaries serving in Legion VII who are attested at Tilurium all but two were buried before the legion received its titles in 42. All are *milites,* apart from one *signifer,* traditionally the standard-bearer in battle, who later became responsible for his fellow soldiers' equipment and savings.[5] Most of the serving members buried elsewhere in the province are found at Salona.

[1] III, 9890 (2828) and p. 217 f.   [2] III, 13250 and p. 459.
[3] Appendices IV, V.   [4] Appendix III.
[5] Epitaphs of serving soldiers in Legion VII buried at Tilurium. Before 42: III, 2716 (*signifer*), 9733, 9734; cf. p. 2269, 2714 (9736), *BD*, 31 (1908), 79, n. 3959A; III, 14931 (Dicmo), 9737, 14932; III, 9738 and *BD*, 26 (1903), 134, n. 3244; III, 2717, 9741, 9742; cf. Betz, n. 40, *BD*, 26 (1903), 130, n. 3321; III, 2709, *BD* 26 (1903), 133, n. 3239. Two are doubtful but may date before 42; III, 2713, 14933. After 42: III, 2715, 13976; cf. *WMBH*, 5 (1897), 351, fig. 10.

Except for one or two doubtful cases most can be associated with the governor's *officium*. Apart from centurions and veterans, sixteen records of Legion VII are attested there, but only nine are definite records of serving soldiers. Three of these, two *signiferi* and one *imaginifer,* were all buried after 42 possibly serving the governor. Of the remaining *milites,* three date before 42, two after then.[1] A fragmentary tombstone of Legion VII at Burnum (occupied by Legion XI) is the only evidence that there was ever a detachment serving there.[2] Conversely, there is good evidence that a detachment of Legion XI C.p.f. was placed at Tilurium after VII had moved away to Moesia.[3] Of other members of Legion VII attested in the province, excluding those serving at *stationes* of *beneficiarii consulares* in the province after the legion had departed, the *miles* buried at Corinium after 42 was probably at home: his tribe is Sergia, which is that of Corinium, while the tombstone was set up not by the usual fellow soldiers but by his wife and daughter.[4] Also in Liburnia at Iader a centurion of VII set up the tombstone of his father who was a magistrate (*IIIIvir i. d.*) of Altinum, the flourishing port on the opposite coast which had close links with Liburnia. Another centurion, of VII C.p.f. and who came from Arretium in Etruria, is recorded at Tragurium on a tombstone set up by his wife who was presumably a native of Dalmatia.[5]

From the above survey it emerges that the men of VII were deployed in only two main centres, the legionary station at Tilurium and the provincial capital Salona, a situation quite different from that which will be shown for Legion XI. The lack of outstations manned by men of Legion VII in the area of Tilurium is perhaps due to the larger number of auxiliary units deployed in the area, at Andetrium, Magnum, and Bigeste, to whom the necessary local police duties could doubtless be entrusted.[6]

By far the majority of the serving soldiers attested for Legion XI are found in the immediate vicinity of the legion's station Burnum (Šuplja Crkva), especially at Ivoševci, two miles to the west where were situated the legionary *canabae*. The

---

[1] Legion VII at Salona before 42: *BD,* 36 (1913), 14, n. 4407A (*eques*); III, 8723, 2071 (both serving soldiers); III, 9711 (uncertain status, but with his own family established at Tragurium). Legion VII at Salona after 42: *VAHD,* 50 (1928–9), 13, n. 5 (centurion, recorded on the epitaph of his freedman); III, 2040, *BD,* 37 (1914), 77, 4576A (*signiferi*); III, 8735 (*imaginifer*), 8760, *BD,* 26 (1903), 193, n. 3150 (serving soldiers). Fragmentary records of Legion VII at Salona: III 14699 (?*miles,* after 42), 8763, 8767, 14248, *BD,* 26 (1903), 189, n. 3228, *BD,* 37 (1914), 65, n. 4656A (eastern recruit, probably serving in Legion VII); III, 3162a (*eques leg. VII C.p.f.*; findspot uncertain, but probably Iader or Salona).

[2] Legion VII at Burnum: III, 14992. A serving soldier of Legion VII (before 42) shared a grave at Narona with his brother, a veteran of the same unit, III, 8487.

[3] Note 3 on p. 101.   [4] III, 2885.

[5] III, 2914 (Iader), 2678; cf. 9699 (Tragurium).   [6] Appendix VIII.

presence of groups of serving *milites* elsewhere suggests detachments on more or less permanent duty. During construction of the railway near Knin (1886–9), 15 miles higher up the river Titius (Krka) where the road over the mons Ulcirus (Strmica) into the interior enters the mountains, there were discovered a number of tombstones of *milites* serving in Legion XI set up on the Kapitul Hill, the majority of them dating after 42. The isolated tombstone from the top of the Strmica pass of a *miles* who was serving after 42 doubtless also belongs to this detachment. There is also a group buried at nearby Mokropolje and Padjine (possibly the *civitas Pasini* of Pliny) about twelve kilometres to the west of Knin. The isolated tombstone from near Promona (Tepljù), beyond Mount Promina near the limit of the *territorium legionis,* suggests that there might have been another detachment there, although for some of this period the place was the station of an auxiliary unit.[1] A few examples of tiles stamped by Legion VII C.p.f. are known from Aequum, and possibly Tilurium also, but their manufacture appears to have begun under Claudius only a few years before the legion was transferred to Moesia. Legion XI C.p.f. had its own works depôt, which presumably produced both tiles and pottery, at Smrdelj 3 miles south of Burnum. Tiles are most plentiful at Burnum, where they can be picked up over the whole area of the legionary fortress; a single example has also been discovered at Tilurium.[2] This is significant since, along with two tombstones (one of a tribune) and a lead seal, it establishes that a detachment of Legion XI C.p.f. was stationed at Tilurium after VII had left.[3] The remainder of the men of Legion XI are attested at Salona.

The most senior serving soldier recorded is the *praefectus castrorum* from Altinum who belongs to the period after 42. His tombstone was set up not far from

[1] Serving members of Legion XI from the area of Knin: III, 9908 (*tesserarius, cornicularius leg. Aug.*), 9904 (*signifer* after 42), Betz, n. 118 (Mokropolje, *cornicen* before 42); III, 6416 (Mokropolje, *eques* after 42); III, 6417 (Strmica pass), 9903, 9906 (14321/4), 13251 (Padjine in Mokropolje), 6419 (9897) (Tepljù, *miles*, presumably of Legion XI), all *milites* after 42. III, 9909 (14321/6) (*miles*, before or after 42). Also three fragments of legionary tombstones, presumably of Legion XI: III, 14321/7 (9910), 14321/25, 14321/8 (9911).

[2] The tiles of Legion VII C.p.f. were seen by the author in 1966 in the collection of the Franciscans at Sinj. All the tiles in Dalmatia stamped by Legion XI bear the titles C.p.f. Most are from Burnum: *WMBH*, 7 (1900), 78, fig. 48 f; cf. *GZMBH*, 26 (1914), 162, fig. 19. Tile-works at Smrdelj: *WMBH*, 7 (1900), 96. At Tilurium: III, 14022; cf. p. 2328/179 and Patsch, *JÖAI* 1 (1898), Bb. 121 f. Tiles of Legion XI have also been found re-used in the fourth century Christian *basilica urbana* at Salona, *BD*, 28 (1904), 159, n. 1089. On military tiles in Dalmatia see now G. Alföldy, *ES*, 4 (1967), 44–51.

[3] Legion XI at Tilurium: III, 2711, cf. *JÖAI*, 1 (1898), Bb. 123 (*tribunus militum*); III, 2708 (9725) (*signifer*). Neither of the above records the titles C.p.f.; cf. Betz, p. 22. Lead seal of Legion XI: III, 13350.

Knin and suggests that he might have been connected with the detachment on the Kapitul Hill guarding the Strmica pass (*mons Ulcirus*).[1] At Burnum a chief centurion (*primuspilus*) is attested before 42 together with a son or brother, also a senior centurion.[2] Of other ranks one centurion is attested after 42, two *signiferi* before 42; another *signifer* who does not record his legion was almost certainly serving in Legion XI, while there is also a fourth of this rank recorded on a fragmentary tombstone. Finally in this group there is a *miles* serving after 42 detached on the staff of one of the tribunes (*beneficiarius tribuni*).[3] A probable total of twenty-three serving *milites* are known from Burnum, five dating to before 42, twelve after that date.[4] In the case of the remainder the legionary titles have either been lost or never appeared on the stone. The higher proportion of men attested after 42 than is the case in Legion VII reflects the legion's longer stay in Dalmatia after the rebellion of L. Arruntius Scribonianus. Nine men of Legion XI (including one veteran) are known at the Knin outpost. In addition to the *praefectus castrorum* mentioned above, there is a *cornicularius legati Augusti* (an important officer on a provincial governor's or legionary legate's staff) and a *signifer*. The presence of a *miles* of Cohort III Alpinorum (stationed later at Andetrium) suggests that, when the legion had departed for Moesia, the garrison post at Knin was taken over by a detachment from the nearest convenient auxiliary station.[5]

The tombstone of a *miles* at Scardona may have been brought down the river Titius from the cemetery at Burnum, or it may indicate that some troops were based at a supply harbour near the mouth of the river (it is not navigable above Scardona).[6] The creation of a *municipium* at Scardona under the Flavian dynasty

---

[1] *SB*, 218, n. 13 (*AE*, 1925, 133) (Zidine near Knin).

[2] The tombstone is fragmentary, III, 14996 (Kistanje): it records L. Cicereiu[s ... f. Ani. F]idus Arim[ino ... and two of his relatives, Cicereius Laevus p[rimipilaris?] leg. XI or possibly p[rinceps], a senior centurion. The other was Cicereius Ascan[ius primipila]ris.

[3] Centurion at Burnum: III, 2834 (9893, cf. p. 2328/12), after 42; *signiferi*: III, 15001 (Rudele), 2832 (cf. p. 1036, n. 9892), both before 42, III, 9899; cf. Ritterling, 1692 (no record of legion), *VAHD*, 51 (1930–4), 235; cf. pl. XXXVII/2 (*AE*, 1940, 178); *beneficiarius tribuni*: III, 14997.

[4] Serving soldiers buried at Burnum. Before 42: III, 6413, 2835; III, 14997/2 (*JÖAI*, 6 (1903), Bb. 86, fig. 16); III, 15000 (14321/13, *BD*, 22 (1899), 49); III, 9892 (add. p. 2832; cf. p. 1036). After 42: *JÖAI*, 6 (1903), Bb. 85, fig. 15 (*AE*, 1903, 303, *SB*, 216, n. 10); III, 2833; cf. pl 2328/161; III, 13263, 14998, 14999; III, p. 43*, 394$^{3-4}$; III, 15004, 14321/19; cf. p. 2328/161; III, 15005/1 (*JÖAI*, 5 (1902), Bb. 1, fig. 1), Betz, n. 144, WS. 24 (1902), 382 (*AE*, 1903, 376); III, 15005, 14994 (legionary title lost, but recruited from Claudian *municipium* Iuvavum in Noricum). Serving soldiers before or after 42: Betz n. 172 (*eques*), III, 2837, *SB*, 216, n. 9 (Betz, n. 171), III, 14991.

[5] III, 14321/5 (9907).

[6] Serving soldier at Scardona: III, 6413 (discovered in church cemetery).

probably removed the need for such an outpost. Of the remainder recorded from Salona two are centurions, both dating after 42, one of whom had held an earlier appointment in the *vigiles* (the quasi-military fire brigade in the city of Rome) before his transfer to a centurionate in Dalmatia. His tombstone was set up by his wife and son. The other rose from the ranks; beginning as a *miles* in Legion VI victrix, then stationed in Germany, he passed to centurionates in VIII Augusta, XIV Germina Martia victrix, from which he was transferred to XI C.p.f. Originating from Aquae Sextiae (Aix-en-Provence), a local recruiting ground for the Rhine legions, his tombstone was set up at Salona by his wife and daughter.[1] Two members of Legion XI (date uncertain for both) are attested in the *officium* of the provincial governor, a *cornicularius* and a *speculator*.[2] A veteran of Legion XI (before 42), who had served as a *speculator* at Salona, was on his retirement adlected to membership of the city council (*ordo*) of Salona as a decurion, no doubt a valuable person to have in one's midst when dealing with the provincial government. His tombstone was presumably set up on his own estate, near the source of the river Vrlika at the north of Imotskipolje.[3] Three, possibly four, *milites* who may have served in the *officium* at Salona, and three fragmentary records of Legion XI (all dating after 42), complete the distribution of men serving in this legion.[4] The young legionary of Legion XI buried before 42 at Alvona has the local voting tribe, and can be assumed to be a native of that city, which became a *municipium* under Tiberius.[5]

When Legion XI C.p.f. left Dalmatia its place at Burnum was taken by IIII Flavia felix. Formed out of the drastic reorganization of some legions by Vespasian after the civil war, it began its existence as the sole legion in Dalmatia. The main evidence for its stay is the eagle bearer (*aquilifer*) buried at Burnum, where a large number of its stamped tiles have been found. Two serving *milites* of the legion are also attested, one at Burnum, another at Salona. The stamped tiles, produced like those of Legion XI at the Smrdelj depot, are found at a number of other centres in the province, including Salona and Asseria, the latter place being close to where they were manufactured. They were used also in the building of

[1] Centurions of Legion XI at Salona: III, 2062 and 8747 (*JÖAI*, 6 (1903), Bb. 83), from Augusta Praetoria; III, 2035, from Aquae Sextiae.
[2] *Cornicularius cos*: III, 8738; *speculator*: BD, 35 (1912), 22, 684B (*Starinar*, III, 1 (1922), 57, pl. 1, 1–2).
[3] III, 1914; cf. p. 2328/121 and n. 4 on p. 112.
[4] Serving soldiers of Legion XI at Salona: III, 2031 (before 42; probably, but not certainly, from Salona); III, 2013, 8740, 2062 (serving soldier or veteran, Forni, 161, n. 2) all after 42. Fragmentary records of Legion XI after 42 at Salona: III, 8768 (12833); III, 8769, 12907.
[5] Serving soldier at Alvona: III, 3052. On the city see Appendix XII, p. 487 ff.

the auxiliary fort at Andetrium, and also at Bigeste.[1] About 86 Legion IIII Flavia felix left Dalmatia and from this period Dalmatia ceased to have legions in the standing provincial army.[2]

Those members of Legions VII and XI who served on the staff of the provincial governor as *beneficiarii consulares,* district officers stationed at important centres throughout the province, belong almost entirely to the period when both legions had left the province and were stationed on the Danube frontier, VII at Viminacium in Moesia Superior, XI at Durostorum in Moesia Inferior. At this time the governor of Dalmatia drew on the legions in other Danubian provinces for the military manpower that he required for his staff, in spite of the government's reluctance to see this practice develop.[3] At the higher level of administration during the first century senior officers of the legion were employed in the governor's most important spheres of provincial government.

One centurion of Legion XI, recorded in retirement on a dedication to Vespasian in 75 as patron of Bovianum Vetus in Samnium, was seconded as prefect of two major peoples in the interior, the Maezaei and Daesitiates. After this he was appointed to the command of Cohort III Alpinorum, then stationed at Andetrium.[4] Doubtless such senior officers were regularly placed in charge of native communities until the government was satisfied that the tribal aristocracies were able to take over their traditional role in an efficient and orderly manner. The other important sphere in which these officers were employed was the settlement of boundary disputes between provincial communities. Officers of both legions were employed, although the majority of the records of these settlements, most of which come from Liburnia, were made by officers of Legion XI. Chronologically these settlements begin in the earliest years of Tiberius and, apart from an isolated example of the late third century,[5] cease

[1] Legion IIII Flavia felix in Dalmatia: III, 14995 (Burnum), *aquilifer*; III, p. 43*, n. 384⁸; cf. V 542 (Burnum); III, 2021 (*WMBH*, 7 (1900), 82, fig. 56) (Salona), both serving soldiers; III, 2004 (*WMBH*, loc. cit.) (Salona), a veteran, also possibly III, 14329 (Čavkić near Založje). Stamped tiles: III, 15110 a–b (*WMBH*, 7 (1900), 79 f., fig. 51) (from Burnum including one from Smrdelj), *BD*, 25 (1902), 136, n. 1309 (Salona); III, 15110 c–e (*WMBH*, loc. cit.) (Andetrium); III, 15110f, *BD*, 23 (1900), 164, *BD*, 26 (1903), 150 (Asseria); III, 14021 (*Röm. Mitt.*, 9 (1894), 233; cf. *WMBH*, 7 (1900), 81 fig., 55, *GZMBH*, 26 (1914), 162, fig. 24). All the tiles are stamped LEG IIII F F.

[2] The precise date of its transfer to the Danube is uncertain, as are the movements of many legions in these years of crisis under Domitian, Betz, 46 ff., G. Alföldy, *AArch. Hung.*, 11 (1959), 116 ff.

[3] Certainly Trajan disapproved of it, Plin., *Ep.*, x, 20. 22.

[4] IX, 2564 (Bovianum Vetus): . . .] *Marcelli* 7 *leg. XI Cl.* [*p. f. pr*]*aef. civitatis Maeze*[*iorum item Daesit*]*iatum.* On this system see also p. 193.

[5] III, 9860 (between Glamoč and Grahovo).

under the Flavians, the latest datable example being of the year 70. When two provincial communities clashed over their boundaries the governor of the province nominated as arbitrators one or more centurions (*iudices dati*), who would then inspect the disputed boundary and propose a settlement (*formula*) for ratification by the governor. When this had been given the settlement would be inscribed on stone pillars set up at points along the boundary in question, some of which have survived. Most settlements appear to have been accepted as final, although there are cases known where after a generation or so the dispute appears to have broken out again, and it was found necessary to restate the original decision or to devise a new settlement.[1]

The settlement recorded between the legionary lands (*prata legionis*) around Burnum and an adjoining private estate was made in the early years of Trajan by the procurator (Ti. Claudius) Augustianus Bellicus.[2] It seems to have been not uncommon for the government to retain control of land assigned originally to a legionary fortress for the upkeep of the troops, even when the legion had been moved elsewhere and the camp was empty. In some cases the land could be used for veteran settlement or the settlement of a *colonia*, as may have been the case when Aequum was founded under Claudius not far from the old station of Legion VII at Tilurium. Although an auxiliary unit remained in garrison there, enough land would be set free for such purposes. This was the case also at Bigeste near Narona. At this place, which was once the site of a large concentration of *auxilia*, the removal of many units late under Augustus enabled the government to release land for legionary veterans (the *veterani pagi Scunastici*) in A.D. 14–15 and allow it to be absorbed into the territory of the colony of Narona.[3]

III *Recruitment of the Legionary Garrison* (see Appendix VI).

In law all recruits to the Roman legions had to be freeborn Roman citizens. Consequently the main sources for recruits in the first century will have been Italy and those provinces, mostly in the West, where dwelt the largest number of communities and individuals who had acquired the citizenship. Apart from this legal stipulation all the available evidence suggests that the Roman legions drew their recruits from the nearest convenient source of manpower. Often there was difficulty in obtaining sufficient recruits, particularly in the eastern provinces, where the number of Roman communities was comparatively small. Conse-

---

[1] Appendix V.

[2] III, 13250; cf. p. 2328/13 and p. 459.

[3] On the legionary *territoria* in general see O. Hirschfeld, *Verwaltungsbeamte*, 143 f. and A. Mócsy, *AAnt. Hung.*, 5 (1953), 179–200.

quently there was a practice which soon became widespread of granting the
civitas to suitable *peregrini* on the understanding that they enrolled in the army
immediately. This device was legal and the citizenship which the recruit obtained would be retained when he retired as a *veteranus* with all the privileges
which that status carried.[1] The normal recruiting age was about 18–20, and very
few were accepted above the age of 25. After the Augustan period the normal
term of service was twenty-five years, the same total for legionaries and auxiliary
soldiers. The men who served for unusually long periods (sometimes more than
thirty-five years) belong to the military emergencies in the later years of
Augustus.

A total of 104 men who served in Legions VII and XI record their origins,
including some who may have joined VII when it left Dalmatia under either
Claudius or Nero. In this category are some men who were settled as veterans in
the Domitianic colony at Scupi (Skopje) in Moesia Superior. That some of these
men joined the legion while it was still stationed at Tilurium is suggested by
recruits from Salona. The number of legionaries for whom the origins are
recorded may be divided into two groups, those who were recruited under
Augustus, Tiberius, and Gaius (total 61), and secondly those who joined under
Claudius and Nero (total 42).

In the first group Italians predominate (34), but it is notable that the rest were
recruited from the eastern provinces, 24 in Legion VII, 3 in Legion XI. The 18
Italians in Legion VII were drawn from a wider area than those in Legion XI.
Legion VII has 5 from Etruria and 5 from Venetia and Istria, 3 from Aemilia,
2 each from Umbria and Transpadana, and one from Apulia. Of the 16 in
Legion XI, 9 are from Venetia and Istria, 3 each from Etruria and Aemilia and
one from Transpadana. This large number of men in Legion XI drawn from the
northeast of Italy may reflect recruitment in the period before 6, when the
legion was for some time in this part of Italy.[2] The Italians in Legion VII were
probably recruited after A.D. 7 when, if arguments advanced above are correct,
that legion became part of the army of Illyricum. The eastern recruits in Legion
VII have been referred to already in connection with the early movements of
that legion (p. 94). Not all of them, however, were necessarily recruited into
the legion when it was stationed in Macedonia, Moesia or further east. There
is no reason why the army in Illyricum should not have continued to draw
some of its intake from eastern sources even well into the first century. The
concentration of forces on the Rhine and in Illyricum in the years after 6 made
heavy demands on the manpower available in Italy and adjacent provinces, and

[1] Parker, *RL*, 169 ff., Forni, 107 f.
[2] It might, however, have been in Moesia before 6, see p. 95.

it would not be surprising if the legion continued to seek recruits from the East.[1]

In the second group, those probably recruited under Claudius or later, Legions VII and XI both continued to draw recruits from the eastern provinces. Not many men are attested for Legion VII in this period, only two from Italy, six from the East, one from Narbonensis, and four recruited locally from Salona. Nineteen Italians are attested for Legion XI, now more equally distributed than in the earlier group, six from Venetia and Istria, four from Etruria, and three apiece from Aemilia, Liguria, and Transpadana. The predominance of recruits from western origins in Legion XI is shown by those drawn from outside Italy: three come from Gaul, two from Spain, and one from Noricum. There are also three men from the East and one local recruit.

Of the communities from which these serving legionaries came, many had received settlements under Caesar and Augustus, either in the form of new colonial foundation composed of discharged veterans, or new settlers added to an existing community. Recruits are known from Forum Iulii, an Augustan colony in Narbonensis, from Caesaraugusta, an Augustan colony in Tarraconensis, and Italica, an Augustan *municipium* in Baetica. Likewise many of the eastern veterans came from colonial foundations: Dyrrhachium and Philippi in Macedonia were triumviral colonies, while Sinope in Pontus was settled by Caesar himself. Recruits are found from Augustus' latin-speaking colonies in parts of Asia Minor, Alexandria Troas and Sebaste in Asia, also Conana in Pisidia, and Ninica in Cilicia. The Galatians represented a good source of fighting men in Central Asia Minor, derived from invading Gauls in the third century B.C., and there is a recruit from further east at Berytus, where M. Agrippa settled a colony about 14 B.C. In conclusion we may repeat an earlier statement than the evidence for recruitment to the legionary garrison of Dalmatia supports the view that the army drew its men from the most convenient sources of available manpower.[2]

IV *Veteran Settlement from the Legionary Garrison* (see Appendix VII).

The problem of finding suitable rewards for the soldiers of victorious armies was never solved by the Roman Republic. The willingness of such men to follow their commanders against the government was due to the belief that only thus would they be certain of obtaining them, and it was one of the underlying causes of the collapse of the senatorial oligarchy and the establishment of the Principate,

[1] In particular in the years after the Augustan Wars when the Danubian legions were hardly an attraction to recruits from Italy.

[2] F. Vittinghoff, 49 ff., and on the eastern cities, A. H. M. Jones, *GC*, 59 ff.

whose authority depended ultimately on the support of the army. The principal fault under the Republic was the complete absence of any machinery to deal with this and similar problems; and it was not the least of Augustus' contributions that he organized the provision of lands or cash grants for retiring legionaries on a sound footing.[1] He created the military treasury (*aerarium militare*), a fund for which the revenues of certain taxes imposed on the Empire as a whole were earmarked. From this source veterans were given discharge grants in two forms, the land grant (*missio agraria*) or the cash gratuity (*missio nummaria*). Initially Augustus' main problem was to dispose safely of the large numbers of soldiers due for retirement from his army after his victory over M. Antonius at Actium in 31 B.C. During the next few years many of these men were settled in colonies in Italy, the western and the eastern provinces. Once this 'bulge' in the numbers due for discharge was past, Augustus was able to evolve a more methodical and less revolutionary system for settling veterans, in particular the men who were enrolled in the legions reorganized after Actium and who, after serving in the great campaigns of Tiberius and Drusus during the years 15–9 B.C., were due for discharge in the years after 7 B.C. According to the *Res Gestae* these troops were discharged regularly with cash payments (*missio nummaria*) in the years between 7 and 2 B.C.[2] After 13 B.C. service in the legions was fixed at sixteen years. Before the soldier received his final discharge (*missio honesta*), however, he was required to remain with the colours for an additional four years as a *veteranus sub vexillo*.[3] Such men were organized in separate cohorts apart from the rest of the legion, with their own special standard (*vexillum*), and under the command of an officer titled *curator veteranorum*.[4] They were exempt from all normal camp duties, and in general were only required to serve actively in the event of an enemy attack or similar emergency. In 6 further changes were introduced; the length of service was increased to twenty years, with an additional five years service as *veterani*.[5] In the years of crisis after 6 the discharges were suspended, and there were many instances of men serving thirty years or more before they received their release.[6]

One question which is difficult to answer is what proportion of discharged

[1] The scale of the problem posed by the land-hungry veterans can be seen from Tacitus' summary account of Augustus' early career, *Ann.*, i, 10: 'cupidine dominandi concitos per largitionem veteranos', and also the ruthless confiscations of land in Italy after the defeat of Brutus and Cassius which led to the bloody war at Perusia in 41 B.C., Syme, *RR*, 206 ff.

[2] *Res Gestae*, 16–17; cf. F. Vittinghof, 23 f.   [3] Cass. Dio, liv, 25, 6.

[4] A *curator veteranorum* who died at Milan in 29 is attested: V, 5832 (*ILS*, 2338).

[5] Dio, lv, 23, 1.

[6] Illustrated by the high *stipendia* of veterans in the Pagus Scunasticus settlement near Narona, p. 112 n. 7.

veterans preferred to return to their homes in Italy or other provinces, as compared with those who chose to remain for the rest of their lives in the vicinity of the legionary stations where they had spent most of their active service. Virtually all the evidence for men who served in the Dalmatian legionary garrison during the first century comes from Dalmatia, and, although it is possible that a sizeable proportion actually did return home, no record has survived of them. It may be assumed that the number of veteran tombstones in Dalmatia is due to the fact that the deceased's comrades ensured that he received the proper memorial a soldier deserved, while this may not have happened in communities far removed from the military centres. However, with such a preponderance of evidence, it would appear that the majority of men preferred to remain in areas where they had served. The organized settlements of veterans from the Dalmatian army were made only within the province, while, with one possible exception, all the veterans settled in the province came from the legions of the province.[1] It is striking that none of the Caesarian or Augustan colonies established in Dalmatia appear to have had legionary veterans among their original settlers; and this must be the explanation for the absence of Illyricum from the list of provinces in the *Res Gestae* to have established veteran colonies.[2] Only one colony is known to have been settled specifically for legionary veterans in Dalmatia, at Aequum (Čitluk in Sinjskopolje), but even in that place there was already a thriving civilian settlement of Roman citizens (*conventus civium Romanorum*);[3] the actual decision, however, to create a colony at Aequum was connected with the removal of Legion VII C.p.f. from nearby Tilurium to Moesia Superior under Claudius or Nero. Some veterans left the province on discharge, but not to return to their homes: Aquileia in Northeast Italy was for some years the military focus of Illyricum and its flourishing commerce attracted many settlers from the legions.[4] For those who preferred to remain in Dalmatia different categories of settlement pattern are recognizable. First there are veterans who remained in the immediate vicinity of their legionary stations, either in the *canabae*, or elsewhere in the *territorium legionis*: secondly there were those who were settled with a land allotment in a collective settlement organized by the government (*deductio*): finally, there are those attested from their place of burial as having settled in the

[1] The exception may be a settlement at Salona of veterans from Legion V Macedonica under Claudius, p. 114 below.

[2] *Res Gestae*, 28: 'colonias in Africa, Sicilia, Macedonia, utraque Hispania, Achaia, Asia, Syria, Gallia Narbonensi, Pisidia militum deduxi'.

[3] III, 2733 (n. 6 on p. 114).

[4] Especially from the Pannonian legions, *CQ*, 56 (1963), 268 ff., and also from those in Dalmatia, Ritterling, 1693.

larger coastal cities, principally Salona, Iader, and Narona. These men may originally have come from collective settlements, preferring to sell their land holdings and settle in the cities, or, and perhaps more likely, some of them received a cash grant rather than land on their discharge.

Comparatively few veterans are attested in the area of their legionary stations. In the period before 42 only one is known at Tilurium, and he appears to have died at the time of his discharge at the age of 44 after twenty-five years service. A veteran who died at Burnum after 42 was only 45 after twenty-four years service, and was presumably still serving with the legion as a *veteranus*. An elderly soldier of Legion XI after 42 describes himself as 'awarded a proper discharge' (d(imissus) [h(onesta) m(issione)]]) and remained with his family in the legionary *canabae*.[1] He does not give an *origo* on his tombstone and it is possible that he may have been born at Burnum. Neither Burnum nor Tilurium became a focal point of settlement, either when the legions were there or after they had departed. Apart from serving soldiers, the tombstones from Tilurium reveal only slaves, freedmen of soldiers and a few Romanized natives.[2] Traders originating from Italy and other provinces are attested at Burnum, but the legion appears to have contributed little to the later growth of the community.[3] At both places most of the soldiers are buried by fellow soldiers nominated as heirs (*heredes*) rather than by families or other dependants.[4] The reason for this is clear: the legionary fortresses were not situated in areas that attracted settlement, while the coastal cities, the natural centres for any part of the Dalmatian coast, were so close and so well-established that it was impossible for other centres to rival them in attraction. When the legions moved to the Danube, far away from the urbanized Mediterranean, the situation was different: there the *canabae* grew rapidly in prosperity and not only attracted most of the veterans, but soon began to furnish the legions with the majority of their recruits. By the third century many of these places had grown into large cities, serving as provincial capitals and, in the fourth century, as residences of emperors.

There are few records from Dalmatia of veterans discharged in the reign of Augustus; this is due partly to the difficulty of dating precisely those members of Legions VII and XI who belong to the period before 42. Undoubtedly

[1] III, 15004/1; the reading is not certain: *L. Val. Maximus Valerio Proclo ann. IXXX leg. XI C.p.f. d. [h.m.] T. Val. Aiae vet* . . . Here the age is read as LXXX (80) rather than IXXX (29).

[2] Civilian settlers at Tilurium: III, 13972, 2723.

[3] There is more evidence for civilian settlement at Burnum than there is at Tilurium: freedmen, III, 13252, 9894 (*Aelonii* from Arretium); III, 9915 (Mokropolje), 9919, 6420. Freeborn Italians: III, 13251, 2841, 2821, 2820, 14321, 14321/26.

[4] Serving soldiers with families at Burnum: III, 9892 (2832), 15004, 15004/1, slaves of soldiers; III, 2834 (centurion of Legion XI), 2838 (*signifer*).

Augustan are the two veterans of Legion XX, which left Dalmatia for Germany in 9. Both were buried in colonies, one in Salona and the other at Iader, and both record on the tombstones their families, freedmen and freedwomen. They may have been discharged with cash gratuities in the years before A.D. 6, but hardly afterwards when discharges were suspended.

A planned settlement of veterans (*deductio veteranorum*) was made under Augustus at the waterfall of Roški-Slap, at a point where the river Titius (Krka) approached the sea. There were then no cities in this area, Scardona, a little further down the river, being a Flavian foundation, as may have been Rider to the east. On the west Varvaria became a *municipium* probably under Tiberius.[1] Further upsteam and around the river was part of the Burnum legionary *territorium*. The epitaphs of three of the veterans were carved on a rock near the road leading to Drniš on the left bank of the river. In addition another veteran was buried at Mratovo, a few miles higher up the Titius opposite Burnum. Three were veterans of Legion XI, the fourth a *centurio veteranorum* who served in Legion IV Macedonica, then probably stationed in Spain. Only two record the number of the years they had served: T. Cillius of Laranda had served no less than thirty-eight years, and died at the age of 70: M. Fraxsanius from Regium Lepidum, on the other hand, had served the regular *stipendia* of twenty-five and died, almost immediately on discharge, at the age of 44. He had been awarded decorations, probably by Tiberius in 9. This settlement may have been made in the years after 9, and some of the men may have been recalled to service with the legions during the great emergency.[2] The centurion of Legion IV Macedonica was obviously connected with these veterans, and his presence suggests that they were still fulfilling some military role. Although final conquest was achieved in A.D. 9 it must have been some years before the roads linking Burnum and Salona were secured. Until the construction of the via Gabiniana between Salona and Andetrium a decade later,[3] the river Titius will have remained a vital link between the legion and the coastal centres, and it may have been the task of the veterans at Roški-Slap to guard this route. At the same time the veterans were granted farms in the neighbourhood. According to his tombstone the veteran buried at Mratovo 'was killed in a field alongside the river Titius in the territory of the Varvarini'.[4] By this time the government had discontinued cash payments and land grants became more common. Not all veterans were satisfied with this and the poverty of the lands offered to them was one of the principal grievances

[1] Appendix XII, p. 487 ff.
[2] Vell. Pat., ii, 110, 7: 'revocati undique et omnes veterani.'
[3] On the programme of road-building after 9 see Appendix IV.
[4] III, 6418 (9896) and below, p. 217.

put forward when the legions in Pannonia revolted after the death of Augustus in 14: what they wanted was a cash sum paid to them in camp on their discharge, but this the government was unable (or unwilling) to provide.[1] In addition to the detachment at Roški-Slap other veterans may have been posted to Asseria, on the road between Iader and Burnum: the evidence is the epitaph of an early veteran of Legion VII buried there.[2]

Veterans of both Legions VII and XI are attested at Salona and Iader before 42: at the latter city there is one from each legion, and at Salona four from each. Another is attested at Siculi (Biač) on the *territorium* of Salona.[3] Some may have been serving in the *officium* of the governor, although only one actually records this. This was C. Appuleius Etruscus who was probably born in Liburnia. He died before 42 and gives no *origo*, but Appuleii were prominent among upper-class families (*honestiores*) in Salona and Liburnia. The erasure of his name on the tombstone may be due to his having supported the rebellion of L. Arruntius Scribonianus. His fourteen-year-old son is recorded, together with his wife who bears the unusual name Cuparia.[4]

By far the majority of veterans known to have been discharged before 42 were settled on the territory of Narona, especially near Bigeste (Humac) in the Trebižat valley.[5] From this place comes a most important document, preserved in two copies, recording a settlement of veterans made in the first year of Tiberius' reign. The text reads: 'Dedicated to the deified Augustus and Ti(berius) Caesar Augustus, son of Augustus, by veterans of the Scunasticus Region to whom the colony Narona allotted lands'.[6] The tombstones of twelve early veterans are known from around Bigeste and from Narona, belonging to Legion VII, all of an early date, and often with many years of service beyond the normal term.[7] The large number of eastern recruits among them led O. Cuntz, following on an earlier suggestion of O. Seeck, to suggest that they were Antonian legionaries absorbed by Augustus in his army reconstruction after Actium, a theory noted

---

[1] In the mutiny of the Pannonian legions in 14 the veterans wanted a cash payment in a lump sum while they were still in the camp, not some indefinite land allotment of dubious quality, Tac., *Ann.*, i, 17: '... sextus decimus stipendii annus finem adferret, ne ultra sub vexillis tenerantur, sed isdem in castris praemium pecunia solveretur'; cf. *CQ*, 56 (1963), 268 ff.

[2] III, 9939.   [3] III, 9712.

[4] III, p. 2328/121 (add. n. 1914): *C. Appuleius Etruscus speculator vet. leg. XI decurio allectus Salona[e] et C. Appuleius Etruscus f. annorum XIIII h. s. s[unt] Cuparia Lup[...*

[5] On the topography of the area see C. Patsch, *Narona*, 23 ff., and pl. I.

[6] M. Abramić, *BIAB*, 19 (1950), 235 f., fig. 2 (*AE*, 1950, 44): *Divo Augusto et Ti. Caesari Aug. f. Aug. sacrum veterani pagi Scunastici quibus colonia Naronit(ana) agros dedit.*

[7] High *stipendia* among Pagus Scunasticus veterans: III, 8487 (33 years), 8488 (30), *JAK*, 2 (1908), 110, fig. 30 (29), Betz, n. 58 (27).

earlier in the discussion of the movements of Legion VII before 6.[1] The dedication from Bigeste (discovered since Cuntz wrote his study) established that they were settled together by the government at the end of Augustus' reign, while the tombstone of L. Riccius L. f. from Pessinus, who died at the age of 60, is demonstrably not earlier than 18, since his recruitment (assuming this to have taken place at the age of 17) cannot have been before the annexation of Galatia in 25 B.C.[2] As has been noted already, the long service of many of these veterans was due to the emergency after 6, and to the desperate shortage of manpower from which the army was then suffering. Similarly, compulsory service for many years beyond the date for official discharge was another of the grievances put forward by the Pannonian mutineers in 14.

There can be no doubt that the veterans around Bigeste are those of Pagus Scunasticus mentioned on the dedication to Tiberius. The details of the settlement are fairly clear. It was a *missio agraria* and the lands for the settlement were purchased (or partly purchased) from the territory of the colony of Narona. The settlement had no connection whatever with the foundation of the colony itself, which had occurred either under Caesar's dictatorship or soon after his death. The dedication set up by the veterans presumably dates from the time when the settlement was actually made, that is in 14. This may be one of the many examples of the strengthening of existing cities by new settlements of veterans on their territories, a device that was not always successful.[3]

The nine veterans of Legion VII from Salona and its territory whose tombstones were set up after 42 were not all necessarily discharged before the rebellion of L. Arruntius Scribonianus in 42 and the departure of the legion to Moesia a decade later. Many who had been discharged from the legion beforehand would not have omitted the legion's new titles from their epitaphs. For instance, the veteran of Legion VII who died at Narona not earlier than 42 aged 60 had served thirty years and might well have left the legion as early as A.D. 29, if

---

[1] O. Seeck, *RM*, 48 (1893), 602 ff., O. Cuntz, *JÖAI*, 25 (1929), 70 ff., Betz, 11 ff. Although the conclusion which Cuntz draws regarding the date when Legion VII reached Dalmatia (not later than 15 B.C., and probably much earlier) cannot be accepted (p. 94 f), there is still a striking coincidence (although the *praenomina* are different) between the *nomina* of these men and some of the army commanders who served M. Antonius during the years before Actium; cf. Alföldy, *Historia*, 13 (1964), 167 ff.

[2] III, 1818 (Narona).

[3] Witness the comments of Tacitus on the attempts to settle colonies of veterans in some of the older cities in Italy, *Ann.*, xiv, 47 (failure of settlements at Antium and Tarentum), *Ann.*, xiii, 31 (Capua and Nuceria strengthened by veteran settlements). The main reason for their failure was that the veterans sold their properties and drifted back to the provinces in which they had served.

he had been recruited at the age of 17.[1] From Legion XI four veterans settled at Salona and died before 42, while two others are known, one at Novae in Imotskipolje, another at Bigeste.

Organized veteran settlements are attested after 42 in two places, at Siculi on the territory of Salona, and in the new Claudian colony at Aequum. According to the Elder Pliny, 'Claudius sent veterans to Siculi' (Biač), which lies on the coast a short distance to the west of Salona, but well within the *territorium* of the colony.[2] Two veterans of Legion XI who died at Siculi after 42 are probably part of this settlement, as may also be the two, possibly three, veterans who died at Salona after 42.

The only instance of veteran settlement in Dalmatia from legions outside it comes from Legion V Macedonica, which was stationed on the lower Danube in Moesia. A dedication was made, probably in the early years of Claudius, by veterans who had served in Moesia under the legate P. Memmius Regulus (35–44) to L. Praecilius Clemens Iulianus their former chief centurion (*primuspilus*).[3] Salona may be his home, since he was *pontifex, flamen,* and patron of the colony. The consular date given for the discharge of these veterans cannot be equated with any known pair of consuls in the *fasti*,[4] but the stone can hardly be later than the reign of Claudius, and if the veterans were discharged during the years 41–44 they could have received land grants (*missio agraria*) in the new settlement at Siculi near Salona.

Colonia Claudia Aequum (Čitluk near Sinj) was founded with a settlement of veterans, at the time when Legion VII left Tilurium, namely either under Claudius, or possibly in the early years of Nero.[5] Before the foundation of the colony a settlement of Roman citizens (*conventus civium Romanorum*) had grown up there, composed of traders and settlers rather than veterans. Sex. Iulius Silvanus was *summus curator* of their quasi-municipal organization in the years immediately before it became a colony, and might obviously expect to play a leading role in the augmented community, composed as it was in part of the earlier settlers, and partly of fresh legionary veterans with land grants. By a vote of the veterans of Legion VII C.p.f. he was the first chosen from the new council (*ordo*) to hold the aedileship.[6] Three veteran settlers are attested in Aequum

[1] III, 1814 (Narona).

[2] Plin., *HN*, iii, 141: 'Siculi in quem locum divus Claudius veteranos misit.' For the veterans attested at Siculi see Appendix VII, p. 469.

[3] III, 8753 (2028). Veterans of Legion V Macedonica at Salona: *BD*, 32 (1909), 59, 3900A. Another, III, 2577, is much later in date, probably third century.

[4] *Q. [L]ut[a]tio Lusio Saturnino M. Seio Verano cos.*; cf. Degrassi, *FC*, 11.   [5] See p. 96.

[6] III, 2733: *Sex. Iu[lius ... f.] Ani. Silva[nus ...] summus c[urator c.R.] suffragio [veteranor. ?] leg. VII C.p.f. aed. [... ab] ordine primus [factus] IIIIvir i. d. pont[ifex ...] in accep[. ...] h.s.h.[n.s.].*

114

and its territory, two of Legion VII, one of Legion XI, all of whom died after 42.

Veteran settlement on the whole contributed little to the development of new cities in the province, but it did in a small way reinforce existing communities, especially Salona and Narona, Aequum was part veteran colony, part civilian settlement, but with this exception the veteran settlements in the hinterland away from the cities contributed little towards the Romanization of the native population.

v *Legions in Dalmatia after the End of the First Century*

There is no evidence to suggest that the Roman government ever again planned to establish a legion permanently in Dalmatia after the departure of IIII Flavia to Moesia about 86. Emergency brought one or more legions for short periods, such as during the Marcomannic Wars, but otherwise the evidence points only to the temporary presence of detachments from legions whose permanent bases were in other provinces. C. Cichorius suggested that Legion I Adiutrix was at Burnum for a short period under Domitian and Trajan.[1] The picture of legionary movements during the wars of this period is confused, and will remain so until more of the Danubian legionary fortresses have been explored and dating evidence for their occupation obtained.[2] The specific evidence for I Adiutrix is a dedication to *Iuppiter Optimus Maximus* set up at Burnum by a *miles* of that legion. However, a new reading of the stone by M. Abramić reveals the man as a *fr(umentarius)*, an appointment held by legionaries in provinces remote from their legionary base and conclusive evidence for the legion not being stationed at Burnum.[3] Other records of I Adiutrix belong to a later date and are discussed below.

Much more certain is the temporary stationing of Legion VIII Augusta in Dalmatia, for which there is a significant amount of evidence including tiles with the legion's stamp. The key piece of evidence is the tombstone of a *miles* at Burnum: he came from Vienna in Narbonensis and had probably served nine years.[4] Until 69 this legion was in Moesia, then in Upper Germany at Argentorate (Strasburg), at which station the Burnum *miles* was almost certainly recruited.[5] Therefore one can exclude a date before 78 at the earliest for this man's

---

[1] C. Cichorius, *Traianssäule*, III, 55 ff., suggests that Legion I Adiutrix can be identified on pl. LXII, fig. LXXXV, and that it is depicted as being in Dalmatia.

[2] The most recent study is by G. Alföldy, *A Arch. Hung.*, 11 (1959), 113–41.

[3] III, 2823; cf. Betz, n. 42.

[4] Betz, n. 228 (otherwise unpublished).

[5] Ritterling, 1647 f.

burial, and probably one before about 86, since up to that date Burnum was occupied without any significant interruption by other legions. The other records are much later in date and do not furnish evidence that the legion itself was based in the province. The fragmentary record of a *duplicarius* at Salona is not earlier than the second half of the second century since his name is Aurelius.[1] Of the three veterans known one belongs to the third century and appears to have returned to his home among the Daesitiates around Sarajevo.[2] The other two cannot be dated but are also men who had returned to their homes, an Octavius at Nedinum and a Trebius at Curicta.[3] However, tiles from Burnum stamped by VIII Augusta suggest that at least a part of the legion was based there, and other examples reveal that they were manufactured at Smrdelj, where the tile works of XI C.p.f. and IIII F.f. also lay.[4] It seems probable that VIII Augusta occupied Burnum when the tile works were a going concern, that is either immediately after XI C.p.f. departed for Italy with the Flavian forces in 69, and before the arrival of the new Legion IIII F.f. at some date early under Vespasian, or alternatively after the departure of the latter for the Danube in 86. Yet this does not rule altogether out a detachment in later period. With the frontier pushed far beyond the Rhine into Germany the permanent station of VIII Augusta at Argentorate enjoyed an unusual tranquillity and was an obvious source of reinforcements for Dalmatia during the Marcomannic crisis. Furthermore, if a detachment were stationed at Burnum then there is no reason why the legion should not stamp its tiles at Smrdelj, which may have still been functioning under civilian control from Asseria or Varvaria. Elsewhere the tiles of VIII Augusta are found at two centres, at Asseria which was the nearest city in Liburnia, and at Bigeste; this was the station of Cohort I Belgarum in the second century, but there is no evidence that men from the legion were ever stationed there or at Asseria.[5] There may have been a detachment in the extreme north of the province as is suggested by the fragmentary tombstone of a *miles* at Alvona.[6]

Definitely attested in the Marcomannic period is the presence of men from two newly-raised legions of Marcus Aurelius. Vexillations from Legions II and III Italica are recorded at Salona on two identical building records in 170 under their original titles II Pia and III Concordia. They rebuilt a length of the north

[1] III, 14692.   [2] III, 8375 (12749).

[3] III, 2865 (*WMBH*, 5 (1897), 339) (Nedinum); III, 3127 (10126) (Curicta, Omišalj).

[4] Tiles of Legion VIII Augusta at Burnum and Smrdelj: III, p. 2328/178, add. 10181/1–2; cf. *WMBH*, 7 (1900), 96, fig. 67 f.

[5] Asseria: III, 10181/2, 13339/1, *BD*, 26 (1903), 150 (seven examples). Bigeste: III, 6435 (10181/1, 13339/2, *WMBH*, 7 (1900), 97, fig. 69, *GZMBH*, 26 (1914), 162, fig. 22) all referring to the same tile from Gradčine near Ljubuški, Betz, 51, n. 121.

[6] III, 3051.

wall of the eastern city (*urbs nova*) at Salona.[1] It is possible that the legions were not yet organized as a fighting force, since the men of both units were under the supervision of a *centurio frumentarius* of Legion II Traiana, who was probably stationed permanently at Salona, although his legion was based in Egypt. The length of wall constructed was 400 feet, much less than what is recorded for two of the four newly-raised cohorts of Delmatae at the same time on similar building records: each of these units built 800 feet of wall including a tower under the supervision of their own commanders (*tribuni*).[2] The protection and defence of Salona was evidently vital during the Marcomannic Wars if new legionary and Auxiliary formations could be spared for building work. Perhaps Marcus Aurelius may have considered the possibility of Salona having to serve as his headquarters if Italy should be completely cut off from the Lower Danube by the invaders.[3]

At about the same time some disturbances were taking place on the eastern fringes of the province. According to his biography in the Augustan History the later emperor Didius Iulianus when governor about 176 successfully defended his province against 'enemies on its borders' (*hostes confines*).[4] These same troubles are recorded in two other contexts. Another general of the period, M. Valerius Maximianus, undertook operations against bandits (*latrones*) on the borders of Macedonia,[5] while the biography of Marcus Aurelius records that 'he made soldiers of the bandits (*latrones*) in Dalmatia and Dardania'.[6]

In addition to detachments from these three legions it appears that men from I and II Adiutrix (whose permanent stations were at Brigetio and Aquincum in Pannonia) were based in Dalmatia under Marcus. Two serving *milites,* one from each legion, are recorded at Bigeste probably under Marcus,[7] while a centurion of I Adiutrix is attested as temporary commander (*praepositus*) in 173 of the Bigeste garrison, Cohort I Belgarum.[8] The same post was also held about the

---

[1] III, 1980; cf. p. 1030 (*ILS* 2287): *Imp. Caes. M. Aurel. Antonino Aug. pont. max. tr. pot. XXIIII cos. III vexillationes leg. II Piae et III Concordiae ped. CC sub cura P. Aeli Amyntiani 7 frumentari leg. II Traian.* Two inscriptions with this same text were found, probably recording the construction of different sections of the wall. One still remains in the wall of the *urbs nova* (p. 360) near the northeast angle alongside III, 6374 (8655).

[2] III, 1979, 6374 (8655), and below, p. 473.   [3] W. Zwikker, 175 f.   [4] *Vita Did. Iul.,* i, 9.
[5] H-G. Pflaum, *Libyca,* 3 (1955), 135 ff. (*AE,* 1956, 124) (Diana Veteranorum, Numidia): 'aucto salario adeptus procurationem, Moesiae inferioris eodem in tempore praeposito vexillationibus et at detrahendam Briseorum latronum manum in confinio Macedon. et Thrac.' The Brysae dwelt on the left bank of the Strymon as far as the river Mestus, Plin., *HN,* iv, 40.
[6] *Vita Marci,* xxi, 7: 'latrones etiam Dalmatiae atque Dardaniae milites fecit.'
[7] *GZMBH,* 26 (1914), 162, fig. 23; cf. Patsch, *Narona,* 68, fig. 31.
[8] III, 1790 (6362, 8484); cf. Patsch, *Narona,* 70, fig. 33.

K

same period by a centurion seconded from I Minervia at Bonna in Lower Germany.[1] The measures taken during the Marcomannic Wars involved not only the stationing of detachments from elsewhere at key centres, but also a stiffening and reorganization of the permanent auxiliary garrison in the province by replacing the less experienced equestrian commanders with legionary centurions.

At about this period also the northern and eastern parts of the province were occupied by auxiliary units. For some time the new Cohort I milliaria Delmatarum was stationed near Užice, while not far away at Jezdinae near Čačak a centurion of Cohort VIII Voluntariorum, normally stationed at Tilurium, set up an official dedication in 197 which suggests the presence there of at least part of his unit.[2] Almost certainly connected with events under Marcus is the concentration of a strong force of auxiliaries, partly of new, partly of old units transferred from elsewhere, in the rich lead-mining area of the Kosmaj hills around Guberevci, a region which may have been included in Moesia Superior or in Pannonia Inferior, but definitely not in Dalmatia.[3] Of the five cohorts attested, four are new formations, II Aurelia nova milliaria equitata c. R.,[4] I(?) Aurelia Dardanorum,[5] I Aurelia n(ova) Pasinatum (?) c. R.,[6] II Aurelia nova Sacorum.[7] One unit, V Callaecorum et Lucensium, had been transferred from Pannonia.[8] The Cohort II Aurelia nova milliaria equitata c. R. is attested in 179, the earliest dated record, and it was still there more than forty years later under Severus Alexander. The other units may have furnished detachments from their permanent stations at Timacum minus (Ravna) and Naissus (Niš) in Moesia Superior.

---

[1] III, 1918 (Vrgorac, west of Bigeste).   [2] III, 8336 (6321).   [3] p. 79 n. 7.

[4] III, 14537 (Stojnik) in 179; III, 14541 (Guberevci), *JÖAI*, 12 (1909), Bb. 189, n. 59 (Stojnik) with title [*Anto*]*niniana* under Caracalla, also *JÖAI*, 7 (1904), Bb. 6, n. 9, dedicated to Severus Alexander.

[5] III, 14700 (Salona), a serving soldier. The unit is either Cohort I Aurelia Dardanorum stationed at Naissus, III, 8251, or II Aurelia Dardanorum at Timacum Minus (Ravna), III, 14576. The deceased, Surus Victoris (f.), is a *peregrinus* and may be one of the recruits mentioned in the Biography of Marcus Aurelius (n. 6 on p. 117).

[6] Only a single problematical record survives for this unit: III, 14545; cf. *JÖAI*, 3 (1900), Bb. 163, n. 63 (Stojnik): [*I*].*O.M.* [. . .*S*]*cribonius Faustus v.e.* (*vet?*) *I Aure. n.* [. . .] *PASINATV* [. . . Premerstein and Vulic (*JÖAI*) connect this unit with the *civitas Pasini*, an inland city of Liburnia mentioned by Pliny, *HN*, iii, 140, cf. p. 218, but not located. At this date, however, recruitment to the *auxilia* from a city in Liburnia is most unlikely, Kraft, 183, n. 1770, p. 101, n. 4.

[7] III, 14217/6 (Guberevci). Wagner, 182, links the unit with Sacida in Southern Dacia, rather than with the perhaps more probable Scythian Sacii.

[8] III, 14542 (Suvodol near Guberevci), a *praefectus coh(ortis)*. The unit appears on diplomas in Pannonia Superior until 154, XVI, 104. Another unit moved from elsewhere was Cohort XVIII Voluntariorum c. R., III, 8162 (6302) (Stojnik).

It is not clear what strategy lay behind these military dispositions within and near Northeast Dalmatia. They are obviously linked with changes over the much greater area of the Danube and can only be understood in such a context. As regards Dalmatia, it appears that the strengthening of the provincial garrison at this period was not always due to external danger but to disturbances within the more remote and less settled parts of the province. Too often it is assumed that the only problem which occupied the Roman imperial army was frontier defence, but the confusion of the Marcomannic Wars shows that dissident elements still remained, and at times of crisis were able to cause considerable trouble to the provincial governments.[1]

Finally a detachment from Legion I Italica (whose permanent station was at Novae in Moesia Inferior) was based at Salona for some time in the early third century. At least twelve serving *milites* are attested, possibly as many as fifteen: all whose names are recorded have the *nomen* Aurelius and they are predominantly Thracian in origin, and one of the tombstones is dated more closely by the legionary title *Severiana* to the reign of Severus Alexander.[2] They do not appear to have been connected with the *officium* of the governor and may have been required for purely military duties, although there is no indication what these might have been.

Later in the third century detachments from neighbouring legions may have been maintained in the northern part of Dalmatia. At Metulum a centurion of II Adiutrix set up a dedication in the reign of Diocletian, while a *miles* of either I or II Adiutrix was buried at Perjašisa near Svojić at a late date.[3] It is possible that the very late *milites* of II Adiutrix buried at various places in the interior (Raetinium, Grahovo, Bistue Nova) had returned home after discharge, but it is perhaps more probable that since none has the title *veteranus* they were serving soldiers who died when on duty at these places.[4] Similarly there are one or two records

---

[1] C. Patsch once announced his intention to publish a study of an insurrection in Northern Dalmatia in the reign of Pius, *WMBH*, 5 (1897), 209, 339 ff., but no such study ever appeared.

[2] III, 12899, with title *Severiana*; III, 2008, 2009 (two serving soldiers), 2010, 2132, 8719, 12898, 12899, 13909, *VHAD*, 50 (1929–30), 14, n. 15 *Sev*[*eriana*], n. 16, *BD*, 27 (1904), 52, 3207 (no legion mentioned, but an Aurelius with the Thracian *cognomen* Mucatra suggests a Thracian serving in Legion I Italica).

[3] III, 10060 (*WMBH*, 7 (1900), 174; *VHAD*, N.S. 9 (1906–7), 91, fig. 213), centurion at Metulum: III, 14333/1 (*VHAD*, N.S. 1 (1895), 156, fig. 99).

[4] III, 10036 (*WMBH*, 7 (1900), 173) (Golubić), Sp. 77 (1934), 19, fig. 26 (Grahovo); III, 12764 (*WMBH*, 6 (1899), 174; *GZMBH*, 26 (1914), 170, fig. 39) (Zenica). The tombstone of the *miles legionis secundes* [sic] *defunctus Bassianis* (Glavatičevo, upper Neretva valley) was presumably set up by his parents, who are named on the stone, after his death at Bassiana in Pannonia Inferior had been reported to them, III, 12799 (8489).

from Salona suggesting that men from Legion XIII Gemina (stationed at Apulum in Dacia) and Legion XIIII Gemina (Carnuntum in Upper Pannonia) also served in these and other detachments.[1]

VI *Legionaries in the Service of the Provincial Governor*

From the Late Republic it was the practice of Roman magistrates to use soldiers under their command for administration and other non-military functions. Later it was accepted that an imperial legate might detach a number of serving soldiers for service as *beneficiarii*. Together with more specialist administrators in the *officium* at the provincial capital, such officers were for a long time the basis of the Roman civil service of the provinces. The men thus appointed always remained technically members of their original unit, even if they spent almost the whole of their military career away from it.[2] With no proper provision for a provincial administration governors came to depend on men from the army to such an extent that Trajan expressed a general disapproval of the practice in a letter to the Younger Pliny while the latter was governor of Bithynia.[3] At what date the system became consolidated into the later fixed hierarchy of ranks and titles is not known. The practice of awarding appointments (*beneficia*) to legionaries is first referred to under Gaius and at least one such appointment is recorded in Dalmatia in the period before 42.[4]

While there is a considerable body of evidence, largely from tombstones, for the organization and titles of members of the *officia* of provincial governors there is little evidence to show what they actually did while serving in these appointments. The normal organization of the *officium* of a provincial governor was administered by a centurion with the title of *princeps praetorii*, but there is no record of any men who held this post in Dalmatia. The only reference to the office is found in the career of the *miles* of Cohort VIII Voluntariorum who served as an assistant to this officer and was later appointed to the post (*statio*) of *beneficiarius consularis* at Doclea, an appointment normally held by legionaries only.[5] Immediately below the *princeps praetorii* were the senior appointments of *cornicularius* and *commentariensis*, with three posts in each grade. These three appointments were classed as *principales* and all possessed their own assistants

---

[1] III, 6549; cf. p. 1510 (two serving soldiers); III, 12896 (both Salona).

[2] For the hierarchy and composition of provincial governors' *officia* see A. v. Domaszewski—B. Dobson, *Rangordnung*, 1 ff.; A. H. M. Jones, *SRGL*, 151 ff.

[3] In this instance troops detached for duty with the *praefectus orae Ponticae*, Plin., *Ep.*, x, 22.

[4] Tac., *Hist.*, iv, 48 (*officium* of proconsul in Africa and of Legion III Augusta at Lambaesis); III, p. 2328/121 (add. n. 1914); cf. n. 4 on p. 112.

[5] III, 12679.

(*adiutores*) who took precedence according to the rank they served. In Dalmatia two *cornicularii* are attested, one from XI (probably before 42) and another whose legion is not recorded: both were at Salona.[1] The *cornicularius* at the Kapitul hill near Knin was probably not a member of the governor's staff at Salona, but held a corresponding appointment in the *officium* of the commander of Legion XI at Burnum.[2] Both men at Salona are of the first century and appear to have been appointed from the legionary garrison of the province. Two *adiutores* of *cornicularii* are attested, both auxiliaries from Cohort VIII Voluntariorum; one was buried at Salona, the other at Tilurium where his unit was stationed.[3] They date to the second century when legionaries were no longer stationed in Dalmatia. The man at Tilurium had completed his term with the legate in Salona and had returned to serve as clerk (*actarius*) in the smaller *officium* of the commander of his own unit. Only one *commentariensis* is known, a *miles* of XIIII Gemina who had previously been a *speculator*, and at his death he had completed thirteen years service.[4] His earlier post was presumably held at Salona; his wife was a native of the province, from either Salona or Liburnia.

Below the three grades of *principales* were the *speculatores*, ten from each legion stationed in the province. As with other grades in the *officium* these posts in Dalmatia were filled by men from neighbouring provinces. Seven *speculatores* are known from Dalmatia, ranging in date from before 42 to the reign of Gordian (238–41). Only a minority are attested in the provincial capital. The earliest, a *speculator veteranus*, was buried near the source of the Vrlika between Salona and Tilurium. After retirement he had been co-opted on to the city council of Salona as a decurion: he gives no *origo* and was probably a native of the province.[5] Two are attested at Iader; one is probably of the early first century, the other, who was from XIIII Gemina, belongs to the late first or early second century.[6] Another is attested at Narona, while of two later examples one at Salona belongs to the late second or early third century, the other at Carevopolje near Josipdol was a member of XI Claudia who set up a dedication to Gordian.[7]

As has been noted already very little is known about what these officers actually did. It is recorded that *commentarienses* and *speculatores* were concerned with custody and execution of the condemned, and it is probable that they carried out

[1] III, 8738 (Legion XI), 8750.

[2] III, 9908 (Kapitul hill, Knin); earlier in his career he had been [*tess*]*erarius*, possibly then *beneficiarius*.

[3] III, 2052 (Salona), *BD*, 26 (1903), 129 (Tilurium).   [4] III, 2015 (Salona).

[5] Note 4 on p. 112.   [6] III, 2910 (9996); III, 2915, with no legion specified.

[7] III, 1809 (Narona), *BD*, 37 (1914), 94, 4692A (*Starinar*, III, 1 (1922), 59, pl. I 3, *AE*, 1945, 88); III, 9401 (*Starinar*, loc. cit., pl. I 4) (both at Salona); III, 3021; cf. 10058, *VHAD*, N.S. 9 (1906–7), 118, fig. 242 (Carevopolje near Josipdol).

instructions from the legate issued by virtue of his *imperium*.[1] Imperial pro-curators, men appointed from the equestrian order who dealt largely with finance, had similar staffs of their own, a military *officium* for judicial duties and a *familia* of slaves and freedmen for finance and accounts. The importance of these senior officers in the provincial administration cannot be over-emphasized: while the consular legate rarely spent more than three years in the province these men often held their posts for a large part of their military service, often in the same province, and will have acquired considerable knowledge of local people and conditions. As time passed these legionaries on detached duty became less and less associated with the fighting formations in which they still served on paper, and as *officiales* were clearly distinguished from men serving with their units. In the fourth century many grades in the civil service bore titles originating from military service, although by then the distinction between military and civilian officials was very clear.[2]

Below the grade of *speculator* were lesser ranks, all private soldiers seconded from their units, *exceptores, exacti* and *librarii*, clerks of one type or another. Only one of these three posts is attested in Dalmatia, an *exactus consularis* of the early third century buried at Andetrium.[3] His appointment came early in his career since he died at the age of 24. The tombstone was set up by an imperial freedman and his mother. He may have been enrolled directly into the Dalmatian *officium* although presumably he still had to be registered in the records of his legion at Viminacium in Upper Moesia. Rather more lowly were the men detached for duty in the governor's personal bodyguard (*singulares consulares*) and in his house-hold as equerries and grooms (*stratores*). For these posts there was no need to draw men from the legions and they were frequently filled by men from the auxiliary garrison of the province.[4]

By far the best documented branch of the provincial administration is the corps of *beneficiarii consulares* who manned posts (*stationes*) in all parts of the province.[5] In the majority of cases these officers are attested on their official dedications of altars to *Iuppiter Optimus Maximus*, sometimes coupled with the

---

[1] See the literature cited by A. H. M. Jones, *SRGL*, 207, n. 66.

[2] A. H. M. Jones, *SRGL*, 164 ff.

[3] *VAHD*, 51 (1930–4), 230, cf. pl. XXXVI, 1 (*AE*, 1940, 177): *D. m. L. Septimio Gratiano mil. leg. VII Cl. exacto cos. v[i]xit ann. XXII[II] d. XI Genialis Aug. n. lib. et Apuleia Salvia filio karis-simo pos.* His mother may have been connected with the Appuleii who were a leading family at Iader and Salona.

[4] *Singulares*: III, 13906 (8725 and 8755), *VAHD*, 53 (1950–1), 226, n. 35; *stratores*: *RS*, 1, 160, n. 14; cf. *VAHD*, 50 (1928–9), 14; III, 2067 (all from Salona).

[5] On the functions of *beneficiarii consulares* see A. v. Domaszewski, *WZ*, 21 (1902), 158 ff., *RM*, 17 (1902), 330 ff.

reigning emperor, the *genius loci* of their *statio* or, as happened at Magnum and Novae, with the *genius* of the local city. Many of these dedications are dated by consuls of the year, and in some cases the month is also given; the usual time was either the 1 April or the 1 August, possibly the dates when they handed their *statio* to their successor. Little is known about the duties of *beneficiarii consulares*, but they probably fulfilled the role of local police officers and superintended the process of collecting taxes.[1] In general they may have occupied a position similar to district officers in colonial territories of European powers during the past hundred years, but in the Roman province the gap between the officer and the people among whom he was stationed had largely disappeared by the end of the second century. Although *beneficiarii consulares* were all legionaries (they are styled *miles leg. . . . b(ene)f(iciarius) co(n)s(ularis)*) there is no evidence that they were engaged solely in military tasks. It was not unusual for such men to be promoted to higher posts in the provincial administration. The only *bf. cos.* who was not a legionary, a *miles* of Cohort VIII Voluntariorum, was appointed to the *statio* at Doclea after having served as assistant (*adiutor*) to the *princeps praetorii* in the Salona *officium*.[2]

As to the siting of *bf. cos. stationes* there is little that can be said beyond indicating their distribution in various areas. Most are known in cities, but the presence or absence of such a post appears to have no bearing upon civic organization: they are found in the early *coloniae* and in Aurelian *municipia* of the late second and early third century. Perhaps most significant is their total absence from Liburnia, apart from the old legionary base at Burnum which after the departure of the legions was retained under imperial administration, at least until the Burnistae achieved municipal status. All *stationes* were sited on or near main roads, but there are no *bf. cos.* records from the three stations of the permanent auxiliary garrison at Andetrium, Tilurium, and Bigeste, and this suggests that in these areas at least some of the duties could be carried out by members of auxiliary units.

The largest number of *bf. cos.* records comes from Salona. Not all had served there, for some of them had completed tours of duty at other posts in the province. Fourteen are known there (including one from Tragurium and one from Klis). Four are veterans from Legion X Gemina and belong to the second century.[3] Of the remaining ten only four specify their legion, two from I

---

[1] M. Rostovtzeff, *SEHRE*[2], p. 738 f., ch. XI, n. 17, emphasizing their policing role in the more unsettled parts of the Empire.

[2] III, 12679 (Doclea).

[3] III, 3158a (findspot not recorded, probably Salona); III, 8745, *BD*, 30 (1907), 39, 3784A (all from Salona); III, 2677 (Tragurium).

Italica, and one each from X Gemina and XI Claudia.[1] All are of the period after the departure of the legions. Of the remaining six at Salona three probably belong to the first century, two to the second. The tombstone of one appears to illustrate the full insignia of a *bf. cos.* in a *statio*, suggesting that at least some of them had been serving elsewhere in the province but were buried at Salona.[2]

In the rest of the province the distribution of these officers can be seen as four groups more or less associated with the major roads of the province radiating from Salona. The first led to Metulum in the north of Dalmatia and then down the Colapis valley to Siscia. No *statio* is found at Andetrium, the fort of Cohort III Alpinorum, but that at Umljanović near Magnum (Balijina Glavica) is attested by seven *I.O.M.* dedications, mostly fragmentary. One set up to the *genius* of the *municipium* at Magnum dates to the late second or early third century. On only two is a legion mentioned, XI Claudia in both cases.[3] The tombstone of a *miles* of V Macedonica attests the *statio* at Burnum.[4] Further north *stationes* were located at Avendo (Crkvina near Brlog) in the Lika polje, Raetinium (Golubić), and Metulum, all important centres of the Iapodes.[5] No *stationes* are attested on the road northward from Burnum over the Strmica pass which led through Drvar and Ključ to the Vrbas valley. However, they do occur on the route from this area to Salona through Livjanskopolje and Glamočkopolje. At Lipa in the former area a *veteranus ex bf. cos. leg. X Gemina* had settled after his service was finished and had been admitted as decurion to the council of the local city. This was probably Pelva which lay somewhere near Livno.[6] Further north there may have been two *stationes* in Glamočkopolje, one at Glamoč and the other at Halapić 7 miles on the road north.[7] The man at Glamoč was a member of XI Claudia; at Halapić an altar was set up by a *bf. cos.* from XIIII Gemina on 1 April

[1] Legion I Italica: III, 2023, Betz, n. 192 (otherwise unpublished); X Gemina: III, 6376 (8656; cf. *Starinar*, III, 1 (1922), pl. II 5); XI Claudia: III, 14703 (Klis); epitaphs with legion not specified: III, 2001; III, 12895 (*Starinar*, loc. cit., 63, pl. 7–8, *FS*, 2, 68, n. 26), III, 8754 (*FS*, 2, 74, n. 80, *ILCV*, 396); III, 8749 *bf.* [*cos.*], *BD*, 30 (1907), 40, 3778A; III, 8743 [*bf.*] *cos.*

[2] III, 12895 (*Starinar*, III, 1 (1922), 63, pl. 7–8, *FS*, 2, 68, n. 26). On the right is represented a writing tablet with stylus box; on the left is a standard with a cross-piece for holding it upright, as with *signa*, while from the cross-piece hang what appear to be two money bags.

[3] *Genius municipii*: III, 14957; Legion XI Claudia: III, 9790, 14959 [? *leg. XI*] *Cl*. Other records at Magnum: III, 14956, 14961, 14962.

[4] *SB*, 216, n. 5, n. 6.

[5] III, 10050; cf. p. 2328/175 (Avendo); III, 15066 (Golubić); III, 3020 (10057) (Josipdol).

[6] III, 9847 (Lipa in Livjanskopolje). For text see below p. 270 n.1 and on the city Pelva, see p. 269 f.

[7] III, 9862, with 13231; cf. p. 2270 add. (Glamoč), *GZMBH*, 39 (1937), 262, 267, dated 1 April 261 (Halapić).

261. Perhaps there was actually only one post in the *territorium* of Salvium (Kamen near Glamoč) and at some period it was transferred from near Glamoč to Halapić. Certainly the dedication at Glamoč is much earlier and may antedate the *municipium* at Salvium. The last post on this road was at Banjaluka on the river Vrbas, which can be identified with Castra of the Itineraries. It is about 14 miles south of the provincial boundary with Upper Pannonia at *Ad Fines* (Laktaši) but was manned by men from the *officium* of the governor of Pannonia.[1]

The third group was not based along a main route but in the lead-mining area around the middle sector of the river Drina. In the south at Plevlje there is a dedication set up in 194 by a soldier from I Adiutrix.[2] To the northeast there are two groups of dedications from Skelani and Lješće on the Drina. They probably represent only one *statio* being only two miles apart and on the same side of the river, for there is no obvious chronological separation between the two. All are official dedications but none is dated: at Skelani one man is from V Macedonica, another from XI Claudia, while in the other group three legions are attested, I Adiutrix, V Macedonica, and X Gemina.[3] It is not certain whether these officers had any connection with the administration of the mines at Domavia which was under the imperial procurator of the Pannonian and Dalmatian silver mines. The only record of a *bf. cos.* from there is a dedication to *Diana Augusta* set up by a man from Lower Pannonia.[4]

The final group of *beneficiarii consulares* was established along the main road from Salona to Doclea near the border with Macedonia. At two places, Tilurium and Bigeste, auxiliary cohorts were in permanent garrison and no *bf. cos.* is known at either place. At Novae (Runović) which lies mid-way between them was a *statio* which has produced the largest number of dedications of any post in the province. A total of eleven are known, two to *I.O.M.,* three to *Genius municipii Novensium,* the earliest being dated to 194. Other dedications include one to *Silvanus Augustus,* made on the 1 of April or August 239. Of the officers who set them up, four came from I Adiutrix, one of whom had served earlier as a *miles* in XIII Gemina, one each from I Italica (a dedication to *Fortuna Redux*),

---

[1] III, 14221 (Banjaluka): *I.O.M. et Genio loci L. Sicinius Macrinus bf. cos. P. s. v. s. l. m.* On the line of the provincial boundary see p. 79.

[2] III, 13847 (Plevlje), dated 194. On the city here see p. 281 ff.

[3] Skelani: *GZMS*, 6 (1951), 308, n. 14 (Šašel, n. 81): Legion V Mac., III, 14219/4: Legion XI Claudia, III, 14219/5, 14219/6; Lješće: III, 14218: Legion I Adiutrix, *GZMBH*, 19 (1907), 437, fig. 9 (*WMBH*, 11 (1909), 146, fig. 46; *GZMBH*, 26 (1914), 175, fig. 49; *AE*, 1910, 214): Legion V. Mac., III, 14219: Legion X Gemina, III, 14219/15: probably XI Claudia. Also at nearby Bajina Bašta: Sp. 98. (1941–8), n. 2, also Voljavica northeast of Ljubovija: Sp. 77 (1934), n. 12: Legion XI Claudia dated 1 October in an unknown year.

[4] III, 12723 (Domavia): *b. cos. P. in.* with no legion recorded.

X Gemina, XI Claudia, and XIIII Gemina.[1] One dedication dated to 195 was set up by a *bf. cos.* of Upper Pannonia.[2] To judge from the dedications mentioned above, the *statio* functioned in close association with the *municipium* of Novae which was founded in the second half of the second century. Moreover, two altars are not dated by the usual consuls, but by the annual magistrates (*IIviri iure dicundo*) of the city. Beyond Bigeste three records attest a *statio* at Narona, including one of a man from XIIII Gemina in 209, and one from I Italica in 225.[3] From there the route moves across the Neretva valley to Stolac in the Bregava valley, where two dedications attest the *statio*.[4] At the final *statio* at Doclea three records are known, one of them fragmentary.[5] Two are dedicated to *I.O.M.* and *Epona Regina*, the Gallic horse and ass deity. One of the dedicators was an auxiliary, a *miles* of Cohort VIII Voluntariorum who was probably a native of Salona, the other a *miles* of I Adiutrix, whose dedication was set up in 187.

Inevitably the evidence for *stationes* of *beneficiarii consulares* is not complete. Yet in spite of this there is a pattern to be seen. Most are situated on the main roads which link Salona and the main cities with the northern parts of the province. There is no evidence to connect their activities with the *cursus publicus*, the imperial post and communications system which was serviced by *mansiones* at regular intervals, nor is their siting linked either with provincial or tribal boundaries or with the *portorium*, the machinery of customs collection. In this Dalmatia was part of the *Portorium Illyrici*, a system which embraced virtually the whole of the Danubian provinces.[6] In general it seems that they represented the Roman government in areas where it could not act conveniently through well-established cities or local military forces. In some cases there were close links between these officers and the communities in which they were based, for instance at Novae, the Livjanskopolje *statio*, and also at Salona. All the evidence seems to suggest that they were alone in their posts, there being no record of any

---

[1] Legion I Adiutrix: III, 1907 (*WMBH*, 8 (1902), 100, fig. 35) dedicated to *I.O.M.* by *bf. cos.* formerly a soldier in XIII Gemina; III, 1910, *I.O.M. et G(enio) m(unicipii) N(ovensium)*, dated by *IIviri quinquennales*; III, 1909, *I.O.M. et G. m. N.* dated to 194; I Italica: III, 1906 [*I.O.M.*]*s. Fort(unae) R[educi] l[eg. I]tal.*; X Gemina: III, 14637; XI Claudia: III, 14638; XIIII Gemina: III, 1911; others III, 14636 (Bublin near Dikovača), III, 14634 (Dikovača), *I.O.M. et G. m.* [*N*?].
[2] III, 12802, *bf. c[os. p]ro P. super.* dated 195.
[3] III, 1780: Legion XIIII in 209; III, 1781: I Italica in 225; III, 1783: previously he had been *optio* in the legion, then appointed *bf. cos.*; the identity of the legion has not survived.
[4] III, 8431; cf. 12789; III, 8435: both Legion XIIII Gemina.
[5] *VAHD*, 50 (1929–30), 67 (*AE*, 1933, 76). Legion I Adiutrix in 187, III, 12679: *mil. coh. Vol. adiu[t]. princ. bf. cos.*, III, 13828: the officer's name is P. Bennius Egregius, possibly connected with the Salona *Bennii*, p. 325.
[6] A. Dobó, *Publicum Portorium Illyrici*.

assistants or other staff. Only a few can be assigned to a particular year, but all belong to the period after the departure of the legionary garrison, most of the dated examples being from the late second and early third centuries. This suggests that many of their duties had previously been carried out by the legions in Dalmatia without any system of special detachment for the purpose. The *beneficiarii consulares* were almost certainly key figures in many areas of the provinces, and often for the mass of the rural population of the interior they must have been the only contact with and visible symbol of the Roman power.

VII *The Social Background of Serving Legionaries and Veterans*

It is not possible to survey the gradual change in the social position of serving legionaries and veterans on the basis of the evidence from Dalmatia alone. Most important was the factor of recruitment, where a great change took place during the hundred years between the middle of the first and the middle of the second century. In the beginning the legions were recruited from a fairly small sector of the Empire, almost exclusively from older Roman cities and veteran colonies, with most recruits coming from Northern and Central Italy, Southern Spain, and Southern Gaul, although a few are known from Roman communities in the eastern provinces. By the middle of the second century legionary recruitment is almost without exception from the nearest convenient source of manpower, and with the great extension of the *civitas* and increase in Roman communities this usually meant local recruitment.[1] There was clearly a considerable difference between the legions and the native population in the first century, a difference that is emphasized by legionary tombstones. Too much importance, however, should not be attached to the external signs of legionary superiority in the first century – fine lettering and well-decorated tombstones. The usual prerogatives and advantages of an occupying garrison are outweighed by the terrible picture of service in the legions given by their spokesman during the mutiny of the Pannonian army in 14. The comfortable existence often depicted as the life of a legionary veteran is a misleading assumption. To have spent much of one's active life fighting the peoples of Illyricum and then, under the title of discharge grant, to be settled as a farmer in a Dalmatian polje was far from pleasant.[2] Elsewhere others were more fortunate: in Britain legionary veterans who had been settled in the Claudian colony at Camulodunum were partly to blame for the

[1] The evidence is collected by G. Forni, *Reclutamento*. For the increasing importance of frontier communities as a source of recruits in the second century see J. C. Mann, *Quint. Cong. Int. Lim. Rom. Stud.*, (Zagreb 1963), 145–50.

[2] For the speech of the mutineers in 14 see Tac., *Ann.*, i, 17, and *CQ*, 56 (1963), 268 ff.

terrible fate suffered by that city during the rebellion of Boudicca in 60, for they had ill-treated the local inhabitants for more than a decade.[1] In Dalmatia there were only a few places where a veteran could settle to enjoy the sort of life he may once have been accustomed to in Italy. By the second century the picture had changed. There was no longer a legionary garrison; the men who served in the governor's *officium* were presumably recruited mostly from the provinces where their legions were stationed. In their time and in that of the few serving legionaries known in the province after 86, there was no longer a clear distinction between the Roman army and the native population. During most of the Principate the interior of Dalmatia was little affected either by recruitment to legions or *auxilia*, or by veteran settlement. It was only in the third century when complete military disintegration was threatening that a central government, whose writ was confined to Italy and the Danubian provinces, had to draw all the manpower it could obtain from such areas as it still controlled. Hence emerged the series of able Illyrian soldier-emperors of the later third and early fourth centuries, who seem to have originated from an area which had not previously appeared in the recruiting records of the army.

The information that can be deduced about the social condition of serving soldiers and veterans is restricted by the details of their own condition which are given on tombstones. In all there are some 200 legionaries attested for the whole period of the Principate in Dalmatia. From the records of these one can see the extent to which serving soldiers were able to establish their own households while still on active service. Until the reign of Septimius Severus they could not legally marry while they were still serving in the army,[2] but unofficial marriages were arranged and these could be regularized in Roman law after discharge. It was from the children of these marriages, often given the birthplace registration *castris* ('on active service'), that the army drew a large proportion of its recruits. It is obvious that the government never actively obstructed soldiers contracting such marriages. Once whole legions had ceased to move regularly from province to province the families of serving soldiers formed an important element in the civilian communities which sprang up rapidly around the legionary fortresses along the Rhine and Danube frontiers.[3] Chronologically the tombstones fall into three groups. The first belongs to the period of the legionary garrison (Augustus to 86), and this can be subdivided into those before and after 42.[4] The second and third are from Trajan to Pius (98–161) and from Mar-

---

[1] The sack of Camulodunum is described by Tacitus, *Ann.*, xiv, 31–2; on the background to the rebellion see Dudley and Webster, *Boudicca*, 44 ff.

[2] Herodian, iii, 5.   [3] See the article of J. C. Mann cited in n. 1 on p. 127.

[4] On the dating value of the legionary titles *Claudia pia fidelis* see Appendix III.

cus Aurelius onwards. For obvious reasons this section does not include men in grades higher than centurion, while within the evidence discussed a clear distinction must always be made between serving soldiers and discharged veterans, whose social and material condition was quite different.

Of the three centurions attested before 42 one was probably a *primuspilus* of Legion XI while his brother, recorded on the same inscription, may have been a senior centurion (*princeps*) of Legion XI: no dependants are mentioned.[1] The other appears at Iader on the tombstone of a magistrate of Altinum on the opposite coast of Italy; this was set up by his son who was at the time a centurion in Legion VII.[2] Six legionary centurions are known from the period between 42 and the Flavian period. One in Legion VII C.p.f. is probably Claudian: he was buried at Tragurium, where he had probably retired and records his wife Iulia Polla, who was probably a native of the province. Another centurion at Salona records a freedman.[3] Of the other four in XI C.p.f. the *praefectus castrorum* had no dependants, while a centurion at Burnum records a freedman. The two buried at Salona have their own households: one married Bennia Sabina, a woman of a good Salona family, while the other records a legal wife (*uxor*) and a freedman.[4]

Twenty-nine legionaries serving before 42 record no family or other dependants. One man was buried by his father who was still serving in the same legion (VII, although the legion is not named on the stone at Tilurium).[5] In four cases tombstones were set up by fellow legionaries who are named, three record fellow soldiers as *fratres,* while another four merely refer to heirs (*heredes*).[6] In four cases

---

[1] III, 14996.   [2] III, 2914.

[3] III, 2678; cf. 9699, *VAHD*, 50 (1928–9), 13, n. 5 (*RS*, 1, 158, fig. 157).

[4] *SB*, 218, n. 13 (*AE*, 1925, 33); III, 2834 (9893; cf. p. 2328/12, *GZMBH*, 7 (1895), 381, fig. 4) (both from Burnum); III, 2062 and 8747 (*JÖAI*, 6 (1903), Bb. 83, also Forni, 161, n. 2); III, 2035 (both from Salona). In legal usage *uxor* denotes a wife acquired under Roman law, while *coniunx* is applied to the wife of a common-law marriage by serving soldiers which was not recognized by the government, Alföldy, *AArch*, 14 (1962), 279.

[5] *BD*, 26 (1903), 130, n. 3321.

[6] Epitaphs with fellow legionaries named: III, 14932; III, 2708 (9725; cf. *JÖAI*, 1 (1898), Bb. 122); III, 9741, *BD*, 36 (1913), 14, n. 4407A (Salona). *Fratres*: III, 9733, 2835 (Burnum); III, 9737. *Heredes*: III, 14997/2 (*JÖAI*, 6 (1903), 86, fig. 16 (Burnum); III, 14931 (Dicmo near Tilurium); III, 9734; cf. p. 2269; III, 2716 (all from Tilurium, except where otherwise stated). Other serving legionaries with no dependants attested: III, 9738 (*BD*, 26 (1903), 134, n. 3244); III, 14933, 9742, 2717, 2714 (9736), 2709 (all from Tilurium), Betz, 172 (otherwise unpublished, with text probably incomplete) an *eques*, probably legionary, *SB*, 216, n. 9; III, 15001, 14993, 14321/13 (15000, *BD*, 22 (1899), 49) (all from Burnum); III, 8436 (Narona); III, 6419 (9897) (Promona, Tepljù); III, 6416 (Mokropolje); III, 6413 (*ILS*, 2258) (Scardona); III, 3052 (Alvona), 2031 (Salona).

freedmen are recorded; one freedman belonged to a *miles* of XIII, who was later transferred to a centurionate in Cohort I Campana.[1] Of the four men with families (one of Legion VII, two of Legion XI, and one of Legion VIIII [?]) only one was buried at Burnum, a *signifer* who shared a grave with his son. This lad, only 18 years old, may perhaps have already joined his father with a view to service in the legion. The remaining three include a *cornicularius consularis* at Salona with his family and a member of Legion VII on a family tombstone at Tragurium.[2] It is clear that before 42 few of the men serving in the legions had formed ties with the local population – or if they had these were not mentioned on their tombstones.

Eight serving men who died after 42 mention no dependants (four of Legion XI C.p.f., two each from Legion VII C.p.f. and Legion IIII F.f.). Except for the two in VII C.p.f. all were buried at or near Burnum.[3] One of the former was buried at Rider and probably belonged to a local family, as may also the *imaginifer* attested at Salona. Nineteen men record on their tombstones either fellow soldiers as heirs or the formula *h(eres) f(aciendum) c(uravit)*: the majority were serving men in XI C.p.f. buried at Burnum.[4] The tombstone of a man in IIII F.f. set up at Salona was arranged for by a fellow legionary who refers to the deceased as *frater*. A *miles* of XI C.p.f. at Salona records his real brother, judging from their common name. On five, possibly six, stones freedmen are recorded (three each from Legion VII C.p.f. and Legion XI C.p.f.), of which five are

---

[1] Serving legionaries before 42 with freedmen: III, 8438, Leg. XIII (Narona); III, 2071, 8723 (both Salona), *BD*, 31 (1908), 78, n. 3939A (Tilurium).

[2] Serving legionaries with families before 42: III, 2832; cf. p. 1036, add. n. 9892 (Burnum); III, 8738 (Salona); III, 9711 (Tragurium), *Inscr. It.*, X, 2, n. 252, *optio* in Legion VIIII, with brother serving in XI (Parentium).

[3] Serving legionaries after 42 with no dependants. XI C.p.f.: Betz, n. 118 (Burnum), 114 (Mokropolje). In both these cases, however, the text as published is incomplete, and there may well be families or dependants recorded. III, 9903 (Knin, Kapitul), 6417 (Strmica); VII C.p.f.: III, 2772 (Rider), 8735 (Salona); IIII F.f.: III, p. 43*, 394/8, III, 14995 (both at Burnum).

[4] Epitaphs of serving soldiers after 42 mentioning fellow soldiers or *heredes*. XI C.p.f.: III, 2833 (cf. p. 2328/161, *WMBH*, 5 (1897), 189, fig. 22); III, 13251; cf. Betz, p. 9, n. 25 (Padjine, Mokropolje); III, 14321/25 (Knin, Kapitul); III, 14997, 14997/1, 14998, 14999, 15005 (*WMBH*, 7 (1900), 76, fig. 47); III, 15005/1 (*JÖAI*, 5 (1902), Bb. 1, fig. 1); III, p. 43*, 394³⁻⁴, *JÖAI*, 6 (1903), Bb. 85, fig. 15 (*AE*, 1903, 303; *SB*, 216, n. 10), WS., 24 (1902), 382 (*AE*, 1903, 376; Betz, 145) (all from Burnum except where otherwise indicated); III, 8740 (Salona). VII C.p.f.: *BD*, 26 (1903), 193, n. 3150 (Salona); III, 2715 (Košute, Tilurium); IIII F.f.: III, 2021 (*WMBH*, 7 (1900), 82, fig. 56) (Salona); legion not survived: III, 14937, 13973 (both Tilurium), *VAHD*, 51 (1930-4), 230 f., pl. XXXVI/2 (*AE*, 1941, 57; cf. III, 9786, better reading) (Andetrium).

found at Salona.[1] Some of these freedmen may have been employed in the *officium*, for instance those of a *signifer* and a *speculator*; the others somehow managed to maintain their households there. There was always the danger that legions stationed too close to wealthy cities would be weakened by the pleasures of the city, and households and freedmen at Salona may be a sign of this, though it would hardly have become as serious a problem as developed with the notorious Syrian legions.[2] Four stones record families, but three of them can be regarded as special cases: a *miles* of Legion XI C.p.f. at Burnum records his real brother: another was born at nearby Aequum and died after only two years service, his mother erecting his memorial: the third, a *miles* of Legion VII C.p.f. at Corinium, was a native of that city where his wife and daughter set up the stone. The fourth had his epitaph set up at Salona by his heiress, though she was not a freedwoman as was often the case.[3] In the case of veterans one looks for a larger number of families and other dependants, but for the early period the evidence does not suggest this. Fifteen who died before 42 record no other persons on their tombstones, eight among them being settled at Pagus Scunasticus near Narona in 14, and three at Roški-Slap near Scardona. The others are from Tilurium, Salona, and Asseria.[4] An Augustan veteran of Legion XX at Salona attests a *familia* of freedmen and freedwomen. Only one of the veterans at Roški-Slap records a freedman.[5] Most of the veterans in this period who record relatives do not have households of their own but attest only members of an earlier or contemporary generation in their own family. A veteran of Legion XI was honoured at Parentium in Western Istria by his own brother, while two generations of the same family and a pair of brothers, also veterans, are the only families attested for the pagus Scunasticus settlement; two veterans (one each

[1] Serving men after 42 with freedmen. VII C.p.f.: III, 14699, 8760, 2040, *signifer*; XI C.p.f.: *BD*, 35 (1912), 22, 684B (*Starinar*, III, 1 (1922), 57; cf. pl. 1, 1–2; *AE*, 1914, 75, *speculator*); III, 2013 (all from Salona), *VAHD*, 51 (1930–4), 7, fig. XXXVII/2 (*AE*, 1940, 178, *signifer*) (Burnum).

[2] As Tacitus, *Ann.*, xiii, 35, describes when the Syrian army was taken over by the stern disciplinarian Cn. Domitius Corbulo in 58.

[3] Epitaphs of serving soldiers after 42 with families. III, 13263 (*BD*, 16 (1893), 49); III, 15004 (both Burnum); III, 2885 (Corinium); III, 3162a (? Salona).

[4] Pagus Scunasticus veterans with no dependants attested: *JAK*, 2 (1908), 110, fig. 30; Betz, n. 66 (otherwise unpublished); *WMBH*, 12 (1912), 132, fig. 60; III, 8488; III, 1815 (Narona). Roški-Slap veterans without dependants: III, 2817 (*ILS*, 2467) *centurio veteranorum* of IV Macedonica; III, 2818; cf. p. 1626; III, 6418 (Mratovo). Other veterans: III, 2913 (Iader); III, 9939 (Asseria); III, 2710 (9726) (Tilurium); III, 2048; *BD*, 37 (1914), 66 (both at Salona).

[5] III, 9885 (Roški-Slap); III, 2030 (Salona).

from VII and XI) appear with families at Salona, while a veteran of Legion XX at Iader has a large family of his own children and freedmen.[1] Most interesting is the *veteranus speculator* of XI buried with his wife and son at the source of the Vrlika not far from Tilurium. After his service on the *officium* he was co-opted decurion at Salona, a good illustration of the social status of an officer in the governor's staff at this time. Moreover he was almost certainly a native of the province.[2]

Eight veterans after 42 have no dependants: four of them were buried at Salona.[3] One became the town clerk (*scriba*), an important officer in the administration of the *colonia*. Two of the others, though they had probably served in Dalmatia, were discharged in Viminacium and one settled in the *colonia* of Scupi (Skopje) in Upper Moesia; the other returned to his home at Heraclea Lyncestis in Macedonia. Three have comrades as heirs: two mention them by name and the other employs the term *heres*.[4] Ten record freedmen, and one of these was a settler at Aequum.[5] Four are attested at Salona, including one each from IIII F.f. and V Macedonica. A veteran at Burnum had one freedman, another at Narona three, including one freedwoman. Three veterans of VII from outside Dalmatia who owned freedmen may be included, two from Scupi and one from Viminacium, among whom one was a native of Salona. Six veterans after 42 are attested with families, including two from Scupi. In Dalmatia one moved to Aequum to settle and records his legal wife (*uxor*). One at Burnum who lived to the age of 80 mentions another veteran who was probably his son and a granddaughter as well. Of two at Salona one mentions a wife (*coniunx*).[6]

Most of the legionaries attested in Dalmatia after the departure of the legionary garrison were either serving on the staff of the provincial governor

[1] *Inscr. It.*, X, 2, 204 (Parentium); III, 1818 (Narona); III, 8487 (Bigeste); III, 9712 (Siculi); III, 2017 (Salona); III, 2911 (Iader).

[2] III, p. 2328/121 (add. n. 1914) and n. 4 on p. 112.

[3] Epitaphs of veterans after 42 with no dependants: III, 2019 *scriba Salonis*; III, 8758; III, 14244/1; III, 8766 (all at Salona); III, 8507; cf. p. 2328/121 (Novae, Imotski); *GZMBH*, 35 (1923), 83 (Bigeste); III, 8199 (Kučeviste near Scupi); Sp. 77 (1934), 31, n. 3 (*AE*, 1934, 216) (Heraclea Lyncestis).

[4] III, 2839 (Burnum); III, 9709 (Siculi); III, 2014 (Salona).

[5] Veterans after 42 with freedmen: III, 14946 (Aequum); III, 8764; III, 2041 both from Legion VII C.p.f.; *BD*, 32 (1909), 59, n. 3900A-V Macedonica; III, 2004; cf. *WMBH*, 7 (1900), 83, fig. 57, from IIII F.f. (all at Salona); III, 2840 (Burnum); III, 1814; cf. p. 1494 (Narona); Sp. 71 (1931), 534; Sp. 71 (1931), 650 (both at Scupi, with *origines* Salona); *JÖAI*, 12 (1909–10), 158, n. 22 (*AE*, 1910, 88) (Viminacium).

[6] Veterans after 42 with families: Sp. 47 (1909), p. 147 (*AE*, 1910, 174); Sp. 71 (1931), 560 (both at Scupi); *VAHD*, 55 (1953), 185, fig. 4 (Gala near Aequum); III, 15004/1 (Kapitul, Knin); III, 9710 with *coniunx*; III, 12909 (both at Salona).

or stationed in Dalmatia in some of the temporary legionary detachments of the later second and early third centuries. Only a minority of those in the *officium* are known from their tombstones: most, especially the *beneficiarii consulares,* are known from official inscriptions of one sort or another. There are very few records of the higher ranks and many of these date to the late second and early third centuries when at least one legionary detachment was stationed in the province.[1] Eighteen tombstones are recorded for the period from Trajan to Pius, twelve of men serving in the *officium*, three of veterans from the *officium* (two at Salona, one at Iader). Three other legionary veterans (two at Salona, one at Narona) were probably also former members of the *officium*, but their tombstones are fragmentary and no record of any such service has survived. The senior rank is a *commentariensis* whose tombstone at Salona was set up by his mother Aebutia Ianuaria and his wife Visellia Iulia. The mother may have belonged to one of the leading families of Liburnia. Of the remainder, six, possibly seven, name families on their tombstones, while the others record dependants. One mentions his slave, who was responsible for setting up his owner's monument. All three veterans from the *officium* record families: a retired *speculator* at Iader mentions his parents, wife (*uxor*), sister, and his brother, a *signifer* in XIIII Gemina. Another records as wife a woman who was probably his freedwoman.[2]

Of the three centurions' tombstones known for the period after Marcus, the centurion of XIIII Gemina at Čakovac records no dependants. The other two are from Salona, one appearing on the tombstone of his wife, the other buried by a fellow soldier (*heres*), after service in I Italica under Severus Alexander.[3] Most of the men attested as serving in the *officium* after Marcus reveal families on their tombstones. An *exactus consularis* who was buried at Andetrium at the age

[1] The (*centurio*) *leg(ionis)* attested on the tombstone of his father, who had been decurion and priest at Salona, may have been serving anywhere, III, 2055 (Salona).

[2] Veterans of the *officium*: Trajan-Pius: III, 8745 *bf. cos.* with wife (Salona); III, 2677 with wife (Tragurium); III, 2915 *speculator* with large family. Legionary veterans: Trajan-Pius: III, 1811 with family or freedmen (Narona); BD, 29 (1906), 12, n. 3311A (*AE*, 1906, 135) with family (Salona); III, 8772 fragmentary but with some dependants recorded. Serving men in the *officium*: Trajan-Pius: III, 2015; cf. p. 2165 *comm(entariensis)* with family; III, 12895; cf. p. 2261 (*FS*, 2, p. 68, n. 26) *bf. cos.* with freedwoman; III, 8749, *bf. cos.* with ? wife; BD, 30 (1907), 40, n. 3778A, *bf. cos.*, with no dependants surviving on the tombstone; III, 6376 (*Starinar*, III, 1 (1922), pl. II 5), *bf. cos.* with brother and wife (*coniunx*); III, 2001, *bf. cos.* with wife (*coniunx*) and daughters; III, 8743, *bf. cos.* with wife (*coniunx*); III, 14706? *cornicularius* with ? wife (all at Salona); III, 14703, *bf. cos.* with son and daughter (Koplice, Klis); III, 2910 *spec[ulator]* with ? family (Iader); III, 14956, *bf. cos.* with ? dependants (Magnum); III, 9862; cf. 13231, p. 2270 add. *bf. cos.* (Gradina near Glamoč).

[3] Centurions after Marcus: *VHAD*, N.S. 9 (1906–7), 95, fig. 204 (Betz, n. 242a); III, 2046, *RS*, 1, 160, n. 5, fig. 167 (*VHAD*, 50 (1929), 14, n. 15) (both Salona).

L

of 24 was the son of an imperial freedman and a local freeborn woman: his own citizenship was received under Septimius.[1] Four of the other six in the *officium* mention families on their tombstones, while that of a *frumentarius* from III Cyrenaica was set up by his freedman. All were buried at Salona except a *beneficiarius consularis,* who was buried at his *statio* in Doclea.[2]

Among the legionaries on detachment duty under Marcus and later, none of those in VIII Augusta record either families or dependants. One of the two men in XIIII Gemina has a *coniunx* and daughter, the other had a fellow soldier as heir.[3] The *miles* of I Adiutrix has no family, but his tombstone was erected by another legionary, from II Adiutrix, who was probably serving in the same detachment.[4] Of those scattered legionaries in the third century only one, a *miles* of II (?) Adiutrix at Grahovo, records a dependant, a *coniunx*; another of the same legion was buried at Ractinium, apparently by a fellow soldier.[5] The only veteran from the *officium* attested is *beneficiarius consularis* at Lipa in Livjanskopolje, who on retirement became a decurion of the local city, probably Pelva, and records a son on his tombstone.[6] Other veterans such as the one of VIII Augusta at Curicta mention no one, while another of the same legion at Nedinum was buried by his *frater,* probably a real brother since he was an Octavius, the leading family of Nedinum.[7] The other three third-century veterans, at Salona (II Italica), near Bihać (I? Italica), and near Sarajevo (VIII Augusta) record wives (*coniuges*) and families of their own.[8]

It is clear that in the early period there were few contacts between the legionary garrison and even the larger coastal cities. Many veterans and serving soldiers are found buried by fellow soldiers, although a minority have their own slaves or freedmen. This lack of contact is perhaps one of the reasons why in later years the Dalmatian cities proved such poor recruiting grounds for the legions and the

[1] Note 3 on p. 122.

[2] Serving members of the *officium* with families after Marcus: III, 2023, *bf. cos.* with daughter; III, 8750, *cornicularius cos.* with wife; *BD,* 37 (1914), 94, n. 4692A; cf. *MZ,* 36 (1941), 15 (*AE,* 1945, 88), *speculator* with family; Betz, n. 192, *bf. cos.,* no dependants, but complete text probably not published (all at Salona); III, 13828, *bf. cos.* with wife (Doclea); III, 2063 (8581, *ILS,* 2370), *frumentarius* of III Cyrenaica with freedman (Salona).

[3] Serving legionaries in Legion XIIII Gemina: III, 12896, with family; III, 6549; cf. p. 1510, with fellow legionary as heir (both at Salona).

[4] *GZMBH,* 26 (1914), 162, fig. 23; cf. Patsch, *Narona,* 68, fig. 31.

[5] *Sp.,* 77 (1934), 19, fig. 26 (Grahovo); III, 10036 (*WMBH,* 6 (1899), 173) (Golubić).

[6] III, 9847 (Lipa in Livjanskopolje), and n. 6 on p. 124.

[7] III, 3127 (Curicta, Omišalj); III, 2865 (*WMBH,* 5 (1897), 339).

[8] III, 8730: *vet. leg.* II Italicae (Salona); III, 10036a (III, 13272; cf. *Starinar,* III, 1 (1922), 60): (I) *Italica* (Brekovica near Bihać); III, 8375 (12749): *veteranus ex leg. VIII Aug.* (Gradac near Sarajevo).

equestrian service, in contrast with other provinces. Even by the end of the first century there were few signs that serving soldiers had made contact with the local population, although it is clear that a larger proportion of veterans had established their own families in the area than was the case earlier in the century. For men of the *officium* in the second and third centuries it was normal to have their own families, and most of their tombstones reveal this. By contrast, few of those men serving in legionary detachments show dependants, which suggests that even in the third century men serving in the provincial army were isolated from the civilian population of the province.

VIII *The* Auxilia *in Dalmatia* (Appendices VIII – IX)

At an early stage in the expansion of the Roman state beyond Italy it was the Roman practice to use contingents from still independent powers in the Mediterranean. Early in the Second Punic War envoys from Syracuse could remind the Senate of how the Republic used large contingents from peoples other than those in the Roman or Latin communities.[1] In the final battle of the Second Punic War at Zama in 202 B.C. the legions were assisted at a crucial point by the Numidian cavalry of King Masinissa, who had only recently become an ally of the Romans through the offices of P. Scipio Africanus, the Roman commander.[2] The fact that Roman strength lay almost exclusively in the heavily armed infantry of the legions never seemed to cause real anxiety to the Roman government, even after such battles as Zama. Political policy was carefully formulated to ensure that in any struggle beyond Italy, Rome would be able to call on some allied help, even when that help was given from self-interest alone. As Rome's system of alliances became more complex and began to assume the aspect of empire so the use of allied forces became an even more vital part of Roman military policy.[3] If the victories of the Roman people could be won without the shedding of Roman blood then for one historian at least the glory of the commander was all the greater.[4]

By the end of the second century B.C. radical changes were taking place in the character and the composition of the legions. The reforms of C. Marius now openly offered the army as a rewarding career to the poorer or landless elements in Roman society, while the enfranchisement of all Italy in 89 B.C. meant that in

[1] Liv., xxii, 35, in 217 B.C.
[2] Liv., xxx, 33 ff.
[3] Cheesman, *Auxilia*, 1 ff.
[4] Note the remarks of Tacitus on Agricola's battle order against the Caledonii at Mons Graupius, *Agr.*, 35. Tacitus' ideas about the desirability of conserving 'Roman blood' seem to be largely an invention of his own, Cheesman, *Auxilia*, 104, n. 2.

future communities which had furnished *socii*, allied contingents which fought under the command of Roman *praefecti*, were now eligible for legionary service.¹ The absence of a regular cavalry arm at this time was marked and on one occasion during his Gallic campaigns Caesar was forced to make his legionaries fight on horseback, so acute was the shortage of reliable cavalry.² During the war with the Italian allies a *turma* of Spanish cavalry serving under Pompeius Strabo was granted the *civitas* for gallantry at Asculum in 89 B.C.³ Some army commanders, especially Caesar and Pompeius, managed to raise contingents from the peoples they had controlled at various times.

Until the time of Caesar the Roman involvement in Illyria was not such as to produce large supplies of fighting men. We know of no occasion where Illyrians fighting as such distinguished themselves in the service of Rome before the end of the Republic. After the removal of Demetrius from Pharos in 219 B.C. both succeeding rulers of Illyria, Scerdilaidas and Pleuratus, offered help in the form of ships to proconsuls operating in Greece but these offers were politely declined because of the universal dislike of Illyrian pirate methods among the Greeks.⁴ In spite of this, their loyalty was recognized, and the alliance with Pleuratus was once compared to that with the great Masinissa. It was another matter, however, when the Romans were in Illyria. During the war against Gentius in 168 B.C. contingents were drawn from the allied cities of Byllis, Apollonia, and Dyrrhachium. There were also some Illyrian allies, notably the Parthini, who provided a force of 2,000 infantry and 200 cavalry under the command of two of their noblemen, Epicadus and Algalsus.⁵ The next time one hears of allied forces in Illyria is during Caesar's proconsulship when he ordered local contingents to assemble and deal with the Pirustae who were raiding Illyria in the southeast, and also the Delmatae who were attacking the Liburnians in the area of Promona. A large number of *auxilia* were also present in the army of P. Vatinius in 44 B.C.⁶ Before Actium Octavianus may have recruited among the Illyrians but, apart from the Liburnian fleet which he incorporated into his own forces, and which played such an important role at Actium, there is no evidence that he ever needed to draw on the considerable manpower of the area while he controlled the resources of Gaul and Spain.⁷

Of the many lasting reforms introduced by Augustus that of the army was one of the most important. Apart from ensuring that the legions were established on

---

¹ See R. E. Smith, *Service in the post-Marian Roman Army*, 27 ff.
² Caes., *BG*, i, 42.   ³ *ILS*, 8888.   ⁴ Liv., xxxi, 28.   ⁵ Liv., xliv, 30, 13.
⁶ Appian, *Ill.*, 13.
⁷ Vegetius, iv, 33 f.; cf. Florus, iv, 11. On the *liburna* see S. Panciera, *Epigraphica*, 18 (1956), 130–56.

a permanent footing, with pay and veteran gratuities now assured from the *aerarium militare,* Augustus transformed the army by the institution of *auxilia.* These were non-citizen cavalry *alae* and infantry *cohortes* raised from the less urbanized parts of the empire which bore permanent titles from the original areas of recruitment.[1] Normally they were commanded by *praefecti equitum* (in the case of cavalry) or *praefecti* and *tribuni* (in the case of cohorts) selected from among suitable members of the equestrian order. Usually they were grouped together as a supplement for the legions, often moving with the same legion from one province to another. These *praefecti* and *tribuni* were technically civilians serving with the army and operated under the supervision of legionary commanders and provincial governors, both appointments which were normally the monopoly of the senatorial order.[2] In the first century the distinction between legions and *auxilia* was considerable, with the legions recruited mostly from Northern Italy and some of the more urbanized provinces, especially from the veteran *coloniae.* The auxiliary soldier served the same term as the legionary, which soon became standardized at twenty-five years, while the reward for the auxiliary on completion of service was citizenship for himself and any family which he had at the time or wife he might take at any time in the future. One bronze tablet recording such a grant survives from the *auxilia* in Dalmatia, dating to A.D. 94.[3]

The institution of the *auxilia* and their incorporation into the standing army was perhaps one of the most successful achievements of all Augustus' administration in the military sphere. From the outset their role in Roman frontier and provincial wars was significant. As early as the war of 6–9 the cavalry of the Thracian Rhoemetalces (still then an independent client ruler) fought against the Pannonians and Dalmatians,[4] while the *auxilia* proper played an important role: according to Velleius Paterculus the great concentration of Roman forces in 7 at Siscia under Tiberius (when the armies of Illyricum and Moesia briefly united, the latter augmented by troops from the East) included more than seventy auxiliary cohorts (nearly the equal of the legions), fourteen cavalry *alae,* more than ten thousand veterans, in addition to a large number of volunteers and the numerous cavalry of the Thracian king.[5] Yet these were still early days in the system and there were dangers. It is worth recalling that the war of 6–9,

[1] Cheesman, *Auxilia,* 14 ff.   [2] The basic study is by E. Birley, *RBRA,* 133–53.
[3] Collected in Volume XVI of *CIL* by H. Nesselhauf (1936, supplement 1955). The Dalmatian diploma is XVI, 38. For the gradual disappearance of the distinctions between legionaries and auxiliaries see J. C. Mann, article cited, n. 1 on p. 127.
[4] Vell. Pat., ii, 112, at the battle of the Volcaean Marshes in 7.
[5] Vell. Pat., ii, 113.

whose outbreak shattered Augustus' schemes for an advance into Central Europe, broke out when the forces demanded from the peoples of Illyricum had been ordered to assemble and assist Tiberius in the campaign against Maroboduus. In spite of this setback the system was continued, and during the first century the *auxilia* played a vital role in such projects as the annexation of Britain under Claudius, and of Dacia under Trajan.

By the second century the distinction between legions and *auxilia* had decreased greatly, although many of the men in the *auxilia* were still non-citizens, except when the men in a unit or the individual had received a personal award of the citizenship for distinguished service in the field. In the fifty years between the accession of Hadrian (117) and the Marcomannic Wars (167) there was comparatively little movement of troops within the Empire. Legions remained in their permanent fortresses and attracted large civilian populations to settlements in the vicinity. The role of the legions became more concerned with administration and construction in the frontier areas, while the chastising of small groups of troublemakers could be entrusted to the more mobile, and also more expendable, auxiliary units. These were dispersed over difficult areas within provinces in forts linked by a network of roads, such as in Dacia Porolissensis or in Northern Britain, or established along the frontiers in the intervals between the legionary fortresses, as for instance along the Danube frontier in Pannonia. Consequently service in the legions, with many building and engineering tasks, tended to become less attractive while the routine fighting was now left to the *auxilia*. The upheavals of the Marcomannic Wars resulted in a few legionary movements, and there were also considerable changes in auxiliary garrisons along the Danube.[1] After the grant of universal citizenship under Caracalla to all freeborn inhabitants of the Empire the distinction in status between legions and *auxilia* no longer existed. Movement of units became a rarity and in some cases the legionary and auxiliary dispositions of the early third century are still repeated in the Notitia Dignitatum, which was compiled in the early years of the fifth century.[2] In many respects the auxiliary units were legions in miniature. Their camps reveal the triple division of a central block with headquarters (*principia*), commandant's residence (*praetorium*), granaries (*horrea*), and the *praetentura* and *retentura* filled with the men's barrack accommodation. The barracks were similar in plan to the L-shaped legionary types providing one block for each century with

[1] Apart from the stationing of the new Legions II and III Italica at Lauriacum (Linz) and Castra Regina (Regensburg), the only major change was the transfer of Legion V Macedonica from Troesmis in Moesia Inferior to Potaissa in Dacia about 170, Ritterling, 1578–9.
[2] As for example along the Hadrian's Wall frontier line in Britain, J. P. Gillam, *CW*², 49 (1949), 38–58.

the centurion's residence at the end. In many instances it can be demonstrated that the auxiliary forts were planned and probably built not by the auxiliary units which occupied them but by the legions.[1]

As might be expected, the development of the *auxilia* in Dalmatia was in the first century closely linked to that of the legionary garrison, and when that departed before the end of the first century the few auxiliary units which remained as a small permanent provincial garrison carried on what military duties were necessary. In one respect, however, the *auxilia* could not replace the legions, and that was in the higher grades of the provincial governor's administration (*officium*). Some men from the *auxilia* were employed, mostly from the citizen unit Cohort VIII Voluntariorum c. R., and the only example of a *bf. cos.* drawn from the *auxilia* comes from this unit.[2]

Sixteen places in Dalmatia have produced inscriptions attesting the presence of auxiliary units and these fall into three distinct groups.[3] First come the major coastal settlements which had become *coloniae* (Iader, Salona, Narona, and Epidaurum). The second group is linked by the military road behind the coast through the legionary fortresses of Burnum and Tilurium to the main concentration of *auxilia* in the province at Bigeste not far from Narona. Along this line were established a number of auxiliary forts, at Promona (Tepljù), Kadina Glavica, Magnum (Balijina Glavica), Andetrium (Muć), and Tihaljina. These are places which can be identified from tombstones as auxiliary stations and where the later civilian community may have begun as the extra-mural settlement (*vicus*) around the fort.[4] Finally, there are four places in the northern region close to the frontiers with Pannonia and Moesia, Raetinium (Golubić near Bihać), Doboj, where the boundary with Pannonia crossed the river Bosna, Užice, and Čačak in the Morava valley near the border with Moesia Superior. It is striking that there is hardly a record of the Roman army in Dalmatia before the third century in that part of the interior where dwelt the fiercest of all the Illyrians who resisted to the last in 9. No record, for instance, is known from the land of the Maezaei (Vrbas and Sana valley), Ditiones (upper Una and Unac valley), Daesitiates (Bosna valley and around Sarajevo, although Doboj may have been on the northern fringe of their territory), Dindari (lower valley of Drina, unless perhaps Užice was on their land). There is no doubt that the final pacification of

---

[1] No excavation has ever taken place on any site occupied by the *auxilia* in Dalmatia, but there is a considerable body of comparative material from other areas, especially Hungary, Britain, and Germany.

[2] III, 12679 (Doclea).   [3] Appendix VIII.

[4] The later city at Magnum may have developed from the *vicus* around the auxiliary fort maintained there in the first century.

these areas amounted to little less than extermination. However, the effects of this may have worn off within one or two generations, and there is abundant epigraphic evidence for a large native population from the late first century onwards. Nor is this absence of military evidence due to neglect by modern researchers. The labours of C. Patsch and D. Sergejevski and others from Sarajevo have furnished us with much epigraphic evidence, and there are few parts of Bosnia or Hercegovina that were not investigated at some time or other during the half century before the Second World War. By contrast the coastal hinterland, from which most records of *auxilia* outside Salona come, has been hardly touched by any serious archaeological investigation. Obviously one cannot conclude that the peoples of the interior felt only very rarely the physical presence of the Roman army; but it does at least seem clear that there was never any plan to construct, in addition to the main roads between Salona and the Save valley,[1] a network of roads linking a large number of auxiliary forts set at intervals of a day's march, a system adopted in other parts of the Roman Empire where the problems of the government were not greatly dissimilar. It was judged better to keep the *auxilia* deployed in a concentration on the Burnum–Tilurium–Bigeste line, supplemented by a few posts on the northern frontier. There is no evidence that this system ever broke down: no serious disturbances are attested in Dalmatia, unlike many more apparently 'peaceful provinces', until the period of the Marcomannic Wars;[2] and it is certain that some interval must have elapsed before the Romans trusted the ruling classes of these peoples with their heritage of authority. The withdrawal of legions and *auxilia* which took place in the later first century was caused less by satisfaction at the state of affairs in Dalmatia than by a more urgent need for troops in other areas. However, by the end of the first century the assimilation of the native upper classes into the hierarchy of the province was already well advanced, and the chance of a major uprising must have seemed very small.

The evidence for the *auxilia* in Dalmatia is best discussed under the heading of individual units.[3] These fall into two distinct groups, those units which were stationed in the province for periods during the first century, and those which remained in the second and third century to form the permanent standing garrison of Dalmatia. Two units are known to have been stationed in Dalmatia only during the war of 6–9, Ala I Parthorum and Cohort XI Gallorum: both almost certainly left in 9 or shortly afterwards. Other units which were probably in the province during this war are the Ala Pannoniorum, Cohorts III Alpinorum, I Bracaraugustanorum, I Campana, II Cyrrhestarum, I Lucensium, Montanorum, VI Voluntariorum c. R., VIII Voluntariorum c. R. Not long afterwards, about

[1] Appendix IV.   [2] See p. 117.   [3] Appendix IX.

15, the Ala Pannoniorum was transferred to Pannonia, following the organization of the Danubian *limes*. Cohort VI Voluntariorum c. R. may also have departed at about this time. The remaining seven units continued in the province until the departure of Legion VII C.p.f. for Moesia under Claudius. It was probably accompanied by the Cohort Montanorum, but this move was compensated by the arrival of a new formation, the Ala Claudia nova miscellanea. It was recruited in the West and moved from Dalmatia to Germany in 70 to join the army concentrating against Civilis. Cohort II Cyrrhestarum may also have departed at this time: all its records are clearly pre-Flavian and all are of men from the original area of the cohort's recruitment. Two units which probably reached Dalmatia early under Vespasian were the Ala (Tungrorum) Frontoniana and Cohort Aquitanorum, both transferred from Germany. With the development of a dangerous situation on the lower Danube frontier in Domitian's early years two units were moved thither from Dalmatia, the Ala (Tungrorum) Frontoniana and Cohort I Lucensium, and these were replaced by two newly-formed cohorts, I Flavia Brittonum and I Flavia Hispanorum. Soon danger turned into disaster and in 86 there was a desperate need for troops on the Danube to fight against the Dacians. Some of these were drawn from Dalmatia, and this time no replacements were sent. This withdrawal coincided with that of the last legion to be stationed in Dalmatia. The *auxilia* which left for the Danube in company with Legion IIII F.f. were all cohorts, I Bracaraugustanorum, I Campana, and probably I Flavia Hispanorum. At this time also, or perhaps a few years later, departed Cohorts Aquitanorum and I Flavia Brittonum: they had certainly left by 94, since on the Dalmatian diploma only the Cohorts III Alpinorum and VIII Voluntariorum are attested. Not many years later this small permanent garrison was increased to three with the arrival of the Cohort I Belgarum, which probably reached Dalmatia about the year 100, and these three units remained in Dalmatia until the Marcomannic Wars. In about 170, when large forces of Germanic invaders had broken through the Danube frontier in Pannonia and Noricum and penetrated as far as Northern Italy, Dalmatia lay very close to the combat area, and for a time provided the only secure communication between Rome and the armies in Moesia and Dacia. Four new cohorts were raised from within the province and two of them, Cohorts I and II milliaria Delmatarum, were stationed in Dalmatia at least until the early third century. Once the Marcomannic emergency passed and the Danubian frontier had been reorganized, the number of units in Dalmatia was reduced to four with the transfer of III Alpinorum to the frontier of Lower Pannonia as a replacement for units overwhelmed during the recent invasions. These four remained in Dalmatia until the confusion in the reign of Gallienus, the only later change being the transfer of

Cohort VIII Voluntariorum to the eastern frontier, probably under Aurelian in about 270.

A striking feature of auxiliary deployment in Dalmatia is the coincidence between sites occupied by auxiliary units and those held in the first century by legionaries and the later system of *beneficiarii consulares* posts. An exception is the route between Salona and Narona which appears to have been held by legionaries alone in the first century. On the other hand the outstation of Legion XI C.p.f. on the Kapitul hill near Knin guarding the Mons Ulcirus (Strmica) pass was also occupied by auxiliaries, although it is not certain whether they were established there after the departure of the legion. A few legionary stations in the south and east of Dalmatia do not appear to have been occupied by auxiliaries at any time.

The occasion when the garrison system was instituted in Dalmatia is still a matter of conjecture, since there is no epigraphic evidence for the army in Dalmatia which can be shown to date before the crucial year 6. Consequently even the earliest picture that exists of the army in the province can be seen only as the reaction of the Roman high command to the war which broke out in that year. Doubtless there were some troops in Southern Illyricum before 6, although it is not certain whether legions were yet established in the camps at Burnum and Tilurium. When the revolt broke out the army of Illyricum was serving under Tiberius far away beyond the Danube against Maroboduus in Bohemia. The only resistance offered to the insurgents came from a group of veterans,[1] possibly in the south of Illyricum, and the vital military bases of Siscia and Sirmium appear to have been virtually unoccupied, being saved for the Romans only by the energy of Messallinus at Siscia and by Caecina who moved out of his province of Moesia into Illyricum. Any attempt to deduce from the epigraphic evidence more than the most general deployment of army units at this period is unlikely to be of any value.

The coastal *coloniae* were accustomed to fighting and saved the Caesarian party in Dalmatia during the civil war with Pompeius. They would also have been threatened by the peoples of the interior when Bato of the Daesitiates moved across the Dinaric Alps to attack the coastal cities late in 6.[2] The danger faced by these cities may be the reason for troops being later stationed there for part of the first century. Accordingly legionary detachments were placed along the coastal route linking Epidaurum, Narona, Salona, and Iader, and probably minor posts at Tragurium, Rider, Scardona, and Asseria. As stability increased, however, these stations were discontinued and the main strength of both *auxilia* and legions concentrated on the inland Burnum–Bigeste line. Only the Marco-

[1] Vell. Pat., ii, 110, 6, and p. 70.   [2] Dio, lv, 29, 4.

mannic emergency brought large numbers of troops back to Salona, specifically to refurbish the city defences, but other troops were still maintained there in the early third century.[1] The key to the Roman army dispositions in Dalmatia was the fortified strategic route running parallel with the coast from Burnum to Bigeste never more than twenty miles from the sea. From Burnum on the fringe of urbanized Liburnia, where it was closely linked by good roads to Asseria, Varvaria, and Iader, the line was linked with the Kapitul hill detachment near Knin on the river Krka, and from there it ran along the east side of Mount Promina to Promona (Tepljù), thence southeastward past Kadina Glavica, Magnum (Balijina Glavica), and Andetrium (Gornje Muć), to the legionary base at Tilurium on the river Cetina at the south end of Sinjsko polje. From there it led through Vrpolje and Imotskipolje to Tihaljina. The terminal point appears to have been the auxiliary base at Bigeste near Ljubuški in the Trebižat valley. All the above-mentioned places held detachments of *auxilia* at some time or other. The greatest strength was concentrated in the sector between Burnum and Tilurium, especially in the difficult country of the Čikola valley to the east of Promona. Bigeste in the south seems to have held as many as four cohorts during the emergency later under Augustus, although most were moved elsewhere not long afterwards. The reduction of the auxiliary units stationed in Dalmatia roughly kept pace with the withdrawal of the legions, but most forts were retained as military posts of one sort or another. Bigeste, Tilurium, and Andetrium were the stations of the permanent garrison, while detachments were maintained at other points. Some *bf. cos. stationes* were established, for instance at Burnum, Magnum, and Novae, and legionaries were introduced during the Marcomannic Wars at Burnum, Andetrium, and Bigeste.[2]

Much later in origin appear to be the military posts in the northern part of the province. Both records from Raetinium and Doboj are Flavian or not much later. The detachments from the Pannonian and Moesian legions at Metulum and the *bf. cos. stationes* at Avendo and Raetinium, all of which were in the territory of the Iapodes, are late in date. The reason why troops were stationed only in the northern part of the interior is not clear, but it is possible that this tendency to move units there from the coastal hinterland, a process which appears to have begun under the Flavians, reflects the experience of the first century when the Bosnian valleys were best controlled more cheaply by fewer forces concentrated in the Save valley. Until the Flavian period the provincial garrison comprised one or two legions supplemented by about half a dozen auxiliary units, but in the early second century it was considered that three cohorts based in the coastal hinterland were sufficient to contain any disturbances that broke out in the

[1] A detachment from Legion I Italica, p. 119.   [2] p. 117 f.

province. Otherwise there is no clear evidence before the reign of Marcus Aurelius that any troop movements made in Dalmatia after Augustus were concerned with problems internal to the province. Normally such movements and transfers were made for reasons connected with other areas.

IX *Recruitment, Settlement, and Social Background of the* Auxilia *in Dalmatia*

As with the recruitment to the legions, so a survey of the areas from which auxiliaries were drawn serves to show the extent of the links formed between the garrison army and urban or rural communities in different parts of the province.[1] The key factor is naturally the amount of local recruitment to units stationed in the province, although in the case of the *auxilia* some factors operated which did not apply to legionary recruitment. With the exception of those units which recruited Roman citizens only, for instance, I Campana and VI and VIII Voluntariorum, all freeborn non-citizens (*peregrini*) were eligible. However it seems to have been the practice at first to seek men either from the original area of the unit's recruitment or from the nearest source of similar manpower. For example only one man is known to have been recruited from Dalmatia into a cavalry unit in Dalmatia (Ala Claudia nova), and he came from the partly Celtic Iapodes, the only likely source of good cavalry in the province. Clearly with the real cavalry[2] one had to have men from areas where horsemanship was practised, and Dalmatia, unlike Pannonia, was not such an area – at least in the first century. Apart from these considerations, the evidence suggests that, like the legions, the *auxilia* were recruited from the nearest convenient source of suitable manpower. The detailed evidence for recruitment to the *auxilia* in Dalmatia is set out in a table (Appendix X) and can best be reviewed in the chronological framework followed there. Dating is fairly reliable for military inscriptions, there being usually sufficient indication in the text and form for a correct date within the four groups adopted.

Beginning with the Julio–Claudian period, the two citizen units, Cohorts I Campana and VIII Voluntariorum, were enrolled originally from Italy, the first named from Campania (all four records are demonstrably from that region), the other from Italy, the only known recruit of the period being from Ariminum.[3]

[1] For auxiliary recruitment to the Rhine and Danube armies see K. Kraft, *Rekrutierung*.

[2] As contrasted with those units of infantry which were part-mounted (*equitata*) and of a lower standard than the proper cavalry *alae*. This distinction is brought out by the remarks of Hadrian in his address to the army at Lambaesis in Africa, regarding the horsemen (*equites*) of Cohort VI Commagenorum, *ILS*, 2487.

[3] On the origin of these units, Kraft, *Rekrutierung*, 87 ff.

A tribune of a similar Cohort VI Voluntariorum serving early under Tiberius came from Atina in Latium. It is clear that Cohort VIII Voluntariorum maintained its original status of being recruited from Roman citizens only, and the fact that it appears on the diploma of 93 along with Cohort III Alpinorum does not necessarily imply that *peregrini* were regularly accepted into it. Such men might have been enlisted during the disturbances of 68, as might be suggested by the wording of the diploma, '*qui peregrinae condicionis probati erant*' (XVI, 38). This practice of accepting only citizens continued in the second century also: only one non-Roman is attested for the Antonine period compared with twelve citizens.[1]

The remainder of the recruits to the *auxilia* in Dalmatia during the Julio–Claudian period came from the area of the Alps or the northwestern provinces of the Empire; in most cases they were men who were drawn from named communities in the Alps, while out of the others two are westerners: the third was the native *Davers(us)* who was the recipient of the diploma of 93. As has already been suggested, the occasion for his recruitment was probably the confused situation which followed the death of Nero in 68. The evidence from Dalmatia for *auxilia* recruitment in the Julio–Claudian period suggests that the population of the province was not regarded as suitable for military service, and that recruits were normally sought from elsewhere.

The pattern remained largely the same in the Flavian–Trajanic period. Five citizen recruits are attested, two from Italy, and three from Noricum, which after the Claudian urbanization programme became an important recruiting area. Among the remainder only one appears to have joined as a citizen, an *eques ex singulari* (governor's bodyguard) of Cohort III Alpinorum who belonged to a family of Salona. Another citizen was a *decurio* in the Ala Claudia nova, while there is a Briton in Cohort I Flavia Brittonum and a German in the Ala (Tungrorum) Frontoniana.[2] Some local recruitment is attested: a Iapodian from Raetinium who joined the Ala Claudia nova had moved with his unit by 74 to Germany where his tombstone was set up. In Cohorts I Belgarum and III Alpinorum single examples of *peregrini* are found, both recruited from native communities within the province. With the fixing of the permanent garrison at three units for most of the second century all recruiting needs could be met from within the province. In the second and third century one can make a distinction between men recruited from the cities (that is men with names of Italian origin, though obviously not necessarily Italians themselves), and men from the native

[1] Compare also the table for the Rhine and Danube armies, Kraft, *Rekrutierung*, 83, with only three *peregrini* out of nearly one hundred serving soldiers attested.
[2] On Nemis, Holder, 2, 710.

peoples, whose ancestry was entirely Illyrian. Here there is a striking difference between the recruiting pattern of Cohorts III Alpinorum and VIII Voluntariorum on the one hand and, on the other Cohort I Belgarum. In the first two units there is an overwhelming proportion of Roman citizens from the urban settler families of the province. In the case of Cohort VIII Voluntariorum there are eleven such men attested in addition to one Italian or westerner, compared with one person recruited as a *peregrinus* and still serving as such. It is the same situation with Cohort III Alpinorum, though in this unit some of the citizens serving come from native communities in the province. There are two westerners and one Norican, while of five from Dalmatia, three belong to urban families, and two have native backgrounds, although only one man is attested as still serving as a *peregrinus*. In the case of the third unit, Cohort I Belgarum, all known recruits are from within the province, yet the ratio between urban families and native recruits is precisely reversed. Six *peregrini* are attested all from purely Illyrian backgrounds, as is probably the only citizen, a junior officer who came from a local city Azina.[1] There is no obvious explanation for this lasting difference in recruiting pattern. The two cohorts which drew most of their recruits from the cities may have required men suitable for administrative posts in the *officium* of the provincial governor, while Cohort I Belgarum stationed much further away from Salona at Bigeste sought only the more basic needs of an army, good physique and a warlike temperament. Not surprisingly a higher proportion of men from Cohorts III Alpinorum and VIII Voluntariorum are recorded with some sort of post under the governor. Cohort I Belgarum has two men who served the governor as grooms (*stratores*), and one centurion who was superintending the Salona theatre (*curagens theatri*). On the other hand, in Cohort III Alpinorum are two members of the governor's personal escort (*singulares cos.*) while Cohort VIII Voluntariorum has men in positions of the administration, two men as assistants to the senior officers of the Salona *officium* (*adiutor cornicularii cos.*), as well as the only instance of an auxiliary as *bf. cos.* at the *statio* in Doclea. The only recruit attested for the new Cohort I milliaria Delmatarum is a *peregrinus* from the native population.

In the last group, those from the period after the Marcomannic Wars, all serving men were Roman citizens, many deriving their citizenship from the universal grant under Caracalla. A considerable proportion of men will have assumed the *nomen* Aurelius at this time. All except two, a westerner and a Pannonian, were probably recruited from within Dalmatia, while, in so far as it is still possible to distinguish a background within the province, the majority came from urban as opposed to native sources; there are four from the latter

[1] III, 8762; cf. p. 2657.

compared with fourteen from city families with Italian *nomina*. The *auxilia* do not seem ever to have been very attractive to people in the interior of the province: most who sought some kind of military career preferred service as marines in the two fleets at Ravenna and Misenum. It is a striking fact also that whereas the reorganization of Septimius Severus brought about a transformation in the recruitment pattern of the praetorian guard and the *equites singulares* at Rome, to the extent of drawing men from the Danubian provinces, especially Thrace, to the virtual exclusion of Italians, Dalmatia itself is very poorly represented compared even with Pannonia.[1]

A study of the age of recruitment shows that the army normally expected to draw men in the age group 18–22, but the available statistics for the *auxilia* in Dalmatia point to recruits of a slightly higher age (at 17:1 man, 18:2, 19:1, 20:2, 23:1, 24:1, 25:4, 26:2, 28:1.)[2] No pattern emerges from one period to another, all ends of the age range being represented at different periods. For the length of service there is less evidence, but it seems that the proper term of twenty-five years was normal, although some auxiliaries in the early first century were retained in service far beyond the normal time for discharge. Four men are attested as having served terms of 29, 31, at least 30, and 35 years, comparable with those of legionary veterans of the same period.[3] No doubt they were just as vociferous in the clamour for release which broke out in Illyricum during the first months of Tiberius' reign.

On the social background of auxiliaries serving in Dalmatia, much less can be said than for the legions, although naturally their tombstones indicate what manner of life they were able to make for themselves while serving in Dalmatia. The rule which forbade all serving men in the Roman army, legionaries and auxiliaries, to contract legal marriage has already been mentioned in the section dealing with the legions (p. 128). The rule was applied also to centurions, the only provision for family accommodation in a fort being in the residences of commanding officers drawn from the equestrian order. These unit commanders were still held to be technically civilians and the main military responsibility for leading auxiliary units appears to have devolved upon the professionals, the corps of centurions. The rule forbidding legal marriage was not as daunting as might at

[1] A. Passerini, 175 ff.

[2] At 17: III, 9816 (3164). At 18: *VAHD*, 56–59/2 (1954–7), II, 82 f., n. 1; III, 9727 (2712). At 19: *JÖAI*, 36 (1946), Bb. 67 ff. At 20: III, 9735; III, 2053. At 23: III, 14246/1. At 24: III, 2016. At 25: XIII, 7023; III, 8491 (6366); cf. *GZMBH*, 26 (1914), 163; *JÖAI*, 36 (1946), Bb. 67 ff.; III, 14934. At 26: III, 9760; *SB*, 217, n. 12. At 28: III, 8495.

[3] 29 years service: III, 9760. 31 years: *JAK*, 2 (1908), 114. At least 30 years: III, 14632; cf. Patsch, *Narona*, 72, n. 5. 35 years: III, 14934. For the long service of legionaries at the same period see p. 112.

first appear: the government did not actually forbid soldiers to set up a house-hold with the women they chose, but the offspring of such marriages could not be Roman citizens, nor would the government accept any responsibility towards the dependants of serving soldiers, a precedent often followed by modern armies. Yet for a local woman marriage with a Roman soldier with his regular pay and reasonable security could be an attractive proposition, always assuming that he was not killed on active service. As in so many aspects of Roman society the law appears to have forbidden what was general practice, but in fact it only refused recognition of any such state of affairs.

In the first century only one man, serving in Cohort VIII Voluntariorum, had his tombstone set up by his wife who describes the deceased man as *coniunx*.[1] The *peregrinus* who was the recipient of the diploma of 93 had a family, all of whom were naturally *peregrini*. The document records his wife, who was from the Deramistae tribe and his son.[2] Others have dependants: a man of western origin in Cohort III Alpinorum has two women as heirs, while a Biturix serving in the Ala Claudia nova was buried along with his sister.[3] The majority of serving men in the *auxilia* during the first century had only their fellow soldiers to attend to the proprieties of burial and provision of a tombstone. This was norm-ally provided out of the common burial fund into which all the soldiers paid a regular contribution from the time of their recruitment, ensuring that even if a man died very early in his term of service he would still receive a proper memorial. In some cases an officer of the unit was named as an heir (*heres*), and five such examples are known.[4] By far the majority, however, were buried by their comrades (*contubernales*), the men with whom they shared daily an eight- or ten-man barrack room. There are eighteen tombstones set up by such men, who are described either as *heres* or *frater*.[5] Only one man had a freedman, signifi-cantly an easterner from Beroea in Cohort II Cyrrhestarum.[6] The evidence for the first century produces a picture of the *auxilia* which corresponds closely to

---

[1] III, 9782; cf. Hofmann, 57; Flavian date from the hairstyle.

[2] XVI, 38, issued to: *pedes Venetus Diti f(ilius) Davers(us) et Madena Plarentis filia uxor eius Deramist(a) et Gaius f(ilius) eius.*

[3] With *heredes*: III, 8495. With sister: III, 2065.

[4] *BD*, 38 (1915), 154 ff. 'arbitratu Sexti Viniusi'; III, 8746, probably an Italian officer, *Sex. Coelius* [. . .]; *JÖAI*, 36 (1946), Bb. 67 *signifer*; *VAHD*, 56–59/2 (1954–7), II, 82 ff., n. 1 *decurio*; III, 8491 (6366); cf. *GZMBH*, 26 (1914), 163 *optio.*

[5] With *heredes*: III, 9816 (3164); III, 9796; III, 9727 (2712); XIII, 7023; III, 2016; III, 14632; III, 8491 (6366); cf. *GZMBH*, 26 (1914), 163; *JAK*, 2 (1908), 114; *JÖAI*, 36 (1946), Bb. 67 f.; III, 9760; Patsch, *Narona*, 75, n. 7; III, 14246/1; cf. *FS*, 2, 67, n. 3; III, 9834; III, 8492, 2745, 13975. With *fratres*: III, 9735, 8486.

[6] III, 14934 *Felix libertus.*

that for the legions, although the legionaries have more slaves and freedmen attested, as one might expect from their higher pay and social status.

During the second century a change took place which resulted in an improvement in the condition of serving men, in as much as relative stability in the army of the province gave the men an opportunity to form more lasting ties with a household. The number of men buried by comrades declines to four, perhaps men whose marriages, if they had contracted such, did not appear on their tombstones.[1] A *decurio* of Cohort I Belgarum had apparently contracted a legal marriage with a local woman (named Appuleia) who calls herself *uxor* on the tombstone.[2] In all other cases where wives are attested this official designation is not employed, but *hospita, coniunx* instead, while reference to the man is as *maritus*.[3] The only other instance of *uxor* in this group appears on a tombstone which may date to the late second or early third century.[4] Both the man, serving in Cohort III Alpinorum, and his wife were named Aurelii, indicating that the right to marry, granted under Septimius Severus, also conferred the privilege of citizenship. In this period only serving *peregrini* are known to have their tombstones set up by their fellow soldiers.[5]

Officers of Cohort III Alpinorum possessed slaves and freedmen, as also did veterans.[6] Although slavery was diminishing in importance in Dalmatia at this time, it is only now that evidence appears for auxiliaries owning slaves. The only serving soldier attested with his own slave appears to have been a native of Salona.[7] This improvement in the social position of serving men during the second century reflects the change which had taken place since the early part of the first century. With recruitment now almost entirely local the ties with the provincial population were much closer, and it may be that a fair proportion of serving men were following the occupation of their fathers, born *in castris* and brought up under the shadow of the camp walls. The difference between the second and third centuries was not very great. With marriages now officially recognized one finds on tombstones *uxor, coniunx*, and even a father-in-law as heir.[8] Slavery was now less widespread, and only one freedman is attested.[9]

---

[1] III, 14935; *VAHD*, 53 (1950–1), 226, n. 35; *WMBH*, 12 (1912), 133 f.; III, 8437.

[2] III, 8762; cf. p. 2657. On *uxor* and *coniunx* see n. 4 on p. 129.

[3] Serving auxiliaries with common-law marriages: III, 9739 *coniux*; III, 14700; III, 2052 *hospita*, 12905 *contubernalis* (?). Veterans: III, 2003, 9708, 14629/1.

[4] III, 2749.   [5] III, 14935?, *VAHD*, 53 (1950–1), 226, n. 35; III, 8437.

[6] Officers' freedmen: III, 8762; cf. p. 2657; III, 1808. Veterans' freedmen: III, 9708, 14629/1.

[7] III, 2045 (Salona).

[8] III, 2067 *uxor*, *GZMBH*, 22 (1910), 181 ff. (*WMBH*, 12 (1912), 136); III, 8376b (*GZMBH*, 26 (1914), 168) *coniux*; III, 3162b; III, 2002, 8729; cf. 14930, with father-in-law as heir.

[9] *RS*, 1, 158, n. 7 (*VAHD*, 50 (1928–9), 13 f.).

The number of auxiliary veterans known from Dalmatia is considerably smaller than that known for the legions, even allowing for the much smaller total manpower. Also, there is not the evidence for organized settlements comparable to those of legionaries near Burnum, Salona, Aequum, and Narona. All those attested appear to have chosen their place of residence individually.

The earliest datable auxiliary veteran is a trooper of the Ala Claudia nova who was probably an original settler in the colony at Aequum where he was buried.[1] Another member of this unit, a *missicius* (probably awarded a discharge after being wounded on campaign), retired to Salona to live with his sister.[2] On the other hand, one cannot assume that the small number of auxiliary veterans attested compared with serving men means that most veterans returned to their original homes, since there is no evidence from these areas. More veterans are attested for the second and third centuries, three in the former and five in the latter. All come from Salona or its immediate vicinity, illustrating how great was the attraction of this flourishing city.[3] This is yet another example of a great drift of people from all areas and all classes in the interior to the greater rewards and attractions of urban life on the coast. Only one man is found at his place of service, a veteran of Cohort I Belgarum buried by his wife (*coniunx*) far away in the north of the province at Doboj.[4] There is no evidence of any veterans being settled with a land grant (*missio agraria*), apart from the cavalryman already mentioned who settled at Aequum. Most apparently received a cash grant (*missio nummaria*) and used it either to buy land or to set themselves up in some form of enterprise. Such money may have been used to buy one or two slaves whose labour as freedmen would ensure a reasonably steady income. Two veterans record such freedmen on their tombstones.[5]

Throughout the Principate the commanders of auxiliary units were drawn from a narrow sector of the social hierarchy, from the Equestrian Order which, as organized by Augustus, ranked immediately below the Senatorial Order on a system of property qualification. Most, though by no means all, came from the cities of Italy or the more urbanized parts of the Empire, especially Narbonensis, Baetica, and North Africa. Many of the equestrian officers attested among the upper classes in Dalmatia belong to first or second generations of Italian immigrant families. The status of these commanders, *praefecti* or *tribuni*, in the army was curious. Normally men who had served a term as decurion or magistrate in their own city could be selected by provincial governors, often through the elab-

---

[1] *BD*, 38 (1915), 154 ff.   [2] III, 2065.
[3] Veterans of second century: *BD*, 37 (1914), 93; III, 2003; III, 14629/1. Of third century: III, 8731; Sp. 77 (1934), 23, n. 35; III, 9708, 12904, 8672.
[4] III, 8376b; cf. *GZMBH*, 26 (1914), 168 (Doboj).   [5] III, 9708; 14629/1.

orate network of family patronage between the senatorial order and the Italian and provincial cities, to serve a term as military tribune in a legion or prefect of an auxiliary cohort. After the time of Claudius the tour of duty (*militiae equestres*) consisted of a more or less fixed rota of posts, beginning with the prefecture of a cohort, the *tribunus angusticlavius* (to distinguish him from the *laticlavius*, senatorial tribune with the broad purple border on his toga) in a legion, and prefect of a cavalry *ala*. These men were not professional soldiers in the majority of cases, and it is unlikely that more than a small proportion served for more than a decade in such appointments, unless they had joined the imperial service with the intention of making it a life's career. For this they had to obtain favourable reports from their superiors before they could reach the higher grades of the imperial hierarchy, the procuratorships and prefectures of the major departments in Rome and the provinces. Many did not seek such a career, and after a suitable term in the army they preferred to return to their estates and enjoy their life in the ruling circles of a provincial city. As has been mentioned already these men were technically civilians and their duties, even when in titular command of a fighting unit, do not seem to have been entirely of a military character.[1]

Turning to the evidence for such men serving in Dalmatia there are twelve unit-commanders or senior ranks of *auxilia* who appear to have originated from Italy.[2] A commander of Cohort I Bracaraugustanorum came probably from Spain, though not from the mountainous area in the northwest where the unit was originally recruited.[3] As might be expected some men were appointed from the appropriate social level in the Dalmatian cities. In the first century a commander of Cohort I Lucensium was such a person from Salona.[4] Naturally both commanding officers and the senior ranks possess more personal dependants, both slaves and freedmen. A change can be detected in the second and third century, with a decrease in the proportion of those of Italian origin.[5] In the third

---

[1] E. Birley, *RBRA*, 133 ff.

[2] III, 8739: *decurio*[*praepositus*?]; *JÖAI*, 36 (1946), Bb. 67 ff.: *signifer*; III, 1810 (*centurio*); XVI, 38 diploma in 94 (*praefectus*); IX, 2564 (Bovianum Vetus): *praefectus*, formerly centurion in XI C.p.f.; III, 9739: *decurio*; III, 8348 (*centurio*), promoted from soldier in Legion XIIII; VI, 31863: *praefectus*; III, 13975 (*centurio*); III, 1742 (*centurio*), *NS*, 1912, 379 (*AE*, 1913, 194) (Rome, via Nomentana): *tribunus*; *Rad*, 339 (1965), p. 129: *tribunus* from Atina in Latium.

[3] III, 1773; cf. Patsch, *Narona* 76. It is unlikely that this man, Ti. Claudius Claudianus, is identical with the legate of that name in Pannonia under Severus, *PIR²*, C 834. More probably he is the man recorded with the same name, and apparently the same prefecture (Cohort I Bracaraugustanorum), at Tudae in Lusitania, II, 5613.

[4] III, 8736.

[5] Italian origin: III, 1918: (*centurio*) I Minerviae, *praepositus coh.*; III, 1979 (*tribunus*); III, 8655 (6374): (*tribunus*); *VAHD*, 51 (1930–4), 225 ff.: *praefectus*, probably identical with the jurist Sex.

century most auxiliary commanders and centurions originated from within the province, three tribunes and six centurions.[1] Of men from elsewhere there are two centurions from the West and one from Beneventum in Southern Italy.[2] The amenities of commanding officers and centurions were quite different from those of the men under their command. An auxiliary unit commander was provided with a fine residence within the fort (*praetorium*) which was modelled on the city house to which he was accustomed in civilian life, including a private bath suite and a generous accommodation for his household. Clearly the intention was to prevent service with the *auxilia* for these municipal worthies disrupting to any noticeable extent the routine of their civilian life.[3] Even centurions in the *auxilia*, whose status was considerably lower than that of the equestrian unit commanders, could sometimes manage to accumulate large sums of money: a centurion of Cohort I Belgarum was commemorated by a tombstone costing 1,000 sesterces, almost a year's pay for a legionary in the second century.[4]

[1] Tribunes: *JÖAI*, 19–20 (1919), Bb. 318, 217; III, 8353 under Commodus; cf. *Sp.*, 98 (1941–8), 485; *Sp.*, 98 (1941–8), 494; V, 707 (*Inscr. It.*, X, 3, 326). Centurions: III, 8756, 9829, 2006; *Sp.*, 77 (1934), 23, n. 35; III, 3163.
[2] Centurions: III, 9724 (2706), from Beneventum; *JAK*, 2 (1908), 113 f.; III, 8336 (6321), both probably from western provinces.
[3] See J. Wilkes in Jarrett and Dobson (ed.), *Britain and Rome*, 121 ff.
[4] *JAK*, 2 (1908), 113 f.

Caecilius Africanus who was active under Pius, *PIR²*, C 18. Western provinces: III, 2746: *centurio* from Celeia in Noricum; III, 14950: *centurio*; III, 14935: *centurio*; III, 3096; cf. *VAHD*, 53 (1950–1), 160 ff.: *centurio*; *WMBH*, 12 (1912), 133 f.: *centurio*, earlier *signifer*; III, 13875: *centurio*.

Chapter 8

The Native Peoples of Dalmatia at the Time of the Roman Conquest

1 *Identity and Location*

The picture of the native population of the Roman province of Dalmatia which can be recovered from ancient literary and epigraphic sources is uneven. Before the end of the fifth century B.C. Greek writers collected facts and names from explorers and traders, and in the following century the establishment of Greek settlements on some of the islands led not only to a much clearer picture of the Dalmatian coastline and its inhabitants, but also to a beginning of exploration and acquaintance with peoples in the interior. Despite this, however, it is only with the military activities of the Romans in the later third century that real knowledge of the interior of Dalmatia begins. By far the majority of written sources which deal with the area rely on evidence that was accumulated during the first century B.C., and there is no doubt that the more remote peoples beyond the Dinaric Alps became known to the Romans and the Classical World as a whole only with the beginning of effective Roman control during the Bellum Pannonicum of 13–9 B.C.

Even with the reasonable quantity of surviving literary sources, not only of the pre-Roman but also of the Empire, the identification and location (except where the evidence is supplemented by epigraphy) of many peoples is far from certain. There are also discrepancies between the different writers, many peoples having moved from one area to another, often splitting into more than one people, although still retaining their original name. Other peoples are sometimes recorded under a collective name without individual details. Finally, some peoples recorded by earlier sources were absorbed into larger groups, and no trace of them survives.[1] Only in a few cases can such changes be discerned: for instance the decline of the Ardiaei is recorded by Pliny, 'once the ravagers of Italy the (V)ardaei are now no more than twenty decuriae'.[2] The absence of once famous names from the Roman provincial organization of the native population is another indication that the Romans discovered that many changes had occurred since they first became involved in the area.

All the peoples recorded by ancient sources as having existed at one time or another in the area of Dalmatia fall into two main groups. The first are those small peoples along the coast identified and recorded by Greek writers before the end of the fourth century B.C. None of them appears after the third century B.C., and their names were only preserved when later writers noted them as once having lived in the area. Along with the names of these peoples are place and river names which also appear to have fallen out of use during the third century B.C. Quite different are the small communities recorded during the Republic in the southeast of the area, along the coast south of Epidaurum, where *oppida* such as Risinium, Acruvium, and Olcinium continued to retain their identity until the end of the Republic, but under the empire were absorbed into either new cities or the larger *civitates*. Such a people were the Illyrian Iadastinoi who dwelt around the river Iadro near Salona. They are mentioned on the Salona decree of 56 B.C. but were soon absorbed into the territory of the *colonia* at Salona.[3] The remainder constitute the second group, peoples who inhabited the Roman province at the Roman conquest, although not all of them were constituted as native *civitates* in the Roman organization. To study the location of all these peoples it will be best to begin with a table listing the evidence from the five principal sources showing the forms in which the names appear and summarizing identifications which are suggested in the Appendix (XI).

The peoples listed in the table can be divided into four groups, on the extent to which they survived as independent groups in the various phases of organization which preceded the final conquest. First, three peoples mentioned by Appian in connection with the wars of 35–33 B.C. are not mentioned by any other source, probably because they were normally accounted as part of larger well-known peoples. Appian took their names from Augustus' record of the war and that writer would have naturally magnified his victories by treating every group he attacked as a separate people. Thus the Posenoi were a community of the Iapodes, since they revolted immediately after Augustus left the territory of that

---

[1] For the peoples of Dalmatia, see Alföldy, *Bevölkerung*, 33 ff., and *Klio*, 41 (1963), 187 ff.
[2] *HN*, iii, 143.
[3] D. Rendić-Miočević, *SA*, 67–81 and above, p. 38 f.

Table of Peoples in Dalmatia by Sources

APPIAN	STRABO	DIO	PLINY	PTOLEMY
—	—	—	Armistae	—
—	—	—	Arthitae	—
Bathiatai	—	—	—	—
[Daisitiatai?]	Daisitiatai	Daisidiatai	Daesitiates	—
Daorsioi	Daorizoi	—	Duersi	Daoursioi
Dalmatai	Dalmateis	Delmatai	Delmatae	—
—	—	—	Deramistae	—
Derbanoi	—	—	Deuri	Derrioi
—	—	—	Deretini	Derriopes
—	—	—	Dindari	Dindarioi
—	Ditiones	—	Ditiones	Ditiones
Dokleatai	—	—	Docleatae	Dokleatai
Glintidiones	—	—	Glinditiones	—
Hippasinoi	—	—	Hemasini	—
Iapodes	Iapodes	Iapudes	Iapudes	Iapudes
—	—	—	Illyrii proprii dicti	—
Interphrourinoi	—	—	Endirudini	—
Kambaioi	—	—	Grabaei	—
—	—	—	Cerauni	Keraunioi
Kinambroi	—	—	—	—
Liburnoi	Liburnoi	Liburnoi	Liburni	—
—	—	—	Labeatae	—
—	Mazaioi	Mazaioi	Maezaei	Maizaioi
Meromennoi	—	—	Melcumani	Melkomenioi
Naresioi	—	—	Naresii	Narensioi
Oxuaioi	—	—	Ozuaei	—
Palarioi	Pleraioi	—	Pyraei	—
Pertheenetai	—	—	Partheni	—
Posenoi	—	—	—	—
Pyrissaioi	Peiroustai	—	—	Piroustai
—	—	—	Sardeates	Sardiotai
—	—	—	Sasaei	—
—	—	—	Scirtari	Skirtones
—	—	—	Siculotae	Sikoulotai
Taulantioi	—	—	Taulantii	—
Ardiaioi	Vardaioi	Ardiaioi	Vardaei	Vardaioi

people on his march through the Pannonians to Siscia.[1] They may be compared to the other communities of the Iapodes attacked at the same time, the Avendeatae of Avendo and others. Similarly the Kinambroi also recorded in the same

[1] Appian, *Ill.*, 21.

context by Appian are the inhabitants of Kinna, a place recorded by the Itineraries on the road between Doclea and Scodra around the northern end of the Lake of Scodra.[1] In the Roman period they, like many smaller communities in the same region, were included in the *civitas* of the Docleatae in the Narona *conventus*. The Bathiatai recorded also by Appian are otherwise unknown: to associate them with the river Bathinus (Bosna) and Central Dalmatia implies far greater conquests than can ever have been achieved by Octavianus in 35–33 B.C.[2] If they did dwell on the Bathinus, they may have been an accessible group of the Breuci or the Osseriates to the east of Siscia, who offered a diplomatic submission to Octavianus when he was encamped there late in the summer of 35 B.C.

The second group are peoples in the southeast between the river Narenta and the Drilo which are well attested as independent communities in the period before the final conquest, but which did not survive as independent *civitates* in the organization of the province. Many had been treated as separate *civitates* in the Republican administration based on Narona and were among the eighty-nine Varro mentions as attending there. After 9 they disappeared into the *territoria* of new coastal cities and larger more viable *civitates*. Many of these are listed by Pliny as inhabiting the area but not in the official *conventus* lists. These peoples are: Interphrourinoi (Endirudini), Kambaioi (Grabaei), Hippasinoi (Hemasini), Illyrii proprii dicti, Labeates, Oxyaioi (Ozuaei), Pertheenetai (Partheni), Palarioi (Pyraci), Taulantii, also the Armistae, Arthitae, and Sasaei. The location and fates of these different peoples are discussed below in the detailed survey of peoples in the province.

Thirdly there are those peoples well-known as independent communities before the conquest and which continued to survive as separate *civitates* in the organization of the Roman province. These are the following, with numbers of *decuriae* and version of their name as given by Pliny:

> Scardona *conventus*: Iapudes, 14 *civitates* of the Liburni.
>
> Salona *conventus*: Delmatae (342), Deuri (22), Ditiones (239), Maezaei (269).
>
> Narona *conventus*: Daesitiates (103), D(a)versi (17), Docleatae (33), Glinditiones (44), Melcumani (24), Naresii (102), Pirustae (not listed by Pliny but probably subdivided into Scirtari (72), Cerauni (24), and Siculotae (24)), Vardaei (20).

[1] *Cinna: It. Ant.*, 339, 3 (18 miles north of Scodra); *Sinna*: Peutinger; *Kinna*: Ptol., ii, 16, 7. Probably Koplice on the east of Lake Scodra.
[2] B. Saria, *Klio*, 23 (1930), 97, n. 3.

Finally there appear in the official lists some names unknown before the Roman conquest:

> Salona *conventus*: Sardeates (52).
>
> Narona *conventus*: Deraemistae (30; formed out of a number of earlier *civitates*), Dindari (33; part of the old Scordisci), Cerauni (24), Scirtari (72), Siculotae (24; all three probably organized out of the Pirustae), Deretini (14). In the case of the Sardiates and Deretini they may be mentioned, but not named, by Strabo when he describes the Pannonian peoples later included in Northern Dalmatia (see below p. 168).

It might seem logical to discuss the detailed evidence for the location of the peoples on the scheme of the *conventus* given by Pliny, which divided the province into three distinct areas. On the other hand, much epigraphic evidence exists for fixing some of the larger peoples, while the study of the considerable body of personal names has revealed clear ethnic differences between one area and another. The picture which has emerged from the detailed studies of such scholars as D. Rendić–Miočević, R. Katačić, and most recently G. Alföldy,[1] suggests the following distinct ethnic and geographical groupings: (i) The Iapodes, (ii) The Liburni, (iii) The Delmatae, (iv) The peoples in the southeast, (v) The Pannonians in Northern Dalmatia, (vi) The Celtic peoples in Northeast Dalmatia, (vii) The peoples of Eastern Dalmatia.

i *The Iapodes.* Ancient authorities are clear about the territory occupied by the Iapodes, at least as regards their western and southern limits. Most sources from Hecataeus[2] onwards mention them, and as far as the evidence goes all their territories were included in Roman Dalmatia. On the west they bordered the Carni of the Julian Alps and the Istri of the Istrian peninsula: to the east they extended into the upper valleys of the Save and the Colapis (Kulpa). The centre of their territory was the area within the mountain ranges of the Velika Kapela and the massive barrier of the Velebit, which separates the barren Lika polje from the Liburnian coastline between Tarsatica and the Ravni Kotari. In the south they extended to the river Tedanius (Žrmanja), where they bordered the Liburni.[3] Within the territory of the Iapodes lay some of the most intractable

---

[1] R. Katačić, *ŽA*, 12 (1962), 95 ff.; 13 (1963), 255 ff.; *Die Sprache*, 10 (1964), 23 ff.; *Simpozijum* (ed. Benac 1964), 9 ff.; G. Alföldy, *BzN*, 15 (1964), 55 ff., and *Bevölkerung*, 20 ff. A recent study of Early Iron Age pins by J. Alexander, *PPS*, 30 (1964), 159 ff., has indicated regional differences similar to those outlined below.

[2] Hecataeus, frg. 97.

[3] Liv., xliii, 5; neighbours of Carni and Istri, Strabo, iv, 6, 1; Albian Mountains (Velika Kapela). For other sources, see Appendix XI below, p. 481 ff.

territory of Europe, with range after range of limestone karst covered by heavy scrub undergrowth and steep valleys with dense forests. There is little doubt that they were the largest single people included in the province, although they did not figure in the great wars of conquest under Augustus. They preserved a quite separate identity against the other peoples of the interior and this is confirmed by finds from their cemeteries and dwelling sites, the distribution of which corresponds fairly well to their territory as described by the literary sources. The typical Iapodian pottery and metalwork has been recognized over an area extending northwestwards from the Lika polje as far as Istria, southwards to the island of Curicta (Krk) in the Quarnerno, eastwards to the river Sana where they bordered the Maezaei, and northwards into the Sana valley.[1] The area revealed by the distribution of Iapodian material is slightly greater than the area which they held at the time of the Roman conquest. The coast from Tarsatica to the river Tedanius was settled at some period by the Liburni: they must have moved northwards to occupy the many small settlements as far as the western side of Istria, at some time possibly in the first century B.C. Pliny refers to earlier writers who describe this part of the coast as Iapodian territory.[2] On the north the lower valley of the river Colapis was the territory of the Pannonians. They did not retreat on all sides, however, and in the northwest appear to have acquired territory in the area of the Okra mountain (towards the Julian Alps). When the Iapodes lost their lands in these areas is not known but their retreat had certainly taken place at the time of Octavianus' campaigns. When Octavianus marched along the Colapis valley for eight days to Siscia he was travelling through the lands of the Pannonians.[3]

With the boundaries of the Iapodes fixed fairly precisely on a combination of literary and archaeological evidence, the main centres of the people within this area can be fixed partly with the aid of inscriptions. These were in the upper valley of the river Una, where leaders of the people in the first century A.D. dedicated a number of altars to Bindus Neptunus at the Privilica spring near Bihać,[4] and among the communities in the Lika polje further to the west.[5] The literary sources speak of the Iapodes being divided into two parts by the Albion

---

[1] V. Mirosavljević, *AI*, 3 (1959), 47 ff., and pl. XXVI. On the settlement pattern see below, p. 349 ff.

[2] Strabo, vii, 5, 4, mentions the 'Iapodian coastline'; also Plin., *HN*, iii, 129: 'Some authors place the Iapydian country on the Gulf of Flanona (Quarnerno).' Tradition links them with Northern Italy, Virg., *Georg.*, iii, 474 ff. For their economic development, U. Kahrstedt, *Nach. Ges. Wiss. Göttingen*, 1927, 33.

[3] Appian, *Ill.*, 22. For their spread to the Okra, Strabo, iv, 6, 10.

[4] Patsch, *WMBH*, 6 (1899), 158 ff.; III, 14325–8, 15064 f., 14324.

[5] Appian, *Ill.*, 16.

Mountain (the Velika and Mali Kapela) with the Cisalpine Iapodes (Avendeatae, Moentini, and Arupini) and the Transalpine Iapodes, more powerful peoples who included the inhabitants of Metulum.[1] Finally the evidence from personal names suggests that the area between the lower valleys of the rivers Una and Sana belonged to the Iapodes and that the latter river was the boundary between them and the Pannonian Maezaei.[2] The picture of the Iapodes presented by the personal names on tombstones is a varied one.[3] Part of the names are thoroughly Illyrian, with one or two particularly common in the territory of the Liburni. These Venetic–Liburnian names among the Iapodes may suggest an earlier stratum still persisting among the population, possibly from the time when the Liburni were much more widespread around the Adriatic. The Illyrian and Venetic names extend east of the Una beyond Bihać and suggest that the Iapodes extended as far as the river Sana. Also common among the Iapodes are Celtic names, found over all parts of their territory, in contrast to those of peoples on the east. The group of Celtic names in the iron-mining district around Ljubija confirms that this area belonged to the Iapodes. This Celtic element in the people was noted in antiquity. Strabo writes: 'they are indeed a war-mad people . . . their lands are poor, the people living for the most part on spelt and millet; their armour is Celtic, and they are tattoed like the rest of the Illyrians and Thracians'. Dionysius of Halicarnassus actually calls them a Celtic people.[4] Although the study of archaeological material from the Iapodes has only just begun some Celtic element has already been detected. Tombstones show a variety of Celtic symbols, circles, rosettes, and triangles in various combinations. Celtic dress can be recognized in the so-called 'Pannonian dress' which appears on figures represented on the tombstone reliefs.[5] Otherwise the amount of Celtic equipment from among the Iapodes is less than might be expected; that which is known from the eastern part of their territory may be the result of more local Pannonian influence, and on the whole the remarks of Strabo quoted above have not been confirmed by recent studies of the archaeological evidence made by Yugoslav archaeologists.[6]

ii *The Liburni.* Like the Iapodes, the Liburni are mentioned by Hecataeus, although their first encounter with the Greeks was much earlier, in the eighth

[1] Strabo, iv, 6, 10, vii, 5, 4; Appian, *Ill.*, 16, 17, 21; cf. Dio, xlix, 35, 1.

[2] Alföldy, *AAnt*, 10 (1962), 8.

[3] Alföldy, *BzN*, 15 (1964), 59 ff.

[4] vii, 5, 4; Dion. Hal., frg. 16 (vol. 7, p. 326, ed. Cary).

[5] I. Čremošnik, *GZMS*, 12 (1957), 232; 13 (1958), 147 ff. (dress and symbols on tombstones). Of 157 fibulae in the Jezerine cemetery 95 were of La Tène date, *WMBH*, 3 (1895), 510. On the Donja Dolina cemetery, Z. Marić, *GZMS*, 19 (1964), 5–128.

[6] See the articles of Z. Marić and S. Gabrovac in A. Benac, *Simpozijum*, 177 ff., 215 ff.

century B.C. when, according to a tradition recorded by Strabo, they were expelled from Corcyra (Corfu) by Corinthian colonists under the leadership of Chersicrates. Other sources speak of the Liburni as extending southward along the coast as far as the Narenta, while, among the islands, Issa and Pharos were once possessions of theirs.[1] On the other side of the Adriatic the Liburni settled in Picenum as early as the fifth century B.C.,[2] just as the Iapodes settled in Southeast Italy, where in Iapygia there is evidence of Illyrian personal and place names.[3] Like the Istri and the rest of the Illyrians the Liburni were known to the Romans as pirates before the end of the fourth century B.C., although the first recorded campaigns made against them did not take place until 129 B.C., under the consul C. Sempronius Tuditanus.[4] Pliny records that Tuditanus explored their territory to its southern limit at the river Titius, and inscribed on a monument: 'From Aquileia to the river Titius 2,000 stades' (about 250 miles).[5] Their final defeat was probably achieved by Octavianus shortly before Actium, in which battle he employed warships (*liburnae*) captured from them to good effect.[6]

The original homeland of the Liburni was the Ravni kotari, a fertile area between the rivers Tedanius and Titius extending inland to the Velebit and the Dinara for a distance of about 30 miles. This was always the most urbanized area of the province. The coast further north between the Tedanius and Western Istria was occupied by a number of different peoples according to the earlier sources,[7] but these were either overwhelmed or absorbed by the Liburni until at the time of conquest they occupied the whole coast from the river Arsia (Raša) in Western Istria to the mouth of the Titius, as well as all the islands of the Quarnerno.[8] Shortly before Caesar's proconsulate they seem to have spread southwards across the Titius: at the time of the conquest the boundaries of one

[1] Hecat., frg. 93; Strabo, vi, 2, 4. On the mainland, Pomp. Mela, ii, 57; and islands, Apol. Rhod., iv, 564.

[2] Plin., *HN*, iii, 110: 'Truentum with its river, the only trace of the Liburnians left in Italy'; cf. iii, 112. The archaeological links are striking; M. Suić, *VAHD*, 55 (1953), 71–101, produces many early Iron Age objects of similar origin from both sides of the Adriatic. Similar links are also suggested from the evidence of Early Iron Age pins, J. Alexander, *PPS*, 30 (1964), 159 ff. Economic links persisted into the Roman period, illustrated by the Tarii Rufi, below p. 330 f.

[3] *Blanda*, X, 125 (Thurii) for Liburnian Blandona, *It. Ant.*, 273, 3; Ptol., ii, 16, 6. *Clampetia* in Bruttium, Plin., *HN*, iii, 132; Mela, ii, 69. On Clambetae see below, p. 211 f.

[4] Liv., x, 2, 4. On the campaigns of Tuditanus see above, p. 32 f.

[5] Plin., *HN*, iii, 129.

[6] Appian, *Ill.*, 16. At Actium, Vegetius, iv, 33 f.; Florus, iv, 11; cf. Grosse, *RE*, 13 (1926), 143 ff.

[7] Appendix XI, p. 481.

[8] Plin., *HN*, iii, 139; cf. 129; Strabo, vii, 5, 4.

Liburnian community, the Varvarini of Varvaria (Bribir), ran in the region of Mratovo on the left bank of the river.[1]

There is more epigraphic evidence for personal names in Liburnia than from any other area of Dalmatia. To some extent the earlier studies of onomastic evidence have distorted the picture by grouping the Liburnian evidence along with the remainder from Pannonia and Dalmatia under the general heading 'Illyrian'. More than anything the names of the Liburnians are Venetic and have the closest links with Northeast Italy, especially Istria, the most distinguishing feature being the termination-*icus*. Some names, for instance *Ceunus*, are peculiarly Illyrian, but only a small proportion of the names from Liburnia appear to be Illyrian, to judge from their wider distribution in the province. The result of recent studies of personal names has been to emphasize the clear differences between one area and another; they have also demonstrated how the term Illyrian was applied more and more widely as larger areas and more peoples became known to the Greco–Roman World.[2] As Pliny records, 'the real Illyrians' (*Illyrii proprii dicti*) were a small people on the coast south of Epidaurum, the centre of the kingdom of Agron and his successors (see p. 15 ff). Greek writers in the fourth century are clear in separating the rest of the peoples along the coast from the Illyrians; only in the Roman period did Illyrian begin to be used as the general term for all the peoples dwelling across the Adriatic until (in the first century A.D.) the process reached its climax, when the Romans labelled the whole area between the Middle Danube and Macedonia as Illyricum.[3] Although there was probably considerable intermixture between peoples in this area the study of the evidence for personal names reflects the more detailed picture given in the earlier sources. It is probably more correct to speak of a Venetic group of peoples around the head of the Adriatic and make a clear distinction between them and the Illyrians. However, of the rest of the peoples of Dalmatia all those which cannot be definitely identified as Celtic or Thracian must be termed Illyrian. Within Liburnia it is possible to make a subdivision between the area north of the river Tedanius and the Ravni kotari: in the northern area Illyrian names are entirely unknown, all being Venetic, while in the Ravni kotari Illyrian names are found in increasing number as one approaches the territory of the Delmatae, especially in the area of Burnum, Varvaria, and Scardona, although even in these areas Venetic names are in the majority. The latter is the earlier stratum of the population, overlaid by the Illyrian Delmatae spreading

---

[1] Promona was once Liburnian, Appian, *Ill.*, 12, 25, but was Dalmatian by the time of Strabo. Varvarini across the Titius: III, 9896 (6418), also p. 217.
[2] Alföldy, *Bevölkerung*, 42 f. On the Veneti, J. Untermann, *Venetische Personnenamen*.
[3] Z. Marić, *GZMS*, 19 (1964), 58 ff., 76 ff.

northwards into the lands of the Liburni, a movement reflected by their attack on Promona during Caesar's proconsulate in Illyricum.[1]

iii *The Delmatae.* The southern neighbours of the Liburni and, it seems, their traditional enemies were the Delmatae, the most numerous people in the Salona *conventus*. Their name was derived from their capital Delminium (Županac), and it was after them that the Roman province which emerged from the division of Illyricum after the final conquest was named. The people are first recorded in the second century B.C. as dependants of the kingdom of Gentius, from whom they revolted. Roman armies invaded their territory in 156–155 B.C. destroying their capital and turning its area into a sheep pasture. They were a fierce people and many of the Roman campaigns under the Republic were directed against them; the final submission of all Illyricum in 9 was signalized by the surrender of their fortress of Andetrium not 20 miles from Salona.[2]

Broadly speaking the Delmatae held the central sector of the coast between the rivers Titius and Narenta; this was by far the most attractive and climatically the most favoured part of the coastline. On the north they were advancing against the Liburni, who had lost Promona but still held some land on the left bank of the Titius.[3] The lower course seems to have had Liburnian territory on both sides, judging from Strabo's remark that the river is navigable as far as the territory of the Delmatae, although this cannot have been very far from the sea.[4] For the northern limit of the Delmatae Strabo is again the principal source: 'and there is the Adrion mountain which cuts the territory of the Delmatae in two parts, one facing the sea and the other in the opposite direction'.[5] The Adrion is the line of the Dinaric Alps which runs parallel with the coast from Knin to the north of Mostar on the Narenta. The part of the Delmatae facing the sea was the area between the two rivers mentioned south of the Dinaric Alps; the other included the high poljes on the watershed between the coastal hinterland and the Bosnian valleys, Livjanskopolje, Glamočkopolje, Duvjanskopolje, Kupreško-polje, and Malovan sedlo. The spread of the Delmatae over this area is confirmed by the evidence of personal names. Their northern limits ran from the Dinara, then southeastward along the mountains Srnetica, Koša gora, Vitoroz, Ljubuša, then towards the Narenta. In the south the Delmatae occupied the major islands in the Manios Kolpos.[6] Not all the land on the right bank of the Narenta was occupied by them. They probably occupied Imotskipolje and the area of the later

---

[1] Alföldy, *BzN*, 15 (1964), 66 ff.

[2] Dio, lvi, 12.   [3] III, 9896 (6418), and above, p. 217.

[4] Strabo, vii, 5, 4.   [5] Strabo, vii, 5, 5.

[6] Alföldy, *Bevölkerung*, 44 f. Personal names attest Delmatae on the islands, for example *Plator* on Solentia (Šolta), *VAHD*, 43 (1920), 111.

city of Novae, although at the end of the Republic the Trebižat valley was still retained by the Ardiaei, in spite of their diminished strength.[1] The principal centre of the Delmatae was Rider (Danilo Kraljice), on the road between Salona and Scardona, which appears to have succeeded Delminium after the latter's destruction in 155 B.C. From this place comes the largest quantity of non-Roman names of any place in the province and it has been analysed in recent years by D. Rendić–Miočević.[2] As might be expected of a place not far from the river Titius there is a considerable quantity of Liburnian names. Smaller numbers of names are also known which are typical of the Iapodes, and of the southeast of the province. There are a few Celtic names, some of which are widely attested among the Pannonian peoples in the northern part of Dalmatia. The closest links of the Delmatae were with these peoples on their northern border, rather than with other groups such as the Venetic peoples or the Iapodes on the northwest, or the Illyrians in the southeast. It has been suggested also that a group of names in the area of Plevlje in the eastern part of the interior can be identified as of the Delmatae, and that these reflect settlements from the Delmatae made by the Roman government during the first century A.D. (p. 176).

iv *The Peoples in the Southeast.* By contrast with other areas of the province which were occupied by large peoples such as the Iapodes, Liburni, and Delmatae, the coastal hinterland between the Narenta and the Drilo was occupied by a considerable number of smaller peoples, most of whom lost their separate identity during the final stages of the Roman occupation. The twenty peoples listed by Pliny were only a fraction of the eighty-nine *civitates* attested by Varro a century earlier at the Narona *conventus*. This part of Dalmatia was populated by the 'real Illyrians', and the evidence from personal names produces a uniform picture with very little influence from other parts of the province,[3] except for a group of Celtic names in the upper Narenta valley around Konjic.[4] In the later third and second centuries B.C. all these peoples were part of the Illyrian kingdom, but with the removal of Gentius they all resumed some form of independence, mostly in some kind of treaty arrangements with the Romans.

The history of the contact between Rome and the Ardiaei in the third and second centuries B.C. has been discussed in an earlier chapter, but by the end of the Republic they had declined to a very small people. This may have been

---

[1] For instance *Messor*, III, 8509 (Postranje near Imotski); *Messila*, III, 1901 (Baška Voda).

[2] *VAHD*, 52 (1950–1), 25 ff. (Supplement); *GZMS*, 6 (1951), 34 ff.; *VAHD*, 55 (1953) 245 ff.; *Zbornik* 1 (1955), 125 ff.; *AI*, 2 (1956), 39 ff.; *ŽA*, 10 (1960), 163 ff; *ARR*, 2 (1962), 315 f.; also Alföldy, *BzN*, 15 (1964), 76 ff.

[3] Typical Illyrian names of the Southeast include *Annaeus-Annaius, Epicadus, Epidius, Pinnes, Plare(n)s, Tatta, Temeia, Zanatis, Ziraeus*; cf. Alföldy, *BzN*, 15 (1964), 86 ff.

[4] *Boio, Bricussa, Iacus, Mallaius, Mascelio*, Alföldy, op. cit., 91.

partly the result of Roman campaigns against them, but may also be due to the Roman policy of detaching all their allies and dependants until only the original core of the tribe was left. According to Strabo they inhabited the mainland opposite Pharos on the right bank of the river Narenta, including the Trebižat valley where later under Augustus a large concentration of auxiliary troops was established.[1] How extensive was the area occupied at the time of conquest is not known but they appear to have suffered from the pressure of neighbouring peoples, such as the Delmatae, and Strabo adds that their land was very infertile; he probably refers to the karst hinterland rather than the fertile lower valley of the Narenta. Their piratical habits continued after 168 B.C., and they were chastised for this by a Roman consul in 135 B.C.[2] The Daorsii (later Duersi) were probably neighbours of the Ardiaei and dwelt on the left or southern bank of the Narenta. In the second century B.C. they produced their own coinage, some of which bears a sea-going merchant ship on the reverse. This would suggest that they dwelt around the lower part of the river, since it is not navigable above the Žitomislići gorge north of Čapljina. Before 168 B.C. they became subjects of Gentius and so remained until they deserted him and made peace with the Romans.[3]

The Pleraeoi (this is the form of their name given by Strabo: other sources give different versions) dwelt on the coast between the Ardiaei and the Gulf of Rhizon; they were probably neighbours of the Daorsi around the lower Narenta. Their land also lay opposite Corcyra Nigra, which suggests that the Pelješac peninsula which juts westward into the Adriatic from east of the mouth of the Narenta belonged to them.[4] The Pleraei also were punished for their piracy along with the Ardiaei in 135 B.C. They are not in Pliny's list of the *civitates* in the Narona *conventus*, although doubtless they were among the eighty-nine recorded by Varro. Their disappearance probably occurred when *coloniae* were established at Narona and Epidaurum, most of their lands being absorbed into the *territoria* of these new Roman foundations. There are very few records of the native population in this area, who were probably dominated by the urban communities composed of new settlers in the *coloniae*.

The Narensii, with 102 *decuriae*, comprised after the Daesitiates (103) the

---

[1] Strabo, vii, 5, 5. On the auxiliaries, see above, p. 139.

[2] Appian, *Ill.*, 10; cf. Liv., *Per.*, lvi.

[3] Hecataeus, frg. 175, records the Thracian *Darsioi*; cf. Patsch, *JÖAI*, 10 (1907), 169 ff., suggesting that at an early date Thracian peoples were widespread on the Adriatic. On their coins and early history see p. 27 and n. 3. They probably dwelt nearer to the coast than the Bregava valley around Stolac, as suggested by Alföldy, *Bevölkerung*, 47.

[4] Strabo, vii, 5, 6.

second largest *civitas* in the Narona *conventus*. Their name suggests that they occupied land in and around the Narenta valley. It is, however, only recorded by the later sources, Pliny, Appian, and Ptolemy, and not by those which record the coastal communities.[1] Consequently they may be located on the middle and upper Narenta. They probably held the whole plain around Mostar, including the Bijelopolje, and to the south may have extended as far as Stolac in the Bregava valley. Although Appian lists them among the peoples whom Octavianus overcame in 34–33 B.C. 'not without some effort', no record of this powerful people has survived from the period of the Roman province. It is possible that they also extended northwards into the upper Narenta valley around Konjic, once held by the Autariatae; here a group of Celtic names suggests the survival of a number of people from this tribe.[2]

After giving the official list of the *civitates* in the Narona *conventus* Pliny adds the names of another group of peoples under the heading: 'Apart from these (peoples in the *conventus* list) the following peoples dwell in the same area (*tractus*), Ozuaei, Partheni, Hemasini, Arthitae, Armistae, and possibly the Cavi'.[3] No *decuriae* numbers are given, and it is not absolutely certain whether they were also all *civitates* in the *conventus*, or whether they were part of others already mentioned, but peoples still identifiable under their own names. Some of them are recorded by Appian among those peoples who submitted to Octavianus, and there is no doubt that they all dwelt in the coastal hinterland south of the mountains of Hercegovina and Montenegro, that is the region of Popovopolje, including Trebinje, Ljubija, and Bileca further north.[4] They may all have been absorbed into the Deramistae, a previously unknown name of a *civitas* with 30 *decuriae* listed in the Narona *conventus*. On the diploma of A.D. 94 a woman of the Deramistae is recorded married to a Daversus serving in Cohort III Alpinorum, and this suggests that the two peoples may have bordered on one another.[5] If the Daversi (or Daorsi) have been correctly located on the lower left bank of the Narenta, with the Pleraei further south along the coast, then the Deramistae probably occupied Popovopolje and its area behind Epidaurum, where the new *civitas* was formed as a more viable unit out of the large number of smaller *civitates* which had been organized during the later Republic. Their name may be connected with the Armistae which appears among Pliny's list of the former *civitates*.

[1] See table, p. 155.

[2] Note 4 on p. 163. On Celtic dress in the area, I. Čremošnik, *Tkalčićev Zbornik*, 2 (1958), 11 ff.

[3] *HN*, iii, 143.

[4] Dedications to *I.O.M. Partinus*, III, 8353, 14613, in Northeast Dalmatia, may be connected with the Partheni, but not the Parthini of Macedonia attacked by Pollio in 39 B.C., above, p. 44 f.

[5] XVI, 38.

The Melcumani with 24 *decuriae* cannot be located precisely, but since they submitted with little resistance to Octavianus they were probably a people in the coastal hinterland.[1] Possibly they bordered the Deramistae on the north, occupying Gačkopolje and Nevesinjepolje, where they would have been the eastern neighbours of the Narensii. Finally come a small group of peoples in the southeast who after the conquest were either made part of the *territoria* of the coastal cities, or included in the *civitas* of the Docleatae based on Doclea (the only *civitas* recorded in Pliny's list for this area) with 33 *decuriae*. Some of them can be associated with places named by the later itineraries along roads in the area. Pliny lists the Labeatae, Endirudini, Sasaei, Grabaei, the 'properly named Illyrians', Taulantii, and Pyraei.[2] To these must be added the Kinambroi of Appian.[3] The Pleraei have already been noted as a coastal people in the region of Epidaurum and Rhizon. The Endirudini, identifiable with the Interphrourinoi of Appian, inhabited Enderon which is a place recorded by Ptolemy on the road between Narona and Scodra, probably somewhere in the area of Nikšić.[4] Like the Kambaioi, the Grabaei of Pliny, they submitted to Octavianus. Neither the latter nor the Sasaei of Pliny's list can be located at all precisely within this general area. The Labeates were the people who dwelt around the Lacus Labeatis (Lake of Scodra), and they too ceased to be independent after the removal of Gentius.[5] The 'properly named Illyrii' were south of the lake around the old capital of the Illyrian kingdom at Scodra. They were absorbed into the territory of the new city, probably a colony, established there under Augustus.[6] Many of the other peoples were made part of the Docleatae, whose centre was Doclea at the confluence of the rivers Zeta and Morača, a few miles north of Titograd, the modern capital of Montenegro. Under the Flavians Doclea became a *municipium*, and it was easily the most important city of southeast Dalmatia, the site of the imperial cult (*Ara Caesaris*), and with its upper classes even dominating some of the older coastal *coloniae*.[7] After their conquest they were increased by the addition of other peoples such as the Kinambroi and the

---

[1] Appian, *Ill.*, 16; cf. Ptolemy's *Melkomenioi*. Von Domaszewski's restoration of III, 8308 (Kolovrat), to read *praef(ectus)* . . .*[civ. Melco]m(enorum)* is unlikely, see below, n. 7 on p. 174. An auxiliary soldier from the people, *Balaterus M(e)li f. civilis Melqumenorum*, is attested serving in Cohort VI Delmatarum at Caesarea in Mauretania, *AE*, 1921, 31.

[2] *HN*, iii, 144.   [3] Note 1 on p. 156.

[4] Ptol., ii, 16, 7: *Enderon*, possibly *Andarva* of It. Ant., 338, 7; cf. *Sanderva* on *Peutinger*, *Anderba*, Rav., iv, 16, 19. On the line of the road, D. Sergejevski, *GZMS*, 17 (1962), 73 ff., E. Pašalić, *Naselja*, 62 ff. The restoration of III, 8370; cf. Evans, *Arch.*, 48 (1884), 91, to *Andarvanor[um]* is doubtful.

[5] Liv., xliii, 19; Caes., *BC*, iii, 25, *Lacus Labeatis*; Liv., xliv, 31, cf. xxix, 3, 5. On the fortress Meteon (Medun) see below, p. 340.   [6] See p. 257.   [7] See p. 260 f.

Endirudini. From their existence as a *civitas* before the Flavian period comes the inscription, from Riječani 20 miles west of Nikšić, mentioning a *princeps Docl(e)-atium*.[1] This place lies on the road between the Nikšić area and Diluntum (Trebinje) and shows that large areas of the hinterland behind Epidaurum and the Gulf of Rhizon were part of the *civitas* of the Docleatae. The Taulantii, named by Pliny somewhere in the hinterland between Epidaurum and Lissus, were one of the most famous peoples who dwelt in that part of the Adriatic. Hecataeus locates them much further to the south around Dyrrhachium, but as Appian lists them among the peoples who submitted to Octavianus they must have been situated somewhere north of Scodra, since that place had been designated at the conference of Brundisium in 40 B.C. as the boundary between the power of Octavianus and M. Antonius.[2] The Taulantii had already once submitted to the Romans when Illyria was invaded in 168 B.C.[3] Their original homeland was probably the coastline south of the Gulf of Rhizon, where they bordered on the Pleraei, as far as Lissus, and including the thin strip of land between the Lake of Scodra and the sea. The disappearance of the Taulantii as a separate *civitas* may have been partly due the organization of cities (called by Pliny *oppida civium Romanorum*) at Acruvium, Butua, Olcinium, and Lissus.

v *Pannonian Peoples in Northern Dalmatia.* Before the Roman provincial boundaries were finally established, and terms such as Pannonia and Dalmatia applied to them, two of the principal sources for the peoples in the area later enclosed within Dalmatia give a picture of the ethnic distribution that portrays more accurately the spread of different peoples. The Romans did not create Dalmatia after a careful analysis of the population and its racial origins but largely as a result of the military needs of pacification, internal security, and communications. Broadly speaking, they ignored the racial distribution of the peoples in the central part of the area which they called Illyricum by fixing the provincial boundary between Pannonia and Dalmatia along the southern edge of the Save valley, and placing such key places as Siscia, Servitium, and Sirmium within Pannonia, despite their main function as military centres during the wars of

---

[1] D. Sergejevski, *GZMS*, 17 (1962), 100 f. (improving *JÖAI*, 12 (1909), Bb. 201, n. 73–4, *Sp.*, 71 (1931), 241–2), locates Salthua at Riječani. The stones record *Agirrus Epicadi f. princeps k(astelli) Salthua(e)*, and *Caius Epicadi f. princeps civitatis Docl(e)atium*, with members of both families:

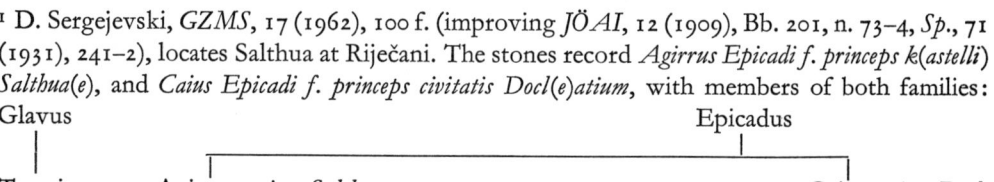

[2] Plin., *HN*, iii, 144; cf. Appian, *Ill.*, 16.   [3] Liv., xlv, 26.

conquest which had been to act as bases in the advance against the powerful peoples to the south in the Bosnian valleys. Why the frontier was fixed in this manner is a puzzle, since there is no easy communication between an army of two legions with its auxiliaries, based on the Adriatic coast and its immediate hinterland south of the Dinaric Alps, and the northern part of Dalmatia. One can only surmise that the intention was to divide the unwieldy command of Illyricum as nearly in half as possible. Ideally the division should have been drawn along the eastern frontier of the Iapodes, and the northern limit of the Delmatae following the watershed between the middle Danube basin and the Adriatic (see above). The objection to this was that Pannonia would be far too large an area to control from a provincial capital in the north of the province.

Before this division was made two writers speak of the peoples later included in Northern Dalmatia as Pannonians, and this is confirmed by the evidence of personal names. Appian (who calls the Pannonians by the name Paiones) and Strabo both use this name as a collective designation for a large group of non-Celtic peoples between the Iapodes, Delmatae, and the middle Danube. Appian writes: 'The Paiones are a great people living on the middle Danube extending from the Iapodes to the Dardanians; they are called Paiones by the Greeks, but Pannonians by the Romans. They are counted by the Romans as part of Illyria, as I have previously said, for which reason it seems proper that I should include them in my Illyrian history.' He also states: 'the country of the Pannonians is wooded and extends from the Iapodes to the Dardanians. On the west they were bordered by the Norici, on the east by the Moesians and the Scordisci.'[1] Noteworthy is the mention of wooded country, clearly a reference to the thickly wooded parts of Bosnia; the location between the Iapodes and the Dardanians refers to land which became later the northern half of Dalmatia. More specific is Strabo who reproduces in greater detail the same pre-conquest tradition as Appian. He describes the 'peoples of the Pannonians who are the Breukoi, Andizetoi, Ditiones, Peiroustai, Mazaioi, Daisitiatai, as well as other smaller peoples as one goes south as far as the lands of the Ardiaioi'.[2] All the peoples in this list, except the Breuci and the Andizetes, were included in the later province of Dalmatia and occur in the *conventus* lists of Pliny. The personal names from the area between the Sana and Drina valleys stand out clearly as a group apart from the rest of Dalmatia. There are some names which are known in other parts, especially the territory of the Delmatae and the southeast, but the closest links are with the Pannonians in Pannonia; this supports the tradition of Appian and

[1] Appian, *Ill.*, 14.
[2] Strabo, vii, 5, 3. On the location of the Breuci and other Pannonians in the Save valley, see Alföldy, *AArch Hung.*, 16 (1964), 254 ff.

Strabo that a large number of Pannonian peoples were included later in Northern Dalmatia.[1]

The Ditiones were the most southerly people in this group. They bordered on the Iapodes and the Delmatae, and can be located in an area of Western Bosnia. One of the military roads built from Salona under the governor P. Cornelius Dolabella led 'to the foot of the mountain of the Ditiones' (*ad imum montem Ditionum*).[2] This was the road through the territory of the Delmatae to the route which led from the area of Knin on the upper Krka across the Strmica pass at the western end of the Dinara mountains, the main route into Western Bosnia. How far the Ditiones extended north from this area is not known, but they may have reached as far as the line connecting Kulen Vakuf at the head of the Una valley, Bosanka Petrovac, and Ključ in the upper Sana valley. It is unlikely that they were ever approached by a Roman army until Tiberius' campaigns in 12–9 B.C., and it was probably through their territory that M. Aemilius Lepidus led the XXth legion southwards on its great march, which probably began at Siscia and ended at Burnum.[3]

The Maezaei with 269 *decuriae* were the largest people in the northern part of Dalmatia, and overall were second only to the *civitas* of the Delmatae. They were probably first conquered by Tiberius in the Bellum Pannonicum, but they joined in the great rebellion of 6 and were finally conquered by Germanicus in 7 operating from Siscia.[4] They lived west of the Iapodes, their common border probably being the Sana valley, and north of the Ditiones. On the east their neighbours were the Daesitiates. How far they extended northward is unknown, but presumably the provincial boundary between the Sana and Vrbas rivers was more or less along their northern limit. Nor can their eastern boundary be located precisely but allowing for the size of the Maezaei they probably extended as far east as the watershed between the Vrbas, and the Bosna valleys west of Jajce, possibly even taking in the Lašva valley around Travnik, where grew up the Flavian *municipium* of Bistue Nova (Han Vitez). In the first century they were ruled directly by an officer of the Roman army; an inscription from Bovianum Vetus in Central Italy records a centurion of Legion XI C.p.f. who was detached to act as *praefectus* of the two *civitates* of the Maezaei and the Daesitiates in northern Dalmatia.[5]

Two smaller peoples may be located in the mountainous area of Western

---

[1] Typical names are: *Bato, Dasius-Dassius-Dasa, Liccaius, Licco-Lica, Scenobarbus, Scenocalus, Scenus*; cf. Alföldy, *BzN*, 15 (1964), 92 ff.

[2] Appendix IV, p. 454.   [3] Vell. Pat., ii, 115.   [4] Dio, lv, 32, 4.

[5] IX 2564 (Bovianum Vetus); cf. n. 4 on p. 104. L. Trebius Exoratus, son of an early legionary veteran, was 'snatched away by Fate in the lands of the Maezaei', III, 6383 (Salona).

Bosnia to the south of the Maezaei, the Sardeates (52 *decuriae*) and the Deuri (22). The former probably dwelt west of Jajce on the northern fringes of the Ditiones in the Pliva valley around Šipovo. A place named Sarnade (or Sarute) recorded by the Itineraries probably at or near Pecka is no doubt connected with them.[1] The much smaller Deuri were probably in the upper valley of the river Vrbas, south of the gorge which begins above Jajce, in the region of Bugojno and Gornje Vakuf. This location would fit the testimony of Appian (calling them Derbani) who makes them neighbours of the Delmatae. They too may have had their name recorded in a place, Derva which is mentioned by Ravennas somewhere to the north of the Delmatae. This people is probably identical with the Derrioi mentioned by Ptolemy:[2] next to them he records the Derriopes, not mentioned by Pliny, but probably to be identified with the Deretini, a small people with 14 *decuriae* in the Narona *conventus*. They must lie to the east of the Deuri, between the Delmatae and the Daesitiates, and if the powerful Narensii extended northward into the upper Narenta Valley around Konjic, then they can be located with reasonable certainty in the Rama valley, a tributary of the Narenta, where was later established the Flavian *municipium* of Bistue Vetus (Varvara near Prozor).[3] The evidence from the personal names in all these areas suggests the presence of Pannonian peoples, among whom were the smaller peoples of the Pannonians, whom Strabo does not name but speaks of as dwelling in the country bordering the Delmatae and the Ardiaei, comprising the Sardeates, Deuri, and Deretini.[4]

Lastly among the Pannonian peoples of Northern Dalmatia were the renowned Daesitiates, whose leader Bato started the great rebellion of Illyricum in 6 and who fought so long against Tiberius and his ten legions, finally surrendering after the fall of Andetrium in 9 to spend the rest of his life in captivity at Ravenna.[5] They can be located accurately on the evidence of an imposing second-century inscription from Bréza north of Sarajevo recording T. *F(lavius)* *Valens* who was *princeps D(a)esitiati(um)*, which places them in Central Bosnia in the area of Sarajevo and the Bosna valley.[6] There is no evidence for their tribal centre but one of the roads built under P. Cornelius Dolabella from Salona into the interior led from Salona to Hedum, a stronghold of the Daesitiates (*a Salonis ad Hedum castel(lum) Daesitiatum*); and, on the ground that the road seems to be heading for Bréza, that place may be identified with *castellum*

[1] *Sarnade*, It. Ant., 269, 3, *Sarute*, Peutinger; cf. Pašalić, *Naselja*, 29.

[2] Appian, *Ill.*, 28, mentioning 'arrears of tribute'. *Derva*, Rav., iv, 19.

[3] Ptolemy's *Derriopes* is probably a confusion with the Macedonian *Deuriopes* of Strabo, vii, 7, 9; Liv., xxxix, 53; Alföldy, *Bevölkerung*, 65, n. 104.

[4] Strabo, vii, 5, 3 and Appendix XI, p. 483.   [5] Suet., *Tib.*, 20.

[6] *Sp.*, 98 (1940–8), 141, n. 10 (Bréza): T. *Fl(avius)* *Valens* *Varron(is)* f. princeps *Desitiati(um)*.

Hedum.[1] To the north they probably reached as far as the provincial boundary which crossed the river Bosna at Doboj, where an auxiliary unit was stationed in the late second and early third century.[2] On the west they bordered the much more numerous Maezaei, and probably did not extend much beyond Stanecli (probably Kiseljak), an important road junction on the middle Bosna some distance above Sarajevo[3]. On the south they were probably neighbours of the Deretini in the Rama valley, while the boundary with the Narensii of the upper Narenta was doubtless on the watershed between the Narenta and the Bosna valleys. This follows the line of the mountains Bitovnja and Bjelašnica, between which runs the key road across the Ivan sedlo linking the Narenta valley with the Sarajevo area. To the east the Daesitiates probably did not reach the Drina valley, home of the Dindari: their common boundary may have run roughly north to south along the mountains Jahorina and the Romanja, not far to the east of Sarajevo.

vi *Celtic Peoples in Northeastern Dalmatia.* In the middle Drina and the western Morava valley there is a considerable quantity of epigraphic material, and the personal names are mostly of Celtic origin, a conclusion confirmed also by the presence in the same area of a large number of Celtic symbols and funeral reliefs on tombstones.[4] The Celtic element in this area extends across the provincial boundary eastward to Kosmaj and Ivanjica in Moesia Superior. It seems reasonable to follow the suggestion of G. Alföldy that these Celtic people are the western part of the Scordisci, a predominantly Celtic people noted for their ability in warfare.[5] The problem of their location and movements over a number of centuries is complicated. In the second century B.C. they were spread over most of what is now Northern Serbia, and Strabo speaks of two groups of the people at this time: the 'Greater Scordisci' in the west dwelt between the river Noaros (probably the Drina) and the Margos (Morava).[6] The attacks which the Scordisci suffered from the Romans and later the Dacians under Burebista (*c.* 60–50 B.C.) seem to have affected only the 'Lesser Scordisci' who dwelt further to the east beyond the Morava between the Illyrians and the Thracians.[7] Probably in 15 B.C. the Scordisci were brought into alliance with Rome, either by fighting or by diplomacy, and gave aid to Tiberius during his conquest of the Pannonian Breuci three years later.[8] Pliny does not locate the Scordisci in

---

[1] Appendix IV, p. 453.   [2] III, 14619 (12759).   [3] Pašalić, *Naselja*, 51.

[4] Typical names are: *Aioia, Andetia, Baeta, Bidna, Catta, Dussona, Enena, Iaca, Madussa, Matisa, Nindia, Sarnus, Seius, Totia*; cf. Alföldy, *BžN*, 15 (1964), 97. For Celtic symbols, I. Čremošnik, *JÖAI*, 44 (1959), 207 ff., *GZMS*, 12 (1957), 232 ff., and on dress, *GZMS*, 11 (1956), 111 ff.

[5] *AAnt. Hung.*, 12 (1964), 107–27.   [6] Strabo, vii, 5, 12; cf. vii, 5, 2.

[7] Strabo, vii, 3, 11, recording Dacian attacks on 'Celts intermingled with Illyrians and Thracians'; cf. Patsch, *Beiträge*, V/1, 42 ff.

[8] *AAnt. Hung.*, 13 (1965), 118 f. and above, p. 61.

Pannonia, Moesia or Dalmatia, but there is little doubt that they still dwelt south of the Save around the Morava.[1] After the organization of Illyricum, the *civitas* of the Scordisci is found in the far southeast corner of Pannonia to the north and east of Sirmium and it is clear that after the conquest of Illyricum they were sub-divided, not only by the boundaries of the three principal Danubian provinces, but also into separate *civitates* within each of those provinces.[2] That organized in Pannonia retained the original name of the people, but in Moesia they are found as the *civitas* of the Celegeri, whose centre is identifiable in the later *municipium Cel(egerorum)* at Ivanjica.[3] Those in Dalmatia were similarly organized and became the *civitas* of the Dindari, with 33 *decuriae* in the Narona *conventus*. The location of the people on the extreme northeast of Dalmatia is established by a *pri[nceps civ(itatis)] Dinda[rior(um)]* from Skelani on the river Drina, in the heart of the area with Celtic personal names and tombstone ornaments.[4] They bordered the Daesitiates in the west, probably extending as far as the Romanja and Jahorina mountains, while to the north and east they reached to the provincial boundary, that is to the river Save in the north, and the border with Moesia in the east, including the Morava valley as far as Čačak.

vii *Peoples in Eastern Dalmatia.*   By far the most difficult peoples to locate in Dalmatia are those who dwelt east of the Drina valley towards Moesia in the east and Dardania in the south. All the remaining peoples listed in the Narona *conventus* by Pliny, the Cerauni, Glinditiones, Scirtones, and Siculotae, must be located in this area. In addition there is the problem of the Pirustae, not named by Pliny, but recorded by Ptolemy in this part of the province. The main diffi-culty is the very small number of inscriptions from this part of the province, especially Northern Montenegro, the area of Novi Pazar, and Northern Albania.[5]

What evidence there is for personal names in this area, including that from the large settlements at Plevlje and Prijepolje, presents a considerable contrast to the Celtic population of the Drina and Morava Valleys, who have been identified with the Dindari, a Roman subdivision of the Scordisci. Some Celtic names are found at Plevlje and Prijepolje, and Celtic influence can be seen on tombstones.[6]

[1] Plin., *HN*, iii, 148, on the Mons Claudius: 'in front of it are the Scordisci, beyond are the Taurisci', that is looking from the Macedonian side.
[2] Ptol., ii, 15, 2; cf. A. Mócsy, *Historia*, 6 (1957), 488 ff.
[3] F. Papazoglu, *ŽA*, 7 (1957), 114; Alföldy, *AAnt. Hung.*, 12 (1964), 122 f.
[4] *WMBH*, 11 (1909), 156, fig. 66; (Skelani): *P. A[elius . . .] pri[nceps civ.]Dinda[rior. . . .]*
[5] Until recent years virtually no archaeological work had been conducted in these areas, apart from occasional visits by Evans, Patsch, and Vulić.
[6] Celtic names include: *Arvus, Belzeius, Cambrius-Cambrianus, Iaritus, Lartus, Madussa*; Alföldy, *BzN*, 15 (1964), 99. On Celtic tombstone ornament, I. Čremošnik, *Tkalčičev Zbornik*, 2 (1958), 11 ff.

By far the majority of the personal names are, however, Illyrian, and there are many names typical of the 'real Illyrian' population in Southeast Dalmatia.[1]

Somewhere in this area must have dwelt the Pirustae: according to Velleius Paterculus they figured prominently as enemies of the Romans in the pacification of the interior of Dalmatia during 9. 'This campaign brought the momentous war to a successful conclusion; for the Pirustae and the Desidiates, Dalmatian tribes, who were almost unconquerable on account of the position of their strongholds in the mountains, their warlike temper, and, above all, the narrow passes in which they lived, were then at last pacified. . .' Strabo records them among peoples of the Pannonians.[2] This was clearly the first occasion when the Romans fought their way into the territory of these peoples, and the earlier recorded contacts with the Pirustae only affected the more accessible communities of this people. Although they appear among conquered peoples in the settlement of 167 B.C. as the Pirustae of the Dassaretii, who were granted *immunitas* (freedom from paying tribute) along with Taulantii and the Daorsii, these are hardly likely to be the same people which Velleius mentions in connection with the fighting in 9.[3] Some of them caused trouble among Roman allies in Illyricum in 54 B.C. but the matter was settled by Caesar without the use of troops, and their conquest 'by a single blow' by Octavianus in 33 B.C. will also have involved those groups of the Pirustae who were accessible from the Adriatic hinterland.[4] There is no need to suggest that the Pirustae as a whole have ever changed their territory between 167 B.C. and 9. They were a large people inhabiting a great mountainous region including Northern Montenegro and Southeastern Bosnia, and it was because of this that the Romans found it impracticable to organize a *civitas* of all the Pirustae. They do not, therefore, appear in Pliny's list of the Narona *conventus* in the area of which they certainly lived. On the other hand Pliny does list some *civitates* which, as happened with the Scordisci further north, had been organized out of the Pirustae: in spite of this they still appear among the peoples of Dalmatia listed by Ptolemy.[5] A large number of Dalmatians were apparently transported to the mining areas of Western Dacia in the early second century A.D., and one of the wax tablets discovered there attests a *vicus Pirustar(um)* at Alburnus Maior, a mining settlement under the administration of an imperial procurator.[6] Another wax tablet records

---

[1] For instance, *Carvanius, Germanus, Larianus, Panto, Pinsus, Pladomenus, Stataria, Testo, Titto, Tritano, Turo-Turus, Vendo, Verzaius,* Alföldy, *BzN,* 15 (1964), 99 f. Similar names are also widespread in the lands of the Dassaretii in northern Albania, R. Katačić, *ŽA,* 12 (1962), 95 ff.
[2] Vell. Pat., ii, 115; cf. Strabo, vii, 5, 3, and above, p. 168.   [3] Liv., xlv, 26.
[4] Caes., *BG,* v, 1, 5 ff.; Appian, *Ill.,* 16.   [5] Ptol., ii, 16, 5.
[6] C. Daicoviciu, *Dacia,* 2 (1958), 259 ff; *vicus Pirustarum*: CIL, III, p. 944 f., tab. viii.

Dasius Verzonis Pirusta ex k(astello) Aviereti(o).[1] There seems little doubt that a substantial proportion of the Dalmatian settlers in the area were from the Pirustae. The fact that they went there as miners points to the Pirustae having lived in the mountainous part of Eastern Bosnia and Northern Montenegro, especially the area of Plevlje.[2] As has been mentioned the Pirustae do not appear in the official schedule of the Narona *conventus* but at least part of them were the powerful Scirtari, a *civitas* with 72 *decuriae* recorded by Pliny. In Ptolemy they appear as the Skirtones, and he places them near to Macedonia,[3] where they can be located in northern Albania beyond Scodra and the Illyrii 'properly named'. A man who had received citizenship after service in the Ravenna Fleet in 152 describes himself as *Scirt(arius) ex Dalmat(ia)*; significantly he has the name Annaeus, very common in Southeast Dalmatia.[4] The Ceraunii (24 *decuriae*) cannot be placed with any precision but their name suggests people who dwelt in mountainous country and they most probably inhabited the area north of the Scirtari in the upper Lim and Tara valleys. Their name is not Illyrian, and most probably is one chosen by the Romans when they organized this *civitas* out of part of the Pirustae.[5] The location of the Siculotae (24 *decuriae*) may, as G. Alföldy has suggested be the large settlement at Plevlje in the Čehotina valley east of Foča, but there are good reasons for rejecting his reconstruction of the later city as the *municipium Aurelium S[icu]lo(tarum)*: a far better reading is *S[p]lo(nistarum)*.[6] These three *civitates* were organized by the Roman government out of the Pirustae, as Alfoldy has suggested; none of them is recorded, either as a tribal name or anything else, before the list of Pliny. It is possible they were still known collectively as the *civitates Pirustarum,* implied by Ptolemy's record of them in Dalmatia, but the expansion of the inscription of a local worthy at Plevlje to *[praef(ectus)] civitatium [Pirustaru]m,* meaning the Siculotae, Ceraunii and Scirtones, must remain problematical.[7]

The Pirustae are called Pannonian by Strabo, and they were presumably among the Pannonian peoples who, according to Appian, bordered on the

[1] III, p. 936 (sale of girl slave), tab. vi; Daicoviciu, op. cit., 263, rejects the earlier reading *Kavieretium*.

[2] 'Mercury the silver worker' (*Mercurius argenti actor*), *VHAD*, 15 (1928), 37 f.

[3] Ptol, ii, 16, 6.

[4] XVI, 100, C. *Valerius Annaei f. Dasius Scirt(arius) ex Dalmat(ia)*.

[5] The name comes from *Keraunos* (thunderbolt) and was commonly applied to high mountain ranges struck by lightning.

[6] Alföldy, *AAnt. Hung.*, 10 (1962), 3 ff., but against, J. Wilkes, *AAnt. Hung.*, 13 (1965), 111 ff. and below, p. 282.

[7] III, 8308 (Kolovrat): P. *Ael(ius) Pladome[nus] Caravantius [praef.] civitatium [Pirustaru]m,* proposed by Alföldy, *Bevölkerung*, 66, n. 134.

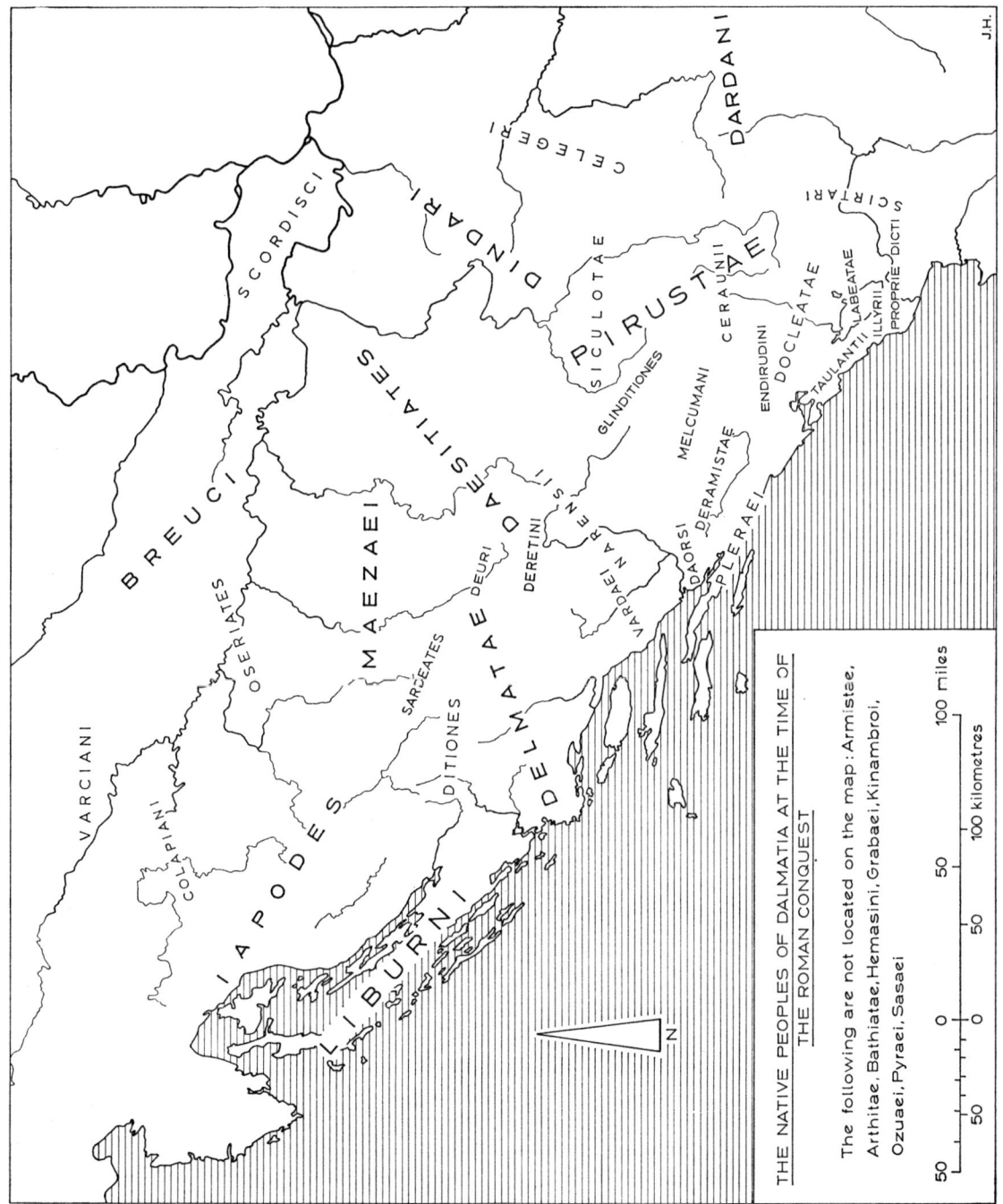

Figure 5 The Native Peoples of Dalmatia

Dardanians.[1] This is supported by the evidence from personal names. Apart from strong Illyrian influence from the neighbouring peoples in Southeast Dalmatia, a Celtic element among the names is probably due to contacts with the Scordisci, or possibly with the Autariatae who may once have been their neighbours.[2] The names found in and around the settlement at Plevlje as studied by Alföldy are similar in origin and their form to those found among the Delmatae south of the Dinaric Alps in the region of Salona.[3] The coincidence is so strong as to suggest a transfer of Delmatae from their own territory to land which had been devastated by the attack on the Pirustae in 9. Such movements may have been necessary to provide land for the new military stations at Tilurium and Andetrium; possibly the Ardiaei were also involved, since they will have lost some of their territory in the establishment of the auxiliary regiments at Bigeste. These settlements were made probably before the movement of Pirustae to Western Dacia after its conquest by Trajan. The name Siculotae, which was probably the name of the *civitas* at Plevlje formed out of the Pirustae, may derive from Siculi (Biač), a place in the territory of Salona where Claudius settled veterans early in his reign.[4]

Finally the Glinditiones, who appear to have submitted, although not without some opposition, to Octavianus in 33 B.C., may have dwelt to the west of Plevlje around Foča in the upper Drina valley. They appear in the list of the Narona *conventus* with 43 *decuriae*. There is no need to suggest any link with the Ditiones far away in Western Bosnia.[5] Although there is very little epigraphic evidence it seems probable that they also belonged to the Pannonian peoples in the north of the province, referred to but not actually named by Strabo as dwelling in the area approaching the Ardiaei further south.

In concluding this study of the political and ethnic geography of the province one may note the boundaries of the three *conventus* into which the administration and the judicial system of the province was divided, and which were based on the three centres of Scardona, Salona, and Narona. The boundary between the Scardona and the Salona *conventus* was that between the Iapodes and the Maezaei, and further south that between the Liburni and the Delmatae. The line will have run northward from the northern boundary of the province near Prijedor and

[1] Strabo, vii, 5, 3.

[2] Southeastern names include: *Annaius, Plares*. Celtic names: *Arvus, Belzeius, Cambrius, Iaritus, Lautus, Madussa, ?Augurianus*. Thracian names: *Bessus, Teres*. Alföldy, *BzN*, 15 (1964), 98 ff.

[3] *Carvanius, Germanus, Lavianus, Panto, Pinsus, Pladomenus, Stataria, Testo, Titto, Tritano, Turo, Vendo, Verzaiius*. The formula of personal names in the area is also similar to that among the Delmatae; Alföldy, *BzN*, 15 (1964), 100.

[4] Plin., *HN*, iii, 141, and p. 114.

[5] A connection was suggested by E. Swoboda, *Octavian* etc., 70 f.

then perhaps southwards up the Sana valley to the boundary between the Iapodes and the Ditiones, around the Strmica pass. South of the mountains it followed the river Titius to the neighbourhood of its mouth, where the Liburnians still retained territory on the left bank of the river. The line between the Salona and the Narona *conventus* is not as certain. In the north it followed the border between the Maezaei and the Daesitiates, the watershed between the Vrbas and the Bosna valleys. From there it followed the great mountain masses between the Vrbas and the Narenta valleys, Vranjica, Čvrsnica, and Čabulja. South of there it followed the boundary between the Delmatae and the Ardiaei east of Novae to reach the sea somewhere in the area of Makarska.

II *Society and Economy*

Although there are numerous references to the peoples of Dalmatia in ancient literature, often with valuable details of information, it is possible to construct only a vague and incomplete picture of their society and economy at the time of their final conquest by the Romans. The information that is available comes from writers of different periods, beginning with Hecataeus in the sixth century B.C. and ending with the Elder Pliny in the middle of the first century A.D. Moreover, much of the evidence which they preserve is only incidental to a narrative of Roman campaigns. For example it is difficult to paint a clear picture of Ardiaean piracy in its social and economic context, although there is abundant evidence of where and when it took place. They were not a people remote from the Ancient World, like the Britons or the Indians, about whom explorers' tales would circulate and be copied. They were known as a people who dwelt in a mountainous area bordering on Greece, renowned as drinkers and warriors, who acquired great unpopularity from their seaborne plundering expeditions.[1] There are few first-hand accounts of the peoples in the area from anyone who actually travelled

[1] In 423 B.C. they were treacherous allies of the Macedonian Perdiccas, Thuc., iv, 125, 1, but normally they were respected as allies or foes, Plut., *Philop.*, vi, 1; Lucian, *dial. mort.*, 14, 2. Agron's campaigns were regarded widely as savage, Pol., ii, 3, 2, and the reputation of the Illyrians was soon widespread, Cic., *ad fam.*, xi, 3: 'semper enim habiti sunt bellicosi'; cf. Tibull., iv, 1 (*Paneg. Messal.*), 107 ff: 'fortis Iapydiae miles'; cf. Liv., x, 2, 4. On the realm of Gentius, Liv., xlv, 43, 4: 'terra marique ferox gens'; cf. Strabo, vii, 5, 4, calling the Iapodes 'war-mad' (*areimanioi*), Vell. Pat., ii, 114: 'ingeniorum ferocia, mira etiam pugnandi scientia', Lucan, *Phars.*, iv, 406: 'bellax gens Curictum'; iv, 530, 'pugnaces Liburni'; Florus, ii, 25, 10: 'in latrocinia promptissimi' of the Delmatae. Another characteristic was their excessive drinking, Theopompus, frg. 40 (*FrGH*, 2 B, p. 543). A much more favourable view was held by the fourth century B.C. Greeks; cf. Pseudo-Scymnus, 422 ff.: 'they are very dutiful and also hospitable, friendly in disposition, and eager to live a most comfortable life'. This chapter owes much to the study of Alföldy, *Bp. Annales*, 4 (1962), 17–26.

there and met them, apart from valuable passages by the scholar Terentius Varro, who may have served there as an officer in the Roman army early in the first century B.C.[1] The main narrative in the *Illyrike* of Appian derives from the Memoirs of Augustus, where little is said about the peoples apart from the quality of the resistance they offered to the advancing Romans.

The great gap is the absence of archaeological evidence. Apart from one or two detailed studies of areas in Hercegovina by C. Patsch, the material remains of the Illyrians have so far told us little about their society or economy: the Delmatae behind Salona were probably the largest people in the province, but not a single site within their territory has been examined. Gradually the picture is changing, however, and in recent years Yugoslav archaeologists have begun to analyse and classify the main ethnic groups of pre-Roman Dalmatia on the basis of evidence already available in museums.[2] The distinction between the Pannonian peoples in the north and the Illyrians in the south is clearly reflected in the archaeological evidence, the former revealing close connections with the Urnfield Culture of the Save valley and further west; the communities in the south are more isolated and external contacts were through the Adriatic and the lands to the south. The Iapodes in the northwest are an identifiable group archaeologically, and their distribution can be shown on a map, but not one of their principal settlements within Dalmatia has ever been examined by excavation. In Liburnia south of the river Tedanius the evidence for the pre-Roman population is more plentiful, with the Liburnian hill-settlements in the Ravni kotari developing into Roman cities: they had already acquired walls built in the Hellenistic fashion before the Romans appeared in the area. The evidence from graves is abundant, especially from the large Liburnian cemeteries around Aenona, but exploration is still continuing there and it may be some years yet before a full picture is available.[3] The evidence to be derived from the study of personal names on tombstones will match the archaeological evidence when more detailed studies have been completed, but already the different regional groups are becoming apparent. Despite this, one must still rely on writers in the Greek and Roman World for a picture of the society of the peoples in Dalmatia at the time of the Roman conquest.

Many authors supply details about the economy of the peoples in Dalmatia. Occasionally it is possible to link some of their general observations with a specific area by consideration of geographical and climatic conditions. Except for the extreme north of the province near the Save valley, there were no large

---

[1] He mentions being in Liburnia, *RR*, ii, 10, 8, and may have served as a legate to Cosconius in 78–76 B.C., Cichorius, *RSt*, 191–3.

[2] See A. Benac, *Simpozijum* (1964).   [3] M. Abramić, *S. Donato* (1912).

areas of land within the province which were suitable for an advanced agriculture, while many areas exclude it altogether. The valleys of Bosnia were thickly forested and as one moves southwards towards the mountains the climate becomes less and less amenable. Some areas in the interior supported an alpine livestock economy, with seasonal migrations between summer and winter pastures, and this would be supplemented by hunting and fishing. South of the mountains the poljes of the Dalmatian karst do contain fertile soil, but in many areas the conservation of the annual rainfall is impossible, although Patsch has demonstrated that parts of Hercegovina were more wooded in the Roman period than they are today.[1] Some areas near the coast were favourable to agriculture, especially around Salona and on some of the larger islands, but in the north the coast suffers from the Bora, a fierce wind which blows down the Adriatic in winter and prevents the accumulation of good tillage or vegetation. In most areas harbours were good and fish are plentiful, but at no time can life on the Dalmatian coast be described in idyllic terms.[2]

Pseudo-Scymnus notes that the livestock of the Liburnians was fertile in producing offspring.[3] From the evidence in other sources it is clear that he is talking about sheep: Varro describes the society of the Liburnian shepherds in a passage that is valuable for information about their social life.[4] According to Strabo, the main settlement of the Delmatae at Delminium, destroyed by Cornelius Scipio Nasica in 155 B.C., and the surrounding area was turned into a sheep pasture. This area probably included most of the polje around Duvno where Delminium has been located, and is very suitable for rearing sheep.[5] Strabo implies that the Romans destroyed an urban centre and reduced it to the size of a small settlement while the plain surrounding it, up to then supporting a large population through agriculture, became the sheep pasture. Most of the products from the area recorded by ancient writers are those of a pastoral economy. According to the Elder Pliny the wool produced in Istria and Liburnia was not suitable for garments with a soft nap, as it was more like hair than real wool.[6] Good cheese was made in the area, and Pliny singles out that made by the Docleatae as among the finest of the alpine variety.[7] He notes also that the island of Brattia was renowned for its goats, but he says nothing of the conditions in which they existed.[8] Pigs

---

[1] Patsch, *Hercegovina*, 9 ff.

[2] Strabo, vii, 5, 10, comparing it with the less favoured east coast of Italy.

[3] 379.   [4] RR, ii, 10, 6–10.

[5] Strabo, vii, 5, 5, mentioning 'sheep pasture' (πεδίον μηλόβοτον).

[6] Plin., *HN*, viii, 191.

[7] Plin., xi, 240; cf. *Expositio Totius Mundi* 53 (*GLM*, p. 119).

[8] Plin., *HN*, iii, 152: 'capris laudata Brattia'.

were also bred in Illyricum, but for Pliny the main point of interest is that they apparently had solid hooves.[1] A reference to horse-breeding in the works of Vegetius, a writer of the fourth century A.D., probably concerns that which took place in the north of Dalmatia.[2] Horsebreeding was not, it seems, ever a major occupation in the province and the native population are not found serving in Roman auxiliary cavalry units. The origin and recruiting ground of the Illyrian cavalry units raised in the third century A.D. were either the Pannonian peoples in Northern Dalmatia or the province of Pannonia north of the Save.

Agriculture was never developed in Dalmatia as highly as it was in neighbouring areas. If the ancient sources are to be believed this was not due entirely to the nature of the terrain. About the (V)ardaei Strabo writes: 'because they pestered the sea through their piratical raids the Romans pushed them back into the interior and forced them to till the soil. But the country is rough and poor and not suited to a farming population, and therefore the tribe has been utterly ruined and in fact almost obliterated'.[3] Many peoples appear to have attempted some form of agriculture, but few were skilled at it. Again the source is Strabo: 'both (Italian and Dalmatian) seaboards in like manner are sunny and good for fruits, for the olive and the vine flourish there, except perhaps in places here and there that are utterly rugged. But in the case of the Illyrian seaboard people in earlier times made but small account of it – perhaps in part owing to their ignorance of its fertility, though mostly because of the wildness of the inhabitants and their piratical habits'. Similarly, 'the Iapodes had poor lands and the people lived on spelt or millet', while on the Pannonian peoples in Northern Dalmatia Cassius Dio writes: 'they cultivate no olives and produce no wine except to a very slight extent and a wretched quality at that, since the winter is very rigorous and occupies the greater part of the year, but they drink as well as eat both barley and millet'.[4] The general absence of the vine struck ancient writers as worthy of note: 'but the whole of the country above this (Dalmatian coast) is mountainous, cold, and subject to snows, especially in the northern part, so that there is a scarcity of the vine, not only on the mountains but also in the plains.'[5] In spite of this a large population managed to exist on the land in Dalmatia, although a bad harvest could bring disaster; for the absence of any surplus production above immediate needs meant a lack of reserves. It was not to no purpose that the Delmatae made offerings and dedicated altars to Silvanus the Harvester (*Silvanus Messor*), a cult of pre-Roman origin.[6] Hunting and fishing were clearly important sources of food, but more exotic products such as snails were enjoyed

[1] Plin., *HN*, xi, 46. [2] Vegetius, *Dig. artis Mulomed.*, iii, 6, 3.
[3] Strabo, vii, 5, 6. [4] Strabo, vii, 5, 10; cf. Dio, xlix, 36, 2.
[5] Strabo, vii, 5, 10. [6] III, 9867 (Rider); *GZMS*, 6 (1951), 51, n. 21 (Rider).

also: an Italian connoisseur who bred them for eating noted that Illyrian snails were remarkable for their size.[1]

Most communities in Dalmatia were self-reliant and there was little which they needed that they could not provide for themselves. The precious salt was often difficult for people to obtain, but within the boundaries of the later province it was available from such different areas as Southern Liburnia, the upper valley of the Narenta, and at Tuzla north of Sarajevo. In the interior there was a sufficient amount of iron ore for local needs, especially in the Sana valley, and the quantity of objects imported from any distance is very small. In the interior there was little to attract the trader, although the deposits of silver in Northern Albania may have attracted the Corinthians to settle on the east side of the Adriatic.[2] On the other hand, the Phocaeans, who were the first of the Greeks to explore the Adriatic, did not exploit their knowledge of the area and soon concentrated their energies on the tin trade with the Western Mediterranean. The gold deposits known in the interior do not appear to have been worked until after the Roman conquest.[3]

The firmest evidence for thriving trade is coinage, and there is little sign of this among the native peoples right up to the final Roman conquest. The coins produced by the Greek cities Issa and Pharos enjoyed a wide circulation among the peoples along the coast and in the immediate hinterland, as also did those of Apollonia and Epidamnus, but few ever travelled far inland.[4] Some Roman Republican issues of the first century B.C. are known from the interior, but are probably the result of Roman settlement along the coast which began about then.[5] The Illyrian kingdom produced a coinage from mints at Scodra and Lissus during the first half of the second century B.C., but after the end of the state in 168 B.C. it ceased altogether.[6] Otherwise the only native Illyrian community known to have produced its own coins were the Daorsii who lived around the lower Narenta (p. 27). Some of their issues carry the relief of a sea-going merchant ship as a reflection of their trading activity. No coinage is attested for the

[1] Plin., *HN*, ix, 173. On hunting see Patsch, *Hercegovina*, 11 f., and the relief from the Crkvina cemetery near Lisičići, *WMBH*, 4 (1896), 269, fig. 39.

[2] O. Davies, *RME*, 239.

[3] According to Florus, ii, 25, Vibius (Postumus), commander in 9 (above, p. 75), 'forced this savage people to dig the earth and melt from its veins the gold, which this otherwise most stupid of peoples seeks with such zeal and diligence that you would think they were extracting it for their own benefit'.

[4] They are found mostly in the hinterland south of the Dinaric Alps, see below, p. 395.

[5] Patsch, *Hercegovina*, 134 f.

[6] On the Illyrian coinage circulating in the south after 135 B.C. see H. Ceka (summarized in *Bibl. Class, Orient.*, 6 (1961), 4 ff.).

Delmatae, a situation which Strabo shows to have lasted up to and probably beyond the Roman conquest: 'the Dalmatians have the peculiar custom of making a redistribution of land every eighth year: and that they make no use of coined money is peculiar to them, as compared with other peoples in that part of the world, although among many other barbarian peoples it is common'.[1] The 'other peoples' mentioned by Strabo were probably the Ardiaei and the Daorsii. It is surprising that no coinage is known to have been issued by the Liburnians, but this may be due to their comparative isolation from the main trade routes of the Mediterranean, at least until the later second century B.C. In trade the Delmatae used barter and, according to Polybius, made the peoples whom they had conquered pay them tribute in cattle and corn.[2]

Whether it was due to a constant problem of overpopulation or just because they were, in spite of their excessive drinking, a hardy people toughened by a rigorous climate and country, their fighting qualities are frequently singled out for praise, culminating in Velleius' description of the last desperate resistance by the Daesitiates and the Pirustae against the Romans in 9.[3] Throughout antiquity the peoples in Dalmatia were dominated by their country's climate and physical character in the basic economy of their food production. No one praises their agriculture, but their cheese and wool were worthy of note. With such a small surplus they attracted the interest of few traders, and between the peoples themselves exchange of commodities was minimal. They could fight and defend themselves, but their isolation from the politics of the Mediterranean World sometimes cost them dear, from the time when they told a Roman consul in the middle of the second century B.C. that affairs in Illyria were 'no business of the Romans'.[4]

The type of economy which has just been described was not likely to encourage the development of large settlements, and this is confirmed by the little archaeological evidence, where few major settlements have been identified, and also by some specific statements in ancient writers. Most of the 'cities' listed along the Dalmatian coast by the early writers were not real cities but small harbours where settlements of a few families made a living by fishing and agriculture. For the interior there is a specific statement from Appian: 'Pannonia is a wooded country extending from the Iapodes to the Dardanoi (p. 168). The inhabitants do not live in cities but scattered through the country or in villages according to relationship. They have no common council and no rulers over the whole nation'. In an earlier section he records that when Octavianus advanced against the Arupini, a community of the Iapodes, 'they moved themselves from

---

[1] Strabo, vii, 5, 5; cf. D. Rendić-Miočević, *GZMS*, 6 (1951), 36.
[2] Pol., xxxii, 9, 4.   [3] P. 173.   [4] Pol., xxxii, 13.

their villages to their city (τὸ ἄστυ), and when he arrived there they fled to the woods'.[1] The city of the Arupini was an Iron Age hill-fort which probably served as a refuge for the whole population in time of emergency. It has been identified by Patsch as a defended enclosure on the Vital hills near Prozor in the northern Lika.[2] Because of its important position on the river Save at the confluence with the Colapis, the settlement at Siscia was prospering before the arrival of the Romans, while the mention of some form of political organization suggests that it may already have acquired the character of a true city.[3] The use of terms such as πόλις and ἄστυ for settlements of this kind is common among ancient writers, and among the later authors both Appian and Strabo describe the settlements of the Iapodes and Delmatae as cities.[4] In the case of Metulum, the principal centre of the Transalpine Iapodes, sufficient is known from Appian's account of the attack by Octavianus in 35 B.C., and also from Veith's identification of it with the Vinčica hill near Munjava, to show that it also was a hill-fort, albeit somewhat more elaborate than Arupium.[5] Similarly, in the case of the Delmatae, Strabo notes that they possessed as many as fifty noteworthy settlements, but only one which merited the title of city was their eponymous capital at Delminium. Their other centres at Synodion, Setovia, Ninia, and even Salona, were fortified strongholds occupied at one time or another by Roman forces. Most places which are recorded as cities in the earlier writers lay in Liburnia or in the Illyrian kingdom: Pseudo-Scylax describes all the settlements along the coast of Liburnia as 'cities',[6] while at a later date Strabo calls Scardona near the mouth of the river Titius 'a city of the Liburnians', and Appian gives the same description to Promona, a chain of fortifications linked to a main citadel on the east side of the Promona mountains (p. 54).[7] From this it is apparent that the widespread labelling of native centres in Dalmatia as cities by ancient writers does not denote a proper urban centre in the classical sense.

In the southeast, however, there may have been centres which did merit the title of city. Most writers refer to cities in the Illyrian kingdom: according to Appian, Gentius in the second century B.C. controlled more than seventy before his defeat by the Romans.[8] Referring to the same period Livy is more precise in

---

[1] Appian, *Ill.*, 22.

[2] Patsch, *Lika*, 30, 76 ff.; G. Veith, *Feldzüge*, etc., 24 f.

[3] Appian, *Ill.*, 22; cf. Strabo, iv, 6, 10, vii, 5, 2, Dio, xlix, 37, 1 f. (*polis*). On the topography, G. Veith, *Feldzüge etc.*, 50 ff. and fig. 7.

[4] Arupium, Terponus, Metulum, Delminium, Synodium, Setovia, Ninia, Salon, all native strongholds described in the writers as πόλεις.

[5] G. Veith, *Feldzüge*, 29 ff., and below, p. 350.

[6] c. 21.   [7] Appian, *Ill.*, 25.

[8] Appian, *Ill.*, 9; cf. Pol., ii, 11, 13; cf. viii, 16, 10.

his terminology: in one place he mentions cities (*urbes*), and in another he divides them into settlements (*oppida*), citadels (*arces*), and strongholds (*castella*). The most important was the royal capital Scodra, 'as it were the citadel of the whole kingdom, the most protected place of the Labeates'.[1] Appian describes it as a city also, and in the first century B.C. it was sufficiently important for it to be the agreed demarcation between the power of Octavianus and M. Antonius after the settlement at Brundisium in 40 B.C.[2] A second city lay south of Scodra at Lissus near the mouth of the Drilo, where an impressive circuit of walls protected the citadel and the harbour on the river (p. 362).[3] Both places served as mints for Gentius, and clearly were the main centres of his power.[4] Other places further north along the coast, Rhizon (Risinium), Olcinium, and Acruvium, were refuges for pirates with safe harbours, although the first two are both called cities before the Roman conquest.[5]

With the exception of Liburnia and the southeast there were no urban centres to speak of in Dalmatia at the time of the Roman conquest. Delminium of the Delmatae may have been once an embryo of city life, as may also have been Siscia among the Pannonians. Otherwise most of the centres which are mentioned were hill-fortifications, possibly the seat of local power but only occupied fully in times of emergency. Such places were the *castellum* Tariona, and the other *castella* which the Elder Pliny lists among the Delmatae, Burnum, Andetrium, and Tribulium (Tilurium), all 'famous for battles'.[6] The *castellum* Hedum (Bréza near Sarajevo) was the terminal point of one of the military roads constructed across the interior soon after the conquest.[7] The settlements of Dalmatians from the interior which were made in the gold-mining area of Western Dacia were similarly organized, to judge from records of two or three different *castella*.[8] Of the different areas within the province Liburnia probably made the greatest advances towards urbanization in the pre-Roman period: it was the first area of the Roman province to become completely urbanized and was soon thick with Augustan and Julio-Claudian foundations. By contrast city development elsewhere was a slow process, with only a few places gaining city status under the Flavian emperors.

The society of the Dalmatian peoples was linked closely to the physical conditions in which they lived, that is in rural communities rather than urban

[1] Liv., xliv, 30 f.; cf. xlv, 26. [2] Appian, *BC*, v, 65.
[3] Praschniker-Schober, 8 ff. [4] J. M. F. May, *JRS*, 36 (1946), 48 ff.
[5] Above, p. 27. [6] Plin., *HN*, iii, 141 f., and n. 1, p. 92.
[7] Appendix IV, p. 453.
[8] Dacoviçiu, *Dacia*, 2 (1958), 259 ff: *k(astellum) Baridusta(rum)*; cf. *Bariduum* on Peutinger Map near Pelva (Livno), III, 1271 (Alburnus maior): *k(astellum) Ansum*, also p. 174 above, *k(astellum) Avieretium*.

centres. One may repeat the specific statement of Appian about the Pannonians in the north of the province: 'they did not live in cities (πόλεις) but scattered throughout the countryside, or in villages (κῶμαι) according to kinship (κατὰ συγγένειαν). They had no common council and no rulers over the whole nation.'[1] Also significant is the remark of Strabo about the peculiar custom among the Delmatae of redividing their land every eighth year.[2] This may have been necessary because of the nature of the lands which the Delmatae cultivated: the fertile parts of the poljes are flooded for some months in every year, and it will have been necessary to adjust the boundaries marked on the land after a certain period had elapsed. On the other hand, Appian's reference to kinship groups among the neighbouring peoples suggests that the lands were held in common ownership by related groups, and as the number of families increased within the community so provision would have to be made for them at regular intervals.

After the conquest the population was organized into *civitates* (p. 156). In Liburnia most of the people became part of new *municipia* established in the early first century A.D. (p. 193), and in the southeast many of the older native communities were absorbed into the new coastal cities (p. 164). In his lists which he copied from an official source Pliny records the number of *decuriae* into which each *civitas* was divided as an indication of its strength; they range in size from the Deretini with only 14 *decuriae* to the powerful Delmatae with 342. It seems reasonable to identify these *decuriae* with the kinship groups mentioned by Appian; the Romans found them still intact and regarded them as a practical basis for local administration. A tombstone set up near Sirmium in Pannonia attests the survival of this society: the epitaph records the deceased's ethnic origin as Amantinus (the Amantini were a people in the area), his *gens* as Undius, of the second *centuria*.[3] A first century dedication from Doclea records two of these *gentes*, both named after male ancestors, *gens Latiniana* and *Epicadiana*, and on a tombstone from the territory of the Daesitiates a man is described as member of a *gens* (*gentilis*).[4] In Liburnia there is recorded a kinship group (*cognatio*), where the descent passed through the female line.[5] In other areas traces of these groups survive in the name-forms of the native population on tombstones of the early Roman period, especially among the Liburni, Iapodes, and the Delmatae.

[1] Appian, *Ill.*, 22.   [2] Strabo, vii, 5, 5.
[3] III, 3224 (Putince near Sirmium). He was drowned in the river at Emona more than four hundred miles away. On the Amantini, Mócsy, *Pannonia*, 76.
[4] III, 14601 (Doclea): *Dis m. sacr. genti Latinianae et Epicadianae*; *Sp.*, 88 (1938), 160, n. 10 (Turbe): [F]*l.* [N]*epos gentilis*.
[5] P. 187, note 1.

In contrast to the simple patronymic formula (personal name with the name of father in the genitive) a native family name appears between the personal name and the patronym. Such names are not widespread, and on most tombstones the simple two-name form is found. This probably reflects the gradual disappearance of the kinship groups, partly as a result of the urbanization in the interior which was continuous after the late first century A.D.[1]

Within the kinship groups were the families, the basis of which was monogamous marriage. There is only one recorded instance of polygamy, in the third century B.C. when king Agron had two wives, Teuta and Triteuta,[2] but the last Illyrian ruler Gentius was married to one woman only.[3] The society of the Liburnians possessed some interesting features which attracted the interest of ancient writers. Pseudo-Scylax records that the Liburnians were ruled by women (γυναικοκρατοῦνται). These were the wives of free men, but they also cohabited with their own slaves and the men of neighbouring districts.[4] This may be a simplification of their society described in more detail by Varro in the first century B.C., when he refers to the sexual freedom of unmarried women in the context of a pastoral society.[5] Another writer who described the Liburnia society is Nicolaus of Damascus: 'the Liburnians have their women in common, and bring up their children all together until they are five years old. Then at eight years old they match up the children to the men and allot one to each on the resemblance to his father. When he has taken a child he brings him up as his own son.'[6]

The family was the small family, comprising the father and mother, and the children. Many examples are set out in full on Roman tombstones, as in the case of a man and his wife who appear with their five children at Visoko in the territory of the Daesitiates.[7]

On tombstones in Liburnia groups of families who shared a common ancestor are attested living together in areas where common cultivation of the land was desirable. From this there developed a common dwelling, with a religious and

[1] D. Rendić-Miočević, *AI*, 2 (1956), 39–51.   [2] Dio, xii, 53, 1.
[3] Liv., xlv, 43: 'Gentius rex cum coniuge (Etleva) et liberis.'
[4] c. 21.   [5] *RR*, ii, 10, 9.
[6] Nic. Dam., frg. 103d (*FGrH*, 2 A, p. 384); cf. Alföldy, *AAnt. Hung.*, 9 (1961), 307 ff.
[7] *Sp.*, 77 (1934), 40, n. 16 (Visoko).

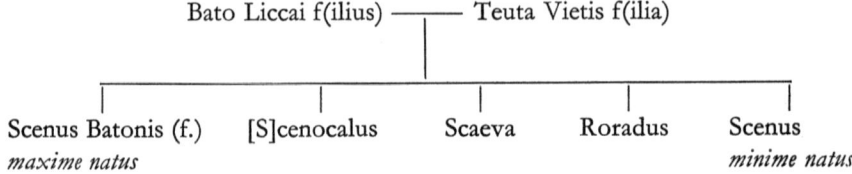

Bato Liccai f(ilius) ——— Teuta Vietis f(ilia)

| Scenus Batonis (f.) | [S]cenocalus | Scaeva | Roradus | Scenus |
| *maxime natus* | | | | *minime natus* |

burial association, comparable to the southern Slav zadruga where groups of families dwelt together on the land in kinship settlements. The Roman name for this group in Liburnia was *cognatio*, and a tombstone from near Varvaria records a *cognatio Nantania*.[1] From this and the information provided by Pseudo-Scylax and Nicolaus of Damascus one can recognize in Liburnia the large family group, where members of the kinship were related through the female line to a common grandmother or great-grandmother. In Roman law *cognatio* denotes relatives on the female side as opposed to *agnati*, relatives on the male side.[2]

The economic background to this society was also piracy, an activity for which the Liburni were renowned in their fast warships (*liburnae*).[3] The comparative sexual freedom enjoyed by the women was part of the life of a community organized for piracy. When the men were absent overseas the women perform a larger role in the economy at home, a state of affairs which Varro describes in the pastoral society of the Liburnians.[4] The leading position of women among the Liburnians is matched further south among the Ardiaei, to judge from some remarks of the historian Theopompus, who wrote in the fourth century B.C., which are preserved in the compilation of Athenaeus: 'the Illyrians dine and drink seated, and even bring their women to banquets; and it is good form for them to drink up to the health of anyone who might be near them. They conduct their husbands home from drinking sessions. The men all live hard lives, and when they are drinking they gird their bellies with wide belts. This they do reasonably loosely at first, but when the drinking becomes more intense they pull their belts in more and more tightly'.[5] The Liburnians were aware of the privileged position their women held among them. A tradition recorded by Servius (the commentator on Virgil) that they believed themselves to be descended from Amazons was probably a local legend, rather than something imported later from outside.[6]

Above the family and the kinship group was the tribe. None of these appears ever to have been anything more than the loosest confederation of scattered communities. There is little evidence for how the individual tribes depicted and maintained their ethnic unity, although some similar pattern of subsistence, social and cultural life was obviously the most important factor. The Iapodes had their national shrine at the spring of *Bindus Neptunus* near Bihać in the

---

[1] D. Rendić-Miočević, *ŽA*, 10 (1960), 165 ff.: '*Marti sac. Turus Longini f. dec. et sacerdotalis pro suis et cognation(e) Nantania de suo (f.) v. s. l. m.*; cf. Alföldy, *AAnt*, 11 (1963), 81.
[2] Gaius *Inst.*, i, 156; Dig., xxxviii, 10, 4.
[3] Note 6 on p. 160.   [4] Varro, *RR*, ii, 9.
[5] Theopompus, frg. 39 (*FGrH*, 2 B, p. 543 = Athenaeus, x, 60).
[6] Servius, *Comm. ad Aeneid.*, i, 243; cf. Alföldy, *AAnt*, 9 (1961), 317 f.

Una valley, and the *principes* of the people continued to make dedications there until the end of the first century.[1] Other peoples may have preserved the tradition of a common descent: there is the Liburnian legend of their descent from the Amazons, while Hecataeus records that they stemmed from an eponymous ancestor Liburnos.[2] Apart from this, it is only on a few occasions, mainly in the time of gravest emergency, that we hear of peoples acting in concert or forming themselves into more powerful political organizations. Sometimes the tribal name was a collective description for a number of quite separate peoples: thus Appian and Strabo list a number of different peoples under the heading of Pannonians. On the other hand some writers record as separate peoples groups which were clearly only individual communities of the larger well-known peoples: in some instances such communities can be connected with places named in the territories of the later *civitates* (p. 154 f). Most remarkable was the failure of the Iapodes to organize any effective resistance against Octavianus in 35 B.C., when the Roman attempted the hazardous march from the coast of Liburnia to the Save valley through the middle of their territory. Only at Metulum, the chief stronghold of the Transalpine Iapodes, was there a gathering of the tribal elders in a council chamber ($\beta o \nu \lambda \epsilon \nu \tau \acute{\eta} \rho \iota o \nu$) at the place which both Appian and Cassius Dio call their capital.[3] To the same extent Delminium was the capital of the Delmatae, although it does not seem to have been replaced by any other stronghold after it was destroyed in 155 B.C. In an emergency there could be leadership: the actions of the two Batos and Pinnes at the outbreak of the great uprising in 6 show that large forces from the Pannonian peoples could be deployed in a scheme of strategy. On a smaller scale Verzo led the united forces of the Delmatae against Octavianus in 34 B.C., but after the defeat at Promona he ordered his troops to scatter to their homes throughout the country.[4]

In the southeast there is evidence for a more advanced political development, due largely to the closer contacts with Macedonia and Greece. In earlier centuries monarchies existed among the Enchelei and the Taulantii in areas which were later to become part of Roman Macedonia.[5] There the central authority was the king ($\beta a \sigma \iota \lambda \acute{\epsilon} \nu s$). The only instance of this within the area of Dalmatia is among the Ardiaei, where a central authority controlled the population and the resources of the coast and hinterland between the Narenta and the Drilo rivers. Here a tribal structure was superseded long before the Romans entered the area,

---

[1] Note 4 on p. 158.　　[2] Frg. 93 (*FGrH*, 1, p. 20).
[3] Appian, *Ill.*, 21; cf. Dio, xliv, 35, 2.
[4] Appian, *Ill.*, 25; cf. p. 54 above.
[5] Pseudo-Scymnus, 420 ff.; cf. Zippel, 12 ff.

and it took place without any great development towards urbanization. The monarchy which arose from the Ardiaei controlled not only that people but others in the area which they had conquered. According to Theopompus they held three hundred thousand people in the condition of helots.[1] The Ardiaean background of the monarchy lessened and all the later writers (Polybius, Livy, Appian, and Cassius Dio) invariably refer to them as Illyrian rulers and to their territory as Illyria. There is a marked difference in social structure between the southeast and the remainder of the province. Among the Ardiaei the king was the sole ruler, and his residence was the capital. He was the supreme authority in peacetime and commanded the army and navy in war, and all foreign policy and treaties were arranged by him. Most of the population he controlled lived in rural settlements and paid him a tribute from which he was able to accumulate a substantial treasure, which fell as a prize to the Romans in 168 B.C.[2]

Alongside the family and person of the king there was an aristocracy. On different occasions Livy refers to *principes* (the same term which appears elsewhere in Dalmatia in the Roman period) and in one instance mentions *nobiles*: Polybius calls the same class potentates (δυνάσται).[3] The relationship between this class and the king is not attested, but they were probably the traditional tribal aristocracy drawn from the chief families of the kinship groups. The Romans removed the king but left their power intact. When the praetor L. Anicius wished to announce the settlement imposed on Illyria after the removal of Gentius he summoned all the *principes* from different parts of the kingdom in order to hold an assembly (*conventus*).[4] With the increasing centralization of political power in the kingdom the role of this class in politics increased, and their separation from the remainder of the population reflects a weakening of the rural kinship organization. The aristocracy of the Ardiaean kingdom, from which men such as Scerdilaidas and Demetrius arose to take over power from the dynasty of Agron as clients of the Romans, is the only class of this type clearly distinguished by the ancient writers among the peoples of Dalmatia. Appian's reference to the council of war at Metulum reveals a gathering of the chief men from the outlying communities of the Iapodes in a time of crisis. At Siscia Appian refers to two classes, the rulers (πρωτεύοντες) and the people (δῆμος). On the approach of the Roman army there was a clash between them, with the leading group wishing to come to terms and the latter wishing

---

[1] Frg. 40 (*FGrH*, 2 B, p. 543).

[2] Tribute: Liv., xlv, 18, xliii, 26; cf. Eutrop., iv, 7, 3. Fortune: Liv., xlv, 43: '27 pounds of gold, 19 of silver, 30,000 denarii, 120,000 Illyrian coins.'

[3] Liv., xxxi, 28; xliv, 31, etc.; cf. Pol., v, 4, 3; cf. iii, 18, 1.

[4] Liv., xlv, 26.

to fight: it is significant that the latter party prevailed.[1] Nothing more is known about this organization at Siscia, but the rulers were clearly quite different from the specially chosen war leaders among the Delmatae and similar peoples. It was always the policy of the Romans to encourage and sustain the power of such tribal aristocracies, to whom much of the task of administering the less developed areas of the province could be entrusted. In almost every instance it was among this class that the first signs of romanization and the classical way of life appear. The grant of citizenship to one of the *principes* of the Iapodes is a sign of such development.[2]

At the other end of the social scale there is evidence for the emergence of depressed classes, and in one instance, of slavery. Theopompus states that the Ardiaei: 'owned three hundred thousand bondsmen ($\pi\rho\sigma\sigma\pi\epsilon\lambda\alpha\tau\eta s$, a Greek equivalent for the Roman *cliens*) as helots'.[3] These were presumably conquered peoples from neighbouring districts employed as forced labour on the land. With a well-developed system of piracy slavery may be expected. According to Polybius queen Teuta brought back slaves to Illyria after her plundering expeditions against Greece.[4] Pseudo-Scylax mentions slavery among the Liburnians (p. 186), and this may also have been the result of organized piracy. Slavery in the Roman province, confined mostly to the coastal cities dominated by settler families of Italian origin, appears in a totally different social context.[5]

From this survey of the society of the peoples of Dalmatia clear differences emerge between the various areas of the province, each with its own pattern of development. In the southeast the tribal system had been superseded by a monarchy which supervised an organized form of naval warfare. The aristocracy became more clearly distinguished from the rest of the population: external land conquests brought a form of serfdom, piracy brought slavery. Among the Liburnians, where tribal society lasted in places into the Roman period, organized piracy was also important and may have provided slaves, but there was little trading with other areas and no political development comparable to that among the Ardiaei. Elsewhere the majority of the native population remained in a tribal society up to, and in many areas long after, the Roman conquest. External contacts were few, and there was an almost total preoccupation with food production, especially livestock. There was little political development and apart from the choosing of war-leaders in time of emergency there was never an

[1] Appian, *Ill.*, 23, and p. 52.
[2] III, 14324.
[3] P. 187, note 5.
[4] Pol., ii, 6, 6; iii, 8, 2.
[5] Alföldy, *A Ant. Hung.*, 9 (1961), 121 ff.

overall political authority. The elders of individual settlements ruled the community but only on a few occasions did they behave as a class or stand apart from the rest of the population. A distinction between rulers and peoples is attested at Siscia, but this is an exception, and no comparable centre is known in the first century B.C. for the Delmatae, the Iapodes, or for the Pannonian peoples included later in Northern Dalmatia.

Chapter 9

The Cities of the Province: Liburnia

For most inhabitants of the Empire the authority which controlled their lives was centred in the local city. In the eastern provinces this would be a Greek *polis*: in the West it would be a Roman colony or *municipium*, or a native tribe whose administration had been organized as a city (*civitas*). For the upper classes in the Greco-Roman World, to live in a city, or at least to take an active role in the life of one, was essential for a person who considered himself civilized. The rule of kings and tribal institutions was a thing of the past and existed only among barbarian peoples outside the limits of the Empire. In the East the process of urbanization was far advanced long before the Romans appeared on the scene. The Seleucids in Syria and the Ptolemies in Egypt, both heirs to the empire of Alexander the Great, relied heavily upon the Greek cities in their areas for administering their realms, while wars between the Hellenistic kingdoms usually took the form of struggles for possession of the Greek cities in the Aegean, Asia Minor, and Southern Syria. Settlement in the many new foundations of these rulers was attractive to the inhabitants of depressed and overpopulated Greece. In the Roman West some areas were rapidly urbanized, Southern Spain (Baetica), North Africa, and Southern Gaul (Narbonensis), on the foundations of existing communities reinforced by large numbers of Italian settlers. These provincial *coloniae* and *municipia*, with their mixed populations, prospered; by the middle of the first century A.D. they were providing many senior army officers and administrators for the emperor's service. Soon they rose much higher: the emperors Trajan and Hadrian came from colonial families of Southern Spain, and Antoninus Pius, Hadrian's successor, belonged to a family which originated at Nemausus (Nîmes) in Gallia Narbonensis.[1]

[1] R. Syme, *CE*, 1-23.

In the province of Dalmatia Greek settlements of any size were confined to the islands, and hardly provided a foundation for the later Roman cities. All the known Greek cities were absorbed in the territories of Caesarian and Augustan colonies. Away from the coast urban settlements had already developed in Liburnia, and this was almost totally untouched by Greek settlement. There the closest ties were with Istria to the northwest and with the east coast of Italy. Within the province the cities fall into three groups clearly differentiated both by geography and by the date of their foundation. By the end of the Julio–Claudian period Liburnia was almost completely urbanized, as also was the littoral between Liburnia and Macedonia. In the Ardiaean kingdom, where the monarchy had led to the growth of a few urban centres, few cities flourished in the Roman period. In areas near the coast the native population advanced very slowly towards city life, less rapidly than the more remote peoples across the mountains in Northern and Eastern Dalmatia. Cities have never flourished in the areas between the coast and the Dinaric Alps and around the mountains of Hercegovina and Montenegro. In the interior city development, or rather the administrative organization of cities with magistrates (*IIviri iure dicundo*) and city council (*ordo*), came very late. The first foundations were not made until the Flavian period and new cities were still being organized in the early third century. In the years following the Roman conquest the native peoples were administered by officers seconded from the Roman army, usually centurions marked out for promotion, who had the title of *praefectus civitatis*. Before the end of the first century they had been supplanted by members of the native aristocracy (*principes*), who by then were judged reliable by the provincial government. These remained in control until the organization of the cities, when their traditional power was disguised by the Roman labels of city government. In some areas the growth of cities was hindered by a system of working the mineral deposits under the close supervision of imperial officials (p. 267 f), who also administered the population dwelling in the mining areas. These were situated in the Sana valley in the northwest and in the middle Drina valley around Srebrenica. It is the lack of epigraphic evidence which prevents the identification of other similar areas, though they must have existed.

1 *Northern Liburnia*

Beginning at the permanent boundary with Italy on the river Arsia the first city of Liburnia was Alvona (Labin). It lay on a neck of land between the eastern branch of the Arsia and the coast of Istria, on the karst plateau at a height of about 1,000 feet. In the pre-Roman period a trading settlement is recorded there in the writings of the geographer Artemidorus of Ephesus (second century B.C.) which list the ports of call for shipping in the area. The city itself was two miles from the coast and the harbour was at Porto Lungo, an inlet linked to Alvona by a road where remains of a Roman settlement have been discovered.[1]

By the early years of Augustus the inhabitants of Alvona, the Alutrenses, had attained exemption from tribute, and when the place became a *municipium*, or Roman chartered town, it acquired the additional grant of Italian status (*ius Italicum*).[2] It was enrolled in the voting tribe Claudia,[3] and inscriptions from the site attest magistrates as *IIviri* and *aediles*. Pliny and Ptolemy give the name of the city as Alvona, but one dedication of the third century (by the *Respublica Albonessium*) and the later geographical sources give the form Albona.[4] The original population of the city was Istrian, but with the growth of the large Roman settlements at Tergeste, Pola, and especially Aquileia, Italian families soon came to predominate. Chief among these were the Gavillii; they belonged to a leading family at Aquileia who had fought for the survival of that colony in the early second century B.C.[5] The number of native families and of non-citizens is small,[6] although native cults such as those of Iutossica and Sentona continued to flourish.[7] The presence of an epitaph of a soldier serving in Legion VIII Augusta suggests that a military post may have been maintained there, perhaps for a short time during the late first century.[8] Most of the population probably lived by agriculture, but some settlers will have been attracted by trade and the good harbour at Porto Lungo. As in many other cities of Liburnia, there is an almost total lack of evidence for the population after the early second century.

Barely five miles along the coast to the north was the next city, Flanona (Plomin) situated at the head of a sheltered inlet. In the pre-Roman period it appears to have been more important than Alvona: Artemidorus records that the gulf at the head of the Adriatic (Quarnerno) was named after Flanona, and it

---

[1] Artemidorus (Steph. Byz, s.v. Φλάνων). On the topography, A. Degrassi, *SVA*, 2, 865 ff., 907 ff.

[2] Appendix XII, p. 487 ff, for the foundation of Liburnian cities.

[3] III, 3047, 3052, 3055, 10067 (3054), 10070 (3059), 10071.

[4] *IIviri* and *aediles*: III, 3054–6; *Alvona*: Plin., *HN*, iii, 140; cf. Ptol., ii, 16, 2; *Respublica Albonessium*: III, 3049 (in 244–9); cf. *Albona* Rav., iv, 22, v, 14; Const. Porph, *DAI*, c. 30.

[5] Liv., xli, 5, 1; cf. III, 3047, 10067 (3054), 3055, 3061.

[6] *Sextus Clitici*: III, 10079; *Benigna* and *Iadestinus*; *AMSI*, 24 (1912), 247.

[7] III, 10074–6, *NS*, 1934, 113.

[8] III, 3051, and p. 116 above. The *miles* of Legion XI was probably a native of Alvona, III, 3052, and above, p. 103.

remained so in the Roman period (*sinus Flanaticus*).[1] The early history of the inhabitants, named by Pliny as the Flamonienses Vanienses, is similar to that of the Alutrenses of Alvona. Exempt from tribute early in the reign of Augustus, the place became a *municipium* under Tiberius enrolled in the voting tribe Claudia, and at the same time acquired Italian status.[2] At Flanona the native population was well established and stood up better to the effects of Italian settlement in the first century. The leading family, however, appears to have been the immigrant Aquillii, but their use of native Istrian names as *cognomina* reveals relations with the older families: this is unusual in the first century, when settler families in general reveal few links with local families and retain their character as immigrants.[3] There were close links with other cities of Istria, including those which lay within Italy. In the late second century a leading citizen of the colony Pola was appointed as imperial commissioner of the city (*curator reipublicae Flanatium*).[4] Older local cults survived, and dedications are known to Ica, Iria, Sentona, and Silvanus. A Romanized version of a local cult of Minerva (*Minerva Flanatica*) was observed also at Parentium on the other side of Istria.[5] Minerva was popular in Istria generally but the spread of the Flanona cult is an indication of the prosperity of that city. The social status of some Flanona families was high: in the late first century an Aquillius was admitted to membership of the city council at the provincial capital Salona, and was later granted a centurionate in the praetorian guard at Rome.[6] As at Alvona there are hardly any inscriptions from Flanona of the later period, although one eastern immigrant is attested.[7] Flanona only features once in imperial history: in 354 the Caesar Constantius Gallus was murdered there on the orders of Constantius II.[8]

The city at the head of the Adriatic was Tarsatica (Trsat near Rijeka). The *municipium* was enrolled in the voting tribe Sergia, and since it appears in Pliny's list of *oppida* its charter may be presumed to have been granted under Augustus.[9] The Roman city was situated on a low hill on the right bank of the river Recina, where the village Trsat perpetuates the name of the ancient city. The pre-Roman centre was in a corresponding position across the river.[10] It has been argued that the establishment of the *municipium* took place not under Augustus but later

[1] Artemidorus (n. 1 on p. 194). On the city see A. Degrassi, *SVA*, 2, 866, 895 ff.

[2] *Claudia*: *JAK*, 5 (1911), 175.

[3] *Aquillii*: 10062 (3038), 3032, 3036 f.; *NS*, 1928, 403 ff.; 1934, 5; cf. Alföldy, *Bevölkerung*, 73.

[4] *Inscr. It.*, X, 1, 88.

[5] III, 3031–2, 3034, *NS*, 1928, 405; Degrassi, *SVA*, 2, 875 ff. (*Minerva Flanatica*).

[6] III, 1940 (Salona).   [7] III, 3041.

[8] Socrates, *Hist. eccl.*, ii, 34, who calls Flanona an island; cf. Degrassi, *SVA*, 2, 896.

[9] Sergia: III, 3027; and Appendix XII below, p. 487 ff.

[10] Degrassi, *SVA*, 2, 931 ff.; cf. *Confine*, 103. Possibly in Pseudo-Scylax, above, p. 4.

under the Flavians or even Hadrian. The tombstone of a non-citizen auxiliary serving in a first cohort of Thracians at Timacum Minus (Ravna) in Moesia Superior was restored by von Premerstein to give an origo *Tarsa[tic]es(is)* and, since the stone belongs to the late first century at the earliest, Tarsatica was therefore at that time a non-Roman community (*civitas peregrina*) and the foundation of the city took place under the Flavians, as A. Degrassi, or under Hadrian, as von Premerstein himself suggested. The problem is removed by the rejection of the restoration: *Tarsa* was a Thracian name, and that area is much more likely to be the origin of a serving soldier in a cohort of Thracians.[1]

The leading family of the city was the Vettidii, two of whom are attested as magistrates (*IIviri*). They were probably immigrants from Italy.[2] Another family of similar origin was the Livii. A member of this family who had served in the praetorian guard at Rome had had his epitaph set up at Tarsatica by his freedman.[3] For religious life there is a dedication set up by a slave to the local cult Sentona.[4]

The two islands Cres and Lošinj lie in the Adriatic not far southeast of Istria and separated by a narrow channel. Together they are nearly 45 miles from north to south, although even at its widest Cres is barely 10 miles across: both islands are well supplied with harbours and areas of cultivable land. In antiquity they were called the Apsyrtides, after Absyrtus the ill-fated brother of Medea in the story of the Argonauts.[5] In the Roman period they supported two cities, Absortium (Apsorus) at Osor in the south and Crexi at Cres in the north,[6] both of which obtained the status of *municipia*. An inscription from Crexi records the building of the senate house (*curia*) with a portico under *IIviri* who held office some year during the reign of Tiberius.[7] The precise find spot is not recorded, but it is certain that it was brought to Osor in the south from some place in the north of Cres island, and the town of Cres seems the only likely place. This record suggests also that the city was founded under Tiberius, while the inclusion of Apsorus in the voting tribe Claudia suggests that the city there was also a Tiberian foundation.[8] The central position of the islands on the Adriatic shipping routes and the excellent harbours attracted traders at an early date, and Greek imports are known at Apsorus.[9]

[1] III, 14579; cf. *JÖAI*, 3 (1900), Bb. 142 and K. Kraft, *Rekrutierung*, 190, n. 1891.

[2] III, 3028 f.; cf. p. 1643, Degrassi, *SVA*, 2, 931.   [3] III, 3027.   [4] III, 3026.

[5] Plin., *HN*, iii, 151: 'also the Apsyrtides named thus by the Greeks after the brother of Medea who was killed there'; cf. Apoll. Rhod., iv, 481 f., Strabo, vii, 5, 5, also in Pseudo-Scylax, see above, p. 4.

[6] Plin., *HN*, iii, 140; cf. Ptol, ii, 16, 13.

[7] III, 3148 (Crexi); cf. III, 15102, 3138–9 (Apsorus), 3147 (Sansego).

[8] III, 3140.   [9] A. Mohorovičić, *Carnuntina* (1956), 95 ff.

Unlike Alvona or Flanona the Italian settlers never seem to have formed a dominant group in either of these cities. One of the magistrates recorded at Crexi has the Roman *gentilicium* Aemilius, but his father has the Venetic name Volso. In the first century A.D. a small detachment from one of the imperial fleets (based at Ravenna and Misenum) may have been based there.[1] The native community at Crexi prospered, and at Apsorus the number of people with the name Iulius reflects the grants of citizenship made under Augustus and Tiberius, although some of the population remained *peregrini* until the second century.[2] Italian settlement and the slavery which these families brought with them are attested.[3] For most of the population agriculture was the basis of their life, with some trade carried on mostly by the immigrant families. As at other cities in the area inscriptions later than the second century are rare, although there is archaeological evidence for building taking place in the later period at Apsorus.[4]

The island Curicta (Krk) lay in the Quarnerno between the Apsyrtides and the coast on Liburnia. The north of the island is separated from the mainland by a channel less than a mile across. Two Liburnian communities are attested there, the Curictae or Culici and the Fertinates or Foretani.[5] In the civil war between Caesar and Pompeius C. Antonius was defeated there by the Pompeians in 49 B.C.[6] An inscription from Krk which may belong to this period records the construction of a defensive wall one hundred and eleven feet long and twenty feet high under the supervision of two local *praefecti*, Turus Granp. Opia. f. and Venetus Lastimeis Hosp. f. It may have been constructed in 49 B.C. when the town was being threatened by the Pompeian fleet under L. Scribonius Libo. The prefects named may have been the quasi-municipal magistrates, or possibly officers specially appointed by Caesar to organize the defence against the Pompeians.[7] Neither the city Curicum, Krk in the south of the island, nor Fertinium, at Omišalj in the north, appear in Pliny's list of Liburnia *oppida*, although their peoples are listed by him as exempt from tribute. They were both probably enrolled in Claudia, and their Roman status may have been granted under Claudius, when they probably also received Italian status.[8] At Fertinium there is an early veteran from Legion VIII Augusta. He was a Trebius, one of the leading families in Liburnia, and he may have joined the legion during the period up to

---

[1] *MZK*, 1905, 294 ff.   [2] *Iulii*: III, 10129 (3141), 10128 (3140). *Peregrini*: III, 3144, 10140.
[3] III, 10129 (3141), 3145, *AMSI*, 30 (1918), 94 f.
[4] A. Mohorovičić, *Carnuntina* (1956), 97 f.
[5] Plin., *HN*, iii, 139; cf. Caes., *BC*, iii, 8; Ptol, ii, 16, 8.
[6] Above, p. 40 f. n. 3.
[7] III, 13295; cf. Degrassi in *ILLRP*, 2, n. 579 note.
[8] Appendix XII.

P

the middle of the first century when it was stationed at Poetovio in Pannonia.[1] There is more epigraphic evidence for the population at Curicum. Italian settlers are recorded as well as native families who received the Roman citizenship under the Julio-Claudians.[2] The magistrates of the city were *IIviri*, and a *IIvir quinquennalis* (the five-yearly magistrates who revised the citizen role in the manner of the censors at Rome), as well as members of the city council (*decuriones*), are attested.[3] Among the local families were the Liburnia Raecii, some of whom rose to membership of the Roman senate in the late second century. Another distinguished citizen was a senior army officer (*protector*) who was patron of the *splendida civitas Curictae* in the middle or late third century.[4] The upper classes of Curicum, in particular the Raecii and Trebii, had close connections with the colony Iader which was the leading city of Liburnia. Trade and manufacturing may have been carried on successfully at Curicum – there is a probable record of a slave – but there is no archaeological evidence from the site to indicate the size or character of the city.[5]

The city of Arba (Rab) lay on a small inlet near the southwest corner of the island which bears the same name, much smaller than Curictae to the north. Like the latter it was separated from the mainland by a narrow sea channel less than 2 miles across. It was given the status of *municipium* under Augustus and enrolled in the voting tribe Sergia: on one of the earliest dated records from Liburnia it is recorded that the defences of Arba were completed in 10 B.C.[6] Its Roman status may have been granted during Tiberius' first administration of Illyricum in 12–9 B.C. At the end of his first years' operations the old proconsular command of Illyricum was superseded by a large imperial command extending from the middle Danube to the Adriatic, and the creation of cities at Arba and elsewhere in Liburnia may be part of the many changes which were carried out at this time.[7]

Magistrates from settler families and from native families are recorded, including the Raecii and the Trebii, and the ruling group seems to have been a mixture of local and immigrant stock. *IIviri* and *aediles* are recorded, and also a number of dedications, probably from statue bases, were set up by the city

[1] III, 3127 (Omišalj).

[2] *Kapii*: III, 13293/a (3133) (Baška); *Lurii*: III, 13298 (Kosljun); *Pitii*: III, 3128 (Curicum). Native familes include the *Raecii*, below, p. 309, and *Oppii*: III, 3131. Enfranchised *Iulii*: III, 3130, 13279 (frgs.).

[3] III, 3128 ff., 13294 (3135).   [4] III, 3126, and below, p. 335 f.

[5] A. Mohorovičić, *Carnuntina* (1956), 95 ff.

[6] III, 10117 (3117): '(... Caesar ...) murum et turres dedit'. *Sergia*: III, 3115, 10121, 13292 (10122).

[7] Above, p. 64.

council to second- and third-century rulers.[1] Nothing is known about Arba from archaeological evidence, but a building record of the later second century provides a telling commentary on the standard of its civic amenities. On 8 November 173, at the height of the Marcomannic Wars, a freedman, C. Raecius Leo, dedicated a plaque to the Nymphs in order to commemorate a civic benefaction he had carried out on behalf of his senatorial patron, C. Raecius Rufus: he had discovered the whereabouts of a supply of fresh water which had once been known but was later forgotten.[2] Another Liburnian family were the Octavii, especially in the south at Nedinum, who also owned property on Arba.[3] Men from the city served in the army and one who joined the praetorian guard returned home after service.[4] In the later period inscriptions become rare and there is little evidence how the city fared. Foreign merchants may have been responsible for the arrival of Mithras,[5] and in the late second or early third century a man who was commissioner of the city (*curator*) dedicated an altar to the Egyptian deities Isis and Serapis at Plevlje in the interior.[6]

South of Arba lies the island Cissa (Pag) which extends for the considerable distance between Arba and the northern tip of the Ravni kotari. Near the head of one of the many inlets is the small town of Časka, where traces of an extensive Roman settlement have been discovered, and which was probably the location of Cissa, one of the *oppida* on islands listed by the Elder Pliny.[7] A dedication to *Divus Augustus* (presumably assignable to the early part of his successor Tiberius' reign) from Vlasčići was set up by L. Quinctius Gallus, an Italian immigrant whose family is to be found among the upper classes of the neighbouring cities Arba and Argyruntum.[8] A most interesting connection is revealed between Cissa and the Calpurnii Pisones, one of the leading senatorial families at Rome under Augustus and Tiberius. A dedication to the exclusive cult Bona Dea was set up at Cissa by Calpurnia, daughter of L. Piso the augur, and granddaughter of Cn. Piso.[9] The latter had fought against Caesar and later joined Brutus and Cassius: although he accepted a consulship in 23 B.C. with Augustus as a colleague he maintained a ferocious independence. His son, who inherited what Tacitus calls the inborn haughtiness of his father, died in 24 after he had been

---

[1] III, 10121, 13292, 2931 (Iader). Imperial dedications: III, 3118 (Marcus Aurelius), 3119 (Iulia Domna), 3120 (Severus), 3121; cf. 10118, p. 2712 (Severus Alexander), 3122 (Trebonianus Gallus).

[2] III, 3116. On the Raecii, see p. 332 f below.

[3] III, 13292 (10122), and below, p. 312.

[4] III, 3114; also a legionary, *JAK*, 6 (1911), 11.   [5] III, 10120.

[6] *GZMBH*, 52 (1940), 20, n. 4; cf. *Sp.*, 98 (1941–8), 287, and n. 106, p. 282, n. 5.

[7] P. Sticotti, *SH*, 179 ff.   [8] III, 3113; cf. *JÖAI*, 12 (1909), 51, III 13293 (Arba).

[9] *ŽA*, 8 (1958), 311 ff., 12 (1963) 387 ff.; cf. *Šašel*, 260.

charged with treason.[1] The family had close links, probably in the form of estates, with other parts of Liburnia and had many connections with different communities around the head of the Adriatic.[2]

Senia (Senj) lay on the mainland opposite Curicta. It possessed an excellent harbour and was one of the few places where a road passed from the coast across the Velebit mountains into the Lika polje. The Roman city was established under Augustus and is listed among the *oppida* by Pliny, but it is not certain whether it was a *colonia* or a *municipium*.[3] Two items of evidence suggest colonial status. In 70 a senator Manlius Patruitus was in exile at a *colonia Seniensis*, the normal adjective for Liburnian Senia,[4] and the latter also possessed a college of Augustales (*corpus Augustalium*), the freedman organization of the imperial cult, which in Dalmatia appears to have been confined to colonies.[5] On the other hand Pliny, who lists all the other Dalmatian colonies including the Liburnian Iader, lists Senia as an *oppidum* which, on the evidence from other places so-named in Liburnia, suggests that it was a *municipium*. A *colonia* could have been established there when it served as the base for Octavianus' operations against the Iapodes in 35 B.C.

The dominant group at Senia seems to have been composed of Italian settler families, particular from Northern Italy.[6] As a class they had wide connections: one held the priesthood of Liburnia (*sacerdos Liburnorum*) in the imperial cult at Scardona,[7] and men from the city served in the praetorian guard at Rome during the second century.[8] In the late second and third centuries new families settled there, not from Italy but from the eastern provinces, including a Jew from Tiberias in Palestine, a Greek from Nicomedia in Bithynia, and another from one of the eastern cities called Neapolis.[9] Others whose families probably originated from the East were two Augustales, both of whom were awarded honorary membership of the Senia city council, doubtless for some unrecorded acts of generosity. One of them records that he came to Senia from the colony Aequum.[10]

---

[1] Tac., *Ann.*, ii, 43; cf. vi, 21, also *PIR*², C, 286, 290.

[2] J. Šašel, *Akt. IV Int. Kong., GLE*, 363 ff. and pl. XVII.

[3] In Pseudo-Scylax, p. 4 above, Plin., *HN*, iii, 140; cf. Ptol., ii, 16, 2. On the site Patsch, *Lika*, 95 ff.

[4] Tac., *Ann.* iv; cf. Alföldy, *AAnt. Hung.*, 10 (1962), 362 f. Much more probable is the Etruscan colony Siena, Plin., *HN*, iii, 51: *colonia Seniensis*.

[5] P. 234.

[6] *Gavii*: *AI*, 2 (1956), 53; *Gessii*: III, 10056; *Verridii*: *VAHD*, 53 (1950–1), 251, fig. 1.

[7] B. Gabričević, *AI*, 2 (1956), 53: L. *Gavius Optatus sac(erdos) Liburnor(um)*.

[8] VI, 2451 (Rome), in tribe Sergia.

[9] III, 10055; cf. Patsch, *Lika*, fig. 44 (Tiberias), fig. 45 (Nicomedia), III, 3019 (Neapolis).

[10] III, 3016–17; cf. *VAHD*, 53 (1950–1), 251.

Arising from the commercial links eastern cults are known, including dedications to Serapis and Mithras.[1] The commercial importance of the city is reflected in the presence of an office of the Illyrian provinces customs area (*portorium publicum Illyrici*) in the second half of the second century. This places Senia on a level of importance with Pola, Tergeste, and Aquileia as a major port in the Adriatic. During the summer months some traffic could have passed through Senia to the interior, northward to Siscia in the Save valley.[2] Because of this commercial activity Senia enjoyed more enduring prosperity than did many other cities in the area. Except for Tarsatica (now modern Rijeka), many of these places around the Adriatic soon slipped into an obscurity from which they have never arisen. Senia went on attracting settlers, and in the third century there is a record of the rebuilding of the city baths under the governor L. Domitius Gallicanus Papinianus (239–41).[3] Excavations carried out since the last war have revealed traces of substantial buildings belonging to the Roman city, including at least one temple near the modern cathedral. Most of the remains are dated to the third and fourth centuries.[4]

Along the coast between Senia and Argyruntum were a number of lesser settlements, each with its small harbour at the foot of the near-impassable wall of the Velebit. Some became *municipia*, at a time when they were dominated by Italian settler families. The first of these was Lopsica (Sv. Juraj) less than 5 miles south of Senia. It was already known to the Greek writers of the fourth century B.C.[5] The region around Lopsica has always been an important timber-producing centre, and large quantities of pre-Roman material are known from there.[6] In the Roman period the Lopsi first of all obtained exemption from tribute and then, with the organization of the *municipium* which probably took place under Tiberius, the additional privilege of Italian status.[7] The names of only a few people who lived there are recorded: two were of native Liburnian origin and received Roman citizenship under Augustus or Tiberius, and they were related to the Liburnian Appuleii, a leading family at Aenona and Iader.[8]

Ortoplinia lay at Stinica, a small harbour settlement which lies on the narrowest part of the channel between Arba and the Liburnian mainland. Although

---

[1] III, 15092 (Serapis), Abramić, *ČZN*, 28 (1933), 148 and n. 2 below (Mithras).

[2] III, 13283; cf. p. 2328/175 (Vratnik near Melnice), a Mithraic cave dedicated by Hermes, slave of C. Antonius Rufus *praefectus vehiculorum*, and also H. Nesselhauf, *Epigraphica* 1, (1939), 337 f., dedication by slave of Ti. Iulius Alexander, both under Pius and Marcus, H-G. Pflaum, *Carrières*, 358, n. 151, 435, n. 174. On the customs posts, De Laet, *Portorium*, 180.

[3] III, 10054, and p. 449 on the governor.   [4] I. Degmedžić, *VAHD*, 53 (1950–1), 251 ff.

[5] Above, p. 4.   [6] Patsch, *Lika*, 103 f.   [7] Appendix XII.

[8] III, 3015; cf. p. 1642, Patsch, *Lika*, fig. 47. Another native commanded an auxiliary unit in the first century, III, 10052.

nothing is known about the people of the place from inscriptions, a cemetery of the Roman period had produced many coins and other small objects.[1] It is included in Pliny's list of *oppida* inhabited by Roman citizens, and it may have received the status of *municipium* from Augustus.[2] Around Ortoplinia were the Iapodes and the names of two of their communities are recorded on inscriptions. The first was found in the Begovača area, across the main ridge of the Velebit and about 10 miles along the road to Kosinj in the Lika. It records an agreement between the Ortoplini and the Parentini over access to fresh water, a precious commodity in this barren area. Kosinj was probably the centre of the Parentini, who are not otherwise recorded.[3] The other settlement was made under the Tiberian governor P. Cornelius Dolabella between the Ortoplini and the Beci. It was found at Jablanac, the next good harbour 2 miles along the coast to the south.[4] The Beci are not attested otherwise, nor is there any record on the stone of what the settlement dealt with.

Twelve miles south of Ortoplinia was Vegium (Karlobag), situated on the sea channel between the mainland and Pag. Only one inscription is recorded from there, on the bronze cremation vessel of a twenty-three-year-old city councillor, L. Sestius Silvester.[5] Nothing is known of the Roman settlement around the harbour, but a little way along the road leading south, between the hamlets Drvešica and Vidovac, some traces of a substantial and expensive Roman building were discovered, with at least three mosaic floors and a wealth of small finds. Part of a statue of an armoured figure in white marble suggests that it might have been a temple to Jupiter. None of the inscriptions fragments found could be restored to add any information, but the coins from the site commenced in the late Republic, suggesting that it was probably constructed in the first century A.D. at the latest. It was built with stamped tiles imported from Italy, and no less than six examples are unknown anywhere else in the province. Quantities of amphora which can be picked up around the town suggest that Vegium was a prosperous community, and this may be due to its road link with the southern part of the Lika polje.[6] Excavation at Vegium may well reveal a small city comparable to the well-known site at Argyruntum a few miles to the south, though not as large as Senia to the north.

The city Argyruntum (Starigrad Paklenica) near the southern end of the Velebit may have attained its status as a *municipium* under Tiberius before the

---

[1] Patsch, *Lika*, 105.   [2] Appendix XII, p. 487 ff.
[3] III, 15053; cf. Patsch, *Lika*, 22.   [4] *Rad*, 339 (1965), 134.
[5] III, 10027; cf. Patsch, *Lika*, 106, fig. 48.
[6] Patsch, *Lika*, 105 ff.; cf. fig. 49; J. Brunšmid, *VHAD*, 5 (1901) 8 ff. On the tile imports see below, p. 499 ff.

year 29, and its voting tribe was probably Claudia.[1] One of three building records dated to the reign of Tiberius records the construction of defences (*murum et turres*), probably in 34–35.[2] The earliest is a dedication to the empress Livia (Iulia Augusta, mother of Tiberius) and was almost certainly set up to her before her death in 29, by a city councillor who wished to celebrate his admission to the city council.[3] His name was C. Iulius Sulla, indicating a recently enfranchised citizen, possibly of native origin. Italian families are attested at Argyruntum, and in the late first and early second centuries men from there served in the praetorian guard.[4] The mother of such a man, who enlisted at the rather late age of 28, received her citizenship under Hadrian: new citizenship grants in the second century are almost unknown in Liburnia, and it is perhaps more likely that this family moved from the interior to Argyruntum some time in the second century.[5]

11 *Southern Liburnia* (fig. 6)

The southern part of Liburnia, between the rivers Tedanius (Žrmanja) and the Titius (Krka), was the most urbanized area in Roman Dalmatia. It comprises a plain bounded towards the interior by a southward continuation of the Velebit and the northern part of the Dinara. Its character is indicated by the modern name Ravni kotari which means 'level corner', and communications within it are easy. The coast has a number of excellent harbours and is sheltered from the worst of the Adriatic storms by the offshore islands Pag, Ugljan, and Pasman. Adjoining the coast there are areas of cultivable land which produce fruit, vine, and olive in quantity, especially in the neighbourhood of Iader. Away from the coast the inland cities of Corinium, Nedinum, Asseria, and Varvaria, were situated on a strip of fertile land between low hills which become progressively higher and more barren as one moves inland.

Aenona (Nin) lies on the coast 8 miles north of Iader at the northwestern tip of the Ravni kotari. It lies on a small island surrounded partly by the sea and partly by marshy lagoons, and is connected to the mainland by two causeways. The site is not a healthy one and until the end of the last century malaria was endemic among the population. In the pre-Roman period Aenona was already an important centre. Extensive cemeteries near the city have been known for

---

[1] Appendix XII below, p. 487 ff.

[2] *JÖAI*, 12 (1909), Bb. 49, also III, 14322; cf. *JÖAI*, 8 (1905), Bb. 57 and 60 (for the correct findspots near the same place).

[3] III, 9972; cf. *JÖAI*, 8 (1905), Bb. 57 for correct findspot.

[4] *Aufidii, Metinii*: *JÖAI*, 12 (1909), Bb. 60; *Quinctii, Turcii*: *JÖAI*, 12 (1909), Bb. 59 (frgs.).

[5] *JÖAI*, 8 (1905), Bb. 57. His grave contained a coin of Hadrian, below, p. 413.

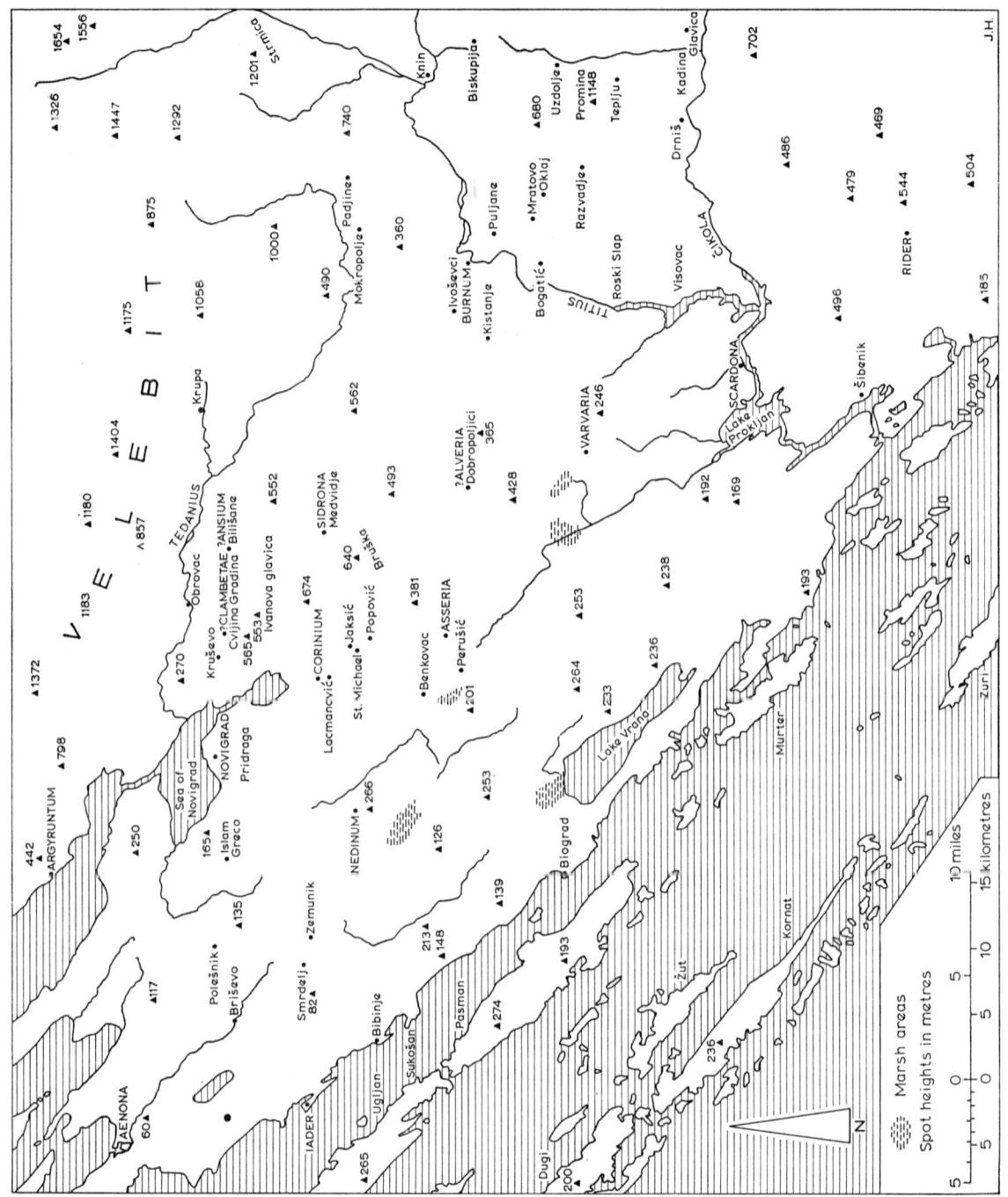

Figure 6 Southern Liburnia

many years, and when their exploration has been completed the material will provide the first substantial quantity of archaeological evidence for the society and economy of the Liburnians.[1] Unlike other native centres in the region, for example Asseria, Nedinum, and Varvaria, Aenona has not produced traces of defences or other structures belonging to the pre-Roman period, all the surviving remains on the site coming from the Roman city. Its municipal status was conferred under Augustus, apparently as early as 16 B.C. when the city council dedicated a statue of P. Silius Nerva, patron of the city, who was proconsul in Illyricum and Northern Italy during that year.[2] A later provincial governor honoured as patron of Aenona was L. Volusius Saturninus (*cos.* 3) who came to Dalmatia early under Tiberius, possibly as the successor to P. Cornelius Dolabella in 20: like many of Tiberius' provincial governors he was left in his office until the end of the reign, when he was replaced by Gaius. He is honoured at Aenona by three dedications, two of which were set up while he was still in the province and the third in the period when he was Prefect of the City under Claudius and early Nero. This office he was still holding when he died in 56 at the age of 93, having been trusted counsellor and friend of all five Julio–Claudian rulers.[3] His patronage will have been a valuable acquisition for Aenona.

The city was enrolled in the voting tribe Sergia and inscriptions attest its magistrates as *IIviri* and *aediles*.[4] Within the city there are extensive remains to be seen of some of the public buildings, built on a lavish scale. The most notable is a forum with temple (*capitolium*), where were discovered in the last century statues of Augustus and Tiberius, the latter in the robes of *pontifex*.[5] Excavators have dated the buildings to the later first century, but the evidence of the statues and early inscriptions suggests that they were some of the earliest buildings of the Augustan city. Unfortunately no complete publication of the excavations has appeared, apart from a report on the temple, and the exposure of the site for many years has caused great damage to the remains. The two causeways linking Aenona with the mainland must have required constant attention: one inscription records that a recently enfranchised Liburnian, C. Iulius Ceuni f. Curticus Aetor, paid for the reconstruction of one of them for a distance of 687 feet. This was carried out under Augustus, since a dedication to Janus Pater by the same man records his decorations received from Tiberius during the war of 6–9: in

---

[1] Aenona is recorded by Pseudo-Scylax, above, p. 4. For Liburnian cemeteries, M. Abramić, *S. Donato*, 14, 81 ff.; cf. M. Suić, *VAHD*, 55 (1953), 71 ff.

[2] III, 2973; cf. 10017 and above, p. 59.   [3] Tac., *Ann.*, xiii and p. 82.

[4] III, 2977; cf. p. 1037, 14322/4, 3158, 2969. Tribe *Sergia*: III, 14322/3, *VAHD*, 52 (1935–49), 55, fig. 1.

[5] M. Cagiano de Azevedo, *RPAA*, 22 (1948), 193 ff.; cf. *JÖAI*, 16 (1913), Bb. 109 f.

addition he was *IIvir* of the city.[1] This is clear evidence for the close relations between the native upper classes of Liburnia and the Roman government during the wars of conquest. The city upper classes of Liburnia and Southern Dalmatia had nothing in common with the aspirations of Bato and the peoples of the interior.

Many native names appear on the inscriptions from Aenona, especially in the early period and often with the *gentilicium* Iulius.[2] Other leading families include the Appuleii and the famous trading family of the Barbii from Aquileia.[3] Most of these families are also attested at Iader. The obvious prosperity of the city in the early period suggests that commerce played a larger role in the economy than in most other cities of Liburnia. Unlike Iader and other cities in the Ravni kotari, Aenona had little fertile land in its vicinity, and the centuriation of Iader's territory approaches to within three miles of it on the south. Economically, if not constitutionally, Aenona seems to have been little better than a village on the territory of the colony. After the middle of the second century the number of inscriptions decreases: two members of the freedman priesthood (*IIIIIIviri Augustales*) are attested, and presumably belong to the organization at Iader, since in Dalmatia the institution is attested in colonies only.[4] With later immigrants from the eastern provinces foreign cults reached Aenona, including Isis and Sabazios.[5]

Eight miles south of Aenona a small tongue of land extends northward parallel with the coast into the 3 mile sea channel between the mainland and the island of Ugljan. This was the site of the colony Iader, a city second only to the provincial capital Salona. Between the peninsula on which the city was built and the mainland is a good harbour. Before the Roman period the place was an important Liburnian settlement, attested by numerous finds of the pre-Roman period. The people were the Iadertini who supported Caesar against Pompey, and by a loan of ships they helped one of Caesar's generals to achieve a victory over the Pompeian fleet. The author of the *Bellum Alexandrinum* praises them for their sterling loyalty to the 'Roman Republic'.[6]

---

[1] *VAHD*, 52 (1935–49), 55, fig. 1; cf. III, 3158, probably the same man.

[2] *Iulii*: III, 3158; *VAHD*, 54 (1953), 208 (3 ex.), *id.* 52 (1935–49), 55; III, 14322/10; *RPAA*, 22, (1948), 198; III, 14322/11.

[3] *Appuleii*: NS, 1936, 481, III, 2977, 14010; *Barbii*: III, 2979. For other Italian families, Alföldy, *Bevölkerung*, 77.

[4] III, 2103; cf. Noll, n. 262, III, 10018 (2978). Both families, *Vettii* and *Tullii*, were well-established in Iader.

[5] *KSp.*, 22 (Sabazios); *VAHD*, 53 (1950–1), 233.

[6] *Bell. Alex.*, 42, see above, p. 41. On Liburnian Iader, B. Ilakovac, *Zbornik*, 2 (1958), 1 ff.; *Radovi*, 4–5 (1959), 466.

At this period settlers from Italy had already begun to arrive at Iader, and before the end of the Republic there may have existed a community of Roman citizens (*conventus civium Romanorum*), of the type out of which the other colonies in Dalmatia are known to have developed. In 35 B.C. Octavianus destroyed the sea-power of the Liburnians, and in his Illyrian campaigns Iader may have served as one of his bases.[1] In 33 B.C. or not long afterwards a colony was established there enrolled in the voting tribe Sergia: there is no reason to believe that it was established before that date, for instance under Caesar. On two inscriptions, neither of which is dated, which record the construction of the colony's defences Augustus is described as 'father of the colony' (*parens coloniae*).[2] The unique record of a *VIvir Iulialis* does not suggest an earlier link with Caesar: more probably it was a general honour for the *gens Iulia*.[3] It has, however, been doubted that Augustus founded any colonies in the province since Illyricum does not figure in the list of the provinces in the *Res Gestae* where Augustus records his foundation of colonies. But these were military colonies (*coloniae militum*) where the embarrassingly large number of expired veterans in the years after Actium were safely settled by Augustus. None of the colonies founded in Dalmatia seems to be of this type. All were founded at existing flourishing settlements, and there is no evidence for veteran settlers at the date of their foundation.[4] Those who do appear were settled not earlier than about 9.[5]

The magistrates of the colony were *IIviri* and *aediles*,[6] while the freedmen colleges connected with the imperial cult are also recorded (*IIIIIIviri, IIIIIIviri Augustales,* and *Augustales*); but there is much less evidence for this class at Iader than at the other colonies in the province.[7] Construction of some of the public buildings and other amenities was probably begun under Augustus. The Appuleii appear to have paid for much of the large forum and temple complex (*capitolium*) which has been exposed in recent years.[8] Building con-

---

[1] Appian, *Ill.*, 16, and above, p. 50.

[2] III, 13264: *Imp. Caesar divi f. Augustus parens coloniae murum turris dedit*; cf. III, 2907 (a later rebuilding); Plin., *HN*, iii, 140; Ptol., ii, 16, 2. *Sergia*: III, 2930, 9997, 1200 (Apulum); XIII, 6827 (Moguntiacum); VI, 221 (Rome). Families in *Tromentina* may be settlers from the older colonies in Dalmatia, Salona, Narona, etc.

[3] *VAHD*, 53 (1950–1), 237 f., n. 9.

[4] Vittinghoff, *Kolonisation etc.*, 124, n. 4.

[5] III, 2911, 2913, 2918 and p. 110 f.

[6] III, 2931, 2932, 2912; cf. 9986, 2920, 2927.

[7] *IIIIIIviri*: III, 2928, 2929, 15047, *VAHD*, 53 (1950–1), 237, n. 9. *IIIIIIviri Augustales*: III, 2921. *Augustales*: III, 2923, 10001.

[8] III, 2904, 2905, altars to *Iuno Augusta* by Appuleia Quinta and her son L. Turpilius Brocchus Licinianus set up outside the *Capitolium*, below, p. 368.

tinued in the first century and an aqueduct was completed under Trajan,[1] and another major project completed probably about this time was a market hall (*emporium*) and square on the north side of the city looking on to the harbour.[2]

Aerial photography has furnished evidence for the territory of the colony. In this limestone country the field boundaries and track lines have changed little since the Roman period; the heaps of stone piled at the edges of the fields have preserved the grid-pattern of land-surveying (*ager centurionatus*), by which the original territory of the colony was organized and distributed in individual lots. The blocks of land (*centuriae*) measured 20 by 20 *actus* (776 by 776 yards) and are identical with those in the colonies at Salona and Epidaurum (p. 226). This gives an area of 200 *iugera* (about 124 acres) which, if the land was of uniform quality, would provide farm allotments (*heredia*) for at least 4 families. The two sets of grid-lines were the *cardines* and the *decumani*. The former ran on a northwest–southeast axis parallel with the coast and with the low limestone ridges of the Ravni kotari, in between which are the strips of fertile land. Except for the immediate area of the city much of the centuriated land is not of good quality, although there is an area of fertile land extending along the coast southwards to Sukošan 10 miles away. Towards the interior there is no obvious limit for the system of centuriation: it crossed the first of the limestone ridges and has been detected as far as the next around Briševo and Smrdelje. The evidence from road alignments on large-scale maps suggests that it might have extended beyond the third of the ridges at Polešnik, more than half-way to the sea of Novigrad on the other side of the Ravni kotari. To the north the system extended to within less than three miles of Aenona.[3]

Off the coast lies the island of Ugljan. The west side which faces out into the Adriatic is quite barren, largely because of the fierce winter storms which sweep down from the north, but on the sheltered east side there is a strip of fertile land which today supports a number of communities, and where vine and olive can be grown. On this land traces of *centuriae* have been discovered laid out on the same grid as the mainland centuriation. Similar discoveries may be predicted on Pasman, a continuation of Ugljan to the south. Both islands were clearly part of the territory of the colony. Further south on the mainland the territory reached

---

[1] III, 2909; also an unspecified project completed by Legions VII and XI under Tiberius: III, 2908.

[2] III, 9987 (2922): 'emporium sterni et arcum fieri et statuas superponi', at a cost of 600,000 sestertii.

[3] Bradford, *Antiquity*, 21 (1947), 197 ff.; *AL*, 178–83, pl. 42–3; M. Suić, *Zbornik*, 1 (1955), 14–17, pl. III–V.

at least as far as Biograd near Lake Vrana, where there is a record of the artisans' guild at Iader (*collegium fabrum et centonariorum*).[1]

The population of the colony in the first century A.D. is attested by a wealth of inscriptions, recording all classes of society from slaves to members of the equestrian order.[2] As one might expect in a colony, Italian settler families domi-nate the upper classes to the almost complete exclusion of native families. Many were probably established there before the colony was founded, and these will have benefited from Caesarian patronage after their loyalty in the civil war. Some of the north Italian families may have arrived with legionary veterans, but none of those who are attested can be dated earlier than the last years of Augustus.[3] Some Italian families specify their original home, and these include Aquileia, Altinum, and Verona, all in Northern Italy.[4] Most of the families seem to have come from this part of Italy, with smaller groups from Umbria and Etruria.[5] Other families reached Iader from cities in Liburnia where they had already become established; in this category were the Raecii and Trebii from Curicum and Arba.[6] Along with the Italian settlers there appeared many slaves and freed-men, the latter developing their own social hierarchy as *IIIIIIviri* and *Augustales*,[7] while there are too a number of people with purely native names or enfranchized *Iulii* and *Claudii*.[8] Settlers increased not only the population in and around the city, but moved also to smaller settlements in the colony's territory. Two modern place names near Iader, Bibinje in the south and the island Ugljan, are derived from the names of Roman estates, *Vibianum* and *Gellianum*, property of the Italian Vibii and Gellii, both of whom are attested on inscriptions at Iader.[9] As at Salona (p. 325) a number of the upper classes at Iader served the emperor as soldiers and administrators, while others amassed sufficient wealth to gain admission to the equestrian order, for which a property qualification of four hundred thousand sesterces was required.[10] At a lower level some joined the

---

[1] III, 9942.

[2] Alföldy, *Bevölkerung*, 79 f.

[3] P. 207, n. 5 above.

[4] *Cossutii* (Aquileia): *VAHD*, 53 (1950–1), 240, n. 14; cf. Šašel 210. On other links between Iader and Aquileia, S. Panciera, *Aquileia*, 86 f. *Elvii* (Altinum): III, 2914, a *IIIIvir* of Altinum with son centurion in Legion VII. *Modii* (Verona): III, 9988 (2937). A man from Teanum Sidicinum in Campania was awarded a public funeral in the colony, *ILS*, 9389.

[5] Alföldy, *Bevölkerung*, 79 f.

[6] III, 9985 (2915), 2918, 2931 and below, p. 309.

[7] Twenty-eight instances of slaves and freedmen, Alföldy, *AAnt.*, 9 (1961), 125 ff.

[8] *Iulii*: III, 9993 (2960, cf. p. 2273), 2952, 10006, 2945, 2962, 2907; VI, 221; III, 2953, 10005, 10015, 2941. *Claudii*: III, 2942.

[9] M. Suić, *Zbornik*, 1 (1955), 16, 31. *Vibii*: III, 2915, 10015. *Gellii*: III, 9991 (2949).

[10] III, 9996a, 9984 (2916), 2932, and below, p. 309.

legions, mostly in the first and second centuries, while a few recruits are attested serving in the praetorian guard and other units at Rome.[1]

Not only was Iader connected closely with Northern and Central Italy, but through her harbour, together with that of Aenona, must have passed most of the trade between the Ravni kotari and the outside world. Furthermore the traffic along the Dalmatian coast between Aquileia and the eastern Mediterranean, as well as the more local traffic with Salona and Narona, may well have used Iader as a port of call. The Dalmatian coast, with its many harbours and islands, was more attractive to the timid sea traffic of antiquity hugging the land wherever possible than the more exposed east coast of Italy. The close links with Salona are reflected by the families from that city domiciled at Iader and holding positions in the city government, including the position of patron.[2] Contacts with the interior were probably few, although there is one with Northern Dalmatia and another with Pannonia. It is unlikely that overland trade outside the Ravni kotari contributed to more than a fraction of the colony's commerce.[3]

After the middle of the second century the number of inscriptions from Iader decreases sharply. Few of the Italian settler families who dominated the city in the first century are now recorded, and the new more pedestrian ruling class came not from one particular area but consisted partly of native families and partly of immigrants from a number of different provinces. The large number of slaves and freedmen associated earlier with the Italian families decreases: *IIIIIIviri* and *Augustales* are almost unknown after the end of the second century. Slaves attested at different places in the territory reflect the tendency of many wealthier families to leave life in the cities and enjoy the self-sufficiency of their estates. In the city the proportion of free workers increased at the expense of slaves,[4] and the association of craftsmen and clothworkers (*collegium fabrum et centonariorum*) is attested by more inscriptions of the later period.[5]

North of the Ravni kotari the sea makes a deep inroad into the land as far as the town of Karin, the site of Roman Corinium. Contact with the open sea is possible through the sea of Novigrad and two narrow channels. Around the smaller sea of Karin there is an area of fertile land, while the site of the city is a

---

[1] XIII, 6827 (I Adiutrix); *RLiÖ*, 18, 16 (XV Apollinaris); III, 1200 (XIII Gemina); cf. III, 14507 (Iader). Praetorians: VI, 32520b, 32519a, l. 8, 32515e, l. 24. Vigiles: VI, 221.

[2] III, 2920, 2932, 9984, 9986 in Tromentina.

[3] *GZMS*, 12 (1957), 121, n. 10 (Gromiljak near Visoko); III, 15139 (Dalj in Southern Pannonia), a man from Iader.

[4] Alföldy, *AAnt*, 9 (1961), 131 ff.

[5] III, 9942 (Biograd); *GZMS*, 12 (1957), n. 10 (Gromiljak near Visoko).

small hill already fortified in pre-Roman times.[1] The place became a *municipium* under Augustus and was enrolled in the voting tribe Sergia.[2] No records of the city institutions have survived, although the many native people with the name Iulius show the widespread grants of citizenship made probably under Augustus. Another group, who probably received the citizenship at the same time, took the name Calpurnius, reflecting the areas's link with the senatorial Calpurnii already attested at Cissa.[3] Not all received citizenship under the Julio–Claudians, however, and some remained non-Romans until the reign of Hadrian.[4] Local cults continued to flourish in the Roman period and few immigrant families chose to settle there.[5] Men from Corinium are attested serving in military units, including the legions, the praetorian guard, and the city police force (*cohortes urbanae*) at Rome.[6]

Somewhere to the northeast of Corinium lay the city Ansium. On the hill Ivanova glavica a boundary settlement between the Ans[ienses] and the Corinienses was set up under the Neronian governor A. Ducenius Geminus.[7] The find-spot is 4 miles northeast of Corinium and the site of Ansium may lie around Bilišane not far south of the river Tedanius. At Kruševo, north of Corinium and west of Bilišane, was found the first or second-century tombstone of a praetorian; although his names are fragmentary his origin seems reasonably certain to be Ansium.[8] North of Corinium one of the main routes which lead from Southern Liburnia into the interior crossed the river Tedanius before climbing over the barrier of the Velebit into the Lika polje. Near the river-crossing was the small settlement Clambetae, named on the Peutinger Map, and to be identified with a typical Liburnian hill-settlement at Cvijina Gradina near Kruševo.[9] A tombstone records the tribe Sergia, and most probably the place was a village (*vicus*) on the territory of Corinium, rather than an independent city in its own right, since the territory of the Corinienses reached up to the river Tedanius (p. 212).[10] Some of the houses excavated on the Cvijina Gradina were built in the

---

[1] Little is known from the site of the city, Abramić, *S. Donato*, 4, 16 ff.

[2] III, 2884, 2885, 9970, and Appendix XII.

[3] *Iulii*: III, 2900, 2885, 2895, 2894, 9977, 9978 (2896), 2897. *Calpurnii* (mostly with native *cognomina*): III, 2886 (Novigrad); III, 2891, 2892; *JÖAI*, 12 (1909), Bb. 33 f.; III, 9976; *JÖAI*, 18 (1915), Bb. 187; III, 2980, 9970, see also p. 199 above.

[4] III, 9975: *Aelia Procula*.

[5] III, 9970–1 (Liburnian Latra). Possible immigrant families: III, 9976 (*Sextilii*), 9968 (*Valerii*).

[6] III, 2885 (centurion in VII C.p.f.); III, 9974 (XI C.p.f.); III, 2888 (praetorian); III, 2886 (*coh. urb.*).

[7] *JÖAI*, 12 (1909), Bb. 30, and below p. 458.

[8] III, 2887: *A. Saufeius P.f. Ca[. . .]max Ansio*, etc.

[9] *Clambetis*; cf. Rav., iv, 16: *Crambeis*.   [10] III, 2884.

first century, judging from a tile of the Pansiana factory made under Nero, but the place did not attract settlers from elsewhere and most of the names on tombstones are native Liburnian.[1] The one or two possible families of Italian origin came from Iader or Corinium, rather than direct from Italy.[2]

The boundaries of Corinium were the subject of arbitration by the governor of the province on at least three separate occasions, from early in Tiberius' reign to late in Nero's. Most of the decisions concerned the boundaries between Corinium and Nedinum (Nadin) 8 miles to the southeast. The first took place under P. Cornelius Dolabella (14–20), although this is known only from a settlement of the Neronian governor A. Ducenius Geminus (63–67) in which it is referred to as the *forma Dolabelliana*.[3] Less than a mile from where this settlement was discovered (St. Michael at Popović, 2 miles south of Corinium) there was found another fragmentary restoration of the old settlement of Dolabella at Jaksić.[4] The position of the boundary marks, more than 5 miles away from Nedinum, suggests that the latter had the lion's share of the good land which lay between the two cities, and this is born out by 'boundary of Nedinum' (*fines Nediti*) carved on a rock near Lacmanović barely a mile south of Corinium.[5] More settlements were required under Gaius; on a stone whose precise findspot is not recorded the boundary between Corinium and Nedinum was once more adjusted.[6] Three separate settlements were made under Nero, one between Corinium and Ansium (p. 210) from Ivanova glavica, and two dealing once more with the Nedinum–Corinium boundary. One of the latter comes from Pridraga, about 4 miles from Corinium on the road to Novigrad in the northwest.[7] The other is the settlement from near Popović which mentions the original made under Tiberius. Thus it is clear that on the south and the east the territory controlled by Corinium did not extend at any point more than 3 miles from the city. On the southeast the Nedinum land reached to within a mile of Corinium. Most of the territory was on the north: here it probably reached to the boundary between Liburnia and the Iapodes along the Tedanius or the Velebit ridge, and will have included Clambetae as a village on its territory.

Nedinum lay on the road between Iader and Burnum, about 12 miles from the former. Listed by Pliny among the peoples in the tenth region of Italy, its inhabitants obtained exemption from tribute early under Augustus and when the *municipium*, enrolled in the voting tribe Claudia, was founded under Tiberius or

[1] *JÖAI*, 8 (1905), Bb. 47, n. 1.
[2] *Peregrini*: *JÖAI*, 8 (1905), Bb. 45, e; also native *Iulii*: *VAHD*, 54 (1953), 211; also *Ostillii*: *JÖAI*, 8 (1905), 44, q. Settlers include *Baebilii*: *JÖAI*, 18 (1915), 186, a; *Gellii*: loc. cit., 187, c; *Maesii*: III, 2884.   [3] III, 9973 (2883), and p. 456 ff.
[4] Betz 34, and below, p. 457.   [5] *JÖAI*, 12 (1909), Bb. 32 f.   [6] III, 2882.   [7] III, 2883.

Claudius, they also acquired Italian status.[1] The territory of the community can be fixed with reasonable accuracy: in the direction of Iader it may have extended as far as Zemunik at a distance of 5 or 6 miles. On the north the Nedinum lands reached to the sea of Novigrad and enclosed the settlement at Islam Greco as a *vicus*: the evidence of the boundary settlements enables the boundary with Corinium to be traced through Lacmanović and Popović.[2] Their neighbours on the southeast were the people of Asseria, which lay near Benkovac less than 6 miles away. No boundary settlements are recorded between these peoples.

In contrast with neighbouring Iader the ruling class at Nedinum was composed for the most part of native families.[3] Those which are found established there may be offshoots from the settlers at Iader who decided to exploit the prosperity of cities in the Ravni kotari during the first century.[4] Enfranchised Iulii are attested, and more clients of the senatorial Calpurnii.[5] The leading family of the city in the first century was the Octavii, from whom emerged the eminent lawyer of the Flavian period C. Octavius Tidius Tossianus L. Iavolenus Priscus.[6] Nedinum retained its Liburnian character: local cults continued to flourish and there are traces of the tribal kinship group (p. 187) and slavery lasting from the pre-Roman period.[7] In the first century men from Nedinum are found serving in the legions, and an Octavius is attested under Augustus serving as centurion in a cohort of Liburnians, an emergency formation probably organized after the crisis of 6. It is another instance of the support enjoyed by the Romans from the

[1] *Claudia*: III, 2864, 2865, 2869, 2871, 2876, 9964, 9965; also magistrates: III, 2870, *VAHD*, 53 (1950–1), 241, n. 8 (III, 2867). Imperial dedications by *ordo*: III, 2860 (Divus Nerva), 2861 (Marcus), 2862 (Severus and Caracalla), 2863 (Valerian).

[2] Above, p. 212.

[3] *Moici*: III, 2858, *Opinii*: III, 2875, *Turranii*: III, 2871; also *Octavii*, n. 6 below, many with native *cognomina*.

[4] *Fulvii*: *VAHD*, 53 (1950–1), 241, n. 18, *Gellii*: III, 2875, *Laecanii*: III, 2877, *Magii*: III, 13260 (9966), 2868, *Mutilii*: III, 9960, *Papisii*: III, 2876, *L. Publicius Macedo Neditanus*, diploma witness in 70, XVI, 11.

[5] *Iulii*: *VAHD*, 53 (1950–1), 242, n. 20; III, 2859, 2872, 2873, *Calpurnii*: III, 2857 and above, p. 199.

[6] III, 2865, 2869, 2872, 2874, and 2870 with stemma of four generations:

Q. Octavius (. . .) aedile, *IIvir III, pontifex*—Quintia Voltisa

C. Octavius Rufus aedile, *IIvir, pontifex*   Octavia Q.f. Secunda—T. Octavius Sex. f. Gracilis aedile, *IIvir*.

Sex. Octavius Sex. f. Celsus—Octavia T.f. Gracilla

Octavia Sex. f. Celsina.

On Iavolenus Priscus see below, p. 332.

[7] *Latra*: III, 2857, 2858, 2859, 15042, 15043.

native upper classes of Liburnia against the peoples of the interior.[1] The magistrates of the city were *IIviri* and *aediles*; most of those who are attested are members of the Octavii family. For its trading contacts Nedinum will have been very dependant on Iader. Commerce does not appear to have been important, and the city probably depended almost entirely upon the products of its territory. Like most other cities in the area Nedinum appears to have declined during the second century, and the number of inscriptions from the second and third centuries is only a fraction of those of the earlier period. A few of those attested were the descendants of earlier families, while immigrants from the Danubian provinces include a leading citizen from Porolissum in Northern Dacia and another settler from Siscia.[2]

Little more than 5 miles southeast of Nedinum was the city Asseria (on the Podgradje hill near Benkovac), the leading inland community in Southern Liburnia. It was one of the Liburnian hill-settlements, situated on the Podgradje hill, 300 feet high, with a commanding view of the surrounding country, a situation similar to those of Nedinum, Varvaria, Clambetae, Sidrona, and Corinium. The pre-Roman walls enclose an area roughly 440 by 170 metres, within which the Roman city developed.[3] The Asseriates received only exemption from tribute, and their city does not appear in Pliny's list of Liburnian *oppida*. Although some of the population acquired the citizenship under Augustus, or Tiberius, the foundation of the city probably did not take place until the reign of Claudius; the main evidence is a priest of a cult to the deified Claudius (*flamen divi Claudii*). The city was enrolled in the voting-tribe Claudia, but it is not known whether Asseria was granted Italian status like the other cities in the Ravni kotari.[4]

The territorial boundaries of the Asseriates had to be settled by the provincial governor on more than one occasion, with the Alveritae in the northeast and with the Sidrini in the north. The first was part of the general regulation and demarcation of boundaries made by Cornelius Dolabella (*forma Dolabelliana*) in the years immediately following the final conquest in 9, but the name of the other people involved in the settlement has not survived. Under the Neronian governor A. Ducenius Geminus a boundary settlement established the claim of the Asseriates to lands extending northwards as far as Bruška, less than 2 miles from the centre of the Sidrini (Gradina near Medvidje), who were the other community involved. The third is the latest dated settlement from Liburnia: found at

---

[1] III, 2865 (le. VIII); *JÖAI*, 36 (1946), 75, n. 3: *T. Octavius C.f. Macer*, etc. (the *praenomen* is certain).

[2] III, 2866, 9962 (*Siscia na(tus)*).   [3] Below, p. 366.

[4] Appendix XII. *Claudia*: III, 15024, 15034; cf. *JÖAI*, 11 (1908), 83; III, 15036/1; *JÖAI*, 11 (1908), 70.

Dobropoljici, it deals with the boundary between the Asseriates and the Alveritae. The latter community are not otherwise recorded, and their centre was probably not far from where the settlement was found. The inscription was set up in the years 69–71, and the arbitrators (*iudices dati*) chosen by the governor were not the usual senior army officers but leading men from the other cities of Liburnia, including a Raecius. Like Nedinium, Asseria appears to have been very successful in the settlement of these disputes.[1]

The picture of the population at Asseria differs from that at Nedinum. Local families did hold leading positions, but so also did Italian immigrants who may have reached there from Iader.[2] The presence of some imperial names suggests recently enfranchised natives, and local cults flourished into the native period.[3] To judge from the city magistrates the ruling group in the city included both immigrant and native families: some of the former may have originated from legionary veterans settled there, in one case before the place became a *municipium*.[4] In the late first century a detachment from the Legion VIII Augusta was based there.[5] Men from Asseria joined the legions, some of whom returned home after service.[6] The most distinguished of her citizens was probably P. Atilius Aebutianus, the praetorian prefect who was appointed and later put to death by Commodus: he was patron of Asseria and was honoured with a statue there.[7] Asseria and its people lived off the produce of its ample lands, which produced crops and supported livestock. Trade also flourished, mainly because the city lay on one of the main routes leading to the interior. At Prekaja near Salvium a family of traders from Asseria is attested.[8] There is also evidence for slaves being owned by both Italian and native families.[9] Few families are attested in the third century: those recorded are descendants of older families. In the later period also there are more people recorded on tombstones in different parts of the territory than in the actual city.

[1] Above, p. 212.

[2] Names in local families include: *Vadicus, Pasinus*: *Diadora*, 1 (1959), 118, fig. 3, *Mamaester*: *VAHD*, 53 (1950–1), 234, f, and perhaps *Trosii*: III, 15033, who may originate from Nedinum, III, 9963, 15045. Upper class families of local Liburnian origin include *Baebii, Caninii, Oppii, Rubrii*; see below, p. 311 ff.

[3] *Iulii*: *VAHD*, 54 (1952), 210, n. 16; III, 15024, 9930 (2850), 9934, 15032, 15031/1. *Latra*: III, 15018, 9939.

[4] III, 9939 (in Legion VII from Verona).   [5] Suggested by stamped tiles, n. 5, p. 116.

[6] III, 15024; cf. *JÖAI*, 11 (1908), 67 (II Augusta); III, 15026 (?tribune in Legion X Fretensis), 15027 (XI Claudia).

[7] *JÖAI*, 11 (1908), 68 ff.=*ILS*, 9001; cf. *Vita Comm.*, vi, 12, PIR², A 1294.

[8] *GZMBH*, 43 (1941), 22 (Prekaja in Una valley): *Vesii Ravonius et Hermes*; cf. III, 9937 (Perušić near Asseria). Also a leading citizen of Salvium at Asseria, Abramić, *S. Donato*, 50 f.

[9] *JÖAI*, 11 (1908), Bb. 66; cf. Alföldy, *Bevölkerung*, 95, n. 153, reading [*liber*]*tu*[*s*].

Nothing is known about the city (*Respublica*) Alveria involved in the boundary settlement with Asseria in 69–71. It was probably somewhere near Dobropoljici, where the Atilii family recorded there may be descendants of a settler family.[1] Little is known about Sidrona, the city of the Sidrini, which has been located on the Gradina near Medvidje, nearly 10 miles to the northeast of Asseria. Its city status is attested by the tombstone of a man who held a magistracy twice, and there are two civic dedications to second-century emperors; but there is no evidence for when it became a *municipium*. Even such a small settlement as Sidrona clearly attracted Italian settler families.[2]

The third city on the same strip of fertile land which supported both Nedinum and Asseria was Varvaria, another Liburnian hill-settlement with defences of the pre-Roman period on the Gradina near Bribir.[3] The Varvarini (or Varvari) appear in the first and second of Pliny's lists; granted tribute exemption early under Augustus they probably acquired a municipal charter under Tiberius and at the same time Italian status.[4] It was enrolled in the voting tribe Claudia, and a number of enfranchised native Iulii and Claudii are attested.[5] Only a small number of inscriptions are known from Varvaria; in the early period the only evidence for city institutions is the tombstone of a man who was city councillor and held a magistracy. Apparently at Varvaria there were not the usual two *IIviri* and two *aediles*, but a college of four *IIIIviri*. Elsewhere this is found only at Salona and Doclea during the first century. A third-century tombstone recording a decurion furnishes the only other evidence for city institutions, but a fragmentary dedication to Trajan in 99 may have recorded some civic building at Varvaria comparable with that which was being undertaken at Asseria in the same reign.[6] Families of native origin predominate at Varvaria, and in some places the native Liburnian kinship groups survived into the Roman period: in one instance the organization had acquired Roman names, a *cognatio* with its own officers (*decuriones*) and priests (*sacerdotales*).[7] Men from the city served in the praetorians and in the fleet during the first and second centuries.[8] The evidence for the city's

---

[1] III, 9902.

[2] *Sidrona*, Ptol., ii, 16, 6; magistrate, III, 2846, also 2844 (to Hadrian), 2845 (L. Verus). It may be also the *Hadra* on the Peutinger Map between Clambetae and Burnum.

[3] F. Bulić, *BD*, 33 (1910), 10; cf. pl. IX, 1, Abramić, *VAHD*, 52 (1935–49), 9 f.; B. Saria, *RE*, 8A (1956), 418 ff.

[4] Appendix XII, below p. 487 ff.

[5] *Claudia*: III, 14514; VI, 32515b, ii, l. 27; XI, 104 (Ravenna). *Iulii*: III, 9883, 9981 (?), *VAHD*, 53 (1952), 246, n. 34. *Claudii*: *SB*, 215, n. 3.

[6] *Diadora*, 2 (1960–1), 183, fig. 1; *SB*, 210, 217, n. 11.

[7] *ŽA*, 10 (1960), 165 ff.

[8] Note 5, under *Claudia*.

enrolment in the tribe Claudia is the tombstone of L. Oppius Secundus, member of a prominent local family, attested at Viminacium as senior centurion (*primuspilus*) and camp commander (*praefectus castorum*) of Legion VII Claudia during the second half of the first century.[1] Although some Italian settlers are attested there,[2] Varvaria was probably too remote to attract traders and depended for much of its prosperity on a fairly extensive territory. This included not only the area on the right bank of the river Titius but also some land across the river in the area of Mratovo opposite the legionary fortress at Burnum. This is shown by the epitaph of an early veteran of Legion XI who was probably discharged before the death of Augustus: 'he was killed in the territory of the Varvarini in the small field alongside the river Titius and the Long Stone.' This place can be fixed precisely since the Long Stone (*petra longa*) is a headland near the river which bears that name today (dugi stina between Puljane and Bogatić).[3] In spite of the attacks from the Delmatae to the south during the first century B.C., the Liburni appear to have held on to some of their territory across the river. Strabo records that the river was the boundary between the two peoples, but this applies only to its lower course below Scardona: thence it probably followed the more natural geographical boundary across the Promina mountains to rejoin the river around Knin. At Oklaj and Razvadje between the river Titius and the Promina fragments of two boundary settlements made under L. Volusius Saturninus are known, but in neither case do the names of the communities involve survive; it can however be assumed that in both instances one of the parties was the Varvarini.[4]

The limit of Varvaria territory in the north was the legionary fortress and later city at Burnum. The later city developed more than a mile to the west of the legionary fortress (Šuplja Crkva) at Ivoševci, where the civilian settlement (*canabae*) had already become established during the legionary occupation: most of the tombstones of serving legionaries come from the cemeteries at Ivoševci.[5] The native people were the Liburnian Burnistae, one of the fourteen *civitates* which were administered through the judicial *conventus* based on Scardona.[6] Many traders were attracted to Burnum, taking advantage of the spending power of the legionaries, and with them came slaves and freedmen.[7] Alongside these immigrants was a minority of native families.[8] Nearly forty years elapsed

---

[1] III, 14514 (Viminacium).   [2] Alföldy, *Bevölkerung*, 86.   [3] III, 6418 (9896) (Mratovo).

[4] III, 9832–3 (both under Gaius), and below, p. 457.

[5] Above, p. 100 f. It appears on the Peutinger Map, also Rav., iv, 16.

[6] Plin., *HN*, iii, 138: *Burnistae.*

[7] *Aelonii* (Arretium): III, 9894 (2840). *Caerellii*: III, 13252. *Orcleci*: III, 9919. *Saenii*: III, 6420; cf. Alföldy, *Bevölkerung*, 87.

[8] III, 14985; cf. *VAHD*, 54 (1950–1), 236, n. 6; Rendić-Miočević, *Onomastika*, 34, n. 32.

between the departure of the legion and the foundation of the *municipium*, which probably took place in the first or second years of Hadrian, to whom the city council set up a dedication in 118. Another reference to the city appears on the tombstone of a decurion of the *municipium Burnistarum*.[1] The Roman government still retained some land near Burnum; a boundary settlement made by a procurator of the province at the end of the first century records the regulation of the limit between part of the old legionary territory (*prata legionis*) and the estates of a private individual.[2] At the end of the reign of Marcus Aurelius the Burnistae are listed among the Liburnian peoples who rebuilt a residence for the provincial governor (*praetorium*) near the *conventus* centre at Scardona. None of the other Liburnians peoples listed by Pliny in the Scardona *conventus*, Lacinienses, Stulpini, and Olbonenses, can be located or otherwise identified.[3] In the list of *oppida* Pliny lists the *civitas Pasini*. It is not recorded by any other source; F. Bulić suggested that it might be located at Padjine in the Mokropolje area a few miles north of Burnum, where inscriptions attested a sizeable settlement.[4]

Finally in Liburnia was Scardona (Skradin) on the north bank of the Titius about 12 miles from the sea. In most of its lower course the river flows through a gorge and is accessible only where the tributary valleys approach the river; Scardona lay at the mouth of one of these valleys, not far from where the river opens out to form Lake Proklijan. Although it was an important administrative centre in Southern Liburnia, and the only settlement of the Liburnians mentioned by Strabo, it did not become a chartered city until the Flavian period (*municipium Flavium*) when it was enrolled in the voting tribe Sergia.[5] The earliest dated inscription from Scardona, probably from a statue base, was dedicated to Nero, son of Germanicus, before 31, collectively by the cities of Liburnia (*civitates Liburniae*); it was presumably set up in connection with the organization of the imperial cult in Liburnia which was based at Scardona (*ara Augusti Liburniae*).[6] In the first century legionaries were stationed at Scardona, and a small detachment of veterans was established nearby at the Roški-Slap waterfall

---

[1] *VAHD*, 54 (1952), 210, n. 19; III, 9890 (2828), 14321/23–4.

[2] III, 13250 (Vedropolje near Uzdolje) and below, p. 459.

[3] III, 2809. A place *Praetorium* appears on the Peutinger Map between Salona and Burnum.

[4] Plin., *HN*, iii, 140; cf. Bulić, *BD*, 14 (1891), 163. Immigrants include the *Cloelii*: III, 9915 (Mokropolje), also imports, M. Suić, *Diadora*, 1 (1959), 95 ff. There is no link with the *coh. I Aurel(ia) Paṣinatu(m) c. R.* proposed by N. Vulić and A. v. Premerstein, *JÖAI*, 3 (1900), Bb. 163. See p. 118.

[5] III, 2809. Tribe *Sergia*: III, 2810, Plin., *HN*, iii, 141: 'Scardona in amne eo (Titius) XII m. pass. a mari'; cf. Ptol., ii, 16, 2; Procop., *BG*, i, 7; Strabo, vii, 5, 4.

[6] III, 2802; cf. 9897. Lost and later republished as a new discovery, *AE*, 1938, 68; cf. III, 2810 *sacer[dos] ad aram Lib[urn.]*, etc.

a little higher up the river.[1] Like Burnum the settlement at Scardona may have attracted settlers because of the proximity of the legion, although it could not be reached by sea-traffic from the Adriatic. The few upper-class families attested there seem to be a mixture of immigrants and native families, with most of the former probably coming from other cities in the province.[2]

[1] Appendix VII, p. 468.
[2] The leading family were the *Turranii*: III, 2810, 2085 (Salona). Enfranchised *Iulii*: III, 2810. Italian families include *Mutilii*: III, 2806; *Petronii*: III, 2802; *Plotii*: *VAHD*, 53 (1950–1), 246, n. 35 (Tarac on Kornat island); *Satrii*: *VAHD*, 56–9/2 (1954–7), 2, 124, n. 3; *Retinii*: III, 2814.

Chapter 10

The Cities of the Province: Southern Dalmatia

1 Salona and the Central Coastline (fig. 7)

The largest and most important city in Dalmatia was Salona (modern Solin), now a small village at the head of the large bay which was part of the ancient Manios Kolpos (Kastelanski Zali, or Bay of Castles from the mediaeval fortresses along the coast).[1] The history of this area before the later second century B.C. is predominantly Greek, concerned with the mainland possessions of Issa at Tragurion (Trogir) and Epetion (Stobreč).[2] Soon after the middle of the second century these places were overrun by the Delmatae, and remained in their possession at least until the campaigns of C. Cosconius in 78–76 B.C. In 118–117 B.C. Salona was already the chief port of the Delmatae when L. Caecilius Metellus Delmaticus spent a winter there,[3] and it remained in their power until it was captured by Cosconius. There is no definite evidence that they recovered possession of it afterwards.[4] Soon Salona was attracting traders and settlers from Italy, and within a generation there was established a flourishing community of Roman citizens with a quasi-municipal organization (*conventus civium Romanorum*). In 56 B.C. an embassy to the proconsul C. Iulius Caesar at Aquileia resulted in the confirmation of Issa's status as a free and allied state (*civitas libera et foederata*). It also appears to have recognized the Greek settlements around the Bay of Salona at Tragurion and Epetion: involved also were the Illyrian Iadastinoi, once enemies

[1] Pseudo-Scylax, c. 23.
[2] Pol., xxxii, 9.
[3] Appian, *Ill.*, 11, and p. 34 above.
[4] The tradition connecting Asinius Pollio with a capture of Salona in 40/39 B.C. can be discounted, above, p. 45.

of Pharos in the early fourth century B.C., who dwelt around the modern river Iadro not far east of Salona.[1]

The events of the civil war have already been recounted (p. 41). The *conventus* at Salona fought well for Caesar; it was the head-quarters of A. Gabinius in 48–47 B.C., and withstood a combined attack by the Delmatae and the Pompeians until the pressure was relieved by P. Vatinius' victory over the enemy fleet at Tauris (Šćedro).[2] The site of the *conventus* was not well protected, either by its position or by man-made defences, and the settlers had rapidly to improvise a timber stockade.[3] In spite of the victory in 47 B.C. it is possible that Salona was for some time once more blockaded by the Delmatae, since during the campaigns of Vatinius against the Delmatae in 45–54 B.C. his headquarters was at Narona, the site of another *conventus* which was probably loyal to Caesar.[4] Salona was probably a Roman base during the campaigns of Octavianus in 34–33 B.C., and even during the last war of conquest in 6–9 the city was endangered by raids across the Dinaric Alps organized by Bato late in 6. The war culminated in the siege of Andetrium (Muć), not 20 miles from the city.[5]

At some time between 47 and 27 B.C. a colonia was established at Salona with the titles *Colonia Martia Iulia Salona*.[6] The chronological limits are certain: in 47 Salona is called a *conventus*,[7] while if it had been founded after 27 B.C. its title would have been *Augusta* rather than *Iulia*.[8] Within these twenty years there are two occasions when the foundation might have been made: by Caesar himself in the years 47–44 B.C. to strengthen his *clientela* and reward the *conventus* after victory in the civil war, or about 34–33 B.C. by Octavianus for similar motives, when the political competition between him and M. Antonius was at its keenest. A number of scholars have argued for one or other of these dates, but often on evidence which is not relevant to the problem.

[1] D. Rendić-Miočević, *VAHD*, 52 (1935–49), 19–34.

[2] *Bell. Alex.*, 44, and above, p. 42.

[3] Caes., *BC*, iii, 9, 2: 'Est autem oppidum et loci natura et colle munitum. sed celeriter cives Romani ligneis effectis turribus sese munierunt.' This implies that the settlers improved on the natural advantages of the site with emergency defences. Yet Salona does not enjoy a well-defended position and the text may be corrupt, with a negative missing from the first sentence.

[4] Vatinius wrote to Cicero from his base there, above, p. 43 f.

[5] Cass. Dio, lvi, 12.

[6] III, 1933 (in 137), *VAHD*, 44 (1921), 23, n. 4853A, the second a dedication to the *Genius coloniae M(artiae) I(uliae) S(alonae)*; also under Diocletian a relief depicts the female *Genius* of the city holding a banner with the letters *M.I.V(aleria) S. F(elix)*, *VAHD*, 52 (1935–49), 279, fig. 1. In the later period the most common designation is *colonia Salonitana*: III, 2026, 2055, 2066, 2078, 2081, 2187, 3199; cf. 10157, 8659, 8864, 10156a, 12196, 14320.

[7] Caes., *BC*, iii, 9.

[8] Vittinghoff, *Kolonisation etc.*, 133, n. 2.

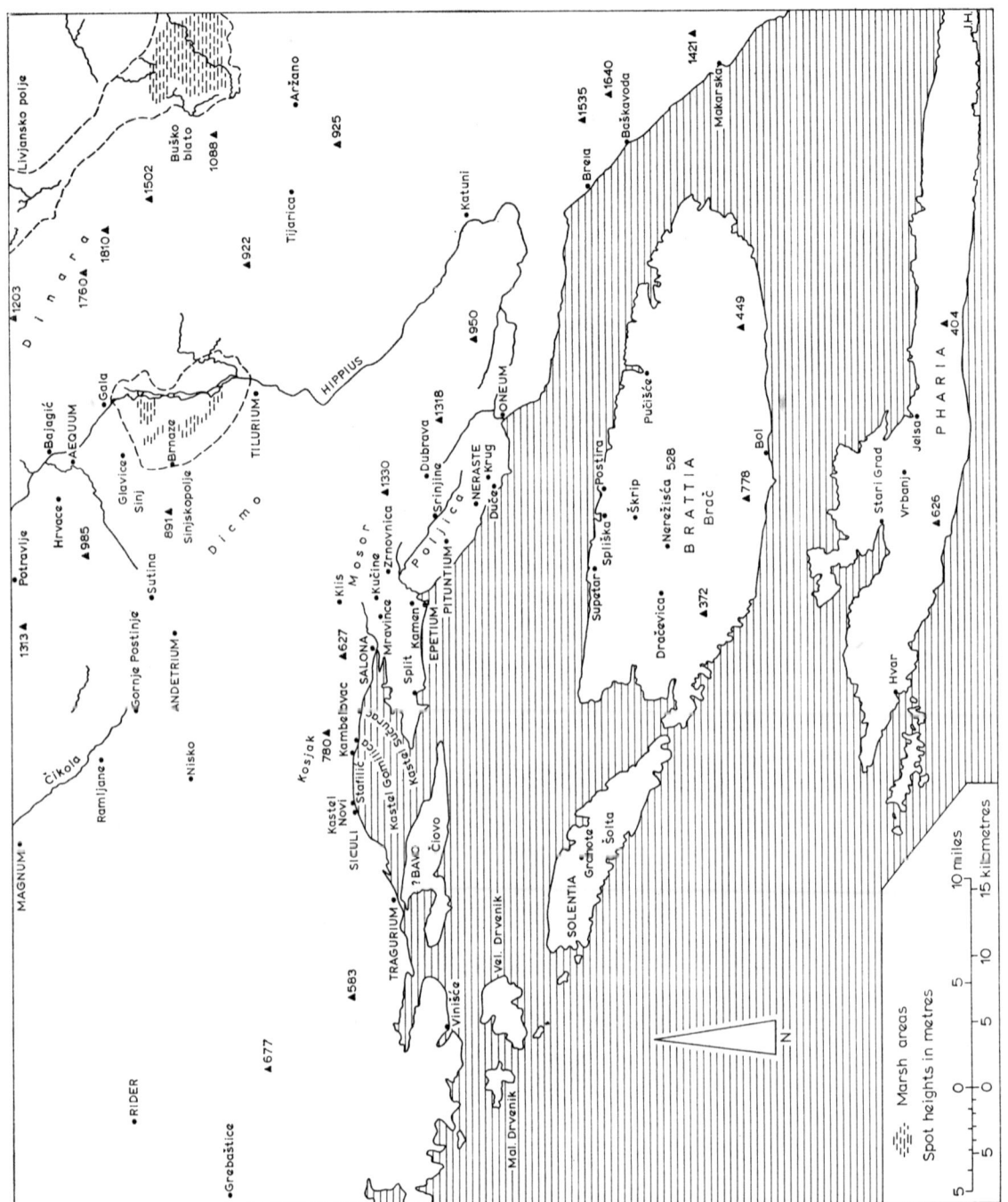

Figure 7 Salona Area

W. Kubitschek argued for the Caesarian date on two grounds, the voting tribe Tromentina in which the colony was enrolled and the fact that an Augustan foundation could be excluded since Illyricum does not appear in the *Res Gestae* among the provinces where colonies were established by Augustus.[1] However, the second reason does not rule out a foundation in 33 B.C. since, as has already been noted in connection with Iader (p. 207), the list in the *Res Gestae* refers to colonies of veterans (*coloniae militum*), whereas all those founded in Dalmatia appear to have been civilian settlements.[2] Most scholars, however, have preferred the later date in the belief that Salona was in the hands of the Delmatae until 34 B.C., when it was recaptured by Octavianus.[3] This is based on a misinterpretation of Strabo where he describes Salona as a 'port of the Delmatae', a situation which existed until its capture by Cosconius.[4] A. Degrassi sought to interpret the history of Salona from the title of the magistrates: *IIIIviri* indicated that Salona was first a *municipium* of Caesar, who then raised it to colonial status, after which the magistrates were called *IIviri*.[5] The evidence does not support this: *IIviri* and *IIIIviri* are both attested during the first and early second centuries A.D.[6] In addition *IIIIviri* are found as magistrates of colonies, for instance at Emona and Poetovio.[7] If there was an abrupt change from one title to the other at Salona, then it probably took place at the end of the first century A.D. (p. 234). In *municipia* both titles are also attested, for instance in Flavian Doclea.[8] Nor does the suggestion of M. Suić that a *municipium* and a *colonia* existed side by side at Salona until the reign of Trajan appear feasible.[9] Another theory which may also be discounted is that of G. Novak, who suggested that a 'Roman' and an 'Issaean' Salona existed together, both gaining autonomy under Octavianus.[10] Issa lost her autonomy after supporting the Pompeians during the civil war, and if it is correct that Salona was founded shortly after the end of that war, all her old territory became part of the colony, while Issa herself probably became a prefecture administered from Salona.[11]

The main problem, touched on by Novak and Suić, is that for some time at

[1] Kubitschek, *IRTD*, 198; cf. *BD*, 14 (1891), 70 f. On the *Res Gestae* passage, B. Saria, *LA*, 1 (1938), 250.

[2] Vittinghoff, *Kolonisation etc.*, 124, n. 4.

[3] Literature in Alföldy, *Bevölkerung*, 123, n. 34.

[4] Strabo, vii, 5, 5: '*Salon, Priamon, Ninia, Sinotion*, both Old and New, which Augustus set on fire' referring only to the last named place, whose destruction is recorded by Appian, while there is no mention of any attack on Salona, above, p. 54, n. 8.

[5] A. Degrassi, *Quattuorviri*, 317 ff.; cf. *Confine, etc.*, 99.   [6] Below, p. 234, n. 1.

[7] III, 10070 (Emona), 4028; cf. Alföldy, *Situla*, 8 (1965), 104 and fig. 2 (Poetovio).

[8] III, 13818 (12680).   [9] *VAHD*, 60 (1958), 11 f., summary 39–42.

[10] *Rad*, 270 (1949), 77 ff.; cf. *Carnuntina* (1956), 117 ff.   [11] III, 2074 and p. 229 f.

least Salona appears to have consisted of two communities. The tribes Tromentina and Sergia are both found among the upper classes of the city,[1] while the plan of the city reveals two areas both surrounded by walls which share one side. The westerly is the *urbs vetus*, with the slightly larger *urbs nova* on the east. The two areas were separated by a wall in which there was a substantial gate (*porta Caesarea*).[2] The two settlements were hardly likely to have been established at the same time. Sergia is a tribe commonly found in Augustan foundations, for instance in the colony at Iader and the *municipium Iulium* at Risinium, both probably established in 33 B.C. or not long afterwards.[3] The settlement at Salona enrolled in Sergia may have been a colony of Octavianus. That in Tromentina is part of an earlier stratum in the urbanization of Dalmatia: the colonies at Narona (*Iulia Narona*) and Epidaurum, both beginning with *conventus* settlements established before the civil war, were probably established by Caesar. The evidence of the tribes and the city plan points to Salona having been a double colony, the *colonia Iulia Martia* of Caesar being reinforced by a second settlement of Octavianus in 33 B.C. enrolled in a different tribe.[4] As has already been noted it is possible that Salona was blockaded, and perhaps even captured, for a few years by the Delmatae after Caesar's death, and the colony of 33 B.C. may have been a re-establishment of the older settlement with new immigrants and some of the old colonists, who may have become refugees at Narona. Such devotion to Caesar's old allies in the Adriatic would be typical of Octavianus at this period.

Not enough study has been made of the city defences of Salona to discover the date of the *urbs vetus* and the *urbs nova*. The fortifications constructed against the Pompeians by the *conventus* were temporary and made only of wood, and these will hardly have formed the basis for the circuits of massive walls which survive today.[5] It is possible that the western *urbs vetus* is Caesar's colony, while the *urbs nova* was that founded by Octavianus. On the other hand, the idea of these two walled settlements being established at so nearly the same time and existing without substantial change into late antiquity is hardly credible.[6] There is some dating

[1] Apart from 22 instances of *Tromentina* in *CIL*, III, there are VI, 30881; *JÖAI*, 6 (1903), Bb. 81 f.; *BD*, 34 (1911), 31; *FS*, 3 (1939), 149; cf. III, 13873. *Sergia*: III, 1978, 2074, 2079, 3079.
[2] E. Dyggve, *RS*, 1 (1928), 14 f.; cf. *HSC*, 1 ff. There seems to be no real evidence for the subdivision of the *urbs vetus* into a Greek *urbs antiqua* and *urbs orientalis*. There can be little doubt that the history of the Salona city defences is much more complicated than has hitherto been supposed, and will only begin to be understood when excavations have produced stratified pottery associated with the different defences.
[3] Above, p. 207 and p. 255.   [4] Alföldy, *Bevölkerung*, 103 f.   [5] P. 358 ff.
[6] Nor is there any evidence for the suggestion of G. Novak, *Rad*, 270 (1949), 81 ff., that the *conventus* existed outside the *urbs vetus* on the west. The *via munita*, III, 2072, was the road leading from the city to the west lined with monumental tombs, below, p. 360.

evidence for the walls. The northern stretch of the walls of the *urbs nova* were built, or rather rebuilt, in 170 at the height of the Marcomannic Wars by legionary and auxiliary troops, while the so-called *porta* Caesarea, by which the two enclosures were linked, was constructed under Augustus and substantially rebuilt under Constantius II in the fourth century.[1] By that time a road had been built along the top of at least part of the dividing wall which appears to have been maintained at its full height. Although possibly not enclosed by a wall until the later second century, the new city on the west was certainly in existence during the first century, probably as part of the colonial foundation.

The plan of the city, measuring east to west 1,590 metres and north to south about 700, and with a wall perimeter of more than 4 kilometres, was curiously elongated. There is no obvious reason for this apart from growth as a ribbon development along the harbour. A reference to this is Lucan's descriptions of 'long-Salona' (*longae Salonae*) which reflects the city's unusual appearance.[2] Some attempt has been made to estimate the city's population. Packed to capacity the Salona amphitheatre held 15,400 people, and if one takes this as a quarter of the population as a whole, as E. Dyggve suggested, then somewhere around 60,000 seems probable.[3] Another figure may be deduced from the capacity of the water supply. On the analogy of Rome, where 300 litres were needed for each person in twenty-four hours, W. Gerber calculated that the flow of water in the Salona aqueduct would meet the needs of at least 40,000. This figure indicates only the people dwelling in or near the city: those in the territory will have relied on other supplies.[4]

The walls of the *urbs vetus* were already in existence when the territory of the colony was surveyed by centuriation, since the *cardo maximus* of the system appears to have been aligned along the west wall.[5] It is possible also that the line of the south wall of the *urbs nova* follows the *decumanus maximus* for a short stretch, the only instance where any part of the city plan coincides with the *decumanus* axis:[6] this suggests that the area of the *urbs nova* was at least defined and settled in the early first century, even if the walls were not yet constructed. There is no evidence when the centuriation of the territories of the Dalmatian colonies was carried out, but most probably it occurred in the years after 33 B.C. With the exception of Pharia (p. 228), all the centuriation systems in Dalmatia were similar. How the settlement of the colony actually took place and what happened to the *conventus* is not known. Presumably all the land was taken over by the govern-

[1] *FS*, 1, 131 ff. and p. 362.   [2] Lucan, *Phars.*, iv, 104.
[3] E. Dyggve, *RS*, 2 (1928), 132.   [4] *FS*, 1 (1917), 140.
[5] M. Suić, *Zbornik*, 1 (1955), 27, fig. 12.
[6] Suggested by Alföldy, *Bevölkerung*, 104 f.

ment and the allocations made to new settlers from Italy and the older settler families, who together made up the population of the new colony.[1]

The territory of Salona was probably the largest of any city in the southern area of the province and also that which can be most accurately defined. Moreover, it was increased on at least two occasions, once in the middle of the first century and also in the Poljica region in the late second century.[2] The limits of the territory away from the coast are fairly certain: the plain around the city is enclosed by the towering cliffs of the mountains Kosjak and Mosor which rise to heights between 5,000 and 6,000 feet, and the only route into the interior is over the pass at Klis.[3] At its greatest extent the territory of the colony reached along the coast from beyond Tragurium in the west to the mouth of the river Hippius (Cetina) at Oneum (Omiš) in the east, a distance of nearly 30 miles. All the islands off the central sector of the Dalmatian coast were included in the territory of Salona.

Within this area there is much fertile land. South of the city the Marijan peninsula is barren and rocky, as is also most of the island Čiovo (probably the Bavo of Pliny) which closes off the bay of Salona on the west. All the cultivable land along this stretch of the coast was divided up by centuriation. Aerial photography has revealed traces of the system from Tragurium to Epetium, and also in Poljica as far as Oneum. The size of the *centuriae* is 20 by 20 *actus* (776 by 776 yards) each giving and area of 200 *iugera*, identical with the systems at Pola, Iader (p. 208), and Epidaurum (p. 254). There are a few traces of the less well-defined subdividing lines (*limites intercisivi*) within the *centuriae* roads of the *decumani* and *cardines*.[4]

Although at first the Salona centuration did not extend westwards beyond Kaštel Stari, the old Greek settlement Tragurium (Trogir) was part of the colony from the time of its foundation. It lay on the sea route north along the coast from

---

[1] See the table in Suić, *Zbornik*, 1 (1955), 29:

	centuriae	*iugera*	colonial families (each with 50 *iugera*, 31 acres?)
Parentium	450	90,000	1,800
Pola	650	130,000	2,600
Iader	50	10,000	200
Salona	80	16,000	320
Epidaurum	50	10,000	200

The Salona territory was larger, with at least 100 *centuriae* (*c.* 400 settler families), apart from the islands and the new centuriated Poljica territory of the later second century, Bradford, *AL*, 190 f.

[2] M. Suić, *Zbornik*, 1 (1955), 18 f.

[3] The southern limit of effective Turkish control in the area during the later Middle Ages.

[4] M. Suić, *Zbornik*, 1 (1955), 1 ff.; Bradford, *AL*, 183–93.

Salona where the channel between the island Čiovo and the mainland is at its narrowest. Originally a possession of Greek Issa it had acquired some form of independence by the time of Caesar's proconsulate, but it probably lost this soon afterwards when, along with its metropolis, it probably supported Pompey in the civil war,[1] for which the penalty was incorporation into the new colony. Pliny's description of Tragurium as 'a town of Roman citizens noted for its marble' does not imply city status; it merely record the status of its inhabitants.[2] The presence of two freedman *IIIIIIviri* from Salona and the lack of any record of municipal institutions among the large number of Roman inscriptions suggests that its legal status was that of a village (*vicus*) on the territory of Salona.[3] In the first century Tragurium may have been administered directly by the Roman army. An early inscription records P. Cloelius, soldier in the auxiliary cohort of Campanians, as 'guardian of Tragurium' (*custos Traguri*), a similar type of control to that attested at a later period by civilians at Pharia and Epetium.[4]

On the site of the modern city of Split an early settlement named Aspalathos (after the aspalathos shrub which grew in the area) in the later geographical sources will have been included in the new colony, while some of the streets in the suburbs of Split are aligned on the boundaries of *centuriae* of the Salona centuriation.[5] Nearby was the second Issaean settlement at Epetium (Stobreč), situated on a small headland with an excellent small harbour 3 miles south of the colony. By an error Pliny lists the Epetini among the island peoples, but the dedication to *Genius Epetinorum* from Stobreč leaves no doubt about the identification. The settlement was entirely enclosed within the Salona centuriation, while two magistrates (*IIIIviri*) and a decurion of Salona confirm that it, like Tragurium, was a village on the territory of Salona, probably administered by a prefect appointed from the city council at Salona.[6]

In the Poljica region between Epetium and Oneum a strip of fertile land between 2 and 4 miles wide extended along the coast up to the main ridge of the Mosor mountains. In this area were three small communities of the Delmatae, Pituntium (Podstrana), Nareste (Jesenice), and Oneum (Omiš). Pliny describes their settlements as *castella*,[7] the usual name for settlements of the native peoples in the province (p. 184). During the first century A.D. they retained their independence. A boundary settlement set up on the road between Nareste and

---

[1] Caes., *BC*, iii, 9; *Bell. Alex.*, 47.   [2] Plin., *HN*, iii, 141; cf. Strabo, vii, 5, 5; Ptol, ii, 16, 9.
[3] III, 2680, 9709 (2676).   [4] III, 8693. On the unit, see p. 144 f.
[5] *Spalathron*: Rav., iv, 16; *Spalato*: Peutinger; *Aspalathos*: Const. Porph., *DAI*, c. 29, 30.
[6] Plin., *HN*, iii, 142; *Genius Epetinorum*: III, 12815; *IIIIviri*: III, 1920, 8525; *decurio*: III, 14230; *praefectura*: E. Polaschek, *RE*, 19 (1938), 1866, who connects it with a Salona lighthouse (*pharos*).
[7] Plin., *HN*, iii, 142: 'the *castella* of *Peguntium* (Pituntium; cf. Ptol, ii, 16, 3), *Nareste*, and *Oneum*'.

Oneum under L. Volusius Saturninus in the reign of Gaius fixed the limit between the Nerastini and Onastini, and a similar settlement was made a few years later between the Nerastini and the Pituntini.[1] In the late second century the territory of Salona was extended to include these communities. Not far from Pituntium a boundary marker of the system records *K(ardo)* I and *D(ecumanus)* II on two of the faces. The date of this extension seems to have been 179, when an inscription from Salona records the construction of a *limes publicus*, one of the roads in the system.[2] At the same time a large number of new families appear settled in the Poljica region.[3]

The major islands opposite Salona within the colony's territory included Pharia (Hvar), Solentia (Šolta), and Brattia (Brač). After the foundation of the Parian colony at Starigrad in the early fourth century B.C. and the later rule of Ballaios in the second century B.C., nothing is known about the history of the island until it was made part of the new colony,[4] and was settled with new colonists. Under Tiberius a magistrate of Salona held also the prefecture of Pharia (*praefectura Phariaca Salonitana*).[5] Only a small number of Roman inscriptions are known from the island, but there is one reference to municipal institutions.[6] Most of the island is barren scrub-covered limestone, except for the fertile plain between Jelsa and Starigrad in the northwest. Here the land is of excellent quality and produces wine and oil of the highest quality: it was this areas which attracted the Greek settlers in the fourth century. The whole area of the plain of Jelsa (roughly 5 by $2\frac{1}{2}$ miles) was divided by a system of centuriation, but with the *centuriae* considerably smaller than those on the mainland. Measuring only 5 by 5 *actus* (585 feet square), they contained only $12\frac{1}{2}$ *iugera*, one sixteenth of the *centuriae* on the mainland.[7] The reason for this difference is clear: the land was of such high quality that it need be distributed only in small quantities. On the neighbouring island of Solentia traces of centuriation have been detected around Grohote, where there is an area of fertile land.[8] Signs have also been noted on the island of Brattia, although there is not much good land there in spite of its great size. Most of the population lives today in small villages around the coast or near the centre of the island. Towards the south the land rises to a plateau, where high-quality marble has been worked since the Roman

[1] Appendix V.   [2] M. Suić, *Zbornik*, 1 (1955), 19, fig. 9; cf. III, 8663 (3157), 14239[4].

[3] Alföldy, *Bevölkerung*, 118.

[4] Before the civil war it may have been controlled by Issa.

[5] III, 14712; cf. 14713. The *praefectura Phariaca* was wrongly associated with a lighthouse by E. Polaschek, n. 6 on p. 227.

[6] III, 3084.

[7] Bradford, *AL*, 191 ff., pl. 47.

[8] op. cit., 193, n. 1.

period. In the early fourth century A.D. it was used widely in the Palace of Diocletian, and even in the imperial baths at Sirmium; today the stone can be seen in
many of the fine Renaissance buildings along the Dalmatian coast. Pliny does not
refer to the marble, but tersely records Brattia as 'famed for goats' (*capris
laudata*). A magistrate of Salona is known from Sv. Elia, 2 miles west of Škrip
and close to the marble quarries. In the second century an auxiliary centurion on
Brattia describes himself as 'superintending the theatre' (*curagens theatri*) – presumably that at Salona; he may have been performing some function at the
marble quarries in connection with the prefecture administration by which
Brattia was controlled from Salona.[1]

In a technical sense the most remote part of the city of Salona was the island
Issa (Vis), the furthest of the offshore islands in Central Dalmatia. Once the city
of Issa enjoyed the friendship (*amicitia*) in the diplomatic sense with the proconsul Caesar: one of his legates, Q. Numerius Rufus, was patron of the city in 56
B.C. and built a portico there at his own expense.[2] In the same year Caesar issued
a decree from Aquileia which re-established Issa's status as a free and independent
state. Yet the city broke with Caesar and supported the Pompeians during the
civil war, probably because of her dislike of the *conventus* of Roman citizens
established close to her mainland territories. In spite of Caesar's praise of these
settlements for their support during the civil war, the behaviour of these people
towards the older communities was often bad enough to make them side with
the enemies of Rome, as did the Greeks who supported Mithridates a generation
earlier. Pliny records Issa as a place inhabited by Roman citizens and notes that
it was under the juridical administration of Salona.[3] Like Tragurium, Issa may
have been at first under military administration. In 20 a military parade ground
(*campus*) was established under P. Cornelius Dolabella. It was dedicated to
Drusus Caesar, the son of Tiberius, who was not, however, present at the dedication. He had been sent to Dalmatia for a short period by his father, but by this
time he had returned to Rome.[4] The voting tribe Sergia is recorded for Issa, and
in the second century a family tombstone from Salona records a decurion of

[1] Plin., *HN*, iii, 152. Marble quarries: III, 10107 (St. Andrea near Splitska); cf. Patsch, *RE*, 3
(1899), 821; *IIIIvir*: III, 13288, cf. p. 2328/18. The centurion *curagens theatri*, III, 3096, may have
been issuing marble for the Salona theatre, B. Gabričević, *VAHD*, 53 (1950–1), 158 ff. On the
centuriation, Alföldy, *Bevölkerung*, 107.

[2] III, 3078 and above, p. 39.

[3] Plin., *HN*, iii, 142: 'petunt (iura) ex insulis Issaei . . .'

[4] *VAHD*, 54 (1952), 41 ff.; cf. pl. II dated late in 20. Drusus was sent to Illyricum in 17,
Tac., *Ann.*, ii, 44, 46, 53, and in 18 dealt with Maroboduus, ii, 62. After visiting Rome he
returned to Illyricum and then returned to Rome again in 20, receiving an *ovatio* on 28 May,
Ann., iii, 19; cf. XIV, 244.

Salona who was enrolled in Tromentina, his elder son, also in Tromentina, decurion of both Salona and Issa, his younger son, enrolled in Sergia, who was decurion of Issa only. This does not denote that Issa was a separate *municipium* but indicates the practice by which some members of the council in Salona were concerned specifically with Issa.[1]

Two Greek cities once existed on the island Corcyra Nigra (Korčula), southeast of Pharia and opposite the peninsula Pelješac, a colony of the Cnidians and a later colony of Issa.[2] In 35 B.C. Octavianus attacked the place as a pirate stronghold. Some inscriptions of the Roman period are known from Velaluka in the west and from the city of Korčula. From the latter place there is a record of a *IIIIIIvir*, but there is no way of telling whether he belonged to the college at Salona or Narona, which is slightly nearer.[3]

There is more epigraphic evidence for the population of Salona at all social levels during the first three centuries A.D. than for any other city in the Danubian provinces.[4] Few cities experienced such consistent prosperity from the Late Republic to the Byzantine Empire. Within the three centuries of the Principate the epigraphical material can be divided into two reasonably distinct groups. The first is those inscriptions which date from the beginning of the colony until roughly the death of Hadrian; the second begins in the Antonine period and lasts to the beginning of the Late Empire with Diocletian and the Tetrarchy at the end of the third century. In most cases the separation of the inscriptions into these two chronological groups is not difficult. Although few of the tombstones are dated by internal evidence, such as an official career or a position in the emperor's service, there is a sufficient number of conventional formulae, including abbreviations, titles, and the form of names, to make the dating reasonably certain within the two chronological groups.[5] Inevitably some may be

[1] III, 2074 (Salona).   [2] Plin., *HN*, iii, 152 and above, p. 8 ff.

[3] III, 3067; cf. *VAHD*, 60 (1958), 125 f.; Appian, *Ill.*, 16.

[4] On the population in general see Alföldy, *Bevölkerung*, 108–18, and on the individual families, *PN* (in the press).

[5] Some general points of dating may be noted. Many early tombstones give the full styles and titles of Roman citizens, *praenomen*, *gentilicium*, filiation, voting tribe, and *cognomen* (if present). Absence of the last is a sure pointer to an early date in most cases. Less reliable are the gradual changes in syntax and the forms of abbreviation. Early tombstones, especially of the soldiers, usually give the deceased's name in the nominative and have the formula *h(ic) s(itus) e(st)*. Also common in the early period is the formula *t(estamento) f(ieri) i(ussit)*. The prefix *Dis manibus* written in full followed by the genitive case belongs usually to about the late first century and the first half of the second century, with the abbreviation to *D.m.* beginning about the end of that period. The use of fulsome epithets is generally late, *incomparabilis*, *indulgentissimus*, *pientissimus*, etc. The formulae for age are not consistent, although *qui vixit* (or *tulit*) *annos*, *defunctus annorum*, and *annos plus minus* are generally indications of late date. Only in a few in-

dated incorrectly by these methods, but such irregular items are few in number and will not alter the picture that emerges from comparative study of the early and later material. The quantity of evidence in the two groups differs greatly. A total of 1,674 inscriptions from the city and its immediate vicinity records 3,086 persons for the first three centuries A.D. Of these only 313 can be assigned to the earlier period (recording 647 persons), while the remaining 1,361 in the later period record 2,439 persons.[1] The population recorded by these inscriptions may be examined under three general headings, origin (including colonial settlers and later immigrants), social structure (composition and role of the ruling class, free proletariat, freedmen and slaves), and the economic and social life of the colony, reflected in the social structure discussed under the previous heading.

The initial wave of Italian settler families which arrived in the Late Republic to join the *conventus* and later the colony was overwhelmingly civilian in character. Veteran settlement did not figure in any of the Dalmatian colonies to the extent that it did in other colonies founded by Caesar and Augustus throughout the Mediterranean.[2] Veterans, mostly of Italian origin, are known to have settled in Salona late under Augustus and also under Claudius, when a settlement made at Siculi (Biač) resulted in an extension of the colony's *territorium* westward beyond Tragurium. With one exception, the settlement of veterans from the Moesian Legion V Macedonica under Gaius or early under Claudius, all the veteran settlers in the first century came from legions stationed in the province, XX under Augustus, VII and XI in the first half of the first century, and IIII Flavia felix under the Flavians.[3] In the later period a number of veterans are known, both from the legions and from the *auxilia*. Some came from the *officium* of the governor based at Salona, while others are recorded from units stationed in the province during the later second and third centuries. A few settled at Salona after service in the Danubian legions, some of whom may have originated from Salona. There is no evidence for any organized veteran settlements during this period, nor do the legionary veterans appear to enjoy the same high social status as some of those in the first century.[4]

In the early first century many families came to Salona from Italy, and more than 188 family names of Italian origin are attested. Many of these can be traced back to Northern, Central, and Southern Italy, the most important areas being Etruria, Umbria, and southern Central Italy. Isolated immigrants are known

[1] Alföldy, *Bevölkerung*, 20.   [2] Appendix VII and p. 107 ff.
[3] Above, p. 114.   [4] Above, p. 134 f.

---

stances does the dating of an individual inscription depend on one of these indications only: invariably a combination of the formulae and abbreviations makes the date reasonably certain.

from the western provinces, and a few Liburnian families spread southwards to Salona and its territory.[1] The native element at this period, attested by native names and by early imperial *gentilicia* signifying enfranchisement at this time, is almost non-existent either in the city or in the territory.[2]

Obviously the process of immigration was continuous, although it lost some of its momentum after the initial phase of colonial development, and it is not possible to see any fluctuations in the arrival of settlers in the first three centuries. On the other hand, there are signs of an increase in new settlers at about the period when the territory of the colony was enlarged by the inclusion of *castella* of the Delmatae at Pituntium, Nareste and Oneum late under Marcus Aurelius.[3] Evidence from the Poljica region in the later period is considerable and indicates a predominance of settler families at the expense of the native population, although there is more evidence for the latter group than in the earlier period. The origins of the later arrivals at Salona are much more varied than those who came in the first century, and the amount of evidence for them is also much greater. More than four hundred family names appear in the later period at Salona: of these less than half are known there in the first and early second centuries.[4] The number of families whose citizenship was derived from grants made by the Julio–Claudian emperors is considerably greater than before: many of them may be new arrivals in the colony. The commonest family name among the population of Salona, as in many other parts of the Empire where native development

[1] Alföldy, *Bevölkerung*, 109, and *PN* (forthcoming). Most families can be linked with different regions of Italy, although only in a few cases with any particular city. Northern Italy: *Laepici* (Istria), *Villii* (Aquileia), also *Africani, Albucii, Cusii, Eubonii, Etuvii, Mescenii, Titidii, Trosii, Verocii, Viscii*. Less certain are the *Agrinii, Octavii*, and *Statii*. The next geographical group is Etruria and Umbria: *Caetennii* (from Volsinii in Etruria; cf. Alföldy, *Eirene* 4 (1965), 43–53), also *Baebidii, Caecinii, Cafatii, Cossonii, Marronii, Petii, Seppieni, Veianii*. The third group, immigrants from Central and Southern Italy, is the largest: *Obultronii* (Casinum), *Caltilii* (Ostia), *Tremelii* (probably from Sipontum), *Concordii* (from Beneventum), also the *Aeronii, Agrii, Ahii, Aprofennii, Atanii, Atatieni, Caesieni, Casinii, Catenii, Cloelii, Dirutii, Ligustii, Offonii, Pacuwii, Papii, Tigidii, Urgulanii, Veii, Verulani*. L. *Albius* Leuga, III, 2073 a magistrate, may originate from Southern Gaul, while another Westerner may be M. *Tauritius* Marcellinus, III, 8753 (2028; cf. p. 1030), of which five examples occur in *CIL*, XIII. The *Volsii*, III, 2167, are probably Liburnian.

[2] Most *Iulii* of the early period are freedmen with Eastern cognomina, *Craterilla, Alexander, Evaristus, Narcissus, Stochas, Noema*; cf. Alföldy, *PN* (forthcoming). Isolated examples of natives include the probably Liburnian *Ceuna*, III, 2043; cf. p. 1031; *Messa*: BD, 37 (1914) 51; *Vendo*: III, 2497; *Epicadus*: III, 14794 (9159). Also a few *peregrini*: *Aeplo*: BD, 29 (1906), 192; *Buccio*: III, 2249; *Messor*: III, 1949; *Tritus Plati f.*: BD, 31 (1908), 55.

[3] III, 3157 (8663); cf. 14239/4 and above, p. 227 f.

[4] Later Salona families include: *Antonii, Cassii, Cornelii, Domitii, Licinii, Petronii, Pompeii, Pomponii, Titii, Valerii*.

came late, was Aurelius, signifying enfranchisement under Marcus, Commodus, or by the universal grant to the freeborn of the Empire (*Constitutio Antoniniana*) under Caracalla in 212. Many other people with this name were probably from native families of the interior, but at this period it becomes difficult to discover ethnic origins from personal and family names. Some of them could well be arrivals from other provinces, in particular from the East (see below). The Italian element in the population is less significant,[1] but there is certainly a group from the western provinces, Africa, and the Danubian provinces, especially Dacia which by the time of the Marcomannic Wars had developed a flourishing economy, with its rich agricultural and mineral resources.[2]

The eastern immigrants are the most obvious. A number of Greek inscriptions at Salona, in no way connected with the earlier Greek communities in the area, reveal these settlers, many of whom bore the name Aurelius.[3] Along with them came eastern deities, Isis, Jupiter Dolichenus, and Mithras, but the most significant and enduring cult from the Orient for the later history of the city was Christianity.[4] The early arrival of this new cult through the middle and lower classes of the eastern cities resulted in Salona becoming one of the greatest Christian centres of the Adriatic and Danubian area.

The transformation of the ruling class of the Mediterranean World from the exclusive senatorial oligarchy of aristocratic families in the late Republic to the widely based circle of Italian and provincial magnates of the second century A.D. is one of the most fascinating themes in Roman imperial history.[5] The history of

[1] Ravenna: III, 2120; *BD*, 34 (1911), 47; III, 8836. Aquileia: III, 8827 (2121); cf. *SA*, 79 f. Urbs Salvia: III, 6382. Bellunum: III, 12925; cf. *SA*, 77 f.

[2] Africa: III, 2127a; cf. p. 1509 (*rhetor natione Afer*), *WMBH*, 9 (1904), 292 ff.; III, 8825; cf. p. 2136, and in general Patsch, *WMBH*, 9 (1904), 298 ff. Spain: III, 2529; cf. Alföldy, *Bevölkerung*, 129, n. 148. Raetia: *BD*, 35 (1912), 6. Dacia: III, 2086 (decurion of Porolissum and merchant), *VAHD*, 47–8 (1927–8), 58, III, 2679 (Tragurium) decurion of Drobetae, *VAHD*, 47–8 (1927–8), 43 f. veteran, *RS*, 1 (1928), 162; cf. *VAHD*, 50 (1930–4), 17; III, 14646 (Kamen) gladiator (*secutor*), and in general, Patsch, *WMBH*, 6 (1899), 262 ff.

[3] *BD*, 25 (1902), 12; Brunšmid, *KSp*, 181; Bulić, *Inscr. Sal.*, 238; cf. III, 1470; *FS*, 3 (1939), 151; *BD*, 25 (1902), 165; Brunšmid, *KSp*, 180. Also *Flavii*: *IGRR*, 1, 552 (veteran of Misenum Fleet); *Claudii*: III, 2152; *Ulpii*: Bulić, *Inscr. Sal.*, 238; *Aelii*: *VAHD*, 47–8 (1926–7), 47 f.

[4] *Serapis*: IX, 3337 (Pescara), *Isis*: *collegium* of Salona, IX, 3338; cf. Kurz, *St. C.*, 4 (1962), 306. *Mithras*: Vermaseren, *CIMRM*, 2, 252 ff. *Dii Syrii*: III, 1961. For the Salona Jewish community, *VAHD*, 49 (1928), 116 ff., also the two fragments possibly from a sacred law involving the Jews and possibly the Christians (*Chrissiani*), Gabričević, *Cong. Int. LGE*, 1957, 77 f., although they may be from different texts, J. Reynolds, *JRS*, 49 (1959), 209. *Magna Mater*: III, 8675 (*cognatio M.M.*), *BD*, 32 (1909), 67. Under Diocletian there flourished an association connected with the worship of the sea deities, *ministri ad Tritones*, K. Kurz, *St. C.* 4 (1962), 301–13.

[5] R. Syme, *Tacitus*, 585 ff.

the ruling class at Salona is a reflection of this process. In the early period the ruling group were drawn from a comparatively small number of families, almost exclusively of Italian origin. They aspired towards the higher levels of the social pyramid at Rome, and from provincial magistracies many were wealthy enough to obtain membership of the equestrian and, in one or two cases, the senatorial order. Such status made them eligible for the higher civil and military appointments in the emperor's service.[1] One can be certain that the wealth of this class was based on the ownership of land, most of which would be farmed by free tenants (*coloni*), or in some cases by bailiffs (*vilici*) controlling gangs of slaves. The flourishing trade and industry of the city was probably controlled by the same class, although indirectly. There is no reason to assume that Salona was unlike other societies in the Empire where the only respectable form of wealth of a gentleman was land and property. In the early period the dominant class in trade and manufacturing were freedmen, some of whom may have been of eastern origin. The wealth and display of this class is one of the striking features of Salona and the other Dalmatian colonies in the first century A.D. In the period up to the middle of the second century slaves and freedmen account for more than one-third of the people attested on inscriptions and, allowing for their lesser opportunities to set up durable monuments, people of slave or freedmen origins may have constituted as much as half of the population, and probably much more in the city itself.[2] The leaders of this class could often rival their patrons with wealthy building and civic display. In prudent fashion the government had devised a suitable outlet for their ambition in the imperial cult of the seviri (*IIIIIIviri*) and Augustales which were reserved for them.[3] Their collective

[1] Magistrates of the first and early second centuries: *IIIIviri*: III, 2073; III, 14712; cf. 14713 (see p. 304), 2075; cf. p. 1509 (*procurator*); III, 8733, 8737 (equestrian army officer), 2079, 2083, 6378, 8813 (?), 8771 (equestrian tribune), 12920, 8524 (1920) (Epetium), 8525 (Kamen), 2049; (equestrian tribune), 8786 (son of freedman); *IIviri*: III, 2072, 1933; cf. p. 1030, 2081, 2087, 1978 (to Divus Nerva), 14249/7, 14230 (?), 8796 (?), 14249/8 (?), 13910 (12918 and 13097) (priest of Divus Vespasianus); *decuriones*: III, 2770 (Rider), 1942 (*augur*), 8789, 2049 (equestrian *praefectus*), 2055 (*sacerdos*, father of centurion), 2026 (equestrian). Other municipal offices: III, 8523 (*augur*), 8788 (*augur*), 2122 (*scriba*=town clerk), 8753 (*pontifex, quinquennalis, flamen, patronus*), 1954 (*quinquennalis*).

[2] Alföldy, *Bevölkerung*, 111. The common practice of using Greek names for slaves and freedmen conceals their real ethnic origins. In the case of those at Salona and in the coastal cities many may be native Dalmatians sold into slavery after the wars of conquest and possible later disturbances.

[3] A portico built to the memory of Claudius in 54 was the work of a freedman of another who was himself a freedman of the provincial governor P. Anteius Rufus, below, p. 444. At the head of the *seviri* was a *magister*, III, 14243/4; *BD*, 37 (1914), 74, although the *flamen Augustalis* was chosen only from the city council families; III, 8733; cf. 14712, 13910. There are no distinc-

and individual dedications are as impressive as any in the colony, and within their own social group they will have seemed as elevated and privileged as the rulers of the city. Some of them will have had their own slaves and freedmen, exploiting them in the same manner as their own families had once been exploited by their owners and patrons.[1]

The clear social stratification recognizable in the first and early second centuries did not last beyond the middle of the second century. Much of the old ruling class was superseded by families generally less distinguished in the imperial hierarchy and of much more varied ethnic and geographical origins. In particular new families arrived from the developing parts of the interior of the province to take their place in the ruling class of the provincial capital, betraying their origins by imperial family names of the second century.[2] At the same time the freedman and slave element so closely associated with the Italian ruling families of the early period now declines markedly in importance. From totalling more than a third of the persons attested for the early period, they now constituted barely a tenth: in the later period few freedmen are attested in the sevirate.[3] The older freedmen families had doubtless by now risen to a higher social level, and the most successful had merged with the real ruling class.[4] With the exception of Poljica, where slavery is attested in households and in agriculture, the importance of the unfree element in the city's economy declined, while the

---

[1] III, 2092, 14661–2 (8791, 9261), 2093 and 2325 (p. 2260), 2096; *VAHD*, 53 (1952), 220 ff.; III, 8803, 14249/3, 8806, 8807.

[2] Members of the *ordo* in the late second and third centuries: III, 2074 (above p. 229 f), 8659, 2076; *BD*, 30 (1907), 75, 3602A; *BD*, 29 (1906), 226 f., 3452, 3451A; III, 12916, 2084; *BD*, 37 (1914), 44, III, 14715–6 (Klis). Also equestrians: III, 2077 (son of imperial freedman *procurator*), *VAHD*, 44 (1921), 30 f., 4780A; III, 2078; *VAHD*, 53 (1950–1), 226 f., n. 36 (father and son); *BD*, 27 (1904), 163, 3370A; cf. *FS*, (1926), 71, n. 52; III, 8713.

[3] In the later period freedmen are attested on 74 inscriptions, slaves on 47, but in the early period the joint total is 63, a much higher proportion of the smaller number of inscriptions, Alföldy, *AAnt.*, 9 (1961), 147 ff.

[4] Some magistrates were descended from freedman parents, n. 1 on p. 234 and 2 on this page.

---

tions to be drawn between the three groups of freedmen *seviri*, while all known members are of freedman origin. *Augustales*: III, 8788; III, p. 2260 (2093 and 2325), 2096, 2098, 8803, 2102, 2104. *Sevir et Augustalis*: III, 1947. *Seviri Augustales*: III, 12917, 2100, 2092, 8786, 2095, 2097, 14717, 8792, 8804, 14249/3 (also an honorary decurion), 8675, 2101, 2103, 8807, 14711, 14249/6, 14718, 2099, 8791, 8794, 8675 (Kučine), 9707 (2676) (Tragurium); *BD*, 30 (1907), 118, 3928A, 37 (1914), 77, 4576A. *Seviri*: III, 6377, 13904, 2094, 8790, 14243/4, 8797, 2097a (2 ex.); III, 8806, 8807, 14663/2 (2 ex.), 8414, 14250, 14719, 2105, 3067, 8524 (1920) (Epetium), 2680 (Tragurium), *VAHD*, 53 (1952), 220, n. 24.

guilds (*collegia*) of independent free craftsmen increased in number and importance.[1]

The imperial government was always very suspicious of associations or clubs that did not relate themselves to the social and political hierarchy. In the Late Republic political clubs were powerful forces exploited by the politicians in the turbulent assemblies at Rome, and in the great cities of the East the mass of the population was given to frequent rioting and other disorders. Less trouble of this kind is attested in the more stable West, until the serious rural disorders of the later second century in Gaul and Spain. We do not know, for instance, whether Trajan would have forbidden a placid city in the West a fire brigade organization as he did Nicomedia in Bithynia, despite the request coming from his own special governor.[2] A number of trade guilds are attested at Salona, each usually relating to a particular craft. They include general craftsmen and cloth-workers,[3] woodworkers,[4] stonemasons,[5] and stevedores,[6] and there was also a veterans' association.[7] Through their own officials (*magistri*) the guilds served their members in many capacities, including organized religious worship. Burials would be properly organized for the deceased, often with tombstones mass-produced in a particular style. Frequently the guilds had as their patron a member of one of the leading families of the city.[8]

In the territory of the colony there is evidence for slavery, both domestic and agricultural, lasting into the third century: in this area there is a significant increase in the number of slaves recorded.[9] Native names are also attested in the territory, apart from Epetium where the population appears to have remained exclusively of Italian and immigrant descent, closely linked to that of the city itself.[10] The change in the population of the Poljica area has already been noted.

[1] Household slaves increase in the later period; *Vernae*: III, 2622, 8888; *VAHD*, 47–8 (1926–7), 33, n. 5157A; III, 8833 (*vernaculus*); *BD*, 37 (1914), 40, 4660 (*vernaculus*); III, 9298 (*vernula*), 9266 (*vernacia*). Also stewards and bailiffs (*vilici*): III, 2134, 13045; *BD*, 29 (1906), 129; *alumni*: III, 2771, 2478, 2374, 2194; *VAHD*, 47–8 (1926–7), 68; III, 8530, 2130, 8547.

[2] Plin., *Epp.*, x, 33 f. Apparently there was a general ban on fire brigades in the eastern provinces, Jones, *GC*, 215.

[3] *collegium fabrum et centonariorum*: III, 8824, 2107; cf. p. 1030, *BD*, 37 (1914), 53; III, 8837 (*patronus* and *vexillarius*), 8819 (*magister*), 14321 (Klis); *BD*, 28 (1905), 153 (*magister quinquennalis*), *VAHD*, 53 (1950–0), 226, n. 36 (equestrian prefect of the *collegium* and patron of Salona), III, 8829, *BD*, 29 (1906), 18, 3339A; III, 8841 (*collegium tignariorum fabrum*, probably wood-carvers).

[4] *coll. dendroforum*: III, 8823.   [5] *coll. lapidariorum*: III, 8840.

[6] *coll. saccariorum* (sack-men): III, 14642–3 (Žrnovnica); *VAHD*, 45 (1922), 7, 4801A.

[7] *coll. veteranorum sive Martensium*: III, 14250/1, also 14242 mentioning a *convivium*.

[8] Note 3 above.

[9] Alföldy, *AAnt.*, 9 (1961), 134 f., probably the result of later immigration from other provinces.

[10] Especially at Srinjine di Poljica near Pituntium, III, 1927; cf. p. 1030, 8551, 1905 (Oneum).

Native families may well have suffered when the better lands were occupied by new settlers from the colony. Among the latter were the Artorii at Pituntium, who held equestrian status under Commodus.[1] In the rest of the territory Italian families, including some legionary veterans, are found in the early period, not only at larger settlements such as Tragurium[2] and Epetium[3] but also in smaller places along the shore of the bay, including Kaštel Novi, Gomilica, Sučurac, and also at Klis to the north.[4] Similar settlements developed on the islands, especially at Pharia and Issa. Here there is little sign of the older Greek population: only Issa retained traces of its Greek character well into the Roman period.[5]

It is clear that Salona supported a large population, much greater than could be sustained by the produce of its territory alone. Its exceptional prosperity must to a large extent have been due to its position as a port on the Adriatic. An outlet for the resources of the interior, it also served shipping passing up and down the Adriatic between Northern Italy and the Eastern Mediterranean. Strabo's contrast between the poor harbours on the east coast of Italy and the good ones of Dalmatia suggests that shipping used the shelter of the many islands which screen the Dalmatian coast from the Gulf of Flanona to Corcyra Nigra.[6] This led to particularly close contact with Aquileia, Salona's only rival in the Adriatic in the later period.[7] During the early period imports which reached Salona from many parts of Italy included pottery, bricks and tiles, glass, metal goods, and luxury objects. In return Salona exported the products of the coast and the interior,

[1] III, 1919; cf. 8513, 14224 (12791) and p. 328 f below.

[2] *Bennii*: III, 2686, *Fundanii, Pomponii*: III, 13970; *Rutilii*: III, 9711; *Stallii*: III, 9707 (2676); *Statii*: III, 2699.

[3] *Aponii*: III, 12815; *Coelii*: *Diadora* 1 (1959), 168 ff.; *Gellii*: III, 8524 (1920); *Petronii*: III, 8524; *Sentii*: *Diadora*, loc. cit.; *Turranii*; III, 8675 (Kučine).

[4] *Antonii*: BD, 35 (1912), 59 (Gomilica); *Aponii*: III, 12938 (9005) (Gomilica); *Fulvii*: III, 8789 (Sučurac); *Oppii*: III, 14316 (Kaštel Novi); *Pomponii*: BD, 32 (1909), 98, 4234A; *Servilii*: III, 13903; *Sextilii*: *VAHD*, 44 (1921), 23, 4852A; *Tarvisii*: BD, 28 (1905), 156, n. 3522A; *Volusii*: III, 14875 (all from Klis).

[5] Settler families; *Solentia*: *VAHD*, 43 (1920), 114; III, 15101 (Liburnian *Raecii*); *Brattia*: III, 3097, 14333/5 (Pučišće); III, 3092; cf. p. 1646; III, 13291, 10114 (3108), 10115, *L. T(itius) Lysonis f. Longinus*: III, 6426 = 10105 probably from an original Greek settler family. *Pharia*: III, 3084; *Corcyra Nigra*: III, 10083 (3066); *Issa*: BD, 15 (1892), 132, also III, 3076, a bilingual dedication to *Mircurius*. An immigrant C. Valius Festus records that he established (*conditor*) the vineyard known after him as *Valianus*, III, 6423.

[6] Strabo vii, 5, 10. There was a *portorium* station at Salona, BD 31 (1908), 142, 3983A.

[7] III, 2133; cf. *FS*, 2 (1926), 67. Also contacts with Sipontum, III, 2083; Croton, *NS*, 1932, 373 (*Salonitanus*), also a merchant at Salona, *VAHD*, 50 (1930–4), 57: 'I have travelled everywhere by land and sea, and returned duly to my native land where now I lie buried.' Other contacts include III, 14641 (*defunctus Aterno*); *VAHD*, 53 (1950–1), 221, n. 26 (*Siponto defunctus*); BD, 39 (1916), 112, n. 446A (*natus Salonis, defunctus monte Gargano*); III, 8821 (*defunctus Ravennae*).

olive oil and wine from the former, timber, minerals, and livestock from the latter.[1] Many inscriptions from Salona itself and from different cities in Italy attested these lines of commerce. As yet no systematic study has been attempted of the large quantity of material recovered by excavation, nor has excavation yet revealed anything about the many activities carried on within the city. One can assume the existence of such occupations as metal-working, shipbuilding, stone-carving, and tile-manufacture, in addition to those crafts already attested by their guilds (p. 236). A distinctive local style can be recognized in tomb-sculpture, but the most expensive items were probably imported from the Eastern Mediter-ranean. In the third century there was certainly one luxury sarcophagus which was manufactured in Attica.[2]

From its wealth of epigraphic and other evidence Salona emerges as more than merely the provincial capital. In Dalmatia no other city compared with it, and its predominance as an urban centre reached far beyond the limits of its own territory. From Salona or somewhere nearby came the greatest man the province produced, the emperor Diocletian. Originating from this cosmopolitan city he imposed a new and enduring pattern of organization on the Empire at the end of the third century. The only emperor ever to abdicate willingly, he retired to his magnificent palace built on the coast a few miles south of the city (p. 387 ff).

11 *The Central Coastal Hinterland*

In the area between the rivers Titius and Narenta and to the south of the Dinaric Alps were a number of settlements of the Delmatae, most of which acquired city status by the beginning of the third century. Economically and socially none of them developed beyond the level of a large village: the land was very poor, and the large cities of the coast, above all Salona, were too close to allow any great development.[3] An aspiring local worthy would soon seek the atmosphere

[1] Wine merchant: III, 2131; timber merchant: III, 12924. Other occupations include engraver (*toreutes*): III, 8839 (possibly from Rome); candlestick maker (*ceriolarius*): III, 2112–13 (easterner); plumber (*plumbaria*): III, 2117. Professions attested include elementary teachers (*pedagogi*): III, 2111; *BD*, 29 (1906), 122, 507B, both freedmen, III, 14731; doctors (*medici*): III, 2123, 14727, possibly both from the East; jurists: III, 8822 (*mag(ister) iuris*), 8836 (from Ravenna); surveyors (*mensores*): III, 2124, 2129 (from Campania); III, 2128 (imperial household slave (*verna*)). Contacts with the interior are attested, some of them unfortunate: III, 6383 (killed in the lands of the Maezaei), 2544 (kidnapped and presumed dead), 9054 (killed by highwaymen, *viatores*). Others from the interior died at Salona, doubtless more peacefully, III, 8339 (Visibaba), 8341 (Požega), 8344 (1671) (Vranjani), Sp. 76, 119 (Plevlje).

[2] *JDAI*, 67 (1952), 31 ff. For Eastern influences in Salona sculpture, K. Prijatelj, *AI*, 1 (1954), 29 ff.

[3] Strabo, vii, 5, 10 and above, p. 180.

of the provincial capital with its greater wealth and opportunities. Eight settlements existed in the region. One was the colony at Aequum (Čitluk near Sinj) founded under Claudius. Settlements of the Delmatae which became *municipia* were Magnum (Balijina Glavica), Novae (Runović near Imotski), and the great settlement at Rider (Danilo Kraljice) between Scardona and Salona. Other settlements were Promona (Tepljù), Andetrium (Muć), and Tilurium (Gardun), all military stations. The first two were occupied by auxiliary units, the third a legionary fortress in the first century and later an auxiliary station.[1] Lastly, in the isolated upper valley of the river Hippius (Cetina) around Vrlika, numerous records of the native population have survived, although there is no certain evidence that a city developed (p. 395 f).

On the border of the Delmatae was Promona, once a chain of fortresses around the eastern foothills of the main Promina mountain. Captured by Octavianus in 34 B.C. from the Delmatae, an auxiliary unit was established on the east side of the mountain at Tepljù north of Drniš in the Čikola valley, the route of Octavianus for his further advance against the Delmatae.[2] Apart from those of the auxiliary garrison there are records of native Delmatae without Roman citizenship, and one or two immigrant families, probably from the coastal cities.[3] The legal status of the native community was that of a country district (*pagus*): a bronze tablet records an agreement or decision about the supply of water for a water-mill which involved the *pagani Prom[onenses]*.[4] Perhaps the settlement was administered from the auxiliary station, which was maintained into the later period. Another auxiliary fort was established nearby at Kadina Glavica, also in the Čikola valley, but there is no trace of the native population, in spite of the continued presence there of the auxiliary unit until the third century. Most probably the area was organized as a *pagus* similar to Promona.[5]

Little more than 5 miles to the east higher up the Čikola valley was a post manned by *beneficiarii consulares,* most of whose dedications were set up at Umljanović.[6] The Illyrian fortress Synodium captured by Octavianus may have been in this area, but the later city was known by the Roman name Magnum and located at nearby Balijina Glavica. The only record for the organization of the city is a decurion and magistrate (*IIvir*); he probably held office in the third century and the Roman citizenship of his family may have been granted under Marcus Aurelius.[7] The station of the *beneficiarii* remained there to play an import-

---

[1] Appendix VIII and p. 470.   [2] Veith, *Feldzüge*, 63 ff.

[3] Native: III, 9839, 14316/6. Immigrants: *BD*, 32 (1909), 49 (*Fabii*); III, 9840 (*Sempronii*).

[4] III, 14969/2.   [5] Appendix VIII, p. 470.

[6] Above, p. 124.

[7] III, 14316/2: *M. Aur. M. f. Luc*[. . .] etc, also a decurion, *SB*, 232.

ant role in the community, and one of them coupled the *Genius* of the city with the official Jupiter Best and Greatest on his votive altar, a dedication found also at Novae (p. 125).[1] Native people from the area were recruited to the Roman army. A non-Roman who gives his home as the city Magnum is found in the late second century serving as a surveyor (*mensor*) of an auxiliary cohort near Mogontiacum in Germania Superior.[2] The citizenship granted along with municipal status to some of the population under Marcus Aurelius was probably confined to the families of city council status. The valley of the Čikola has little fertile land and an unpleasant climate. Magnum was unlikely ever to develop into a large settlement, and what prosperity it enjoyed may have depended on its position on the main land route between Salona and Southern Liburnia.

At a place not far beyond the head of the Čikola valley, where the road to Aequum crosses a low ridge into the Sutina gorge, was the great native stronghold of Andetrium (Gornje Muć), besieged and captured by Tiberius in 9.[3] Following this it became a base for auxiliary units on the road between Burnum and Tilurium. Not far from here took place the ambush of Caesar's legate A. Gabinius in 48 B.C., and his name was later commemorated by the via Gabiniana from Salona to Andetrium, built by Legion VII in 17.[4] Some native people with the Roman citizenship are recorded from the late first century onwards, while estates in the area were owned by families from Salona and Aequum.[5] One of those recorded was a decurion of Aequum: he lived and was buried on his lands near Andetrium, and it is possible that some of the land in the area which was not required for the auxiliary garrison was included in the territory of that colony.[6]

The principal settlement of the Delmatae, at least at the time of the Roman conquest, appears to have been Rider (Danilo Kraljice), inhabited by the Riditae, less than 10 miles from Scardona. The native stronghold lay on the steep-sided hill (gradina), but early in the Roman period this was abandoned and the settlement established in the fertile valley.[7] The earliest record of its organization is the epitaph of a *princeps* of the Delmatae whose family obtained Roman citizenship under Claudius,[8] a time when such grants were restricted to a very select

[1] III, 14957. Recorded on Peutinger and by Ravennas, iv, 16: *Magnum*.
[2] XIII, 6538 (Mainhardt): *Maximus Dasantis f. . . . c(ivis) Dalmata ex municipio Magn(o)*.
[3] Dio, lvi, 12.   [4] Appendix IV, p. 453.
[5] III, 9783 (*Flavia*), BD, 31 (1908), 83, Sutina (*Aelius*); BD, loc. cit. (*Aurelius*). Immigrants: III, 2747, 2743 (*Fabericius*). Slave: III, 9792 *Agricola Iul(iorum) servus*.
[6] III, 9783. His age 10 is certainly an error on the stone. On the *Bennii*, see below, p. 325.
[7] D. Rendić-Miočević, GZMS, 6 (1951), 49 ff.
[8] III, 2776: [*Ti. Claudio? . . .*] *principi Delmatarum ann. XXII Claudia Tib. fil. [. . ., also *Diadora*, 1 (1959), 233, n. 9; cf. fig. 9: *Ti. Claudius Firmus Ti. Claudi Triti f. Firmus ann. VII*.

number of persons, and the development of the settlement as a whole was very slow. Neither the place nor its people are recorded by Pliny. The settlement appears to have been organized as a village (*vicus*) under the control of *magistri*, at least during the time when the Delmatae as a whole were controlled by a Roman or a native prefect.[1] For some part of the first century a small legionary detachment was maintained there.[2]

Rider advanced only very slowly towards achieving full city status, perhaps because so few settler families chose to settle there, although those that did arrive held leading positions in the community.[3] Rider is rich in records of the native population, and only a small proportion have any Latin names. The form of the names is also entirely native, usually appearing as a personal name with the name of the father in the genitive.[4] It is not known when Rider became a city (*municipium* of the Riditae as it is styled), but this is unlikely to have taken place before the Flavian period, and the grant of city status appears to have been Latin Status of the lesser grade (*Ius Latinum minus*), in which only the magistrates (*IIviri*) acquired their citizenship automatically, the councillors (*decuriones*) remaining non-Romans (*peregrini*).[5] The universal grant of citizenship in the early third century is reflected by the number of Aurelii; later immigration is attested, including some families of eastern origin. Neither trade nor manufacturing, however, appear to have been important and the economy was probably entirely agricultural. There is some trace of slavery among native families.[6] At the highest level some of the old native families, descended from the tribal *principes*, may have retained their position after the city was founded; the *princeps* of the *municipium* of the Riditae may have been the member of such a family, although he bears the Latin name Petronius.[7]

At a point where the river Hippius leaves Sinjskopolje to enter the hills behind Oneum was the legionary fortress Tilurium. After the departure of the legion in the middle of the first century an auxiliary regiment was permanently stationed

[1] III, 9865 (6410).   [2] III, 2772.

[3] III, 2770, also decurion of Salona.

[4] D. Rendić-Miočević, *GZMS*, 6 (1951), 49 ff.

[5] Mommsen, CIL, III, p. 363. III, 2774: *IIviri qq., princeps municipii Riditarum*; III, 2026 (Salona): *IIvir qq.* and *dispunctor* (auditor), *BD*, 38 (1916), 45 (Srinjine di Poljica): *IIvir* and *decurio*. Non-citizen *decuriones*: III, 2773, 2775, 6411; cf. *Germania* 34 (1956) 237; III, 2770, *ARR*, 2 (1962), 329, n. 4: *dec(urio) et pr[inceps municipii] Riditaru[m* . . .]; III, 12815a (Perun between Pituntium and Nareste); III, 6371 (Pituntium): *IIvir*.

[6] Eastern settlers: III, 2784 (*Eutychus*), 2777 (*Malcio*), also the worship of Mithras, *VAHD*, 53 (1905-1), 216, n. 11. Slavery: *GZMS*, 6 (1951), 53, n. 5, 51, n. 3, 59, n. 14 (freedwoman); III, 9872 (*verna*). The *collegium fabrum*; III, 2026, is probably that of Salona, Alföldy *Bevölkerung* 97.

[7] III, 2774.

there. A small civilian settlement grew up near by, but on the whole veterans did not choose to settle there. Some families along with their slaves did arrive, but by the second century the main centre in this area was the colony Aequum at the other end of the polje.[1] A record of a guild of bronzeworkers at Tilurium probably belongs to the college at Aequum.[2]

The only colony known to have been settled in Dalmatia after Augustus was at Aequum (Čitluk in Sinjskopolje). The date of foundation is not certain but its title *Claudia* indicates the reign of Claudius (41–54).[3] It was enrolled in the voting tribe Tromentina, to judge from serving soldiers who name Aequum as their home town.[4] Before the establishment of the colony, which probably took place when the legion left Tilurium for Moesia, there was a community of Roman citizens (*conventus*) already established there. Some families probably arrived from Salona, and these appear enrolled in the voting tribe Sergia, one of those attested in the colony.[5] The specific evidence for the *conventus* appears on the tombstone of the settler Sex. Iulius Silvanus (his tribe Aniensis establishes that he was an immigrant), who may have been a legionary veteran from Tilurium. For a time he was chief commissioner of the Roman citizens settled there (*summus curator civium Romanorum*), when they may have been established on lands controlled by the legion. When the colony was created he was the first to be elected aedile, by the veterans of the Legion VII C.p.f., and later became one of the magistrates (*IIIIvir*) and also priest (*pontifex*).[6] His family was to rise much higher over the next century: Sex. Iulius Severus, probably his grandson, was Hadrian's best general, and his son Cn. Iulius Verus held a similar position in the following generation.[7] The original population of the colony was a mixture of civilians and veterans, the latter receiving their discharge gratuities in the form of a land grant (*missio agraria*) in the colony. Tombstones record a veteran of Legion XI Claudia and a cavalryman from the Ala Claudia nova.[8] Like the earlier colonies

---

[1] Above, p. 110 n. 2.   [2] *BD*, 26 (1903), 131, n. 3114: *co[lle]gium [ae]nia[torum]*?

[3] *Colonia Claudia Aequum*: III, 1323 (Zlatna, Dacia), 4376 (Arrabona), 15004 (Burnum); III, 2026 (Salona). The colony is not mentioned by Pliny, although he does record the Claudian veteran settlement at Siculi (Biač) above p. 114.

[4] XIII, 6828, 6830, 6831, 6833 (all in I Adiutrix); *RIB*, 486–7 (II Adiutrix).

[5] III, 2730, 9767; *SB*, 233, n. 1, 234, n. 2. Also the senatorial *Iulii*, see below, p. 321 ff.

[6] III, 2733: *Sex. Iu[lius . . . f.] Ani. Silva[nus] summus c[urator c. R.] suffragio [? veteranor.] leg. VII C.p.f. aed[ilis ab] ordine primus[factus . . .] IIIIvir i. d. pontifex [. . .* The title of summus curator is found also in Gaul, XII, 1721, 1900 (Lugdunum). *Sex. Iulii* and tribe Aniensis are common in Gallia Narbonensis and Silvanus may originate from there, Alföldy, *ES* (forthcoming).

[7] Below, p. 321.

[8] III, 9761 (Hrvace), 14946 (Glavice); *VAHD*, 55 (1953), 184, n. 4 (Gala); *BD*, 38 (1915), 154, 4633A (Sinj), also above, p. 114 f.

along the coast Aequum attracted many settler families, but few of them appear to have arrived directly from Italy. Most came through the larger cities, especially Salona which was barely 20 miles away.[1] There are a few of the native Delmatae recorded, but the ruling group seems to have been composed exclusively of settlers. At a lower level some men left Aequum for service in the legions and in the fleets at Ravenna and Misenum.[2] Civilians from the colony are found in other provinces as traders, especially in Dacia where the links with Dalmatia were particularly close.[3]

There is no evidence for centuriation, nor are there any other precise indications for the extent of the colony's territory. As has already been suggested (p. 109), there was probably a connection between the removal of the legion from Tilurium and the creation of the colony. This released land which could be issued to veteran settlers and incorporated into the territory of the colony. On a lesser scale this happened at Bigeste early under Tiberius, when veterans were settled after the transfer of *auxilia* and their lands incorporated into the territory of the existing colony at Narona (p. 112). In the case of Aequum most of the polje around Sinj was probably made part of the colony's territory. It will also have included small communities of the Delmatae, such as the Osiniates of the Sinj area recorded on a dedication.[4] How far the lands of Aequum reached along the Hippius valley above Hrvace is not known, but it seems unlikely that an area occupied by native people only and with no settlers attested was included in the colony, and there is some evidence that one of the settlements near Vrlika became a city in its own right. To the west the territory reached as far as the area of Andetrium, to judge from the estates of a decurion who was buried there.[5] Economically the colony depended on the produce of its territory. Slavery is attested in the early period: most of the slaves recorded were owned by veterans or settler families.[6] It is not certain to what extent the colony maintained its prosperity in later years, but there is little indication that the commercial or

---

[1] On the Aequum families see below, p. 305 f.

[2] P. 242 n. 4 above. Also in Legion XI C.p.f., III, 15004 (Burnum), 14214/11, 1.

[3] III, 1323 (Ampelum), 1109; cf. p. 1390 (Apulum); III, 1596 (Val) all *honestiores*; III, 1262 (Verespatak), 1223 (Apulum), 1407 (Kiskalan): *pagus Aequensis*. Also in Liburnian Senia, above, p. 200.

[4] *VAHD*, 51 (1930–4), 157, dedication to [?I.O.M. et G]*enio Osini(atium)* by P. Rapidius *signifer*. The place may be connected to Sinotion (Synodion), above, p. 41.

[5] III, 9783.

[6] Freedmen: III, 2734, 9766, 9771, 9777, 9778 (all Aequum), *BD*, 26 (1903), 127 (Bajagić); *VAHD*, 55 (1953), 185, fig. 4 (Gala); III, 14946 (Glavice). Sevirate: III, 2734, 9765, *VAHD*, 55 (1953), 258, n. 6 (Glavice), *BD*, 34 (1911), 56, n. 4060A (Salona): . . . IIIIIIv[*ir co*]*l. Aequ*[*ensium . . . orna*]*to orn*[*amentis decurionalibus*], an honorary councillor.

industrial life of Aequum approached anything near the level attained by the major coastal cities.

The long stretch of the Hippius valley above Sinj appears to have been inhabited throughout the Roman period by native Delmatae. Vrlika and its vicinity has produced a large number of native tombstones, comparable with those of Rider.[1] Roman citizenship was not granted to any people dwelling in the area before the second century. At this time men were recruited to serve in auxiliary units and, during the third century, in the praetorian guard at Rome.[2] There is no definite evidence for the political organization of these settlements. In the first century a boundary settlement from Šušnjar between Vrlika and Koljane records the Barizani and the Lizaviates, small communities of the Delmatae similar to the Promonenses and the Osiniates.[3] They also may have been administered as *pagi*, subject to the control of a Roman prefect or native *principes* selected by the governor. The first-named people may be linked with Bariduum, a place recorded on one of the routes depicted on the Peutinger Map. As with Magnum in the Čikola valley a city may have been organized there under Marcus Aurelius; the only trace of city institutions is a *quinquennalis* of unknown date.[4] The name of the city may have been Setovia, a stronghold of the Delmatae captured by Octavianus and to be located somewhere in the area west of Aequum. At Rider a decurion of *Set(ovia?)* is recorded.[5] He was not a Roman citizen and the city may have received the same grant of Lesser Latin Status (*Ius Latinum minus*) that was granted to Rider.[6]

Southeast of Aequum and Sinjskopolje was the polje of Imotski, separated from the coast between Oneum and Makarska by ridges of mountains which rise in places to more than 4,000 feet. Although the only definite evidence is the base at Gradac near Posušje, it is likely that Novae (Runović) was a post on the military route between Tilurium and Bigeste in the first century. The only record of the Roman army in the vicinity of Novae is a third-century record of the Cohort I Belgarum at Tihaljina, which lay more than 10 miles south of the city along the road to the unit's permanent base at Bigeste.[7] Apart from some legionary veterans settled in the first century (p. 112) all the civilians recorded on tombstones in the area are natives, none of whom received citizenship before the

[1] Patsch, *WMBH*, 7 (1900), 119 ff. and below, p. 395 f.

[2] III, 13201 (Koljane near Vrlika).

[3] Below, p. 458 f. Few of the names of the *castella* among the Delmatae have been preserved, for example a marine from *Castrum Planae*, XI, 76.

[4] III, 14967 (Kievo).

[5] *GZMS*, 6 (1951), 57, n. 10 = Šašel, 185 (Rider).

[6] Suggested by Mommsen, *CIL*, III, p. 363.

[7] III, 12810.

middle of the second century. At first Novae was a post manned by *beneficiarii consulares* which was still maintained there after the city was established, probably in the reign of Marcus Aurelius.[1] The earliest record is a dedication recording the rebuilding of the bridge over the river Tihaljina at Kamenmost in 170, paid for by the city.[2] A few years later the Novenses, along with the people of Rider and Delminium, paid for the building of the bridge over the Hippius at Tilurium. It is possible that the territory of these three cities all met at this important river crossing where one of the main roads into the interior passed over the river.[3] At Novae the *beneficiarii* held an important position in the city and often coupled the city of Novae with their official dedications to Jupiter Best and Greatest. One dedication is dated by consuls to 194; another of about the same period is dated only by magistrates of the city (*IIviri quinquennales*). Three of the recorded magistrates have the name Aurelius.[4] Most probably the Novenses, one of the communities of the Delmatae, occupied most of Imotskipolje and may have extended southeastwards along the river Tihaljina towards the auxiliary post at Bigeste; on the southwest they reached to the coast around Makarska, in spite of the difficult nature of the country.[5]

III *Narona and the Southern Coastline* (fig. 8)

From the time of the earliest contacts between Dalmatia and the Greek World the river Narenta (Neretva) was a major trade route between the Adriatic and the interior. Before the fourth century a Greek trading post (*emporion*) was established near the mouth of the river;[6] its importance increased with the growth of the settlement at Narona (Vid), the only city of the Dalmatian coast which could rival the provincial capital Salona to the north. Indeed, before the organization of the province late under Augustus, Narona was probably the more important centre of the two for the Romans. On the other hand, its prosperity seems to have declined by the late second century A.D., when it was completely overshadowed by Salona to the north and by newer native communities which were developing rapidly as cities. The main reason for this decline was probably its position, a low hill on the west side of the marshy delta of the Narenta. The

---

[1] At least one altar was dated by magistrates, III, 1910 and above, p. 125 f.

[2] III, p. 2328/121 (1913), also fragmentary dedication to Pius, possibly by the city; III, p. 2328/121 (add. 1912).

[3] III, 3203; cf. p. 1651.

[4] III, 1910, 1892 (Zaostrog). T. *Aelius* Messor, III, 8509 (Postranje), may have obtained citizenship from Pius. *Septimii*: III, 8508, 8511.

[5] III, 1892 (Zaostrog).

[6] Theopompus in Strabo vii, 5, 9; cf. Pseudo-Scylax, c. 24.

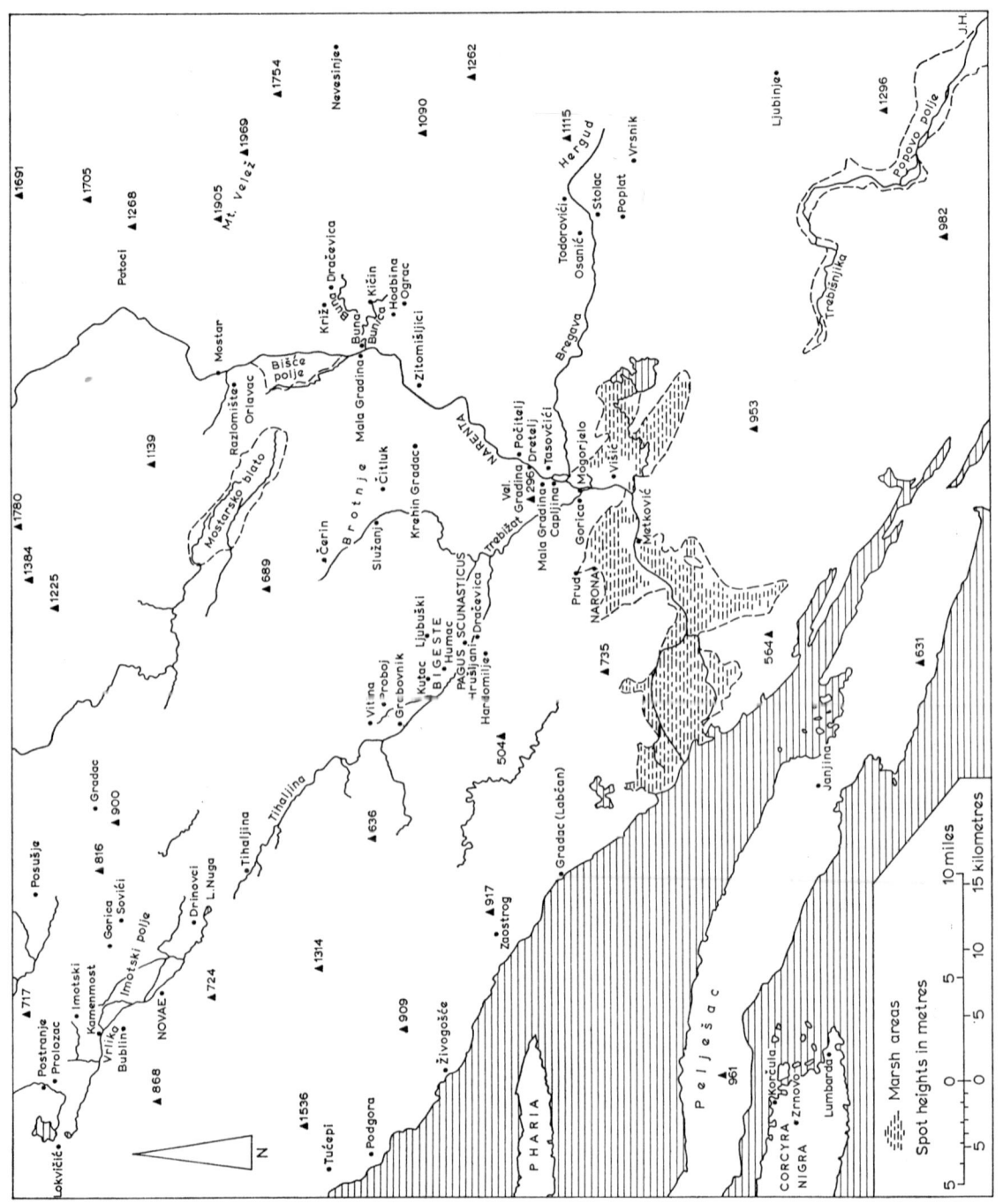

Figure 8 Narona Area

246

area is frequently flooded and is unhealthy in the summer; there is no proper harbour for coastal shipping near the city (unless the river has changed its course radically since ancient times). Thus it enjoyed poor facilities by comparison with other coastal cities. The modern centre of the area is on the opposite side of the river at Metković, a place which has become a byword in Dalmatia for primitive conditions.[1]

In the late second and first centuries B.C. it was Narona which attracted settlers and traders from Italy. Originally on land controlled by the Pleraei or the Ardiaei, it fell under Roman influence after the defeat of Gentius, while Salona remained continuously in the hands of the hostile Delmatae until at least the early seventies B.C. The growth of Salona took place later; under Caesar's dictatorship Narona was still the main Roman centre, used as a base by P. Vatinius in his campaigns against the Delmatae in 45–44 B.C. and possibly later by P. Servilius Isauricus.[2] Unlike Salona, where the only certain epigraphic evidence for the pre-colonial period is the Greek decree of 56 B.C. involving Issa and her territories, Narona has produced a number of inscriptions belonging to the period of the *conventus*, including one which records the quasi-municipal organization of the settlement. Built into the houses of the modern village, like many of the Narona inscriptions, is a record of the building of a defensive wall with towers under the four officials of the *conventus*, two *magistri* and two *quaestores,* replicas of the normal *IIviri* and *quaestores* (or *aediles*) in a proper city. One of each pair of magistrates is a freedman.[3] The only one with a *cognomen* is the freedman *quaestor* who has the native name Epicadus. It is tempting to connect the defences which he and his colleagues built with the civil emergency when the Dalmatian *conventus* fought for Caesar against Pompey, and were rewarded with colonial status, although Narona is not mentioned in any of the episodes of the civil war in the Adriatic. The freedman *quaestor* P. Annaeus Epicadus also built a temple to Liber Pater, possibly on behalf of his patron, indicating the position already attained by freedman in the Narona *conventus*.[4] This cult lasted at Narona: a temple was built there for it by the auxiliary unit in garrison at Bigeste under Marcus Aurelius.[5] Not only was the Narona settlement already functioning as a city, but it was also the centre of the Roman administration under the Republican proconsuls, the seat of the judicial circuit (*conventus*) where, according to Varro, as many as eighty-nine peoples (*civitates*) were accustomed to attend.[6] The influx of Italian settlers was not confined to the city itself: at Tasovčići, a few miles

[1] *WMBH*, 12 (1912), 68 ff.; Patsch, *Beiträge*, VI (1933).

[2] Patsch, *Narona*, 23, fig. 12.

[3] III, 8423 (1820).

[4] III, 1784.   [5] III, 8484 (1790, 6362).   [6] Plin., *HN*, iii, 142 and below, p. 484 f.

higher up the Narenta on the opposite bank, the Papii brothers recorded on stone the victory of the triumvir Octavianus and the recovery of Sicily in 36 B.C.[1]

Some time before 27 B.C. Narona became a colony (*colonia Iulia Narona*).[2] Dedications set up by *seviri* while Augustus was still alive rule out any later date for its foundation, for instance under Tiberius, which some have suggested.[3] The historical context for the foundation is similar to that of the others along the Dalmatian coast, reward to loyal partisans after the civil war and a strengthening of *clientela*.[4] The colony was enrolled in the voting tribe Tromentina, suggesting that it was founded at the same time as the earlier settlement at Salona, that is during the last years of Caesar.[5] All the evidence suggests that the colony was not settled with legionary veterans, but rather civilians.[6] One may doubt whether the new settlers were greater in number than the people already established in the *conventus*. Veterans did settle at Narona, or rather in its territory, at the beginning of Tiberius' reign, when the mutiny of legions in Illyricum forced the government to release men who had served long past their proper time of discharge. A group of long service veterans from Legion VII at Tilurium were settled at Pagus Scunasticus in the territory of Narona not far from Bigeste. There is no evidence to connect this settlement, made in 14 or 15, with the foundation of the colony as a whole. The lands near Bigeste were issued to these men as their belated discharge grant (*missio agraria*).[7] Other veterans are attested in the reign of Claudius, and it is possible that they were part of another organized settlement similar to that at Siculi on the territory of Salona.[8] Neither of these settlements had a great impact on the colony, which was already dominated by families originating mainly from Central and Southern Italy, many of them represented by a large group of rich freedmen.[9]

A few families may have arrived from Northern Italy, including the Aquillii who may be linked with a family of the same name established at Flanona.[10] Altogether about fifty-six families can be connected with different parts of Italy:

[1] III, 14265: *Imp. Caesari divi f. Sicilia recepta C. Papius Celsus M. Papius Kanus fratres.*
[2] *Iulia Narona*: BD, 33 (1910), 106 (early in 193); *colonia Naronit(ana)*: BIAB, 16 (1950), 236= Šašel 113 f.; cf. III, 12695, *colonia Narona*: Plin., HN, iii, 142; Ptol., ii, 16, 7.
[3] III, 1769; *VAHD*, 54 (1952), 165, fig. 7, pl. XI=*Šašel* 107 (12–8 B.C.).
[4] As suggested for Salona, p. 221.
[5] III, 1851; cf. p. 1029; III, 1868; cf. p. 1029, GZMBH, 36 (1924), 87 ff.; III, 14623/2 (8451), Janjina on Pelješac; cf. *VAHD*, 55 (1953), 234, n. 48.
[6] F. Vittinghoff, 124, n. 4.   [7] Abramić, BIAB, 19 (1950), 235 f. and above, p. 112 f.
[8] GZMBH, 35 (1923), 83 (Vitina); III, 1811, 1814, 1812 (probably an auxiliary).
[9] Alföldy, *Bevölkerung*, 136 f., n. 27.
[10] *Aquilii*: III, 1770 (*sevir*), 8448. On the family, see p. 195.

some can be connected with individual cities, for instance the Bovianii who originated from Bovianum Vetus in the Samnite country.[1] The majority of Italian family names occur with those of freedmen, often on expensive dedications. They had probably been established at Narona to conduct business and control land on behalf of their patrons who remained in Italy. This is the best explanation for the small number of leading families recorded, when compared with those of their freedmen. As at Salona in the early period, there is no record of the native population at Narona, apart from the official of the *conventus* who had the Illyrian name Epicadus (p. 247); most probably they were expelled from the Lower Narenta when the power of the *conventus* was increasing.[2] The few magistrates of the colony recorded belong mostly to Italian settler families. Both *IIviri* and *IIIIviri* are attested,[3] and the change from the former to the latter magistracy may have taken place about the end of the first century, as appears to have happened at Salona (p. 223). The voting tribe Tromentina is not widely attested: few of the upper classes bothered to record their voting tribe on tombstones, and one retained his old tribe Aniensis.[4] This lack of uniformity, unlike at Salona or Iader where all the upper classes were either in Tromentina or Sergia, is another indication that the population of the *conventus* remained dominant after the colony was established. A change took place in the composition of the ruling group in the later first century, when the Flavian rulers gave citizenship to some of the native population in the hinterland. A second-generation citizen T. Flavius Laedio, son of T. Flavius Blodi f., was *IIIIvir* and aedile of Narona at the end of the first century.[5] This family may have been aristocrats of the Narensii and are recorded at their home at Stolac in the Bregava valley. The wealthy families of Flavii at Doclea in the south also entered the ruling circle at the same time, and they were overshadowing the older settler families both in Narona and the other coastal cities. Compared with those of Salona or Aequum the upper classes of Narona did not advance into the imperial hierarchy of the

[1] III, 1800 (*sevir*).

[2] *P. Annaeus Epicadus*, below, p. 299; *P. Mucius Dasius*, *VAHD*, 55 (1953), 261 f., n. 12, on a collegiate *IIIIIIviri* dedication.

[3] III, 1822: *A. Annaeus A.f. An. Flaccus flamen Augustalis IIIIvir II quinqu. IIIIvir i. d. praef. i.d. ex dec. dec. pontif. IIIIviri*: III, 1774, 1832 (son of freedman); *VAHD*, 55 (1953), 234, n. 48 (III, 8451 = 14623/2) Janjina on Pelješac; *GZMBH*, 37 (1925), 87 ff. (son of *sevir Augustalis*, Žitomisljići). Enfranchised *Flavii* at Stolac, below, n. 5; III, 14626. *IIviri*: *VAHD*, 54 (1952), 166, fig. 8. *aediles* and *decuriones*: *BD*, 33 (1910), 110 (possibly of freedman origin); III, 8443, 8441, 8444, also a (*h*)*aruspex*: *BD*, 33 (1910), 109, also auditor (*dispunctor*) from Bistue in the interior: III, 8783, cf. p. 2326; and two noble ladies in priesthoods: III, 1796, 6361.

[4] *Aniensis*: III, 1822.   [5] *GZMS*, 3 (1948), 168, pl. I (Stolac).

equestrian and senatorial orders, although in the first century they did enjoy for a time the patronage of the Neronian governor A. Ducenius Geminus. The only senator recorded from the city was M. Lusius Severus, but he appears to have performed no office within that order.[1]

To judge from the number and quality of their dedications the freedmen of Narona outshone members of the city council and magistrates in their display. Many records of this class are corporate dedications by the *seviri* of the freedman imperial cult, which was established under Augustus. There are variations in the titles attached to this office: many are called *IIIIIIviri* only, while some have the additional abbreviated title *M.M.*, which has been expanded to *Magister Mercurialis*, emphasizing the importance of commerce to this class. There are only two records of *IIIIIIviri Augustales*. In the early second century the cult was brought up to date to include the Flavians and Nerva with the omnibus title *Augustalis Flavialis Titialis Nervialis*. A *flamen Augustalis*, who may have been the head of this cult, was a leading member of the city aristocracy.[2] Compared with the other colonies there is little evidence for trade-guilds of free workers (*collegia*). The only record of the usually common craftsmen's guild (*collegium fabrum*) is a first-century dedication to a freedman *sevir*.[3]

Although the inscriptions reveal Narona as a thriving centre with a wealthy freedmen class, there is no evidence for the size or character of the city itself or for any of its major buildings. Nor is there any indication that Narona was a manufacturing centre: the only trade attested is that of stonemason (*lapidarius*).[4] However, the large quantity of imported goods at Narona and around the Narenta valley suggests that the import and export traffic between the hinterland, interior, and the Adriatic, was the main basis for the city's prosperity in the early period.[5] Similarly, the decline of the city in the second century may have been partly due to the decrease of this trade with Italy. Few third-century inscriptions are known, although there is a record of the rebuilding of the municipal winter

---

[1] *JAK*, 2 (1908), 96; III 1786. *Lusii* are common at Narona (17 persons).

[2] Patsch, *JAK*, 2 (1908), 90 f. *Seviri*: III, 1825, 1826, *JÖAI*, 15 (1912–13), Bb. 77, n. 1; III, 1828, 1830, *VAHD*, 55 (1953), 261 f., n. 12; III, 14223/1, Patsch, *Narona*, 37, n. 5, fig. 17, op. cit., 91 f., n. 6, fig. 50; III, 1824; cf. Patsch, *Narona*, 88; III, 14625/1, 8442, 8443, 1835, 1793, 1831 also possibly 1802. *Seviri m(agistri) M(ercuriales)*: III, 1827, 1798, 8440; cf. Patsch, *Narona*, 87, n. 2, fig. 46; III, 1800, 1775, 1770, 1792. *M(agistri) M(ercuriales)*: III, 8421 (1801), 1769; cf. 1833. *Seviri Augustales*: III, 1832, *GZMBH*, 37 (1925), 87 ff. (Žitomisljići). *Augustalis*: III, 1851; cf. p. 1029. *Augustalis F(lavialis) T(itialis) [N(ervialis)]*: III, 14624/1. *Sevir Augustalis Flavialis Titialis Nervialis*: III, 1768, 1835; cf. 1797. *IIIIvir (ter) flamen Augustalis*: III, 1822, also *seviri* a the head of the youth association (*thiasus iuventutis*): III, 1828.

[3] Patsch, *Narona*, 91 f., n. 7, fig. 51: *C. Iunio C. l. Cisso IIIIIIviro collegium fabrum*.

[4] III, 1777.   [5] Below, p. 411.

baths (*thermae hiemales*) in 280 by a senior army officer who orginated from there.[1] Some later immigrants are attested, including some from the eastern provinces and from Africa, while the Artorii from Salona are also attested.[2] Unlike the other coastal cities Narona has produced few traces of enfranchised native families with names such as Aelius or Aurelius. This was due not to the conservatism of the government towards the population of the area but rather to the lack of attraction of Narona as a place to settle in.[3]

There is no evidence for centuriation in the territory around Narona. The lower Narenta valley is marshy and there is little arable land. The only major area is further north in Bijelopolje around Mostar. Otherwise the land is in such small pockets and so irregularly distributed that delimitation by centuriation was probably impracticable. The Narenta valley below Mostar with its major tributaries the Bregava and Trebižat were all included in the territory of the colony. The area is a compact unit and in later centuries formed the main part of the Hercegovina principality with its capital at Mostar. Further south the land around the mouth of the Narenta and the Pelješac peninsula was also part of the city; in the latter a magistrate of the colony is attested at Janjina.[4] To the west much of the land around Ljubuški, including the pagus Scunasticus where veterans were settled under Tiberius, was included in the territory of Narona, except for the area around Bigeste where an auxiliary fort was maintained into the third century. To the east the Bregava valley around Stolac also belonged to the colony, to judge from the Flavii there who were magistrates.[5] No other city is known to have existed in this area, and all the native peoples appear to have been annexed to the colony under the Flavians, including the Pleraei, Ardiaei, and the Daversi (Daorsii).[6] Some of the early Italian settlers chose to live in the country: the Papii brothers at Tasovčići were probably landowners, as also were the Safinii, one of whom appears among the officers of the *conventus* in the first century B.C.[7]

The economic position of the city in relation to its territory changed considerably over the years. As the long distance trade, in particular that with Italy, tailed off so more goods were produced locally. The freedmen who were so promi-

[1] III, 1805; cf. p. 2328/119.

[2] III, 8425 (1846) and below, p. 328 f.

[3] *Aelii*: III, 1839, 12798a (married to a *Safinius*); III, 12789 (8431), Stolac. *Aurelii*: WMBH, 9 (1909), 266 (Potoci, dedication to Mithras).

[4] Note 3 on p. 249.

[5] Note 5 on p. 249.

[6] The Daversus on the diploma of 94 (XVI, 38) could have been born in the territory of Narona.

[7] On the *Papii* and *Safinii*, see below, p. 298 f.

nent in the first century are almost unknown by the end of the second, the more successful being by then absorbed into the ruling class as established landowners. There also appears a tendency for the wealthy families to move away from the city and live on their lands in various parts of the territory; and a number of those attested in the city during the early period now appear in different parts of the countryside.[1] Of all the Italian-dominated cities on the Dalmatian coast, Narona appears to have had the least impact on the native population. In its early years all the families, with perhaps one or two exceptions, were immigrants, settlers and traders. When the economy of the city declined, the city had no natural advantages such as a local community or a sea-port, as Iader and Salona had, to fall back on. In other cities new people were settling during the second century, both from other provinces of the Empire and from the interior of Dalmatia, whence a considerable movement of the native upper classes can be observed. Although such people can be discovered at Narona, they did not arrive in sufficient strength to halt the decline of the city.[2] The last reference to the place is when delegates from its church attended the Salona provincial councils in 530 and 533.[3] After that it disappeared into obscurity. For much of the Middle Ages it lay on the border between Dalmatia and Hercegovina, a no-man's-land between the Turks and the Adriatic coast, like the deserted Salona to the north.

The third of the colonies in Dalmatia bore the Greek name Epidaurum. The small headland south of Dubrovnik may have been a trading post frequented by merchants, but there is no evidence that it was ever an established Greek settlement. The place is first recorded as a stronghold (*praesidium*) of Caesar during the civil war, attacked by the Pompeian fleet in 47 B.C. but saved by the intervention of P. Vatinius.[4] Like other places along the coast it may have been occupied by a community of Roman citizens, although no record of them survives on the inscriptions. According to Pliny, Epidaurum was a colony and tombstones reveal that it was enrolled in the tribe Tromentina.[5] The foundation was probably part of Caesar's programme to reward his allies in the Adriatic. As at the other colonies, there is no evidence that veterans were settled there; all the families attested appear to be civilian settlers.[6] A small military post was maintained at Epidaurum in the early first century, drawn from the citizen auxiliary

[1] Alföldy, *Bevölkerung*, 138 f.
[2] *BD*, 33 (1910), 106 f., dedication to Jupiter Dolichenus under Pertinax in 193 by Flavius Faladus and Domitius Apollinaris. Also other eastern cults, *Isis*: III, 1864, *Mithras*: III, 1783, 1788; cf. p. 1029, also Patsch, *WMBH*, 6 (1899), 209.
[3] Farlati, *IS*, 2, 10; 4, 184; *Naronitana ecclesia.*   [4] *Bell. Alex.*, 44 and above, p. 42.
[5] Plin., *HN*, iii, 143; cf. 144; III, 12695 (Doclea). *Tromentina*: III, 8407, 1755, 1748, 1745; *Syria* 30 (1953), 278, fig. 2 (Marcius Turbo, see below, p. 327).
[6] Vittinghoff, 124, n. 24 and above, p. 207.

units, Cohorts VI and VIII Voluntariorum. The only closely dated record is of a tribune of the former unit, L. Purtisius Atinas (from Atina in Campania), under the governor P. Cornelius Dolabella (14–21). It appears to be an official dedication or building record and names the two magistrates (*IIviri*) of the colony, both from settler families.[1] Seven of these are attested altogether, including one *quinquennalis*, and there are single instances of decurions and aediles.[2] No members of the freedman associations are known, but the *Augustales* and *seviri* together received donations from one of the colony's leading citizens.[3] In the early period the ruling class consisted of Italian settler families, although the exclusiveness of this group is less marked than at Salona or Narona.[4] Some of the families may have reached Epidaurum from these places, but one or two families have names which suggest native origin, and their entry into the ruling class before the end of the first century is unusual for a city outside Liburnia. The Pomentini (attested otherwise only at Dyrrhachium) and the Marcii may be examples of such families; from the latter came Hadrian's great praetorian prefect Q. Marcius Turbo.[5]

Once Epidaurum may have been a great coastal city, but in late antiquity parts of it were submerged beneath the sea. Along the southern part of the Dalmatian coast the land appears to have subsided more than 2 metres in places. During the last few years underwater exploration in the Bay of Cavtat has shown that considerable remains of the city exist beneath the Adriatic, but these discoveries await proper publication.[6] There is no evidence for the original size of the city, but it is unlikely that it compared with any of the larger colonies to the north. In the first century it was the centre for the imperial cult in Dalmatia,[7] although a separate centre existed for Liburnia at Scardona (p. 218). As Epidaurum declined in the second century the burden of the cult became too great for the city, and it was transferred to the new Flavian *municipium* of Doclea, some of whose leading citizens were already beginning to dominate the older coastal cities.[8]

The territory of the colony probably included the coast from the area of the

---

[1] G. Novak, *Rad*, 339 (1965), 129 and below, p. 473.

[2] III, 8407: *quinquennalis*, 8408, 1747, 1748, 1750.

[3] III, 1745.

[4] *Anuleni*: III, 1750; *Fulvii*: III, 1739; *Saenii*: *Rad*, 339 (1965), 129; *Statii*: III, 1757 (below, p. 302); *Varii*: III, 1755; *Vibii*: XVI, 14 (diploma witness in 71); III, 1750.

[5] *Pomentini*: III, 1748; cf. *LE*, 533, n. 12; also in Dyrrhachium, III, 622, probably of the Epidaurum family. *Marcii*: III, 1755.

[6] *Chron. Min.*, 1, p. 239; cf. Evans, *Archaeologia* 48 (1884) 18. For underwater exploration, E. Falcon-Barker, *passim*, with useful endpaper maps.

[7] III, 1741; cf. *Rad*, 339 (1965) 128.   [8] III, 12695 and below, p. 260.

lower Narenta, where it may have bordered on that of Narona, to the northern edge of the Gulf of Risinium around Hercegnovi. Within this area there is much fertile land, but it is not concentrated in one area as is the case around Iader and Salona. There is good land in the valley of Konavli, which extends for 10 miles south of the city and is closed off from the sea by a low range of hills. A system of irrigation which ran the whole length of Konavli and supplied water to the city reservoir was studied by Evans in the last century, who discovered the record of a magistrate buried with his family at Ljuta in the south end of Konavli.[1] At least around the city the land was divided by centuriation on an identical system of *centuriae* to that used in the other colonies of Dalmatia. Little is known about the extent of the system: only a few aerial photographs have been published, and the *limites* of the *centuriae* have been almost obliterated by later cultivation.[2]

Little is known about Epidaurum in the later period. Some families are recorded, and the magistrate at Ljuta suggests that the wealthy preferred to move away from the city and live on their estates in the country, as happened at Narona. The cult of Mithras became well established at a number of places near the city, which may have been the result of immigration from the East.[3] Despite the natural disasters Epidaurum survived as an urban community and its bishop attended the Salona provincial council in 533. About 615 Epidaurum was destroyed by the invading Slavs and Avars: the population of the Roman city were led by the bishop John to a refuge further north along the coast where the great mediaeval trading city Ragusa was founded.[4]

On the coast between Epidaurum and the river Drilo Pliny lists six places as settlements of Roman citizens' (*oppida civium Romanorum*), Risinium, Acruvium, Butua, Olcinium, Scodra (not a coastal settlement strictly speaking, but on the lake named after it), and Lissus on the provincial boundary with Macedonia.[5] Four of them are attested as chartered cities: for the two smallest places, Butua (Budva) and Olcinium (Ulcinj), there is no evidence.

The city of Risinium (Risan in the Gulf of Kotor) was situated at the northern extremity of one of the arms of the great bay which in antiquity was named after it (*sinus Rhizonicus*). Virtually sealed off from the interior by high mountains, sea transport has always been vital to the settlement.[6] It began as Rhizon, a settle-

[1] Evans, *Archaeologia*, 48 (1884), 37 ff.; cf. III, 8408 (Ljuta).
[2] M. Suić, *Zbornik*, 1 (1955), 20, pl. VIII.
[3] *Mithras*: Evans, op. cit., 19 ff.; cf. *GZMS*, 8 (1953), 275 ff.
[4] Const. Porph., *DAI*, c. 29, 215 ff.; cf. Farlati, *IS* 6, 4–35.   [5] *HN*, iii, 144.
[6] Strabo, vii, 5, 3; cf. Ptol., ii, 16, 3. On the site, Evans, *NC*, 20 (1880), 235 ff. *Archaeologia*, 48 (1884), 39–52.

ment of the Illyrian pirates in the third century B.C. of the Ardiaean kingdom. After the defeat of Gentius in 168 B.C. the Rhizonitae were granted freedom and immunity from taxation (*libertas et immunitas*) for timely desertion to the Roman side.[1] Later it was one of the centres controlled by the Illyrian ruler Ballaios, and there is no evidence that this remote centre ever attracted the attention of Greek traders or settlers. Its early history is entirely Illyrian.

There may have been a small Roman community established at Risinium already in the first century B.C. from which the city developed. An inscription from Doclea gives the title of the *municipium* as *Iulium Risinium*, while tombstones from the city reveal that it was in the voting tribe Sergia.[2] The probable date for its foundation is in the years before 27 B.C., perhaps when Octavianus completed his Illyrian campaigns in 33 B.C. It may even have been a colony, if a reading of a tombstone from Rogatica in the territory of the Daesitiates inscribed *dec(urio) c(oloniae) Ris(inii)* is correct.[3] Italian settler families from Central and Southern Italy are attested, and there are also one or two native families recorded.[4] In the first century the ruling class was exclusively Italian in origin: some of them held equestrian rank and senior military appointments.[5] In the second century the ill-fated senator L. Lucceius Torquatus, commander of Legion III Augusta in Africa in the years 167–9, set up a metric dedication recalling the 'Aeacian Walls' of his native city Risinium and the native deity Medaurus which thrived there.[6] There is not enough fertile land around Risinium to support anything more than a small community, and trade from shipping must have been important to the settlement. There were contacts with the interior: a decurion is found at Rogatica (see above), and the freedman Manlius attested at the road centre Kiseljak near Sarajevo probably belongs to the Risinium family of that name.[7] They may be linked to members of the Adriatic shipping guild at Ostia (*corpus maris Hadriatici*) in which a family of the same

[1] Liv., xlv, 26.

[2] III, 12695 (Doclea); *Sergia*: III, 1717, 6359; cf. p. 1491, 8392 (1730), 8393 (1732), 8403 (1738); XIII, 6852, *ILS* 2638 (Aquileia, *primuspilus* of Legion XIII Gemina; cf. Alföldy, *Bevölkerung*, 149, n. 85).

[3] III, 12748 (2766b, 8369), Rogatica: *T. Cl(audius) Maximus dec. c(oloniae?) Ris(inni?)*, etc. Rejected by Patsch, *WMBH*, 11 (1909), 182, fig, 132, although *Claudii* are rare in the interior, but are known at Risinium, III, 8359; cf. Alföldy, *AAnt.*, 9 (1961), 129 f., n. 35.

[4] *Serveni*: III, 8402 (also at Doclea, III, 12701). *Tifatii*: III, 12785 (1738), both from Southern Italy. *Minidii* (Ostia): III, 8398; cf. *LE*, 362. Native *Plaetorii*: III, 8399, 8392 (1730).

[5] III, 8403 (1738), 1717, 6359 (centurion); *ILS*, 2638 (n. 2 above); XIII, 6852 (?centurion in Legion II Adiutrix).

[6] Below, p. 323 f. On Medaurus, *MZK*, 1903, 171, fig. 41 (Greek dedication at Risinium); Patsch, *JÖAI*, 6 (1903), Bb. 71 ff.   [7] III, 8379; cf. p. 2256 (Kiseljak); cf. III, 1717 (Risinium).

name is recorded.[1] Other immigrant families in the eastern part of the interior, especially at Plevlje, may have come from Risinium,[2] and in the later period traders from the eastern provinces are found in that city.

Acruvium (Kotor), situated in another extremity of the Gulf, probably also began its existence as a pirate stronghold of the Ardiaei. In 167 B.C. the Agravonitae were given freedom and immunity from taxation, in the same manner as the Rhizonitae, and the place is also recorded later by Pliny as a settlement of Roman citizens.[3] The presence of Italian settler families and freedmen suggests that trade was important. Not far to the south, however, the plain of Grbalj contains an area of fertile land which the city may have shared with Butua, the next city to the south. Acruvium was also enrolled in the tribe Sergia, with *IIviri* as magistrates. It may have been a colony, also like Risinium, but the reading of the key inscription at Doclea is uncertain.[4]

Butua on the Adriatic coast probably began as a Greek trading settlement and a calling place for coastal shipping, but by the third century it was in Illyrian hands. Its inhabitants are not mentioned in the settlement imposed on the area by the Romans in 167 B.C., and the only record of it in the Roman period, apart from the later geographers, appears in Pliny.[5] A few of the population, most with Illyrian names, are recorded. The only settler family recorded is the Statii, probably a branch of the family established at Risinium.[6] No inscriptions record the people or the status of Olcinium, although its inhabitants the Olciniatae figure in the settlement of 167 B.C. It was situated on a small promonotory extending from the coast south of the Lake of Scodra. The coast in this area is much less of a mountain barrier than further north between Butua and the Gulf of Kotor.[7]

The most southerly coastal city was Lissus (Lješ) near the mouth of the Albanian Drin. Until 167 B.C. it was the principal base of the Illyrian kingdom,

[1] VI, 9682 (Ostia); cf. XIV 409.
[2] *Caesii*: WMBH, 12 (1912), 127, fig. 52. *Egnatii*: WMBH, 12 (1912), 126, fig. 51; 127, fig. 52. *Paconii*: WMBH, 12 (1912), 124 f., fig. 49, 50. At Risinium, III, 8400. Immigrants; III, 8401, (Iader), 1719 (Cilicia); *VAHD*, 47–8 (1926–7), 73 (Alexandria); III, 1723 = 8390, also *AEM*, 9 (1886), 27 (two Greek tombstones, possibly brought to Risan from elsewhere as ship ballast).
[3] Plin., *HN*, iii, 142; cf. Ptol., ii, 16, 3.
[4] III, 1711 (*IIviri*); *Sergia*: III, 1710, 1711, 1738 (Prevlaka). III, 13829 (cf. Sticotti, *Doclea*, 179 f., n. 53, fig. 138): *Fl. Urso DC AQR*, etc. Sticotti reads *do(mo)* but the C is clear on his own publication. Possibly *d(e)c(urio)* suggested by Hirschfeld (*CIL*, III) is better than *d(ecurio) c(oloniae)* preferred by Alföldy, *Bevölkerung*, 149, n. 78. Freedman association: III, 1713 (*Clodii*).
[5] Liv., xlv, 26; Plin., *HN*, iii, 144; Ptol., ii, 16, 3.
[6] III, 6338 (*Statii*). Native families: *GNUBK*, 4 (1938), 35 f. (not accessible): *Ternia Baia, Iulia Temus*.　　[7] Praschniker-Schober, 82 f., fig. 100.

and was one of the places where Gentius issued his coins.[1] By the time of the civil war Roman settlers had arrived, and the place was a well-organized *conventus* helping Caesar against the Pompeians. As at Salona and Narona, fortifications were constructed during the emergency against the Pompeian fleet.[2] The site of the city is a low steep-sided hill near the mouth of the river. On the hill was the acropolis with walls extending down to the water to protect the harbour at the foot of the hill.[3] The only evidence for city organization is an early *IIvir quinquennalis* who supervised the rebuilding of the city walls, no doubt under Augustus. He may have been a first-generation immigrant from Italy, to judge from his tribe Arnensis which is otherwise unknown in the province.[4] Other inscriptions record the freedmen Didii and a civic dedication to Caracalla.[5]

Lastly in the southeast was the city of Scodra (Skhöder), on a low steep-sided hill at the south end of the lake which is named after it. Protected by rivers on both sides it was once the citadel of the Illyrian kingdom, and was captured by the Romans in 167 B.C.[6] In 40 B.C. Scodra was fixed by the treaty of Brundisium as the boundary between the power of Octavianus and Antonius.[7] There is virtually no evidence for civic institutions from the city itself, but at Doclea a leading citizen in the early second century was priest in the colony of Scodra ([*p*]*on*[*t*]. *in col. Sc*[*o*]*dr*.). It may have been a foundation of Octavianus in the late thirties B.C. after he had received the surrender of the peoples in the area.[8] From the city itself the only evidence for its status is a civic dedication to Septimius in the first year of his reign.[9] No immigrant families are attested there, or in the vicinity: all the names recorded on tombstones are of enfranchised natives of the second and third centuries.[10]

A visit to the sites of these six cities leaves the impression that, with the exception of Lissus, they never developed into urban centres of any importance. Compared with the coastal cities further north archaeological remains are meagre and of poor quality, even allowing for the almost total lack of research carried out in the area. It is curious that the area of Dalmatia where the erosion of tribal

---

[1] *JRS*, 36 (1946), 49 ff.

[2] Caes., *BC*, iii, 26 ff.; cf. Appian, *BC*, ii, 59; Plut., *Ant.*, 7; cf. Plin., *HN*, iii, 144; Ptol., ii, 3, 16; Strabo, vii, 5, 8.

[3] Praschniker-Schober, 14 ff. and below, p. 362 f.

[4] III, 1704: *L. Gavius Arnn(ensis)*.

[5] *Didii*: Praschniker-Schober, 22, fig. 31; Patsch, *JÖAI*, 10 (1907), Bb. 102 (MS source overlooked by *CIL*, III).

[6] Liv., xlv, 8.   [7] Appian, *BC*, v, 65.

[8] III, 12695 (Sticotti, n. 26), now destroyed.   [9] *JÖAI*, 10 (1907), Bb. 101, n. 1.

[10] *Sp.*, 71 (1933), 335; also at Vuksanlekić: III, 14601 (above, p. 185); III, 14602 (*Plaetorii*). Freedmen of immigrant *Cassii*: III, 14600; cf. Praschniker-Schober, 95, fig. 112.

society by political development and outside influence had been most marked was far from becoming the most urbanized in the long term. There can be no comparison between this area in the southeast and the wealthy, highly urbanized, Ravni kotari of Southern Liburnia. The old tribes of the region which were absorbed into the territories of the Roman cities (Illyrii, Labeatae, Taulantii and others) contributed little towards their development, except perhaps as Risinium and Scodra. They may once have been colonies founded by the Romans (only Scodra is certain), but they were so insignificant that Pliny did not know of their status.[1]

iv *Southern Coastal Hinterland*

Few areas of Dalmatia must have appeared so inhospitable and unattractive to settlement as the karst hinterland of Southern Hercegovina, especially around Popovopolje. Away from the coast there is mile upon mile of bare limestone hills separating the few pockets of fertile land. Even today the area is one of the least inhabited parts of Yugoslavia, apart from the even more desolate mountains in the north of Hercegovina and Montenegro. The coast between the river Narenta and Epidaurum was occupied by the Pleraei. Behind them were a group of small peoples, once a part of the Narona *conventus*, but under Augustus they were probably absorbed into the newly-created *civitas* of the Deramistae.[2] Only one city is known to have existed in this area, a late *municipium* named Diluntum. The major centre of the area today is at Trebinje, but the sole record of the city, the tombstone of a decurion of native origin from Trebimlje, suggests that the city was somewhere around the western end of Popovopolje, possibly at Ljubinje a few miles to the northeast.[3] On the main road between Narona and Scodra the Antonine Itinerary and the Peutinger Map record Diluntum (or Daluntum) 25 miles from Narona, somewhere about the western end of Popovopolje.[4]

---

[1] Their colonial status is accepted by Alföldy, *AAnt.*, 10 (1962), 363 ff.

[2] Plin., *HN*, iii, 143 and above, p. 165.

[3] *GZMBH*, 47 (1935), 17; cf. pl. IV: *P. Aplius Pla*[. . .]*sus . . . dec*(*urio*) *m*(*unicipii*) *Dil*(*unti*). The name is native; cf. III, 2501 (Salona).

[4] The routes are not the same:

It. Ant. 337, 4 ff.	Peutinger
Narona	Narona
	XXII
XXV	Ad Turres (cf. Rav., iv, 16)
	XIII
Dalluntum	Diluntum

The former is the direct route through Hutovo and into the west of Popovopolje. The Peu-

It is not surprising that the area did not attract many settlers to move inland from the more amiable sea coast. The few inscriptions known in the area reveal only native families, who did not begin to receive Roman citizenship until the reign of Hadrian. There is no evidence for when the city at Diluntum was founded, but the tombstone of the decurion is probably not earlier than the late second century. One settler family owned property in the area, however: from the crossing of the river Trebišnjica at Kosijerevo a few miles north of Trebinje a boundary settlement made under the Flavian governor L. Funisulanus Vettonianus was carved on a nearby rock face. A centurion of Legion IIII Flavia felix fixed the boundary between the lands of the Vesii family and another party, possibly the *civitas* of the Deramistae. A freedman of this family is attested at Narona, and they may have reached this part of the province from Asseria, where they were well established.[1]

Like the Deramistae, the Docleatae were an agglomeration of smaller peoples probably organized in the late Republic. They were not a large group (only 33 *decuriae*) but their city Doclea (Dukljia north of Titograd) is the best known city of Dalmatia away from the coast. Before the *municipium* was organized under the Flavians the Docleatae were controlled from native strongholds (*castella*) in different parts of their territory by the tribal aristocracy (*principes*) who together formed the council of the people as a whole.[2] From Riječani, on the western border of their territory, two members of this ruling class are recorded: Gaius son of Epicadus, who was a *princeps* of the *civitas* of the Docleatae, and his brother Agirrus, *princeps* of the *castellum* Salthua, which can be located at Šuntulja near Riječani, on the main Roman road between Narona and Scodra.[3] Although the Latin language was used by the ruling class, the family were still non-citizens (*peregrini*) and date before the Flavian period, when the *municipium* was founded and the citizenship widely conferred.[4]

---

[1] *AI*, 5 (1964), 93 ff. *Vesii*: III, 1797 (Narona) and above, p. 125
[2] On this system of administration, see above, p. 193.
[3] *GZMS*, 17 (1962), 100 f., and above, p. 167, n. 1.
[4] A *Docleas* was serving in Cohort V Delmatarum in the late first century, XIII, 7509 (11962), Moguntiacum.

---

tinger route follows the Bregava valley to Stolac then southeastwards to Ljubinje. To locate Diluntum at Stolac, as D. Sergejevski, *GZMS*, 17 (1962), 111 f., is most unlikely since it was part of Narona, above, p. 251, and Trebimlje is much better, as E. Pašalić, *Naselja*, 62 f., where a native family is attested, *Šašel*, n. 106 (Ljubomir):

Ziraeus Plarentis f. *m* Annaia Zanat(is) f.

Plarens Ziraei f.   Zanas Ziraei f.

The site of the city was already occupied in the pre-Roman period. It lies at the confluence of the rivers Zeta and Morača, the two major rivers of Montenegro which flow into the lake of Scodra a few miles to the south. In plan it is an irregular quadrilateral and on three sides the settlement was protected by the two rivers and a dry flood channel. Along the short stretch where the site was open two parallel ditches gave protection. In the Roman period the city acquired a stone wall, repaired on numerous occasions, which still stands in places to a height of more than 15 feet.[1]

The city (*municipium*) was established under the Flavians, possibly by Titus (79–81) to whom a posthumous dedication was set up by a magistrate (*IIIIvir*) of the city.[2] The dedication probably belongs to the earliest years of the city, since *IIIIviri* were almost immediately superseded by *IIviri*, and apart from this instance all the known magistrates bear the latter title.[3] The majority of the ruling class bear the name Flavius and belong to the voting tribe Quirina, indicating a wholesale grant of citizenship to the upper classes on the founding of the city. Doclea soon became the most important centre in the southeast, overshadowing Epidaurum (whence it acquired custody of the imperial cult) and other coastal foundations of the early period such as Risinium and Scodra. The position of Doclea in the second century is reflected in the great wealth of the leading family, M. Flavius Fronto with his wife Flavia Tertulla (his *praenomen* Marcus indicates that he is at least a second-generation citizen). He and his wife were responsible for building the basilica, and probably the whole forum complex (p. 371), which they dedicated to the memory of their son M. Flavius Balbinus who died at the age of fifteen.[4] The unfortunate youth was also commemorated by an equestrian statue which his parents had gilded, and the city council had already voted him a pedestrian statue and a public funeral after he had obtained 'every honour that was permitted by law'.[5] Another text records the impressive list of magistracies and priesthoods held by his father Flavius Fronto at Doclea and other cities in the southeast: he was priest (*sacerdos*) in the colonies Narona and Epidaurum, *IIvir quinquennalis* in the colony Scodra, *IIvir* in Julian Risinium while in his own city he was *IIvir quinquennalis*, controller of the craftsmen's guild (*praefectus collegii fabrum*), and priest of the city's founder Titus (*flamen divi [Titi]*).[6] The entry of the native upper classes enfranchised in the late first century

---

[1] Sticotti, *Doclea*, 45–64 and below, p. 363.

[2] III, 12680 (Sticotti, n. 9), also to *Divus Traianus*: III, 12681 f.

[3] *IIviri*: III, 12695, 8287, 8287e; cf. 12678, 12679 (?), 12699; *VAHD*, 50 (1928–9), also III, 12690 (*scriba qu(aestorius)*); *Sp.*, 71 (1931), n. 4 (Andrijevica).

[4] III, 12692; cf. 13819 (Sticotti, n. 22).

[5] III, 13280 (Sticotti, n. 23).   [6] III, 12695; cf. p. 2253.

to the city ruling classes has already been noted at Narona with the Flavii from Stolac, but nothing elsewhere in the province, apart from two similar careers at Salona, compared with the position achieved by this leading Doclea family in the older Italian settled coastal cities.

In Doclea Flavii predominate: out of 126 persons attested on inscriptions in the city during the Principate, 28 have the name Flavius; one or two native families are also found (Epidii and Plaetorii).[1] Families of Italian origin did settle at Doclea, and probably reached there from the nearby coastal cities, especially Epidaurum, Risinium, and Narona. Its prosperity rested mainly on the products of its territory: Pliny singles out for special praise alpine cheese made by the Docleatae. Some traders may have been attracted to the flourishing new centre, especially when the coastal cities in the southeast began to decline. Not all the population were enfranchised under the Flavians. Some in the area received citizenship under Hadrian, and during the second century immigrants were arriving from cities further afield, including Salona and Iader.[2] A fragmentary statue base suggests that the city may have enjoyed the patronage of a senatorial family in the second century, and in the third century there was at least one member of the equestrian order among the ruling class.[3]

[1] *Epidii*: III, 8287 and p. 300 below. Also Sticotti, n. 29; cf. III, 12691, p. 2252 (decurion); III, 1707=8282; *CIL*, III, p. 13*, n. 110* (Sticotti, col. 201). Adopted *Epidii* with *Flavii*: III, 12680=13818 (Sticotti, n. 9); III, 12696 and 14218/8 (Sticotti, n. 57); also *T. Cassius Valerius Epidianus* with native mother *Epidia Tatta*, Sticotti, 15 f., n. 45. *Plaetorii*: *VAHD*, 50 (1928–9), 70, n. 8=Sp., 71 (1931), n. 297 (east of Tuzi near Podgorica).

[2] *VAHD*, 50 (1928–9), 65, n. 1; cf. *Sp.*, 71 (1931), n. 124 (Salona); III, 8291 (*Iadestinus*), slave of *Baebii*; III, 12701, 13833 (Zlatica, east of Doclea). Other immigrants: III, 12704 (Gaul); *JÖAI*, 11 (1909), Bb. 202; cf. *Sp.*, 47 (1909), 189, *Verrii* and *Silvii*; cf. Alföldy, *Bevölkerung*, 151, n. 119. Eastern Immigrants: III, 12708, 13822 (12702): *artis Graecae grammaticae peritissimus*.

[3] III, 12690, 13826 and below, p. 320.

Chapter 11
Cities and Citizenship in the Interior

1 *The Interior*

As has been noted already the province divided easily into distinct geographical areas. In each of these the growth of cities and the spread of Roman forms including the citizenship followed a different course according to the nearness of Italy and the natural advantages of the countryside. First was the coast with its excellent harbours, fertile soil, and mild climate; here the wealthy coastal cities attracted large numbers of settlers, especially from Italy in the first century A.D. Next was the immediate coastal hinterland up to the high watershed between the Adriatic and the Bosnian valleys. Most of this is the waterless limestone karst with remote poljes in the main difficult to approach, and where travel was hampered by seasonal flooding. Here the native society remained little affected by the outside world, and urban centres did not appear until the later second century at the earliest. This was partly due to the poverty of the area but also to the proximity of the coastal cities, which were always an attraction to any of the local upper classes with wealth and ambition. Quite apart from these two areas were the peoples in the northern part of the province, ethnically Pannonian and much closer to the Save and Danube valleys.[1] The mountains in between were the great problem for the Roman army under Augustus, and pacification was only assured when roads were constructed to link the Adriatic with military centres in the Save valleys. The northern part of the province (modern Bosnia with part of Western Serbia) was densely wooded and the rivers too often flow through steep and winding gorges to be important for organized transport. In this area there was an abundance of minerals (gold, lead, and iron) while among

[1] Strabo, vii, 5, 3 and above, p. 167 f.

262

the rich forests there were areas of fertile land in the larger valleys. The remoteness of this area from Salona and the other larger cities enabled local centres to flourish and acquire Roman status more rapidly than settlements in the coastal hinterland. A few of the upper classes from the interior did enter the ruling circles at Salona and elsewhere, and numbers of traders, and possibly settlers, made the difficult journey across the Dinaric Alps into the high valleys and plateaux of the interior to exploit the increasing prosperity of the mining and other settlements. Most striking is the predominance of Salona in contacts with the interior. The road system, developed originally from purely strategic motives, was partly responsible for this. Travellers between other coastal cities and the interior must often have found it necessary to pass through Salona.

Compared with the coastal cities, or even with parts of the hinterland, the amount of epigraphic evidence for the cities and population of the interior is small. Throughout the Principate some 420 inscriptions record the names of 667 persons, less than is known for the comparatively small area of Southeast Dalmatia, and barely one-seventh of the total from Salona.[1] The majority are tombstones of the native population, among which the upper classes form an unrepresentative proportion. In some areas there is a shortage of good stone, plentiful along the coast, and tombstones were set up in perishable wood. Even in the mining settlements, which have produced large numbers of the known inscriptions, there is no evidence for their population comparable to the wax tablets from the Dacian gold-mines.[2] The great lack is once again archaeological exploration. Scholars such as C. Patsch and the late D. Sergejevski traversed most of Bosnia and Hercegovina and virtually everything that is known about the area, in addition to the collections of inscriptions, is due to the work of these two. On the other hand, neither was able to complete more than field surveys of the different areas. Barely half a dozen sites have been examined by excavation to an extent that has yielded archaeological and historical evidence to supplement the picture formed by inscriptions. Thus while large numbers of 'Roman sites' can be listed even in remote areas such as the poljes of Livno and Glamoč, little can usually be said about the history or economy of these settlements, apart from the obvious inferences from discoveries of imported objects, or find lists of Roman coins. Some excavations have been conducted since the war, notably by I. Čremošnik and the late E. Pašalić; the former scholar has begun the systematic study of Roman pottery in Northern Dalmatia, while the latter has added much to our knowledge of roads and associated settlements, especially those concerned

---

[1] Alföldy, *Bevölkerung*, 20, listing 89 inscriptions (115 persons) in the earlier, 331 (552 persons) in the later.

[2] III, p. 921–60.

with mining. It is certainly no reflection on either of these scholars that evidence from detailed excavation is so small: what exists is due almost entirely to them.

There is no attested historical or regional connection between any of the cities in the interior and the native peoples described by Pliny in the middle of the first century, in so far as the locations proposed in an earlier chapter (pp. 167–177) are roughly correct. Cities in the interior are known by the name either of the place, or of the people who lived in the settlement where the city was later established. In no case can the territory of a city be identified with that of one of the earlier peoples (*civitates*) listed by Pliny. Thus although Salvium, Pelva, and Delminium were cities organized from the Delmatae, no ethnic title appears in the city name as, for instance, at Doclea with the *Respublica Docleatium*.[1] The cities are therefore best examined by geographical areas, rather than by the territories of the native peoples, whose precise location must remain conjectural. Seven regions of the interior can be distinguished: the Lika polje, the Una and Sana valleys, the high poljes north of the Dinaric Alps (Livno, Duvno, Glamoč), the Vrbas valley, the Bosna valley (including the upper Narenta valley around Konjic), the Drina valley and its tributaries, and the Morava and its tributaries.

i *The Lika Polje.* Apart from Appian's references to communities of the Iapodes attacked by Octavianus in 35 B.C. the main evidence for settlements in the Lika comes from the Antonine Itinerary and the Peutinger Map. The latter records stations along a road which crosses the Velebit from Clambetae in Liburnia into the Southern Lika and then continues northward as far as Siscia, with a branch road recorded by both to Senia on the coast opposite the north end of the Lika.[2] Sixteen miles inland from Senia, Avendo can be located at Brlog. Patsch identified traces of a Roman settlement which had also been occupied continuously since the early Iron age.[3] It was the settlement of the Avendeatae, the first people attacked by Octavianus. There is no evidence that the place became a city. Only one family is recorded, of whom one member betrays Hadrianic citizenship while the other was a member of one of the priestly colleges in the ancient Latin tradition at Laurentum and Lavinium, which often included members of the senatorial and equestrian orders.[4]

The next place attacked by Octavianus was Arupium of the Arupini, which lay 10 miles along the road from Avendo and can be located at Prozor near

[1] III, 12692; cf. 13819, 13280 and above, p. 260.
[2] The Antonine Itinerary records only the route between Senia and Siscia, 273, 7–274, 7, while that through the Southern Lika appears on the Peutinger Map only.
[3] Patsch, *Lika*, 29, 90 ff.; also Strabo, iv, 6, 10; vii, 5, 4.
[4] III, 10051; cf. Patsch, *Lika*, 91, fig. 39.

Otočac. The pre-Roman settlement lay on the nearby Vital hill.[1] The earliest evidence for the city is a civic dedication to Nerva in 97; similar dedications are known to Marcus Aurelius as Caesar (145–61), Decius (249–51), and Florianus (276).[2] There is one fragmentary record of a magistrate (*IIvir*). At Salona P. Aelius Rastorianus arrived from the interior with numerous city offices including a quaestorship at Arupium.[3] A few miles to the southeast were two shrines dedicated to Mithras, each with its cult relief.[4] The third people attacked by Octavianus were the Moentini; their settlement does not appear on the road lists and may be at Humac near Brinje, where imported Roman tiles have been discovered.[5] The other sites on the main roads in the Lika can be located only roughly. The road-junction Bivium was near Janjca at the source of the river Gačka.[6] The next place was Romula, near the crossing of the Kapela mountains whence the road passed down the Glina valley to Siscia, crossing the frontier at Velika Kladuša (*ad fines*), a post manned by men from the Pannonian legions.[7]

[1] Patsch, *Lika*, 30, 76–8; also Strabo, iv, 6, 10; vii, 5, 4.

[2] III, 3006 (Nerva), 3007 (Marcus as Caesar), 15084/2 (Decius), 15086 (Florianus). III, 10046 (3008); cf. p. 2328/173 is not Augustan. Another probably honoured Pius, III, p. 2328/147 add. 10047; cf. Patsch, *Lika*, 74, fig. 25.

[3] III, 8783 (Sučurac), cf. p. 317; III, 3009.   [4] Patsch, *Lika*, 82 ff.; *CIMRM*, 2, 254 f.

[5] Patsch, *Lika*, 29, 111 f.; cf. Strabo, iv, 6, 10; vii 5, 4. A perfume merchant (*seplasiarius*) is attested, III, 15088. On the imported tiles see below, p. 500.

[6] Patsch, *Lika*, 31; cf. 5, fig. 6.

[7] There is some confusion in the sources about the route south from Siscia into Dalmatia:

Peutinger	It. Ant. 259–60	It. Ant. 273–4
Siscia	Siscia	Siscia
xx		xxi
Ad Fines	xxviiii	Ad Fines
xiiii		xiiii
Quadrata	Quadrata	Quadrata
xiiii		xiiii
Romula	xxviii	Romula
x		x
Novioduno	Novioduno	Bivium
on to Emona		x
		Arupium
		xviii
		Avendo
		xx
		Senia

The last is that between Siscia and Senia across the Northern Lika. If this followed the other route given in both the sources to Emona, in order to avoid the marshes south of Siscia, then Bivium must be located somewhere in the Colapis valley, which is much too far north to tally

There is no evidence to indicate how much of the Lika was included in the city of Arupium: it may have included all three centres of the Iapodes in the late first century. Enfranchised native families (Iulii, Flavii, and Aelii) are attested in the area, with Aurelii in the south near Gospić.[1] There is some evidence for settler families at Arupium, while the cult of Mithras suggests foreign traders, who were particularly well established at Senia on the coast not far away.[2] Virtually nothing is known of the Southern Lika. Places on the road which ran to the south from Bivium cannot be located precisely. Epidotion was probably at Kvarte in the west, Ancus at Kula near Osik, where inscriptions attest a settlement. Finally, Ausancalio was at Medak, not far north of the Velebit. Nothing is known of these places, neither of their status nor of their population. The area is not fertile and in many places water is in short supply: closed off from the coast and from the interior by high mountains the Lika remained, like the rest of the hinterland further south, a backward area with no large settlements and with few attractions to immigrants from outside.[3]

In the third century there was a military post at Josipdol in the hill country south of Karlovac. The earliest record is under Septimius Severus and the latest a dedication under Diocletian by a centurion of the Pannonian Legion II Adiutrix to *Iuppiter Optimus Maximus* and the *genius* of the *municipium* Metulum.[4] This solved the vexed problem of the location of Iapodian Metulum, their stronghold attacked by Octavianus. It has been identified nearby with the large hill-fort on the Viničica hill.[5] Apart from the garrison only Aurelii are known in the area, indicating late development.[6] There is no evidence for the date of the city. In the third century a commissioner (*curator*) of the city is found at Plevlje far to the east.[7]

ii *The Una and Sana Valleys* (fig. 9). The centre of the *civitas Iapodum* in the first century was at the Privilica spring near Bihać, where the Una valley broadens out into a fertile plain. Many native settlements are known in the area, but only the cemeteries with hundreds of burials and grave goods have been excavated. In the war of 6–9 the Iapodes were grouped with at least part of Liburnia under the administration of a Roman army officer, but control soon passed to native rulers (*principes*) appointed by the Roman administration who

[1] See below, Appendix XIII.
[2] Also a dedication to *Iuppiter Conservator Dolichenus*, III, 10044, set up by an Octavius.
[3] Patsch, *Lika*, 30 f.   [4] III, 10060 (Čakovac): *I.O.M. et genio loci m(unicipii) Met(uli)*, etc.
[5] Veith, *Feldzüge*, etc., 29 ff. with map.   [6] Below, Appendix XIII.   [7] Note 5 on p. 282.

with the distances recorded to Senia. Mócsy, *RE*, supp. 9 (1962), 662, accepts this explanation, although it involves rejecting the Antonine Itinerary route into Dalmatia to Senia on the coast.

acted as governors of the people (*praepositi* or *praefecti*). Most are non-citizens although one records his receipt of citizenship from Vespasian (69–79).[1]

It is possible that Bihać is Raetinium, a native stronghold attacked by the Romans in 8–9. A trooper of the Ala Claudia nova in Germany, Andes Sexti f(ilius), calls himself citizen of Raetinium (*civis Raetinius*) and all the five known instances of this name come from Bihać or its vicinity, while a decurion of the same unit is also attested there.[2] On the other hand, Bihać was the centre of the Iapodes, and after their conquest by Octavianus there is no evidence that they were involved in the war when Raetinium was captured.

Of the peoples in the interior the Iapodes retained their separate culture for longer than most, although the upper classes were becoming rapidly romanized during the later first century. There is evidence for a villa economy in the plain around Bihać; the area is also rich in timber and is today one of the most prosperous parts of Bosnia. Yet in dress, as depicted on tombstone reliefs, and in material goods, they retained their traditions. One cannot speak of Iapodian art, since the quantity of evidence is small, but their sculpture and metalwork has an originality and freshness not found elsewhere in the interior, where too often people attempted imitation of classical motifs and techniques which they did not fully understand.[3]

Until the road over the Strmica pass (*mons Ditionum*) was completed in 47–48 the Una valley was barely accessible from the coast.[4] On the other hand a number of Iulii with simple Latin *cognomina* indicates that already citizenship was being conferred at an early date in the Bihać area, while a small number of purely Iapodian names were adapted as *gentilicia* for other new citizens, probably in the first century.[5] Instances of slavery are found among the wealthier native families, and the presence of foreign traders is indicated by two freedmen of a Liburnian family at Prekaja.[6]

The river Sana flows into the Una at Bosnian Novi, the frontier between Dalmatia and Pannonia. The area is very rich in iron ore deposits which were worked extensively in the Roman period, especially in the area around Stari Majdan, under the control of a government official (*procurator ferriarum*) based in the area

[1] On the military administration see above, p. 104, and on the native *praepositi* and *praefecti* above, p. 158.

[2] XIII, 7023 (Mainhardt). *Andes* in Dalmatia: III, 14012 (Bihać), 14013 (Jezerine), 10035 (Golubić); III, p. 2328/171 (3001, 10024) (Kula in Lika); III, 13249 (Knin), 10033 (Golubić) a decurion of Ala Claudia nova.

[3] I. Čremošnik, *GZMS*, 11 (1956), 133 f.; 13 (1958), 121 ff.; 14 (1959), 103 ff.

[4] Appendix IV, p. 454.   [5] Alföldy, *Bevölkerung*, 159, and for the *Iulii*, below, p. 493.

[6] Freedmen *Vesii*: *GZMBH*, 43 (1931), 22, probably from Asseria, above, p. 215. Slaves: Sp. 93 (1940), 135, n. 1–8 (Golubić).

around Briševo and Ljubija. Altars to Terra Mater, patron deity of miners, were set up by the procurator and his overseer (*vilicus officinae ferrariae*) who was a freedman or perhaps a slave. They were set up on 21 April, probably every year. The nine altars which survive belong to the period between 201 and the reign of Gallienus (253–68). The first includes the only record of the leaseholder (*conductor*) who actually operated the mines on a contract arrangement with the

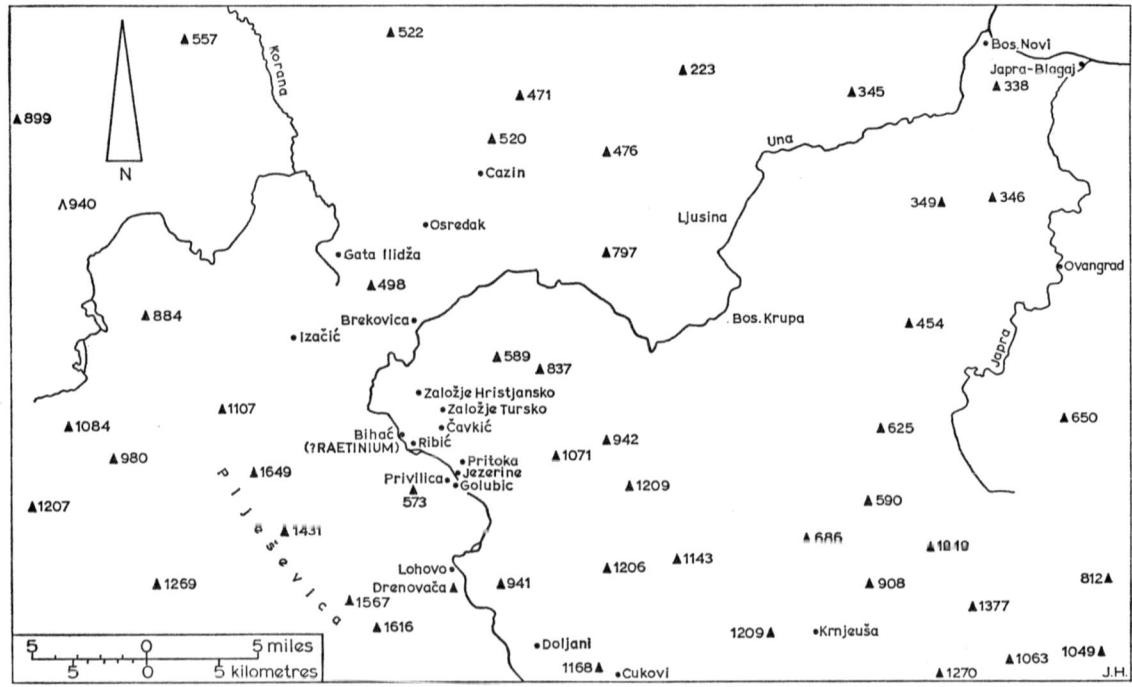

Figure 9 Bihać and Una Valley

imperial mining administration, but he was superseded by the procurator before 209. There is no obvious reason for why 21 April should be chosen for the annual dedication: possibly it was the day on which the mining was first officially organized in the area.[1]

There is no evidence for any city existing in this area, although the mining continued into the sixth century.[2] Some of the labour force may have been criminals sentenced to the mines instead of to capital punishment (*damnati ad metallos*), but not surprisingly all the people known from inscriptions are free,

[1] D. Sergejevski, *GZMS*, 18 (1963), 85 ff.; E. Pašalić, *GIDBH*, 10 (1959), 321 ff. A *bf. cos.* of the Pannonian Legion X Gemina may have also been concerned with the mines administration, *GZMS*, 12 (1957), 117, n. 8 (Zašelak Miloševići near Prijedor).

[2] Cassiod, *Variae*, iii, 25 f. and below, p. 424.

mostly with citizenship conferred by second-century emperors. Instances of immigrants are known at Blagaj, a little to the west of Bosnian Novi.[1]

iii *Livno, Glamoč, and Duvno Poljes* (Pelva, Salvium, and Delminium) (fig. 10). North of the Dinaric Alps, which cut the territory of the Delmatae in half, were three large poljes each with cities which grew out of settlements of the Delmatae. The northern limit of this people was the watershed of the Bosnian valleys. In the poljes of the Dalmatian karst there was usually only one main centre, and this was the only place likely to acquire city status. Although such a place may have been the residence of the local members of the tribal aristocracy, none of these centres was likely to grow to the size of even a small city. This was not always due to poverty or under-population but to the need for the people to live along the edge of the polje surface at the foot of the hills, opposite to the land they cultivated. For some months, when much of the polje was flooded in the winter and early spring, transport from one settlement to another would be difficult. Consequently it was never possible for a settlement to grow up in a polje to a size to compare with Flavian Doclea in the middle of its plain.

Across the Dinaric Alps north of Aequum and Sinjskopolje was Livjanskopolje, with its centre Livno on slightly higher ground at the southeastern end of the polje. The area is fertile, and at an altitude of more than 2,000 feet the climate is much healthier than that of the coastal hinterland to the south. The polje is the largest in the region with an area of more than 160 square miles. The city of Livjanskopolje was Pelva and is probably to be located at modern Livno. It is named on the Antonine Itinerary route between Salona and Servitium which passed across the polje from the Prolog pass over the Dinara (3,600 feet high; *In Alperio* on Peutinger, 8 miles from Aequum).[2] From there it passed to Salvium, the city in Glamočkopolje. A number of Pelva decurions are found in the different settlements of the polje;[3] one is at Grkovci in the far north, while others are attested at Gubin in the north and Vašarovin on the opposite side to Livno,

[1] *Campanii*: GZMBH, 51 (1939), 12, possibly from the Salona family, below, p. 308.

[2] The route given by *It. Ant.*, 269, 7 ff., between Salona and Servitium passes through Pelva (Livno) and Salvium (Glamoč) and is 153 Roman miles long, while the shorter (125 m.p.) Peutinger route misses both cities by a more direct line across Livno and Glamoč poljes, Pašalić, *Naselja*, 18 ff.

[3] *WMBH*, 11 (1909), 120, fig. 10 (Grkovci); *GZMBH*, 40 (1928), 91 f. (Vašarovin and Grkovci); III, 9848; cf. *WMBH*, 11 (1909), 125, fig. 13 (Gubin near Provo); Sp. 77 (1934), n. 28 (Bastaši). The restoration of *GZMS*, 6 (1951), 301, n. 1 (Grkovci) to read *d(ec.) m(un). S(alviae)* is doubtful; cf. Šašel n. 168. The man is an immigrant *Trosius*, probably from Liburnia, Alföldy, *PN* (forthcoming).

where a *beneficiarius consularis* settled and became a decurion of the city.[1] Many of the population received citizenship under Hadrian, for most are Aelii with the *praenomen* Publius.[2] Local traditions, as revealed by tombstone sculptures, endured throughout the Principate. The small cremation chest with inscriptions on the decorated sides, often with incised geometric pattern reminiscent of

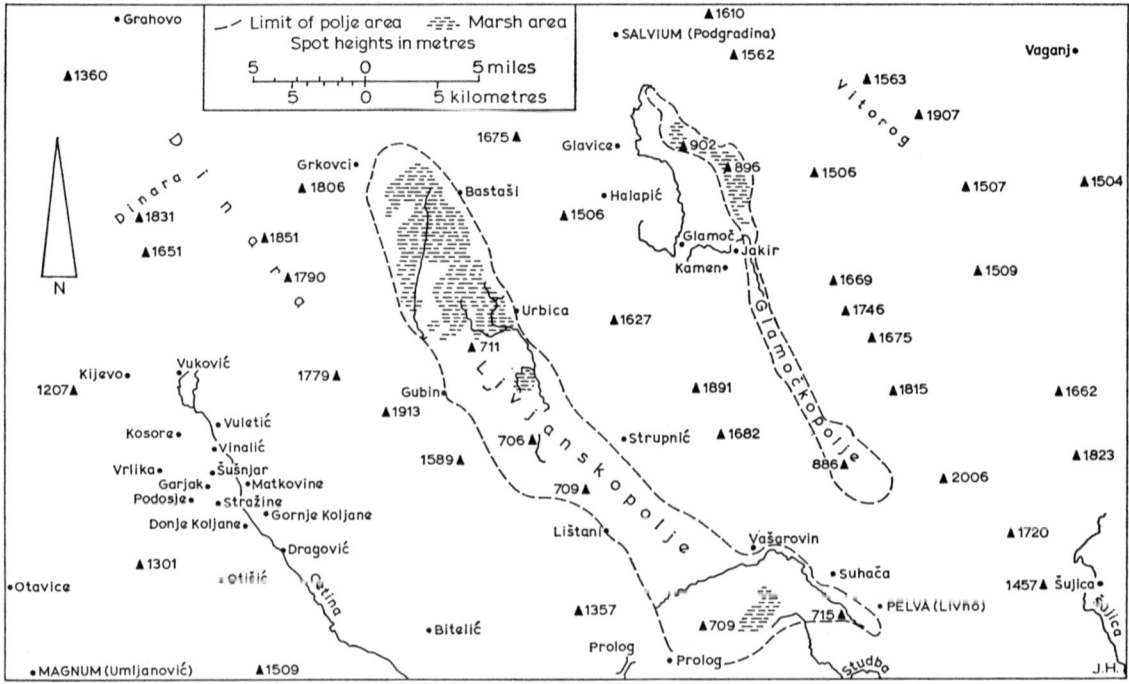

Figure 10 Upper Cetina Valley, Livno and Glamoč Poljes

some Celtic ornamentation further east, is common throughout the polje.[3] Few immigrants are attested, and all the city councillors of Pelva were of native origin. In the third century men were recruited from the area to serve in the legions of Pannonia.[4]

Eighteen miles north of Pelva was Salvium (Podgradina near Kamen) in Glamočkopolje.[5] Most of the immediate area of the city is above 3,000 feet and the economy is alpine with large stretches of grazing for cattle, although the

[1] III, 9847; cf. p. 2165, *WMBH*, 11 (1909), 123, fig. 12 (Lipa): *M. Nasi[d]i[u]s Se[c]undus dec. mun. vet. [b]f. c[os.] leg. X G.*, etc.

[2] Appendix XIII.

[3] *WMBH*, 11 (1909), 118 ff.; *GZMBH*, 40 (1928), 97; 42 (1931) 20 ff.; 50 (1938) 91 ff.

[4] *Sp.*, 77 (1934), 19, n. 26 (Grahovo): *miles* of I or II Adiutrix.

[5] Located by the studies of Sergejevski, *GZMBH*, 39 (1927), 255 ff.; 40 (1928) 87; 45 (1933), 7 ff.; 54 (1942), 172. Previously Patsch had located Salvium at Grkovci.

marshy basin is 500 feet lower to the south. The route from Livno is difficult and Glamoč is one of the most isolated areas of Bosnia, shut off on the north by the high mountains around the head of the Vrbas and Pliva valleys. The history of Salvium and its peoples is similar to that of Pelva. Widespread grants of citizenship were made under Hadrian, but a few Aurelii are known.[1] The city (*municipium*) was probably organized under Hadrian also; in the middle second century an auxiliary soldier serving in Germany records that he came from the *municipium* Salvium. As a non-citizen he was legally an inhabitant (*incola*) on the territory of the city.[2] Men continued to be recruited to the army from Salvium during the third century.[3] Three members of the city council are known; the two whose names are recorded were both Aelii. The third, who was *princeps* of the city, belongs to the third century and had obtained equestrian rank.[4]

Both Pelva and Salvium may have developed ties with the coastal cities, especially with Salona to which they were linked by the main road from Servitium. One of the Salvium decurions was buried at Salona, and the cult of Mithras may have reached there through traders from the coastal cities, or possibly through the legionaries attested there in the third century.[5]

The third city in the northern half of the territory of the Delmatae was Delminium, their eponymous capital, attacked and destroyed by a Roman army in the middle of the second century B.C. The site of the Roman settlement is on the Lib planina near Županac in Duvanjskopolje, southeast of Livno.[6] The polje is smaller and less fertile than Livno or Glamoč, although at an altitude of about

[1] Appendix XIII.

[2] XIII, 6538 (Mainhardt): *Ba[t]o Beusantis (f.) optio (coh. ? Asturum) ex muni[c]ipio Salvi[o]* in the middle of the second century; cf. Kraft *Rekrutierung*, 168, n. 1093c. The city is named by Ptolemy, ii, 16, 6: Σαλουία.

[3] III, 9861 (Gradina): *Ael. Titus ex protectore.*

[4] *GZMBH*, 40 (1928), 87, n. 9, fig. 7 (Podgradina); III, 14249/2 (Sučurac near Salona): *Ael. Capito dec. municip. Salvio natus Starue*, etc., born in the village of Starue in the territory of Salvium; cf. *JÖAI*, 2 (1899), Bb. 111 f., possibly the *Sarute* on the Peutinger Map. In the fifth century a leading citizen was buried at Rider, *BD*, 28 (1905), 48; *GZMBH*, 39 (1929), 260, n. 9 (Kamen): *princ(eps) m[unicipii . . .*, possibly connected also with the Dalmatian mines administration.

[5] Mithras: *GZMBH*, 45 (1933), 7, n. 2. In the later period a citizen of Salvium was buried at Asseria, p. 215 above, n. 8. A boundary stone from the region records a settlement between the cities Salvium and Stridon (*i[nt]e[r] Salvia[t]as e[t] S[tr]ido[n]enses*) under the *praeses* Constantius, later Augustus. Stridon was the birthplace of St. Jerome, near the boundary of Dalmatia and Pannonia, Hieron. *de viris ill.* 135. In the early fourth century it was part of Pannonia, when its bishop attended the Council at Nicaea in 325, Mansi, 2, col 696. The problem of locating Stridon has occupied many pages but with little result, Mayer, *Sprache*, 323.

[6] Originally located at Tilurium (Gardun) but now almost certainly at Županac in Duvjanskopolje, Patsch, *WMBH*, 9 (1904), 171 ff.; cf. *JAK*, 2 (1908), 103 f.

2,700 feet. The city lay on the north side of the polje, but there is virtually no evidence of its history or organization. A forum partly excavated by C. Patsch produced fragments of an official dedication which could belong either to Hadrian or to Antoninus Pius.[1] From Mokronoge a little to the north of the city a dedication to *Iuppiter Optimus Maximus* may record a decurion of the city but the reading is uncertain.[2] The city was in existence by 184 when its inhabitants joined with the people of Rider and Novae in paying for the repairing of the bridge across the river Hippius (Cetina) at Tilurium (p. 97 f). This was probably the point at which the territories of the three cities met, while the road which led from Salona to the eastern interior crossed the river at Tilurium and passed through Aržano into Duvanjskopolje.[3] Little is known of the population; apart from Aelii there are instances of Flavii and Ulpii, as well as later Aurelii.[4] There are immigrants attested, but these could well have reached Delminium from other parts of the interior rather than the coastal cities.[5]

iv *The Vrbas Valley.* Both Statius and Martial refer to gold being obtained from Dalmatia, and Florus records a story that some gold-mining was organized by Vibius Postumus almost immediately after the final conquest in 9.[6] Apart from a reference in the Elder Pliny to a large find being made at the time of Nero, there is little evidence that gold-mining ever flourished in Dalmatia on the same scale as the iron in the Sana valley or the argentiferous lead in the Drina valley around Domavia.[7] However there was an imperial administration of the gold-mines, apparently based at Salona, where a slave secretary (*commentariensis*) of the department is attested.[8]

[1] *WMBH*, 9 (1904), 177, fig. 3 and below, p. 371.
[2] *GZMS*, 12 (1957), 109, n. 1: *I(ovi) Cap(itolino) Victor(i) dec(uriones) D(e)l(minensium) c(ivitatis) v.s.l.m.* but rejected by Pflaum, ap. *Šašel*, n. 167. A decurion appears at Zbanica near Županac, III, 14229, also a dignitary of Novae, III, 13887.
[3] III, 3202 in A.D. 184. The route linked Salona with Bistue Vetus in the Rama valley, and is recorded on Peutinger: Salona-xvi-Tilurio-xxii-Ad Libros-ix-in monte Bulsinio-vi-Bistue vetus, leading on to Domavia. Mons Bulsinius is Ljubuša between Duvno and the Rama valley.
[4] Appendix XIII, p. 494.
[5] A Celtic *Mattonia Tertia*: III, 14320/2; cf. Holder 2, 478, also *Sest(ius) Onesime*: III, 14320/1; cf. Alföldy, *Bevölkerung*, 163, n. 73. One person perished in Pannonia with his two sons, III, 9740; cf. 13185 (Letka) photo in Patsch-Ballif, *Strassen*, pl. IX, fig. 17. Along with others in the territory of the Delmatae the Delminium church appears in the Salona provincial council of 532, see below, p. 432, 434.
[6] Statius, *Silvae*, i, 2, 153; iii, 3, 90; Martial, x, 78, 5; Florus, ii, 25 and above, p. 181 n. 3.
[7] Plin., *HN*, xxxiii, 67. Traces of gold panning are known in the Vrbas valley, Davies, *RME*, 186 ff.
[8] III, 1997 (Salona).

The Vrbas valley is attractive to settlement in two areas, around Jajce and the Pliva valley to the west, and in the upper part around Bugojno. This latter area was probably part of the territory of Bistus Vetus which lay at Varvara near Prozor in the Rama valley across the mountains to the southeast.[1] Between Bugojno and Jajce the river flows through an impressive gorge more than 15 miles long. The Jajce area was close to the road between Salona and Servitium. This does not travel along the Vrbas valley until Banjaluka, where the river begins to leave the hills and enter the Save valley. North from Glamoč the road crosses some high ground to Sarnade (Pecka at the source of the river Sana) through Stinica to Leusaba (near Han Bunari, where a Roman bridge still survived early this century) and Lamate (near Šlivno), and then on to the Vrbas at Castra (Banjaluka). This was a small military post not far south of the frontier with Pannonia at Laktaši (*ad fines*).[2] Most of this road was used as one of the major routes in this part of Bosnia until the advent of modern transport. The hills are not impassable, and to follow the winding course of the Vrbas would have nearly doubled the length of the route in that sector. A number of side roads link the road to various centres in the valley to the east, including the mining area around Majdan and Mrkonjićgrad, northwest of Jajce. Here copper and some gold was worked, but there is no evidence where the chief settlement was, nor for any system of administration, apart from the official at Salona.[3] Near Šipovo in the Pliva valley was a large settlement occupied in the Roman period. A reference to city councillors from Šarići near by indicates that the place became a *municipium*, but there is no evidence for the name of the city.[4] An identification with Splonum, the stronghold captured in 9 and later attested as the *municipium Splonistarum*, is not supported by any evidence, and there is good reason to believe that it may be the city at Plevlje to the east.[5] The city at Šipovo was probably organized in the second century, perhaps under Hadrian, and the enfranchised native families of the place are mostly Aelii or Aurelii. It may, however, have been established already under Trajan, if it was responsible for a dedication to the governor C. Minicius Fundanus (*cos.* 107), one of the cultivated friends of the Younger Pliny.[6] It is possible that the mines in the area was administered from this place and this contributed to its prosperity, if we may judge from some

[1] A tile stamped BISTVE[S] is known from Crkvina near Bugojno, J. Petrović, *GZMS*, 15–16 (1961), 230, fig. 1. On the settlements in the Upper Vrbas valley, Patsch, *WMBH*, 6 (1899), 237 ff.; *GZMS*, 13 (1958), 267; 15–16 (1961), 229 ff.

[2] Pašalić, *Naselja* 21–9 and maps 1–2.   [3] Pašalić, *GZMS*, 9 (1954), 55 f.

[4] III, 13982; cf. Patsch *WMBH*, 12 (1912), 137 ff., Sergejevski *GZMS*, 7 (1952), 41 ff.

[5] Thus G. Alföldy, *AAnt. Hung.*, 10 (1962), 3 ff., but against J. Wilkes, *AAnt. Hung.*, 13 (1965), 111–25 and below, p. 282.

[6] On the names in this area see Appendix XIII, and on C. Minicius Fundanus, p. 445 f.

items of high-quality sculpture which have come from the site. Settlers were attracted there, more probably along the main road from Salona, rather than from Pannonia to the north.[1]

In the wild hill-country south of Jajce the long valley of the Jany reaches far into the mountains. At Vaganj near the head of the valley a boundary settlement was made between two communities. It is the only first-century settlement known from the interior, and was set up under the ill-fated governor L. Arruntius Scribonianus, who attempted rebellion against Claudius. A centurion of Legion VII settled the boundary between the Sapuates and the [. .]matini. Sapua is listed by Ravennas in the interior, and the other people could possibly be the inhabitants of Lamatis, although this place is usually located near Bunari far to the north, on the Antonine Itinerary route a few miles south of Banjaluka. The two peoples were probably communities of the Maezaei or possibly the Sardeates, their smaller neighbours on the south.[2]

v *The Bosna Valley* (including Lašva Valley and upper Narenta).   The major settlements in the Bosna valley and its tributaries lay in five areas, Crkvenica at Doboj, Zenica and the Lašva valley around Travnik, the Sarajevo area around the source of the Bosna, the upper Narenta around Konjic and its tributary the Rama. The Bosna valley is not suitable for travel into the interior between the Save valley and Zenica; but it becomes increasingly broader until the plain around Ilidže, into which the river emerges in full volume from the foot of the mountain Igman. One of the few military stations maintained in the interior was at Crkvenica near Doboj where the river Spreča flows into the valley from the southeast.[3] Around was the wooded countryside of Northern and Central Bosnia, not as forbidding as further south, but an area where political control was difficult to maintain and where the population has always proved stubborn and resistant, both to military invaders and higher material culture. The post was retained at Doboj into the third century, presumably for the purpose of controlling this area. Apart from a few records of people in the civil settlement (*vicus*), there are no records of the native Daesitiates.[4]

A city existed at Vitez in the Lašva valley not far from Travnik, the old Turkish capital of Bosnia. Three inscriptions name it as Bistue, and it can be identified

[1] III, 13981; cf. *WMBH*, 12 (1912), 146 (*Aeneas Proclianus*, possibly from the East), 140, fig. 65 (*Sex. Iulius Gracilis*, possibly from Aequum where *Sex. Iulii* are attested); *GZMBH*, 38 (1926), 157, fig. 2 (*L. Publicius Telesphorus*, possibly from Salona).
[2] III, 9864a, see Appendix V. *Sapua*: Rav., iv, 19, and on *Lamatis*, Pašalić, *Naselja*, 28 f.
[3] III, 14619 (12759) and p. 143.
[4] III, 8376b, 14222, veterans with families. Also worship of Mithras, III, 14222/1.

with Bistue Nova on the main route recorded on the Peutinger Map between Salona and the Bosna valley.[1] The territory of the city included not only the Lašva valley but also the middle part of the Bosna around Zenica. Two of the magistrates (*IIviri*) and decurions are recorded there, in the remains of an early Christian church, while the third comes from Fazlići in the hills north of Travnik. There is no doubt, however, that the city itself was situated at the important river crossing Vitez.[2] The city was Flavian *municipium* and Flavian citizenship is common among the leading families. At Salona the native aristocrat P. Aelius Rastorianus held a number of offices in cities of the interior, including decurion, *IIvir*, and *IIvir quinquenalis* of both Bistue Vetus and Bistue Nova.[3] Other families were enfranchised later; Aelii and Aurelii appear on the tombstones of leading families.[4] Bistue attracted settlers from the coastal cities and from the Danube valley.[5] A mystery cult is known and men were recruited to serve in the Pannonian legions.[6]

In the plain west of Sarajevo there was a settlement at the warm springs of Ilidže, a curative spa already in the Roman period to judge from a series of elaborate bath buildings which have been excavated.[7] The name of the spa is recorded only in the abbreviated form Aquae S. . . . Although excavation has demonstrated that the place was developing in the first century A.D., the only record of the community as a whole is a dedication to Diocletian by the *Respublica Aq(uae) S.* . . .[8] A senatorial family of the early third century, the Catii, are attested at Ilidže but it is not clear whether one of them was governor of Dalmatia at the time, owned property in the area, or was merely seeking a cure from the hot springs. There is no evidence that they were a Dalmatian family, and they certainly did not originate among the native Daesitiates of the region.[9]

---

[1] III, 12765, 12766 with 12762; cf. *GZMBH*, 44 (1932), 36 f. (Zenica); III, 12761 (Fazlići). It may be the *Ibisua* of Rav., iv, 19.

[2] On sites in the region, C. Truhelka, *WMBH*, 1 (1893), 273 ff. (Zenica); 3 (1895), 227; D. Sergejevski, *GZMBH*, 44 (1932), 35 ff.; *WMBH*, 3 (1895), 243 ff. (Fazlići); 2 (1894), 66 f.; 3 (1895), 229 f. (Mali Mošunj).

[3] III, 8783; cf. p. 2136, 2326 (Sučurac) and below, p. 317 n. 3.

[4] Appendix XIII, p. 495.

[5] *Pompeii*: III, 8380 (Vitez). One at Salona records a man who died in the territory of the Maezaei, III, 6388. Some traces of gold working are known in the area, Davies, *RME*, 188 f.

[6] *WMBH*, 9 (1904), 230, fig. 106 (lead plaque from Vitez). *Miles* of II (Adiutrix): III, 12764 with *GZMBH*, 44 (1932), 46 f.

[7] *GZMS*, 14 (1959), 113 ff.

[8] D. Sergejevski, *GZMBH*, 52 (1940), 15: *Imp. [C.] C. Valer. Diocletian. p.f. invi[c]to Aug. R.P. Aq. S.*

[9] D. Sergejevski, *GZMBH*, 52 (1940), 15 f., n. 1 and below, p. 335.

In the remaining territory of the Daesitiates there were no large settlements of the Roman period. The various *castella* continued to be inhabited by local ruling families, and as might be expected they were the first of their people to receive Roman citizenship. The only known Flavius is the *princeps* of the Daesitiates at Bréza north of Sarajevo. This was probably one of the major settlements of the people, Hedum *castellum*, the terminus of a strategic road built soon after 9 from Salona to the Bosna valley.[1] Apart from members of this class, most remained non-citizens until the later second century. Ulpii and Aelii are attested, but the latter are much less common than among the Delmatae to the south. Most are Aurelii, some with the *praenomen* Titus, indicating a grant under Marcus Aurelius.[2] Immigrant families are known; at Kiseljak the Manlii, who probably came from Risinium, have already been noted.[3] The main attraction was probably trade rather than acquisition of property, but it is possible that some people acquired estates which were rented out to tenants (*coloni*), rather than worked directly by slaves as seems to have been the practice in the Salona area.[4]

The main route to the south and southeast from the Sarajevo area passes across the watershed of Mount Ivanjica into the upper valley of the Narenta around Konjic.[5] From there until the confluence with the Rama, where the river turns south into a gorge through the high peaks of northern Hercegovina, the valley is broad and fertile, and from excavations carried out in this area before it was flooded for the Jablanica hydro-electric system many Roman settlements along this part of the valley are known. Mostly they are small farms which reached their peak of prosperity in the later second and early third centuries.[6] The most remarkable discovery in the area, however, was made at the end of the last century near Konjic when a Mithraeum was excavated and a fine set of ritual reliefs discovered. One has the Mithraic tauroctony on the front and a ritual

---

[1] Appendix IV, p. 453.

[2] Appendix XIII, p. 495.

[3] III, 8379; cf. p. 2256 and above, p. 255.

[4] III, 13858 (Ilidže): *Apollin[i] Tadeno Charmidis col. d.d.* Here col(*onus*) or tenant is better than col(*oniae servus*); cf. Alföldy, *Bevölkerung*, 162, n. 53. By the third century much of the land in this area may have been concentrated in the hands of landowning families, such as the Catii at Aquae S. or the Claudii at Skelani and the Flavii at Maluesa, all of senatorial rank. Across the border in Moesia Superior were the large estates of the senatorial *Furii* (*domus Furiana*) around Ulpiana (Lipljan), in particular C. Furius Octavianus consul in the early third century, *JÖAI*, 6 (1903), Bb. 26 ff.; cf. *PIR²*, F 580.

[5] Along this important route from the coast to the interior were a number of large settlements, at Fojnica, Visoko, and Pazarić: *WMBH*, 4 (1896), 248 ff.; 5 (1897), 131 f.; 6 (1899), 264 ff.; 9 (1904), 233; *GZMBH*, 10 (1919), 97; cf. Pašalić, *Naselja*, 46 f.

[6] *GZMS*, 12 (1957), 143 ff. and below, p. 401 f.

banquet scene on the back, carved in a local style.[1] The dedicator was probably a
trader, like L. Antonius Menander from Aphrodisias in Caria who set up a similar
monument at Vratnica near Lisičići; other traders were probably responsible for
introducing the cult to such remote areas as Glamočkopolje.[2] The area around
Konjic was probably inhabited by the Narensii, but there is no sign that the
people were ever included within the city of Narona. Indeed compared with
Salona and other coastal cities there is very little evidence of contacts between
Narona and the peoples of the interior. This is probably due to the slow development of most of the area, beginning in the second century at a time when
Narona already seems to be in decline. The Konjic area may have been part of
the city Bistue Vetus in the Rama valley to the northwest. The native people of
the area received citizenship first in the second century, Aelii and Aurelii being
the commonest names.[3]

Across the watershed from the head of the Vrbas valley was the Rama valley
which runs southeast through the mountains to join the Narenta near Slatina.
At the head of the valley was the only city in this area Bistue Vetus, which three
records of magistrates (*IIviri*) and decurions locate at Varvara near Prozor.[4] The
area is remote from the Narenta valley but is linked by road with Duvanjskopolje to the west. Although this may have been the territory of the Deretini there
is virtually no evidence for the population or the economy. The magistrates of
the city (*municipium*) were Flavii and all appear to belong to the same family,
although the mother of one was an Aelia. All were of native origin. The Rama
valley formed most of the city's territory, but the discovery of a stamped brick
Bistue[s] at Bugojno indicates that part of the upper valley of the Vrbas was also
included within it.[5]

vi *The Drina Valley (including Plevlje).* The Drina valley is longer than the
other Bosnian valleys and with its tributaries the Lim and Piva is very different
in character. The hills are steeper and less rounded than further west; in the
south above Foča the forest is mostly coniferous, with areas of open grassland,
especially in the Čehotina valley around Plevlje.[6] The largest and most flourishing centre in the valley was Domavia (Gradina near Srebrenica), the centre of the

---

[1] *WMBH*, 6 (1899), 186 f.; 9 (1904) 243 f.; *CIMRM*, 2, n. 1896 with figs. 490–1.
[2] III, 13859; cf. *CIMRM*, n. 1893, fig. 488. On the style of the sculptures, B. Gabričević, AI 1
(1954), 37–52.
[3] Appendix XIII, p. 495. *Petronii*: III, 14617/1 (Čerići); *GZMS*, 9 (1954), 219 f. (Lisičići), who
may have arrived from Salona.
[4] *WMBH*, 11 (1909), 105 ff.; cf. D. Sergejevski, *GZMS*, 44 (1932), 36, also III, 8783.
[5] Note 1 on p. 273.
[6] Patsch, *WMBH*, 4 (1896), 275; 12 (1912), 120 ff.; Evans, *Archaeologia*, 49 (1885), 25 ff.

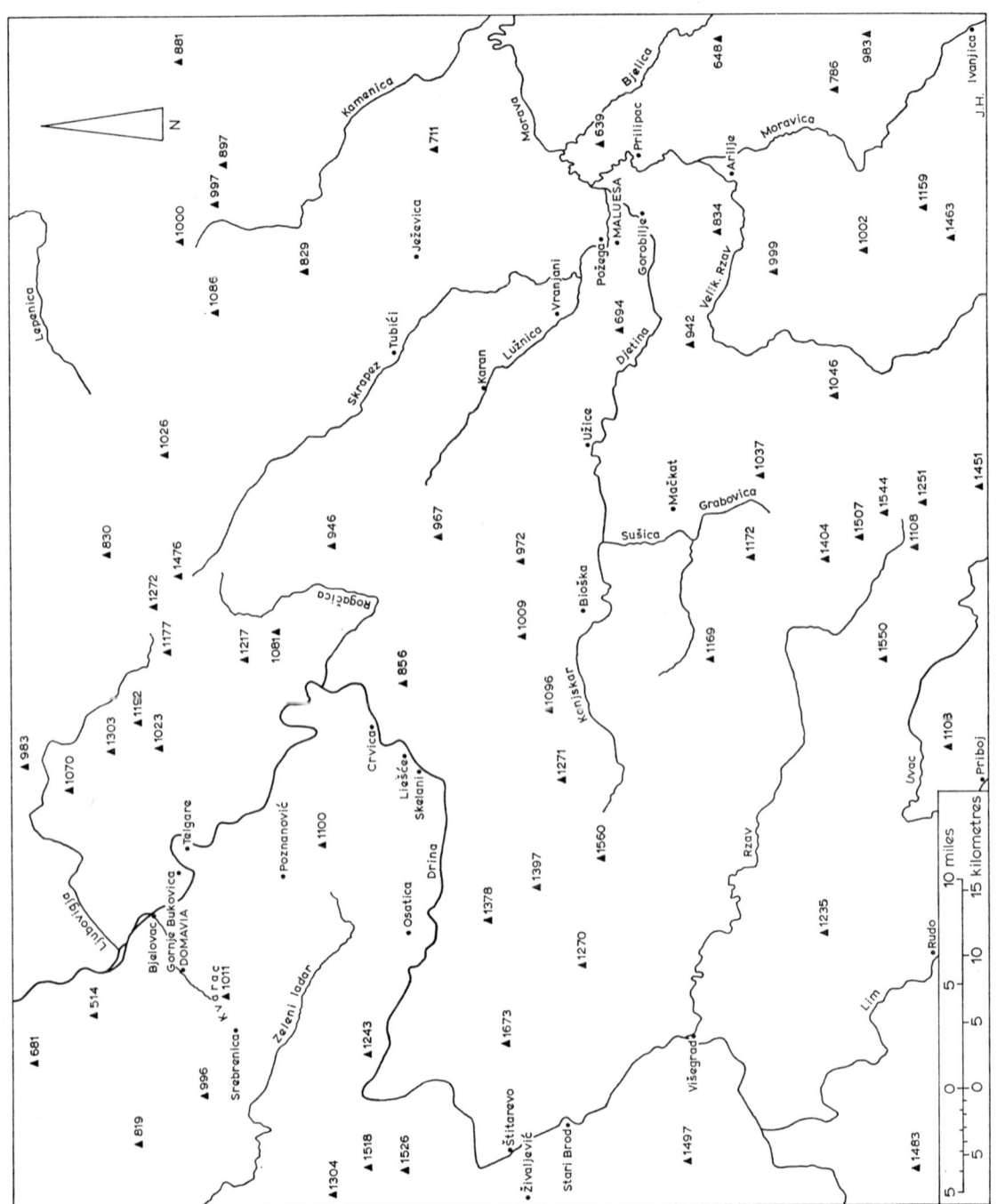

Figure 11 Domavia and Maluesa

278

Dalmatian lead-mines in the Roman period. The settlement is not actually in the Drina valley but at the head of a small tributary on the north side of mount Kvarac (fig 11). In the mediaeval and early modern periods the centre was at Srebrenica on the other side of the mountain. The area is densely wooded and the hills rise to about 3,000 feet. When the mining actually began in the region is not known but the main period of prosperity for the Roman settlement was in the first half of the third century. Mining on a large scale probably began under Marcus Aurelius, when the mining administration was reorganized and a procurator installed there. Extensive traces of Roman working are to be seen; at the end of the last century W. Radimsky discovered the principal buildings of the settlement and a number of interesting official dedications and building records. There were two main buildings, the basilica and an elaborate bath-block.[1] The mines were controlled by equestrian procurators, of whom the names of seven are known from dedications. After Marcus the Domavia mines were controlled in conjunction with those of Pannonia, although there is no evidence whatsoever that there were any mines in that province. The title of the procurator at Domavia was usually *procurator argentariarum* (or *metallorum*) *Delmaticarum et Pannoniarum*. This officer is only known in connection with the argentiferous lead at Domavia; the iron-mining administration in the Sana valley was administered quite separately. Alongside the wall of the basilica there were set up dedications to individual procurators, mostly in the early third century. One praises the *bonitas* and *integritas* of the procurator L. Domitius Eros, while C. Iulius Silvanus Melanio is described as patron of the city (*patronus municipii Domaviani*). The first reference to the city is on a dedication to Severus Alexander and Iulia Mamaea (222–35) by the council (*ordo*), supervised by the procurator Iulius Tacitianus.[2] The city was already in existence in 218, however, when it (*Respublica Domaviana*) rebuilt the market hall (*macellum*) after a disastrous fire. The same procurator mentioned in connection with this work, Valerius Super, was also concerned with providing a water supply for the baths two years later.[3] The city may have been founded slightly earlier than this, however, as is suggested by two dedications to Severus and Caracalla; they are fragmentary, but are almost certainly civic dedications.[4] There is no evidence to suggest that it was in

---

[1] W. Radimsky, *WMBH*, 1 (1893), 218 ff.; 4 (1896), 202 ff.; cf. Davies, *RME*, 19 1 f; Pašalić, *GZMS*, 9 (1954), 47 ff. On the buildings see below, p. 372 ff.

[2] On the mines organization, H-G. Pflaum, *RE*, 33 (1957), 1253. Earlier the procurators were *sexagenarii*, with a salary of 60,000 sestertii; later the status of the appointment was raised to *centenarii* (100,000). For a list of the known officials, see Pflaum, *Carrières*, 3, 1063.

[3] III, 12733 (8363), 12734. Also III, 12732: *municipium Domavianum*, and a decurion far away in the southeast at Sočanica, III, 8297: *M. Aurel. Felicianus dec. mun. D(omavianum)*.

[4] III, 12726; Sp. 93 (1940), 144, n. 12.

existence before this period. Some time between Severus Alexander and Trebonianus Gallus Domavia was given the status of colony; a dedication to the latter ruler and his son Volusianus was set up by the city council (*ordo decurionum*) of the col(*onia*) *m*(*etalla*?) D(*omaviana*).[1] The city continued to prosper into the later third century. The baths mentioned in 220 had fallen into a dilapidated state by 274 when they were restored to their former condition (*pristina forma*) by the procurator Aurelius Verecundus.[2] The native population gained citizenship in stages during the second century, and the settlement at Domavia attracted families from other parts of the province and elsewhere. Included among them were the famous Barbii, originally from Aquileia; new families also came in from the East bringing the eastern cult of Sabazios.[3]

In the Drina valley south of Domavia a city existed at Skelani close to the *statio* manned by *beneficiarii consulares* at Lješće.[4] Citizenship was conferred on some of the population as early as Claudius or Nero, the earliest instance of enfranchisement in the interior. Possibly the grants were made in connection with gold-mining under Nero, although the only archaeological evidence for this is much further west in the Vrbas valley. Only a minority received citizenship at this time, however, and other grants were made at intervals until the early third century.[5] Sometime before the middle of the second century a city was established at Skelani, possibly with the name Gerdis. The earliest evidence is a civic dedication in 158, but a few years later the magistrate (*IIvir quinquennalis*) T. Flavius Similis records that in 169 he was the first member of the council to have a statue of himself set up in the city basilica.[6] Two other magistrates are attested, one of whom was also magistrate (*IIvir*) at the city Maluesa in the Morava valley further east.[7] The Flavian citizenship of its magistrates suggests that it may have been one of the earliest cities organized in the interior, like Bistue Vetus and Nova further west. In the third century some of the leading families had become very wealthy, and still maintained slave labour on their

---

[1] III, 12728–9.   [2] III, 12736.

[3] On citizenship see Appendix XIII, p. 495. *Barbii*: III, 12743 (Poznanovići south of Tegare). Other families include the *Caninii*: III, 12742 (8364) (Zvornik); *Catilii*: III, 12722 (8362); *Papinii*: III, 8365 (Selanac); *Salvii*: III, 12744 (Bjelovac). Sabazios is attested by a bronze votive hand, *GZMS*, 15–16 (1961), 203 ff.

[4] Patsch, *WMBH*, 11 (1909), 140 ff. On the *bf. cos. statio* see above, p. 125.

[5] Appendix XIII, p. 495.

[6] III, 14219/7, 14219/10 dedicated on 26 April, the 58th birthday of Marcus Aurelius.

[7] *WMBH*, 11 (1909), 155: *IIv*[*i*]*rali fu*[*n*]*cto*, 149: . . .]*IIv*[*i*]*r. q*[*q*]. *Gerd*(*is*) *i*[*tem*] *m. M*(*al.*) *l.p.* connected by Patsch with the *Gensis* on the Peutinger Map in the area. Alföldy, *Bevölkerung*, 161, n. 22, prefers to read: *q*[*q. sa*]*cerd*(*otalis*), although the *G* is clear on Patsch's drawing, ibid., 149, fig. 54.

estates; about this period also the Claudii reached equestrian and even senatorial rank.[1]

In the middle Drina valley southwest of Skelani a city existed at Rogatica near the Prača valley in the hill country east of Sarajevo.[2] The tombstone of a decurion at Rudo, in the Lim valley southeast of Višegrad, records a *muni-(cipium) Fl(avium)*, probably the city at Rogatica.[3] Two of the other magistrates are Flavii, the other an Aelius.[4] The city lies close to the main road from the Sarajevo area to the Domavia mines, but there is no indication that the city was ever concerned with mining. That contacts existed with the coastal cities is suggested by the tombstone of a decurion from Risinium. Not far to the south a small military detachment controlled the important crossing of the Drina at Goražde, and possibly mines in the area, which were worked extensively during the Middle Ages.[5]

After Domavia the other major settlement in the Drina valley was at the confluence of the rivers Vežeznica and Čehotina.[6] Together with the Lim valley around Bijelopolje this was the northern part of the former Sandjak of Novipazar, one of the most inaccessible parts of the interior, shut off from the south and the southeast by the mountains of Montenegro and far from the main centres of Bosnia. Although a Roman road is known to have approached the place from Novipazar in the east there is no record of it on any of the Itineraries,[7] while the name of the place, if the identification with Splonum proposed below is correct, is not recorded by any written source. Even today the area is remote and isolated from the rest of the interior. Lead is mined in the area and the extensive deposits of lignite are the main source of fuel.[8] Apart from brief visits

[1] Slaves and freedmen: *WMBH*, 11 (1909), 157, n. 25, fig. 68 (freedwoman); III, 14219/13 (slaves of a Flavius Silvanus; cf. III, 14219/14) both in third century. Senatorial *Claudii*: *WMBH*, 11 (1909), 152, n. 19, fig. 59–60 (architrave fragment): [? *in memoriam Claudii* . . .]*avii eq. R. c.v.* [. . . *patris et* . . .]*matris c.f. Cl. Cla*[. . . For other *Claudii* at Skelani see Appendix XIII, p. 495

[2] Patsch, *WMBH*, 11 (1909), 181 ff.; Pašalić, *Naselja*, 70 f.

[3] *Sp.*, 77 (1934), 16, n. 19; cf. *ŽA*, 7 (1957), 118; 8 (1958), 332 on the reading: *D.m. T.F. Silvanus dec. m(?) muni(cipii) Fl(*. . . There is no evidence for the existence of a separate city at Rudo, assumed by Pašalić, *Naselja*, 70.

[4] III, 8366: *P. Ael. Clemens IIvir* (perhaps the same man who is called *veteranus* on another dedication; III, 8367), III, 12747 (8368): [*T.] Fl. Alba[n]us II[vir q]q.* both dedications to *I.O.M.*

[5] Risinium decurion, n. 3, p. 255.

On the settlements see below, p. 353 f, and on the inscriptions Evans, *Archaeologia*, 49 (1885), 25f.; Patsch, *WMBH*, 12 (1912), 102 ff.; *Sp.*, 98 (1941–8), n. 285–313.

[7] III, 10163 milestone (Čičjapolje near Bijelopolje).

[8] On the mines Davies, *RME*, 191, also the dedication to Mercury the silver worker (*Mercurius argenti actor*), above, p. 174, n. 2.

by Patsch, Evans and one or two others, no archaeological research has been conducted in the area.

None of the population obtained Roman citizenship before the reign of Hadrian. Most have the names Aelius, from Hadrian or Antoninus Pius, or Aurelius which only appears with the *praenomen* Titus.[1] These probably received citizenship from Antoninus Pius, but the title of the city *municipium Aurelium* indicates that Marcus was the benefactor. On the other hand, the earliest official record from the city is a dedication to L. Verus as Caesar (138–61).[2] No mention of the city survives on the stone, but it seems probable that, as Alföldy has suggested, it was organized in the last years of Antoninus Pius and completed under Marcus. When the majority of the local people took the name Aurelius, Marcus and Verus were ruling, but they kept the *praenomen* Titus in memory of Antoninus Pius. The name of this city is a problem. One of its leading citizens in the second century was prefect of the city but unfortunately its name has been partly obliterated on his inscription: *praef(ectus) i(ure) d(icundo)* [*mun(icipii)*] *Aureli S[.]lo.*, which is best expanded to *S[p]lo(nistarum)*, the city Splonum captured during the ruthless pacification of the area in 9, when the Roman army for the first time entered the territory of the Daesitiates and the Pirustae.[3] Apart from this, on tombstones of magistrates and decurions the name of the city is usually abbreviated to *municipium S. . . .*[4] Moreover, an altar at Plevlje records an immigrant who was commissioner (*curator*) of Splonum and a number of other cities elsewhere in the province.[5] All the administration of the area appears to have been in the hands of the magistrates and decurions. Apart from a *beneficiarius consularis* in 194, and another at Komine, there is no record of any government official who might be concerned with mining in the area.[6] Possibly the workings were controlled from Domavia further north.

Virtually nothing is known about the economy of the city at Plevlje, although slaves of native families are attested late in the Roman period, presumably work-

---

[1] Appendix XIII.   [2] Sp. 98 (1941–8), 298.

[3] III, 8308; cf. the drawing by Evans, *Archaeologia*, 49 (1885), 44, fig. 21 (Kolovrat in Lim valley); *D.m.s. P. Ael. P[l]adome[n]o* [. . .] *Caravantio* [. . .? *praefectus*] *civitatium* [?*Pirustaru*]*m praef, i.d.* [*mun.*] *Aureli S[p]lo(nistarum) Pantoni coniugi eius viva parentibus pientissimis A[e]l(ii) Titus Lupus et Firminus h.p.c. h.s.f.* On the restoration of the Pirustae see above, p. 174, n. 7, and on the location of Splonum, literature cited in n. 6, p. 174 above.

[4] III, 8309 (1708, 6343), 8298 (Kolovrat); III, 8310 (6344); cf. Sp. 98 (1941–8), 300, *Starinar*, 1950, 183 (Džurovo); III, 8301 (6341; cf. 2275), *WMBH*, 12 (1912), 127, n. 11, fig. 53.

[5] *GZMBH*, 52 (1940), 20, n. 4, fig. 4; cf. *Sp.*, 98 (1941–8), 287 (Komine): *Serapidi et Isidi M. Ulp. Gellianus eq. R. cur(ator) Arbensi(um) Metlensi(um) Splonistar(um) Maluesati(um).*

[6] III, 13847.

ing on the land.¹ On the other hand, the place was sufficiently prosperous to attract people from the coastal cities, especially those of the southeast.² The only immigrant from abroad was M. Ulpius Gellianus, an equestrian who was the commissioner of some Dalmatian cities including Splonum. He is the only Ulpius attested here and his dedication to the eastern deities Serapis and Isis suggests he was an immigrant from one of the oriental provinces.³

vii *The Morava Valley* (fig. 11).   That part of the upper Morava valley with its tributaries which was included in Dalmatia was inhabited by a Celtic population, probably part of the old Scordisci, organized as the *civitas* of the Dindari. The people retained their old traditions in dress, portraiture, and decoration on stone, well into the Principate and they were slow in adopting even the outward forms of Roman life.⁴ The main settlement was Maluesa (Visibaba near Požega) which the became the city (*municipium Maluesatium*) of the area incorporating the territory of the Dindari.⁵ Although there are a few Flavii, Ulpii, and Aelii, the majority are Aurelii. The Aelii have the *praenomen* Titus or Publius, indicating enfranchisement from Hadrian and Antonius Pius respectively, while the Aurelii have Titus. There is one instance of a Publius Aurelius.⁶ This picture is one of steady citizenship grants throughout the second century, rather than a sweeping grant on one occasion as is known elsewhere with the Flavii at Doclea or the Publii Aelii among the northern Delmatae. There is virtually no trace of immigrant families, and all the known magistrates (*IIviri*) of the city are of native origin.⁷ The only person connected with the city from outside Dalmatia was the commissioner (*curator*) of some Dalmatian cities at Plevlje including Maluesa.⁸ This is the only record of the citys' name in full. At Maluesa itself it is recorded once as *m(unicipium) Mal(uesatium)* but in most cases it is abbreviated to *M.*⁹ The limit of the city's territory on the east was the provincial boundary with

¹ A bailiff (*vilicus*) is known at Kolovrat: *Sp.*, 98 (1941–8), 335, also a freedman (*libertus*) at Beran: III, 13832; cf. *Sp.*, 71 (1931), n. 11.
² For instance from Risinium, n. 2, p. 256.   ³ See n. 5 above.
⁴ See literature cited above, n. 4, p. 171.
⁵ In general, F. Papazoglu, *ŽA*, 7 (1957), 114 ff.
⁶ III, 14607/1 and Appendix XIII, p. 496.
⁷ *IIviri*: III, 8339, 8340 (Karan); III, 8324 (1672) (Požega); III, 14613 (Bioška), 8354; cf. *Sp.*, 98 (1941–8) 487 (Mačkat); *decuriones*: III, 8343 (Vrutci), 8344 (1671) *def(unctus) Salona, Sp.*, 39 (1903), 88 (Tubići); *sac(erdotalis)*: *Sp.*, 75 (1931), 598; cf. 98 (1941–8), 486 (Mačkat), also fragments: III, 8341, 8345, *WMBH*, 11 (1909), 149, fig. 54 (Skelani, see n. 7 on p. 280), 155, fig. 65 (Skelani).
⁸ Note 5 on p. 282.
⁹ III, 8343 (Vrutci): *Ael. Victor dec. m. Mal.*

Upper Moesia at Čačak where a small military detachment was maintained.[1] Although the mines are not far from the city there is no evidence that they played any role in the economy of the city.[2] The Serbian Morava is more fertile than the Drina valley to the west, but it is remote from the main centres of Dalmatia, and its natural outside contacts are with Moesia and the Middle Danube. Most of the members of the city council are found buried in different parts of the city territory, suggesting that most of their life was bound up with farms and estates away from the city. A large number of sites inhabited in the Roman period, mostly farms and smaller places, are attested by surface remains around the city, but so far none has been excavated. Some slaves are attested working on the estates of wealthier families, and at least one of the families may have been rich enough to gain admission to the senatorial order.[3]

II *City Development and the Spread of Citizenship*

With the possible exception of Liburnia, no part of Dalmatia had developed cities able to continue as flourishing political societies within the Roman province in the manner of the Greek cities of the Eastern Mediterranean. No large native settlements are known to have passed immediately into the form of a Roman provincial city without at least some major development involving a new settlement or an upheaval in the native pattern of life. This does not mean that the class structure of Dalmatian society was ever changed drastically – at least in the purely native cities – and men whose families appear with recent citizenship, together with the trappings and labels of municipal office, were merely performing the role within their communities which their ancestors had carried on for generations before the Roman conquest.

The signs of political development among the native peoples before the Roman period have already been examined in an earlier section (pp. 182–186), and from that it is clear that the growth of cities in the province owed little to previous political development. The clearest instance of this is the old Illyrian kingdom of Agron in the southeast. Some of the centres, Scodra, Risinium, Lissus, etc., were cities at an early date, but this was due entirely to Italian settlement during the Late Republic rather than to the Illyrian population. Similarly the cities of the central coastline owed virtually nothing to the Greek cities on the islands. Further north the Iapodes appear with a semblance of political

---

[1] Appendices VIII, IX.

[2] An official of the provincial financial organization (*arc(arius) f(isci) Dalm.*) is the only evidence for the government outside the city organization, *Sp.*, 47 (1909), p. 183 (not accessible).

[3] III, 8350 (Karan): *D.m. Fl. Tattae libertae et nutrici def. an. l. Fl. Prisca c(larissima) f(emina) et Dazieri vil(ico) vivo p.*, also III, 8351 (Gorobilje) a *s[ervus]?*

organization, but none of their settlements became cities before the end of the first century A.D., nor did they ever rival later cities in the northern part of the province.

Liburnia is the exception. All the cities which existed on or near the coast between Western Istria and the Ravni kotari had become *municipia* before the end of the Julio–Claudian period, apart from Scardona in the extreme south. The delay there may have been due to the nearness of the Delmatae and also of the legionary fortress at Burnum, and the position of the latter in the administration of the few non-Roman communities of inland Liburnia and the Iapodes. In Liburnia the old hill settlements of the Liburni rapidly became cities in physical reality with temples, baths, and fora.[1]

The main factors which governed city development in the first two centuries of the Principate were much more geographical and economic than any position attained in the pre-Roman period. At the same time there is a coincidence between the geographical divisions of the province and the spread of cities under different rulers, almost as if the various regions came to exist in a social and economic hierarchy awaiting their turn for official sanction and approval of city status. The earliest phase of city development involved the granting of privileges to settlements of Italian colonists along the coast of Dalmatia, Salona, Narona, Epidaurum, and the smaller cities further south. They were virtually extensions of Italy, and they remained dominated by the Italian settler families for three or four generations after the colonial period. In none of these places does any native element appear, apart from Narona where one or two native families are found at an early stage, while the large number of freedmen there suggests that it was different in social character from the other colonies. The reasons for their establishment are varied. The Italians were attracted main by greed: a new land to be exploited under the umbrella of Roman armies, a local population to be dispossessed and exploited. Sometimes the Italian settlers met with disaster. In the early eighties B.C. king Mithridates of Pontus had no difficulty in finding allies in Greece to join against the hated oppressors. Eighty thousand Italians in the Eastern Mediterranean paid with their lives for more than half a century of oppression and cruelty.[2] The situation along the Dalmatian coast may have been similar, where the settlers had to contend with both the native Delmatae and the older Greek settlements such as Issa and her possessions. Civil war assured their

---

[1] For example at Asseria, below, p. 366 f.

[2] 'Such was the awful fate that befell the Romans and Italians in Asia, men, women, and children, their freedmen and slaves, all who were of Italian blood; by which it was made very clear that it was quite as much hatred of the Romans as fear of Mithridates that impelled the Asiatics to commit these atrocities', Appian, *Mith.*, 23.

future. All were supporters of Caesar and were strengthened and rewarded with colonial status by Caesar and Octavianus. For supporting Pompey the Delmatae were attacked and Issa lost her independence. The Italians were now secure with Roman armies to protect them, and the Adriatic was secured for Caesar and his heir.

Only at the end of the first century A.D. do the Italian families begin to be displaced by natives in their monopoly of magistracies and council membership. The settler families can easily be identified in the first century. Their wealth was based on the ownership of land and property and the control of trade, at a time when traffic with Italian ports was at its height. In the second century the new men appear: when they arrive their prestige is great, for they often hold a plurality of magistracies in the newer cities of the interior. Like their predecessors in Italy the Roman colonies began as defensive bastions against the native peoples, who in the first century were fierce warriors with a primitive economy. On the other hand, the northern part of the province developed fairly rapidly with little or no Italian settlement and with ruling classes exclusively of native origin.

While the precise date of many cities in Liburnia is uncertain, most were certainly established under Augustus, Tiberius, or Claudius. Liburnian society, based partly on organized piracy, had already displayed signs of political development with slavery and large settlements, especially in the Ravni kotari. These cities, together with those in the Quarnero, did attract Italian settlers, but as communities already well established, not as pioneers in the midst of hostile natives as further south. The only place where Italian families were dominant was Iader, and even here native families are found from the earliest period. In no cities of Liburnia, and in only one of Dalmatia, do legionary veterans appear as original settlers: they are found later under Augustus, Tiberius and Claudius, when they were attracted to wealthy and flourishing communities. Otherwise organized veteran settlements appear only on land near military stations made available by the government. The exception is Aequum, a colony established under Claudius after the departure of Legion VII from Tilurium. Here legionary and auxiliary veterans were settled, but even so the basis of the community was an established settlement of civilians, from whom some of the early magistrates of the city were drawn. This is the only veteran colony known in the province and was only possible after the major change caused by the permanent transfer of a legion from the provincial garrison.[1]

There is a clear distinction between the Julio–Claudian cities of Liburnia and

[1] On veteran settlements see above, p. 107 ff.

Dalmatia and the others which grew in the coastal hinterland and interior of the province. While there is no evidence for any consistent policy to spread Roman habits and political forms in the manner of a missionary, the government were eager to allow the maximum local autonomy and to entrust the duties and, more important, the cost of local government to the local people, preferably an oligarchy chosen on a property qualification. In this field Dalmatia made only slow progress during the first century but by the early third century, when all the known cities were in existence, the province can be described as an urbanized area unlike neighbouring provinces. The basis of city development was the organization and control of the native *civitates* and it is necessary to examine this process before examining the growth of cities under different emperors.

When Rome acquired her complicated network of alliances and 'friendships' in the Mediterranean she would normally deal with two categories of political institutions, kings (*reges* – βασίλεις) and cities (*civitates* – πόλεις) or in a few cases leagues of cities. The monarchs were often tolerated long after the time when effective Roman control could have been established, either because the ruler was a loyal and valuable ally, or because the territory or the population was so unattractive to Romans that they preferred to leave well alone. The Ptolemies were traditionally friends and lasted until Cleopatra; Herod, in spite of his notorious changes of allegiance, was allowed to rule the difficult nation of the Jews, while the Thracian kings were tolerated, in spite of frequent dynastic disputes, because their lands and people were a daunting problem for a Roman government.

As the peoples of Dalmatia became gradually absorbed in a system of administration they were each regarded as separate entities and for the most part were left under the control of their native aristocracy.[1] At first the Roman government preferred to deal with small political units; Varro records eighty-nine *civitates* being administered from Narona in the late first century B.C.[2] The individual communities are officially described as *civitates*, implying city status in the strictly legal sense, but which were in reality units of tribal society. They varied greatly in size, and under Augustus the government preferred to create larger *civitates* from groups of smaller ones, as happened with the Narensii, Deramistae, and Docleatae.[3] These would be more viable units of local government, in cases where peoples near the coast were not included in the territories of the coastal cities. For the major peoples of the interior subdued in 9 the ethnic units were retained in the form of *civitates* with members of the native aristocracy (*principes*)

---

[1] Even in 8 Bato of the Breuci was allowed to rule his people after the surrender, Vell. Pat., ii, 114.

[2] Plin., *HN*, iii, 142 and above, p. 163 f.   [3] Above, p. 165.

ruling as officially appointed administrators (*praepositi, praefecti*) from their own individual centres (*castella*), but this was only made effective after a long probationary period. Most of the larger peoples in the interior had submitted only after conquest by the Roman army, and in the early part of the first century A.D. they were ruled directly by the governor through senior officers seconded from the provincial army. For administration they were divided into three circuits (*conventus*) for justice, taxation, and the levying of troops, a system which had already provoked them into open revolt in 6.[1] Two of the *conventus* centres were major colonies, Salona and Narona, while the third was Scardona in the extreme south of Liburnia.

As well as the powerful Iapodes, Scardona administered the fourteen *civitates* of the Liburni, not all of whom are named by Pliny. Compared with the cities of the Ravni kotari they were insignificant places, probably far from the coast around the foot of the Velebit and the Dinara mountains. Under Tiberius the *civitates Liburniae* set up a dedication to Nero son of Germanicus who died in 31, and they were still under the same administration in the late second century.[2] In the last years of Marcus Aurelius the Liburnian communities paid for the rebuilding of the *praetorium*, an official residence where the governor or his representative held his court at intervals during the year and gave out judgements on disputes.[3] The stone is fragmentary but records one of the peoples named by Pliny, the Burnistae. Further north much of the territory of the Iapodes was included in the territories of new cities founded during the second century, with grants of citizenship and the institution of city magistracies on the Roman pattern; these reduced the area controlled from the tribal centre at Bihać.

In the northern part of the province the great peoples in the Salona and Narona *conventus*, Maezaei, Daesitiates, Delmatae, retained their identity, but their political unity was rapidly eroded by the promotion of individual places to municipal status, beginning in the late first century. The fierce and isolated Pirustae disappear into three new *civitates* in the mountains of the southeast interior, as also do the powerful Scordisci in the northeast: only one of their communities, the Dindari, was included in Dalmatia, the others being in Pannonia and Moesia.[4]

Although there is evidence for the framework and titles of the system by which these native communities were governed, very little is known about how this worked in reality and how the new external control affected the various classes within the native population. For the Roman government in the first century A.D. the crucial problem was the loyalty of the ruling classes: if this could not be

[1] Dio, lv, 29, 1–2.   [2] III, 2808; cf. 9897 (p. 1035) and above, p. 218.
[3] III, 2809.   [4] Alföldy, *AAnt.*, 12 (1964), 107 ff. and above, p. 171 f.

gained then a large army would be required in the province and direct military control of much of the population retained. After 9 nothing is known of events in Dalmatia, for the next few years, but this does not necessarily indicate the end of disturbance. It is significant that military administration remained throughout the Julio–Claudian period, and that removal of the single legion of the provincial garrison in the late first century was forced on the government by crisis on the Danube frontier. Some of the officers who administered the peoples are known: under Augustus an equestrian controlled part of Liburnia together with the Iapodes.[1] The practice of grouping different areas and peoples under one command was continued: under Nero, or possibly Vespasian, a centurion of Legion XI Claudia controlled the Maezaei and the Daesitiates together, indicating also that the command followed local political and military needs and not the *conventus* organization.[2] From this appointment the officer was promoted to command the auxiliary Cohort III Alpinorum stationed at Andetrium, where his duties may have been similar with regard to some communities of the Delmatae. The change from military to civil administration appears to have been made under the Flavians. Men who remembered the great rebellion of 6–9 were now dead or removed from power by old age. Careful government (and some of the early governors were men of immense prestige and great ability) ensured loyalty among the native upper classes. The change can be observed among the Iapodes. At their centre near Bihać the *principes* of the tribe set up altars to *Bindus Neptunus* at the Privilica spring near Golubić. Some of these have the title *praepositus* (one instance of *praefectus* is known), indicating an official appointment which was accompanied by a grant of citizenship.[3] Among the Docleatae in the southeast native leaders are attested: one who calls himself *princeps* of the *civitas* of the Docleatae may have held an official appointment.[4] Elsewhere the change in authority under the Flavians took a different form, with the creation of new cities out of areas of the tribal territories, in the Lika polje (Arupium), among the Daesitiates (Bistue Nova, Rogatica), Dindari (Skelani), and the Docleatae. In spite of these changes the native *civitates* still remained the organization for large parts of the interior, but as the process of urbanization was accelerated under Hadrian and his successors, so the old tribal units began to disappear. In the middle of the second century a recruit to the auxiliary regiment at Bigeste would still describe himself as Maezaeus, and the *princeps* of the Dindari at Skelani belonged to a family whose citizenship came from Hadrian, as did another at Kolovrat near Plevlje who may have been *praefectus* of the *civitates* formed from the Pirustae.[5] There is no evidence for the details of the final reorganization

[1] V, 3346 and above, p. 159 f.   [2] IX, 2564.   [3] III, 14324.
[4] p. 167, n. 1 above.   [5] p. 174, n. 7 above.

which must have taken place in the third century, although it is likely that universal citizenship under Caracalla meant the end of the native *civitates*, the newly enfranchised population being attached to the cities as part of enlarged territories.

It was the Flavians who began the urbanization of the interior, while completing that of the coastal area with Scardona. Elsewhere Flavian *municipia* are known at Arupium in the Lika polje, the two cities Bistue Vetus and Nova, and the cities in the Drina valley at Rogatica and Skelani. In addition Doclea became a city, probably under Titus, and Rider of the Delmatae probably acquired a Latin status.[1] Not all the foundation dates are certain: only Scardona and Rogatica are called *municipia Flavia*, and there is no doubt about Doclea. In other cases the dates are based upon the citizenship conferred on the few known families holding magistracies. The reason for these foundations is not obvious: they did not prosper to the extent of later cities in the interior.

Under Hadrian the northern communities of the Delmatae gained city status, Pelva, Salvium, and probably Delminium in the northern poljes; in the lands of the Maezaei a city was established at Šipovo in the Pliva valley. In Liburnia the old civilian settlement at the legionary fortress Burnum became a *municipium*, although the old native *civitas* lasted beside it into the late second century (p. 218). Under Marcus cities appear in two areas, the Delmatae south of the Dinaric Alps and the mining settlements in the eastern interior. In the former area Magnum, Novae, and possibly the upper Hippius valley around Vrlika, acquired municipal status, as also did Diluntum further south in Popovopolje. With the great coastal cities so close at hand, however, none of these places developed to any size. In the interior Domavia and Plevlje became cities at the end of the century, as also did Maluesa in the Morava valley and the spa resort Aquae S. at Ilidže near Sarajevo. In the extreme north the old Iapodian stronghold Metulum was retained for a long period under military control but had become a *municipium* by the end of the third century.

Thus Dalmatia became an urbanized province with altogether more than sixty cities. Some areas appear to have remained permanently under military control, such as the northern part of the Daesitiates around Doboj and the Delmatae around Andetrium, Tilurium, and Bigeste, or under procuratorial administration, as in the case of the mines in the Sana valley. In other remote areas, such as the southeast interior between Plevlje and Doclea, not even the semblance of city organization could be expected to develop, and there is no evidence to indicate how these areas were administered in the third century. Possibly they were remote parts of cities such as Municipium S. or Domavia, (p. 279) administered

[1] Thus Mommsen, *CIL*, III, p. 363.

by municipal *praefecti* in the manner of the Dalmatian islands which were part of Salona.[1]

Since there were no Greek cities, apart from the unfortunate Issa, existing in Dalmatia at the time of the Roman conquest, all the cities of the province adopted the titles and internal organization common to most cities in the Latin West. Apart from Issa and Greek minorities in the larger coastal cities, Latin was spoken throughout the province; there is evidence, however, that the native language was still spoken in the second century A.D.[2] The city dealt with the provincial government as an autonomous entity: through it taxes were paid, roads were built, and the official life of the province, the provincial cult, and deputations to the emperor were organized. Civic duties were imposed upon its inhabitants, and as long as there was no large-scale waste of money or flagrant corruption the governor was prepared to leave well alone. The larger cities were successful, well established by Italian settlement in the first century, and there seems to have been no miscalculation about the reliability of the native aristocracy in the interior as happened in Britain in the years preceding the rebellion of Boudicca. In the later period commissioners (*curatores*) are known for a number of cities in the province, in Liburnia and in the interior.[3] In the first stages of this system they were senators sent by the emperor to enquire in a discreet manner into internal affairs, in particular local finance, while attempting to respect long acknowledged independence.[4] Later they were chosen from members of the provincial aristocracy, and their control of local affairs became tighter, as their duties included ensuring that city councillors met their obligations and that money earmarked for public projects was wisely spent and reached its proper destination intact.[5]

There is no evidence for any real difference in status between *coloniae* and *municipia* in Dalmatia. Theoretically colonies were settlements of Romans, new foundations with their constitutions modelled closely on that of the city itself. In Italy they were used to relieve overcrowding in Rome and to garrison conquered territory in various parts of Italy. Later the institution was employed to solve the problem of disposing of dangerously large numbers of time-expired

[1] A decurion of Domavia was buried at Sočanica near the provincial boundary with Moesia Superior, III, 8297.

[2] Mayer, *Sprache*, 12 f.

[3] Above, p. 282, n. 5, below p. 316; also attested in the later period is the office of auditor (*dispunctor*), III, 8783 of Narona, found otherwise only in Mauretania, *ILS*, 5728, etc.

[4] Note the advice given by the Younger Pliny to a friend who was going to 'set in order the constitutions of free cities' in Achaea, *Epp.*, viii, 24. On the origin and development of this system, A. H. M. Jones, *GC*, 136 ff.

[5] As the Younger Pliny was doing in Bithynia, *Epp.*, x, 15 ff.

legionary veterans, especially by Caesar and Augustus. In Dalmatia only Aequum falls into this latter category, the others being composed of civilian settlers drawn from all parts of Italy.[1] *Municipia*, on the other hand, were existing native settlements granted citizenship and Roman status, although it appears that they could retain their own laws and internal organization.[2]

In some of the colonies the magistrates were a college of four (*IIIIviri iure dicundo*) chosen annually from members of the city council, which normally numbered about one hundred. On their election they paid a sum of money to the city, to be used for public amenities and civic expenses. Some gave banquets to their colleagues on the council to celebrate their election, and gave gifts to the various trade guilds and corporations in the city.[3] The college of four magistrates is found in the first century at Salona, Narona, and Aequum, but at the end of the first century was superseded by a college of two (*IIviri iure dicundo*) with two junior magistrates (*aediles*) acting as their assistants. In the other colonies only *IIviri* are known. Apart from isolated cases of *IIIIviri* at Varvaria in Liburnia and Doclea, all the *municipia* in the province had *IIviri* and *aediles* (or quaestors) as magistrates. Every five years magistrates were chosen to revise the citizen role and their ownership of property, in the manner of the censors at Rome. Usually the men chosen for this role were ex-magistrates and when they held office for this purpose they bore the title *quinquennalis*. These are the outward titles of municipal worthies, attested proudly on many tombstones. There is no way by which one can get behind the labels and trappings of office and study the realities of power and influence within the cities. The rise and fall of Dalmatian families cannot be described in anything more than the barest outline from a haphazard selection of tombstones, and the real life at the top of local cities remains hidden.

Within the framework of city government the imperial authorities tolerated and even encouraged a number of associations and trade guilds. In the large cities the freedmen had their own association linked to the imperial cult, which was closely linked to the city hierarchy. This was their substitute for membership of the city council: in Dalmatia freedman associations are found almost exclusively in the coastal colonies where their strength was considerable.[4] The close association with emperor-worship satisfied the government that regular surveillance could always be exercised over such groups. They were more cauti-

---

[1] According to Suetonius, *div. Iul.* 42, Caesar settled eighty thousand citizens in overseas colonies.

[2] Gellius, *NA*, xvi, 13, 4–5, quoting some remarks of Hadrian.

[3] The misuse of these payments is described by Pliny, *Epp.*, x, 39, 5.

[4] Outside Liburnia they are known only in Salona, Narona, Aequum, Rider, and Doclea. For the function and variety of these guilds see Waltzing, *Études*, etc.

ous in their attitude towards the trade guilds (*collegia*) composed of free independent craftsmen and traders. This class had vested interests to protect and in some
cities was often responsible for major disturbances. The urban mob which had
caused such trouble in Rome were not runaway slaves and criminals but often
free artisans and shopkeepers, the 'wretched and half-starved poor' who suffered
constantly from shortages of food and tyranny of magistrates.[1] The extent they
could go in order to protect their interest is seen in the first century A.D. when
St. Paul's preaching at Ephesus appeared as a threat to the magic of the great
goddess. This aroused the anger of the guild of silversmiths who made their
money from selling expensive miniatures of the shrine to visitors. Their leader
Demetrius and his followers managed to break up a civic meeting in the theatre,
forcing Paul and his party to leave for Macedonia.[2] The commonest association
of this type known in Dalmatia was the guild of smiths and clothworkers.

The grants of city status to native communities in the interior have already
been discussed in an earlier section, (p. 290) but it will be worthwhile completing
a study of urbanization with a brief survey of the spread of citizenship throughout the province in the two and a half centuries between the proconsulship of
Iulius Caesar and the universal grant of citizenship under Caracalla. This falls
into two phases; the earlier ends with the Julio–Claudians when Roman citizenship was valuable for personal status, especially in the eastern provinces. Here
St. Paul provides another good illustration. The announcement that he was a
Roman citizen soon changed the attitude of the authorities in Jerusalem who had
arrested him. The main routes to the citizenship were loyalty to the ruling
emperor (or earlier to a proconsul) and service in the army. The Republican
clientela spills over into the Principate: just as the Domitii secured citizenship for
their friends and clients in Narbonensis, or the Fabii in Spain, so the Iulii of Gaul
have been favoured by the Julian House in the Republican tradition.[3] The only
instance of a senatorial connection with Dalmatia reflected in citizenship grants
are the Calpurnii Pisones in Liburnia.[4] The second phase begins with the Flavians
and lasts through the second century, most grants being made under Hadrian,
Pius, and Marcus Aurelius. Now citizenship was associated with the founding of
cities, which was often accompanied with widespread grants to the native population.

From Republican times it was a common practice for foreigners to adopt
Latin names. A full Roman citizen had the *tria nomina*, *origo*, filiation and voting

[1] P. A. Brunt, *PP*, 35 (1966), 3–27.
[2] *Acts*, xix, 24–40. On the legal aspects of the incident, A. N. Sherwin-White, *Roman Society*,
etc., 83 ff.
[3] Badian, *FC*, 309, 313 f.   [4] p. 331.

X

tribe, the last named now an anachronism. The emperor Claudius is recorded to have forbidden *peregrini* to usurp Roman names as if they were citizens.[1] The citizenship of some peoples was of doubtful origin and for the north Italian Anauni Claudius had to approve a retrospective grant to confirm their assumed Roman status, since a strict application of the law would have produced great hardship and many legal difficulties.[2] In practice grants of citizenship were made by the provincial governor acting on instructions from the central government.[3] The governor would also be required to maintain an up-to-date register of all Roman citizens in his province. The most rapid adoption of Roman name-forms appears in the Venetic area of Liburnia and Western Istria. It is not always certain that a native of the province is a Roman citizen or whether he had adapted the more developed onomastic formulae of the area to the *tria nomina* of the Roman pattern. In the case of city magistrates there is no doubt of their citizenship; in the first century when the problem is greatest most give their Roman names in full with filiation and voting tribe. Some groups such as the men who served in the imperial fleets at Ravenna and Miseum are known to have enjoyed Latin Status, an inferior grade of citizenship. From the time of Vespasian they received this status and usually adopted the three Roman names, instead of their native names which betrayed their origin, but as *Latini* they could not show filiation and voting tribe.[4] Other classes may have received the same status, such as the ruling classes of Rider among the Delmatae and possibly the *principes* of the Iapodes at Bihać, some of whom have *nomina* adopted from native names.[5]

The vast majority of enfranchised natives bear names of emperors: in the interior virtually the whole of the native population are Flavii, Aelii, or Aurelii. The name Iulius was conferred under Caesar, Augustus, Tiberius, and Gaius, and most native people with this *gentilicium* are in the *municipia* of Liburnia especially in the northern part of the Ravni kotari.[6] A few are known from the Dalmatian colonies, especially in the territory of Salona and Narona. The foundation of these, however, did not involve any widespread grants of citizenship, as the majority of their populations were Italians who settled there. Virtually all

[1] Suet., *Claud.*, 25. The process was already widespread in the first century B.C., Cic., *Verr.*, v, 112.

[2] *ILS*, 206.

[3] When Pliny asks Trajan to grant Roman citizenship to his Alexandrian doctor, *Epp.*, x, 5 f., it was necessary for the emperor to write to the Prefect of Egypt where a register of native-born Roman citizens was kept, F. Schulze, *JRS*, 32 (1942), 78 ff.; 33 (1943), 55 ff.

[4] Starr, *Roman Imperial Navy*, 71 ff.

[5] *Licinus Teuda, Proclus Parmanic(us), T. Loantius*; cf. Alföldy, *Bevölkerung*, 179 f.

[6] The most extensive grants appear to have been made in the Corinium area, p. 211.

the Iulii with *praenomina* are Caii Iulii; grants with this name occurred only under Caesar or Augustus: citizens created under Tiberius are not attested. Grants under Claudius and Nero usually involve the name Claudius, and it is only the former who is known to have had an active policy of political advancement, especially in Gaul where he was born and spent his earliest years.

The colony at Aequum did not apparently involve any grants of citizenship to the native upper class of the area, although this did not happen at Asseria and Varvaria, Claudian cities in the Ravni kotari. An isolated group of Claudii occur at Skelani in the Drina valley, but there is no obvious reason for this grant to a remote settlement in the interior. Geographically the impact of Julio–Claudian citizenship was slight and for the most part confined to the coast.

As with the cities, it is only in the Flavian period that the spread of citizenship made an impact on the peoples of the interior. Significantly, there are no Flavii in Liburnia. In the southern hinterland the Docleatae appear to have been enfranchised at one sweep, and a little further north the newly enfranchised upper classes around Narona proceeded straightway to civic office in the colony.[1] In the north there were four Flavian cities, in all of which the magistrates are Flavii. At none of these places, however, were the grants universal, for later Aelii and Aurelii are attested. A sole Cocceius at Skelani is the only legacy of Nerva's brief reign and Trajan's principate reveals no cities founded but rather a scatter of individual grants at Bihać, the Sana valley, Bistue Vetus and Nova, Aquae S., Skelani, Rogatica, and Maluesa. In the hinterland they are found in the upper Hippius valley around Vrlika.

Hadrian's reign marks the greatest advance and, apart from the new city at Burnum where Aelii are attested, all his grants were made in Northern Dalmatia, ignoring the coastal hinterland inhabited by the southern Delmatae. The largest proportion of Aelii is found at Pelva, Salvium, and Delminium, all three presumably Hadrianic foundations. Hadrianic Aelii have the *praenomen* Publius. There are some with Titus indicating grants from Antoninus Pius, but in the interior they appear only at Municipium S. and Maluesa. T. Aurelii are also attested at these places, as well as at Aquae S. and in the Konjic area. They belong to Marcus, and the city at Plevlje (*municipium Aurelium*) was certainly established in his reign. By contrast Aurelii with Marcus' own *praenomen* are found in any number only at Maluesa. Cities under Marcus or later were established in the coastal hinterland, and their peoples enfranchised. The numerous Aurelii without *praenomina* could have received citizenship from Marcus, Commodus, or under the universal grant (*Constitutio Antoniniana*) of Caracalla in

[1] Above, p. 251. For Flavian and later grants of citizenship in the interior see Appendix XIII p. 497.

212.[1] Septimii received their citizenship under Septimius Severus: his name appears on one tombstone at Osatica near Skelani. Other instances at Vrlika may reflect grants to *peregrini*, although the name also appears among Italian immigrants to the coastal cities and may derive from them.

[1] On the many problems surrounding this enactment see now Chr. Sasse, *Constitutio Antoniniana*.

Chapter 12
The Upper Classes

1 *The Municipal Aristocracy*

The inscriptions which record people and families living in Dalmatia deal largely with families of substance, often holding official positions in the cities or among the native communities. This is especially true of the interior. Tombstones in the Roman fashion were an expensive innovation in this region, and when one sees large ornately carved family epitaphs, such as those common at Municipium S. or Maluesa, there is no doubt about who these people were in social terms, even if no official status is recorded.[1] Elsewhere in other cities of the interior (Bistue Vetus, Rogatica, and Skelani) virtually all the tombstones are demonstrably of wealthy families holding office in the different cities.[2] In only one or two areas is there a larger proportion of ordinary people, for instance at Pelva and Salvium in the limestone areas north of the Dinaric Alps, and Doclea in the southeast; in the latter place, however, families of decurion status are also strongly represented. This is the reason why many of the observations already made about city development, population, and citizenship appear to be concerned largely with upper-class families. Only the coastal cities furnish evidence for their populations at all social levels. Here one can study the different classes, especially in their origins and their changing fortunes over two and a half centuries. The two aspects which can be studied most clearly are the pattern of immigration into Dalmatia during the Principate, and the origins and composition of the upper classes. The two come together as a study of the Italian families established in the coastal cities. One group can be examined separately, those who rose above pro-

---

[1] For instance the Plevlje inscriptions illustrated in *Sp.*, 98 (1941–8), n. 285 f.
[2] All the known families at Bistue Vetus were members of the city council, above, p. 277.

vincial society into the imperial hierarchy by membership of the senatorial and equestrian orders. They are worthy of detailed study since the Dalmatian contribution to the imperial aristocracy is one of the few means available for comparing Dalmatia with other areas of the Empire. Comparison of the number of senators from the Spanish, African, or Gallic provinces with those from Dalmatia over three centuries indicates clearly how the wealthiest families measured up to magnates from elsewhere, while their origins within Dalmatian society can sharpen the picture of the differences in the development of different areas and cities within the province.

The Italian immigrant families are best examined under three headings: Republican families, all of whom are at Narona, Italian families in Dalmatia, and Italian and native families established in Liburnia. In most cases the names of these families are not so common (for instance Valerii, Antonii) as to make their distribution meaningless, and, when one examines the spread of various *gentilicia* in the different cities, it is striking in how many instances names attested in more than one city occur in the context of other upper-class families. The starting point must be those families which were of city-council status. These were the *honestiores* separated by later Roman lawyers from the *humiliores*, or mass of the population, for different treatment before the law.[1]

i *Republican Settlers.* While it is probably true that a number of the settler families known in Dalmatia became established there in the Late Republic, only five occur in dated contexts, all at Narona which was the main Roman centre at the time. On the building record set up by officers of the Narona *conventus* four families are recorded; two of these are freedman families and two freeborn, for the officers were drawn in equal numbers from both classes.[2] The name of the freeborn *magister*, Q. *Safinius* Q. f., is not attested widely in the province: at Narona L. Safin(ius) Quartus was a *magister Mercurialis*, that is, the holder of a freedman priesthood which under Augustus was incorporated into the *seviri Augustales*.[3] Another example is from the territory of the colony and dates to the second century, to judge from his wife who was an Aelia.[4] Linked to them may be a *Safius* who was *IIIIvir* and aedile at Narona: he has the same *praenomen* and

---

[1] By the third century they are clearly distinguished in criminal law, Mommsen, *Strafrecht*, 225, 481, but the distinction is already implicit in the edicts of second-century emperors. *Humiliores* suffered penalties such as execution or penal servitude in the mines, while the corresponding penalty for the *honestiores* was exile (*relegatio*), usually to an island. On the emergence of class-distinctions in Roman Law, G. Cardiascia, *Rev. hist. de droit français et étranger*, 28 (1950), 305 ff., 461 ff.

[2] III, 1820 and above, p. 247.

[3] III, 1801.   [4] III, 12798 (Čitluk in Brotnopolje).

cognomen as the priest nor is his name found elsewhere in the province.[1] Other Safinii occur at Salona and Iader and may belong to the Narona family.[2]

The freedman *magister* is L. *Marius* L. l. Apart from Narona the name is found at Salona, Iader, and Aequum, with numbers of freedmen mentioned. At Iader Maria Q.f. Paulla was of city-council status, and her brother M. Marius Paullus had married into the Salona Albucii.[3] In the first century L. Marius Fortunatus joined the local Legion IIII Flavia felix and his tombstone at Salona records that he died while still a serving soldier.[4] The freeborn quaestor was Q. *Marcius* Q. f. possibly a member of the family which was also settled at Epidaurum and from which originated Hadrian's praetorian prefect Q. Marcius Turbo.[5] At the latter colony they were city councillors and their freedmen appear in the sevirate at Aequum.[6] The freedman quaestor was P. *Annaeus* Q. l. Epicadus, the earliest record of this leading Narona family. His *cognomen* Epicadus shows him to be a native Illyrian from the southeast. On behalf of his patron he also dedicated a temple to Liber Pater, a cult that later became well established at Narona.[7] Eight records are known of the Narona Annaei, of whom the most eminent was A. Annaeus A. f. An(iensis) Flaccus *flamen Augustalis, IIIIvir i.d. quinquennalis* (twice), *IIIIvir i.d.*, prefect of the city and priest (*pontifex*).[8] His tribe Aniensis reveals him as an Italian immigrant, while the accumulation of honours suggests that he may have lived to an advanced age. A *sevir* of the family is known under Augustus: he was related to an immigrant with the unusual name *Lacutulanus*, originating from Central Italy.[9] Two other *seviri* of the family are known, one of whom was honoured with a funeral by the young men's guild (*thiasus iuventutis*).[10] The only member of the family recorded elsewhere in the province is the commander of one of the new cohorts of Dalmatians which rebuilt a section for the Salona city walls in 170.[11] He is almost certainly a local appointment from the Narona branch of the family. The fifth of the Republican families was the *Papii*. The brothers C. Papius Celsus and M. Papius Kanus recorded the recovery of Sicily (*Sicilia recepta*) by Octavianus on a stone set up at Tasovčići.[12] The name is known in Latium, and is also attested among the leaders of the Samnites in the fourth century B.C.[13] Apart from two freedmen at Salona, all the

[1] III, 14626.   [2] III, 2935 (Iader); *BD*, 32 (1909), 67, n. 3945A (Salona).

[3] III, 2926 (Iader), 1965 (Salona).   [4] III, 2021.

[5] Below, p. 327.   [6] III, 1755 (Epidaurum), 9765 (Aequum).   [7] III, 1784.   [8] III, 1822.

[9] Definitely Southern Italian are IX, 4179 (Amiternum); X, 824 (Pompeii); X 5484 (Aquinum); cf. Schulze, *LE*, 358.

[10] III, 1801, 1828; cf. p. 1494. Other *Annaei* come from Narona and its territory, III, 1841, 8446a, 8447, 1842.

[11] III, 6374 and above, p. 117.   [12] III, 14625.

[13] Liv., viii, 10 f.

records of Papii in Dalmatia come from Narona.[1] Their social status was high, judging from Papia L. f. Brocchina who was priestess of the empress Livia after her deification under Claudius (*sacerdos divae Augustae*).[2] There may be a link between the Narona Papii and the Iader Appuleii, because the unusual *cognomen* Brocchus occurs among them.[3]

    ii *Italian Families Established in Dalmatia under the Empire.* The few Italian families which became established in more than one of the Dalmatian cities are all attested at Salona; this suggests that Salona was the place where many of the leading groups in the province first established themselves. If so, it would appear likely that many of the dominant families arrived in Dalmatia under Augustus rather than earlier, by which time Salona had overhauled Narona as the major coastal centre. Families which moved from Salona inland to newer communities include the Turranii at Flavian Scardona, Rutilii at Rider, and the Cassii and Novii families at Doclea, another Flavian city. *Cassii* at Salona held equestrian rank in the first century and their continued dominance is reflected by a later Q. Cassius [. . . . .]*IIvir* of the colony, probably a descendant of the equestrian Cassius Constans; a man with the same name from Aternum on the opposite Italian coast, who recorded that he was a member of the guild of worshippers of Serapis at Salona, also belonged to this family.[4] Salona has thirty-five persons recorded, many of them freedmen, and they last well into the third century. In the interior they reached to Municipium S. and the Sana valley[5] but away from Salona the only city where they became well established was Doclea. There the decurion Q. Cassius Aquila is found married to an Epidia Celerina, from one of the leading native families of Doclea.[6]

    Clodii appear at Salona in overwhelming numbers compared with their distribution elsewhere. Forty-three persons are attested, many of them freedmen. Elsewhere, apart from one example at Asseria, they appear only at Acruvium, where C. Clodius C.f. Serg(ia) Vitellinus was *IIvir* of the city and an equestrian who had served on the jury-panels at Rome. A family of their freedmen is also known there.[7] At Salona a *signifer* of Legion VII C.p.f. whose name is lost has a freedman who was a *sevir*, and may have been the ancestor of a first-century magistrate (*IIIIvir*) C. Clodius C.f. Serg(ia) Fadienus.[8] Many of the Clodii freed-

---

[1] III, 9258, 14824 (Salona), 1869; *JÖAI*, 15 (1912), Bb. 77.
[2] III, 6361.   [3] III, 9982 (Iader).
[4] III, 8737; cf. *BD*, 34 (1911), 10, n. 4111A and below, p. 325; IX, 6106 (Amiternum).
[5] *Starinar* 1950, 183 (Džurovo); III, 13238 (Mrkonjićgrad).
[6] III, 8287 (Vuksanlekíc).   [7] III, 1711, 1713 (Acruvium).
[8] *BD*, 37 (1914), 77, n. 4576A; III, 2079.

men were *seviri*, and another at Narona probably belongs to them.[1] The origin of the Clodii is obviously Italian, and they reached Salona by movements of individual families. The name is a famous senatorial one but there is no evidence for that branch having any link with the province. Similar to the Clodii are the *Egnatii*. There is a decurion at Risinium, C. Egnatius C. f. Serg(ia) Marcellus, and at Salona there is L. Egnatius L. f. Cn. nep. Cn. pronep. Tro(mentina) Clemens, decurion and augur.[2] The half dozen other records from Salona are mostly of freedmen. In Risinium they were connected with the important Statii, and at Aenona a dedication to the Liburnian deity Latra was set up by Egnatia C. f. Paullina, a lady of high social status; her brother Egnatius Secundus may be the man with the same names attested at Iader.[3] The Iader Egnatii were also probably linked to the Salona family: Egnatia Quinta at the latter place is probably identical with one with the same names at Iader.[4] Away from the coast members of the family are found at Municipium S. and Skelani, probably as traders.[5]

Fulvii were *honestiores* at Salona and Epidaurum: in the latter city there is Q. Fulv[ius. . . . . .] IIvir, married to a Taria, and who was probably related to an army veteran.[6] At Salona there are two of this class, a decurion with his family and a Fulvia married to an aedile.[7] They may be connected to a soldier of Legion XI with this name who originated from Philippi.[8] Their freedmen appear at Salona, some of them in the second century.[9] but there is no evidence for any link between the Dalmatian Fulvii and the governor Fulvius Maximus at the end of the second century.[10] Elsewhere a Fulvia was married to a soldier in the provincial garrison from Cohort VIII Voluntariorum at Andetrium who came from Cemenelum in Gaul.[11] In Liburnia they appear at Nedinum (and this may reflect the link with the Tarii at Epidaurum who were a Nedinum family) with an aedile enrolled in the local tribe Claudia.[12]

The *Iunii* also appear at Salona and Epidaurum. At the latter place [I]un(ius) Epidianus was *IIvir*, and his *cognomen* indicates some native ancestry.[13] A *sevir* is known at Narona, while at Salona M. Iunius Iustus in the second century was

[1] III, 2095, cf. 8583 (Salona); *VAHD*, 55 (1953), 262 (Narona).
[2] III, 1758; cf. 8403 (Risinium); III, 1942 (Salona).
[3] III, 2971 (Aenona).
[4] III, 2311 (Salona); III, 9944, 2906 (Iader).
[5] *WMBH*, 12 (1912), 127, n. 10, fig. 52; 126, n. 9, fig. 51 (Plevlje); Sp. 93 (1940), n. 16 (Skelani), possibly a *bf. cos.*
[6] III, 8408; cf. n. 1739.
[7] III, 8789; *BD*, 26 (1903), 140, n. 3119.   [8] III, 2031.
[9] III, 2144 on the tombstone of P. *Ael. P. lib. Satyrus*; cf. also III, 8590 (2109).
[10] XIII, 8007; cf. p. 448.   [11] III, 9782.
[12] *VAHD*, 53 (1950–1), 241, n. 18, re-reading of III, 2867.   [13] III, 1747.

decurion, *IIvir* and *pontifex* and one of the freedmen was a *sevir*.[1] Virtually all the Iunii known in Dalmatia came from Salona (fourteen persons attested) and, apart from those already noted, the only other instance is a decurion in Cohort III Alpinorum at Kadina Glavica.[2] The *Statii* were *honestiores* at Salona, with an aedile and *IIvir* who was also priest of the deified Vespasian. A *quinquennalis* is also attested, and a *sevir* in the family appears to have obtained membership of the city council, a rare instance of bridging the social gulf between even the wealthiest of freedmen and members of the ruling class.[3] Elsewhere Statii are common only at Risinium, with nine persons recorded and two at neighbouring Butua.[4] One of the Risinium Statii was a praetorian decorated by Trajan for service in Dacia and then appointed as centurion to the Spanish Legion VII Gemina.[5] This may be a case of an Italian family becoming established in a smaller city, here Risinium, before achieving status at Salona.

Although there are many *Titii* at Salona (thirty-seven persons including two legionary veterans) only one (an unusually low proportion) is recorded in the city council, C. Titius C.f. Vel(ina) Primus who was *IIIIvir* in the first century.[6] His tribe is foreign to Dalmatia and shows him to be a first-generation immigrant. Some of the many records of this name in the later period may be an adaptation of the native Illyrian Titus, which is common in parts of the interior.[7] Elsewhere a Titius is decurion at Iader, M. Titius M. [f.] Ser(gia) Marinus, and isolated examples occur at Asseria and Sidrona.[8] It is possible that some of the Titii of Salona may be descended from early legionaries of eastern origin, for instance M. Titius who was trooper in Legion VII under Augustus, and originated from Isinda in Pisidia.[9] Another family which may have military origins, though at a later date, was the *Domitii*. An imposing dedication of a temple in 137 records P. Domitius Potens as one of the *IIviri*. A veteran of Cohort III Alpinorum appears with the same names at Salona; another with the *nomen* is L. Domitius Valens, a veteran of Legion V Macedonica.[10] Domitii are unknown at Salona in the first century, but in the later period twenty-one are known, including numerous freedmen. Elsewhere they are very rare, apart from a Domitius Apollinaris who was *sacerdos* in Narona at the end of the second century and may

[1] Patsch, *Narona*, 92, n. 7; cf. III, 8458, 2081, *BD*, 30 (1907), 118, n. 3928A.

[2] III, 2759.   [3] III, 13910, 1954, 14249/3 (Salona).

[4] III, 1717, 1733, 6360, 8393 (1732; cf. p. 1028), also at Aquileia T. *Statius P. f. Serg(ia) Marrax*, *primuspilus* of Legion XIII Gemina, *ILS*, 2638; III, 6338 (near Butua).

[5] III, 6359.   [6] III, 2092.

[7] Alföldy, *PN* (forthcoming), for distribution among the Delmatae.

[8] III, 2930 (Iader), 15020 (Asseria), 9925 (Sidrona).

[9] *BD*, 36 (1913), 14, n. 4407A.

[10] III, 1933, 2003; *BD*, 32 (1909), 59, n. 3900A (Salona).

be of eastern origin.[1] *Lurii* are known in two centres only, Salona and Risinium (with one at Acruvium). Like the Statii they may have become established first at the latter place. One of the witnesses on the Salona diploma of A.D. 70 is P. Lurius Moderatus Risinitan(us), and the family are attested there on two tombstones and on another at nearby Acruvium.[2] They appear in the upper classes at Salona, where Luria Hygia was the daughter of a man of city council status.[3]

The last family in this category is the *Petronii*; they are unusual in being found not only in a number of city councils in Dalmatia but also in Liburnia. At Salona they were *IIIIviri* in the first century and their freedmen, probably of native origin, are found in the sevirate.[4] A Petronius also appears in the same context at Narona,[5] and since this is the only record of the name there, in contrast with the seventeen persons at Salona, he may well belong to the Salona Petronii. Elsewhere they were leading citizens at Scardona, where one commemorates his election as augur.[6] They occur also at Iader and in the far north at Alvona, where the name is borne by a native, Vesclevius Petronius Triti f.[7] They are also one of the few probably immigrant families who settled at Rider.[8]

About half a dozen families of Italian origin are found established at Salona only. The *Albii* were magistrates there in the first century and their survival in this class is indicated by the marriage of Albia Crispina to P. Aelius Rastorianus, a man of native origin from the interior who held numerous municipal offices at Salona and elsewhere in the middle second century or later.[9] He is a striking example of the entry of native families into the Salona ruling circle and their acceptance with a marriage alliance. The Albii may have reached Salona from Aquileia or Istria, but their interests in Dalmatia involved Salona only: all nine persons with the name are found there.[10] The *Albucii* have a similar distribution. At Salona a family tombstone records a father and his two sons. The former was decurion of Salona and its dependency Issa, the elder son decurion of Salona only and the younger son of Issa only (p. 229 f). The last was enrolled in the tribe Sergia, while his father and elder brother were in the older Tromentina.[11] Other Albucii are known as decurions and their freedmen appear as *seviri*.[12] They were

[1] *BD*, 33 (1910), 106, see above, p. 252, n. 2.
[2] XVI, 14; III, 1725 f. (Risinium), 1715 (Acruvium).   [3] III, 1971; cf. 13006, 14809 (Salona).
[4] III, 8525; cf. p. 2323 (Epetium), 8799, 2079a (with native *cognomen Dasius*).
[5] Patsch, *Narona*, 89, fig. 47.   [6] III, 2802 (Scardona).
[7] III, 2950, 10009, 10010 (Iader), 3058 (Alvona); also III, 9935 (Asseria).
[8] III, 2772 (Rider), a veteran of Legion VII Gemina.
[9] III, 2073, 8783 and below, p. 317.
[10] *BD*, 33 (1910), 55. One has the South Gaulish *cognomen Leuga*, III, 2073, cf. Holder, 2, 197 ff.
[11] III, 2074.
[12] *BD*, 30 (1907), 87, n. 3809A; III, 2100; cf. add. 8586, 2166, 2167, 8868.

connected to other Salona families of substance: Albucia C. f. Pontia was married to a Marius, and a *sevir* of the family was married to a Tullia, who was possibly a member of the household of the Salona family of that name which attained equestrian rank in the second century.[1] Their wider trading contacts are indicated by a dedication to *Dea Suria* by one of their freedmen. They probably came originally from Northern Italy where the family is common: in other areas it is fairly rare.[2]

One of the leading families at Salona in the early years of the colony were the *Anicii*. L. Anicius L.f. Pactinas was *IIIIvir quinquennalis* and also *praefectus quinquennalis*, that is acting deputy, of the honorary magistrates Drusus Caesar Germanicus and the Tiberian governor P. Cornelius Dolabella, *pontifex* and *flamen* of the empress Livia (Iulia Augusta). Within the city he was prefect of the artisans' guild and also held the Pharia prefecture. Found near his epitaph is that of another Anicius with the same *cognomen* (which is of Etruscan origin) but a a different filiation. He also held high office in the colony, *IIIIvir quinquennalis*, and *IIIIvir* as well as prefect of the artisans' guild.[3] Apart from one instance at Acruvium there are no other records of the family in Dalmatia, although it does appear at Aquileia.[4] The isolation of this family is interesting, with no freedmen and no descendants attested. Neither of these Anicii records family or household on his tombstone; this suggests that both died without issue.

Caesii are found in various places in the interior, including Plevlje, but their main centres were Salona and Risinium.[5] A freedman *sovir* of the family, C. Caesius C. l. Amaranthus, was married to Clodia P. l. Blanda, and the same stone records his patron C. Caesius C. f. Tro. Vindex, aedile and *IIIIvir*, married to a Cornelia P. f. Clementilla, an equestrian family of Salona.[6] A freedman *sevir* at Narona, M. Caesius M. l. Primus, is the only record of the family there and he may belong to the Salona Caesii.[7] A small group were at Risinium, and at Tragurium a Caesius was married to a Bennia, another leading Salona family of equestrian rank.[8] They may have had military origins, from L. Caesius L. f. Cam(ilia) Bassus from Pisaurum, a veteran of Legion VII who died before 42 after settling at Salona.[9] The *Nassii* were another Italian family established at

[1] III, 1965, 2100.

[2] III, 1961. *Albucii* were a leading family at Mediolanum, Chilver, *CG*, 107.

[3] III, 14712 f. and above, p. 228.

[4] III, 8387 (Acruvium), Calderini, *Aquileia*, 450.

[5] *WMBH*, 12 (1912), 127, n. 10, fig. 52 (Plevlje); also Sp. 77 (1934), 33 (*Castellum Salthua-Riječani*) with cognomen *Epidianus*.

[6] III, 8786. On equestrian *Cornelii* see below, p. 325.

[7] Bulić, *Povodom* (1931), 98 = *AE*, 1932, 82.

[8] III, 1720–2 (Risinium), 2688 (Tragurium).   [9] III, 2014.

Salona. The diploma of A.D. 70 records a local witness M. Nassius Phoebus Salonit(anus).[1] In the city Q. Nassius Q. f. Tro. Certus Draco was aedile and *IIIIvir* and married Tullia Intuma, member of a family which held equestrian rank in the second century.[2] One of their freedmen, Nassius Iulianus, is attested as *sevir Augustalis* and another, M. Nassius Sotericus, was a friend of a wine merchant at Vranjic, a small village on the Bay of Salona.[3]

The last and most numerous of the Salona families was the *Vettii*; sixteen persons are attested there, compared with nine scattered in other cities along the coast. Two *honestiores* are known. T. Vettius Augustalis was decurion, aedile, quaestor, and *IIvir*, as well as patron of the artisans' guild. From the evidence of the magistracy he dates to the second century, and the other is of the same period, L. Vettius L. f. Serg. Catulus, a *IIvir* who set up a dedication to divus Nerva, presumably under Trajan.[4] This inscription is the earliest dated instance of a Salona *IIvir* and indicates the approximate period when *IIIIviri* were superseded by *IIviri*. It also suggests that the Vettii did not come to Salona as *honestiores* from Italy, but were men who rose from the lower classes locally during the first century: the *cognomen* Augustalis is hardly a fashionable one. The freedmen with this name attested in the sevirate are of an earlier period than the magistrates, and may be the latters' ancestors rather than their contemporary dependants.[5] A military origin is possible: the earliest Vettius is Q. Vettius Hospes from Suessa in Campania, serving in the Cohort I Campana under Augustus.[6]

The Salona families held a position of power and wealth which extended far beyond the confines of their native city. Even allowing for the large numbers of inscriptions at Salona and its territory, the number of these families and their wealth indicate their power, which is in strong contrast with the local families in the other cities. It is also significant that when their members appear in the other cities they are either freedmen or related to local council families. Other cities did produce families of note, Aequum the most outstanding of all, but none of the Italian settler families compared with those of Salona in their contacts with other cities.

Claudian Aequum has a group of families which, apart from the senatorial Iulii, had few contacts elsewhere in the province. One family was the *Calpurnii*.

---

[1] XVI, 11.   [2] III, 1083. On the *Tullii* see p. 336.

[3] III, 8792; cf. p. 2328/126, 2131 (Vranjic), an Italian family. The name is found in Central Italy, Schulze, *LE*, 275.

[4] III, 2087, 1978.

[5] III, 2104; cf. 8588: *T. Vettius Fortunatus Augustalis*; III, 2103.

[6] III, 14246/1.

Apart from an equestrian officer at Salona, at Aequum Calpurnia Crispina was married to a *IIvir* who died before entering on his office.[1] Elsewhere Calpurnii only appear around Corinium in Southern Liburnia as dependants of the senatorial Calpurnii Pisones.[2] The *Naevii*, apart from a freedman at Salona, are confined to Aequum. The individual at Salona was *magister* of the *seviri* corporation, and may belong to the Aequum family.[3] Their estates were at Potravlje, where M. Naevius Firmus, decurion, aedile, and *IIvir*, appears with his family, and another tombstone records that Q. Naevius Simplex, decurion and aedile, was married to a Domitia Marcella.[4] Almost certainly related to them was T. Naevienus Seneca, decurion, aedile, and *IIvir*, who was buried at the same place. Another of the family is attested trading at Skelani in the interior.[5] Naevienus Seneca was related to the third leading family of Aequum, the *Seccii*. Apart from a freedman at Salona, all persons known with this name in Dalmatia are found at Aequum. Naevienus Seneca was married to Seccia Pudentilla. Other members of the family were C. Seccius Cn. f. Serg. Marcellus and C. Seccius C. fil. Serg. Aper who commemorated their magistracies with a banqueting hall and portico. A number of freedmen and women are known: Seccia Silvia at Hrvace, and five freedmen and a freedwoman on what was probably a building record rather than a tombstone. They spread to Rider, where one of them is known. The name is rare and is of Celtic origin.[6] They are not natives of the area and they may well be descendants of an immigrant at Aequum, probably an auxiliary veteran settled there under Claudius.

The population of Narona appears quite different in character from other cities of the province, where small numbers of Italian settler families can be identified as dominant in the political and economic life of their communities. Many names are attested at Narona, some of them very uncommon and unknown elsewhere in the province. The two provincial families were the Annaei, who appear in the Late Republic and had native Illyrian connections, and the Lusii, who may be later arrivals and who rose to senatorial rank probably not before the third century.[7]

The origin of the *Publicii* may be as municipal slaves. Isolated members of the family are found at Iader and Asseria[8] but their absence from the upper classes at Salona suggests that they were of little account there. At Narona (?) Publicius

[1] III, 8736 (Salona), 9763 (Aequum).   [2] Below, p. 331.   [3] III, 14243/4 (Salona).
[4] *SB*, 225, n. 3–4.   [5] *VAHD*, 55 (1953), 257, n. 4.
[6] III, 9767, 9777–8 (Aequum), *VAHD*, 51 (1950–1), 225 (Rider). Holder, 2, 1423, cites examples from Noricum, III, 5671, 11480, and Narbonensis, XII, 4151: *Seccia Secci fil. Secundina*: cf. Schulze, *LE*, 20, 227.
[7] On the *Annaei*, p. 299 above, *Lusii*, below, p. 334.
[8] III, 2902 (Iader), 9941 (Asseria).

Q. f. Nicephorus was aedile and *IIIIvir* and his *cognomen* points to a freedman origin.[1] Another is attested as decurion and his daughter's name Ilurica indicates a native ancestry.[2] Publicii are common in the Narona sevirate as late as the second century[3] but apart from these examples only one instance is known at Narona, compared with nineteen persons attested at Salona. Few of the other Narona families whose members appear as magistrates were of any account and there are few records of them otherwise. This emphasizes the picture of Narona as a declining community with few families of any substance lasting there after the first-century period of Italian settlement. The family of T. *Mevius* T. f. Tro. Celsus, aedile and *IIIIvir*, probably came from Southern Italy, to judge from the distribution of his name. Only one other instance of it is recorded in Dalmatia: at Iader, Mevia Felicula was married to the decurion M. *Caton(ius)* Varus.[4] A second family is that of Q. *Veturius* Secundus, decurion at Narona in the second century. The only other record of the name is an *eques* at Salona who had served in a praetorian cohort at Rome: his marriage to an Aelia dates him also to the second century.[5] An interesting fact about the Narona population is the lack of connection between the few attested families of *honestiores* and the large number of freedmen who are known there. This is quite different from what we find at Aequum or Salona where two or three people attested in the city council are regularly accompanied by numbers of freedmen and other dependants. Many of the Narona freedmen were clearly working for patrons elsewhere, in other Dalmatian cities or even in Italy. This is the only explanation for the numerical dominance of this class in the colony. In the time of P. Vatinius the proconsul, Cicero enquired about his runaway slave last seen at Narona.[6] How did he arrive there and who reported to Cicero that he was seen there? Clearly it was already a major trading centre of the coast. Italian families were interested in Narona, not as a place to settle but for its commerce which made them send their freedmen there.

Finally *Vibii* are fairly common at Salona and Narona but only in Epidaurum do they appear as magistrates. P. Vibius P. f. Urbicus records the building of a water reservoir, and at Narona they appear in the sevirate.[7] In Istria they were related to the Aquilii, the leading family at Flanona, and other examples are known at Iader and Arba.[8]

[1] *BD*, 33 (1910), 110.   [2] III, 8441.   [3] III, 8442, 14624/1, 14625/1.

[4] III, 1868 (Narona) with *IIIvir* instead of *IIIIvir* on MS copy, 2924 (Iader).

[5] III, 8444 (Narona), 8765 (Salona).

[6] Cic., *Epp. ad fam.*, v, 9, 11, where he suggests that Vatinius could have him for his triumph if he should catch him.

[7] III, 1750 (Epidaurum), 1770, 1835 (3 ex.) (Narona), 8806 (Salona).

[8] III, 3032 (Flanona), 10015 (Iader), 10123 (Arba).

The difference between Salona families and those of other coastal cities is emphasized by a number of city magistrates at the latter who provide the only examples of their names found in the province. Only one at Salona falls into this category: D. *Campanius* L. f. Tro. Varus, aedile, *IIIIvir*, *IIIIvir quinquennalis*, *augur*, *flamen*, and prefect of the artisans' guild. He may belong to a Campanian family but is not likely to be a first generation settler as his tribe suggests that he was a native of Salona.[1] Only one other record of the name appears in the province, a trader at Blagaj in the Sana valley.[2] An interesting group of families is found at Epidaurum. Unlike families at Risinium, who are often well attested elsewhere, they are restricted to this one city. A *IIvir* P. *Anulenus* Bassus who superintended the building of the city reservoir is the only record of his family. Another magistrate was M. *Pomentinus* Turbo who appears with his son and daughter.[3] There is no other record of the family in the province, but one appears at Dyrrhacium further south along the coast. The name is rare and elsewhere is found only in Rome and Africa. Those at Epidaurum may be a native family, to judge from their *cognomina* (Boria, Turbo). One of these appears with Q. Marcius Turbo in the early second century. The name of another magistrate, dated to the reign of Tiberius, was C. Saenius, found otherwise only at Narona.[4] The *Cipii* of Acruvium were almost certainly a family from Ostia, where twenty-six examples are known.[5] Three persons are recorded at a high level in the city: Sex. Cipius G. fil. Serg. Firminianus, with his father and cousin who were both called G. Cipius Aper, gave banquets to the city councillors – possibly to celebrate their election.[6] They are the only Cipii found in the province. In the far south only one family is known at Lissus, a *IIvir* L. *Gavius* Arn(ensis). He lived under Augustus and may belong to one of the original *conventus* families.[7] Veterans of Italian origin, from Florentia and Brixellum, with this name are known at Burnum, and three persons are attested at Salona in the later period.[8]

iii *The Upper Classes of Liburnia.* The leading families in the Liburnian cities are different from those of the coastal cities of Dalmatia. In the north the population was Venetic and linked closely to Northeast Italy. There is no clear distinction to be made between Italian settlers and natives in this region, and a large proportion of recorded families reveal native Liburnian names. There is settle-

[1] III, 8787; cf. X, 3940 (Capua).
[2] *GZMBH*, 51 (1939), 12.
[3] III, 1750, 1748; cf. III, 622 (Dyrrhachium).
[4] G. Novak, *Rad*, 339 (1965), 129 (Epidaurum); *SB*, 218 f. (Narona).
[5] *CIL*, XIV, index p. 509, 776; R. Meiggs, *Ostia*, 323, for their role in the shipping guilds.
[6] III, 1710.   [7] III, 1704.
[8] III, 15000 (14231/13), 2837 (Burnum), 9108; cf. *BD*, 37 (1914), 43, 4601A (Salona).

ment by Italian families, especially in the Ravni kotari, but only in the colony Iader did they constitute the dominant group. The one senatorial family of Liburnian origin arose from a native family in Arba.

The Liburnian name *Raecus*, latinized to *Raecius*, appears in a number of cities in Liburnia, and apart from two examples at Salona, is not attested elsewhere in the province.[1] On Crexi the magistrate Q. Fonteius Raeci f. was married to Volsouna Oplica Plaetoris filia and reveals Raecii as *honestoires* in the early first century A.D.[2] The examples at Salona are Raecia Maria married to the native Aplius Karus, and on the island Solentia there is P. Raecius [. . . . .] Liccaius, a typical Liburnian name. The *Trebii* were related to the Raecii, although originally they may have been immigrants from Italy. At Iader M. Trebius Proculus was an equestrian and magistrate in his own city Arba, a few miles to the north.[3] His daughter Trebia Procula was married to Q. Raecius Rufus, senior centurion (*primuspilus*) of the eastern Legion XII Fulminata in the late first century.[4] The veteran of Legion VIII Augusta, L. Trebius Paulus, was a recruit from the family in the later first century and returned to his home at Fertinium (Omišalj) on Curicta.[5] An early generation of the Liburnian Trebii may be the 80-year-old veteran of Legion XI C. Trebius C. f. Firmus. He records neither *origo* nor voting tribe and it is possible that his family were already established in Iader at an early date, since he must have been born before 38 B.C. Another Liburnian may be the L. Trebius Secundus, camp prefect of Legion VII, who arranged a boundary settlement between two communities of the Delmatae in the first year of Gaius: he also records no origin or voting tribe. Another early veteran was L. Trebius L. f. whose son L. Trebius Exoratus died at the age of 12 in the lands of the Maezaei.[6]

The third great family of Liburnia were the *Appuleii*. Unlike the Raecii and Trebii who seem to have been based in the northern part of Liburnia, their centre was Iader and they may be either an Italian family, or perhaps one of native origin. There could be a link with Sex. Appuleius, legate in Illyricum in 8 B.C.[7] At Iader the status of the family is indicated by the young equestrian C. Appuleius C. f. Serg. Balbinus who was *pontifex* but died at the age of 21: his mother Epidia Celerina came from a native background not in Liburnia.[8] At Aenona there is Appuleius P. f. Fronto, aedile and *IIvir quinquennalis*, possibly a member of the Iader city council.[9] The most impressive records of the family

---

[1] III, 2501 (Salona), 15101 (Solentia). [2] III, 3149 and below, p. 332 f.
[3] III, 2931. [4] III, 2917 (Iader) and below, p. 333.
[5] III, 3127. On Legion VIII Augusta see above, p. 115 f.
[6] III, 6383 (Salona), 8472 (Krug di Jesenice), 2918 (Iader).
[7] *PIR*, A 961 and above, p. 66. [8] III, 9997. [9] III, 2977; cf. p. 1037.

are two gigantic altars dedicated by Appuleia M. f. Quinta and originally placed in the centre of the Iader forum, but which now support columns in the church of S. Donatus which is built directly on to the paved surface of the Roman forum. One was dedicated to Jupiter Augustus, the other to Juno Augusta, and they were set up jointly by the lady and her son L. Turpilius Brocchus Licinianus. His names (and those of his father) are not found elsewhere in the area and they were presumably both Italians.[1] As with the wealthier Salona families, their freedmen are attested: a T. Appuleius T. l. Antigonus dedicated to the Liburnian deity Anzotica, and Appuleia Quinta also refers to her own household.[2] Another member of this family may be the early legionary veteran Appuleius Etruscus who retired to membership of the Salona council after service on the governor's staff.[3] He records neither voting tribe nor origin, which is rare for a legionary under Augustus or Tiberius. His descendants appear to have retained their position: L. Appuleius Montanus was a decurion of Salona and also magistrate of Aequum, while his wife was an Octavia, possibly one of the leading family at Nedinum.[4] Elsewhere in Liburnia Appuleia Marcella appears in a group of ladies at Lopsica, some of whom were of native origin.[5] A L. Appuleius L. f. Serg. Iadestinus serving in Legion I Adiutrix had probably once been a *peregrinus* serving in the fleet; his citizenship and the *cognomen* may have been due to an Appuleius holding a city magistracy in the year of his enfranchisement.[6]

The fourth and last of the equestrian families of Liburnia was the *Vettidii*. Their centre was also Iader, where the equestrian C. Vettidius C. f. Tro. Maximus was *pontifex*, *IIvir quinquennalis* and patron of the colony; to judge from his tribe he was not a native of Iader and he may have originated from Salona where a single Vettidius is attested.[7] A family of the same name were magistrates at Tarsatica. A *IIvir* Vettidius Nepos appears with his son of the same names, and another tombstone records C. Notarius Vettidianus Secundus, *IIvir* and priest (*sacerdos*) of Augustus. Vettidius Nepos refers to him as brother (*frater*) and he was probably born a Vettidius and adopted later by a C. Notarius Secundus, a name not otherwise attested in Dalmatia.[8]

The family of M. *Autronius* D. f. Atratinus, an equestrian attested on two inscriptions at Iader, is not known otherwise in the province, and the variation of *praenomen* suggests he may date to the early first century A.D., an original settler from Italy.[9] *Dellii* were established at Iader, another family of Italian origin. Q.

---

[1] III, 9994 (6566), 9982 (2904); cf. 2905.   [2] Degrassi, *SVA*, 1, 498 f.; *AE*, 1938, 31.

[3] III, 8506; cf. p. 2328/121 and above, p. 112, n. 4.   [4] III, 8721.

[5] III, 3015; cf. Patsch, *Lika*, 104, with a native *Iulia C.f. Tertia Toruca*.

[6] XIII, 6827 (Mogontiacum); cf. Ritterling, *legio* 1385.   [7] III, 2932.

[8] III, 3028–9 and above, p. 196.   [9] III, 9999, 10000.

Dellius appears with honorary (although not actual) city council membership, and he may be identical with the wealthy freedman Q. Dellius Q. l. Fuscus attested on a tombstone. The family may have originated from Aquileia, where six of them are known.[1] A rare link with Narona is attested by M. Caton(ius) Varus decurion at Iader and married to Mevia Felicula, who may be related to a Narona magistrate. He was probably an isolated trader or settler from Northern Italy, and there is no other record of the family in the province.[2]

Most of these families were based at Iader and reflect the Italian domination of that city. Families in the other cities reveal much more native background, especially in Northern Liburnia, the home of the Raecii. *Baebii* are common in many parts of the Empire; in Dalmatia most of the instances of the name are at Salona (thirteen persons including freedmen). In Liburnia the name appears with native families, for instance L. Baebius Opiavi f. Ser. Oplus Malavicus, decurion and *IIvir* at Arba, and married to Seia Opli f. Tertulla. Another Baebia was married to a decurion and *IIvir*, while a third appears as aedile in Aenona, Q. Baebius [.] Zyprius.[3] All these were probably living in the first century; most of the Salona Baebii date to the second century or later. Elsewhere in Liburnian cities they are found connected with families of quality: at Corinium a Baebius was married to an enfranchised Calpurnia, and at Asseria a Baebia was connected to the *Oppii*, a leading family there and at Varvaria.[4]

The *Decidii* were probably from Northern Italy, and appear at Apsoros and Salona. In the former place M. Decidius M. f. Maximus was aedile, *IIvir*, and *augur*, but those at Salona do not appear to have enjoyed comparable status,[5] and they may be a different Aquileian or Istrian family.[6] L. Fonteius Q. f. Rufus was *IIvir* at Crexi and like his colleague [C.] Aemilius Volso(nis) f. Ocla(tinus) was of Liburnian origin and linked to the Raecii through Q. Fonteius Raeci f., who may be the former's father. The filiation is right and Rufus is a *cognomen* of the Raecii in later generations.[7] The freedman L. *Valerius* Agathopus at Senia was honoured with city council membership and may be connected with the Valerii of Apsorus, where Valerius Oclatinus was aedile and *IIIIvir quinquennalis* in the first century, but more probably he was an immigrant from the East.[8] The family of L. *Magius* Neus, honoured with a public funeral at Apsorus, was connected with the *Lartii* at Apsorus and Nedinum. In the former city Magius'

[1] III, 2921, 9998; cf. Calderini, *Aquileia*, 490.   [2] III, 2924; cf. Holder, 3, 1150.
[3] III, 10121, 13293 (Arba), 14322/4 (Aenona).
[4] III, 2890 (Corinium), 15030/1, 15036/1 (Asseria).
[5] III, 15102 (Apsorus), 9025, 3177 (?) (Salona).
[6] Nine ex. at Aquileia, Calderini 489 f., also Pola, *Inscr. It.*, X, 1, 592a, e, b.
[7] III, 3148, 3149, also L. *Fonteius L. f. Salona*: V, 2711 (Ateste), III, 9401 (Salona).
[8] III, 3138 (Apsorus), 3017 (Senia).

wife was Lartia T. f. Magia and a daughter was Magia T. f. Maxima, possibly by her mother's earlier husband.[1] At Nedinum C. Lartius Sabinianus, *officialis* of Nedinum, was married to Magia Maxima, possibly the step-daughter of the Apsorus magistrate.[2] Otherwise Lartii are found only at Salona.[3]

At Alvona the *Gavillii* probably originated as colonists in Aquileia. In 178 B.C. two leading colonists were Cn. and L. Gavillius Novellus who took the initiative in a raid against the troublesome Istri.[4] The family prospered and are attested in their city with numerous tombstones but they also spread to other cities in the area.[5] Three tombstones record six members of the family at Alvona. Sex. Gavillius Sex. f. Germus, aedile and *IIvir*, is attested along with his daughter T. Gavillius C. f. Claud. Lambicus, aedile and *IIvir*, who was awarded a public funeral, with his wife Taelia Volsetis f. Quarta and son P. Gavillius P. f. Cla. Maximus, also aedile and *IIvir*.[6] In spite of their Aquileia connection the Alvona Gavillii married locally and bear native *cognomina* such as Germus and Lambicus. No other members of the family are known in the province nor are there any other records of the Alvona upper classes.

The *Octavii* of Nedinum were linked to the eminent Flavian–Trajanic senator and jurist C. Octavius Tidius Tossianus L. Iavolenus Priscus.[7] They appear in the city on two tombstones, one recording Sex. Octavius Sex. f. Cla. Constans, *IIvir* and *pontifex*, while the other reveals three generations of the family as magistrates, and indicates marriage with a native woman in the first generation and later intermarriage, apparently with cousins.[8] An Octavius was *IIvir* and priest at Iader, C. Octavius Montanus, and another was decurion at Arba, P. Octavius [.] f. Serg. Cirtus.[9] There are few of them elsewhere: at Salona an Octavia Rufina was married to an Appuleius who was of city-council status. These may be members of the Liburnian families from Iader and Nedinum.[10] At Nedinum the Octavius who was veteran of Legion VIII (Augusta) was probably a recruit from Nedinum in the later first century who returned to his home on retirement.[11]

A leading family of Flavian Scardona was the *Turranii*. The name is common in Northeast Italy and is perhaps Venetic in origin. Their distribution is interesting with isolated examples at Flanona, Corinium (Clambetae) – a native family –

[1] III, 3137.   [2] III, 2868.
[3] III, 2414 (Salona), 2679 (Tragurium).   [4] Liv., xli, 5, 1.
[5] V 1553, 1234, 1235, 1052b, 34, 1126 (Aquileia), 338, 351 (Tergeste). Also in Noricum: III, 4920, 11539 (Virunum).
[6] III, 10067 (3054), 3047, 3055; also 3061.
[7] His Nedinum origin is suggested below, p. 332.
[8] III, 2869, 2870.   [9] III, 2927 (Iader), 13292 (10122) (Arba).
[10] III, 8721.   [11] III, 2885 and above, p. 116.

Nedinum, and Salona.[1] In Scardona T. Turranius T. f. Ser. Seda[tus], decurion
and *IIvir*, was priest at the altar of the imperial cult in Liburnia; this was an
onerous duty but fortunately based in his own city, where he was honoured with
a statue.[2] At Salona T. Turranius T. f. Verus, aedile of Scardona, appears with
his household, and a freedman of theirs was a member of the Salona sevirate.[3]
Another Turranius was aedile at Nedinum, while at Roški-Slap waterfall on the
Titius not far above Scardona a praetorian *evocatus*, C. Turranius C. f. Severus,
may be one of the first members of the family to become established there.[4] He
dedicated a stone to the Liburnian deity Latra, who was very popular in the
Ravni kotari, especially around Corinium in the first century.[5] It is possible that
this family came through Liburnia to reach Scardona and Salona. They are restricted to the coastal cities mentioned and no record of them is found elsewhere
in the province.

A few names appear in single cities, often with no relatives or other dependants. In many cases the names are uncommon and can be tied down to certain
areas of Italy. As might be expected, most of these Italian immigrants come from
Iader. C. *Arrenus* C. f. Tro. Maximus was aedile in the colony and also records his
freedman C. Arren(us) Dionysius. The name is not attested elsewhere in the
province, and the only instance known in the Danube area is from Moesia Inferior, but it is found in a number of places in northern central Italy. His tribe is
not that of the city, and he may be an original immigrant from Italy, rather than
one who moved northwards from Salona.[6] Q. *Asisienus* Q. f. Tro. Agrippa,
aedile, *IIvir* and priest (*pontifex*), who was honoured by the council and people of
Iader, was also an immigrant with the same anomalous tribe. His name derives
from the Umbrian city Asisium (tribe Sergia) but there is no reason to believe
that he came from there. It is the only recorded instance of the name in Dalmatia.[7]
An Italian immigrant at Iader was T. *Elvius* Maximus, *IIIIvir* of Altinum, a
city on the Italian coast a little to the west of Aquileia. His son was T. Elvius
Salinator centurion in the provincial legion some time before 42. This
reflects an interesting link between the upper classes of an Italian city and
Dalmatia. Presumably the father found some scope for his commercial
operations, with his son serving as an officer in the provincial garrison. Two

[1] III, 3045 frg. (Flanona); JÖAI, 8 (1905), Bb. 46: *T. Dasantis f. Verus* (Corinium), III, 2871
(Nedinum); BD, 37 (1914), 93; 32 (1909) 70; III, 8839, 9942 (Salona).
[2] III, 2810.   [3] III, 2805, 8675 (Kučine).
[4] III, 2870 (Nedinum), 2816 (Roški-Slap).   [5] III, 15018 (Asseria).
[6] III, 2910 (Iader); cf. 7518 (Barboşi near Galaţi in Moesia Inferior). In Italy: V, 2073 (Feltria),
6954 (Taurini); IX, 5067 (Interamna), 5276 (Hispellum); XIV, 3951 (Nomentum), NS, 1900,
575 (Rome).
[7] III, 2920.

of their freedmen, Elvius Felix and his son of the same name, occur at Asseria.[1]

At Iader *Melia* Anniana constructed the market hall of the colony opposite the north harbour in memory of her husband Q. *Laepicus* Q. f. Serg. Bassus. His name is Venetic, and probably originated in Istria.[2] His wife's name was Celtic and she may have come from further west in Northern Italy. The name of the man is found at only one other centre; at Salona C. Laepicus Secundus was married to Maria Rectina, whose family held high position at Salona and Narona.[3] The *Caninii* were an Italian family at Asseria. L. Caninius T. f. Cla. Fronto, *IIvir* and priest (*flamen*) of the deified Claudius, was a leading citizen in the earliest years of the city, where a fragmentary tombstone records another member of the same family.[4] Apart from a praetorian at Corinium and a family of Caninii at Doclea, two freedmen appear at Salona.[5] Only one *Cinius* is known in Dalmatia, Cinius Genialis who restored the statue of Janus Augustus at Aenona on behalf of the council and his fellow citizens.[6] Another family with a rare name is the *Pitii* of Curicum, where P. Pitius P. f. Marullus was decurion. The family probably originated from Southern Italy, and another family of them appears settled at Carnuntum; in Italy two examples are found at Baiae.[7] At Sidrona a *IIvir* Q. *Cestius* Q. filius Proculus who held the magistracy twice was probably an immigrant from Northern or Central Italy. To judge from the names of his daughter he probably married a native woman after his arrival in Liburnia.[8] Other cities of Liburnia reveal isolated families which originated in Italy; often they held local city magistracies and were invariably families of property. An example is L. *Sestius* L. f. Ser. Silvester at Vegium, a decurion who died at the age of 23. It is the only record of the name from Liburnia, but later Sestii appear at Salona.[9]

Liburnia reveals a different type of family in the ruling class of its cities. At the top the equestrian and senatorial families are predominantly of native origin, and other families who dominated individual cities (Gavillii at Alvona, Octavii at Nedinum) invariably have native names among their members. A few Italian families do appear, often quite isolated and with few descendants, and most are found at Iader. This is a quite different picture from Dalmatia where the settlers

---

[1] III, 2914 (Iader); *VAHD*, 54 (1952), 210, n. 17 (Bukovica).

[2] III, 2922; cf. 9897, also Untermann 77.

[3] On *Melius*, Holder, 2, 538 f.; *Laepicus*: III, 2431 (Salona). On the *Marii* see above, p. 299.

[4] *JÖAI*, 11 (1908), Bb. 70, n. 12; cf. 66, n. 6.

[5] III, 2884 (Clambetae), 8288a (Doclea); *BD*, 38 (1914), 88, 4671A (Salona).

[6] III, 2969.   [7] III, 3128 (Curicum), 4518, 8964 (Carnuntum); X, 2367, 2850 (Baiae).

[8] III, 2846. It occurs in the East: III, 416 (Ephesus), 12322 (Samothrace), and tiles in Noricum: III, 13552/21 (Ovilava), 12014/198 (Virunum).

[9] III, 10027 (Vegium), 2605, 9341 (Salona).

rapidly established themselves and their wealth is reflected by the large number of freedmen in the first and second centuries, while branches of the families, especially those at Salona, are found among the upper classes of other cities along the coast and at one or two native centres in the hinterland, such as Doclea. It may be that Liburnia, apart from Iader, was more an agricultural area with fewer outside contacts than were Salona and the other cities, where trade was of great importance and contacts with Italy and other areas much greater.

iv *The Rise of the Native Families.* The spread of Roman citizenship among the native population of Dalmatia has been discussed in an earlier section (p. 293) together with the political development of the interior. On the other hand, a brief survey of the political development of the native people, especially the upper classes, and their gradual approach to equality with the Italian settler families, is the best way to examine the composition of the ruling classes during the second and third centuries, when the greater conformism in nomenclature makes the study of origins less precise. Enfranchised *Iulii* appear in large numbers only in Liburnia, especially the northern part of the Ravni kotari. At Aenona the wealthy C. Iulius Ceuni f. Serg. Curticus Aetor was generous to his own city and also received decorations for service in the war of 6–9. He made a dedication to Janus Pater Augustus. At Iader Iulia Tertulla who was related to a native named Turus was priestess of Diva Augusta, the empress Livia, probably under Claudius when she was deified.[1] Ti. Iulii enfranchised by Tiberius are much less common than Caii Iulii; two appear at Asseria, one a decurion the other probably centurion in Legion II Augusta.[2] Other enfranchised Iulii appear as magistrates in Curicum and Apsorus, and at Argyruntum; most of them can be dated to the reigns of Augustus or Tiberius.[3] The largest number of Iulii with native *cognomina* and peregrine filiations was at Corinium, an Augustan city; Iulia C. f. Oia, Iulia Iaefi f. Secunda, Iulia Virno, C. Iulius Ceuni f. Acirrus. At Lopsica we find Iulia C. f. Tertia Toruca, who was related to the Iader Appuleii. Others are known at Nedinum, Aenona, and Asseria.[4] Elsewhere there is very little sign of enfranchised Iulii. The Sex. Iulii at Aequum were Italian immi-

[1] III, 3158 (findspot uncertain); *VAHD*, 52 (1950–1), 55, fig. 1 (Aenona); Abramić, *S. Donato*, 50, n. 30, related to a Turus.

[2] III, 2850, 15024 (Asseria), also *Ti. Iulius Optatus*, who paid for the repairing of the Augustan walls at Iader, III, 2907 and above, p. 207, n. 2.

[3] III, 3130 (Curicum), 2147 (Apsorus-Sansego), 9972 (Argyruntum) under Tiberius.

[4] *Iulia C. f. Oia*: III, 2895, *Iulia Iaefi f. Secunda*: III, 2896, *Iulia Virno*: III, 2897, *C. Iulius Ceuni f. Acirrus* (with Liburnian family): III, 2900, *Iulia C. f. Tertia Toruca*: III, 3015; cf. Patsch, *Lika* 104; also at Nedinum, *C. Iulius Picusi f. Ceunus*: III, 2859 dedicated to Latra; III, 14322/10 (Aenona), 15032 (Asseria).

grants, not native Delmatae. Only at Narona are there some freedmen *seviri* who may belong to enfranchised natives, although none of the latter are actually recorded. Iulii are not found in the upper classes of any of the Dalmatian cities, apart from Iulia Tertulla married to a decurion at Risinium.[1]

Claudii reveal no widespread grants: the emperor's experience of the province in A.D. 42 was hardly likely to help its development. A *princeps* of the Delmatae at Rider bears this name,[2] as do the Claudii at Skelani who were another enfranchised native family, possibly of Celtic origin, who rose to equestrian and senatorial status in the late second and third centuries. Another at nearby Rogatica was member of the Risinium city council.[3] Apart from a few instances in Liburnia and the native peoples around Doclea no widespread grants were made to the people of the hinterland until the end of the second century A.D. The advance of the wealthier members of native families from the interior into the ruling circles of the coastal cities can be studied from the tombstones of a few individuals.

The power of the Doclea *Flavii* has been discussed already (p. 260): Flavius Fronto was dominant not only in his own city but also in Narona, Epidaurum, Risinium, and Scodra, and his influence was great over a large area of Southeast Dalmatia. Another member of the Doclea Flavii appears in the city council of Acruvium. Their entry into the ruling class of the cities in this area appears to have been rapid and complete.[4] Similarly, the Flavii from Stolac entered the Narona council immediately they received the citizenship.[5] The entry of other Flavii from the interior into the Salona council is indicated by T. Flavius T. fil. Tro. Agricola who, apart from membership of the Salona council, was a councillor at Aequum (possibly his home), *IIvir quinquennalis* and auditor (*dispunctor*) at Rider, and commissioner of the city Splonum. At the end of his tombstone appears a tribunate in Legion X Gemina p. f., which appears to have been added subsequently. A later person was T. Fl(avius) Herennius Iaso, equestrian, city councillor, priest (*pontifex*), aedile, and prefect of the artisans' guild, all at Salona. His son, who bore the same names, was a *v(ir) e(gregius)* and patron of the colony. They may well belong to a native family from the interior, although they reveal no connections with the cities in that area.[6]

The *Ulpius* Gellianus who dedicated an altar to Serapis and Isis at Municipium S. was commissioner of a number of cities in the interior (Splonum, Maluesa,

---

[1] III, 1775, 1833, 1769 (Narona), 1738; cf. 8403 (Risinium).
[2] III, 2776; cf. p. 1035 (Rider), 1769; cf. p. 1494 (Narona). [3] III, 12748 (2766b, 8369).
[4] III, 12692; cf. 13819 and above, p. 260. [5] *GZMS*, 3 (1948), 168.
[6] T. *Flavius T.f. Tro. Agricola*: III, 2026; cf. p. 1030, T. *Fl. Herennius Iaso*: *VAHD*, 53 (1952), 227, n. 36.

Metulum) and the city at Arba. The dedication suggests that he may have been an eastern immigrant rather than a native of the province.[1] At Salona M. Ulpius M. f. Sabinus was an equestrian and magistrate (*IIvir*) of the colony, probably in the second century, and a freedman of Trajan appears in the Narona sevirate.[2] It is clear that by the middle of the second century enfranchised families were well established in the upper classes of the coastal cities. The first signs appear at Narona and other cities in the southeast; Salona, with its much larger population and greater number of Italian settlers, may have resisted the newer families for a longer period, and, when they were admitted, it was only the wealthiest men from the interior, with interests in a number of cities, who could afford to undertake the expensive business of city office. Those who do appear at Salona are not men who became powerful within particular tribal areas but those whose interests were often widely scattered in different parts of the interior. An example is P. Aelius Rastorianus in the late second century, who still retained a native *cognomen* after Hadrianic citizenship. An equestrian, he was decurion and *IIvir* in Salona, *quinquennalis* in Bistue Vetus and Bistue Nova, auditor (*dispunctor*) of Narona, quaestor of the cities Azina, Splonum, and Arupium.[3] It is an impressive collection of offices in all parts of the province, mostly in the central interior, but also in the Lika polje, as well as Salona on the coast. This is an example of the changing character of city aristocracies, a process which seems to have been complete by the end of the second century; significantly there are few records of *Aurelii* of this status, although Aurelii, almost certainly enfranchised Delmatae, appear as magistrates in Salona and Aequum.[4] The appearance of these people from one of the most backward areas of the province at this level marks the final closing of the gap between 'Roman' and 'native', at least in the upper reaches of society. The names of many of the Italian families survived; intermarriage with newer families, natives from the interior and immigrants from

---

[1] *GZMBH*, 52 (1940), 20, n. 4, fig. 4=Sp. 98 (1941–8), 287 and above, p. 282, n. 2.

[2] *BD*, 37 (1914), 75, n. 4574A (Salona); III, 1792 (Narona).

[3] III, 8783; cf. p. 2136, 2326 (Sučurac): *D.m. P. Ael. Rastoriano eq. p. decur. IIviro et qq. munic. [Bis]tuatium dis[p. ci]vitat. Naron[. . .] q. municipp. Azina[tium] Splonistarum Ar[upin?] et Ael[i]ae Procili[anae?] defunct. ann[. . .] Albia Crisp[ina coniugi] incompara[bili et fi]liae infelicissim[ae] et sibi.* Here Kubitschek's reading *municipp. Azina[tium* is preferred to Hirschfeld's *municip. Pazina[tium* in CIL. A *civitas Pasini* is named by Pliny, *HN*, iii, 140, in the interior of Liburnia and may be located at Padjine in Mokropolje, Alföldy, *Bevölkerung*, 88. Better is *Azina* which is an *origo* on a praetorian list at Rome, VI, 2388, frg. 9: *vic. Azin.*, while a tombstone at Salona, III, 8762, gives *Azinas* as either a *cognomen* or an ethnic. Thus there was probably a place Azina, earlier a *vicus* which had become a *municipium* by the late second century. Not, however, the *Assino* of Rav., iv, 19, suggested by Mayer, *Sprache*, 65.

[4] III, 2078 (2 ex., one a *T. Aurelius*) (Salona); III, 9750 (Aequum).

elsewhere, enable them to hold on to their property and their social position in the more cosmopolitan ruling circles of the later period.

Above the city families stood the imperial hierarchy, senators and equestrians. Of the second category, men who record themselves as merely 'of equestrian status' (*equo publico* or *eques Romanus*) have been included along with the local aristocracy. The senators and equestrians active in the imperial service, and therefore rising in status, can be isolated as the top segment of the pyramid of provincial society. What is important for this study is not so much the incidental character and chronology of their careers, but their roots in the society of Dalmatia. Are they descendants of Italian settler families alone, or of the more mixed population of the late second and third centuries? The senators and equestrians from Dalmatia will be examined not in the context of the senatorial government as a whole, but as it were from the underneath, by considering their provincial origins and the type of development in the province which produced them. At the same time the interests of outside senatorial families will be considered; these may have arisen in a number of ways, by campaigns, governorships, political associations (*clientelae*), or the ownership of property.

II *Senatorial and Equestrian Families in Dalmatia*

It is to be expected that the people who entered the senatorial and equestrian orders in the first and early second centuries would originate from the coastal cities of Dalmatia, or the urbanized area of Liburnia. There is no evidence for any Dalmatian native rising through military ability alone to the highest level in this period, as did Trajan's formidable Moorish general Lusius Quietus.[1] From the cities dominated by Italian immigrants one expects to find men beginning as legionary centurions or equestrian commanders on the road to higher officers, including the well-paid procuratorships, with the hope of securing even higher social status for the next generation. The promotion of such men and the advancement of their families could depend on a number of factors, but the most important was personal patronage, usually by a senator at Rome who could press the claims of his friends on the emperor himself. Ability obviously counted, but it only became paramount after the Marcomannic wars, when it was vital that generals should be able to win battles if called upon. Earlier it had been family connection and the prestige of a patron that usually counted in the end. Pliny writes to army commanders to seek posts for his young friends, but rarely does he give any assessment of the man's ability for the post.[2]

[1] Who came from that part of Libya not under Roman control, Themistius, *Or.,* xvi, p. 250 Dind.
[2] As with Voconius Romanus, Epp., ii, 13, x, 4, for whom he sought the *latus clavus* from Trajan. He may have been unsuccessful, Syme, *Tacitus,* 83, n. 5.

The first Roman senator to have taken more than a passing interest in the area was C. Iulius Caesar, as proconsul from 58 to 50 B.C., but he never found an opportunity to visit the coast for any length of time. He may have been responsible for some individual grants of citizenship, and his legate Q. Numerius Rufus is found conferring amenities on Issa in 56 B.C., doubtless on the instructions of the proconsul.[1] Caesar's interests in the area resulted in the strengthening of the Italian settlements; although no individuals are known to have been promoted by him, as happened in Spain with Cornelius Balbus from Gades who became his private secretary.[2] With the Principate and more settled conditions it would be the greater senatorial families who provided the links between the province and the central government, mostly through governorships or property in the province. A group of senatorial families are attested in this role: none of their members was born in the province but their role in advancing the careers of families of the coastal cities may have been crucial.

P. Servilius Isauricus was consul twice, in 48 and in 41 B.C., and a supporter of Caesar.[3] He may have been proconsul of Illyricum as Octavianus' man in the years after the Treaty of Brundisium, just as Antonius' man C. Asinius Pollio went to fight the Parthini in Northwest Macedonia. A statue was set up to him at his base Narona,[4] but it does not belong to the period of his proconsulship, and may be a recollection by the colony of an association with an old Republican family, set up in the first or second century. Freedmen Servilii appear at Narona.[5] Otherwise there is less evidence for connections between senatorial families and the Dalmatian cities, than with those of Liburnia. In the last year of Tiberius, Pontius Fregellanus was expelled from the Senate. At Salona C. Pontilius Fregellanus was honoured with a statue as consul and patron of the colony. The origin of the *cognomen* is the Latin city Fregellae, destroyed after rebellion in 125 B.C. Some of the families who scattered throughout Italy retained the name of their old home as a traditional *cognomen*. Nothing else is known of the man at Salona. If he is identical with the man named by Tacitus then he regained his seat in the Senate and also proceeded to hold the consulship although there is no record of him in the Fasti. No records of the Pontilii are known in the province, but freedmen Pontii appear at Salona.[6] Finally a Hadrianic senator of some eminence appears to have a connection with Salona. P. Coelius P. f. Serg.

[1] III, 3078 and above, p. 39.

[2] Cic., *Pro Balbo*; cf. Syme, *RR*, 72.   [3] *MRR*, 2, 371.

[4] Patsch, *Narona*, 23, fig. 12 (III, 1858; cf. p. 1494): *P. Servilio Isaurico cos.*[. . . Ligatures on the stone suggest a much later date for the stone.

[5] III, 1768.

[6] III, 8715 (Salona), Tac., *ann.*, vi, 48; cf. Syme, *JRS*, 39 (1949), 13 f. On the *Fregellani*, Degrassi, *SVA*, 1, 527 ff.

Balbinus Vibullius Pius was consul ordinarius in 137; he was the son of a consul under Trajan. His appointment to patrician status and a priesthood of Trajan suggests a close relationship to the ruling house. His career up to the consulship is recorded on a text at Rome dedicated by the citizens of an unknown community; it is devoid of major military commands and heroic deeds on the frontiers and suggests that he spent most of his time in the emperor's circle. Newer families without prestige of ancestors or noble connections, such as the Iulii of Aequum, command armies and win victories in order to establish themselves in the oligarchy. Coelius' father was suffect consul in 111 and he may have been close to Trajan and Hadrian through a common origin in Southern Spain.[1] A number of tombstones at Salona record his freedmen and slaves.[2] Altogether eighteen persons with the name Coelius are attested, and of those with *praenomina* only one is not a Publius Coelius. A governorship is possible, for members from households of earlier governors are attested, L. Volusius Saturninus, and L. Arruntius Scribonianus, and the governors of Dalmatia are unknown at the period when Coelius is likely to have been there.[3] On the other hand, even for a possibly lengthy tenure under Antoninus Pius, the number of Coelii is too great; he must have owned property in the city to have maintained such a large household there.[4] Only one other external contact with a Dalmatian city is attested for this time, not in a coastal city but in the new city at Doclea. A statue base records a man with a number of different names: Cn. Sertorius Brocchus Aquilius Agricola Pedanius Fuscus Salinator Iulius Servianus.[5] Some second-century senators are known with multiple names, indicating previous marriages of the family and inheritance of property.[6] All the names of the man at Doclea belong to people who lived in the late first or early second century. He was probably known as Cn. Sertorius Brocchus and was doubtless the descendant of a Claudian senator with those names.[7] Aquilius Agricola is not an attested senatorial combination, but the others all refer to one ill-fated family who were at one time very close to Hadrian. Cn. Pedanius Fuscus was consul in

---

[1] VI, 1383; cf. *PIR²*, C 1241 and below, p. 446. His father was P. Coelius Apollinaris, *PIR²*, C 1239.

[2] III, 2295; cf. 2294, 2561, 13295 (Salona), 2687 (Tragurium).

[3] Also Alföldy, *BJ* (forthcoming). On the staff and households of other governors see above, p. 83 ff.

[4] There seems to be no real basis for the statement in the *Vita Pii*, v, 3, that he kept governors in office for long periods; cf. A. R. Birley, *Coroll. Mem. E. Swoboda*, 48 f.

[5] III, 13826; cf. Sticotti, *Doclea*, 173, n. 35, Alföldy, *BJ* (forthcoming).

[6] An extreme case is Q. Sosius Priscus, *cos. ord.* 169, with thirty-one other names, *ILS*, 1104.

[7] *PIR*, S 394; cf. Groag, *RE*, 10 (1919), 890; 2A (1923), 1753, also R. Syme, *Historia* 17 (1968) 89 f.

118 and was at one time considered by Hadrian as a successor. He married Julia, Hadrian's niece and the daughter of Domitia Paulina and Iulius Ursus Servianus, consul for the third time in 134.[1] Two years later the family perished under the suspicion of conspiracy, Iulius himself at the age of ninety, and his grandson Fuscus, son of the consul of 118 and born in that year.[2] In what way the man at Doclea was connected with this family is not certain. No official post or personal status is recorded, but he may be a second-century senator who inherited some of the family's property, and who governed Dalmatia sometime in that century.

None of the links between senators and the Dalmatian cities can be demonstrated to have aided the advancement of Dalmatian families. The greatest family which came from the province during the Principate was the Iulii of Aequum. The first member known is the original Italian settler from Italy, Sex. Iulius [Sex.] f. Ani(ensis) Silvanus. He was chief commissioner of the settlement of Roman citizens (*conventus*) at Aequum, and on the establishment of the colony under Claudius was chosen by the veterans as one of the first magistrates; there is no evidence, however, that Iulius Silvanus was himself a veteran.[3] The next member of the family is Sex. Iulius [Sex. ?] f. Severus, probably the grandson of the magistrate.[4] Nothing is known of his real father but he probably owed more to his adoptive father Cn. Minicius Faustinus, the consul of 116. Afterwards Severus' full names were Cn. Minicius Faustinus Sex. Iulius Severus and appear on his career inscription at Burnum. There is no apparent reason why it should have been set up there rather than his home at Aequum, where all other records of the family are found. He appears there on two other inscriptions, in both cases with the *praenomen* of his adoptive father.[5] A detailed study of his long career in the service of the emperor would be out of place, but some general observations tell us something about the kind of man he was. He was a military man: according to Cassius Dio he was Hadrian's best general.[6] At an early age he may

---

[1] On Pedanius, *PIR*, P 144, Iulius Ursus Salinator, *PIR*², I, 631.

[2] Dio, lxix, 17, 1–2; *Vit. Had.*, 23, 3, 7–8; 15, 8; 25, 8. Groag restored a fragmentary *cursus* from Salona, *BD*, 37 (1914), 42; cf. *PIR*², C 692, to record L. Cestius Gallus Cerrinius Iustus Lutatius Natalis, whose career up to the consulship, probably under Marcus and Verus, is preserved on a *cursus* at Volturnum, X, 3722. The order of the offices on the Salona fragments fits well with his career, but there is no record of any status or connection in the province. *Cestii* are recorded among *honestiores* in Liburnia, III, 2846 (Sidrona); cf. Alföldy, *BJ*, (forthcoming).

[3] III, 2733 and p. 242, n. 6.   [4] *PIR*², I, 576, and now Alföldy, *BJ*, (forthcoming).

[5] *PIR*, M 431; cf. J. Morris, *LF*, 86 (1963), 41. III, 2830; cf. p. 1059 (Burnum): [*Cn?*] *Minicius Faustinus* [*Sex?*] *I*[*uli*]*us* [*. . .f*]*il. Serg. Severus*, Abramić, *BIAB*, 16 (1950), 237, fig. 3 (Aequum): *Cn. Minicius Faustinus Iulius Severus*, ibid., 239, fig. 4 (Aequum): *Cn. Iul. S*[*everus . . .*]. Generally he is *Sex. Iulius Severus*, for instance in the consulship, XVI, 68.   [6] Dio lxix, 13, 2.

have been selected for promotion by Trajan, possibly after service as a young legionary tribune in the Pannonian Legion XIV Gemina Martia victrix. His next two posts, quaestor, or assistant to the proconsul, in Macedonia, and the archaic office of tribune of the plebs he acquired as a nominee (*candidatus*) of the emperor. His career continued to prosper under Hadrian, and after the praetorship he held two appointments which confirm Dio's judgement on his ability, legate of his old Legion XIV at Carnuntum and then governor of the new province Dacia, a crucial military command which he held from about 120 to 126. This was an unusually long tenure: he succeeded the great Dalmatian Q. Marcius Turbo and may have been retained for political as well as military reasons. After a consulship he moved to major commands in Moesia Inferior (129–31), Britain (130/1–133), and then to a special command in the Jewish rebellion where he achieved his greatest triumph. For his services he was awarded the insignia of a triumph 'for successful campaigns in Judaea'.[1] Later he was the regular consular governor of Syria. Retirement, possibly to his home in Dalmatia, may have enabled him to help younger men from the province to aim at a similar career, although the only such man attested for the next generation is his son (or possibly nephew) Cn. Iulius Cn. f. Verus. Nothing more than his *tria nomina* is attested and his precise relationship to Severus remains uncertain. His home was Aequum, where his *cursus* was set up by the citizens (*Aequenses municipes*).[2] With the support of Severus the career of Verus shows signs of favour: instead of a quaestorship in a province Verus remained in Rome as *quaestor Augusti*, a favoured appointment involving reading imperial dispatches and documents to meetings of the Senate. His military tribunate was spent in the eastern Legion X Fretensis, probably when it was part of the army commanded by Iulius Severus in Palestine. After praetorship he commanded Legion XXX Ulpia victrix in Lower Germany and was then appointed controller of the ancient state treasury in Rome (*aerarium Saturni*). His consulship probably came in 151 and he then governed Lower Germany and Britain; in the latter command he probably achieved the victory attested on coins in 155 and may have been responsible for some re-organization of the northern frontier. Unlike Severus, however, who could spend the rest of his life in retirement during the placid reign of Antonius Pius, the experience of Verus was needed in the increasing difficulties of the next reign. In 163–6 he went to the East as governor of Syria to

---

[1] III, 2830: *huic [senatus a]uctore [imp. Tra]iano Hadrian[o Au]g. ornamenta triu[mp]halia decrevit ob res in [Iu]daea prospere ge[st]as [d.] d.*; cf. *BIAB*, 16 (1950), 239, fig. 4.

[2] III, 8714 and 2732 (*ILS*, 1057 and 8794) (Aequum): *Cn. Iulius Cn. fil. Verus.* There is a gap of two or three lines between the surviving fragments of the *cursus* recording the highest posts, the *comes* of L. Verus in the East and the raising of Legions II and III Italica, *PIR²*, I, 618.

act as adviser on the staff of the younger emperor L. Verus against the Parthians, and when the crisis on the Middle Danube was threatening he supervised the raising of two new legions, II and III Italica, from Northern Italy in 166–7.[1] He lived on to the end of Marcus Aurelius' reign but died in 179, before he could assume the second consulship which had been earmarked for him in 180.[2] If he was about 20 years of age when tribune in Legion X Fretensis in 134 then he will have lived to about 66. These two men are the only leading figures from the cities of Dalmatia, men who rose through military ability from the aristocracy of an obscure colony to be the leading generals of the Empire in successive generations. Together their careers spanned a long period. Severus could remember Trajan's great conquests and the confident advance into Dacia and Parthia, while Verus lived to see a different world, the emperor Marcus Aurelius desperately defending the northern frontier of the Empire against the Marcomanni and their allies. During the Principate no other men from the province compare in prestige with the Iulii from Aequum. A fragmentary career inscription from the Salona amphitheatre records the earlier part of a senatorial career which shows every sign of imperial favour, nominations for the tribunate of the plebs and the praetorship and then a legionary command. He is probably a native of the province, but could be a second-century governor.[3]

A younger contemporary of Cn. Iulius Verus came from Risinium. At Lambaesis in Numidia M. Lucceius Torquatus Bassianus (or Cassianus) set up dedications as legate of the Legion III Augusta in the years 167 and 169. In one he speaks in a verse of the Illyrian war god Medaurus and the walls of his home city Risinium.[4] Apart from an isolated instance in the Lika polje the name Lucceius

---

[1] III, 199=*ILS*, 5864 (Antilebanon). On the raising of the new legions see H-G. Pflaum, *Carrières*, 164 bis, on Ti. Claudius Proculus Cornelianus who was sent *ad dilectum cum Iulio Vero per Italiam tironum II leg. Italicae*. The recruitment took place in Italy, J. C. Mann, *Hermes* 91 (1963), 485 f.

[2] P. *Durae Europos* 23 (Final Report, 1959, 128, n. 25, l. 14).

[3] *BD*, 37 (1914), 33, n. 4303A=*AE*, 1922, 36 and below, p. 450. He could be a governor but recently Alföldy, *BJ* (forthcoming), has suggested that he may be a son of Sex. Iulius Severus, and possibly a brother of Cn. Iulius Verus. He served the military tribunate in Legion I Italica, stationed at Novae in Moesia Inferior, which Iulius Severus governed about 128–30, and may have been chosen by the latter for his first military post. If this is correct his command of Legion XXX Ulpia victrix falls about 141–3 as successor of L. Aemilius Karus, Alföldy, *Legaten*, 30, n. 38.

[4] L. Leschi, *Libyca*, 2 (1954), 171–81 in A.D. 169; VIII, 4208=18496, 2348=17866, 2581=*ILS*, 4881 in 167, the last with a poem:

Moenia qui Risinni Aeacia, qui colis arcem
Delmatiae, nostri publice lar populi
Sancte Medauro domi e[t] sancte hic . . .

On Medaurus see above, p. 255.

is not found anywhere in the province, but presumably he comes from an Italian family settled at the city in the first century.[1] He may be the same man as ?M. Lucceius Torquatus who a few years before was legate of the proconsul of Asia and city commissioner at Ephesus. After the Lambaesis command he advanced to a consulship, forecast in the Lambaesis dedications and held probably late in 169 or in 170. Late under Commodus he was Prefect of the City; he is attested in office in 190, but soon afterwards he was put to death, and the official condemnation of his memory which ensued (*damnatio memoriae*) caused his names to be erased on his earlier dedications.[2]

Fortune has preserved the origins of the Iulii at Aequum and Lucceius Torquatus at Risinium. At the same period that their families were becoming established other Italian families were holding equestrian appointments in the emperor's service, usually after a period of service on the city council and the holding of a magistracy. The men who appear in these imperial appointments can be divided into different groups; some were the sons of professional career officers, mostly centurions, but a few were centurions promoted to equestrian rank late in their active life. If they were still active they could yet have time to reach the more lucrative higher posts in the order, such as the procuratorships. Both these categories of equestrian officers add up to only a minority of those attested. Most of those recorded are the municipal worthies who spent short tours of duty with the army as unit commanders. Most of them would be in their early thirties and usually had little previous experience. This does not mean that they were totally incompetent, since their duties do not appear, in normal times at least, to have been predominantly military, but involved administration for which their city-council background made them well suited. Fighting and discipline was handled by the centurions, who normally remained in the same units for much longer periods. The equestrian commanders played an important role in the command structure of the Roman army throughout most of the Principate, and only disappeared along with senatorial commanders in the crisis of the third century. Men holding these appointments, commander of an auxiliary unit or tribune in a legion – which were usually held in a combination of three posts (*militiae equestres*) following on in order of seniority – were technically civilians, and unlike the professional centurions were not assured of a permanent career. Promotion to higher offices depended on reports from their superior and on any patronage which they could invoke on their

[1] *Lucceius*: III, 15085 (Arupium). His father may be *M. Lucceius Felix*, procurator in Dacia Apulensis at an unknown date, III, 1437; cf. p. 1407 (Sarmizegethusa).
[2] CIG 2977 (Ephesus); cf. *RE*, 13 (1926), 1561 f., where the *praenomen* Π is wrongly read instead of M. As *praefectus urbi*: *AE*, 1941, 56, death: *vit. Com.*, vii, 6, about 190.

behalf.[1] Most of the men attested in this category lived in the first or early second centuries and, with one or two possible exceptions, all came from the coastal cities, seven from Salona, two from Iader, and one each from Epidaurum, Risinium, and Acruvium.

At Salona P. Bennius Sabinus was *IIIIvir*, *IIIIvir quinquennalis*, augur, and priest of Augustus in the city. At some stage in his career he commanded Cohort II Lusitanorum equitata. A unit with these titles is attested in Egypt, but another of the same name may have been stationed in a western province.[2] Other Bennii are known: Bennia Sabina was married to a centurion in Legion XI Claudia who later commanded the sixth cohort of the Rome fire brigade (*vigiles*), while other Bennii appear among the city council at Aequum. Their ancestor may have been a soldier in a citizen auxiliary unit, Cohort VIII Voluntariorum, who was *beneficiarius consularis* at Doclea. The name is probably Italian and commonest in the south.[3] A Calpurnius was commander of an auxiliary cohort after promotion from legionary centurion. His unit was the Cohort I Lucensium, stationed in the province under Augustus and Tiberius, while his tribe Tromentina shows that he was almost certainly a native of Salona.[4] Q. Cassius Constans, also a native of Salona, commanded Cohort IIII Voluntariorum in Pannonia after he had held municipal magistracies. His tombstone was set up by his freedman only, but the family remained in the Salona ruling class well into the second century.[5] Another Salona citizen was legionary tribune and earned decorations from Tiberius, presumably for service in the war of 6–9. His family, the Cornelii, were well established in the city and many of their freedmen are represented.[6] Q. Ennius [. . . . .] commanded the local auxiliary Cohort III Alpinorum at Andetrium some time in the first or early second century, and is another instance of a local man holding a post in the provincial army.[7] Q. Servilius M. f. Pal-(atina) Pacuvianus was not a native of the city but did hold a magistracy there. He commanded the Cohort I Morinorum in Britain. The Servilia M. f. Copiesilla at Salona was probably the daughter of the equestrian's son Servilius Copiensis,

[1] Birley, *RBRA*, 133 ff., disposing of earlier notions that such officers were 'almost amateur soldiers'.
[2] III, 8733. On the cohort, *RE*, 4 (1901), 312 f.
[3] III, 2062 and 8747; cf. Kubitschek, *JÖAI*, 6 (1903), Bb. 83 (Salona); cf. III, 9783 (Aequum) and above, p. 129, III, 12697 (Doclea).
[4] III, 8736 (Salona). On the cohort see below, p. 473. *Calpurnii* were members of the city council at Aequum, III, 9763.
[5] III, 8737 and above, p. 300.
[6] III, 2018. He held the early military *praefectura fabrum* twice, *Cornelii*: III, 8768, 8686 (Salona), 9971 (Aequum), 1792 (Narona): *IIIIIIvir magister Mercurialis*, 2936 (Iader); *AE*, 1940, 6 (Aenona).
[7] III, 8739, also an *Ennius* at Corinium, III, 2881.

Z

while another member of the same family may be Q. Servilius Statianus, centurion of Cohort I Belgarum at Bigeste.[1]

At Iader L. Geminius Montanus commanded the Cohort I Sebastenorum which was stationed in Judaea, but he does not record any city magistracy or other member of his family. A freedman with these names is known at Salona, and the tribe Tromentina suggests that the equestrian may have come from there rather than Iader. The name of another equestrian officer at Iader is not preserved nor any details of the appointments he had held.[2] At Pharia L. Rustius Picens is described as *trib(unus) mil(itum)* and *praefectus equitum*. The name is unknown elsewhere in the province and he was probably an Italian, possibly the man who was the first commander of a cavalry unit later known as the Ala (Gallorum) Picentiana.[3] At Epidaurum M. Annius M. f. Triarius was probably *tr(ibunus) mil(itum)* but there are no further details of his appointment. He may have been commanding troops at Epidaurum in the early first century, where a military post was still maintained under Tiberius.[4] At Risinium and Acruvium two equestrians, both city magistrates and from well-known families, did not hold military appointments but spent a period at Rome serving on the jury panels drawn from their order.[5]

After equestrian posts attached to the army could come lucrative positions as imperial procurators handling revenues and superintending offices; these could lead eventually to the three great prefectures of the praetorian guard, the Rome corn supply, and Egypt, the latter controlling an army and province of a size normally reserved for consular senators.[6] There is only one person known to have achieved such posts from the Salona upper classes in the first century. L. Antonius L. f. Tro. Firmus, aedile, and *IIIIvir*, held two official appointments, *praefectus fabrum* and then imperial procurator. No details are given of his procuratorship: it is certainly not the province of Dalmatia, since he was a native of Salona.[7]

---

[1] III, 2049. The cohort was sometime in Britain, XVI, 48 (in 103), also in *Not. Dign. Occ.*, xl, 52. Other *Servilii*: III, 13903, 8756 (centurion of Cohort I Belgarum). For other fragmentary records of equestrian officers, most with municipal offices and equestrian tribunates: III, 14707, 12906, 8780, 8771, 8770.

[2] III, 2916, The unit was in Palestine under Pius, XVI, 87 (in 139). Other *Geminii*: III, 14711 and *BD*, 26 (1903), 10, n. 3206; *VIvir* [*Aug.*]. The family of his friend Aufidius Postimus were city councillors at Salona, III, 2076, 2078.

[3] III, 10094; cf. E. Stein, *Beamte u. Truppenkörper*, 147, although a Gallic origin is possible; cf. p. 471.

[4] III, 8406. Hirschfeld (*CIL*) prefers to read *tr. mil.* rather than *pr(aefectus) mil(itum)*. He may have commanded the Cohort VI Voluntariorum stationed at Epidaurum under Tiberius, below p. 473.

[5] III, 1711 (Acruvium), 1717 (Risinium). On the families see above, p. 300 ff.

[6] E. Birley, *RBRA*, 133 ff.   [7] III, 2075.

Lastly in this group of first-century equestrians from the coastal cities of Dalmatia, apart from Liburnia, is the remarkable career of Q. Marcius Turbo from Epidaurum. Most of the known equestrian officers from the province obtained posts in the *militiae equestres* directly from membership of their city councils and magistracies. As has been noted, this did not offer permanent appointment, and there is no evidence that these local dignitaries wished for anything more than a brief tour of duty with the colours. To be certain of a permanent post it was better to obtain a legionary centurionate (a direct commission was possible for the right person) and then to reach the higher equestrian posts through promotion from senior centurion in a legion (*primuspilus*), a position normally held for one year only. In social terms a legionary centurion was below an equestrian officer, however inexperienced, but when it was necessary to seek efficient officers for the highest posts, the experience of a legionary centurion was often decisive. Naturally a legionary centurion relied much more on his own ability than might an equestrian officer enjoying the patronage of powerful families. Q. Marcius Q. f. (Fronto) Turbo (Publicius Severus) came from Epidaurum. He probably belonged to the Marcii who are attested in the city council there, while his *cognomen* Turbo, which may be of native origin, occurs in another upper-class family.[1] He began as legionary centurion, and is attested in Legion II Adiutrix at Aquincum in the period 103–7. After rising to *primuspilus* he was appointed to command of the Misenum fleet, in which position he is attested in 114. This was one of the few occasions during the Principate when the Italian fleets participated in a military enterprise: in this case they conveyed Trajan to Antioch to begin his Parthian campaign. While on this commission a career inscription was set up to Turbo at Cyrrhus not far from Antioch.[2] He had already held other posts, including three tribunates at Rome, in the city fire brigade (*vigiles*), mounted imperial guard (*equites singulares*), and the imperial guard (*praetoriani*). By now Turbo had attracted the attention of Trajan or one of his advisers, and the further posts he held involved active service, suggesting that he was still in his forties. In 117 a major revolt of the Jews in Cyrene and Egypt was crushed by Turbo holding a special command.[3] With the accession of Hadrian his career moved rapidly upward. It is conceivable that the friendship between the two men had been formed in the last decade of the first century, when Hadrian was a young senatorial tribune in Legion II Adiutrix and Turbo an able young cen-

[1] *Marcius*: III, 1755 and above, p. 299; *Turbo*: III, 1748.
[2] As centurion: III, 14349/2 (Aquincum), prefect of Misenum Fleet: *Syria*, 30 (1953), 247–78 = *AE*, 1955, 225, also fleet diploma XVI, 60 (Sardinia). On his career see Pflaum, *Carrières*, n. 157, R. Syme, *JRS*, 52 (1962), 95 for his descendants.
[3] Eusebius, *HE*, iv, 2.

turion of good family. The early months of Hadrians' reign were difficult. Opposition to his policy from some of Trajan's generals may have turned into conspiracy, and four consular senators were put to death, the worst incident in relations between Princeps and the Senate since the last years of Domitian. Then Turbo was *procurator* (governor) of Mauretania and was called by Hadrian to govern two Danubian provinces, Pannonia Inferior and Dacia: for this he was given the same status as the prefect of Egypt.[1] There were probably good military reasons for this appointment, in addition to the shortage or reliable senatorial generals. Within two years Turbo was summoned to Rome as praetorian prefect, an appointment he held for fifteen years. His diligence and efficiency were famous, although like so many other friends of the emperor his relations with Hadrian appear to have become strained in later years. Nevertheless after his death he was commemorated with a statue in Rome, an almost unique distinction for an equestrian at this time.[2]

There is no evidence that Turbo had any children of his own. He appears to have adopted the two sons of T. Flavius Longinus, member of the councils of a number of Dacian cities, possibly during the time he was governing Dacia. Adoption by such a person made senatorial status assured if sought after. The elder son was probably T. Flavius Longinus Q. Marcius Turbo, suffect consul in 145 and governor of Moesia Inferior ten years later, while the younger was probably the equestrian T. Flavius Priscus Gallonius Fronto Marcius Turbo, a *procurator* of Mauretania under Antoninus Pius. Neither appears to have any connection with Dalmatia.[3]

The Artorii owned property in the Poljica area of the Salona territory in the late second or third century. They were a family of Italian origin, possibly from the south, but there is no definite evidence when they became established at Salona.[4] None are known in the first century and their position may derive from the distinguished army officer and administrator L. Artorius Castus, attested on two inscriptions from Pituntium,[5] perhaps of the late second century. Like Turbo he began as a legionary centurion with posts in Legions III Gallica, VI

---

[1] *Vit. Had.*, vi, 7. He received the status (*titulus*) of Prefect of Egypt *quo plus auctoritatis haberet*. The special command did not include Pannonia Superior, where L. Minicius Natalis was retained in office, II, 4509=*ILS*, 1029 (Barcino).

[2] Praetorian Prefect: III, 1462, 1551 (Sarmizegethusa); Dio, lxix, 18; Fronto, i, 256H; *vit. Had.*, xv, 7.

[3] *PIR*[2], F 305, 344; cf. Syme, *JRS*, (1962), 95.

[4] III, 9226, 2520 (Salona), 8476 (Krug di Jesenice), 8425 (Narona). In CIL the distribution (V:4, IX:7, X:12, XI:14, XIV:7) suggests an origin in Central or Southern Italy.

[5] III, 1919; cf. 8513, 14224 (12791) (Pituntium); cf. Pflaum, *Carrières*, n. 196, whose dating is accepted here.

Ferrata (both in the East), II Adiutrix at Aquincum, and V Macedonica, which was probably then stationed at Potaissa in Dacia. After a period as temporary commander (*praepositus*) of the Misenum Fleet he was appointed camp prefect of Legion VI victrix at Eboracum in Britannia, in effect deputy commander. From this post he was sent as field commander (*dux*) of a task force drawn from two of the three British legions to deal with trouble in Armorica (Britanny), whose independent population had often caused trouble to the imperial authorities.[1] There is no evidence to date the career of Artorius Castus precisely, but for an equestrian to be entrusted with such a mission was, although not unparalleled, very unusual, and he may have been an appointment of the praetorian prefect Perennis early under Commodus. He is known to have used equestrians in preference to senators as legionary commanders, a practice which probably contributed to his downfall in 185.[2] Artorius Castus' last post was in Dalmatia, as special governor (*procurator iure gladii*) of Liburnia. No other person is attested as holding such a post, which must have represented an infringement of the power of the consular senator governing Dalmatia. It may have been another appointment made by Perennis. Even allowing for the confusion which must have followed the Marcomannic Wars one would hardly have expected trouble in Liburnia, the most urbanized area of the province. At this time he may have acquired property at Salona and have retired to live there when his appointment in Liburnia ended. He has no connection with the city recorded on his inscriptions, nor are any relatives mentioned. A contemporary of Artorius Castus was P. Atilius Aebutianus, praetorian prefect early under Commodus and executed at the instigation of Cleander who was appointed in his place. Atilius appears as patron of Asseria and exhibits the titles of a senator *c*(*larissimus*) *v*(*ir*). No other connections with the area are known, nor is there any evidence for his earlier career.[3] Identification of a person's origin on the basis of name alone is often hazardous, but there is good reason to believe that Q. (Claudius Ferox) Aeronius Montanus, procurator of Mauretania attested in 158 and 162, was born at Salona in a family of Italian origin.[4] The name Aeronius is not common, and the only concentration is at Salona, mostly freedmen. Nine examples are recorded there,

---

[1] *dux legg* [. . .]*m Britanici* <*i*> *arum adversus Arm*[*oricanos*]; cf. *Vit. Com.*, xiii, 6, for disturbances in Britain, Germany, and Dacia.

[2] *Vit. Com.*, vi, 2. Ritterling, *legio* 1610, dates Castus to the third century.

[3] *JÖAI*, 11 (1908), Bb. 68, n. 11, fig. 46 = *ILS*, 9001 (Asseria), *vit. Com.*, vi, 12, for his death. *Aebutii* were in the council at Aequum, III, 2730, and are attested at Salona, III, 2015, 8853, 2140, 14251/1; *BD*, 33 (1910), 43, 4319A; III, 8819 frg.

[4] *PIR*[2], A 974 gives the older reading of the name as *Apronius*, but see Chatelain, *ILM*, 62 (add. VIII, 21825) on 1 February 162 (Volubilis); *AE*, 1948, 115. I owe the suggestion of a Dalmatian origin to E. Birley.

and the only *praenomen* which appears with the family in Dalmatia is Quintus. Nothing else is known of his career.[1]

Dalmatian senatorial and equestrian families in the first and second centuries have their roots mostly in the Italian settler families of the coastal cities and their descendants. Only in the case of Marcius Turbo is there good evidence for some native ancestry, a peculiarity of the Epidaurum upper classes. Liburnia presents a different picture: no senatorial or leading equestrian families are known among those of Italian origin, and after the exceptional career of L. Tarius Rufus the only senatorial family from the area were the Raecii, whose background is predominantly native. They reached that status only in the second half of the second century, but in the first century a number of senatorial families are known to have had connections with the area.

The earliest senator of Dalmatian origin may be the Liburnian L. Tarius Rufus, consul in 16 B.C. The Elder Pliny records that he rose from very humble origins to the consulship by his outstanding military ability, and that later he amassed a considerable fortune, some of which he invested by purchasing derelict estates in Picenum. He was still alive in 24 when he was superintendent of the Rome water supply. His first exploit that is recorded was to command part of the fleet for Octavianus at Actium in 31 B.C. After a proconsulship in Cyprus he held a command in Macedonia about 17–16 B.C. before he achieved a suffect consulship. The family did not prosper later, however: according to Seneca his son was exiled under Augustus to Massilia, and he may be the L. Tarius Rufus attested at Vienna among the friends of a local equestrian. Tarius Gratianus, a praetorian senator who perished in 35, was probably the consul's grandson and is the last known senator of the family.[2]

Families of native Tarii at Nedinum suggest that he may have originated from that area. The name Tarius appears to be of Liburnian origin and can be linked with the 'ancient land of the Tariotae' (*antiqua regio Tariotarum*) and the Tariona *castellum* located by Pliny somewhere in Southeast Liburnia. As G. Alföldy has argued, he was probably a young Liburnian nobleman whose skill as an admiral

[1] Schulze, *LE*, 111, cites X, 8256 (Minturnae), XIV, 4091, 39 (Praeneste), *Q. Aeronius Antiochus sevir August. et qq*: XIV, 4140 (Ostia). In Dalmatia: III, 9882, *VAHD*, 53 (1950–1), 245, n. 29 with native *cognomen Ieta* (Varvaria), III, 2161, 8864, 6384, 6385, 12917 (Salona), eleven persons altogether.

[2] Humble origins: Plin., *HN*, xviii, 37. At Actium: Dio, l, 14; cf. Veget., iv, 33. *Curator aquarum*: Front., *de Aq.*, 102. In Cyprus: *IGR*, III, 952 (Paphos); cf. Groag, *RE*, 4A (1932), 2320 f. Attested at Amphipolis as *pro pr(aetore)*: *AE*, 1936, 18, and he may be the Λούκιος Γάιος who dealt with an invasion of the Sarmatae in 16 B.C., Dio, liv, 20, 3. He may have been Augustus' legate in Macedon, Syme, *RR*, 391, n. 1. On the younger (Tarius Rufus), Seneca, *de Clem.*, i, 15, 2 ff.; cf. XII, 1872 (Vienna), Tac., *Ann.*, vi, 38.

was appreciated by Octavianus for the Liburnian ships which he used at Actium. The gratitude of the princeps was shown by a place in the Senate in the census of 29 B.C., and a consulship in due course.[1]

The best recorded senatorial connection with Liburnia involves the great family of the Calpurnii Pisones, one of the few Republican families who remained active at the centre of government during the Julio–Claudian period.[2] Their influence, which was in the form of estates and clients, centred on the island Cissa and the northern part of the Ravni kotari, especially Corinium. In the former place Calpurnia, daughter of the ill-fated L. Piso the augur (*cos.* 1 B.C.) who died in 24, set up a dedication to the exclusive Roman cult of the Bona Dea. The same lady is recorded on two other dedications, both identical, but nothing more than her name and that of her father is preserved.[3] The family obviously owned some property there. Not far to the south at Corinium a number of Calpurnii appear with native *cognomina* and are obviously first generation citizens, Calpurnia C. f. Ceuna, and Calpurnia Volaesa, enfranchised through the influence of the Pisones.[4] Their Adriatic interests were not restricted to Liburnia. L. Piso Caesoninus (*cos.* 58 B.C.) was first *IIvir* of Pola along with L. Cassius Longinus, brother of Caesar's assassin.[5] Early under Claudius a Piso governed Dalmatia, probably L. Calpurnius Cn. f. Piso the consul of 27.[6]

[1] A Liburnian origin for the early *Tarii* must now be preferred after the detailed analysis of the name by Alföldy, *BJ* (forthcoming), in preference to the earlier suggestion of an origin in Picenum suggested by R. Syme, *SH*, 227, and followed by J. Wilkes, *BJ*, 166 (1966), 652. There can be little doubt that the Nedinum *Tarii* were a native Liburnian family: III, 2877, 2878, with *M. Tar[i]us C.f. Triera Tariae*, the last name being probably an *origo* in the lands of the Liburnian Tariotae, where Pliny records the *castellum Tariona*, *HN*, iii, 141. The amphorae stamped *L. Tarius Rufus* at Aquileia and in the vicinity (*NS*, 1930, 439; cf. V, 8112, 78) and in Siscia (III, 12010, 30) derived from the wine or oil exports from the family estates in Picenum, while the *Tarii* in Rome were the consul's freedmen or their descendants: VI, 37805 *domus L. Tari Rufi*; cf. VI, 14160b, 27106, 27107, 37489, 36475, 38297, 5727 all *L. Tarii*. A freedwoman also appears in Alvona, III, 3060 (10071).

[2] Alföldy, *BJ* (forthcoming); Šašel, *Akt. IV kong. gr. u. lat. Epigr.* (1964), 363–7, with pl. XVIII.

[3] P. Sticotti, *SH*, 179; Šašel, *ŽA*, 12 (1963), 387 ff.

[4] III, 9976: *L. C. Agapetus, Maximus, Polio*, 9970: *Q. C. Sex. f. Ser(gia) F[. . .]*, *JÖAI*, 18 (1915) Bb. 187: *[Cal]purnius [. . .]*; III, 2891, 2892, cf. 2857: *C. C.f. Ceuna*, 9763: *Calpu[r]nia Crispina*, 2891: *C. C.f. Oepla*, *JÖAI*, 12 (1909), Bb. 33, n. 5: *Kalpurnia Peculiaris*, 2890: *Calpurnia Ter[i]u[ll]a*, 2886: *Calpurnia Volaesa*, *JÖAI*, 12 (1909), Bb. 33, n. 6 (Zelengrad).

[5] *Inscr. It.*, X, 1, 65, 708, probably in 42 or 41 B.C.; cf. Degrassi, *Confine*, 65 f. After the death of Germanicus in the East Cn. Piso broke his journey back to Rome and remained for a time in Dalmatia where he hoped to gain some support from Drusus, who was then supervising affairs in Illyricum. Piso returned to Ancona by sea and had probably been living on the family estates in Liburnia, Tac., *Ann.*, iii, 7 ff.

[6] III, 12794 and below, p. 443. Another Augustan senatorial family who probably owned estates

The most eminent jurist of the Flavian era was L. Iavolenus Priscus, suffect consul in 86, and in Dalmatia he was connected with the Octavii of Nedinum. A career inscription set up there by his close friend P. Mutilius P. f. Cla. Crispinus records his senatorial career from the command of Legion IIII Flavia felix, at the end of Vespasian's reign or under Titus, when it was stationed at Burnum, up to his proconsulship in Africa not long after 101.[1] Here his full names are given as C. Octavius Tidius Tossianus L. Iavolenus Priscus, although otherwise he is always known as L. Iavolenus Priscus. His friendship with Mutilius Crispinus of Nedinum (the tribe Claudia shows that Mutilius was a native) could have been formed when he commanded the legion at Burnum, probably for a period of three years. Most have assumed on the evidence of the names Tidius, Tossianus, and Iavolenus that he originated in Umbria, probably in Iguvium, but there is still the link suggested by the names C. Octavius with the Octavii of Nedinum, the leading family of that city.[2] It is most unlikely that such a family were acquiring citizenship under the Flavians; on the contrary there are indications (absence of *cognomen*, repetition of municipal magistracies) that the earliest of the Nedinum Octavii date to the period of Augustus. It seems reasonable to conclude that the lawyer was born in Nedinum, probably early under Claudius, with the names C. Octavius Priscus and that his more familiar names were acquired through adoption, as G. Alföldy has argued. Like some of his contemporaries, he dropped his original family names, although these were well remembered in Liburnia and proudly recorded by a Nedinum friend.[3]

A later Liburnian family of senatorial rank were the Raecii, who reached that status in the second half of the second century. Their name is Venetic, and especially common in northern Liburnia and Istria. A *IIvir* of Crexi under Tiberius was the son of a non-Roman Raecus.[4] The next recorded member of the family

---

[1] III, 9960; cf. p. 2168 (*ILS*, 1015, and *add.* p. CLXXIII), PIR², I, 14, Alföldy, *BJ* (forthcoming). He may have been *adlectus inter praetorios* in Vespasian's censorship, and thus held no earlier senatorial offices. On the chronology of his career see Alföldy, op. cit.

[2] Thus Syme, *SH*, 227, W. Kunkel, *Herkunft*, etc., 138 ff., J. Wilkes, *BJ*, 166 (1966), 652 f., the last assuming the Nedinum *Octavii* to be descendants from his household in later years. *Mutilii* are attested also at Varvaria: *VAHD*, 53 (1950–1), 244 and Scardona: III, 2806. *Iavolenus*: XI, 5865 f., and *Tidius*: XI, 5901–3, are attested at Iguvium.

[3] On the Nedinum *Octavii*, see p. 213 above. The earliest member of the family was Q. Octavius (no *cognomen*) who was three times *IIvir* of the city, almost certainly in its early years under Augustus or Tiberius, III, 2870.

[4] III, 3149 (Crexi); cf. *Recus Sentius*: III, 9958 (Nedinum).

---

in Liburnia were the A. Caecinae from Etruscan Volaterrae, if III, 2967 (Iader) can be read *A. C[a]ecinae A. Caecin[a] A.f. parenti*; cf. Alföldy, *BJ*, (forthcoming).

is the centurion Q. Raecius Q. f. Cla. Rufus, whose home was probably Curicum; he became *primuspilus* of the eastern Legion XII Fulminata and was decorated during a long career by Titus in Judaea and by Trajan in Dacia. His wife was Trebia M. f. Procula, the daughter of the equestrian M. Trebius Proculus, a magistrate at Arba.[1] This Raecius was probably the grandfather of C. Raecius Rufus of Arba, a senator, whose freedman provided a new water-supply for the city on behalf of his patron in 173. A few years before Raecius held the post of superintendent of sacred buildings (*curator aedium*) at Rome.[2] Compared with the Aequum Iulii they are hardly distinguished and no more of this family are attested at this level. Their background was entirely Liburnian, with no sign of adoptions or links with established senatorial families in earlier generations. They rose from city-council status to equestrian rank through service in the army, and then to membership of the Roman senate. This was not a meteoric rise compared with other provincial families and may have taken six generations. On the other hand one must never undervalue the rank of Roman senator: although the Raecii were probably undistinguished in the hierarchy of the Roman Senate, in Liburnia they were a great family whose friendship and patronage would be much sought after.

By the end of the second century the distinction between the families of the coastal cities and the native population of the interior had largely disappeared, at least among the upper classes; nevertheless the majority of the senatorial and equestrian families attested in the third century appear in the coastal cities, mostly at Salona and Narona. In the former city C. Valerius C. f. Trom. Respectus Terentianus was a young man of senatorial family (*clarissimus iuvenis*) who died after holding his first office in the senatorial career, one of the ten who assisted in fixing legal damages (*Xviri stlitibus iudicandis*). His tribe reveals him a native of Salona and through his mother Caedicia L. f. Luc[illa] Crispinilla he was probably related to a consular family at Rome. She was related to Lucia Lorenia Cornelia L. f Crispini Crispina, a *clarissima puella* and probably the daughter of L. Lorenius L. f. Crispinus, member of the Arval Brethren (one of the leading priestly colleges at Rome reserved for senators) in 241 and suffect consul sometime before 244.[3] Also at Salona a fragmentary *cursus* records a man who was

[1] III, 2917, 2931 (Iader). On the *Trebii* see above, p. 309.

[2] III, 3116 (Arba): *Nymphis Aug. sacrum C. Raecius Leo aquam nullus antiquorum in civitate fuisse meminerit inventam impendio ex volunt. C. Raeci Rufi c. v. patron[. . . de]dicavit [Severo e]t Pompeiano II cos. VI Idus Nov.* (8 November 173). *Curator Aquarum*: VI, 360 in A.D. 166.

[3] III, 1989 and 1990; cf. *JÖAI*, 6 (1903), Bb. 81 f.: *C. Valerio C.f. [T]rom. Respe[cto] Terentiano clarissimo iuven[i XVviro] stlit. iudicand. [. . .] Caedicia L.f. Luc[illa] Crispinilla mate[r] infelicissima an[. . .* At Rome Lucia Lorenia Cornelia L. f. Crispini Crispina *clarissima puella* (VI, 1448) was probably the daughter of L. Lorenius L. f. Pal. Crispinus, *frater Arvalis* in 231, VI, 2108, 7, and

commissioner of public works (*curator operum publicorum*) and commissioner of the aqueducts and of the harbour at Minucia (*curator aquae et Minuciae*). The holding of these last posts together fixes the date probably between Commodus and Elagabalus, but there is no apparent reason for the dedication, which was set up by the city of Salona, unless his home was in the city.[1] One senator is attested at Narona, M. Lusius Severus who is described as *clarissimus vir*. The family is well known at Narona, with three freedmen *seviri* out of a total of twenty-one people with the name. Nothing is known of his career or background and there is no reason to connect him with the other senatorial Lusii attested in the second century.[2] No active senatorial families are known to have come from the interior of the province, nor is there any evidence that any of those attested in the coastal cities had moved south in an earlier generation from the native upper classes. Neither C. Minicius Fundanus, a governor under Trajan who may

[1] A. Betz, *VAHD*, 56–59/2 (1954–9), 85, n. 3, pl. IX, 2: . . ./. . .] *cu*[r]*ator* [*ope*]*rum publicorum* [*cur*]*ator* [*aqua*]*e et* [*cur*]*ator* [*Min*]*uciae* [R. P.] *S*(*alonitana*). For the division of these posts, H-G. Pflaum, *BJ*, 163 (1963), 232 f. The good quality of the lettering make a possible date in the period between Philip and Diocletian much less likely than the earlier period, Alföldy, *BJ* (forthcoming). Another native of Salona in the third century may be Cornelia Salonina, the empress of Gallienus. From the distribution of her *cognomen* it may be that in the third century it was very fashionable in the Dalmatian capital, where seven examples are attested, *BD*, 31 (1908), 145, n. 3986A, III, 2506 (8638), 13897 (12954), 14239/6 (9354); *BD*, 28 (1905), 133, n. 3440A; 37 (1914), 81; 33 (1910), 38, n. 4165A, III, 3182a (findspot uncertain), with others at Viminacium (a Dalmatian, III, 6300), III, 3323 (near Lussonium), IX, 3465 (Peltuinum), and a Christian lady at Aeclanum, IX, 1392. Also connected with Salona was probably her relative P. Cornelius Saecularis *cos. II ord.* in 260, for whose *cognomen* there are six examples at Salona: III, 2189 (8605), 2259, 2547, 12940, and 2386 (Klis), 14655 (Srinjine di Poljica); cf. Alföldy, *BJ* (forthcoming).

[2] III, 1768 (Narona): *M. Lusi Severi c. v. Modestus lib. templum ex voto restituit*. Other *Lusii*: III, 1775, 1798, 8426 (1855), 1856, 1872; *SB*, 218 f., III 1863, 1787, 1877, 1806, 1862, 1788, 8420, altogether 23 persons. A much earlier senatorial link for Narona is suggested by Claudia Aesernina *sacerdos divae Augustae*: III, 7196. The Empress is Iulia Augusta (Livia) the wife of Augustus who died in 29 and who was deified by her grandson Claudius in 42. The lady at Narona is probably one of the *Claudii Marcelli Aesernini*, descended from the man whose father defended Aesernia during the Italian War in 90 B.C., Munzer and Groag, *RE*, 3, (1899) 2770 f., n. 232–3. The latter's son was *consul ordinarius* in 22 B.C., and his own grandson was probably the man with the same names who was praetor in 19. Heir to the large fortunes of the family, he was regarded as one of the best orators of his generation, Tac., *Ann.*, xi, 7; cf. *PIR*², C 928, Alföldy, *BJ* (forthcoming).

suffect consul before 244, VI, 1447; cf. VI, 31657, Barbieri, *Albo*, n. 1089, 2112. The young Valerius could be the son of the Severan general C. Valerius Pudens. Another member of the family at Salona is Valeria Respectilla: *BD*, 39 (1916), 105, n. 4288A; cf. Alföldy, *BJ* (forthcoming).

have been patron of the city at Šipovo in the Pliva valley,[1] nor the third-century Catii at Aquae S. were natives of the province.[2] Further east the native Claudii at Skelani and the Flavii at Maluesa did attain senatorial rank. One of the former appears as *clarissimus vir*, the son of an *eques Romanus*, while the status of the latter is represented by Flavia Prisca, a *clarissima femina*, who is mentioned on the tombstone of her nurse (*nutrix*) Flavia Tatta.[3]

The equestrians from the province in the later period reflect more clearly the changes which had been taking place in the composition of the upper classes during the decades following the Marcomannic wars. The old Italian settler families with city magistracies and one or two appointments as equestrian unit commanders appear no longer, and in their place is a group of more professional character and whose origins within the province were more humble. Often they are Aurelii, and probably originate from the interior. One of the earliest was T. Flavius Agricola, whose municipal career has been discussed already (p. 316) and who was tribune in Legion X Gemina.[4] One of the few third-century equestrian officers whose family appears also as city councillors was Desidienus Aemilianus, a unit commander on the frontier in Northern Britain attested in 258. The name is rare and appears elsewhere only in a third-century city-council family at Salona.[5] A good example of the change in character of the equestrians also comes from Salona: a procurator M. Aurelius Hermes was an imperial freedman, but his son M. Aurelius Hermogenes was an equestrian and, although he died aged only twenty, he had already been aedile at Salona.[6] At Narona M. Aurelius Valerius, a *vir egregius* and member of the emperor's military staff (*protector lateris divini*), rebuilt the winter baths of the colony and gave a banquet for his fellow citizens in 280. He was probably a native, from a remote part of the Narona territory where the population was not enfranchised until the late second or early third centuries.[7] Another *protector* appears at Curicum in

---

[1] *GZMBH*, 38 (1926), 155, and p. 445 f.

[2] *GZMBH*, 52 (1940), 15 = *AE*, 1948, 241; cf. Barbieri, *Albo*, n. 988, Alföldy, *BJ* (forthcoming).

[3] III, 1986; cf. 8572, p. 1031 *Casconia Marcella* and daughter with the same names at Salona, III, 8350 (Karan) and for *Claudii* at Skelani, see above, p. 281.

[4] III, 2026 = *ILS*, 7162.

[5] *RIB*, 1589 (Vercovicium); III, 12916 (Salona): *C. Desidienus Proculus dec. col. S[a]loni[t]anor.*; cf. 9028: *Desidiena Profutura*.

[6] III, 2077: *D.m. M. Aureli Hermogenis eq. Rom. dec. aedili cur(?). def. an. XX d. III M. Aurel. Augg. lib. Hermes proc. piissimo filio.*

[7] III, 1805; cf. p. 2328/119 (Narona): *Thermas rei p. hi[emales ...] populo in ruinam [... di]lap[sas] M. Aur. Valerius v. e. ducen[ari]us ex protectorib. lateris divini de frugalitate IO[... aedifi]cavit et lavantes rei p. tradidit epulum quoque c[i]vibus suis ea die praebu[i]t Messala e[t] Grato cos. dedicante M. Aur. Tiberiano v. p. praes. prov. Delm.*

Liburnia. His name has not survived, but his holding of the three tribunates at Rome (*cohortes urbanae*, *vigiles*, and praetorians) dates him probably to the middle of the third century. He was patron of 'the most splendid city Curicta' (*patronus splendidissimae civitatis Curictarum*) and was honoured there with a statue for his outstanding generosity (*ob insignem eius benevolentiam*).[1] There is no evidence that any of the equestrian mines-procurators either those in the Sana valley or at Domavia, were of native origin. One was honoured in the latter place by his close friend (*amicus praestantissimus*) M. Aurelius Ru[sti]cus who was also a *vir egregius ducenarius*; he may originate from the province and was possibly an earlier procurator at Domavia.[2] One is known from the interior, a *procurator metallorum* on an elaborate fragmentary epitaph at Salvium, which mentions other military appointments.[3] Finally there is no doubt about the native origin of Caecilius Bato, prefect of Cohort XV Voluntariorum in Germania Inferior attested in 197–8. His *cognomen* suggests that he came either from the Delmatae or the Pannonian peoples in the north, possibly the Daesitiates. Caecilii are known at Salona; Caecilia Logiana was the daughter of an *ementissimus vir* and married the equestrian Tullius Callipianus.[4]

Such are the people from the province who achieved a place in the imperial hierarchy. There is very little continuity from the earlier to the later period, and only in one or two instances is it possible to trace the advance of a family over more than two generations. There is no steady rise of provincial magnates, as in Africa, Spain, or Southern Gaul.[5] The Iulii were important people by any standards, but had no connections with the native population. There was not the wealth to sustain rising families away from the coast, nor does there appear any tendency for property to accumulate in the hands of a few very powerful families, as appears to have happened elsewhere in the western provinces during the later period.

[1] III, 3126; cf. 10125.
[2] III, 8361 (Domavia).
[3] *GZMBH*, 39 (1927), 260, n. 9 (Kamen).
[4] XIII, 8824=*ILS*, 9178 (Roomberg near Leiden); for distribution of Bato see Alföldy, *PN* (forthcoming). *Caecilia Logiana*: III, 8713.
[5] On the African families, M. G. Jarrett, *Historia*, 12 (1963), 209 ff.

Chapter 13

City and Country

1 *The Pattern of Native Settlement*

The main type of settlement inhabited by the native population of Dalmatia was the fortified hill settlement, and remains of these are to be seen today in almost every part of the province. In some areas they represent the only discernable traces of the population before the Roman conquest. From what has been said in Chapter 8 about the organization of the native peoples, it is clear that these hill settlements, today often called gradina, were the political and economic centres of the population, and against an external invader such as the Romans provided the physical focus of opposition. In the three Roman wars in the area for which we have any details, that in 156–155 B.C. against the Delmatae, in 34–33 B.C. against the same people, and the great rebellion of 6–9, final victory came with the reduction of the hill-forts where resistance had been concentrated. Although none of the well-known strongholds has been examined archaeologically, places such as Metulum, Terponus, Delminium, Raetinium, Splonum, and Andetrium had major fortification able to withstand the formidable siege techniques of the Roman army. As for the Veneti in Gaul or the Cantabri in Spain, warfare for the Dalmatians meant holding out in a fortress, while the invader dissipated his energies with futile attacks in a terrain where supplies were difficult.[1]

P. Vatinius, Caesar's proconsul in Illyricum during 45–44 B.C., was a commander of energy and ability; yet he found the hill-forts (*oppida*) of the Delmatae difficult to attack and admitted in a letter that all his gains in a campaigning

[1] Compare the guerrilla tactics and the use of isolated strongholds by the Spanish tribes against Augustus, A. Brancati, *Augusto e La Guerra di Spagna*, 70 ff. On the fortresses of the Veneti in Northwest Gaul, see Wheeler and Richardson, *Hill Forts*, *etc.*, 18 ff.

season would be lost with the onset of winter. He believed that he had earned the triumph he claimed, but was frustrated by having no solid achievement to show in Rome. The sufferings of an invader in the Dalmatian karst are well known. When Tiberius was blockading Andetrium in 9 the Roman army found the task unrewarding enough to talk of mutiny. There was no sign of victory, even though the place was barely a day's march from Salona and the Adriatic.[1]

i *The Illyrian Kingdom* (fig. 12). The best preserved examples of native strongholds in the province are in the southeast, in the area of the old kingdom ruled by Agron and his successors. Although the walls of Lissus (p. 362) are of native origin they belong to the history of urbanization and Roman city development, rather than to that of native Illyrian strongholds. In 213 B.C. Philip V of Macedon made one of his few energetic attacks against Roman clients on his western borders. He captured Lissus, thus obtaining a naval base on the Adriatic, and the higher stronghold Acrolissus, more than 1 kilometre to the east at the summit of the Mali Šelbuemit (410 metres). The place has great strategic value, controlling the main north–south route from the Lake of Scodra down to the hills behind Dyrrhachium. On the hill extensive remains survive of the fortifications attacked by Philip, enclosing the small summits at each end of the ridge.[2] On the west side the slope is precipitous and no fortification was required. To the east, however, the approach is easier and the defences extended some way down the hill, enclosing an area of about 80 by 300 metres. Little survives of the curtain wall, except at the corners where greater stability was necessary, especially at the north and south. Around the north are remains of three projecting rectangular towers, while the longest stretch of surviving wall on the south was 100 metres long. Here no traces of towers were discovered, but the strengthened southern angle served the purpose of a turret. The southern summit was separated from the rest of the enclosure by a cross-wall, which survives for 25 metres with a gateway facing south. The construction technique is similar to that of the Lissus city walls, and there can be little doubt that they were part of the same complex. If the Acrolissus was not held, Lissus itself would be virtually indefensible, a situation confirmed by the Macedonian attack. Since the Acrolissus could not be taken by direct assault, Philip encamped between the two strongholds and after feigning flight from a skirmish with the city defenders, he was able to lure the small garrison from the Acrolissus, eager for their share of plunder. Immediately a concealed force took the stronghold and the city fell the next day with little effort by

[1] Dio, lvi, 13, 1 ff.
[2] Praschniker-Schober, 23 ff., figs., 35 ff. Capture of Acrolissus: Pol., viii, 15, 16 and above, p. 21 f.

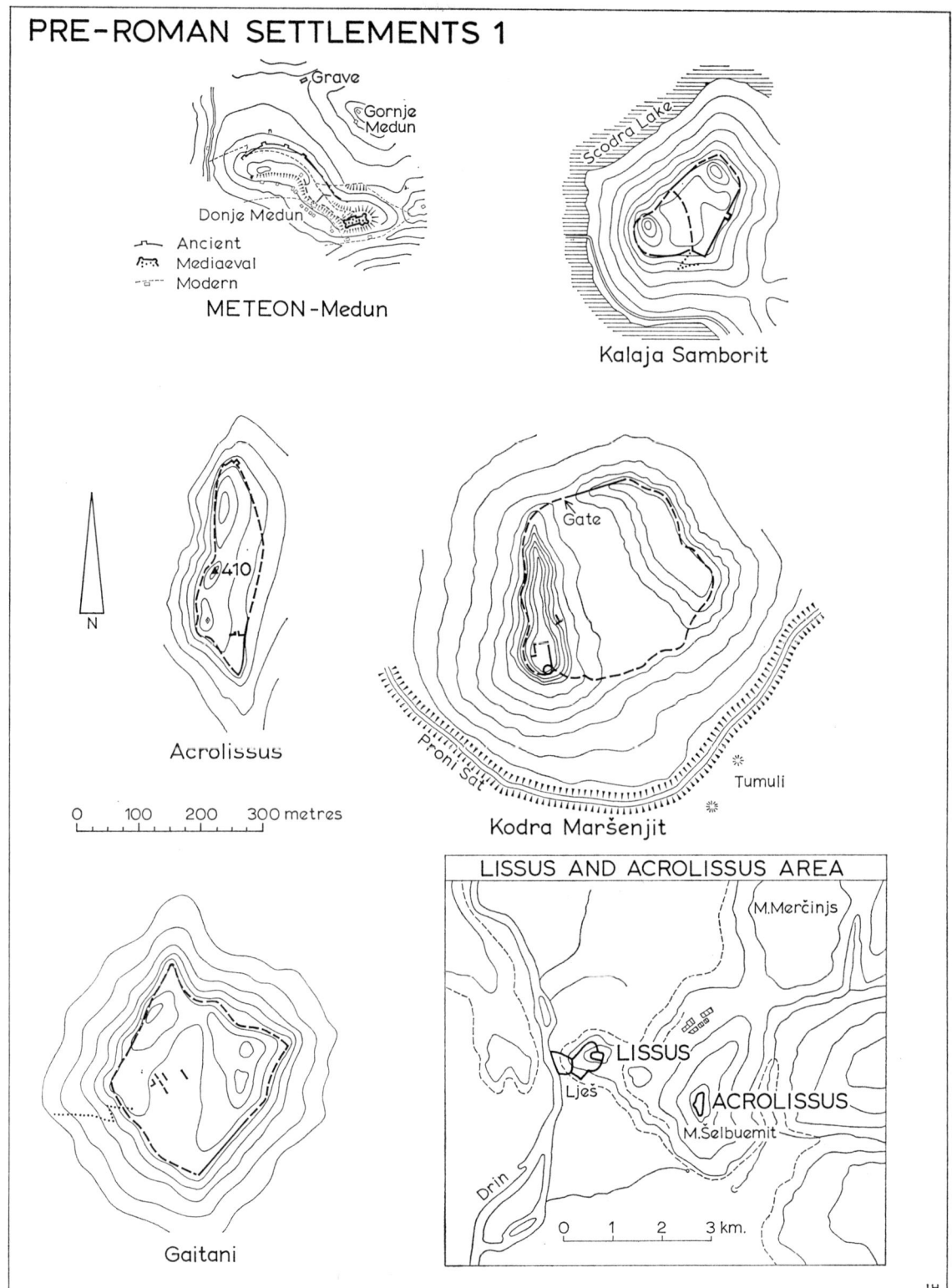

PRE-ROMAN SETTLEMENTS 1

Grave

Gornje Medun

Donje Medun

⌐—⌐ Ancient
▭▭ Mediaeval
⌐—⌐ Modern

METEON-Medun

Scodra Lake

Kalaja Samborit

N

▲410

Acrolissus

0 100 200 300 metres

Gate

Proni Sat

Tumuli

Kodra Maršenjit

LISSUS AND ACROLISSUS AREA

M.Merčinjs

LISSUS

Lješ

ACROLISSUS

M.Šelbuemit

Drin

0 1 2 3 km.

Gaitani

J.H.

Figure 12 Pre-Roman Settlements 1 (Lissus)

the Macedonians. After the Roman conquest the Acrolissus was abandoned, but the defences of the city were retained into the first century B.C. for protection against sea attack (fig. 15). For this purpose the Acrolissus was of little use, and it appears to have remained unoccupied until a tower was built on the southern summit in the Middle Ages.

Because of its close association with the city Lissus, the Acrolissus was not a typical stronghold in the Illyrian kingdom. Gentius' capital Scodra later became a Roman city and remains today the chief town in Northern Albania. Traces of the Illyrian defences can be detected beneath the mediaeval walls, and reveal a construction similar to Lissus.[1] North of the Lake of Scodra was Gentius' fortress Meteon (Medun). This occupied an east–west ridge, with steep slopes on the south; at the east end it rises to a small peak 586 metres above sea level.[2] From dolnje Medun at the foot of the hill an ancient track climbs up to the ridge at a point where the remains of the Illyrian stronghold can be identified, although the main area of the hill is now occupied by a mediaeval fortification. Apart from near the ancient road entrance no wall was necessary along the south side, but along the north a wall survives for more than 150 metres, with four projecting towers spaced about 24 metres apart. Only two courses of the Meteon wall survive, but it is clear that its construction was similar to that at Lissus, lines of dressed limestone blocks with a rubble core, and like the latter probably dates to the third or early second century B.C. In the small quantity of pottery found there were some Greek imports.

These three places were the major centres of the area, the residences and strongholds of the Illyrian kings. Below the king were the tribal chiefs (*principes*), whose power would be based on other strongholds within the kingdom. Some of these have been identified along the east side of the lake of Scodra. Seven kilometres south of Scodra the hill-fort Gaitani enclosed a square with sides of more than 250 metres.[3] The defences were built of dry stone walls, and some trace of dwellings was found inside the area. Less impressive than the royal strongholds and exhibiting much less Greek influence, the Gaitani defences would nevertheless require a powerful attack before they would yield. The small quantity of Greek and Roman pottery found there indicates that it remained occupied from at least the third century B.C. until well into the Roman period. Gaitani is typical of a number of these hill settlements near the main road between Doclea and Scorda along the east side of the lake, at Kodra Maršenjit, Kalaja Hotit, Kalaja Šamborit. All of these have produced small quantities of Greek and Roman pottery, indicating that it was a long time before they were abandoned by the

[1] Praschniker-Schober, 8 ff., figs. 12–14.
[2] Op. cit., 3 ff., figs. 6–11.   [3] Op. cit., 86 ff., figs. 102–4.

local population. They were the native *castella* inhabited by the native *principes*, as for example those of the Docleatae at Salthua (Riječani) before the foundation of Doclea.

With their stone construction and projecting towers most of these fortifications were built in imitation of Lissus and similar centres. Although they do not extend to the south of Lissus (ending approximately at the southern limit of the Illyrian kingdom), they are common along the east coast of the Adriatic as far as Istria, where a large number of comparable hill-settlements (castellieri) have been identified.[1] The principal feature is a hill-settlement, usually a single defensive circuit around a hill with two summits. In the Dalmatian coastal region there are signs of the same stone building-techniques as used further south, but none of these places has yet been surveyed or excavated, apart from a small group around Knin.[2] These show many features found in the area around Scodra and Lissus, such as single lines of defences with external towers, but their construction is much simpler with no trace of dressed masonry.[3]

ii *The Territory of Narona* (fig. 13).   North of the Illyrian kingdom the Narenta valley never developed any independent political power. The easier route to the hinterland and the interior was an invitation to the Greek trader and settler, and later to the Roman conqueror. Native fortifications are known in the middle Narenta valley around Mostar, but there is no such clear picture of the social and political structure of pre-Roman society in the area as is provided by the strongholds around Scodra and Lissus. No pre-Roman site is known in the vicinity of Narona, a city which may have begun as a trading post (*emporion*) in Greek times. A few miles upstream from Narona the hills close in on the river and at this point on the same bank is Čapljina, dominated by the two hills Velika and Mala Gradina. On the summit of the latter are substantial traces of stone defences, rough masonry with no courses or regular size of stone. The wall survives for a length of 28 metres, 1.20 thick, and to a height of 3.30 metres.[4] The area enclosed by the defences cannot have been large, but was sufficient to control the river passage from its height of more than 200 metres. Although the majority of finds made on the surface are of Roman date, the native origin of the defences is certain. Some other pottery of a type well-attested in the Narenta valley was found, white fabric with grey-brown colour-coating and painted decoration, attested also at

---

[1] On the Istrian castellieri, see Marchesetti, *Castellieri Preistorici*.

[2] A group in the Ravni kotari were identified by L. Jelić, most in the area south of Iader near to the coast; cf. Praschniker-Schober, 87. For other sites in the area of Knin see W. Büttler, 21 *BerRGK* (1931), 183–98.

[3] W. Büttler, op. cit., pl. 32, n. 2.   [4] *WMBH*, 12 (1912), 80 f., fig. 10–11.

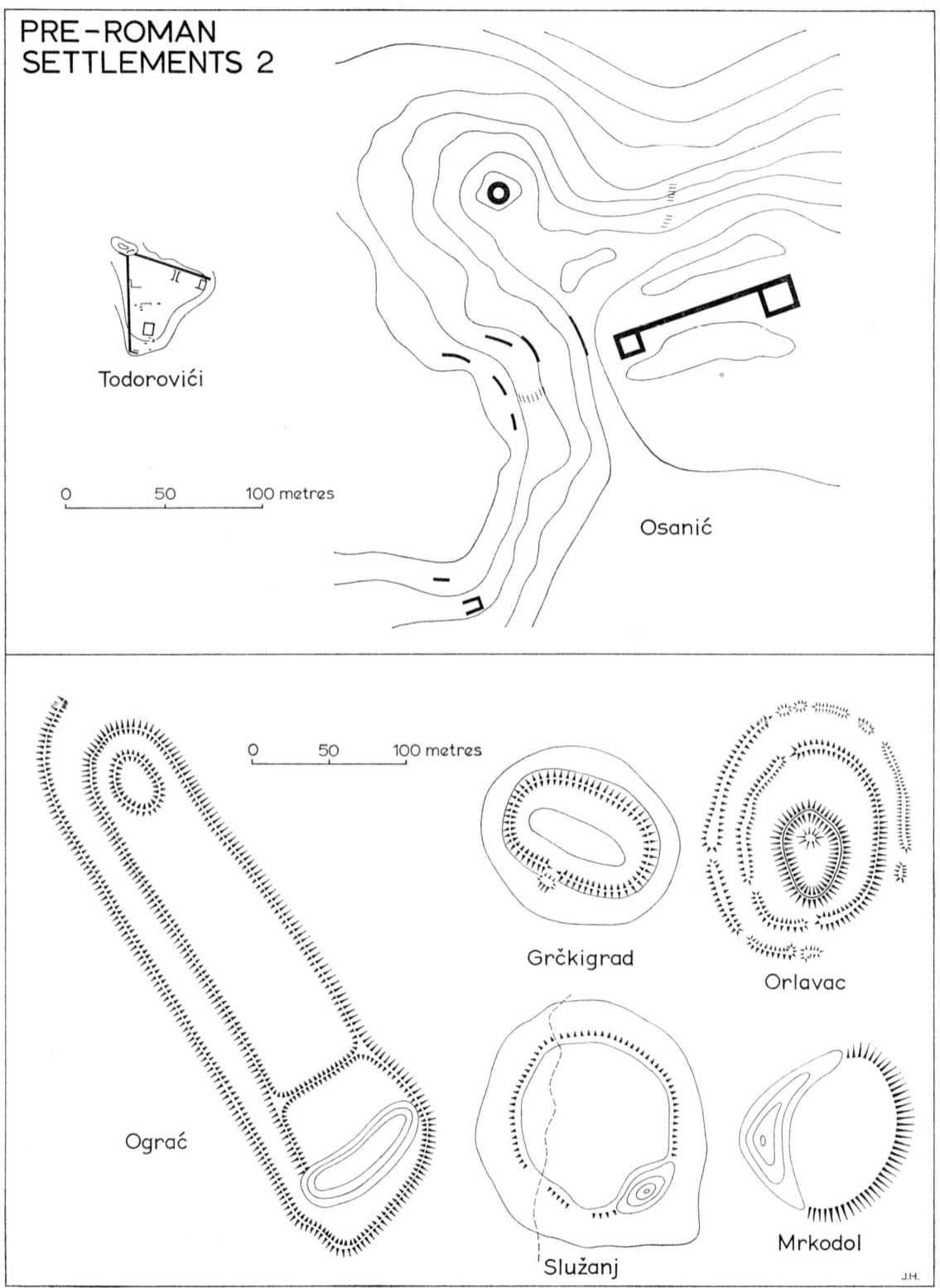

PRE-ROMAN SETTLEMENTS 2

Todorovići

0   50   100 metres

Osanić

0   50   100 metres

Ograć

Grčkigrad

Orlavac

Služanj

Mrkodol

J.H.

Figure 13 Pre-Roman Settlements 2 (Narenta valley)

Osanić near Stolac (p. 345) and at Narona. The Roman tiles and amphora-lids attest the trading links of the Čapljina settlement with Italy during the second and first centuries B.C. Coins of Dyrrhachium and Apollonia are known from there, while in a large deposit of Roman Republican issues the latest coin has been dated to between 29 and 25 B.C. How important Čapljina was politically is not known, but it was only one of a number of such settlements along the Narenta which flourished and grew as trading centres until Narona eventually established its predominance with Italian settlement, and later colonial status.

The Lower Narenta is separated from the plains around Mostar by the Žitomisljić gorge, above which the river has always been impassable to shipping. Consequently external trade will have had less effect on the area, and the political organization was less influenced by outside contacts. A survey by W. Radimsky at the end of the last century recorded a number of hill-settlements in the Bišćepolje region south of Mostar.[1] A native hill-fort on the Mala gradina (fig. 14) dominates the area around the confluence between the Bunica and the Narenta. On a steep-sided hill nearly 200 metres high three tumuli are cut through by the stone wall of the settlement, which is also preceded by an earthen defence. Mortar was used in the construction and the thickness varies from 1 to 2 metres. Large quantities of tiles from the Roman period suggested to Radimsky that a native hill-fort with earth defences had been superseded by a stone Roman stronghold. Around the foot of the hill were extensive surface traces of Roman building materials, suggesting a settlement contemporary with the stone defences.

South of the river Buna and on the edge of the plain was the largest hill-fort in the region, but with no traces of stone defences. The Ograc hill settlement near Hodbina (fig. 13) measures 102 by 49 metres. The entrance begins at one end of the enclosure but is screened by a rampart for the whole length of the defences before access is gained to the interior. Rapid excavations suggested that it was a place of refuge only rather than a permanently occupied settlement. The defences were made from heaps of loose stones, the only available material short of a masonry wall since little timber is available in the vicinity. Between the river Buna and its tributary the Bunica was a third hill settlement, situated on the Kićin hill (fig. 14). Here the defences were much more elaborate than at Hodbina. A circular rampart of loose stones crowned the top of the hill (170 metres); outside this were traces of two other roughly concentric lines of defence, but only on the side of the hill away from the Bunica which flows past its foot. On the west of the Kićin settlement was a lower hill Gorica, where were discovered traces of dwelling huts built from rough stone. They were circular in plan, with diameters of

[1] *WMBH*, 2 (1894), 3 ff., with general plan fig. 1.

about 3 metres and walls about 1 to 1.5 metres thick. Considerable quantities of pottery were found on the surface; other finds included a quernstone for grinding corn. Two distinct types of pottery were present and identified by Radimsky. The earlier was made in a fabric of various colours and matches closely the pottery of the Istrian castellieri, which began in the Neolithic and Bronze Ages and lasted well into the Roman period. All the pottery from Kićin in this group is pre-Roman and of an early date in its type. The second type of pottery appears in a much finer fabric and imitates some of the more common Roman pottery forms, especially the amphora and other large storage jars. Radimsky concluded that Kićin was a major permanent settlement occupied continuously from the Bronze Age until the period when Roman imports were reaching the Narenta valley in quantity. North of the river Buna on the eastern edge of the Bišćepolje was the hill-fort at Križ (fig. 14). A single rampart enclosed an elliptical area around the summit, and another defence closes off a small area on the north side. Altogether the enclosure measures 76 by 65 metres; all the ramparts are of loose stones heaped together. A limited excavation produced some pottery and fragments of a quernstone, suggesting permanent occupation at some period.

Apart from Kićin, the settlements in the Mostar region show few contacts with the outside world. Most appear to have been abandoned at the time of the Roman occupation; nor did any of them grow into a centre in the Roman period, except perhaps the Mala gradina opposite the confluence of the Narenta and the Buna. The whole region around Mostar and Bišćepolje was included in the territory of Narona. Not all the native settlements are found in the plain close to the major rivers. The route between the Narenta crossing at Mostar and the Mostarsko blato is dominated by the Gradina Orlavac near Razlomište (fig. 13) at an altitude of 473 metres.[1] The stronghold is elliptical, roughly following the contours of the hill. An inner stone wall survives to a height of more than 3 metres, enclosing an area 56 by 37 metres. Outside this circuit, in which no trace of the entrance can be discerned, were two lines of fortifications made from loosely heaped stones, the inner with three entrances and the outer line incomplete, possibly unfinished. Overall the complex measures 155 by 126 metres. The site may not have been inhabited permanently, since no trace of occupation was discovered. A similar site in the Mostar area was Služanj at the southern end of Brotnjopolje (fig. 13) on the main route between Mostar and Ljubuški.[2] The defences enclose a flat-topped hill 264 metres high, with a circular rubble wall 110 metres in diameter and surviving to a height of 2.5 metres. On the southeast side was a stone mound, built at the same time as the main defence as a protective bastion. Compared with the other strongholds in the Narenta valley the

[1] *WMBH*, 5 (1897), 270 f.   [2] *WMBH*, 5 (1897), 270 ff., fig. 9–10.

Služanj defences are very simple and the area had few contacts with the outside world. In construction it has much more in common with the hill-settlements further north around Delminium and Pelva (p. 348).

Nevesinjepolje lies to the east of Bišćepolje, separated by the 2,000-metre Velež mountain barrier. Near the village of Šlivlje, to the west of Nevesinje, is a small hill-fort (fig. 13) called Grčkigrad (Greektown) on a hill 1,193 metres high.[1] A rampart of limestone blocks heaped together enclosed an area roughly 74 by 37 metres. On the south side the entrance was screened by a short stretch of rampart, similar to the *tutulus* in Roman marching camp. A large quantity of hand-made pottery from the interior suggests that this was a permanently occupied settlement.

Apart from the city itself, one of the most flourishing centres in the Narona territory was Stolac in the Bregava valley, which flows into the Narenta from the east at Čapljina. Its prosperity in the Roman period is surprising since Stolac is an isolated place with few natural advantages and a most oppressive summer climate. However, the wealth of its settler and native families is demonstrated by houses with a high standard of luxury (p. 398). In the vicinity of Stolac are some of the most impressive native fortification of the Narenta area. Across the river was Osanić, where the site of the Roman settlement is easily identifiable on the ground, near the foot of a hill with two summits both nearly 300 metres above sea level. Both reveal considerable remains of stone fortifications.[2] Across the main summit a stone wall, built in the rusticated style, linked two square towers of different size (fig. 13). They are 54 metres apart and the wall linking them is 2 metres thick. The individual stones are large, averaging 2 metres long and 1.2 metres across, and these rest upon four foundation courses each 90 centimetres deep. Both the towers project towards the south; the smaller on the west is 11 metres square overall, the other 15 by 14 metres. The area around the wall was thick with fragments of Roman tiles and mortar, although these belong to later Roman buildings on the site and not to the original defences. Elsewhere on the hill are traces of circuit walls, apparently sealing off the approaches from the west, where a track leads down to the Rotimlja valley. The other summit of the Osanić hill is crowned with a circular defensive enclosure 11 metres in diameter, with a similar type of wall construction 2 metres thick. The defences at Osanić show a similar construction to those around Lissus and Scodra, but the plan is quite different and not paralleled elsewhere in the province. The two towers linked by the curtain wall suggest rather a place to control a subject population than a refuge for the local people in time of danger, as was the case with the hill strongholds around Mostar. The walls may have been constructed under Greek

[1] *WMBH*, 2 (1894), 56, with plan fig. 4.   [2] *WMBH*, 2 (1894), 36 ff., fig. 1–5.

influence, and the site was clearly inhabited into the period when Roman building materials and techniques were spreading through the area. The place was
perhaps the residence of the chief native family, or families, at Stolac; when
granted Roman citizenship and admitted to the ruling circle of Narona they
changed their pattern of life and built some of the fine Roman houses near the
river Bregava at Osanić and Stolac.

Not far south of Stolac along the road to Ljubinje is the hill Vrsnik which
dominates the village of Poplat and, although only 514 metres above sea level,
rises 464 metres above the level of Stolac. Its summit is crowned by one of the
largest hill-forts known in the region.[1] The defences, a series of concentric
ellipses, consist of five elements, at the centre of which is a stone cairn (gromila)
7 metres high and 25 metres across, and adjacent to it a circular enclosure 42
metres in diameter. These two elements were enclosed by three rings of defences,
the outer line measuring 371 by 269 metres with a total area of 7.8 hectares (19.3
acres) – nearly the same as the Liburnian city Asseria. The labour of building
these fortifications on top of the hill was immense, and it is strange that excavation yielded no evidence for any occupation. As Radimsky suggested, with such
an isolated yet prominent position and curious plan it may have had a religious
importance, similar to the holy mountain of the Dacians mentioned by Strabo.

East of Stolac the Hergud plateau rises steeply for more than 1,000 metres from
the level of the river. An enemy could establish himself there for a long period;
only one path leads up to the plateau from the valley, and this is controlled by
the hill-fort at Todorovići, at a height of 250 metres.[2] The top of the hill is
triangular and a stone wall protects two sides (fig. 13), the third side remaining
unprotected for no apparent reason. Inside the fort were a number of rectangular
buildings, for which manufactured tiles and pottery indicate a Roman date;
some graves within the defences almost certainly belong to a period after the
fortress was abandoned. For a Roman fortification Todorovići is untypical.
There is no evidence for date; it could represent a refurbishing of an old Illyrian
stronghold during the insecurity of the Late Empire.

At Gradac near Posušje the road from Mostar to the Duvno region begins its
ascent to cross the Dinaric ridge. In the early first century A.D. it was a key military post, part of the strategy against the peoples of the interior organized during
the war of 6–9. The Roman site is attested by a wealth of stone remains and iron
objects, and consisted of a rectangular building measuring internally 69 by 55
metres. Above this site, on the Kulina hill, was an oval enclosure measuring 100
by 70 metres.[3] The walls were built of mortared stone and they override a native

---

[1] *WMBH*, 2 (1894), 53 f., fig. 1.   [2] *WMBH*, 1 (1893), 296 f., fig. 68.
[3] *WMBH*, 3 (1895), 258, fig. 1–2. A similar site existed nearby at Babingrad, 4 (1896), 178, fig. 29.

tumulus. To judge from the pottery found on the site the defences were of native origin, and formed one of the many Illyrian strongholds which held out against Tiberius and his generals in the hard fighting of 8–9.

iii *The Southern Delmatae.* No plan or survey exists of any major settlement of the Delmatae south of the Dinaric Alps. The great fortresses 'ennobled by battles' at Tilurium and elsewhere were later occupied permanently by units of the Roman army. Although the site of the Andetrium stronghold (Gornje Muć) is easily identifiable no survey or plan has yet appeared. Near Aequum the old native hill settlement seems to have survived, probably because it was never concerned in the wars of conquest. There was a major fortress on the citadel of modern Sinj, centre of the Osiniates, which commands the point where the river Hippius emerges from the hills into the Sinj polje. Further west lies the hill-fort at Rider, which preceded the low-lying settlement of the Roman period. The stronghold (Danilo gornje) was defended by stone walls of much cruder construction than those in the Illyrian kingdom to the south. Large quantities of native pottery can be picked up on the surface, but the hill is small and cannot have held an enclosure more than 50 metres square. Synodium may be identified with one of the many strongholds in the country behind Andetrium, but no certain identification is possible. Similarly the complex of defences on the Promona hills, once Liburnian but captured later by the Delmatae, can be identified and understood from Appian's account of the attack by Octavianus in 34 B.C. On the smaller peaks (Appian's 'sawteeth'), which screen the eastern side of the hills, traces of Illyrian fortifications and Roman siege-works have been noted by Veith.[1] No evidence exists for any settlement on these hills and the site belongs more to the history of Roman conquest than to the pattern of settlement in the pre-Roman period.

In the central and northern regions of Dalmatia studies of the settlement pattern of the native population are available for three areas, the Duvno region including Delminium, the Bihać area and the Sana valley. All three were made by Radimsky, and in some places he was able to obtain evidence by trial excavation. Although his reports, for the most part published more than seventy years ago, provide little more than a distribution of the chief sites with outline surveys, they still constitute the best local studies of the native settlement pattern available for the northern part of the province.

The Duvno polje around Županac encloses an area 20 by 9 kilometres at an altitude of 860–900 metres. The river Šuica flows into it from the north and merges into the flood basin south of Županac. As in most of the poljes of this

---

[1] Veith, *Feldzüge*, 63 ff.

area the pre-Roman settlements (gradina) are very common, and spread evenly through the inhabitable areas of the plain.[1] Forty-one hill-forts were recorded, all of roughly the same dimensions. As permanently occupied settlements Radimsky suggested that each supported a population of about 200, making a rough total for the pre-Roman population in the area of 8,200, slightly less than half the population of the Županac region at the beginning of this century. Most of the settlements were on hills or plateaux which could be defended in an emergency, but none of them is on any high peak or isolated from the fertile land in the polje, as was sometimes the case in the Narenta valley. Ideally a promontory was chosen for the site, and the enclosure was formed by a rampart sealing off the settlement from the hills behind. No defences were built from dressed masonry; usually they were of heaped stones collected together from the area. Another feature common to the sites, which has already been noted elsewhere, was a mound incorporated into the rampart at the highest point of the site, to serve as a citadel and watchtower. None of the defences were built to withstand a serious attack: there was never more than a single rampart, nor were any elaborations incorporated into the entrances, the traditional weak point in such enclosures. There was a concentration along the east side of the polje between Sarajlije and Mandinoselo, with no less than six sites in this line. A typical site is the Mrkodol gradina (fig. 13). A rocky plateau juts out from the hills to form a precipice, where no defence needed to be built. On the inner side the plateau was sealed off by an elliptical rampart 101 metres long; the outer dimension is about 70 metres.

The fate of these polje settlements in the Roman period is interesting. The majority (34) reveal no trace of Roman occupation-material and were apparently abandoned, more through their inconvenience to the local population than pressure from the Roman authorities, since, unlike those strongholds around Mostar and Stolac, none of them could have been regarded as a threat to Roman control. These were not the people who fought on to the end in 9: they had been the Daesitiates and the Pirustae of the wooded valleys to the north and east. Seven of the settlements in the Duvno region provide definite evidence from pottery and coins that they remained occupied into the Roman period. Radimsky interpreted this as Roman military occupation designed to secure some of the strategic roads in the Županac region. There is little evidence to support this view. Roman military sites have long been identified in the hinterland south of the Dinaric ridge and their character recognized. It was not usual for a Roman army to occupy piecemeal a large number of small native strongholds on grounds

[1] From the survey by Radimsky, *WMBH*, 4 (1896), 136 ff. The complexity of Roman roads in the Duvno area suggests a large population, Pašalić, *Naselja* map at end.

of security. None of the Duvno settlements occupied in the Roman period reveals definite traces of military occupation, in the form of tiles and tombstones, as do those military stations further south. The new roads which came with Roman control facilitated movement and soon began to attract settlement. Native settlements in the more isolated parts of the polje, for example those along the east side, were soon abandoned, but those which were situated close to the roads grew and prospered.

Doubtless the other poljes in the area (Livno, Grahovo, and Glamoč) would reveal a similar picture if they were examined with the same care. One stronghold which belongs to a quite different category is the Vidoši hill fortifications 6 kilometres southeast of Livno.[1] Unlike the Županac settlements it is not on the edge of the level polje but in the hills at the head of the river Studba which flows westward into Livjanskopolje. A roughly circular area was enclosed by a single rampart, and two outlying ramparts branched out to the northwest and the south (fig. 14). The usual defensive mound was at the junction between the latter and the main enclosure. Later the defences were strengthened by a stone wall and the settlement remained occupied into the Roman period. Again Radimsky suggests that the stone defences represent Roman military occupation, but this is unlikely. All the occupation of the Vidoši hill was by the native population: the improvement of the defences became necessary because of its isolated position.

iv *The Bihać Area.* Evidence for the origin and development of hill-forts in this area is provided by the excavations carried out on the Čungar hill near Osredak in the Cazin region.[2] In the wide plain of the river Una a number of native sites have been noted, with a distribution similar to those in the Duvno area. The Cazin site has produced pottery similar to that from the Istrian castellieri. Beginning as a small settlement in the Neolithic period it remained occupied to the end of the Hallstatt Iron Age (about 500–400 B.C.), but appears to have been abandoned long before the Roman period. The main finds of later Iron Age material in the Bihać region come from the large cemeteries, in particular that at Jezerine near Golubić.[3] In this vicinity twenty-six settlements have been identified.[4] Although no larger in area than those further south, they possess more elaborate defences, with ramparts carefully planned to suit the terrain. Most have

---

[1] *WMBH*, 4 (1896), 189, fig. 7–9.   [2] *WMBH*, 4 (1896), 73 ff., fig. 1 ff.
[3] For the Jezerine cemetery, *WMBH*, 1 (1893), 195 f.; 3 (1895), 39, with map on page 40. On Donje Dolina, the Save valley pile-dwelling, see *WMBH*, 9 (1904), 1 ff.; 11 (1909), 1 ff., and now Z. Marić, *GZMS*, 19 (1964), 1–82.
[4] Radimsky, *WMBH*, 4 (1896), 101–12.

single ones, but at the gradina Drenovača near Lohovo, and Crnkica gradina near Cukovi, traces of multivallate defences have been observed. Virtually no finds are known from these sites, some of which probably remained occupied into the Roman period. None of them was a major centre, and if Raetinium has been correctly located in the Bihać region, then it may be one of these small centres. The impact of Roman rule is not difficult to see. By the second century the wealthier families of the area had settled on estates in the plain close to the river Una and had built their houses as *villae rusticae* in the Roman fashion. As in the poljes to the south, no major urban centre developed in the area, and there is no evidence that this was due to lack of encouragement from the provincial government.

Bihać lay in the territory of the Iapodes. When attacked by Octavianus their resistance centred on their chief stronghold at Metulum, not far from Ogulin in the hill country west of Bihać. On the isolated Vinčica hill an impressive series of fortifications once occupied the whole of two plateaux, an area more than 1,000 metres long and 200 metres wide. The scale of these defences is far greater than at any other site in the area; the identification with Metulum is established by an inscription of the Roman period, while Appian's description of the stronghold, 'situated on a thickly wooded mountain, on two ridges with a narrow valley between them', fits the Vinčica perfectly.[1] There is little trace of the ancient defences today, but it was possible for Veith to identify on the ground the route by which Octavinus led the desperate Roman attack on the main entrance of the stronghold. Under Roman rule the hill was abandoned and a new settlement grew up at Čakovac in the valley on the southeast, where a detachment of troops, drawn partly from the Pannonian legions, was maintained in the third century. A similar pattern is found for the hill settlements of the Iapodes in the Lika, all of which can be shown to be superseded later by Roman communities on more convenient sites in the plain.

In the Sana valley north of Bihać, Radimsky identified a group of hill settlements with defences more impressive than those further south, including stone walls and dwelling towers.[2] Roman tiles and other building materials led Radimsky to designate them as Roman military fortifications, but this is unlikely, and some of them, for instance the stone strongholds at Sastavci south of Sanskimost or the Ovangrad in the Japra valley west of the Majdan hills, were clearly native centres.[3] In many respects Northern Bosnia was more difficult to control than the more mountainous areas further south. If the Roman army did occupy key military sites in the area, and this nowhere happened before the later second

[1] Veith, *Feldzüge*, 29 ff.   [2] *WMBH*, 1 (1893), 203 ff.
[3] *WMBH*, 1 (1893), 207 and fig. 2; 214, fig. 6.

century, it was due to military threats from outside, such as the invading Marco-manni. The region west of the Sana valley was a major iron-producing area, and it might have been necessary to provide some protection by the reoccupation of old native strongholds with small military detachments. The wealth of the area appears to have increased rapidly with the Roman conquest and gave rise to an increase in the population: compared with seven pre-Roman sites, twenty-one are attested which began in the Roman period, a growth clearly due to the iron industry.

v *The Interior* (fig. 14). Less is known about the pattern of settlement in East and North Bosnia. Exploration and detailed field work is not easy in this part of the province and little has been carried out. The principal settlement area which has been studied comprises the astonishingly wealthy cemeteries at Glasinac, half-way along the road between Sarajevo and Višegrad. The site is an isolated plateau not far east of the Romanja plateau (1,300 metres), and is covered with groups of small hill-forts; below the settlements were twenty-five groups of burial tumuli, each group containing several hundred burials.[1] In them the bodies were laid for burial on platforms of stone slabs and then surrounded with rings of smaller stones. The total number of burials was more than 20,000, of which sixty per cent were inhumations and thirty per cent cremation with the remainder mixed. The thirty hill-forts on the plateau are all simple in plan, with one rampart and a single entrance. They lacked the citadel common to those in the Duvno region and generally were much less elaborate than Iapodian sites around Bihać. Most of the remains are pre-Roman in date, but the cemetery certainly remained in use well into the Roman period. There is no evidence whether the Glasinac settlements represent an important political group; perhaps some of the main strongholds (*castella*) were inhabited by the rulers of the Dae-sitiates. No comparable community developed in the Roman period, apart from a small city at Rogatica to the east. The comparison between the ancient and modern population appears similar to the estimate for the Duvno region. At the beginning of this century 24,000 people dwelt on the Glasinac; the excavators' estimate for the population in the late Iron Age is 10,000, slightly less than half. Like Jezerine and the Iapodian cemeteries, it was a burial ground for a large area, but there is no evidence that it had any special religious character, as some have suggested. The cemetery was in use for a long period, beginning about 900 B.C. and later receiving imported Greek objects manufactured in the fifth century B.C.

Apart from the Glasinac, one major native settlement in this area has been

[1] Fiala, *WMBH*, 4 (1896), 1 ff., for summary of the site.

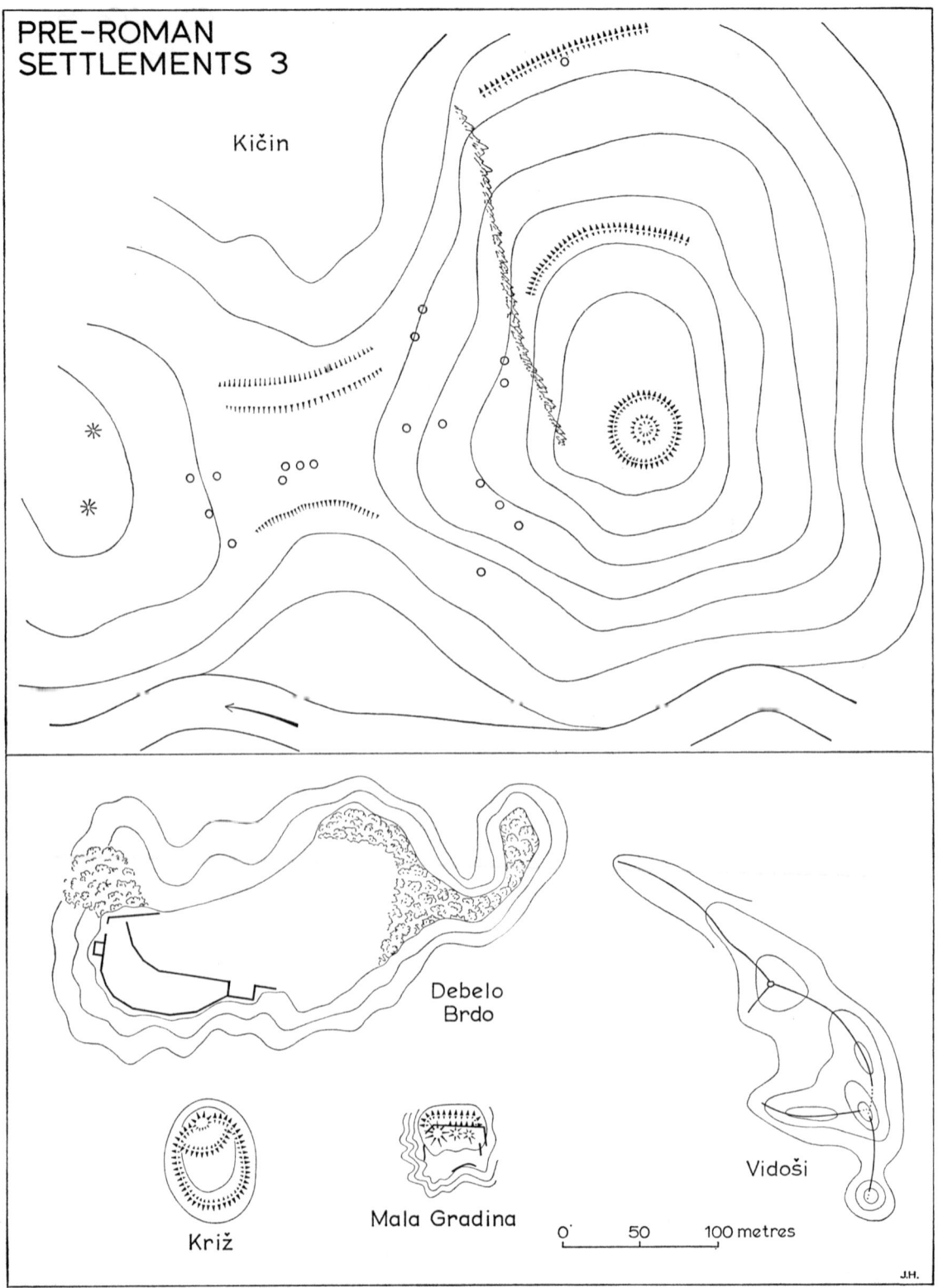

Figure 14 Pre-Roman Settlements 3 (Interior)

excavated, the Debelo brdo near Sarajevo.[1] To the south the city of Sarajevo, which lies in a narrow valley not far from the source of the river Bosna, is dominated by the Trebević mountains (1,629 metres). The Debelo brdo is a western spur of this massif jutting into the Sarajevo plain and protected on all sides by steep cliffs, except on the southwest where two lines of fortifications were constructed in stone (fig. 14). Another may have originally protected the north side, but erosion and landslips have removed virtually all trace of it. The defences consisted of stone walls bonded with mortar. They do not appear to have comprised a serious obstacle to an attacker, since they were never more than 2 metres high. The main wall was constructed in short, straight sections and there were two projecting rectangular towers, one in the outer wall, and a larger in the inner at the point where it is joined by the outer defence. An unprotected gateway was situated in the outer wall not far from the northwest corner. No trace of structures were discovered within the enclosure – presumably they were of timber – but the ground near the stone walls was more than 2 metres deep in occupation material of both pre-Roman and Roman date, including flint and bone artefacts, pottery, bronze, and iron. Bronze Age pottery and artefacts and late La Tène brooches indicate the range of dated material, but the absence of the Hallstatt early Iron Age material suggests a gap in occupation.

The excavator Fiala envisaged the Debelo brdo primarily as a refuge; any community wishing to control the plain of Ilidže around the head of the Bosna must occupy the place, and the range of material found there shows that this is what happened. Fiala also saw the stone defences as a sign of Roman military occupation, but this is very doubtful. It is striking that only three Roman coins were discovered among the vast quantity of material, two illegible third-century issues and a bronze of Justinian I. The Roman occupation may have involved some military control, possibly in association with a tile-works at Satorište, a few hundred yards to the northwest, where graves of the Roman period were discovered. In plan this stronghold resembles some of the larger Istrian castellieri, and its situation compares closely with strongholds in the Mostar area and North-western Bosnia. While it is very different in character from the settlements in the Duvno region, the construction and planning of the stone defences are not unlike those at Osanić near Stolac. Many objects were imported to the Debelo brdo, especially in the La Tène late Iron Age. Brooches and other adornments, including obsidian, amber, and glass beads, all appear in great quantity and variety.

None of the hill-settlements in the interior noted above stands in a close relation to a later Roman city. An exception to this may be the city at Plevlje, for which the only detailed description and plan was made by Evans nearly a cen-

[1] *WMBH*, 4 (1896), 38 ff.; cf. 5 (1897) 124 ff.; 6 (1899), 128 ff.

tury ago.[1] The modern town is situated on the north side of a plain near the head of the Čehotina valley. The site of the Roman city is near the confluence with the Vežeznica, close to the village of Vidre, where extensive remains of Roman buildings and debris can be seen over a large area. Higher up the valley, about 2 kilometres south of the city, is the hill Sveti Ilija (St. Elias). The numerous inscriptions and sculptures found on the site near Vidre are classical in style with good lettering and many of them belong to upper-class families, while those from the hill-settlement are much cruder and have a large proportion of Illyrian names. The site was never abandoned until Turkish times: coins of the Byzantine period have been found there and the hill is still crowned with a small Serbian Orthodox church from which the hill takes its name. It seems that the native settlement, Splonum, if the identification proposed earlier is correct (p. 282), was on the Sveti Ilija hill; it declined in prosperity but remained occupied while a new city developed in a more spacious site in the plain near Vidre. This is the only purely native site in the interior which has produced substantial traces of its community in the Roman period, including tombstones in Latin.

11 *The Cities Compared*

Virtually all the cities which grew and prospered in Southern Dalmatia were on, or very close to, the coast, and most enjoyed the advantages of a good harbour. Obviously most of the traffic between these cities was carried by water, for such a mountainous coastline made land-travel tedious and expensive. The Adriatic is safe for coastal shipping during most of the year, apart from occasional periods of stormy weather. Even then the islands of the Quarnerno and the screen of smaller islands which protect the coast between the Ravni kotari and Pelješac peninsula give a great measure of shelter from the fierce north wind (Bora) which blows down the Adriatic during the winter months. It is significant that neither Scardona nor Narona, the only two major cities in the area which grew up at some distance from the sea, appears to have maintained its prosperity into the later period. Scardona was 11 miles from the sea on the river Titius and its role today has been taken over by Šibenik, the mediaeval centre which lies on the large salt-water lake through which the river flows into the sea. By far the best harbour facilities were enjoyed by the provincial capital Salona, at the head of its large bay shut off by the peninsula Marijan to the south and to the north by the island Čiovo, which is separated from the mainland only by a very narrow sea-channel at Tragurium. The ancient Salona was abandoned in the early

[1] Evans, *Archaeologia* 49 (1884), 29, fig. 10; also Patsch, *WMBH*, 4 (1896), 276 ff.; 8 (1901), 115 f.; 12 (1912), 102 ff.

seventh century when the arrival of Slav and Avar invaders forced the Roman population to seek refuge in the old palace of Diocletian a few miles to the south on the open sea shore. The central part of the Dalmatian coastline runs on an almost east–west axis. To the north the peninsular of St. Nicolas (*promunturium Diomedis*) protects the region of Salona, including the islands Pharia, Brattia, and Corcyra Nigra; this contributes to the closeness of the places throughout the centuries. Elsewhere there were many good harbours, as Strabo records,[1] but there were other factors which prevented their settlements developing beyond the level of villages, as most of them remain today. On the west side of Istria, Albona and Flanona were isolated cities at the head of fiords cutting into the waterless karst plateau. The north Liburnian coast is shut off from the interior by the Velebit mountains which fall steeply into the sea for a distance of nearly 100 miles. Even cities such as Senia cling to the foot of the rocky coastline, while many of the smaller places to the south which obtained city status in the first century can barely be approached from the land. The wealth of Liburnia lay in the plain of the Ravni kotari, which itself was shut off from the interior by a southward continuation of the Velebit and the Dinaric mountains. Iader has an excellent, although small, harbour, and a considerable part of its wealth was derived from its own territory as well the trade between inland Liburnia and Italy.

There are good harbours south of the Narenta. Epidaurum on its small peninsula developed more than one harbour before being overwhelmed by the sea, probably in the fourth century A.D. The deep recesses of the Gulf of Kotor provided ideal secluded anchorages, too secluded indeed, and more suitable for pirate strongholds than bases for Adriatic sea trade. The surrounding mountains prevented all but the lightest traffic with the interior. Near the mouth of the Drin, Lissus enjoyed a good harbour, but the river is an unreliable channel and not always suitable for larger vessels. Lissus was never an important port of call for coastal shipping and most of the long-distance traffic from Istria and northern Italy would probably call at Iader or Salona, and then pass on directly to Apollonia, Dyrrhachium, or Corcyra (Corfu). Across the Adriatic the two principal sea routes given in the *Itinerarium Maritimum* were from Ancona to Iader (105 miles) and from Aternum to Salona (185), with a third from Sipuntum to Salona (185 miles).[2] The major part of the traffic with Italy passed through these two ports.

The coastal cities developed where they did because of harbours and the trade they attracted from the interior, but only those with substantial territories of

---

[1] vii, 5, 10.

[2] *It. Marit.*, 497, 2, 3, 8 (p. 78, ed. Cuntz).

good land grew to any size. The cities which developed in the hinterland between the coast and the Dinaric ridge and those in the northern valley developed purely because of local conditions and resources. One or two centres did grow out of early Roman military stations, but these were the exception. Cities at Burnum, Magnum, and Novae began as extra-mural settlements around forts or from *stationes* manned by *beneficiarii consulares*. As a colony of discharged Roman troops, Aequum was an external creation and was able to prosper because of the generous grants of land made to it by the Roman government. On the other hand, Doclea appears to have grown from an existing native settlement, well-protected at the confluence of two rivers but away from the major roads which lead from Narona to Lissus. It had no direct contact with the sea and very few external outlets, in spite of the dominant position attained by upper-class Doclea families in Southeast Dalmatia.

In the poljes further north Pelva and Salvium grew up on the main road between Salona and Servitium, but they never became real urban centres; most of the population dwelt in small hamlets around the edge of the poljes, often far apart and sometimes inaccessible for some months of the year. Cities developed where communications were best; in this respect the impact of Roman rule was much greater in the northern part of the province than in the south where urban centres had already begun to develop. Most of the cities in the three major valleys of the north were established on new sites, and conveniently situated for the main roads. In this category are the city at Šipovo in the Pliva valley and Bistue Nova in the Lašva valley. In neither area has any major pre-Roman site been identified; both the Roman centres are on new sites very close to the river. The spa resort at Ilidže lies close to the river Bosna, in the wide plain near its source. Excavation on the site have only produced traces of the spa buildings and there is no indication that a large proportion of the native population was attracted to settle there, abandoning their more remote strongholds such as the Debelo brdo (p. 353) which continued to be occupied into the Roman period. A major centre of the Daesitiates was Bréza, north of Sarajevo; this is probably to be identified with the Hedum *castellum* which was the terminal point of one of the early military roads from Salona to the interior. No trace of the settlement is known and it is possible that the richer land around Ilidže attracted some of the people although some of the native upper-class families were still at Bréza in the middle of the second century A.D. Further east all the Roman cities, apart from Maluesa and the mining centre Domavia, lay in the valleys of the Drina or one of its major tributaries. Most of the settlements around Zvornik and Bijelina in the Drina valley are close to the river, as are the cities at Skelani and at Rogatica in the Prača valley. The city at Plevlje was more isolated near the head of the Čehotina valley; it was the only major centre of the interior so far removed from a major river.

Until more excavation, rather than surface field work, has been carried out the picture of the beginnings of urbanization in the province must remain far from complete. Until one of the city sites has been examined and its earliest phases studied very little can be said about the growth conditions for cities in the northern part of the province. On the other hand, the fairly plentiful epigraphic evidence suggests that city life in the physical sense began quite suddenly, along with grants of legal status and Roman citizenship. Some of the old hill-settlements remained occupied throughout the Roman period, but the wealth and administration of the interior soon became based in the new cities, except among the Iapodes, where no great changes appear to have taken place. Further east the growth of cities in the lands of the Daesitiates, Pirustae, and Dindari in the late first and second centuries A.D. had a profound effect on the upper classes and their pattern of life.

The cities on the coast grew and prospered from earlier communities. In spite of political changes brought about by Roman conquest, Italian settlement, and the civil wars, the cities near the coast grew rapidly, and from the very beginning the prosperity of the area was dependent upon them. By contrast, the development of cities in the interior was due partly to pressure from the Roman government and initially they were grafted on to the tribal society of the native peoples. None of these foundations is known to have become a compact urban centre, with the full range of public buildings, organized street-plan, and city defences. For the most part all that is known about these centres is one or two isolated buildings with no signs of the proper civic amenities such as large baths, water supply, or city drainage. Insecurity in the fifth and sixth centuries brought about their decline and eventually their total disappearance. None of them was defended and the appearance of invaders within the Empire drove the population back to the old hill-forts, many of them abandoned centuries before. The large number of mediaeval hill-fortresses in Bosnia represents this pattern of life, the natural reaction of the population when freedom from attack was not guaranteed by a powerful authority such as the Roman army.[1] Conditions of the time and local material advantage determined the siting of the cities in the interior, rather than any imagined political considerations. In the long term, however, the Roman cities in the interior were failures. None of them are great centres of population today. Sarajevo, Banjaluka, Travnik, Jajce, and Zvornik owe noth-

[1] For example Visućgrad near Šipovljani in Northwest Bosnia, *WMBH*, 4 (1896), 174 ff., and the fortress constructed in the ancient defences at Meteon (Medun) in the southeast, Praschniker-Schober, 5, fig. 7.

ing to earlier Roman settlements. Places such as Bistue Nova, Maluesa, and the city at Šipovo are now almost deserted or little more than villages. The mining centres remained occupied for their mineral wealth, but even at Domavia the silver deposits were later worked from a centre at Srebrenica in the next valley rather than Gradina, the site of Domavia.

Few of the cities in Dalmatia have been explored extensively by excavation. Salona, with its wealth of Christian remains, has always been the principal attraction to scholars, the leading city of the province on a site which has not been built on since the place was overrun by the Slav invaders in the early seventh century. By contrast, until the disastrous bombing raids during the Second World War destroyed much of the mediaeval city of Zadar, virtually nothing was known of Roman Iader, still the leading city of the region. Since the destruction archaeological research has yielded new evidence for the city defences, its street plan, and some of its principal buildings. Apart from the few cases where city buildings have been excavated and planned, the most prominent remains of ancient cities to survive above ground are the defences, some of which are preserved to near their original height (fig. 15). Nowhere can the magnificent walls of Dubrovnik be rivalled among the Roman cities, but the provision of walls and the character of the defences throw some light on their early history and later physical development. Three cities on the Dalmatian coast still retain circuits of Roman walls which are nearly complete, or which can still be clearly traced on the surface, Salona, Lissus, and Doclea. In Liburnia the best preserved defences which have been studied are those at Asseria.[1]

The walls of Salona were built in the first and second centuries A.D. The problems of the two separate enclosures (fig. 16), the earlier western *urbs vetus* and the eastern *urbs nova*, have already been discussed as they affect the history of the colony (p. 224 f.). In their present state they represent the remains of a much altered complex of defences, beginning with the walls of the original Caesarian colony and ending with the major reconstruction carried out by the Byzantine general Constantianus after he had recovered Salona from the Goths in 536. The

[1] The following table indicates the areas enclosed within city walls (where known):

Iader	1,700 by 800 metres	136·0 hectares	(326·0 acres)
Salona	1,590 by 700 metres	94·4 hectares	(233·3 acres)
Doclea	800 by 300 metres	24·0 hectares	(59·3 acres)
Lissus	710 by 255 metres	17·85 hectares	(44·1 acres)
Aequum	410 by 330 metres	13·0 hectares	(32·1 acres)
Issa	265 by 360 metres	9·54 hectares	(24·7 acres)
Asseria	440 by 170 metres	8·0 hectares	(19·8 acres)
Argyruntum	220 by 150 metres	3·3 hectares	(8·2 acres)

For the walls of cities not discussed in the section see below, n. 3, p. 367.

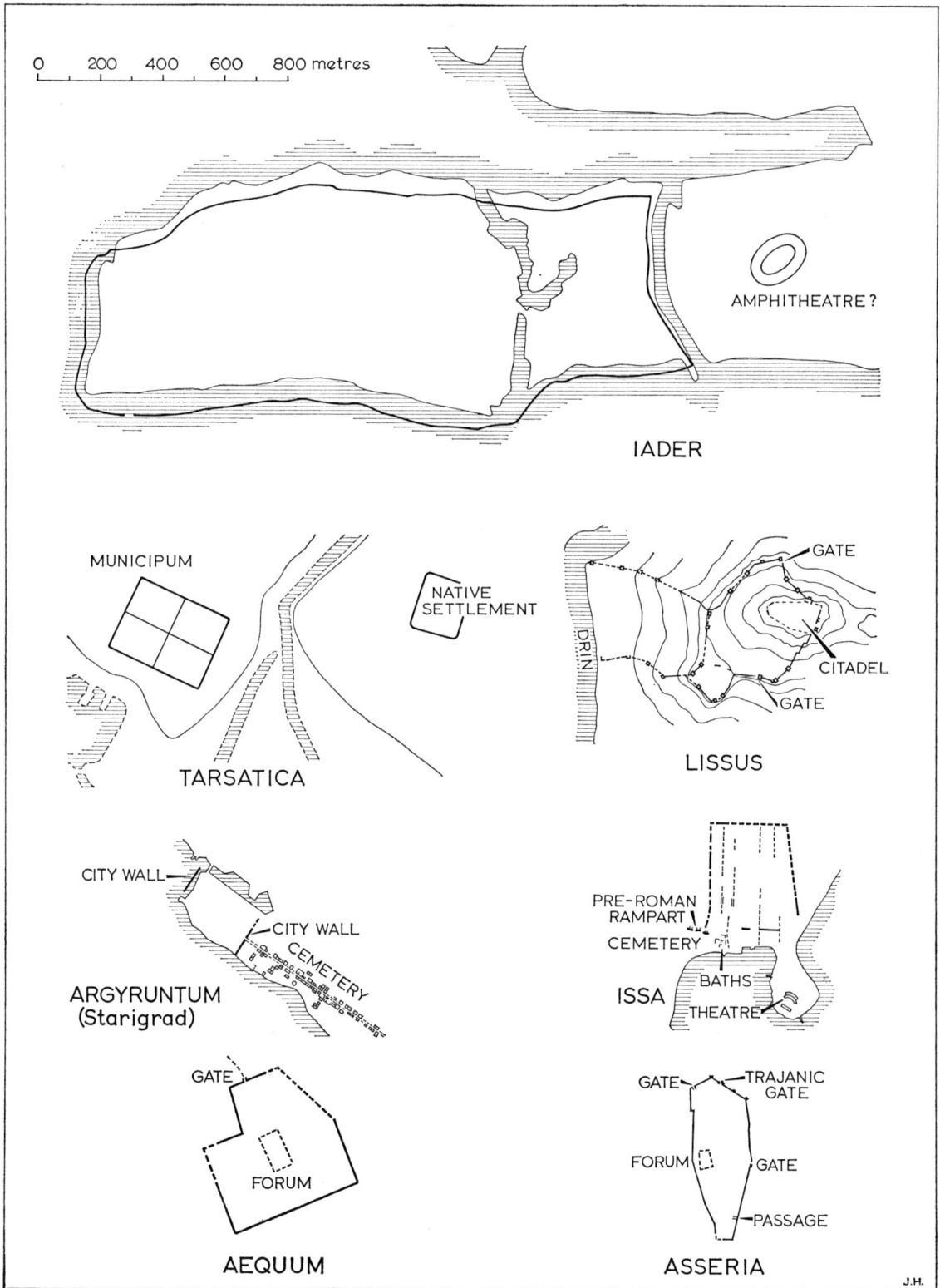

0   200   400   600   800 metres

AMPHITHEATRE?

IADER

MUNICIPUM

NATIVE
SETTLEMENT

TARSATICA

DRIN

GATE

CITADEL

GATE

LISSUS

CITY WALL

CITY WALL

CEMETERY

ARGYRUNTUM
(Starigrad)

PRE-ROMAN
RAMPART

CEMETERY

BATHS

THEATRE

ISSA

GATE

FORUM

AEQUUM

GATE

TRAJANIC
GATE

FORUM

GATE

PASSAGE

ASSERIA

J.H.

Figure 15 Outline Town Plans

north sector of the walls of the *urbs nova* still exhibits the building records of the Marcomannic emergency in 170. Another major reconstruction is attested under Theodosius II in the early fifth century, followed by the last rebuilding in 536.[1] Along the north wall of both enclosures, the sectors which faced attacks from the interior, ninety-two towers and turrets were added to the face of the wall. The rectangular towers belong to the Theodosian reconstruction, while the triangular ones were added in the sixth century.[2] Few detailed statistics are available for the Salona walls. Part of the west wall was examined at the end of the last century when sectioned by the construction of the railway between Split and Knin. Here the breadth was found to vary from 3.95 to 4.25 metres, and the construction was of massive smoothly dressed blocks of limestone. Most of this part appears to have been a later rebuilding, to judge from the incorporation of sculptured stones, probably from tombstones. Along the south the line of the walls can be determined in the marshy ground near the sea, and it is clear from the irregular course followed by the walls of the *urbs vetus* and *nova* that both were built along the shore-line, but apparently with no open quay or harbour buildings. In the northwest corner the amphitheatre is enclosed by the walls, probably a later modification when it served as a defensive bastion of monumental size.

Diligent search has been made for traces of an earlier period of fortifications. Some hundred metres west of the *urbs vetus* M. Abramić excavated a strip of ground alongside the road which led from the west gate, prior to the reconstruction of the modern road. Alongside the road on the north was a Roman cemetery which is named on a tombstone as the '(funeral) garden of Metrodorus' (*hortus Metrodori*). It was an area enclosed by a wall of monumental masonry, with individual blocks more than four metres long, within which were marked out by dividing walls a number of family burial plots.[3] It was suggested that this was part of a pre-Roman defensive wall, associated with the hypothetical Greek Salona. In spite of the monumental masonry, nothing in the remains suggests that it was part of a defensive enclosure, nor is there any evidence for a Greek Salona as implied by Abramić. Although there are traces of an Illyrian settlement on a hill near by, probably belonging to the Iadastinoi, there is no hint of any defences which can be dated earlier than the foundation of the colony. In the double circuit of walls there were six gates.[4] The best preserved gate in the whole

[1] Theodosian reconstruction: III, 1984; sixth-century: Procop. *BG*, i, 7, 36 and below, p. 426.
[2] For excavations and interpretations of the Salona walls, Abramić, *FS*, 1, 4 ff.; E. Dyggve, *RS*, 1, 18; and in general E. Ceci, *Salona Pagana*, 72 f., and pl. 27.
[3] Abramić, *VAHD*, 52 (1935–49), 1–18. The *hortus Metrodori* is mentioned on a tombstone, III, 2207. The theory of an earlier Greek city was accepted by Dyggve, who deduced a north–south wall across the *urbs vetus*, *HSC*, fig. 1, 4–6.
[4] Ceci, *Salona Pagana*, 73 f., with plan plate iv, 2.

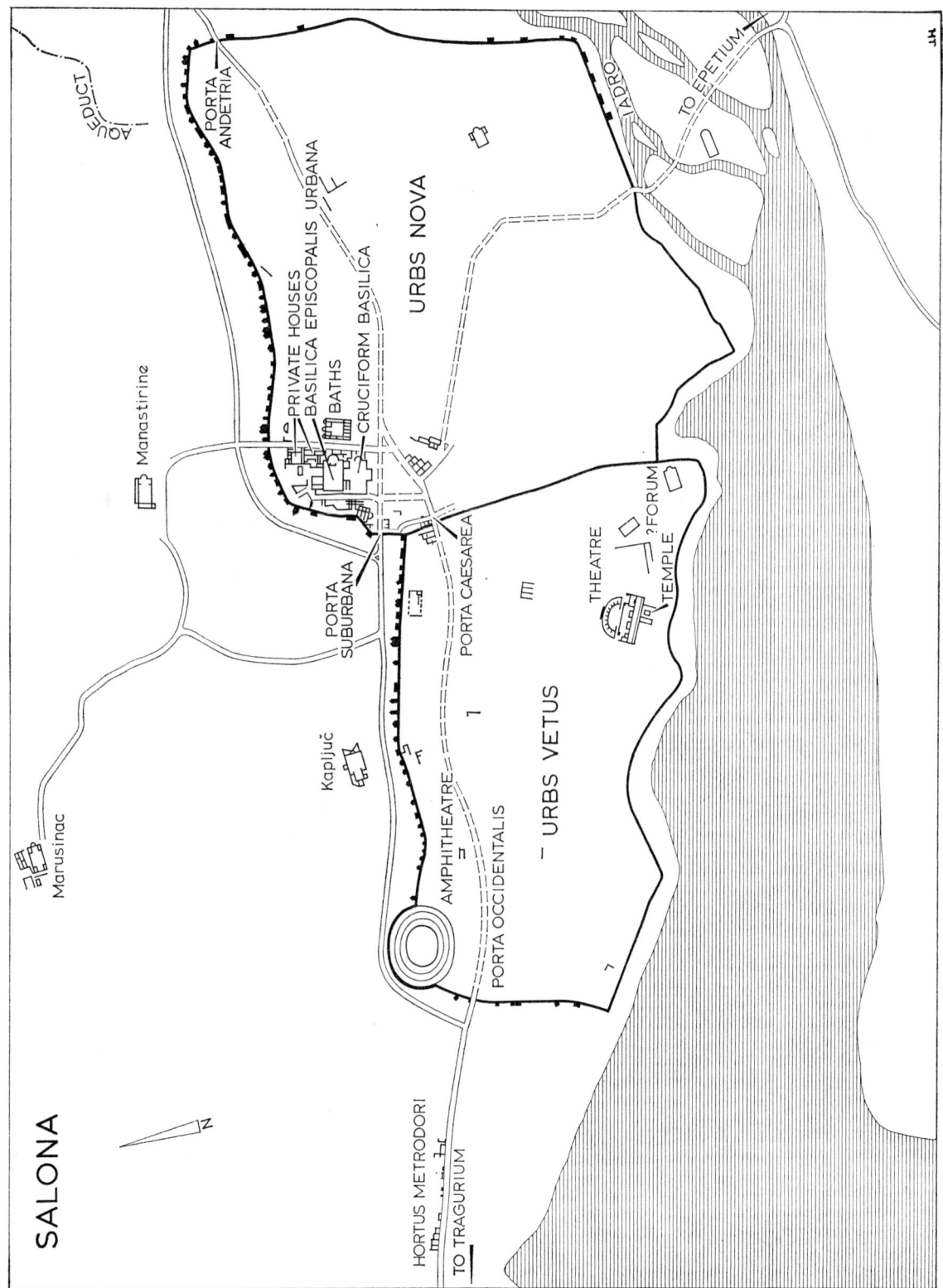

Figure 16 Plan of Salona

province is the Salona *porta Caesarea* (fig. 21) which has an unusual plan.[1] The city wall on either side of the gate still runs near its original height. It lay not in the defences of the double city but in the north of the east wall of the *urbs vetus*, later the dividing wall between the two parts of the double city. This wall survived into the later period, when a road was constructed along the top of it between the two enclosures. In the gate a single passage was provided for wheeled traffic, and on either side were two passages for pedestrians, each 1.3 metres wide. The surface around the gate was paved with stone flags. In the front on either side, later within the *urbs nova*, were two eight-sided towers, only one of which survives above foundation level. They were built as independent structures and were not bonded in with the wall. Typologically the plan of the gate is early, and the original building took place about the time of Augustus, although most of the masonry surviving in the superstructure belongs to the middle of the fourth century, when it was reconstructed under Constantius II.[2] To the north the *porta suburbia* in the northwest angle of the *urbs nova* was probably for pedestrians only, being 2.75 metres wide, although it was approached from the east by a full-width street.[3] Towards the interior of the province the principal route led over the pass at Klis to Andetrium. The road, the *via Gabiniana*, was built originally by the army under Tiberius and led out of the city through a single-passage gate in the northeast corner of the *urbs nova*. This is the only gate which can be linked with a major road leading from the city. The *porta surburbia* gave pedestrian access to an area off the north side of the *urbs vetus*. Here there is evidence that settlements had grown up around the walls at an early date, and in the fourth century there were established the great Christian martyr shrines at Manastirine, Marusinac, and Kapljuć. The gate in the southeast corner of the *urbs nova* was the only exit which led towards the harbour, which Salona must have possessed; it gave access across the mouth of the river Iadro towards Epetium on the coast to the east of Split.

Although they do not remain such impressive ruins as those at Salona or Doclea, the walls of Lissus (fig. 15) were some of the most ambitions fortifications of any city in the province. They enclose not only the city alongside the river Drin but also the citadel on a nearby hill 180 metres high. The much higher Acrolissus (p. 338, fig. 12) was the major fortification in the area of the city and about two kilometres inland; it was captured by Philip of Macedon in 213 B.C.[4]

---

[1] W. Gerber, *FS*, 1, 131 ff.

[2] Augustan inscription: H. Kähler, *VAHD*, 51 (1930–4), 13, fig. 5. For fourth-century rebuilding, III, 8710; cf. Gerber, *FS*, 1, 132, fig. 243. All the names of the gates are modern inventions.

[3] Gerber, *FS*, 1, 119 ff.   [4] Praschniker-Schober, 14 ff.

The perimeter of the walls is more than 2,200 metres. Although there is a wall which divides off the citadel from the remainder of the city the whole complex appears to have been part of one constructional programme. The curtain wall is faced with blocks of limestone about half a metre square and has an average thickness of 3.5 metres, slightly narrower than the Salona wall. Even along the moderate slopes the courses of masonry were laid horizontal, and tapered away towards the foundations in a manner reminiscent of the old polygonal techniques, although the construction is quite different. The faces of the stones have been worn away by exposure, apart from one of the towers where the masonry dressing is still to be seen in its original condition. The entire circuit of the Lissus walls is protected by towers all built at the same time as the walls; most measure between 8 and 10 metres across and project, according to their siting, from 1.5 to 8 metres beyond the face of the wall. At almost every angle the curtain wall changes direction at a tower, each separate stretch of wall being built in a straight line. Two gates survive, both leading into the citadel, on the north and east sides. Below in the city there must have been two gates, on the north and south sides, for the road along the river Drin which led to Scodra. There is no evidence for the date of these fortifications; Caesar records that he furnished Lissus with defences, probably late in his proconsulship, and an inscription records wall-building taking place under the direction of a city magistrate, perhaps early under Augustus.[1] An earlier date is possible. Lissus was a stronghold, in fact the principal sea base, of the Illyrian kingdom and was a mint for Gentius. He must have fortified the place in the second century B.C., and was responsible for the original plan of the walls, which were later refurbished under Caesar and Augustus.

The most impressive remains of city walls in the province are those at Doclea.[2] They enclose an area surrounded on almost all sides by natural chasms up to 20 metres deep, the rivers Zeta and Morača, and the Širalja torrent bed. Only for a short distance of 400 metres does the wall face out upon level ground, and at this point a double ditch system was added to compensate (fig. 17). To follow the lines of these natural defences the walls take an irregular course in the shape of a trapezium, although where possible the curtain wall was built in straight lengths with frequent changes of direction. No plan of any gate survives, but the position of the main gate is established by the main street of the city and a gap in the surviving wall, while the existence of a smaller entrance on the south is indicated by the traces of a bridge across the chasm of the river Morača.

Unlike at Lissus, two periods of construction can be detected in the Doclea walls, the later additions being some external towers on the north side facing the

[1] Caes. *BC*, iii, 29; III, 1704.　　[2] Sticotti, *Doclea*, 45–64.

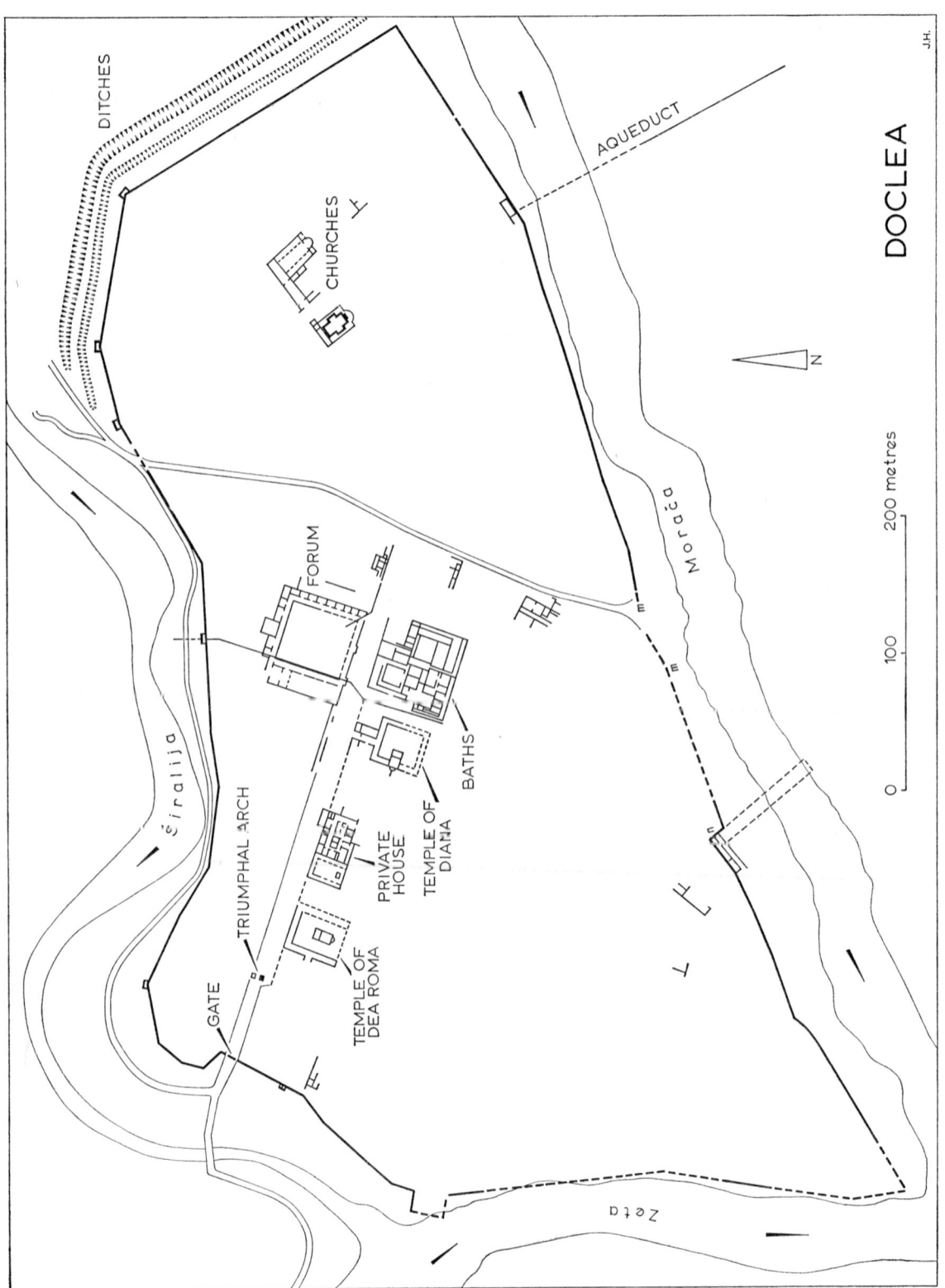

Figure 17 Plan of Doclea

Širalja torrent bed, in that part of the defences which faces the interior. In breadth the wall varies from 2 to 2.3 metres and in height to the parapet-walk from 3 to 6 metres. In some sectors the stability of the wall was a problem, and a concrete foundation was laid to a depth of 1 metre, half a metre wider than the full width of the standing wall. The stone for the walls and the lime for the mortar had to be carried from some distance, the limestone probably from Spuž, higher up the Zeta valley on the road to Nikšić. The masonry of the wall is small, 25 by 33 cm., and dressed smooth, but the later external towers are built from larger rusticated blocks measuring 1.7 by 0.6 metres. Along the inside face of the wall there were sockets for horizontal beams to accommodate a wooden platform set half-way up the side of the wall. As at Salona and Lissus, there were no traces of an earthen bank built up against the inside of the wall.

The main gate was in the west wall a little to the north of the Širalja mouth, where the road from Diluntum and Narona entered the city. This was a branch from the main route and the city itself is not listed on any of the road lists for the province. At a width of more than 15 metres the road which entered the city was unusually wide, but nothing is known of the plan or construction of the gate, apart from a door lintel discovered in debris near by. On each side the wall makes an inward turn towards the position of the gate. This part of the defences appears to have been constructed or reconstructed in times of emergency since it contained no less than twenty inscriptions, including six imperial dedications originally set up by the city in the forum basilica. The latest is dedicated to Valerian in 254 and indicates that some of this building may have taken place during the insecurity of the third century, although a much later date is possible.[1]

Thus cities in the south reveal simple defensive circuits of walls with towers, elaborated in some cases over more than six hundred years. It is striking that the type of fortifications which a city required remained much the same; apparently little adaptation was felt to be necessary to suit changes in techniques of warfare. The Lissus defences were a formidable enclosure with external towers built at one period which, apart from repair when necessary, remained unchanged until the end of the Roman period. The Salona defences grew in stages. Elaborate gateways, more ornamental than defensive, were further elaborated in the later period, while rows of external towers were added along the north side when real danger threatened in the fifth and sixth centuries. The Doclea walls were built last of the three, and were later improved by external towers, probably at the same time as those at Salona. Tactically Doclea was the most protected, but it had the serious disadvantage of being away from the sea coast and could therefore be easily blockaded by a land force advancing from the interior.

[1] III, 12684–13823; cf. Sticotti, *Doclea*, 163, n. 18, fig. 112.

The inland cities of the Ravni kotari, Corinium, Nedinum, Asseria, Varvaria, and the others, were all provided with defences before the Roman conquest and these survived as city defences into the late Roman period. Best preserved are those at Asseria and Varvaria, but only the former have been examined in detail. The site of Asseria is a steep-sided hill with a plateau measuring 440 by 170 metres (fig. 15), all of which is enclosed by the irregular oblong of the walls.[1] It is constructed from two lines of rusticated masonry set about 4 metres apart with the intervening space filled with rubble set in mortar. The height of the courses varies according to the terrain from 0.3 to 0.8 metres. Three gates led into the city, two on the short north side where the city's hill is linked to a range of hills on the northwest. The third is on the east side and is flanked by a tower which projects 3.6 metres beyond the wall. The gate passage is 1.28 metres wide; earlier visitors to the site noted that its archway was intact, at least until the middle of the nineteenth century. Not far south of this gate a narrow passage 0.8 metres wide led through the wall; it is not clear what its function was.

The main gate and the strongest part of the fortifications were on the north, which was the area where any attack on the city could be expected. Here the wall incorporates four square external towers, built as an integral part of the pre-Roman Liburnian defences. In the northwest corner a small gate 4 metres wide was inset from the outside face of the wall by nearly 12 metres. All these features were part of the fortifications of Liburnian Asseria. The construction technique was no doubt adapted from Greek originals or possibly from the strongholds in the old Illyrian kingdom to the south. In the time of the Roman city the only alteration was the insertion of a monumental gate in the style of a triumphal arch under Trajan (fig. 21). It is set at an angle to the line of the wall so that it stood across the axis of the main north south street in the city. Part of one projecting tower was sliced away to accommodate the new entrance, indicating that the times of danger when the defences were first built were long forgotten. Although it had been almost entirely destroyed it was possible for the Austrian excavators to produce a complete plan and reconstruction from the architectural debris in the area. A single passage more than 4 metres wide was flanked by two square foundations giving a total width for the whole structure of 13.48 metres. Across the front of the gate were six half-columns, three on either side of the passage. At the rear four of the six columns were free-standing, only those nearest the entrance being half-columns. All were topped with Corinthian capitals. The building and dedication of the gate were recorded on two panels set in the front over the entrance, above and below the architrave. The upper records the dedication to Trajan at the end of 113, the lower the name of the local worthy L. Laelius

[1] H. Liebl and W. Wilberg, *JÖAI*, 11 (1908), Bb. 17 ff., with plan fig. 2.

Proculus, who paid for it and gave a civic banquet to celebrate the occasion.[1]
Below the architrave and above the vaulting of the arch were two sculptured
bull heads; in the same positions on the back were two bearded male heads with
horns and animal ears.[2] Totally irrelevant to any consideration of defence, this
gate proclaims the security of the Empire by its resemblance to a triumphal arch;
its siting at an angle to the wall seems indeed to emphasize its non-military
character. Some time later the gate passage was narrowed with the needs of
defence once more in mind, and the rest of the walls were doubtless refurbished.
Nothing is known about the fate of Asseria in the late sixth and early seventh
centuries at the time of the Slav and Avar invasions.

The principal buildings to be found in a typical Roman provincial city were
fora, temples, and baths, usually incorporated into the central blocks of a
street grid-plan. The evidence for internal planning in the cities of the province
is scanty, although Iader and probably Salona had planned street-grids. At the
former aerial photographs and excavations provide the evidence. In the case of
Salona, the confusion of later buildings has obliterated the original plan, but the
irregular growth of the city and the haphazard positioning of the gates do not
suggest an original overall plan (fig. 16). In Liburnia Tarsatica and Argyruntum certainly had regular street plans, but in Dalmatia Issa is the only centre (fig.
15) which has yielded extensive traces of a street-grid.[3] The colony at Aequum
was a planned city: as far as was possible on the site the walls followed a regular
plan, and the forum is placed symmetrically in a central position at the end of the
street which leads into the city through the main gate. At Doclea the main street
ran in a straight line across the irregular area enclosed by the defences, with all
the known buildings fronting on to it and separated into *insulae* by side streets;[4]
there is no evidence how the rest of the city was planned. Not even the main
public buildings at Asseria were aligned on a regular plan; the forum is near the
edge of the plateau against the city wall (fig. 15), and the rest of the known
buildings are distributed in an irregular scatter (fig. 19). The Asseria plateau
was too uneven for a regular plan to be feasible – although in other provincial
cities it was often used in most unsuitable locations – and no attempt was made

[1] *JÖAI*, 11 (1908), Bb. 71–4, fig. 49–50.

[2] *JÖAI*, 11 (1908), Bb. 41, fig. 21–2.

[3] Apart from those discussed above, cities where at least some part of the city walls and plan
is known include Aequum: *JÖAI*, 16 (1913), Bb. 139, fig. 37; Narona: Patsch, *Narona* 9 ff., and
plate II; Iader: Brunelli, *Zara*, 124 ff., and Suić, *Zbornik*, 2 (1958), 20 ff., fig. 4 f.; Issa: B. Gabričević, *Urbs*, 2 (1958), with plan; cf. Novak, *Vis*, fig. 27 ff.; Tarsatica: a plan of a rectangular
enclosure (with no scale) is published by A. Degrassi, *Confine*, pl. VI; Aenona: M. Cagiano de
Azevedo, *RPAA*, 22 (1948), 193 ff.

[4] Sticotti, *Doclea*, plan; cf. fig. 17.

to produce one. The cities where grid plans are known were all early Julio–Claudian foundations, Argyruntum a Tiberian *municipium*, and Iader an Augustan colony (fig. 15). Both were probably planned as new settlements when the government granted them walls. The old *conventus* settlements in the south (Salona, Narona, Lissus, etc.) were not disturbed in this way. There is no evidence for any planning in the interior. The only city for which a settlement plan is available is the Domavia mining settlement (fig. 19), where the chaotic arrangement of building in the narrow glen reflects the rapid growth it achieved during the late second and early third centuries.

Pride of place in a Roman provincial city was given to its administrative centre, the forum. This was usually a rectangular area at the centre of the city, paved or gravelled, which occupied a complete street block and was enclosed on three sides by colonnades. Around the outside were often ranges of rooms designed as shops or offices. The principal buildings of the forum complex were normally placed along that side of the open forum opposite the main entrance. These consisted of the city hall (*basilica*), a number of smaller rooms including the council chamber (*curia*) where the local senate met, and other rooms for legal and financial administration. In some forums a civic shrine, containing imperial statues and other civic dedications, was also part of the complex. In appearance and function the provincial *fora* of this type closely resemble the headquarters (*principia*) of a legionary fortress, and indeed appear to be derived from it.

The most imposing forum known in Dalmatia was not of this type. Recent excavations have begun to reveal the Iader forum to be a double precinct. An oblong court with two entrances, each set about the middle of the long sides, more than 180 metres long and 130 metres wide, represents two elements. In one half was the open market area of the forum surrounded by colonnades with the city *basilica* across the end; the other contained a classical temple (*capitolium*) and altars. The complex is similar to the fora of some Gallic cities built in the later first century A.D.[1] The eleventh-century church of St. Donatus is built directly upon the stone paving of the Roman forum, and in its foundations are incorporated many sections from pillars, Corinthian capitals, and parts of the two monumental altars dedicated to Juno Augusta.[2] Of the temple little survives, but excavations have revealed that it was part of the original complex and was set on a high podium. For the area of the city, at its greatest 1,700 by 800 metres, the Iader forum is unusually large. It is the only double precinct known in the province; all the other forums are of the simpler single-enclosure type described

[1] To be published by Dr. M. Suić.
[2] Brunelli, *Zara*, 128 ff., figs. 45–50.

above. The Iader forum is certainly Julio–Claudian, possibly Augustan; the *basilica*, however, across the southeast side was not part of the original plan, but was a later addition along with other alterations of unknown date. Fora of the more orthodox type are known in four cities of the province, Asseria, Aequum, Delminium, and Doclea (fig. 18), the last being the best preserved, with the *basilica* walls standing more than three metres high. The Asseria forum was built in the middle of the first century A.D., while that of Delminium was dedicated under Hadrian or Antoninus Pius.

Only the rear part of the Asseria forum (fig. 18) is preserved, but enough remains to indicate its size and character.[1] Overall the building was 70 metres wide but the open area in the middle was only 28.6. Behind this was an area of paving raised above the level of the courtyard which gave access to the buildings at the rear. These consisted of a narrow transverse corridor which opened into a series of chambers 8.9 metres wide across the rear of the entire building. The central three of these were really a hall more than 40 metres long, the partitions being no more than wide arches. It is not certain whether this was the city *basilica*, since on either side of the open forum were aisled halls. Only the stylobate survives to indicate the columns in both halls, but the debris produced considerable architectural remains including Corinthian capitals. The decoration and construction of the forum was similar to that of the triumphal arch at the north gate. Like the gate it was built by a magistrate, L. Caninius Fronto. His priesthood of the deified Claudius (*divus Claudius*) dates him to the middle of the first century.[2]

The Aequum forum occupied the proper central position in the city (fig. 15), but it was built slightly off the alignment of the main street of the colony, which indicates that the building of the forum and the planning of the street grid were not carried out at the same time.[3] Overall it measured 90 by 60 metres and consisted of an open paved courtyard flanked on three sides by colonnades and shops (fig. 18). The way in from the street was an elaborate two stage entrance; along the back of the enclosure was a raised podium, also paved, but there was no sign of the *basilica*. Behind the raised area was a range of rooms which formed the centre of the colony's administration. Two stairways entered the central room which measured 9 metres square; this was most likely the senate house (*curia*). On either side were other rooms, one of which contained imperial statues and was the centre of civic cults. There is no epigraphic evidence for the date of the Aequum forum, but the city has produced some tiles stamped by Legion VII C.p.f. (the only site in the province to have done so); these may

---

[1] *JÖAI*, 11 (1908), Bb. 47 ff.   [2] *JÖAI*, 11 (1908), 70, fig. 47.
[3] E. Reisch, *JÖAI*, 16 (1913), Bb. 135 ff.

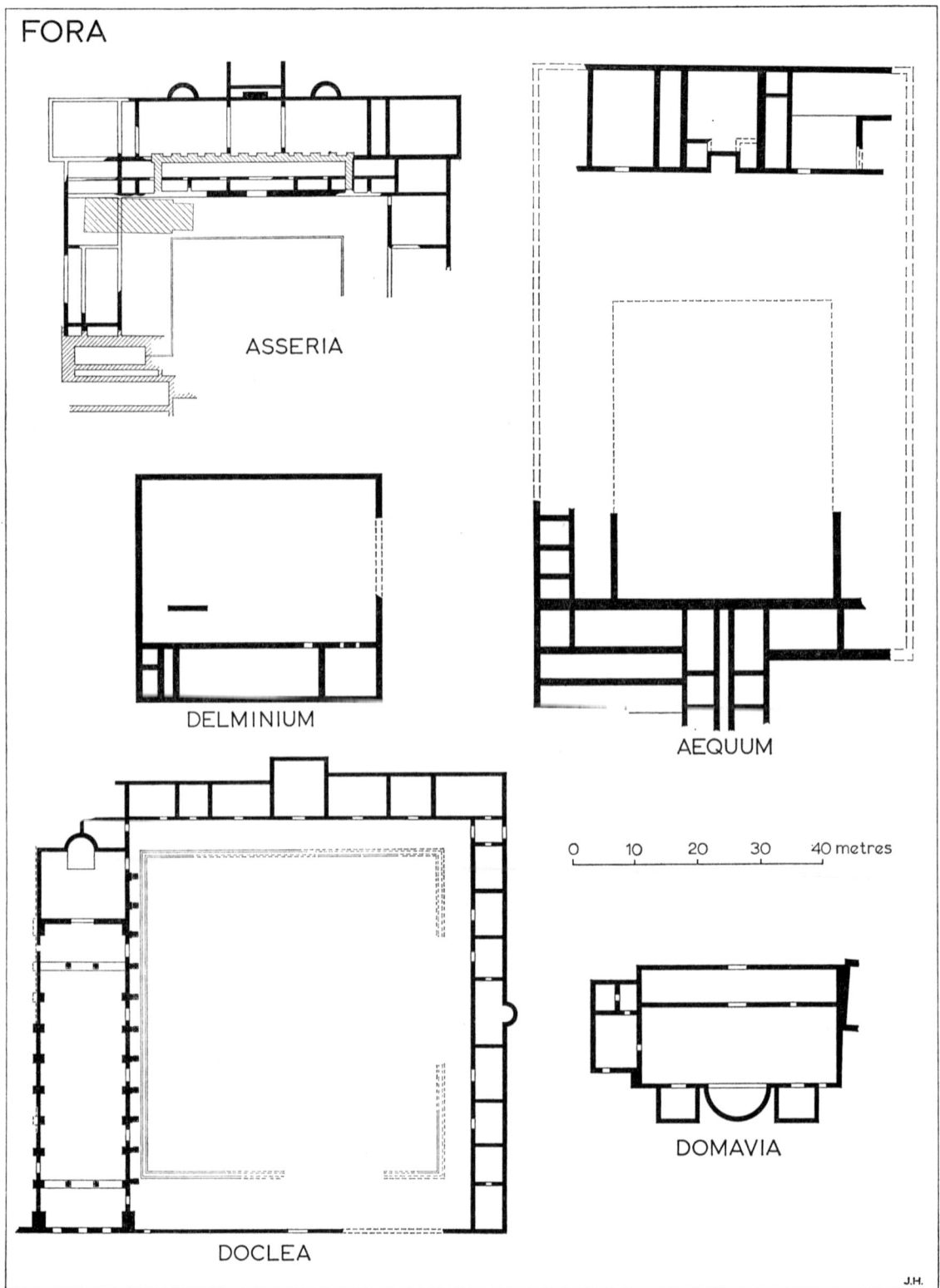

FORA

ASSERIA

DELMINIUM

AEQUUM

0   10   20   30   40 metres

DOCLEA

DOMAVIA

J.H.

Figure 18 Fora

have come from the forum and if so would indicate that it was built when the colony was founded under Claudius.[1]

The Doclea forum measures 60 by 55 metres.[2] A gravelled open area was bordered by shops along the east side, and on the north was the range of official rooms, including the senate house 8 metres square, the floor of which was raised 1.5 metres above the open forum. Along the west side was the *basilica* (fig. 18). This was divided into two chambers, the larger 50 by 13 metres, with a single row of columns across each end. To the north was a smaller room, 13 by 10 metres, with an apse in the north wall enclosing a tribunal. Used for emergency building near the main city gate (p. 365) were statue bases dedicated to third-century emperors, the earliest to Severus Alexander in 226–7 and the latest to Gallienus in 257–60.[3] The forum was probably built in the late first or early second century, and was paid for by the family of Flavius Fronto and his wife Flavia Tertulla who dedicated it to the memory of their son Flavius Balbinus. Although the four fora described above were in different types of city, an Augustan colony, a native Liburnian city, a Claudian military colony, and a Flavian *municipium* at Doclea, all of them were on or very close to the Adriatic coast. Further north only one city has produced evidence for its forum, Delminium in Duvjanskopolje.

The Delminium forum (fig. 18) is small, only 41.8 by 37.4 metres, and the simplest of those known in the province.[2] The masonry is crude and the courses are uneven in depth; the corners of the building were strengthened by large vertical blocks. No tiles were used in the construction, nor were there any in the building débris, and consequently the roof was probably of stone slabs. Inside more than three-quarters of the area was occupied by a paved open space. There were no colonnades or buildings around the wall, and the only feature in this part was a rostrum. A cross wall separated an area on the south 7.55 metres wide which was divided into rooms of varying size, a main chamber 24.2 metres long which served as the city *basilica*, and a smaller chamber of 8.2 metres, adjoining which was the senate house. Both the *basilica* and the senate house were entered directly from the open area of the forum, but the entrance to the latter appears to have been blocked soon after it was built. This was because a northward facing entrance let in the prevailing wind during the winter, and it was necessary to install a fireplace as well as to create an entrance through the *basilica*. The picture of the Delminium senate huddled together in the draughty council chamber illustrates the character of the inland cities, and it is likely that the councillors

[1] Seen by the writer (1966) in the Franciscan collection in Sinj.
[2] Sticotti, *Doclea*, 105 ff.   [3] Sticotti, *Doclea*, 160 ff., nos. 13–18.
[4] Patsch, *WMBH*, 9 (1904), 171 ff.

may have felt some doubts about the desirability of the grand new building which they had been expected to pay for after their community had been granted city status. Some fragments of a bronze statue were discovered, but the architectural remain suggests that compared with Asseria or Doclea it was a building of very modest pretensions. The surviving fragments from the dedication record an emperor with a *tribunicia potestas* renewed at least twenty times; this was almost certainly either Hadrian or Antoninus Pius. It is only in the reign of the former that Roman citizenship begins to appear among the native population of the area (p. 295).

Apart from these examples there is virtually no evidence for the main civic buildings in the Dalmatian cities. What may be part of the forum at Salona (fig. 16), a double precinct similar to Iader with a *capitolium* temple, has been identified in the southern part of the *urbs vetus*.[1] At Domavia the senate house, or possibly the residence of the imperial procurator, has been excavated (fig. 18). It may, however, have been the forum since the dedications to individual procurators found there were mostly set up by the city council of Domavia, while the absence of any open forum area can be explained by its position in a steep-sided valley.[2]

In the limestone karst the provision of water is a problem throughout most of the year (p. xiii). Cities in this area, even those on the coast where many karst rivers finally flow out, would have to make provision for drinking water as well as for irrigation. Such projects will have come very high among the building priorities in the cities of Southern Dalmatia. The finest surviving aqueduct is that at Salona.[3] The source was the river Iadro which comes from the foot of the Mosor mountains; from there the water was channelled towards the city, entering a little to the north of the northeast gate (*porta Andetria*). At intervals along the course of the channel towers were added to regularize the flow. Gerber calculated that the aqueduct supplied more than two and a half million gallons a day when the flow was normal; by Roman standards this was sufficient for at least 40,000 people. The aqueduct is still in use today. When the city was abandoned it was diverted to carry water to Split, a function which, in a reconstructed form, it continues to fulfil. A colony with a large population like Salona could afford the ideal solution for the water problem, but it was quite different for the smaller cities. In the remote area of the Western Lika behind Senia two small communities of the Iapodes and the Liburni disputed access to a precious supply of fresh water, and the same happened at Promona near the river Titius.[4] On the islands,

---

[1] Ceci, *Salona Pagana*, 75 f., and III, 8817 mentioning the *curia*.
[2] Radimsky, *WMBH*, 1 (1893), 228 ff.   [3] Gerber, *FS*, 1, 139 ff.
[4] III, 15053; cf. Patsch, *Lika*, 22 f.; also III, 14969/2.

the small settlement at Časka on Cissa (Pag) built its own aqueduct,[1] although further north the *municipium* on Arba does not appear to have enjoyed an adequate supply until a new source was located and channelled in 173.[2] The permanent auxiliary garrison found it necessary to construct a water tower for the needs of its base at Tilurium,[3] and both Epidaurum and Doclea could afford to channel water from a long distance in ample quantity. The Epidaurum aqueduct was more than 15 kilometres long and as well as filling the city reservoirs also irrigated the Konavli area. Doclea (fig. 17) lay in the middle of a plain and was forced to bring its water from a mountain spring more than 14 kilometres away.[4] Whether Iader had an adequate water supply in the first century is not known, but the need to provide a new aqueduct under Trajan suggests the insufficiency of the existing supply.[5] There will have been great hardship away from the large cities, as there is occasionally today, for people in the karst hinterland, especially in areas such as the Lika, the upper Cetina valley, Imotskipolje, and above all the poljes of Popovo, Nevesinje, and Gačko. Here the rain water is carefully collected and where possible wells are dug. Despite many other factors the water problem was probably the greatest hindrance to the growth of communities above the level of a large village. By contrast Northern Dalmatia has abundant supplies of water, along with many other advantages. The rivers flow smoothly for long distances, quite different from the irregular torrents which pour into the Adriatic from the karst; moreover, there are many warm springs of mineral water in Central and Northern Bosnia. No aqueducts are known here, nor is the building of any attested on inscriptions: the site of the settlement had only to be chosen wisely and no problem would arise.

Some of the cities will have boasted large and expensive temples. The imperial cult was the chief focus of the province's loyalty and this was divided into two areas, that of Liburnia centred at Scardona, and of Dalmatia centred first at Epidaurum then later at Doclea. Only at the last place is there any evidence for the cult temple. A small single-chamber classical temple was fronted by two columns only. Overall it measured 14 by 9.4 metres, the podium being 1.32 metres high.[6] The chamber (*cella*) housing the cult was nearly square, 7.55 by 7.4 metres, with a small apse in the end wall. It was surrounded by an enclosure (*temenos*) fronting on to the main street near the site of the triumphal arch (fig. 17). On the architrave of the temple was a relief of *Dea Roma*, the personification of the imperial city, and fragments from an imperial statue were also found. Not far away from

---

[1] P. Sticotti, *SH*, 181.   [2] III, 3116; and above, p. 199.

[3] *VAHD*, 51 (1930–4), 225 = *AE*, 1940, 176.

[4] Evans, *Archaeologia*, 48 (1884), 37 ff.; Sticotti, *Doclea*, 39 ff.

[5] III, 2909.   [6] Sticotti, *Doclea*, 63 ff.

the west gate was discovered the dedication to the deified Titus (*divus Titus*) which probably came from a temple-statue. At Salona there was a temple in the southern part of the *urbs vetus* not far from the site of the forum. Though only part of the foundations survives (fig. 16), it was possible for the excavators to determine the various building-phases through which the building had passed.[1] It was built in the classical style during the first century and matches closely the temple of Augustus at Pola, set on a podium 1.75 metres high, and measuring overall 15.12 by 8.92 metres. In the second century the building of the theatre made some changes necessary: steps were added to the podium and the entire temple surrounded by a stone wall to form an ambulatory 3 to 4 metres wide. The *cella* was square with sides 8.38 metres, while the forehall was screened by four columns. The building of the theatre alongside the temple did not affect the function of the temple. In the early fourth century changes were made which included the addition of a new façade and an elaborate portico. The capitals were Roman Corinthian. The original first-century shrine may have been a shrine to Augustus, to judge from the fragments of sculptures discovered.

Most of the cities along the coast had classical temples. At Doclea a second temple was dedicated to Diana and was set in its own enclosure (fig. 17), while another smaller temple in its enclosure was attached to a large private house, perhaps that of the Flavii, fronting on the main street.[2] The temple in the Iader forum precinct was very similar to those at Salona and Pola and was certainly an original part of the Iader forum. The smaller cities could not have afforded such buildings, although at Vegium remains of a substantial building a little outside the town at Drvešica may have been part of a large temple of Jupiter, to judge from fragments of a monumental statue.[3] Another classical temple is known at Aenona: this was an early building and housed monumental statues of Augustus and Tiberius; unfortunately no complete publication of the excavations has been produced.[4] Inland, at the Liburnian settlement Clambetae (Cvijina gradina) there was a small temple.[5] Remains of the stylobate indicate that the podium was more than 1 metre high: it measured 6.65 metres wide and was partitioned into a forehall (*pronaos*) 3.5 metres deep and a *cella* 6.6 metres. Four columns formed the façade on the east side, where traces of steps were also noted. It was built of rectangular blocks in courses more than 1.5 metres high; while the column bases had simple mouldings. Statue fragments and part of a

[1] F. Weilbach, *RS*, 2 (1928), 11–32.
[2] Sticotti, *Doclea*, 85 ff. (Diana temple), 75 ff. (private temple).
[3] Patsch, *Lika*, 107 f.
[4] *RPAA*, 22 (1948), 193 ff.
[5] Colnago and Keil, *JÖAI*, 8 (1905), 34 ff.

stone eagle with the head turned to one side reveal that it was dedicated to Jupiter.

Only in two cities are there remains of the large private houses such as would belong to the wealthier families of city-council status. Such a residence would normally be rectangular and consist of rooms arranged around the four sides of a courtyard, including the main entrance hall (*atrium*), dining room (*triclinium*), as well as bedrooms, kitchens, and servants' quarters. At Salona there were houses of this type in the northwest corner of the *urbs nova*, which were destroyed when Christian churches were built in the first half of the fourth century. When the houses were first constructed they were neatly located within the city street-grid, but a long time before the fourth century the area had begun to be occupied by a jumble of irregular buildings. One large house near the northwest corner of the episcopal church had at least sixteen rooms and overall measured 30 metres square (fig. 19); another was located to the north, between the first house and the north wall of the city.[1] A row of houses in the same area was built along the inside of the west wall, one of which had a private bath suite of more than five rooms. In this area the city street-grid still survives, but the pressure for space had obviously become very acute during the third century. Further west, in the *urbs vetus*, private houses occupied the area north of the street which passed into the *urbs nova* through the *porta Caesarea*, one of which had more than fifteen rooms. Most of these houses show a high standard of living, with fine mosaic floors, painted wall-plaster, a private water-supply from the municipal aqueduct, and hypocaust heating. Small-scale excavations at Iader, Senia, and Narona have revealed details of similar private houses from the first to the fourth century.[2] At Iader the picture is similar to that in Salona, with rebuilding taking place over more than three centuries, mosaic floors, hypocausts, and porticos being built and dismantled as the houses passed through various changes of plan and ownership.

The most elaborate town-residence known is at Doclea (fig. 19). Facing on to the main street opposite the forum was a private residence which incorporated domestic quarters with a temple in its own enclosure.[3] This rectangular house contained more than twenty rooms around the courtyard, and overall measured more than 30 by 23 metres. In a corner was a private bath-suite where a dry-heat room (*laconicum*) was available in addition to the usual steam-heat facilites (*caldarium*). Its prominent position in the city, together with the private temples,

[1] Gerber, *FS*, 1 (1917), 100 f.
[2] Iader: B. Ilakovac, *VAHD*, 60 (1958), 43 ff., and p. 367, n. 3 above; Senia: Ivica Degmedžić, *VAHD*, 53 (1950–1), 251 ff.
[3] Sticotti, *Doclea*, 79 ff.

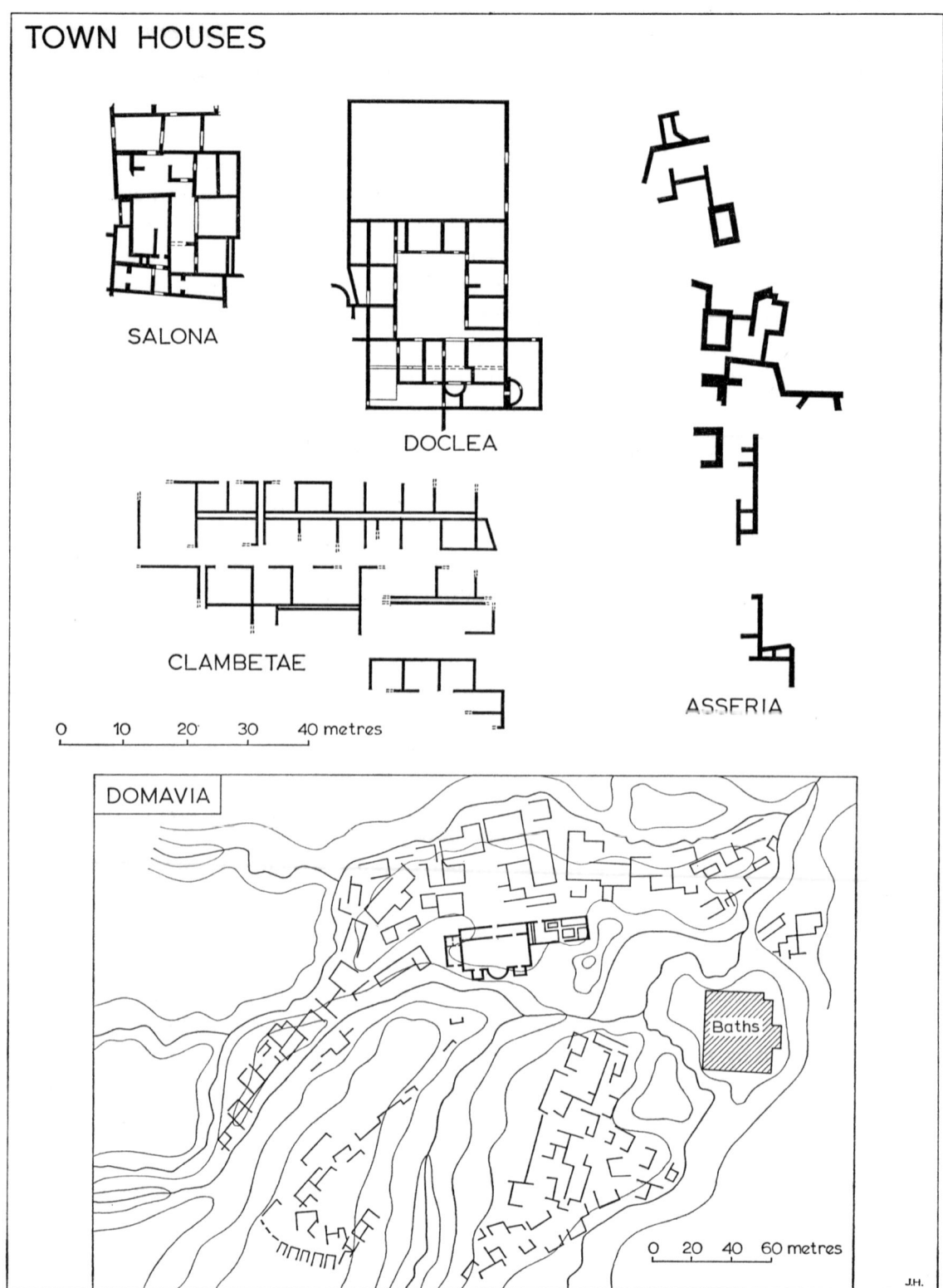

TOWN HOUSES

SALONA

DOCLEA

CLAMBETAE

ASSERIA

0   10   20   30   40 metres

DOMAVIA

Baths

0   20   40   60 metres

J.H.

Figure 19 Town Houses

leaves no doubt that this was the residence of one of the wealthiest families, probably the Flavii who built the forum. Elsewhere at Doclea there are traces of town-houses, but none compares in size with this example. At Asseria a scatter of small buildings is known in the area to the north of the forum, but no single structure can be identified (fig. 19). One of them included a small bath-suite, but the plan of this and the other buildings is so chaotic as to make clear that no systematic street-grid was ever imposed.[1] By contrast, at nearby Clambetae a remarkable instance of uniform planning is known within the settlement (fig. 19), where three rows of buildings were separated by parallel streets.[2] The lines of small buildings are possibly shops, open fronted structures facing on to the street. In plan they resemble the barrack blocks in a Roman auxiliary fort, at one end a room 20 metres square adjoining two rows of eight smaller rooms measuring 4 metres square. The small settlement on the Smokovac gradina at Krupa was enclosed by a wall at least 6 metres thick.[3] In plan the settlement was rectangular and the few buildings known inside, small houses and shops, were all aligned along the same axis as the surviving stretches of the wall.

The evidence from Dalmatia reveals the full range of urban buildings, and it demonstrates clearly the different character of the cities. There are Salona and Iader, full of wealthy buildings constantly being altered and repaired and with the pressure of living space within the city becoming progressively more acute. The original regular plan of houses and shops within the street-grid was lost with the expansion and rebuilding of three centuries. By contrast Doclea reveals its neat layout of buildings in the central area almost untouched by later alterations (fig. 17). At Salona the great expansion of Christian building impinged on a densely occupied residential area, but at Doclea the churches were in another part of the city and left the old pagan buildings at the centre completely untouched.[4] Elsewhere there is the confusion found at Asseria, where the site made formal planning impracticable; symmetry and a neat plan, however, are found in the smaller settlements at Clambetae and Krupa, neither of which were cities. At Doclea few major buildings were added after the building of the city centre, but in the older coastal cities apart from the changes made to the existing buildings, the addition of new amenities such as the amphitheatre and theatre at Salona involved many changes in the areas where they were built. At Domavia the houses were small single rooms, most not more than 5 by 3 metres, and they are crammed together on the two level areas in the steep glen of the Sase river

[1] Liebl and Wilberg, *JÖAI*, 11 (1908), Bb. 53.
[2] Colnago and Keil, *JÖAI*, 8 (1905), Bb. 40 ff.
[3] *JÖAI*, 12 (1909), Bb. 37 ff., fig. 11 ff.
[4] Sticotti, *Doclea*, 137 ff.

(fig. 19). More than 120 have been traced on the surface and most of them probably date to the third century.

The city baths (*thermae*) played a greater role in the daily lives of citizens than it is possible to visualize today. Every city was equipped with this amenity, and their maintenance and supply of fuel was one of the heaviest burdens which could fall on the members of the city council. Civic benefactions often took the form of new baths or the repair of existing ones: Narona was fortunate to have a new set of winter baths (*thermae hiemales*) paid for and inaugurated with a civic banquet by one of its own citizens who had risen to high rank in the army during the second half of the third century.[1] Senia may have received a similar gift; there a fragmentary inscription records the building of the city baths (*balneum*) under Gordian III (239–41).[2] The Roman bath system was simple, although some of the largest baths were very complex structures offering a considerable variety of facilities. After undressing one entered the room with a cold bath (*frigidarium* and then passed on to the rooms heated by a hypocaust system, usually the warm room (*tepidarium*) and the hot room (*caldarium*). After perspiration the oil applied to the bather as cleansing agent was scraped off and the process was completed in the cold room with a plunge in the bath to prevent catching cold. Such services could be provided by a simple range of rooms heated by furnaces against the outside of the building; this is the usual type of baths found near the small Roman forts along the northern frontiers. The main city baths were intended for much more than the simple bath routine, and many cities had more than one set of baths, each comprising an involved complex of heated and cold rooms together with numerous ante-rooms, passages, and lounges where food was often provided. Elaborate decoration, including wall paintings, and mosaic floors, are common in such buildings which are best understood by studying the well-preserved baths at Rome or Pompeii, or at Lepcis Magna in North Africa.

Two city baths of the most elaborate type are known at Salona and Doclea (fig. 20). In the interior there is an elaborate set of baths at the Domavia settlement (fig. 20), designed specially to serve the needs of the mining population who worked in the cramped galleries of the silver mines. Many of the miners here were not slaves or criminals, but specialists whose good health and well-being were a necessary care of the mines administration. Here the baths were paid for by the government, but in a city they were provided from civic funds or through the generosity of wealthy citizens, and provided a useful amenity for the community at a nominal charge. They were administered by an agent (*conductor*) on behalf of the city. Under his charge would be a staff consisting of public slaves, attendants, stokers, and general maintenance men.

[1] III, 1805.   [2] III, 10054.

What was probably one of the city baths at Salona lay in the northwest corner of the *urbs nova*, next to the site of the main churches built in the fourth and fifth centuries.[1] It was a rectangular block measuring 40 by 30 metres and faced to the south, while on the west side it impinged on to one of the principal north–south streets (*cardines*) in the city (fig. 20). In plan it is typical of city baths in Mediterranean cities. One entered through a vestibule into an open courtyard surrounded by a portico from which the principal rooms were entered, including the main undressing room (*apodyterium*) There were separate bath suites on either side, that on the east side being the more elaborate with provision for not only steam-heated rooms but also the fierce dry-heat room (*laconicum*), the use of which was often prescribed as treatment by physicians. Although the materials employed were of a high quality the standard of construction was poor, but this may be due to the many renovations which were carried out over the years. Both the walls and floors of the heated rooms were covered with marble; the floor of the cold room was merely paved. The principal heated room (*caldarium*) was subdivided to provided two levels of heat, and the double door leading from the adjacent warm room (*tepidarium*) was hinged to the wall at an angle, so as to ensure that one of the doors always remained shut. The usual features of bath-house construction were discovered, hypocaust floors on pillars of tiles, thick insulating wall-plaster rendered with a variety of colours and walls with jackets of box flue-tiles. There is no evidence for the date when the Salona baths were built, but they certainly remained in use well into the fourth century, after the Christian churches had been built.

More than half of the Doclea baths have been examined.[2] They occupied an area 65 metres square and faced the forum across the main street (fig. 17). It included two separate bath systems, and although only the baths in the western part have been examined there is no doubt that the facilities were equal to, if not better than, those available at Salona (fig. 20). The entrance was from the main street opposite the forum. The vestibule was a large hall and contained two niches for statues. From here access was gained to the two systems, probably the men's and the women's baths, which were entered from separate waiting rooms. In the west the men's baths were grouped around an open courtyard surrounded with a portico similar to that at Salona. In the baths themselves the warm room had a mosaic floor, and most of the walls were inlaid with marble. Three separate water tanks, for hot, warm, and cold, enabled the temperature of the water in the hot room to be adjusted easily. In the same part of the building were rooms which may have been used for reading and exercise. The women's bath has not been examined but the outline plan suggests that it was identical to the men's in

[1] Gerber, *FS*, I, 109 ff.   [2] Sticotti, *Doclea*, 98 ff.

BATHS

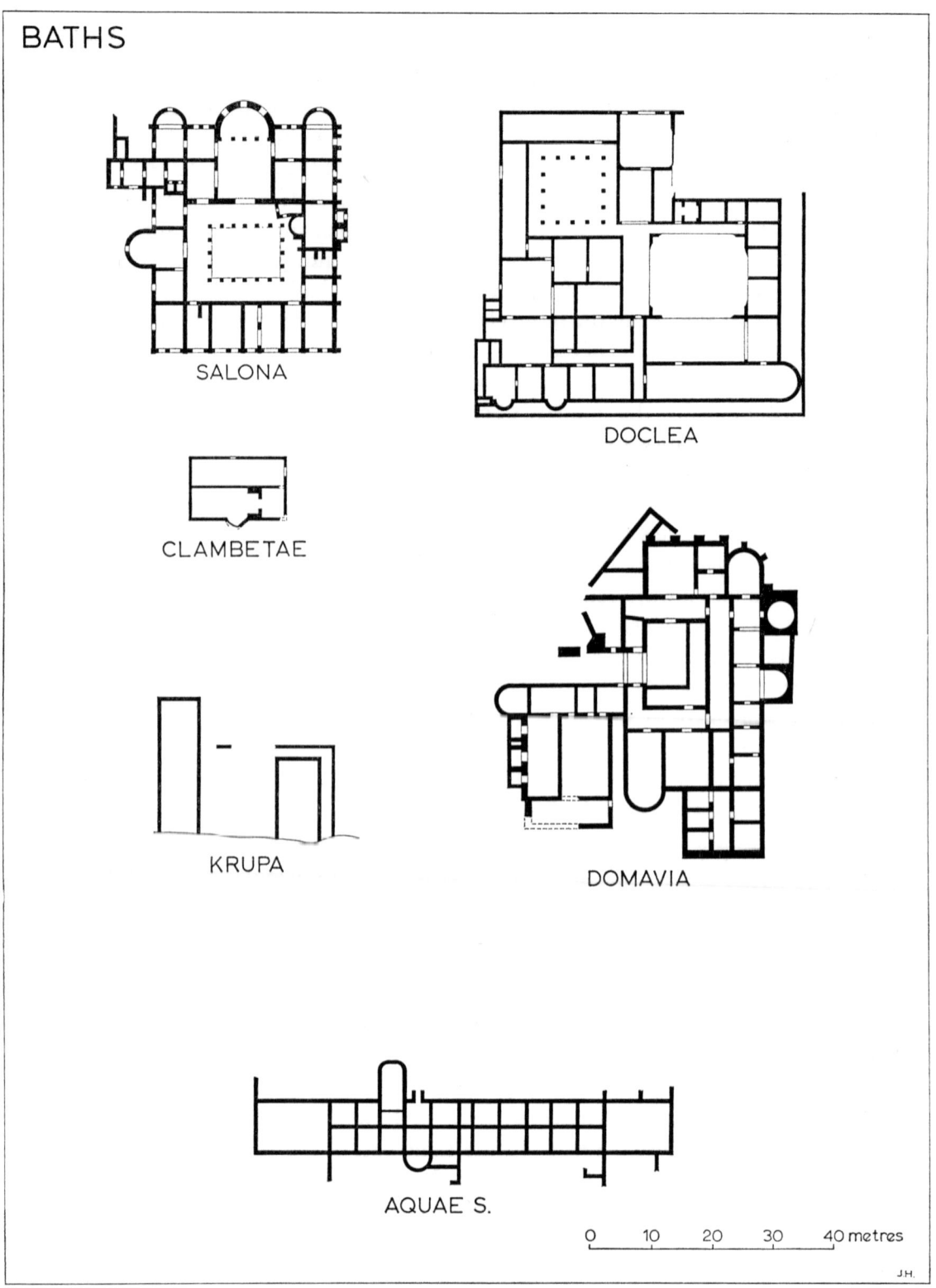

SALONA

DOCLEA

CLAMBETAE

KRUPA

DOMAVIA

AQUAE S.

0   10   20   30   40 metres

JH.

Figure 20 Baths

the west part of the building. An open courtyard with portico was surrounded by a series of heated rooms, with the hot room along the rear of the building.

The two city baths described above furnish a comparison between the civic amenities in different cities of the province. The Doclea baths were more elaborate than those at Salona, and suggest that the latter's facilities were not always superior to those in other cities. On the other hand, the Doclea baths, like most of the civic buildings, appear to have been the enterprise of a small group of wealthy families in the early years of the Flavian city. The fact that the Doclea baths survived almost untouched by later alterations suggests that the great period of civic building was a brief one, whereas the northwest part of the Salona *urbs nova* reveals an intricate palimpsest of structures lasting from the second to the fourth century.

Elsewhere in the coastal area little is known about the baths in the smaller cities. Ruins of an elaborate city bath-complex at Issa (fig. 15) have been traced on the surface,[1] and in the Ravni kotari the baths of two small settlements, neither of them cities, have been excavated at Clambetae and Krupa (fig. 20). At the former place they measured overall 16 by 10 metres.[2] Across the front was the undressing room, behind which was a range of three rooms, a cold and two heated ones. There was no dry-heat system and only the bare essentials were provided for visitors. Apart from a mosaic floor in the undressing room, the building was devoid of any decoration or embellishment. Not far to the east the small settlement at Krupa on the gradina Smokovac was enclosed by a wall; here the bath block was 100 metres away alongside the Orahovaca stream.[3] It consisted of two separate buildings, a rectangular room 45 by 15 metres (the front has been eroded away by the stream) with a mosaic floor which was the undressing room. Alongside this, and built as separate structures, were traces of the hot and warm rooms both of which, like the undressing room, were aligned end-on to the stream. In construction they were more elaborate than the Clambetae baths and were probably typical of the modest bath-suites built by the small inland Liburnian hill-settlements.

In plan the Domavia baths are the most elaborate known in the province, consisting of more than fifty rooms (fig. 20). They were paid for by the mines administration: in 220 a procurator supervised the provision of a new water supply, and in 274 rebuilt them after they had fallen into a dilapidated state. Coins found during excavation of the baths indicate that it was in use from the beginning of the third century until at least early in the fourth.[4] Two structural

[1] See the plan by Gabričević, *Urbs*, 2 (1958).
[2] Colnago and Keil, *JÖAI*, 8 (1905), Bb. 37 ff.
[3] Abramić and Colnago, *JÖAI*, 12 (1909), Bb. 40. [4] Radimsky, *WMBH*, 4 (1896), 207 ff.

phases have been identified: the earlier comprised a single range of rooms, three waiting, two cold, a warm, and a hot room, totalling seven rooms in all. This simple set was enclosed entirely within the later baths. Apart from the main heated rooms with all necessary facilities, these included a separate women's block of more than ten rooms, an open courtyard surrounded by corridors, and on the north a set of rooms where food was provided. The baths were entered by a monumental doorway with vestibule, where the building inscriptions were originally set up; among the special rooms was the cloakroom in the woman's bath where 33 coat hooks were found attached to the wall. The two heated rooms in the main bath-suite were adorned with mosaic floors. An unusual feature of the Domavia baths is the large number of small rooms, some hardly more than cubicles. They may have been reserved for resident officials in the administration and city dignitaries, since it would have been difficult to build and maintain another bath-suite on the site of Domavia.

A unique settlement in the province which developed into a city was the curative spa Aquae S. . . . . at Ilidže near the source of the river Bosna. It had become a city before the end of the third century, though before this the sulphurous waters had already been attracting senatorial visitors. Excavations carried out in 1893 and from 1955 until 1958 have revealed substantial traces of the spa buildings. The buildings around the source of the waters were discovered first when the modern spa building was being constructed at the end of the last century.[1] They extended over an area of at least 55 by 50 metres, although it was possible to uncover only a few of the rooms. The standard of comfort was very high, with numerous mosaic floors, painted walls, and finely carved imported Corinthian capitals. Coins from the building begin in the second century, but the period of greatest prosperity appears to have been the first half of the third century. Since it was built directly on the source, it was clearly the principal building of the spa; however, the foundations of another block on the south side indicate that it was not the only one near the springs. More recent excavations have revealed a courtyard house and the hospital, where those who came to the spa for treatment would be accommodated.[2] The house contained more than thirty rooms, most of them opening on to the portico around the courtyard. One or two of the larger rooms had mosaic floors but most were of simple concrete (*opus signinum*); the roof was tiled with locally manufactured *tegulae* and *imbrices*. The history of the building is similar to that of the main spa; beginning with a modest structure in the second century, it was enlarged in the first half of the third century and continued in use during the fourth century at least until the

[1] J. Kellner, *WMBH*, 5 (1897), 131 ff.
[2] E. Pašalić, *GZMS*, 14 (1959), 113 ff.

reign of Valentinian I (364–75). The excavator suggested that it began as a private residence, but was later converted and enlarged to serve as the administrative centre for the hospital. This was close by and included wards and treatment rooms for the sick (fig. 20). At one end there was a small bath block with a range of twelve small rooms extending to the northeast with four on the other side, measuring overall 70 by 15 metres. Most of the individual rooms had mosaic floors with a geometric pattern, but otherwise it was a simple structure. This was the hospital (*receptaculum*) were patients lived and were treated. It was built later than the other buildings, in the third century, and remained in use during the fourth. There are numerous traces of similar buildings in the vicinity, many with mosaic floors and painted walls. The settlement was clearly an attraction to the local population, although the specialist tasks carried out may have been the work of men brought from the cities in the south. Very little evidence survives for the people of the settlement, and the wealth of the main spa building suggests that it may have been a commercial venture, possibly controlled by business-men from elsewhere. The standard of building is far higher than anything else in the region. The money spent would never be recovered from the native population, but from wealthy patients ordered there by their physicians.

The finest surviving monuments of Roman Salona are the two principal centres of pleasure and entertainment, the amphitheatre and the theatre. The oval amphitheatre with its arena is partly enclosed in the city walls at the northwest corner of the *urbs vetus* (fig. 21); the semicircular theatre lies in the southern half of the same enclosure facing across the bay (fig. 16). Both have been excavated and detailed monographs have been published by Einar Dyggve and his Danish colleagues in the second volume of *Recherches à Salone*. During the Republic it was the practice at Rome to erect temporary stands and arenas for major displays and shows, until Cn. Pompeius built the first stone theatre. Amphitheatres also spread, and during the first century A.D. most of the western cities acquired arenas surrounded by banks of stone seats.[1] A similar type of building was also used by the Roman army near their permanent legionary fortresses: here the purpose was tactical demonstrations and training in weapon techniques, although doubtless they were also used for entertainment. In the main frontier centres at Carnuntum and Aquincum on the Danube, the legionary fortress and the civilian city each had their own amphitheatre, both about the same size and similar in plan. Amphitheatres in the Empire fall into two types; the earlier were arenas surrounded by solid banks on which there were rows of seats to which access was gained by stairs and ramps from the outside. The military amphitheatre of Legion II Augusta at Isca Silurum in Britannia was of this

[1] L. Friedländer, *Roman Life and Manners* 2, 40–90.

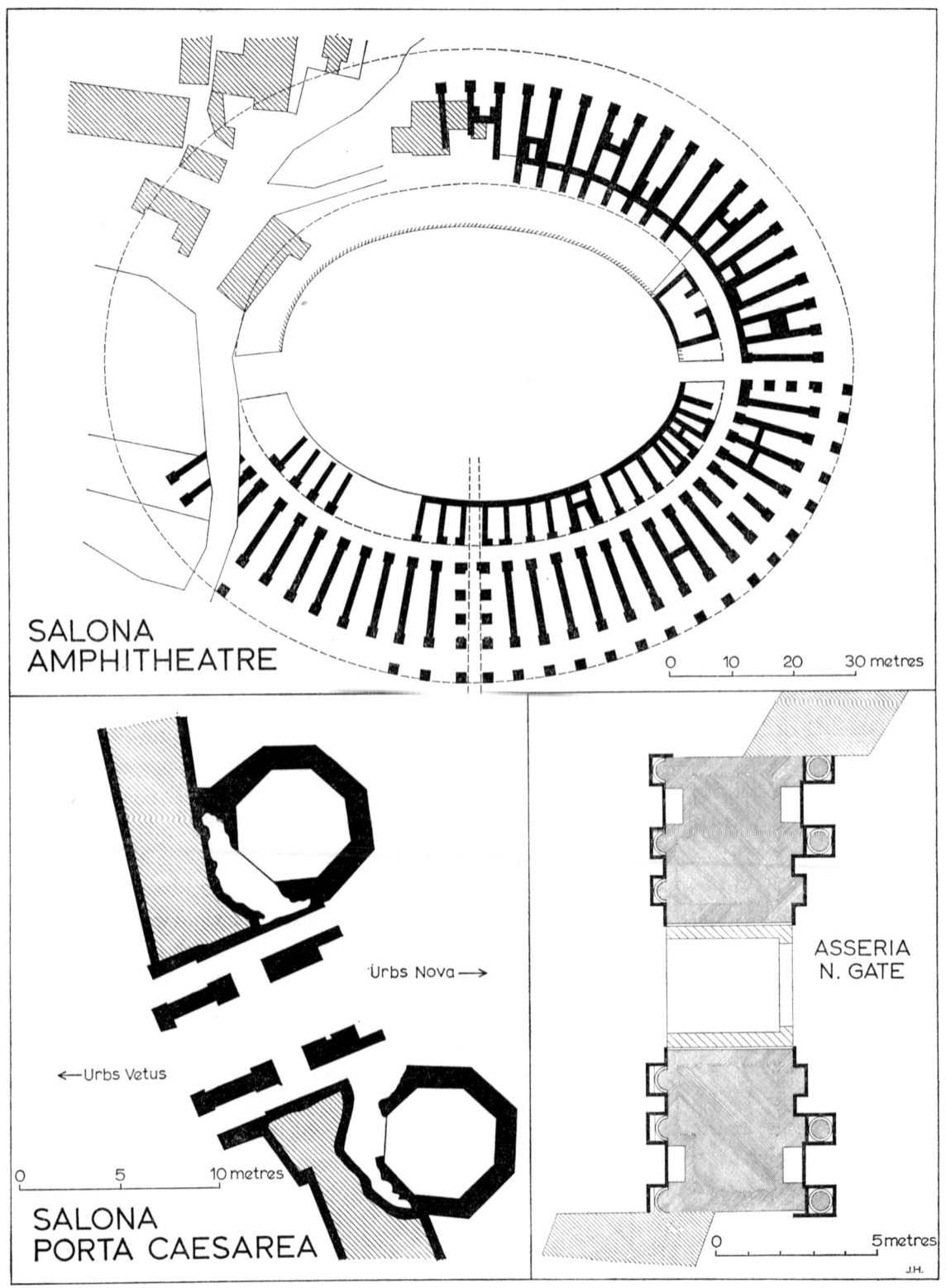

SALONA
AMPHITHEATRE

0   10   20   30 metres

Urbs Nova →

←Urbs Vetus

ASSERIA
N. GATE

0   5   10 metres

SALONA
PORTA CAESAREA

0   5 metres

J.H.

Figure 21 Salona Amphitheatre, Asseria and Salona Gates

type. The second type is exemplified by the great Flavian Amphitheatre at Rome which was inaugurated under Titus or the more modest structure at the Istrian colony Pola. Here the banks of seats were in steep rows built above a super-structure of radial walls, providing scope for corridors within the structure to give access at two or more levels. The Salona amphitheatre was of the second type and from the remains it was possible for Dyggve to produce a complete reconstruction. After the destruction of Salona it remained the most prominent ruin on the site and according to the historian Thomas the Archdeacon survived almost intact until the thirteenth century.[1] Later centuries have seen much stone robbing; although the ground plan is still complete the external walls and the seats have largely disappeared.

Overall the amphitheatre measured 125 by 101 metres, the arena was 62.5 by 40 metres, and the superstructure was carried on sixty-eight radial walls. Three concentric enclosure walls provided two ambulatories. Within the area there were two main banks of seats (*maeniana*). Allowing for the space taken up by the entrances (*vomitoria*), the passages between each block, and the 'royal box' near one of the entrances, the capacity can be calculated. In the front bank were four-teen rows, in the rear sixteen: allowing a space for each person of half a metre the total seating capacity was 13,380 to which can be added standing room for at least 2,000. Compared with those of other provincial cities the Salona amphi-theatre is about the average size. There are few statistics available for seating capacities; Capua apparently held 42,000, Pompeii only 12,800. The front rows were invariably reserved for city dignitaries and others of substance, and doubt-less they would have required more space and comfort than those occupying the second bank. The total of 15,000 for Salona may represent about one quarter of the adult population. Little is known about the history of the building. It appears to have been built about 170 and was completely renovated about the end of the third century; it was still in use at the time of the persecution under Diocletian. Parts of the monumental inscription from the podium survive, but only individual letters. It was at least 19 metres long and may have recorded an act of individual civic generosity, but no reconstruction is possible.

The arena was the place for spectacles, chiefly the hunts with wild beasts (*venationes*) and the combats between professional gladiators, men who fought with the net and trident (*retiarii*) or the sword (*secutores*). These entertainments would be paid for by city councillors or magistrates to celebrate their holding civic office or entering the city council. The names of gladiators who fought in the Salona arena are attested in their small cemetery nearby. There was Rapidus 'the Aquileian' (although his real home was Bellunum) who died in hospital after

[1] *Historia Salonitana* of Thomas the Archdeacon, c. 7 ff. (ed. Fr. Rački, Zagreb, 1894).

his sixth combat. There was the Dacian swordsman Amabilis who had thirteen fights before he died 'not by the hand of man'. Another swordsman, hero of five fights, had the misfortune to be killed by a bandit at the age of 22. Fighting gladiators are popular motifs for decoration. From the amphitheatre a stone frieze portrays two naked wrestlers locked in combat: one has a firm head hold on his opponent who from his kneeling position attempts a leg lock. Another scene shows a large wolfhound fighting with a bear.

The theatre had already a distinguished history before it reached the Roman World. Like the amphitheatres the theatre at Rome began as temporary wooden structures: Vitruvius speaks of many such temporary erections at Rome during one year.[1] It was Pompeius who constructed the first permanent theatre in Rome after his eastern triumph. The Greek theatre centred on the *orchestra*, the circular area used by actors, but the Romans reduced this to a semicircle incorporated in the auditorium and often used it for additional seating accommodation. As they appear in provincial cities theatres were semicircular, with an elaborately adorned back wall to the stage (*scaenae frons*) rising to the same height as the seating enclosure. In some cities of the northwest, for instance Paris and Verulamium, a different plan was adopted, with a circular *orchestra* and enclosing seat accommodation. With a lateral stage this may have served as both theatre and amphitheatre.[2] These belong to the fringe of the Roman World and the true Roman theatre is exemplified by those at Sabrata and Lepcis Magna in Tripolitania, and at Arausio (Orange) in Gaul. These were quite different from the classical Greek theatres and most of the performances were the much less elevated Roman burlesque.

At Salona much less survives of the theatre than of the amphitheatre.[3] It was smaller than that at Arausio, being 65 metres wide compared with the latter's 95. Part of the semicircular seating survives with the lower half of the stage façade. The central part of this latter feature was dominated by an arch and a recess, but few other remains survive. It was constructed about the same time as the amphitheatre, about 170. No other buildings of this type are known in the province. An eighteenth-century traveller observed remains of the amphitheatre at Aequum, but no trace has been observed since.[4] The few traces of the Issa theatre (fig. 15) suggest that it might have been of the Greek type, with a simple curved bank of seats facing on to an open arena.

[1] *De Architectura*, v, 7.
[2] Verulamium: K. Kenyon, *Archaeologia*, 84 (1935), 213–61; Paris: P-M. Duval, *Paris Antique*, 180 ff.
[3] Bulić, *BD*, 34 (1911), 63–6; cf. *RS*, 2, preface.
[4] Fortis, *Viaggio in Dalmazia* (second ed. 1774), 77; cf. *JÖAI*, 16 (1913), Bb. 136.

III The Palace of Diocletian

The retirement of Diocletian from supreme power in 305 is an event unique in the history of the Roman Empire. No other emperor gave up the purple willingly to enjoy a comfortable retirement and die in peace as a private citizen. Diocletian was born in 246 in or near Salona and his twenty-one years of rule (284–305) marked the beginning of a new epoch in the history of the Roman World. For his retirement he had built a palatial residence on the Adriatic coast a few miles south of his native city, where he spent the last ten years of his life indulging his passion for gardening until his death in 315. In 307, when his successors found themselves in difficulties, he refused a request to return to power and severed all connection with the controlling of the Empire. After his death Diocletian's 'villa' (this is the description which later writers employ) reverted to the state, and although members of the imperial family occasionally resided there, part of it was put to more practical use as a textile factory.[1] Much later the security of its massive walls and its position on the open coast attracted refugees from Salona, which was finally destroyed by the Slavs in the early seventh century and ceased to exist as a city. Within the walls of the Palace mediaeval Spalato (modern Split) grew up and today the irregular streets of the old city reveal traces of the Palace at many points, although the majority of the surviving remains are concealed by the later buildings, small houses, merchants' palaces, and churches: many of these are fine examples of different periods in architecture.

The first systematic study of the remains was made by the English architect and designer Robert Adam. During his visit in July 1757 he made drawings of the remains, in spite of the hostility of the local population, and his work (published in 1764) preserves many details which have since been obscured by later buildings or even destroyed altogether. The main studies were carried out in the first decade of this century by two architects, the Austrian G. Niemann and the Frenchman E. Hébrard, the latter in association with the historian J. Zeiller. Until the systematic exploration of the underground chambers in the southern area, undertaken during the last decade by the city authorities of Split,[2] the two publications of these scholars (1910, 1912) formed the basis of our knowledge of the construction and planning of Diocletian's residence.

[1] Eutropius, ix, 28, and Prosper of Aquitaine (*Chron. Min.*, 1, p. 448) both record Diocletian's death in his *villa* at Split. The textile workshop (literally *gynaecium*, a place where women worked) is mentioned in *Not. Dign. occ.*, xi, 48: *procurator gynaecii Jovensis, Dalmatiae Aspalato*. Members of later imperial families attested there include a woman descended from Constantine I, *FS*, 1, 79, n. 96. A gold brooch found there belonged to the same family, III, 10195, 1.
[2] J. Marasović, *Urbs*, 4 (1961–2), 24–54; T. and J. Marasović, *Diocletian Palace* (Zagreb 1968).

The site was well chosen, a small inlet to the east of the Marijan peninsula which screens the Bay of Salona from the open sea. Recent evidence from excavations near the Peristyle have revealed architectural fragments dating to the first and second centuries A.D., but it cannot be assumed that these came from buildings on the site before the fourth century, since the Palace incorporated a variety of re-used material, including whole columns brought from Egypt.[1] Late Roman geographers name the place as Aspalathos (from which the modern names Spalato and Split are derived): the aspalathos was a thorny shrub which grew in many of the eastern provinces and in Illyricum, whose essence, according to the Elder Pliny, was used for a variety of perfumes and scented oils.[2] The Palace was completely isolated in antiquity, there being no trace of any buildings in the vicinity.

No literary or epigraphic source supplies details for the construction of the Palace, either for the architect who planned it or for the date when it was completed. The name Zotikos has been found carved at different places in the building but nothing is known about him or his work. This oriental name and the discovery of Greek initial letters carved in unobtrusive places suggest that the Palace was built by eastern craftsmen brought there for the purpose. Although some decorative parts of the building reveal imported materials, much of the construction incorporates limestone from the quarries on Brattia and from Seget near Tragurium. The former is found in the main central buildings, including the Peristyle, the Mausoleum, and the Temple; it is a white stone which stains black, while the latter was used at the north gate (*porta aurea*, a name bestowed in the Middle Ages) and is a softer honey-coloured material. Roofs were of tile. That which survives on the Mausoleum was built partly from tiles from a local factory with the stamp DALMATIA, which were possibly produced solely for use in the building. Older products were also used, including some from the first and second century Q. CLODIUS AMBROSIUS factory near Aquileia. Decoration throughout the Palace appears to have been extensive but not over-lavish. The principal rooms in the south had mosaics on the walls and floors. The building was apparently completed in time for Diocletian's retirement in 305. During his stay at Salona in the previous year he was probably already living there when four members of his bodyguard were martyred for their Christian faith (p. 429).

There are no obvious precursors for the Palace: its unique purpose as a home

---

[1] Four sphinxes were brought from Egypt and set up around the Mausoleum, including one of Rameses II (18th Dynasty, thirteenth century B.C.), another of Tutmoses III (fifteenth century B.C.), and a third of Amenhotep (Memnon) (18th Dynasty, *c.* fourteenth century B.C.), cf. Bulić-Karaman, *Palast*, 46–9.

[2] Note 5 above, p. 227. The aspalathos is mentioned frequently by the Elder Pliny, *HN*, xiii, 18, etc.

for a retired emperor is reflected in a quite unparalleled arrangement of buildings within a strong defensive wall. In appearance this latter feature must have given it the character of a military camp built in the fashion of the age. In plan it is an irregular quadrilateral facing the sea with the long axis aligned roughly east south-east–west northwest. The east and west sides measure 216 metres: the shorter sides are unequal, the north, facing inland towards Salona, measures 175 metres, while the longer south side at the water's edge measures 180 metres. The irregu-larity was due to the narrower area of level ground away from the sea. The area enclosed by the walls is 2.9 hectares (7.56 acres) and in 1926 it held a population of 3,200 inhabitants. The walls were designed to provide a level walk around the perimeter: on the north they are 17 metres high, on the south 24. Along the south front was a gallery screened by an arcade of columns. To break the monotony of this façade there were three loggias, one at each end, and a third placed centrally above the south gate (*porta argentea*) which led to a small jetty on the water. The rest of the perimeter was undecorated, presenting an unbroken surface of smooth ashlar.

Three main gates, each flanked by octagonal towers, were set roughly mid-way in the north, east, and west walls. The southern entrance (*porta argentea*) led from the waterside directly into the cellars beneath the private apartments in the south of the Palace: the gate itself was no more than a simple doorway. The most imposing is still the main entrance in the north (*porta aurea*) with a single passage 4.17 metres wide. Set in the outside face of the wall above the entrance was a series of niches crowned with arches: they may have held statues of the emperor and his family. The east (*porta aenea*) and the west (*porta ferrea*) were similar in plan but much less can be seen of them today. The east gate was des-troyed in the Middle Ages, probably during a Turkish attack in the thirteenth century, while the west gate is now almost totally enclosed by houses on either side of the entrance. Little has survived of the gate towers: their usefulness in mediaeval warfare was negligible and their building stone was valuable.

The perimeter wall was strengthened at the corners by four square towers, with sides of 12 metres, and which stood 4 metres higher than the curtain wall. The two northern towers are still preserved, and that on the northwest is still inhabited. The southeast tower is the best preserved, but the southwest was demolished in the sixteenth century. All these features were to be found in mili-tary forts built in the first half of the fourth century, but apart from the protec-tion which any building isolated in the open country would require there is no suggestion that the needs of military defence were important to the architects. More probably they were meeting Diocletian's demands for seclusion in spacious luxury: all his private apartments were invisible from the land, and the only possibility of seeing the retired emperor in his garden was from a boat moored some distance away from the south façade. The military character of the outside walls was later a real benefit to the inhabitants of Split, from the time when the first refugees arrived there in the seventh century until the departure of the Turks from the fortress at Klis in the nineteenth.

Within the walls the area was divided by two main thoroughfares, both lined with open colonnades. The main division was the paved street between the east and west gates, corresponding to the *via principalis* in a military fort: south of this line were the principal buildings, the Mausoleum, the Temple, and Diocletian's private apartments. The north part was divided by a second road, the equivalent of the military *via praetoria*, which led from the north gate: this area probably contained the accommodation for bodyguard and other staff. Opposite the junction of these roads was the Peristyle, an open area 24 by 13.25 metres lined on either side by a colonnade. This was dominated by the entrance to Diocletian's residence on the south, an imposing façade with a pediment resting on four columns of crimson granite. From the moment one entered the Palace by the north gate the attention was held by this entrance: the colonnades on either side of the Peristyle continued the line of columns on either side of the road. The Peristyle was not a continuation of the road but rather an open space separating the two major structures between the east–west road and the private apartments. On the east is the octagonal Mausoleum (inside it is circular) surrounded with its own portico, and originally enclosed within a rectangular colonnaded enclosure (*temenos*) appropriate to a building which would hold the mortal remains of the deified emperor, and measuring 39 by 35 metres. Here the body of Diocletian was placed in 315: fifty years later a tomb-robber forfeited his life for stealing the emperor's purple shroud.[1] In a similar enclosure entered from the west side of the Peristyle was a temple, probably dedicated to Diocletian's personal deity Jupiter, measuring externally 10 by 9 metres. Except for the façade of columns and the triangular pediment which have disappeared altogether, the building has survived undamaged and now serves as a baptistery. It is one of the best preserved examples of a small classical temple, with an intricately decorated doorway. Inside the elaborately carved barrel-vault of the ceiling is preserved and matches closely that in the temple of Venus and Rome in Rome. Apart from these two sacred buildings little is recorded of any structures inside the Palace apart from Diocletian's own living quarters.

If the Mausoleum and the Temple are the most impressive single remains of the buildings to be seen today, it is the southern part of the Palace, where the emperor's private apartments were ranged behind the southern façade, that will

[1] Amm. Marc., xvi, 8, 4; cf. Sidon Apoll., xxiii, 495.

one day provide the most impressive evidence for the scale of the building. South of the Peristyle the floor was raised above the original ground level which sloped towards the sea: behind the south wall this level was more than 10 metres above the ground. Of the buildings on the upper floor level no trace now remains except for the circular Vestibule, 12 metres across and 17 high, which was entered from the Peristyle. It was constructed from courses of masonry alternating with bands of tile courses rising to the circular vault. Light was admitted through small windows high in the walls, and at ground level there were four semicircular niches which may have contained statues of the household gods (*penates*). The upper part of the wall was inlaid with a glass mosaic of geometric pattern. Behind this nothing survives today of the suites of halls and vestibules where Diocletian spent his retirement. The people of mediaeval Split used the material for building their houses but they did not break through the raised floor. The accumulated rubbish of centuries filled and protected the underground chambers beneath: these are now revealing evidence for the plan of the building at the upper level. The clearance of the debris during the last decade has revealed almost the entire plan of the private apartments, but it is not yet possible to determine the precise function of the different suites, comprising halls, vestibules, and corridors, which have been revealed.

IV *The Countryside*

In a province such as Dalmatia control of the land would be divided broadly between two authorities, the imperial government and the local autonomous city. Although it is not possible to draw the boundaries everywhere precisely between the two categories there is no doubt that a very large proportion of the province was controlled by the cities as their *territoria* or, until the middle of the second century, by the remaining native *civitates*. In a legal sense the *territorium* was part of the city and there is no evidence for any significant distinctions between residents in the urban centre and people who lived in the country, at least as regards justice and taxation. An inscription at Salona refers to 'citizens and resident (aliens)' (*coloni et incolae*) in what appears to be a formal designation of all the freeborn residents in the colony along with the magistrates and city councillors, but there is no distinction between dwellers inside the walls (*intramurani*) and those outside (*extramurani*). Not all the population would necessarily be on the same legal footing as regards Roman citizenship: in some instances the creation of a *municipium* brought citizenship at first only to the wealthiest families, while the mass gained it later over two or three generations. Much of the land in the city *territoria* would be owned by families of city-council status and was farmed for them by tenants (*coloni*), whose personal freedom was unrestricted until the fourth century when legislation was issued to bind them to their tenancies by hereditary obligation. Apart from the areas near the coastal cities dominated exclusively by immigrant families there is no evidence that slavery was ever widespread in agriculture, and what there was appears to have declined to insignificance by the middle of the second century; this is paralleled by the similar decline of urban industrial slavery and the growth of free guilds of craftsmen (*collegia*). There is nowhere any detailed evidence for the pattern of landownership, but it is clear that in the newer communities of the interior enfranchised families, such as the Flavii in Doclea and the Aelii at Salona with a plurality of city offices, possessed considerable fortunes in the form of land. There was no other source for their wealth. That small proportion of the land which did not form part of city territories would be controlled by the imperial government, usually under two quite separate headings, as provision for the needs of the army and imperial estates, including the exploitation of minerals. In the case of the army a broad strip of territory must have been provided for the military stations between Burnum and Bigeste, with the largest areas around the legionary fortresses at Burnum and Tilurium. These 'lands of the legion' (*prata legionis*) were not necessarily returned to the native population after the unit was moved and the fortress abandoned, but if it was of reasonable quality it could be used for settling colonies of discharged veterans, as happened at Aequum under Claudius, when Legion VII C.p.f. was moved to Moesia. It could, on the other hand, be retained indefinitely under the administration of the imperial procurator, who may have leased lands through an agent (*conductor*) to local landowners. This happened at Burnum, where the old legionary lands were still maintained intact nearly twenty years after the legion had left.[1] There is no evidence that the emperors or members of their families owned large estates in the province. The only well-attested foreign landowners are the Calpurnii Pisones, but their lands were all included in the territories of the Liburnian cities where they were situated. Some estates in Liburnia manufactured their own building tiles; the names of others are preserved in place-names in the territory of Iader. A recently-discovered boundary settlement from near Trebinje, made under the Flavians, records a decision of the governor involving the Vesii family who were not native to the area.[2] This is an exception and all the other known settlements of this type involve either cities in Liburnia or communities of the Delmatae around Salona.

[1] III, 13250; and below, p. 459.
[2] D. Sergejevski, *AI*, 5 (1964), 93 f., citing also another boundary settlement at Gačko, *GZMBH*, 43 (1931), 222.

Only two major mining regions are known, the Sana valley iron-mines around Ljubija and Briševo, and the Domavia silver-lead-mines in the Drina valley. Both were administered by resident equestrian procurators, and, while they controlled the resources of the area above and below ground, cities were unlikely to develop. The mining settlement did acquire the title of a city in the third century, but its independence must have been circumscribed by the presence of the procurator, and if we may judge from the dedications to the *bonitas* and *integritas* of some, the relations of the city with others were not harmonious.

Climate and geography made the pattern of life in the rural areas of the province differ widely. In the coastal cities, dominated for the most part by immigrant families, much of the land had been surveyed on a grid system and allotted to settlers. The native population in these areas which had survived the terrible wars of conquest had no share in their life for generations. In one instance, the expansion of the Salona territory into the Poljica area drove out the Delmatae and it was settled by Salona families and new immigrants after being resurveyed. At Aequum the lands passed directly to legionary and auxiliary veterans as well as to the few Italian settlers already established there. They will not have been well disposed to the native population, and the place remained a community of settlers for generations. An early legionary veteran was settled on lands apparently among the Delmatae near the west end of Imotskipolje. The name on his tombstone was erased in antiquity, possibly by people he terrorized (p. 112). In the Narenta valley few settler families are known, compared with freedmen-traders, although some lived on estates. The Papii brothers who are recorded in 36 B.C. at Tasovčići (p. 248) were immigrants, probably Narona colonists. These and other families who owned estates appear to have lived on them from the earliest years of the province. Elsewhere it is only in the second half of the second century that the landowners' preference to leave the city and live on their lands can be detected.

Away from the coast the native population lived scattered throughout the land in small settlements, the villages (κῶμαι) spoken of by Appian and other writers. In the karst the settlements were scattered around the edges of the poljes, while in the valleys to the north most lived close to the bank of the river. Some of these settlements may have grown and acquired city titles as the urban centres for the area, but it is clear that this process had little effect on the mass of the population. Only the few people actively concerned in the city government moved to the city from their old strongholds, as happened at Doclea. In many cases the city never acquired any position of dominance over its own territory. At Bistue Nova some of the leading families are found buried at Zenica on the Bosna, more than 20 miles from the urban centre at Vitez in the Lašva valley.

393

More striking is the evidence from Maluesa in the northeast (p. 283). Most of the tombstones, especially those of the wealthier families, are found at different places in the city territory, with only a few from the urban centre at Visibaba near Požega. The same situation existed in the Bihać area: here the fertile plain around the river Una supported a large population but no urban centre developed as an attraction for the wealthier families.

When one turns to examine the evidence for rural settlement the paucity of archaeological evidence allows no more than an outline survey. In a few areas large houses built in the Roman fashion have been uncovered and planned; these are the *villae rusticae* upon which were centred the large estates. Such places are known in the upper Narenta around Konjic and also the Bihać area; a few scattered examples are also found in the interior. None is known in the territories of the coastal cities, with the exception of Narona. A good illustration of a rural area in the karst hinterland near to the coast is Imotskipolje (fig. 8), the territory of the city Novae (Runović). Like many of the poljes it is cut off from neighbouring areas by limestone mountains, except on the southeast where it is linked to the Trebižat valley and thus to the Narenta.[1] The source of water is the Vrlika which rises in the northwest corner of the polje near Proložac whence it flows to the polje basin, the marshy lake Nuga near Drinovci. Later the same river reappears as the Tihaljina and finally as the Trebižat which reaches the Narenta a short distance above Narona. In autumn the waters rise rapidly, with torrents flowing erratically across the plain. This made it necessary to secure communications by maintaining the bridges in good repair, many of which stand for most of the year over dry torrent beds. In 1890 a local priest arranged for the three hamlets of Gorica, Sovići, and Drinovci to construct a bridge across the Plavilo stream, a modern analogy for the rebuilding of the Hippius (Cetina) bridge at Tilurium by Delminium, Novae, and Rider together in the late second century. There the co-ordinating influence was the provincial governor. The floods come to the polje regularly and traditionally begin to disappear on 20 July, although naturally the extent of the flooding can vary from year to year. Snow is very rarely seen, and the polje experiences neither of the prevailing winds of the Adriatic coast, the winter northern Bora or the summer Sirocco. Today the area has few trees, but a traveller in 1717 mentions the dense woodland around Imotski. Contacts with the coast have never been close: the route to the sea is difficult and the only area for settlement in that direction is the line of the coast road between Salona and Narona, where more than a dozen settlements of the Roman period are known, many of them included in the territory of Novae.

[1] Patsch, *WMBH*, 8 (1902), 61 ff.

Roman conquest brought a military road through the area, linking Tilurium and Bigeste. It was completed under Tiberius, as is shown by the building record of 26–7 from Lokvičić, where the road makes the steep descent into the polje from the north.[1] Before the Roman period the main line of travel was the trade route which linked Imotski with the Adriatic through the Trebižat and the Narenta valley. It was flourishing in the Hellenistic period: twenty-three coins of Apollonia and Dyrrhachium of the third and second centuries B.C. have been found in the region. The Roman road crosses the Vrlika at Kamenmost (Stonebridge) and joins together the two halves of the polje. An inscription records that it was rebuilt in the second century. From Imotski a road led across the hills to Delminium in Duvjanskopolje, where at least one of the leading Novae families owned estates. In the polje the road continues towards Gradac near Posušje, a military centre in the early first century. By the end of Tiberius' reign legionary and auxiliary forts linked by road had established complete control over the lands of the Novenses.

In contrast to the people of the upper valley of the Cetina, the Novenses were rapidly affected by Roman forms and ideas. Among religious dedications the cults of Diana, Silvanus, Ceres and the Triviae (guardians of crossroads), and Fortuna Redux are attested, apart from the official dedications to Jupiter Optimus Maximus. Christianity arrived in due course: the church at Bublin is one of those recorded at the Salona provincial council of 532. A striking feature is the large number of settlements occupied in the Roman period over the whole region. Apart from the city Novae at Runović, there were more than a dozen small settlements along the south side of the polje, although none of them has yet been excavated. The region was once part of the Delmatae and was later included in the city of the Novenses. This may have extended from the sea coast around Makarska as far inland as Duvjanskopolje, although the north part around the Vrlika source was part of the Salona territory, to judge from the early settlement of legionary veterans. Chance finds from some of the small settlements indicate a good standard of life for some of the population, column bases at Sovići, late La Téne brooches and buckles from Gorica, imported building bricks at Kamenmost, and altars from Bublin and Novae.

The picture is quite different in the upper valley of the Cetina around Vrlika.[2] Between the source of the river and Koljane there are two small poljes, the Cetinsko nearer the source, and the Vrlika a short distance to the south (fig. 10). Below Koljane the river flows in the narrow valley southeastwards to Sinj. Two

[1] III, 8512. On the road in detail, Patsch, *JAK*, 2 (1908), 97 ff.
[2] Patsch, *WMBH*, 7 (1900), 119 ff. On the native settlements around Kievo, W. Büttler, 21 *BerRGK*, (1931), 185–7.

small communities of the Delmatae in this area, the Barizani and the Lizaviates, were involved in a boundary dispute at Šušnjar settled sometime in the middle of the first century A.D. (p. 458), but there is no evidence that a city ever developed in the area. As is the case today most of the settlements are located around the edges of the polje, when the modern centre is now at Vrlika. The higher slopes supported livestock, the lower ground around the villages agriculture and viticulture. The native population remained unaffected by Roman rule for nearly two centuries. Most of the tombstones record *peregrini* with Dalmatian names and, apart from an isolated Septimius family, the only Roman name recorded is Aurelius. Patsch suggested that the population in antiquity was greater than it was at the beginning of this century. By a rapid survey he identified four major settlements, Koljane gornje, Stražine, Lastve–Sevače (Vuletić), and Kievo, and eleven smaller sites. Although Roman gods appear on dedications, such as Silvanus (with his own well supported shrine at Stražine), Diana, Liber, Jupiter, Juno, and Janus, there are fewer signs of Roman influence than at Novae. The tombstones do not follow the normal Roman practice: out of seventeen examples the formula *dis manibus* (to the departed spirits) appears on only three.

Apart from the mining areas the parts of Dalmatia most attractive for settlers were the rich lands in the territories of the coastal cities. Numerous tombstones in these regions attest families of Italian origin, in the Ravni kotari, the Salona territory, and especially the Narona territory in the Narenta valley. Only in this last area is there archaeological evidence for the country houses on the estates of these landowning families. The lower Narenta was thickly settled in the earliest period and imports are found in large quantity. The settler families appear to have been completely dependent on Italian imports for manufactured articles. There is no doubt about the considerable wealth of these families, and the *villae rusticae* of families similar to the Safinii and Papii have been excavated. There was a fine estate at Dretelj near the Narenta opposite the estates of the Papii at Tasovčići.[1] No plan of the house is preserved, but it was lavishly equipped with hypocaust-heating, mosaic floors, and marble veneer on the wall as well as painted plaster. The land around the house is very fertile and the perfect site chosen for it suggests the privilege of a wealthy landowner. It was built in the early first century A.D., using imported building tiles from the Italian PANSIANA and M. C. CHRESIMUS factories. The land grew cereal crops, and a number of quernstones were discovered in the ruins of the house. Many estates of this type existed at Čapljina, Tasovčići, Dretelj, and Počitelj, as well as in the smaller valleys of the Trebižat and the Bregava. Narona prospered by the Italian trade

[1] Patsch, *WMBH*, 9 (1904), 278–80.

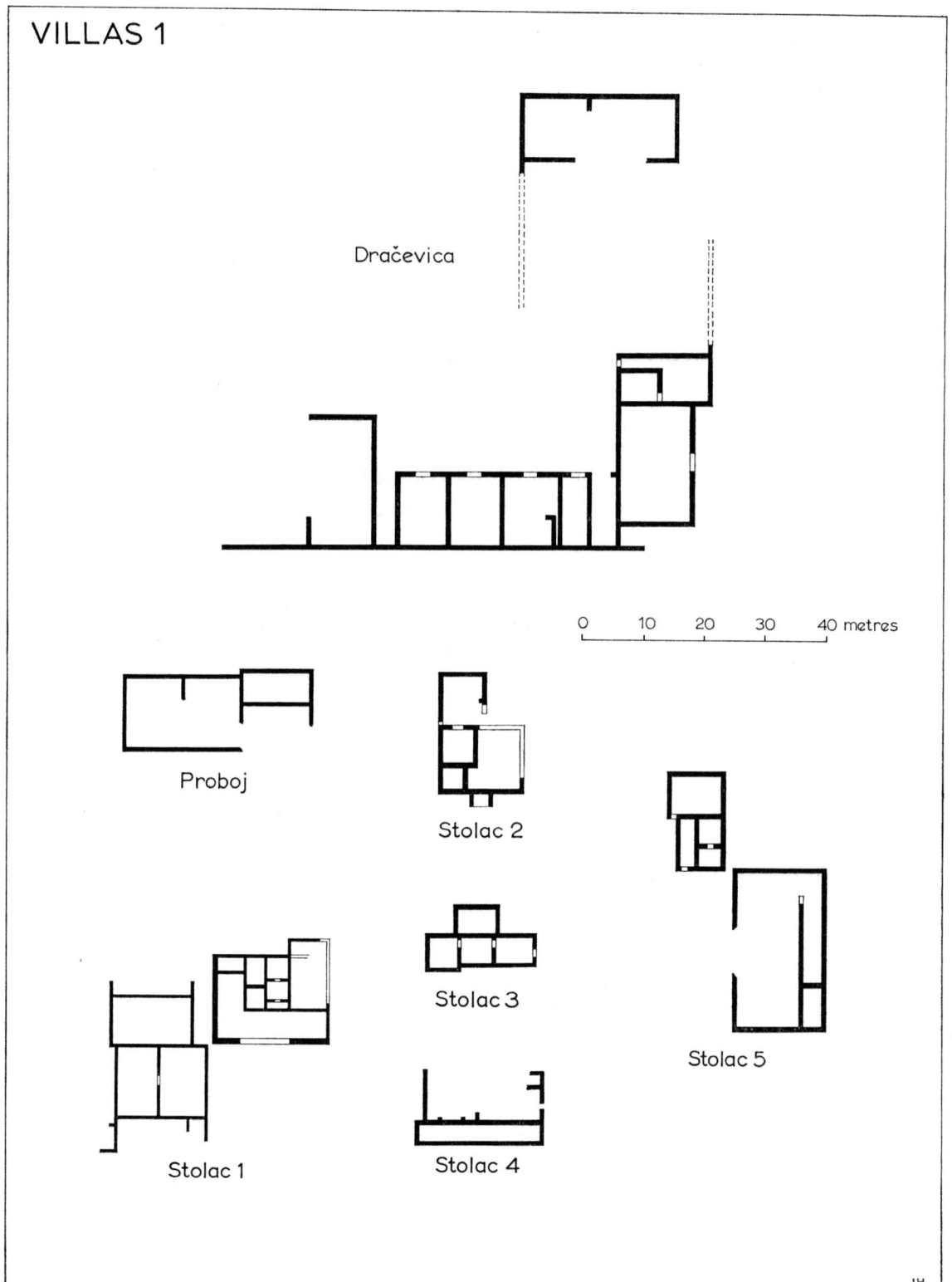

VILLAS 1

Dračevica

0   10   20   30   40 metres

Proboj

Stolac 2

Stolac 3

Stolac 1

Stolac 4

Stolac 5

J.H.

Figure 22 Villas 1

with its territory, but when this declined in the second century it did not prosper as much as Salona or Iader. There was a large house at Dračevica (fig. 22) in the most fertile part of the Trebižat valley around Ljubuški.[1] Part of this area was occupied by the auxiliary Cohort I Belgarum at Bigeste (Humac), but some of the government land had been given over to Narona under Tiberius and settled with legionary veterans. The villa consisted of ranges of rooms around the three sides of an open courtyard. Although less than half of the plan is recorded, the ten rooms known indicate a house occupying an area more than 60 metres square. Coins found in clearing the surface debris do not date before the middle of the second century, but the use of large quantities of imported Italian building tiles from the first-century PANSIANA and C. TITIUS HERMEROS factories suggest that the original house on the site was built in the first century. The latest coin is of Julian (361–3); and the end of the villa came with a disastrous fire, possibly the result of a barbarian raid in the last decades of the fourth century. Other houses of the same type are known at Proboj, Hrušljani, Kutac, and Ljubuški. No details of their plans have been published but their use of large quantities of imported tiles suggests that they began as the *villae rusticae* of settler families in the first century. Not all the houses were country mansions on the scale of Dračevica. The house at Proboj was a simple building with only four rooms, and no mosaics or heated rooms.[2] Although most of the coins found there date to the fourth century, the use of stamped building-tiles from the Salona factory of L. MALTINIUS ABASCANTUS suggests that it began in the first century. It was less favoured than other sites: water had to be carried from the nearest source more than 200 metres away. The Brotnjopolje between Mostar and the Trebižat valley reveals a similar pattern of settlement, with large country houses at Čerin, Čitluk, and Krehin gradac. The lands here were owned by Narona families, among whom the Livii and Safinii are attested.[3] Like the remainder of the Narona territory the area has produced large quantities of imported goods, but its period of greatest prosperity appears to have been in the second rather than in the first century.

A way from the Narenta valley the only major settlement on Narona territory was at Stolac in the Bregava valley. The excavation of ten groups of buildings near the modern town has yielded much evidence for the standard of living enjoyed by the upper classes in the Roman period. In spite of its oppressive summer climate Stolac attracted a number of settlers in the first century, and it is probably this class who built the fine houses and exploited the land during that

[1] Fiala, *WMBH*, 5 (1897), 163–5.   [2] Fiala and Patsch, *WMBH*, 3 (1895), 280–3.
[3] Fiala, *WMBH*, 2 (1894), 59 ff.; Patsch, *WMBH*, 9 (1904), 280–4. On the Narona families, see p. 298 f.

period. On the other hand, the arrival of enfranchised native families in the Narona ruling class under the Flavians suggests that in the long run the settlers were not as dominant at Stolac as they were around the city.

Most of the houses excavated were simple in plan (fig. 22) with a small number of rooms.[1] In some cases the farm buildings were kept quite separate from the dwelling house, but none of them is likely to have been the centre of a large estate. Mosaic floors are common: one had four, of which the largest was 6 by 4 metres. The motifs and patterns were traditional: one exhibits the common design of four female figures in the corners representing the seasons of the year enclosed in triangular panels. In an adjoining room was an early floor-pattern of intersecting arcs and curves in an elaborate design. Three of the houses are known only from their bath blocks, the most durable part of any Roman building, but the standard of building was high. In one cold room was a striking mosaic of the Cretan Labyrinth in a geometric maze pattern, with a fierce portrait of the Minotaur in the central panel.[2] Much of this bath block was decorated with painted wall-plaster and marble inlay. The date of the Stolac houses is not attested from the excavations, but the widespread use of imported Italian building-tiles (PANSIANA, SOLONAS, T. VETTIUS AVITUS, Q. CLODIUS AMBROSIUS, Q. GRANIUS PRISCUS, etc.,) suggests that the earliest buildings belong to the first century; all the coins recovered from the surface, however, belong to the fourth century. All the buildings were farms: large numbers of quernstones, all of the rotary type, and quantities of iron sickles and bill-hooks were discovered. There was no trace of any manufacturing or industrial activity, and in its period of prosperity it is clear that the settlement depended greatly on imports from Italy. The landowners of Narona appear to have chosen to live on their estates from the beginning, even in the more remote areas of the territory such as Brotnjopolje and Stolac. The city was dominated by mercantile and settler families until the end of the first century. Like the territory of Iader or Salona, it was one of those regions to which the Elder Pliny's remark about Narbonensis could be applied: 'more like Italy than a province' (*Italia verius quam provincia*).[3]

The southern region of Hercegovina belongs to the Mediterranean World, with all its advantages of climate, rich produce, and the sea. Its drawbacks were the scarcity of fertile land, the oppressive heat in summer which scorches much of the vegetation long before autumn, and the severe shortage of regular supplies of water. Beyond the great peaks of the Prenj mountains which rise to more than 2,000 metres is the long upper valley of the Narenta around the modern town of

[1] Stolac: Fiala, *WMBH*, 1 (1893), 284 ff.; Fiala and Patsch, *WMBH*, 3 (1894), 272 ff.; 5 (1897), 168.
[2] *WMBH*, 5 (1897), 168 ff., fig. 9–11.   [3] *HN*, iii, 31.

Konjic. The valley is fertile, especially in the stretch between Lisičići and Ostro-
žac to beyond Podhum. There is a small strip of agricultural land, large areas of
grass pasturage, and hills covered with many square miles of birch and deciduous
forest. In addition to the Narenta many tributary valleys (Rakitnica, Trešanica,
Neretvica, Rama, Doljanka, Bjela, and Idbar) have the same conditions and
ensure a plentiful water supply from the mountains which retain snow until July.
The valleys produce fruit and some wine, while the upland pastures, especially
the Visočića and Radoblje plateaux, were used by the shepherds from the karst
country beyond the mountains to the south for pasture in the summer. At the
beginning of the present century as many as 50,000 beasts were brought to these
areas in one season. The region was linked to the coastal area by two routes, the
difficult passage down the gorge of the Narenta north of Mostar and the longer
but more practical route north from Mostar across the Porim mountains into the
upper Narenta at Lipeta Karaula west of Glavatičevo and then down the valley
towards Konjic. This was the main route to the area in the Roman period
(attested by third-century milestones); while the Narenta gorge was only prac-
ticable after the construction of the narrow-gauge railway and the more recent
road. Not surprisingly the area supported a large population, possibly as many
as the 22,000 who lived there in the early part of this century. In the Narenta
valley nineteen Roman sites have been identified, eight of which were large
settlements. Little is known about the composition of the population, which was
probably a mixture of Illyrian Narensii and Celtic Autariatae. The region was
not isolated in the pre-Roman period, and coins from Apollonia and Dyrrhachium attest links with the Greek world in the third and second centuries B.C.[1]

In the Roman period tombstones attest classical influences spreading among
the population, as also do dedications to classical deities. The amount of immigration from the coast was small and there are few families with Italian names.
In the third century some eastern traders reached the region, and one who came
from Caria in Asia Minor dedicated to Mithras near Konjic. Before the area was
flooded by the Jablanica hydro-electric scheme, excavations were carried out on
some sites around Lisičići, which revealed a group of *villae rusticae* of a type quite
different from those around Narona. Three were found spaced 300 metres apart
along the north bank of the river (fig. 23).[2] The largest of the three consisted
of an eight-roomed building about 30 by 20 metres. The others were smaller and
of different plan. One was a small house 11 by 9 metres placed against one of the
walls of an enclosure 80 by 60 metres. Architecturally the building was simple,

[1] Patsch, *WMBH*, 9 (1904), 235 ff.
[2] I. Čremošnik, *GZMS*, 10 (1955), 132 ff.; 12 (1957), 143 ff., with map of the three sites, 157,
fig. 9. For comparable sites in Germany, *BJ* (1928), 132–4, figs. 60–1.

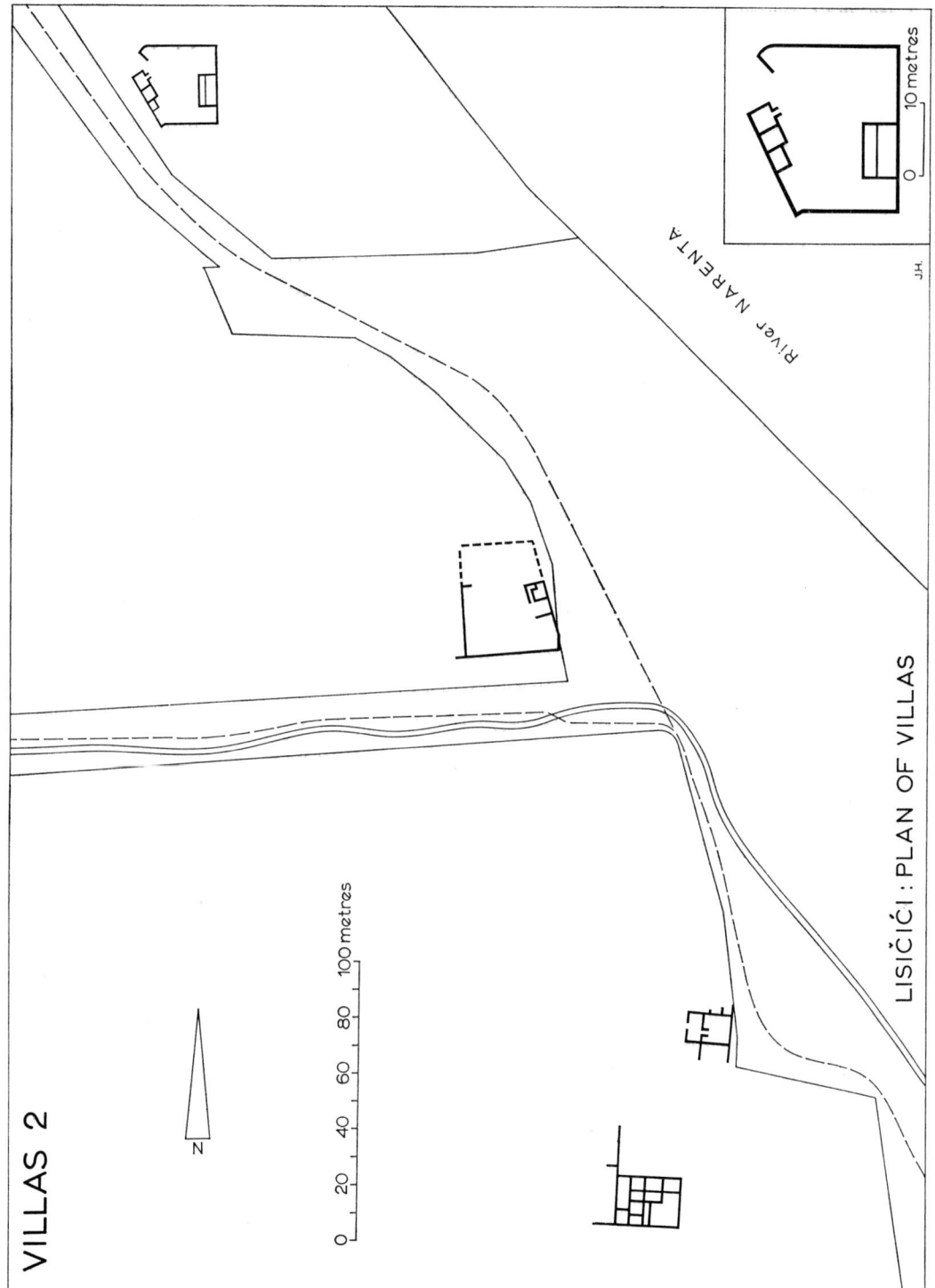

Figure 23 Villas 2

with poor quality marble on the walls and no mosaic floors. The third, the smallest of the three, included a kiln which made tiles for use on the farm. It did not stamp the products nor were any imported tiles used in the buildings. Similar groups of farms spaced at three hundred metre intervals occur at intervals of three to five kilometres along the bank of the Narenta in this sector. What outside contacts the people enjoyed is not attested in the remains found in the farms, but near the third of the villas mentioned above, at Vratnica near the foot of the Gostijeranj hill, was discovered a Mithraic relief dedicated by the merchant from Aphrodisias in Caria. This was not the only offering to Mithras from the area, and at least two of the grottoes in the hillside were used as temples to Mithras.[1]

These farms were occupied by natives of the area, and the enclosures around the farm-buildings indicate that livestock was important in the economy. This type of pastoral farm is well attested in other European provinces, especially in Noricum, Raetia, and Gaul. They manufactured pottery locally; the iron implements, with incised Celtic decoration, are similar to examples found in Northern Dalmatia. The farms date to the third and fourth centuries and reflect the gradual spread of Roman farming-techniques into the more remote areas of the province. The cemetery of this community was across the river in the tumulus Crkvina, where numerous Roman tombstones have been found. All the burials were inhumations and among the grave-goods the pottery matched precisely that found in the farms across the river, although this cemetery was also used in the pre-Roman period.[2] The tombstones reveal a knowledge of Latin but there are no official positions or indications of social status. Hunting was a popular occupation and one stone from the cemetery has a fine relief of the chase, with the huntsman and his hound cornering a deer which has climbed a small tree. The farmstead communities in the upper Narenta valley are probably typical of the interior in the areas where there was good pasture but where conditions never favoured the growth of a city. There is no doubt that in the Roman period Konjic was the centre of the area as it is today: it stands at the junction of the Narenta valley and the route over the Ivan pass to the Sarajevo area. Traders settled there, and one of them constructed a small Mithraeum using a portable double-sided cult relief, which showed the tauroctony on the front and the ritual banquet on the rear.[3] To judge from the coins found in the debris it flourished for most of the fourth century.

---

[1] *WMBH*, 4 (1896), 252; cf. 9 (1904) 250; *CIMRM*, 2, n. 1893, fig. 488.

[2] Patsch, *WMBH*, 4 (1896), 266 ff.; cf. I. Čremošnik, *GZMS*, 12 (1957), 156 ff.

[3] Patsch, *WMBH*, 6 (1899), 186 ff., plates X a, b, and fig. 20; *CIMRM*, 2, n. 1895–6 and figs., 489–91. A fine marble head from a larger than lifesize female statue is also known from Konjic; *WMBH*, 4 (1896), 272, figs. 42–3.

Portraits on the tombstones reveal something of the clothing and characteristics of the people.[1] Many carry reliefs of two people, crudely carved, although the individual features can usually be recognized. The women wear a long plain tight-fitting tunic with long sleeves. It is fastened on the shoulders with large brooches (*fibulae*), while the waist is pulled in by a girdle fastened at the side or the back. Married women have their heads covered with shawls, but maidens have their long hair uncovered. In the case of the men no difference in dress is apparent between different age groups. They wear a long-sleeved tunic, with a cloak covering the left hand and arm and fastened on the right shoulder by a brooch. All have their hair cut short, and apart from the brooches as dress-fasteners, the only jewellery which appears is earrings worn by women. The latter are depicted on their tombstones in their best clothes, but it does not appear to have been the custom to wear jewellery such as bangles, necklaces, or rings. No details can be recognized of the brooches, except that the women's were large and ornate, while those worn by the men were smaller and more utilitarian.

In the northwest the wide plain around Bihać in the Una valley supported an advanced agriculture in the Roman period, similar to that of the Konjic area. There is no evidence that any city developed in the region, and the native *civitas* of the Iapodes was still flourishing at the end of the first century A.D., as is shown by the dedications at the Privilica spring. The land was covered with small farms, most of them situated on small hills close to the river. Although the Roman citizenship came early to some families and there are traces of slave-owning among the native families, the Iapodes remained conservative towards Roman influences, more so than the people around Konjic. Their tombstones reveal many pre-Roman features, though the large cemeteries at Ribić, Jezerine, and Glubić, remained in use well into the Roman period.[2] There is little detailed archaeological evidence for individual settlements, but the small courtyard house (21 by 9.6 metres) at Založje is probably typical of the area.[3] The Založje (fig. 24) house had its own bath block and was very similar in plan to the larger house in the group at Lisičići. Farms of this type have been traced at Huduri, Izačić, Gata Ilidža, Brekovica, and Tutnjevac (Bjeline).[4] At the first-named place three houses are spaced at regular intervals along the river like

[1] Patsch, *WMBH*, 9 (1904), 240.

[2] Čremošnik, *GZMS*, 13 (1958), 121 ff., summarizing earlier work.

[3] Založje: *GZMS*, loc. cit.; J. Rankovići, *GZMS*, 10 (1955), 137.

[4] Huduri: *WMBH*, 7 (1900), 58 ff. (Jezerine-Pritoka cemetery); Izačić: *WMBH*, loc. cit.; Gata Ilidža: *GZMS*, 11 (1956), 127; Brekovica: *GZMS*, 11 (1956), 132; cf. *WMBH*, 7 (1900), 46; Tutnjevac (Bjeline): I. Čremošnik, *Članci*, 1 (1958), 37–51.

those along the Narenta at Lisičići. There is less evidence for the dates when they were built, but what is known suggests that they were occupied during the third and fourth centuries. There is one house which does not belong to this series. Twenty miles downstream at Ljušina, north of Bosanska Krupa, was a large house with at least twenty rooms (fig. 24), ranged around the three sides

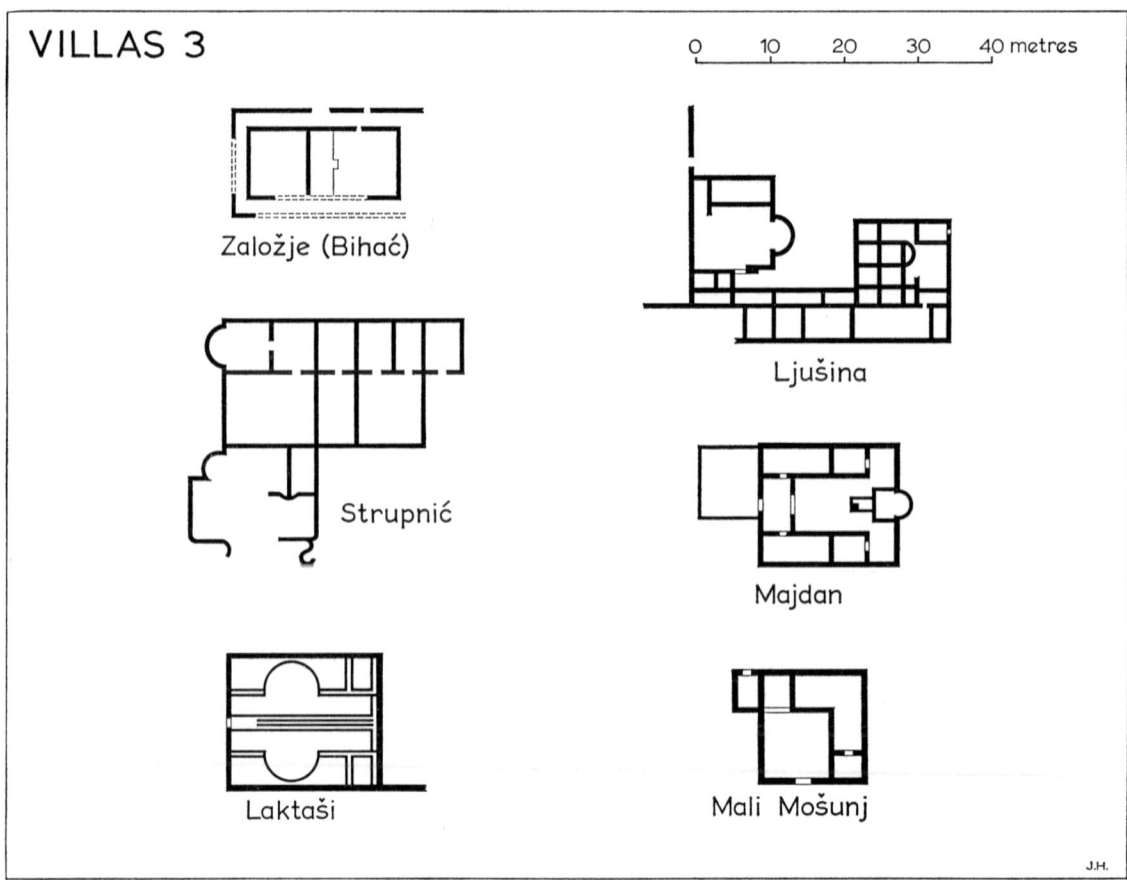

Figure 24 Villas 3

of an open courtyard.[1] Six domestic rooms opened off a corridor, from which a large quantity of locally manufactured pottery and iron agricultural implements were recovered. Although the house had windows of green and yellow glass and included some columns, there were few signs of real luxury, no mosaics or painted plaster. The large quantity of animal bones from the debris included ox, horse, goat, and fowl. The house was built in the fourth century and may

[1] Čremošnik, *GZMS*, 14 (1959), 137 ff.; cf. *WMBH*, 2 (1894), 69.

have been the centre of a large estate owned either by a member of the imperial family or by a wealthy absentee landowner, and was possibly administered by a steward (*vilicus*), an appointment which is attested in other parts of the province (p. 224).

Apart from these two areas where systematic excavation has revealed a clear picture of rural settlements and their economy little is known about the country-side in the rest of the interior. The poljes occupied by the Northern Delmatae will not have supported many large estates, although one may have been based at Strupnić in Livjanskopolje (fig. 24) where a house with more than thirteen rooms was occupied in the fourth century.[1] It consists of a row of small rooms flanked by three large rooms as well as others not completely planned, and it compares closely with the house at Ljušina near Krupa. In the northern valleys there may have been many large houses of this type. At Majdan near Varcar Vakuf, on a tributary of the river Vrbas, a curious building with a basilican plan (fig. 24) has been identified as the centre of an estate.[2] It consists of a rectangle 18.6 by 16 metres with an almost circular apse in the end wall. The plastered walls were decorated with geometric patterns. On either side of the main chamber were two pairs of rooms, while the apse was flanked by double columns. A similar type of building is known at Laktaši (fig. 24) close to the provincial boundary with Pannonia.[3] Overall it measured 21.2 by 17.6 metres but little else can be deduced from the published remains. It was probably the bath block of a much larger building, to judge from the large variety of box and flue tiles; on the other hand, the absence of any water supply in the area led the excavator to suggest that it was a dwelling house. A house of more orthodox plan, roughly square with an *atrium* and four rooms (fig. 24), is known at Mali Mošunj in the territory of Bistue Nova.[4] One of its rooms was heated by a hypocaust; the earliest coin it produced is of Iulia Mamaea (222–35). Nothing is reported about the material discovered in these places, but their economy was probably based on a mixture of livestock and agriculture. At the last-named site a cow-bell bears out the suggestion of livestock. The Mali Mošunj house was part of a small settlement, but this was probably no more than a small group of houses like those around Bihać and Lisičići.

The archaeological surveys which have been made and the large quantities of agricultural implements and other finds leave no doubt that in the Roman period the Bosnian valleys were thickly populated and in some areas intensively exploited. All the cities which existed there during the Empire have probably been

[1] Patsch, *WMBH*, 11 (1909), 127 f.   [2] Radimsky, *WMBH*, 3 (1895), 248 ff.
[3] Kellner, *WMBH*, 1 (1893), 254 ff.
[4] Truhelka and Patsch, *WMBH*, 3 (1895), 229 ff.

recognized from the size of the area occupied, but not all can be identified by name, for instance Šipovo in the Pliva valley. The many small settlements identified by surface remains could be large isolated houses at the centre of estates, although there were probably fewer of these than the small mixed farms of the type known in the Narenta and Una valleys.

Chapter 14
The Pattern of Trade

It may be that the extent to which the Pax Romana enabled free movement throughout the Empire has been exaggerated. Few people could travel long distances within the Roman World unless they were sponsored by some public body or were following a traditional route as established traders. Wasteful journeys at public expense by provincial city dignitaries to congratulate the emperor on his birthday or the anniversary of his accession were criticized by Trajan. Land travel was especially expensive and in some provinces very difficult and dangerous (it is an illusion to assume that the Roman Empire provided a universal rule of 'law and order'); moreover the cost of transport made the movement of many classes of goods prohibitive. Nor did the Roman army build roads across such areas as the interior of Dalmatia in order to increase the profits of merchants or facilitate the economic development of more backward areas. Only the privileged few were entitled to enjoy the benefit of the imperial transport system (*cursus publicus*) with its maintained posting stations (*stationes*) and guest-houses (*mansiones*). Even for provincial governors authorization to use this was restricted by the central government at Rome and a pass (*diploma*) was not always freely granted on request.[1] A great proportion of travel was always undertaken by water, by river or coastal voyages, wherever possible. The long coastline of Dalmatia with its many harbours has always drawn the area towards close contacts with Italy and the Mediterranean, while the mountainous country inland hindered contacts and tended to separate the regions both politically and economically.

[1] The Younger Pliny felt that he had to be careful when using such permits, *Epp.*, x, 120. Normally they were not available to private persons, however eminent.

The Pattern of Trade

Most of the trade which can be studied from archaeological evidence took place between the larger coastal cities and the chief ports along the east coast of Italy, Pola, Aquileia, Altinum, Ancona, Aternum, as well as with Rome through its port at Ostia. These were the main routes of long-distance trade, and through regular voyages, which forged close links between the Dalmatian and Italian cities, contacts between the trading guilds of the different ports became established. By contrast the volume of trade between the coastal cities and the interior was small. A few families of traders are known from tombstones in the north, but the archaeological evidence suggests little contact.

In the Adriatic coastal region the pattern of trade is clear, at least during the first century A.D. Manufactured goods from Italian workshops were imported to the Dalmatian cities in exchange for foodstuffs, livestock, minerals, and a few manufactured articles such as cloth. Much of the traffic was in the hands of shipping guilds (*corpus naviculariorum*) and passed mostly through the main ports. The growth of this trade was closely linked with the establishment of the Italian communities during the Late Republic. The spread of these imports was restricted; most are only found at the sites of the older cities and not in the adjacent hinterland, except in the Narenta valley, where Italian settlements were more widespread and the rivers facilitated inland transport. The main natural resouces of the coast are wine and the olive, both of which were exported mainly to Italy. The traders are illustrated by a wine merchant (*negotiator vinarius*) in the territory of Salona and an oil merchant (*negotiator olearius*) at Iader,[1] and the trade itself by the numerous amphorae found in many ports of the coast; these were large earthenware storage or transport jars which were used in Dalmatia from about the middle of the first century B.C., especially at Narona where many deposits have been found.[2] Fruit was probably another export, especially from the Liburnian Ravni kotari. Timber was a great resource of the province but most was in remote areas where transport was expensive. A timber merchant is attested at Salona (*negotiator materiarius*), and the deforestation of the karst hinterland may have begun already with the growth of the timber trade near the coast in antiquity.[3] Then the major timber-producing region was the Lika polje behind the Velebit mountains: a specialized product was the barrel, which was already being manufactured and exported in the middle of the first century B.C.[4] Another export was marble. Stone from Corcyra Nigra was used in the early military buildings at Gradac near Posušje;[5] in the fourth century the Brattia marble quarries near Škrip were worked to obtain columns for the new imperial

[1] III, 2131, 2936.   [2] Patsch, *JAK*, 2 (1908), 91, fig. 5.   [3] III, 12924.
[4] Patsch, *Lika*, 103, referring to Lopsica.
[5] Fiala and Patsch, *WMBH* 3, (1895), 259.

baths at Sirmium,[1] as well as for the Palace of Diocletain (p. 388). Such a supply was quite exceptional, and only the government can have contemplated transporting large quantities of marble for such a distance. Apart from these items the natural resources of the coast were few when compared with those of the interior. Such products as the Gentian medicinal herb noted by Pling, which grew wild in the southeast, or the murex fish, which was dried and used to produce the dye for imperial purple, will have had little impact on the economy of the area.[2]

A major asset was livestock. The Delmatae once demanded tribute in cattle from their subject peoples, and away from the coast almost every Roman site that is excavated reveals bones and examples of cowbells which suggest that herds were widespread.[3] The climate of the karst made necessary seasonal migrations of the type already mentioned between the southern Narenta and the high pastureland around Konjic (p. 400). Scatters of coins far away from settlement sites attest the scale of these migrations, mostly between the karst and the uplands to the north. The herds and flocks were of cattle, sheep, or goats. In addition there has always been a large population of wild goats whose effect on the vegetation has been disastrous.[4] Some of the by-products were exported, especially leather, but the cloth produced was too coarse for anywhere but the home market (p. 179). The minerals produced in Northern Dalmatia (iron, gold, copper, lead, and silver) had little impact on the pattern of trade. They were exploited by the government and the main effect of this was the growth of the mining settlements, and therefore markets with large purchasing powers, in some more remote parts of the interior. Gold is not found in quantity, and much of the gold jewellery discovered in tombs appears to have come from outside. Little wine was produced in the interior, and what there was proved barely drinkable. The mass of the population drank *sabaium*, a powerful drink brewed from grain.[5]

The later second and third centuries saw the interior gaining in prosperity, but with few external trade contacts. The coast still attracted Italian trade, but the proportion of foreign commerce from elsewhere was increasing, and the overwhelming dominance of Italian exports had passed away. In most places tile-kilns produced their tiles unstamped and for local use only, while the im-

---

[1] III, 10107 from the quarries near Splitska.

[2] On the Gentian plant, Plin. *HN*, xxv, 71; also the murex fish used for the purple dye in the imperial textile factory at Split (*bafium*, *Not. Dign. occ.* 22); cf. Patsch, *Hercegovina*, 142 f.

[3] Patsch, *Hercegovina*, 141, fig. 79–81 (from Lib planina, Proboj, and Grahovnik-Otunj near Ljubuški).

[4] Patsch, *Hercegovina*, 27 ff.

[5] 'A drink of a type made from cereal and water and called *sabaium* in the barbarous speech of Pannonia and Dalmatia', Jerome, *Comm. on Isaiah*, vii, 19 (292); cf. Amm. Marc., xxvi, 8, 2, in 365.

ported sigillata pottery from Italy and Gaul was replaced by local products, much of which was made in imitation of the older imported forms. In particular there was the orange sigillata manufactured in the Narona area from the early third century onwards in large quantities. It is found in a villa at Visići near Čapljina, where there appears to have been a factory. In the interior it is common, being found at Duvno, Bihać, Konjic, Travnik, Doboj, and Šipovo, and also further afield at Siscia and Sirmium in the Save valley.[1]

Archaeological evidence for close links with Italy in the first century consists mostly of durable items such as building bricks manufactured and stamped by the Italian factories, amphorae, and pottery, much of which was also marked with the makers' names. The pattern of Greek trade which preceded this was quite different. Imports from the Aegean are known in the large cemeteries of the interior at Glasinac, Donja Dolina, Sanskimost, and also at Gorica in Imotskipolje. All these were luxury articles of metal ware, helmets, greaves, and weapons. In the coastal cities this trade was obviously greater, but virtually nothing of its remains have been published, an exception being the fine Hellenistic jewellery at Butua.[2]

It is strange that it was commercially profitable to export building tiles from Italy to Dalmatia. Yet this was certainly the case during the first century A.D. A brief visit to almost any site along the coast will reveal the imports in large quantities, but the number decreases sharply even a short distance inland. Only a minority of the stamps have been published, although the products of more than one hundred factories have been identified, virtually all located in Italy. Most are stamped with the *tria nomina* of Romans, in some cases obviously freedmen who directed the factory on behalf of their patrons. The largest number of published tile-stamps is at Salona, where the compilations in the *Corpus Inscriptionum Latinarum* have been supplemented by the inventories made by Bulić. There is little evidence how the business of tile-manufacture was organized. In many parts of Italy they were made by large estates for local use, and very few stamps have a distribution throughout the peninsula. Factories which produced them for general sale and export were near the east coast, especially in Istria, Aemilia, and Picenum. These are the places which produced the exports for Dalmatia, and virtually none of the stamps attested in the province was manufactured outside this region. There is no evidence who owned and controlled the output of these factories. The PANSIANA factory was nationalized under Augustus and its products are the commonest, although a small group of other factories are almost as common. Many of the smaller factories may have been owned by landed pro-

[1] I. Čremošnik, *GZMS*, 17 (1962), 115–40; and on Roman coarse pottery, 16 (1961), 189–202.
[2] D. Rendić-Miočević, *Opusc. Arch.* (Zagreb), 4 (1959), 5–47.

prietors (since they would obviously control the raw materials) who were eager to share in the great commercial prosperity of such centres as Aquileia.[1] The trade in amphorae was obviously different. These reached the province through the wine and oil trade, and most of them were used on the short sea voyages across the Adriatic. Some of the products attested can be paralleled at Pompeii, and many of the jars themselves are found at Brundisium, whence they obviously began their journey to Dalmatia. Presumably they were used for carrying wine or oil from Dalmatia to Italy, as well as for carrying the same products in the other direction. The only published group of amphora stamps in the province is that compiled by Patsch in the Narona area; it reflects the principal trading links with South and Central Italy. In the first century, Italian factories dominated the market for good quality household pottery, as much as they did with building-tiles and amphorae. The main centre of pottery-production in the first centuries B.C. and A.D. was at the old Etruscan town of Arretium, whose products took over the Dalmatian market for quality pottery from the Apulian products which had been imported from the third century B.C. Arretine pottery is common throughout the coast, and a wide range of stamps is represented among those which have been published. The earliest imports were the black Arretine sigillata, soon replaced by the orange-red products. In time Arretium was rivalled and eventually surpassed by the South Gaulish factories which soon took over the northwestern markets. Coarse pottery was also imported, but this trade did not last long. In the Narona territory it appears to have been displaced by products from the interior by the second century A.D.[2]

Pottery and building materials were only part of the imports from Italy. This trade was temporary and was closely linked with the predominance of Italian settlers in the coastal communities. Manufactured articles of more specialized categories, bronze wares, jewellery, lamps, and amber, were imported in large quantities, especially during the first century. Although the quantity of this trade diminished it was a more durable contact than the shipping of pottery and building materials, lasting into the second and third centuries A.D. The best-documented group of these imports which has been studied in an archaeological context comes from the cemetery of Argyruntum, the small town in Liburnia. This was excavated and described by A. Colnago and M. Abramić shortly before the First World War.[3] The land south of the city is poor and today is water-logged, although in the Roman period it was dry. A street 4 metres wide led from the south gate of the city towards the fertile area of the territory around the

---

[1] Chilver, *CG*, 176 ff.   [2] Appendix XV.
[3] Abramić and Colnago, *JÖAI*, 12 (1909), Bb. 45–112, the only detailed study of small finds from Liburnia.

river Paklenica. For a distance of more than half a kilometre on both sides of the road was an uninterrupted series of rectangular grave plots, enclosed by low walls and separated by passages less than a metre wide (fig. 15). Some of the plots were divided by partitions, and most of them enclosed an area of from 30 to 40 square metres. Within these areas were buried stone vessels often covered with a single tile, sealing the ashes of the deceased. The cemetery contained only cremations and around each burial were the personal possessions of the dead, most of them articles imported from Italy, arranged by their families. The date of the various burials within one plot were always different, to judge from the coins placed in the funerary urns. The grave plots belonged to the wealthier families, and around them were the graves of humbler folk, sometimes with a few but mostly with no grave goods. There are few traces of the epitaphs from the cemetery. Some fragments of the Liburnian type of tombstone (*cippus Liburnicus*), a circular gravestone topped with a pine cone and with the epitaph inscribed in a panel on the side, were found in the corners of some grave plots, but the material of these monuments was so useful in building that few were discovered intact.

A total of 400 cremations were discovered, of which twenty-five were contained in cylindrical cysts; there were a few rectangular examples. Occasionally the grave-goods were placed inside the vessel, but they were usually laid out carefully near by. From the coins placed in the graves the expansions of the cemetery along the road can be traced. Those nearest to the city have mostly Julio–Claudian coins, with a few of the Republican period (the earliest dated to 90 B.C.); those half-way along the road have Flavian and early second-century issues, while the graves furthest removed from the city have only the small badly-minted coins of the third century. None of the graves was later than the reign of Diocletian. This may have been due to a change in burial custom, or possibly to some natural disaster. Sinking of the coastline did occur in the fourth century, and is well attested at Epidaurum, and this may have caused the abandonment of the Argyruntum cemetery.

The most flourishing period was the late first and early second centuries, the date of the graves with the richest selection of personal possessions. Invariably these include lamps, brooches, glass vessels, and rings. The mens' graves contained weapons, scrapers, fish-hooks, and dice, while in the womens' graves were jewellery, toiletry articles, and many trinkets of amber. There were a few pottery vessels manufactured locally. The amber came in the form of finished articles from Aquileia where it had been brought from the Baltic, and the bronze vessels were probably imported from the Capua factories. Even the tiles used as grave-covers were stamped products of the Italian factories. One of the graves can be identified. The tombstone of the praetorian C. M(. . . .) Severus[1] came from a grave containing a coin of Hadrian, and some of his personal military equipment was found in the grave. None of the contents of the cemetery were specially produced as grave-goods, but were used regularly by the deceased in their daily lives. The lamps had all been used, the rings and jewellery had been worn frequently, and the various implements also show signs of wear and repair. The praetorian was not the only soldier buried in the cemetery. One grave contained a medallion belonging to a certain L. Valerius, soldier in the century of Proclus, who may have been a legionary. There were also three pendants from his uniform, one with a deity standing in an archway, also *phalerae*, gilded bronze discs awarded for gallantry and part of the soldiers' ceremonial parade dress. These had been worn and then placed as an offering in the grave of their owner.

This picture could probably be repeated by excavation in many of the cemeteries around the coastal cities, although the small finds at Argyruntum were well preserved because of the water-logged ground. They were graves of the city families; one or two may have been of city-council status, but overall there is very little sign of a great variation in wealth between the different families. The Narona area has produced quantities of similar finds, but not in carefully excavated contexts nor as well preserved. There is some fine glass from Stolac,[2] and glass beads and armlets are common finds in the area. An interesting group of imports are the small statuettes of gods and goddesses, among which Diana and Mercury were particularly popular. These are found not only on the coast but also in the more remote areas. There is a fine example of Diana the Huntress with flowing cloak and weapons from Taleza near Trebinje in Popovopolje.[3] Among the precious metals silver is the commonest, although there is no sign that it came from the provincial mines, and the large ornate silver brooches, finger-rings, and earrings, probably reached the area as finished products. It is generally striking that there are no finds reported of ingots from the provincial mines, or even lead pigs which are fairly common in other provinces. In the Narona area some of the most expensive jewellery belongs to the later period, such as the jewellery of a wealthy Christian lady which was buried hurriedly at Hrveca along with late sixth-century gold coins.[4] The steady demand for good knife blades, arrow heads, lance tips, and spears was probably met from supplies produced locally in the province.

---

[1] *JÖAI*, 8 (1905), Bb. 57 = *AE*, 1905, 165.
[2] *WMBH*, 1 (1892), 285 ff., pl. I a–b; also in the Stolac houses, p. 399.
[3] *WMBH*, 12 (1912), 155 ff., fig. 97–8.
[4] *BD*, 25 (1902), 197 ff., pl. XII; *BD*, 35 (1912), 112 f., pl. XXI, fig. 5.

From the pattern of trade that can be deduced with this meagre evidence clear differences emerge between different areas within the province. In the cities of the Dalmatian coast, apart from Liburnia, the business of trading was always an important occupation. Large quantities of manufactured articles were brought fairly cheaply by sea from Italy, in exchange for which the products of the city territoria, and to some extent those of the interior, were exported. This trade was in the beginning in the hands of the Italian settler families, using their freed-men in the cities as agents. In Liburnia, with its less marked distinctions between settler and native, the economy was based more on agriculture and, with the exception of Iader, commerce appears to have been less important. The land and its products were important, as witnessed by the zealous attention paid to fixing city boundaries. What industry there was appears to have been purely for local needs, and the population as a whole appears to have been less dependent on Italian imports. Immigration from Italy in this region was much more localized, and most families became established first at Iader. The land was worked almost entirely by free labour, and the native hill-cities in the Ravni kotari soon pros-pered far ahead of the smaller settler communities along the Dalmatian coast. In the Augustan period, before people thought in terms of provincial boundaries, Liburnia may have been regarded as somehow part of Italy; certainly the popu-lation was ethnically close to that of Istria and much of the Tenth Region. Because of this the area retained its native Liburnian character. The social organ-ization, the type of gravestone, and the native name forms all point to this persis-tence of the native character. Liburnia was assimilated to the Roman World long before the Augustan wars, and its people were aiding Caesar in the civil war side by side with the settlers further south. Gradually this individuality seems to have disappeared, although it is to be admitted that this impression is due to the striking lack of inscriptional evidence for the people in the second century and later.

Behind the two coastal regions was the hinterland south of the mountains. Few areas were thoroughly Romanized. The army had little contact with the native population and in any case most of it had been moved elsewhere before the end of the first century. City development here was slow compared with areas further north. Only under Marcus Aurelius did cities become widespread, and these did not increase the few commercial and cultural contacts with the outside world. The severe physical conditions prevented any great change in the primi-tive agricultural and pastoral economy throughout the Roman period. In the interior the long-term economic prospects were much better than for the coastal hinterland, although communications were difficult in many areas. Industry developed for local needs, since the cost of transporting building materials and pottery from the coast was prohibitive, but the natural resources of the area were such that it was soon exporting to the south, especially timber and live-stock. In spite of this, many areas in the interior remained almost untouched by outside influence, not necessarily because of the poverty of the land but because travel was difficult and journeys usually circuitous. In these areas, parts of Iapodian territory, the headwaters of the major rivers, and the mountain massif between the Drina valley and the Adriatic in the southeast, some of the population will hardly have been aware of their status as provincial citizens of a world Empire. They still spoke their native language, and had little contact with the new cities growing up in the larger valleys. Disturbances and economic changes in the Empire during the late second and third centuries brought them more into contact with the outside world, and one of the results of the military fragmenta-tion of the Empire in the emergency of the third century was large-scale army recruitment in this and similar areas in the Danubian lands, which replaced the old veteran colonies and frontier cities along the Danube that had supplied the army hitherto. A result of this was the series of great Illyrian soldier-emperors in the late third and fourth centuries, many of whom were sons of peasants from re-mote areas who worked their way to the top through sheer ability as soldiers and administrators.

At the same time the predominant position of the coastal cities was declining. Socially their ruling classes lost their Italian settler character, and the quantity of imported goods fell away markedly after the early second century. This process can be seen in those products which can be studied archaeologically, while the growth of local industry is reflected by the increasing importance of the trade guilds (*collegia*), especially in Salona. Perhaps it is not so much a process of decline in one area while counterbalanced by prosperity in another, as the level-ling out of the clear-cut social and economic distinctions of the first century A.D. In the third century and later it is possible to claim that Dalmatia was less pros-perous, but on the other hand what prosperity there was may have been shared more evenly among the different strata of the provincial population. New domi-nant social groups do arise, but they are never as powerful as the urban ruling classes in the first century. In the interior some families (p. 316) reach the highest social class, with membership of the senatorial and equestrian orders, presumably on the basis of lands gathered together into large estates over many years.

Chapter 15
Dalmatia in the Later Empire

1 *From Diocletian to the Ostrogothic Conquest*

In the middle and later third century the Empire suffered invasion on almost every frontier. The central military government, with its carefully balanced defensive deployment of the legions and *auxilia* along the northern and eastern frontiers, was shattered by a situation which had been often feared but never realised, the simultaneous advance of external peoples such as the Alamanni, Franks, and Goths. The collapse of large sectors of the Danube frontier brought the province once more into the main current of Imperial history for the first time in nearly three centuries. Along with other areas of the interior, Dalmatia provided the manpower, and not least the generals and emperors, by whom the Empire was rescued from near disintegration, and who were responsible for beginning the transformation of the Principate into the Later Roman Empire of the fourth, fifth, and sixth centuries. The large number of army units with Illyrian titles which appear in the later official lists were raised at this time, not from the old provincial cities or frontier towns, but from the interior areas which were neither urbanized nor much affected by the higher life of Roman cities. The men who were responsible for rescuing the Empire, Claudius II (Gothicus), Probus, and Aurelian were all of Illyrian origin, while the greatest of them, Diocletian, was born somewhere in the territory around Salona. When he abdicated in 305 he retired to his palace which he had built for himself on the Adriatic coast a few miles south of Salona. There is no evidence that Dalmatia suffered greatly from the barbarian invasions of the third century, while the cities in the south, screened on the north by the mountains, do not appear to have suffered at all.

Diocletian's provincial reorganization subdivided the larger provinces into

416

smaller units, and set in hand a progressive separation between the military and civil authority, each with their quite separate hierarchies of command.[1] Dalmatia was little affected by this provincial reorganization except for a small area in the southeast, to the east and south of the Gulf of Kotor, which was included, along with territory from other adjoining provinces, in a new province Praevalitana centred around Doclea and Scodra. It resembles very closely the territory of the old Illyrian kingdom. The remainder of the province remained intact with the provincial capital still at Salona.[2]

Under the rule of the Tetrarchy, the collegiate rule of two *Augusti* and two junior *Caesares*, Dalmatia was controlled by the eastern Caesar Galerius and, after 307, by Licinius. After the death of Constantine I in 337, who had united the Empire once more under his sole rule, there was a division between his sons, in which Constans obtained Dalmatia as part of Illyricum.[3] The civil wars which took place during the middle of the fourth century did not impinge on the province. The great military route leading from Northern Italy down the Save valley to Serdica (Sofia) and Constantinople was the main axis for these struggles, as much as it had once been designed for communications and army deployment along the frontier. Dalmatia had long been a backwater from this route, and the old military roads between the Adriatic and the Save valley appear to have fallen into disuse.

Within Dalmatia little is known about life in the province after the end of the third century. Except at Salona, the quantity of inscriptions decreases sharply from this time, apart from a few sarcophagi in the northern valleys. However, the vitality of rural life in the northern part of the province is attested by St. Jerome who was born in the unidentified city Stridon somewhere near the Pannonian border.[4] Coins of the Later Empire are common throughout the interior, and the prosperity of the mining communities continued through the fourth century. Little is known about any military dispositions within the province. In the southeast are two late fortresses, at Nikšić and Vigu in Praevalitana.[5]

---

[1] A. H. M. Jones, *LRE*, 42 ff.

[2] Both appear in the Verona List: *Privalitana* (249, v, 8, ed. Seeck), *Dalmatia* (249, vi, 4), compiled between 312 and 314.

[3] Euseb., *vit. Const.*, iv, 51; Aur. Vict., *Epit. de Caes.*, 41, 20.

[4] Jerome, Letter vii to Chromatius, Jovinus, and Eusebius (Migne, *PL*, 1, 340): 'In my homeland, in the ordinary country, the belly is the god, and the man who lives for the day is wealthier than the richer man.'

[5] Nikšić: Evans, *Archaeologia*, 48 (1884), 86; Vigu: Praschniker-Schober, 13, fig. 19. The building at Mogorjelo, near Čapljina in the Narenta valley, is not a military fortification but a country residence, built in a manner similar to that of Diocletian's Palace, H. Vetters and E. Dyggve, *Mogorjelo* (1966), 53 ff.

The death of Theodosius I in 395 marks the final separation between the eastern and western halves of the Empire, and their interests soon began to diverge. Although Justinian was to reconquer many of the western Mediterranean provinces, including Italy, in the middle of the sixth century, this was merely a temporary recovery, and the overstrained resources of the East were unable to prevent many of the new conquests being rapidly overrun by new invaders, Lombards, Slavs, and the armies of Islam. The experiences of Illyricum illustrate well the finality of the division which occurred at the end of the fourth century. Four centuries earlier the Triumvirs M. Antonius and Caesar Octavianus had partitioned the Roman World between them with the division fixed along the mountains of Montenegro and northern Albania. In 395 Dalmatia was part of the West, included in the Diocese of Illyricum, and was controlled by the praetorian prefect in Italy, while the new Praevalitana was part of the eastern Empire's Diocese of Dacia within the praetorian prefecture of Illyricum.[1] Once more the Balkan peninsula formed the division between the two halves of the Roman World, emphasizing the increasing separation of interest between Rome and Constantinople.

In the year of the death of Theodosius I the Visigoths, who had been settled some years before in the Illyrian provinces, rebelled and, although the western ruler Stilicho advanced later to confront them in Northern Greece, they had already reached part of the Adriatic coast and attacked its cities during the latter half of 395.[2] At the same time the western Empire claimed Illyricum, again through Stilicho acting for the western Emperor Honorius, the ineffectual son of Theodosius; this claim, however, was resisted strenuously by the East ruled by Theodosius' other son Arcadius, who also was controlled by a series of generals and court officials throughout most of his reign (395–408). In the years 414–15 Salona may have been briefly controlled by the East; the death of Honorius in 423 without male heir brought an expedition from Constantinople to the west to install his nephew Valentinian III under the influence of his formidable sister Galla Placidia. Salona was captured by the Admiral Arduba in 425, who had been placed in command of the expedition by the eastern ruler Theodosius II. After this success he rebuilt the city walls.[3] Although his expedition against the usurper John at Ravenna was a failure, the latter was soon removed by diplomacy and Valentinian III was installed as the legal Augustus in October 425.

---

[1] *Not. Dign. occ.*, ii, 31; *or.* iii, 19.

[2] Claudian. *In Rufin.*, ii, 36 f; Jerome, *To Heliodorus* (Migne *PL*, 1, 609) *Ep.* lx, 16; cf. Egger, *FS*, 2, 43. The Manastirine cemetery was ransacked then, although a tombstone was set up on 4 July in that year (FS, 2, n. 116).

[3] III, 1984.

The West paid a price for this help. Its claims to eastern Illyricum were abandoned and on the marriage of Valentinian to his cousin Licinia Eudoxia in 437 a substantial part of western Illyricum was transferred to the East, including most, if not all, of Dalmatia.[1]

The reign of Honorius witnessed massive invasions of the Empire by northern peoples, and large areas of the West were lost for ever to the central government. The collapse of the Danube frontier, and the position of Dalmatia as a frontier zone between East and West, laid the province open to barbarian attack. In 395 the Goths reached Salona, as did also the Marcomanni and the Quadi, old enemies repeating their exploits of the time of Marcus Aurelius more than two centuries before. At this time cities in the north of the province were destroyed, including St. Jerome's birthplace at Stridon.[2] The effect of these raids can be seen in the province. At this time the city at Šipovo appears to have been abandoned by its inhabitants who fled to some of the old hill strongholds in the area.[3] Few of the Roman cities in the north were built on defensible sites, and none is known to have possessed circuits of walls: when attack threatened flight was the only sensible course, for the invaders were unlikely to waste their time and energy on capturing hill-forts. The long north–south valleys of Bosnia invited the Goths to pillage but the Dinaric watershed prevented them reaching the Adriatic cities in any force.[4] Salona and her sisters were secure behind their walls, although no troops were stationed there or in the other cities, and the only military presence may have been in the forts at Nikšić and Vigu mentioned above (p. 417). The imperial textile factory at Bassiana in Pannonia Inferior was transferred for safety to Salona,[5] while large numbers of the civil population of Pannonia and Northern Dalmatia, and some from Italy escaping from the invasion of Alaric, fled to the protection of the Adriatic coast. Alaric is believed to have contemplated organizing an area of German settlement based on Northeast Italy, Noricum, and Dalmatia.[6] The refugee problem caused great difficulties for the government, which had to issue a directive in 415 about the supervision of their movement by government officials.[7]

---

[1] Bury, *LRE*, I, 221 ff., esp. 226.

[2] Jerome, *de viris illustr.*, cxxxv (Migne, *PL*, 2, 755); cf. *Comm. in Sophon. proph.*, i, 2 f. (Migne, *PL*, 6, 1341). The land was ravaged again in 397, Jerome, *epist.* lxviB, 14, to Pammachius (Migne, *PL*, 1, 647).

[3] Suggested by D. Sergejevski, *GZMS*, 7 (1952), 56 f.

[4] The Augustan Shore (*litus Augustum*), as Merobaudes calls it, *Pan.*, I, frag. IIB, 7 ff. (*MGH*, AA 14, p. 10).

[5] *Not. Dign.*, occ. xi, 46: *procurator gynaecii Bassianensis, Pannoniae Secundae—translati Salonis.*

[6] Zosimus, v, 48.

[7] *Cod. Theod.*, VI, 29, 12 (8 January 415).

In spite of this the middle of the fifth century saw Dalmatia, or rather the Adriatic coastline, a comparatively tranquil backwater still intact from invasion or Germanic settlement. A haven for refugees at all social levels, it was never under the effective control of either the East or the West, unless an imperial fleet actually happened to be present at Salona. Except for the Vandals, the German tribes could not operate on the sea effectively, and Dalmatia was not an attractive place to approach by land from the north, when compared with Italy, Southern Gaul, or Spain, and was certainly nowhere near as wealthy as any of these. It is not surprising that this isolation led to the emergence of an independent political power based on Salona, which lasted from 454 until the Ostrogothic conquest of Italy. The general (*comes rei militaris*, later *magister militum*) Marcellinus came from an aristocratic pagan Roman family and was appointed to command in Dalmatia by the great patrician Aetius.[1] When in 454 the latter was murdered by Valentinian III, Marcellinus refused allegiance to the western government. Militarily he was secure, with a powerful fleet based at Salona and his own local forces. These were recruited from the Huns, but they could be supplemented from the great resources of manpower in his sphere of authority. He had no opposition to fear, and never needed to usurp the imperial titles, or issue coins in his own right, although his ambitions were clearly directed towards rule in the West. With his almost complete security from external attack (only one barbarian raid from the north is attested during his rule),[2] it was possible for Marcellinus to play for a few years an independent role in western affairs.

When chaos broke out in Italy after the murder of Valentinian III in 455, Marcellinus kept himself detached from affairs to the west. Procopius records that he was offered the imperial crown in 458 by the Gallo-Romans before they accepted Ricimer's nominee Majorianus.[3] When he was requested by Majorianus to assist against the dangerous Vandals, Marcellinus agreed and advanced to Sicily. The Vandals had already mastered the sea and were even threatening Dalmatia.[4] Marcellinus overran Sicily with little difficulty, but he was unwilling to join in a struggle for power with Ricimer and soon withdrew to his province,[5] which he now ruled with the blessing of the eastern Emperor Leo I, enjoying the anomalous title of 'commander of both (infantry and cavalry) forces and patrician' (*magister militum utriusque militiae et patricius*).[6] In 467 Marcellinus was

---

[1] Procop., *BV*, I, vi, 7; cf. Marcell, *com.* on 448 (*Chron. Min.*, 2, 90). On his career, W. Ensslin, *RE*, 14 (1928), 1446 ff., n. 25.

[2] Jord., *Get.*, liii (ed. Mommsen, p. 274)

[3] Procop., *BV*, I, vi; cf. Sidon. Apoll., *Epp.*, i, 11, 6.

[4] Victor Vittensis, *de persec. Vandal.*, I, 51 (*MGH*, AA, 3, i, p. 13).

[5] Priscus, frg. 29 (*FHG*, IV, 103).   [6] Ensslin, *RE*, 14 (1928), 1447.

once again operating in Sicily, but was murdered on the orders of Ricimer. His death and absence from Dalmatia led to a Suevian invasion under King Hunnimund.[1]

The separate existence of Dalmatia did not cease with the death of Marcellinus but was continued under Julius Nepos, the son of his sister and a certain Nepotianus, who was recognized by Leo in 473 as 'commander of forces in Dalmatia' (*magister militum Dalmatiae*).[2] In Italy Glycerius had been appointed emperor by Gundobad, the Burgundian successor and nephew of Ricimer, who had died late in 472. This emperor was not recognized by Leo: Nepos marched to Italy, deposed Glycerius, and was appointed Augustus with the approval of Leo. In place of Gundobad he appointed as patrician Orestes, who in his younger days had been secretary to Attila. Although he achieved some success in Gaul, he was deposed by Orestes in 475, who returned him to Dalmatia and replaced him with his own young son, the unfortunate Romulus, nicknamed Augustulus or 'little emperor'.[3] When he had removed Glycerius, Nepos disposed of him by installing him as bishop of Salona, a place where he could be kept under surveillance.[4] When he himself was also relegated to Dalmatia, Nepos complained bitterly about his retirement to Zeno, the new emperor in Constantinople. Meanwhile Orestes and his son were removed by Odovacar, who sought from Zeno a confirmation of his position in Italy, the title of *patricius*. Zeno replied that he should seek his authority from Nepos, who was still the legal ruler in the West. At the same time, however, he gave a measure of approval to Odovacar and the latter was satisfied with what amounted to *de facto* recognition. Odovacar ignored Nepos in Salona, who lived on in Diocletian's Palace until he was murdered in 480, the last legal emperor of the western Empire. The imperial status of Nepos was more than an illusion supported by himself and acknowledged indifferently by Zeno, who anyway had too many troubles of his own to care much about the West. It has recently been demonstrated by J. P. C. Kent that Italian coins were struck in his names not only during his actual reign in Italy (23 June 474 to 28 August 475), but again after September 476 until his assassination on 9 May 480, the true date of the formal disappearance of the western Empire.[5] There seems little doubt that the Dalmatian ruler was acknowledged as emperor by Odovacar, who avenged the murder of Nepos by an invasion of Dalmatia in the following year to put the assassins to death. These were Victor and Ovida; they could well

---

[1] Marcell, *com.* on 468 (*Chron. Min.*, 2, 90); cf. Cassiod., *chron. ad* 468 (*Chron. Min.*, 2, 158).
[2] Cod. Just., VI, 61, 5 (1 June 473); cf. John of Antioch, frg. 209, 2 (*FHG*, IV, 618 f.); Marcell, *com.* on 474 (*Chron. Min.*, 2, 91); Malchus, frg., 10 ex (*FHG*, IV, 119).   [3] Bury, *LRE*, 1, 404 f.
[4] Anon. Vales., (*Chron. Min.*, 1, 306 f.); Marcell, *com.* (*Chron. Min.*, 2, 91) implies that he never even reached Salona.   [5] J. P. C. Kent, *Coroll. Mem. E. Swoboda*, 146 ff.

have acted under the orders of Glycerius, the ex-emperor who was still living on as bishop in Salona.[1]

Under Gallienus in the middle of the third century the senatorial order was excluded as a body from holding army commands and was replaced by a more professional class of equestrian soldiers and administrators. Although Dalmatia had no standing army after the first century, apart from three regiments of *auxilia* and occasional legionary detachments, its governor had continued to be chosen from senators of consular rank, men who were considered generally eligible for the larger frontier provinces with armies of two or more legions. Now, however, these consular governors were replaced by equestrian *praesides* with the title *vir perfectissimus*. The earliest attested is Aurelius Marcianus in 277; his successor was probably M. Aurelius Tiberianus, attested in 280.[2] Between 282 and 284 the governor was Flavius Valerius Constantius, later Caesar in the West and father of Constantine I.[3] Under Diocletian M. Aurelius Iulus was *praeses* during the great persecution of the Christians, when Domnio, bishop of Salona, and others suffered martyrdom.[4] A later governor was Flavius Iulius Rufinus Sarmentius (337–50), whose name appears on the rebuilt *porta Caesarea* at Salona.[5] Both he and Aurelius Iulus were of senatorial rank with the title *vir clarissimus*. Last attested is Apollonius Phoebadius, possibly a governor in the fifth century.[6] The procurator remained an important official, but the only individual known in the office was a man who had been recalled from retirement.[7]

In the fourth century the provincial governor was served by an *officium* similar to that of the Principate, although they were no longer men on detached duty from the legions. Their titles, as listed by the Notitia Dignitatium (*Occ.* xlv) record the same officers, the *princeps officii, cornicularii, tabularii, commentarienses,* and *adiutores*, along with other subsidiary grades described as *cohortalini*. During the independent rule of Marcellinus based at Salona, the civil and military authority were once again centred in the same person, a *comes rei militaris*, later *magister militum Dalmatiae*. To this period probably belongs the tombstone of Flavius Valerius, *centenarius* (the later equivalent of centurion) in a unit of archers.[8] In the fourth and early fifth centuries finance was controlled by the *comes largitionum per Illyricum* (secretary of the treasury in Illyricum), along with

---

[1] Auct. Havn. in *consularia Italica* on 475 (*Chron. Min.*, 1, 309); cf. Marcell, *com.* on 480 (*Chron. Min.*, 2, 91); Jordan. *Rom.*, 45; cf. *Getica*, xlv.

[2] III, 8708, 1805.   [3] *Vit. Cari* 17, 6; cf. Anon. Vales. I, 1 (*Chron. Min.* 1, 7); III, 9860.

[4] III, 1938 = 8565; cf. BD, 37 (1914), 118 ff. Other doubtful *praesides* under Diocletian are recorded in later sources, Dacianus and Tarquinius, Farlati, *IS*, 1, 677, 1, 112.

[5] III, 1982, 1983, 2771.   [6] *BD*, 32 (1909), 1 ff.

[7] III, 8712; cf. Egger, *FS*, 2, 73, n. 74.   [8] *BD*, 33 (1910), 59, n. 4122.

a *rationalis summarum Pannoniae Secundae, Dalmatiae et Saviae*. In charge of the pro-vincial treasury at Salona was a *praepositus*.[1] Under these officials came also the state factories, textile factories (*gynaecii*), and dye works (*bafii*), which were based mainly at Salona, together with the mines-administration. There is no longer epigraphic evidence for administrators of the mines in the Sana valley or at Domavia. The latest procurator in the latter dates to 274; the iron-mines, how-ever, were apparently still in operation in the early sixth century.[2]

Taxation was applied on the basis of Diocletian's reformed system of land and poll-tax (*iugatio et capitatio*), which was calculated on the basis of a regular but complicated census assessment, a much fairer way of raising state revenue than the cruder systems applied in the Principate.[3] Under Valentinian the new sales tax of four per cent introduced in the western Empire (one *siliqua* for a *solidus*, hence the name *siliquaticum*) was administered by a separate bureau of officials, and remained in force under Ostrogothic rule.[4] There is no trace of city or local government organization after Diocletian. No records of *IIviri* or *decuriones* survive. The citizens who had regarded membership of the local senate as a desirable privilege found themselves treated in imperial laws as a class (*curiales*) liable to this as a duty by hereditary obligation. Even in the third century govern-ment nominees had interfered extensively in city government as *curatores*, mainly to control and regulate the unwise squandering of local revenues and the corrup-tion which appears to have been endemic in any building project. By the time of Diocletian every city had a permanent *curator*, usually chosen from the citizen body, but very soon his position was overshadowed by the *defensor civitatis*. This office was revived by Valentinian I (364–75) with the original purpose of protect-ing the mass of the populace from the exactions of the wealthy landowners when squeezed by the government to pay their taxes.[5]

ii *Dalmatia under the Goths*

The death of Nepos in 480 brought Dalmatia once more under the legal sovereignty of the emperor in Constantinople, who remained the titular ruler of the area until the destruction of the imperial city by the infamous Fourth Crusade in 1204. The later Slav kingdoms of Croatia and Serbia both formally acknowledged this rule, and the attachment to East Rome remained strong among the *Romani* who survived along the coast and in the hinterland long after

[1] *Not. Dign. Occ.*, xi.   [2] *Not. Dign. Or.*, xiii, 11 records a *comes metallorum per Illyricum*.
[3] A. H. M. Jones, *LRE*, 61 ff.   [4] Cassiod., *Variae*, iii, 26 and below, p. 424.
[5] A. H. M. Jones, *LRE*, 726 f. A *princeps coloniae* with the status of *vir perfectissimus* is attested at Narona, probably in the late fourth century, III, 9540; cf. Egger, *FS*, 2, 77, n. 89.

conquest by the Slavs had removed any effective control by the Emperor.[1]

Odovacar asserted his authority over Dalmatia in the year following the death of Nepos, acting on behalf of the Emperor. Nothing is known about his administration in the area, and very soon his position in Italy was threatened by the approach of the Ostrogoths under Theoderic. Coming from the east they advanced past Sirmium and along the Save valley into Italy, and there followed a terrible war between the two leaders which culminated in one of the many sieges which Ravenna experienced during its history. The war ended in 493 with the murder of Odovacar by Theoderic himself, during which time Dalmatia remained under the control of Constantinople, where the emperor Anastasius had succeeded Zeno in 491. In 504, however, Dalmatia, along with the province Pannonia Secunda around Sirmium, was confirmed as part of the kingdom of Theodoric (d. 526) and something like a stable administration began to function not only along the coast but also in some areas of the interior.[2] The principal evidence for these years is the correspondence of the Ostrogothic rulers preserved in the works of the learned Italian senator Cassiodorus; in these letters Theoderic is revealed as an active administrator in the tradition of the ablest Roman emperors.

The Gothic territory in Illyricum was divided into two areas, Dalmatia (along with Savia) and Pannonia Sirmiensis. Each was ruled by a leading Goth; in Dalmatia he had the title of *comes Dalmatiae et Saviae*. He controlled both the Gothic forces and the Roman population between which there was a strict separation, the right of intermarriage being forbidden. In spite of Theoderic's attempt at impartial administration, relations between the two communities were bad. The settlement of Goths in the province involved the requisition of one third of the land in Dalmatia. The *comes* in Dalmatia was Osvin, who remained in control under Theoderic's successor Athalaric.[3] In 508 a special official, the *comes* Simeonius, was sent to organize the collection of the *siliquaticim* and also to check on other irregularities, including excessive taxation and embezzlement. At the same time he was instructed to enquire into the workings of the iron-mines, still controlled by the *comes sacrarum largitionum*. Like the Romans the Gothic rulers retained some lands for their private revenues, which were administered by the *comes* of the *patrimonium*.[4] Along with the iron-mines the state workshops were still in production; other facilities such

---

[1] F. Šišić, *Povijest Hrvata*, 1, 166.

[2] The Sirmium region (Pannonia II) was confirmed to the Italian kingdom in 504, Cassiod. *chron.* (*Chron. Min.* 1, 160); cf. Ennodius, *Pan.* (*MGH*, p. 211); Jordan. *Getica*, lviii.

[3] Cassiod., *Variae*, ix, 9; cf. viii, ix, 8. On the career of Oswin, *RE*, 18 (1942), 1854.

[4] Cassiod., *Variae*, iii, 25, 26.

as sea transport, fishing, and salt pans were administered by *tribuni maritimi*.[1]

The main problem confronting the Ostrogoths was religious; they were Arians ruling an Orthodox people. It was here that Theoderic's greatest qualities as a ruler were displayed, for he took infinite pains to see that some sort of working relationship replaced the mistrust which normally existed between the two groups. The church was now well established as a power in Dalmatia, especially at Salona; and under bishop Honorius II (525–50) the new cruciform basilica was built (p. 431), while two provincial synods met at Salona under his chairmanship in 530 and 533. There is no evidence for the number or distribution of Gothic settlements in the province. Their coins have been found in the Narenta valley, a silver piece of Vitigis at Narona, and another of Athalaric from Labčan–Gradac at the mouth of the river.[2] A runic inscription on a church at Bréza (*castellum Hedum* of the Daesitiates) may belong to the period of Ostrogothic rule: it is certainly of Germanic origin.[3]

The death of Theoderic and the succession of Athalaric under the guidance of his mother Amalaswintha does not appear to have reduced the standard of administration under the Ostrogoths.[4] In Constantinople the following year saw a change of ruler which was to have disastrous results for Ostrogothic rule in Italy. The new emperor Justinian was soon planning the recovery of the West, in particular Italy and North Africa. The energy of the new ruler was soon felt when he created a new city close to the site of his birthplace, Justiniana Prima (Caričingrad) west of Naissus in Moesia Superior. He created there a new Metropolitan see, and placed under its control not only Sirmium and Singidunum, but also the province Praevalitana and its principal bishopric at Doclea.[5] In 535 the attack on the Ostrogoths was set under way. The main force sailed to Sicily under Belisarius, destroyer of the Vandals in Africa a few years before. In such an undertaking Dalmatia could not be ignored, and accordingly in the same year Mundus was sent as *magister militum per Illyricum* to eliminate Gothic power there.[6] He soon defeated the Gothic forces and occupied Salona.[7] New forces were sent from Italy under Asinarius and Grippa to ensure the recapture of Salona, which could be a vital possession to hold during a protracted war in Italy. Although at the time there were negotiations taking place between the Ostrogothic king Theodahat and Justinian, the imperial force defeated the

---

[1] *Gynaecia*: Cassiod., *Variae*, i, 2; also a *comes patrimonii*: vi, 9, 5. *Tribuni maritimi*: xii, 24.
[2] Patsch, *Narona*, 101 f., f.
[3] Gr. Čremošnik and D. Sergejevski, *Novitates Musei Sarajevoensis*, iv (1930); cf. Arntz-Zeiss, *Runendenkmäler*, 1, 143–54; also 146, note 2 for a tile of Theoderic.
[4] Cassiod., *Variae*, ix, 8–9.   [5] Just., *Nov.*, XI (14 April 535); CXXXI, 3 (18 March 545).
[6] Procop., *BG*, i, 5, 2.   [7] ibid., i, 5, 11.

Goths, but only at the cost of the loss of their leader Mundus, who had impetuously led a rapid pursuit of the enemy in revenge for the recent death of his son Mauricus in a skirmish. The loss was serious enough to make the imperial forces evacuate Dalmatia, although the Gothic forces did not immediately reoccupy Salona because of the attitude of the provincials, but remained in the nearby strongholds,[1] until the arrival of new forces enabled them to recover the city (about March 536).[2]

This defeat was soon reversed. The Constable (*comes stabuli*) Constantianus moved northwards from Dyrrhachium with a powerful force, while at the same time Belisarius was ordered to begin the assault on Italy. Constantianus landed first at Epidaurum: the Goths could not defend Salona with its damaged fortifications, withdrew to Scardona and eventually retreated back to Ravenna by June 536.[3] The imperial forces occupied Issa and then Salona. Constantianus ordered a complete rebuilding of the defences, and also surrounded part of the city with a defensive ditch. Gothic hopes of recovering it were now very slight.[4] The accession of Vitigis to the Gothic throne gave little cohesion to their defence of Italy. As a subordinate, for instance under Theoderic against the Gepidae around Sirmium, he was excellent, but as a leader and strategist he was poor. He sent an expedition to Dalmatia under Asinarius, who had been there with the forces in 536, and Vilegesils. While Asinarius moved northwards into Savia to recruit more Germans, Vilegesils marched southwards along the Liburnian coast to be defeated by imperial forces at Scardona (537), probably while attempting to cross the river Titius. From there he retreated to Burnum, where he rebuilt the defences of the old legionary fortress. Meanwhile Asinarius moved south and managed to institute a blockade of Salona by land and sea. Constantianus was now well prepared for this and defeated the Gothic fleet in the Bay of Salona. Although this made their chances of success much smaller the Goths still maintained their land blockade vigorously.[5] For Dalmatia the victory in 537 was the turning point, and never again did the Goths make a serious attempt to take Salona.

There was a raid into Dalmatia in 549 when Vitigis' abler successor Totila sent Indulf, who had once served under Belisarius, across the Adriatic with a strong land force. He landed on the coast a few miles south of Salona at Mouicurum (Makarska), captured two small towns, and slaughtered the population. From there he moved to Laureatum (the site is unknown but was probably on the coast not far south) where he compelled an imperial force which had been sent against him under Claudianus to flee back to Salona. The invaders were no

[1] ibid., i, 7, 1–10. [2] ibid., i, 7, 27. [3] ibid., i, 7, 26–37; 15, 15, advancing as far as Liburnia.
[4] ibid., i, 7, 36. [5] i, 16, 7–18.

longer interested in conquest, however, and appeared glad to return home laden with booty, although the capture of some strongpoints across the Adriatic might well have been useful to Totila in preventing the movement of imperial forces through Dalmatia into Northern Italy.[1] Late in 550, when Justinian was planning a major offensive against the troublesome Totila, an imperial army wintered at Salona under the *magister militum* Johannes, and early in the next year he led a seaborne attack on Ancona, and defeated the Gothic fleet. However, by this action, he had exceeded his instructions, and later the commander-in-chief Narses took the forces on to Italy and eventual victory, while Johannes remained behind in Illyricum to recruit new forces.[2]

The Ostrogothic control of Dalmatia was exercised through a Goth with the title *comes Dalmatiae et Saviae* and the rank of *vir illustris*. He ruled the Goths in the province as a general commanded his soldiers, and there were two *principes* to assist him. Civilian authority over the Roman population still rested in the provincial governor (*praeses*), later called a *consularis*, who had some responsibility for raising taxes.[3] Under the Gothic *comes*, there were other officials commanding individual places, such as the *comes* of the island Curitana and its city Celsina (Curicum) in Liburnia.[4] Virtually nothing is known about the men who held these posts in the province: Osvin was *comes* under Theoderic and Athalaric, while a certain Epiphanius is attested as *consularis*. The old imperial taxation system appears to have been maintained intact. Cassiodorus mentions the raising of the *siliquaticum* sales tax with its own bureau of officials headed by the *comes siliquarus* Simeonius, and Theoderic himself appears to have made a serious attempt to get the old iron-mines in the Sana valley into production again. After the reconquest Justinian reconstituted the praetorian prefecture of Illyricum. The title of his governor in Dalmatia was *proconsul*, recalling the titles of some of the first Romans to enter the region in the Republic. A *proconsul* Marcellinus is attested at Salona on another man's tombstone, and a letter of Pope Gregory establishes that he was holding office in 599.[5]

III *Christianity*

The most striking development in Dalmatia during the Late Empire was the spread of the Christian religion, signified by the massive building programme of churches and martyr shrines at Salona, which now dominated the coastline even more than it had done during the Principate. The Christian monuments of Salona rival those of any other city in this part of the Empire, and as a place for

[1] ibid., iii, 35, 23–30. [2] ibid., iii, 40, 27; iv, 21, 5–9; 22, 1; 23, 4–42; 26, 11.
[3] Cassiod., *Variae*, v, 24.
[4] Cassiod., *Variae*, vii, 16. [5] III, 9527, an official elected locally.

the study of early Christian archaeology it is second only to Ravenna.[1] The wide appeal of Christianity during the third century was part of a change in the religious life of the people within the Empire, a change which brought into prominence many cults of eastern origin, offering salvation to the individual and requiring initiation into a congregation of believers who performed regular and elaborate ritual in their shrines. Egyptian Isis and Serapis reached the west in a form modified by the Greeks; another of the most widespread cults was that of Mithras, the Persian god of light, whose triumph over evil was signified by his legendary slaying of the bull (tauroctony).[2] This scene is the most common representation among the cult-sculptures which have been found in Mithraic shrines. Its distribution in the province suggests that it was introduced by, and remained largely confined to, the trading communities especially the immigrants from the eastern provinces.[3] An early pair of Mithraic dedications were set up near Senia by officials of the Illyrian customs system. Mithraic caves are known around Arupium in the Lika and also in the south near Epidaurum. The greatest concentration of Mithraic sculptures is found at Salona, where most dedications were to *Deus Invictus Mithras*. There are a group of Tauroctonies, dedicated mostly by imperial officials or eastern traders. The latter group were responsible for the Mithraic shrines in the Narenta valley around Konjic. One was dedicated by L. Antonius Menander whose home was at Aphrodisias in Caria. Mithras was a rival of Christianity, and the latter's propagandists make some of their bitterest attacks against it. In general it seems to have died out rapidly early in the fourth century when Christianity became fashionable, but the Konjic Mithraeum continued to flourish as a place of worship throughout the fourth century. Later it was apparently deliberately desecrated, possibly under Theodosius I, when pressure from the church was increasing against the more blatant survivals of pagan cults.

The first Christian mission reached the province in the time of the Apostles. In verses 18–19 of Chapter 15 of his letter to the Romans St. Paul writes: 'For

---

[1] Excavations in Salona have been carried out for more than eighty years. The programme was initiated by Bulić, who was later joined by Austrian scholars, the results of whose work was published in *Forschungen in Salona*, 1 (1918), 2 (1926), and 3 (1939). During the twenties the work was continued by E. Dyggve and his Danish colleagues, who examined not only the Christian centres but also the amphitheatre, whose work was published in *Recherches à Salone*, 1 (1928), 2 (1933). An early study of the growth of Christianity in the provinces is by J. Zeiller, *Les origines, etc.* (1906), while the archaeological evidence is surveyed by E. Dyggve, *HSC*, (1951).

[2] The evidence for Mithras in Dalmatia is collected and illustrated in *CIMRM*, 2, 252–70.

[3] B. Gabričević, *AI*, 1 (1954), 37 ff., who concluded that an eastern origin for many of the sculptures is unlikely, and that all the obvious external influences derive from the military centres of the Danube frontier.

I will not dare to speak of any of those things which Christ hath not wrought by me, to make the Gentiles obedient, by word and deed, through mighty signs and wonders, by the power of the spirit of God; so that from Jerusalem and round about unto Illyricum, I have fully preached the gospel of Christ.' He did not visit the province on his voyage to Rome, but his pupil Timothy was sent to Dalmatia according to the second letter addressed to him.[1] A much later tradition makes the rebellion of Furius Camillus Scribonianus in 42 coincide with the arrival of St. Peter in the province.[2] Salona's importance as a large Mediterranean port will obviously have attracted Christian preachers, although there is no evidence about individual missionaries before the end of the third century. In the oldest bishop-lists the first name is Domnio (or Domnius).[3] It has been suggested that Venantius, whose image was placed in the mosaics of the Lateran baptistery by Pope John IV in the seventh century, was an earlier bishop. A possible emendation of the text of *Liber Pontificalis* could read that he was martyred among the Delmatae in the third century, but there is no other evidence to support this.[4]

Diocletian was probably living in Salona when the martyrdoms took place there. In 304 Domnio suffered death in the amphitheatre on 10 April, along with four Christian soldiers from Diocletian's personal bodyguard, and a priest called Asterius.[5] They were buried in the martyrs' church at Kapljuć outside the Salona walls close to the amphitheatre where they died.[6] An altar-cover of a reliquary records the name of Domnio and fixes the precise day of his death. After the abandonment of the Kapljuć shrine the remains of the martyrs were transferred to the Manastirine basilica. Another martyred at this time was the fuller Anastasius who left his home in Aquileia with the intention of seeking martyrdom in Salona, where he was drowned in the bay with a millstone around his neck. He was interred at the third martyrs' basilica at Marusinac, a few hundred metres north of the city.[7]

Domnio came from Nisibis in Mesopotamia, and probably arrived in Salona

---

[1] II *Tim.*, 4, 11. Its authorship is not certain. There is no evidence to support the suggestion that Paul was shipwrecked on Dalmatian Melite (Mljet); cf. *BD*, 36 (1913), suppl. 1.

[2] Orosius, *Hist. adv. paganos*, vii, 6.

[3] The identity and chronology of the Salona bishops is given by Bulić, *Kronotaksa solinskih biskupa*, suppl. *BD*, 35 (1912).

[4] Bulić, *Kronotaksa*, 15 ff. on *Liber Pontificalis*, 1, p. 330 (ed. Duchesne); cf. Egger, *FS*, 2, 51 f. On the Lateran mosaics see below, p. 435.

[5] *Chron. Min.*, 1, 738. The date is established by III, 9575; cf. *FS*, 2, 75, n. 81.

[6] Brønstedt, *RS*, 1, 33 f. Their names are recorded on the border of a reliquary cover, III, 8874 = 12839; cf. *FS*, 2, 108, n. 285.

[7] Egger and Dyggve, *FS*, 3, 131 ff.

along with a group of his countrymen during the late third century, one of many similar missions which came to the west at this period.[1] The eastern origins of the new faith are reflected in the architecture of some of the earlier Christian buildings, whose decoration and construction reveals clear traces of Syrian influence.[2] At the same time as Domnio there probably arrived his nephew Primus, who succeeded him as bishop. He survived the persecution, and appears to have died a natural death in 325, when he was buried in the Manastirine basilica, where his sarcophagus is preserved with its epitaph. He was largely responsible for building this shrine, which soon became the chief burial-place for the Salona community during the fourth century.[3] The Milan Edict tolerating Christianity which was issued in 313 caused a rapid increase in this community, and soon afterwards the first church was built within the city, the *basilica urbana* in the northwest corner of the *urbs nova*.[4] Little is known about the Salona bishops during the fourth century except their names. The successor of Primus was Maximus I, who appears among the signatories of the letter sent by the Serdica Council (342) to absent eastern bishops.[5] The traditional Roman list gives his successors as Theodorus II, Petrus II, and Leo. Nothing is known about the first two, but the third is the Leontius Salonitanus mentioned in a tract published against St. Ambrosius.[6] The next two were Gaianus (d. *c.* 391) and Sympherius (d. 405), both attested by their sarcophagi with epitaphs in the Manastirine basilica.[7] Sympherius, along with his successor Hesychius, was responsible for rebuilding the episcopal basilica on a grand scale, where their work is commemorated by an inscription set into the mosaic floor.[8]

In the early fifth century the bishop of Salona was involved in the struggle against the Arian Heresy, a doctrine which arose in the east and to which many of the Gothic peoples were converted before they entered the Empire. Pope Zosimus addressed Hesychius in 418 as metropolitan, but the title archbishop (*archiepiscopus*) is not attested for the Salona diocese until more than a century later in 527. Although there is no certain evidence it seems reasonable to follow

---

[1] He came from Antiochia, almost certainly Nisibis on the Mygdon, Farlati, *IS*, 1, 414; cf. Egger, *FS*, 2, 52.

[2] Dyggve, *HSC*, 80 ff.

[3] III, 14897; cf. Egger, *FS*, 2, 76, n. 82; *RE*, 22 (1954), 1996.   [4] Egger, *FS*, 1, 89 ff.

[5] Mansi, 3, 126. He may be recorded on a fragmentary tombstone, III, 14925 = Egger, *FS*, 2, 91, n. 155.

[6] *Disertatio Maximini contra Ambrosium* (Kaufman, *Texte und Untersuchungen zur altgermanische Religionsgeschichte* 1, 87).

[7] Egger, *FS*, 2, 90 f., n. 153–4; 92 f., n. 158, 161.

[8] Egger, *FS*, 1, 89 f: *Nova post vetera coepit Synferius, Esychius eius nepos cum clero et populo fecit.* The tomb of bishop Hesychius is known from the Manastirine shrine, *FS*, 2, 94, n. 169, fig. 58.

the suggestion of Bulić that this elevated status came from the Patriarch at Constantinople rather than from Rome.[1] The episcopate of Hesychius marks not only the greatest period of importance of the Salona church within the Christian World, but also the greatest period of building in the city. Apart from the city basilica mentioned above, new basilicas were built for the old martyr shrines at Kapljuć and at Manastirine, and above all the new shrine of Marusinac, more secluded than the other two, where the martyr Anastasius had been buried. From the changes which took place in the early fifth century Egger has been able to deduce new patterns in the social structure and organization of the Salona congregation of the period.[2] People of all social classes were buried at the two shrines immediately outside the walls of the city (Kapljuć, Manastirine). The bishop and the wealthier members of the church were buried inside the basilicas in large stone sarcophagi close to the tomb of the martyrs, while the poorer people were buried around the outside of the shrine in simple graves constructed from roof tiles or even broken *amphorae*. Although there is no doubt about the sharp social distinction between rich and poor, there was still a feeling of belonging to the same community, and all were sharing in the blessings of the martyrs' proximity at the time of judgement. At the centre of his flock was the bishop with his clergy. The rebuilding of Marusinac under Hesychius brings a quite different atmosphere. It was never intended that any but the wealthiest should be buried there, and the practice of interring the bishop there marks the emergence of a clear division between the church hierarchy and wealthy people on the one hand, and the mass of the congregation on the other. Although the Salona church never again attained the position it had held under Bishop Hesychius, it had now become a major landowner, and its extensive properties are attested in papyri of the fifth and sixth centuries.

The independent rule of Marcellinus and Nepos (p. 420), together with the installation as bishop of the ex-emperor Glycerius, cannot have had a beneficial effect on the Salona church. The Salona list of bishops gives an interregnum after Glycerius until Honorius I, who built the cruciform basilica in the city alongside the cathedral, where his monogram has been discovered.[3] Correspondence with Pope Gelasius in 493, however, records disturbed conditions in the Salona church. Apparently the heresy of Pelagius, once sternly resisted by St. Augustine and his followers, was widespread in the province. Demands that he should act resolutely against the heresy as metropolitan of the province produced a surprised reaction from Honorius, indicating that relations with Rome

[1] Farlati, *IS*, 2, 78; cf. Abramić, *FS*, 1, 8 and Bulić, *Kronotaksa*, 43 ff.
[2] Egger, *FS*, 3, 105; cf. Dyggve, *HSC*, 73.
[3] Egger, *FS*, 1, 91; cf. Dyggve, *HSC*, 26.

were poor at this time.[1] Under Ostrogothic rule church affairs appear to have been conducted without interference. The expansion of the Orthodox Church with new bishoprics and the holding of provincial synods continued during the first half of the sixth century unaffected by Arian rule. Yet the conflicts between Goth and Roman may have involved church affairs, and the dominance of the former must surely have helped the spread of Arianism. E. Dyggve has suggested that a basilica with its own baptistery which he excavated within the city must be separate from the main church buildings and was probably the Arian cathedral.[2] No Arian bishop or clergy are attested in Dalmatia, but it is possible that some of the many names in the traditional list may be those of Arian bishops There is certainly a larger number for the length of time than is usual.

The main events under bishop Honorius II (528–47) were the two provincial synods held in the cathedral at Salona, of which the *Acta* are preserved in the history of Thomas the Archdeacon (d. 1268).[3] The first took place in 530 and the second was held on 4 May 533. They furnish some of the only detailed information about the organization of the church in Dalmatia outside Salona. The church of Dalmatia included not only that province but also Savia to the north; with the capture of Sirmium, and the flight of its metropolitan to Thessalonica, Siscia came under the control of Salona. At the first synod there attended, apart from Honorius of Salona, Ioannes of Siscia, Andreas of Iader, Titianus of Arba, Marcellus of Narona, Fabricius of Epidaurum, Constantinus of Scardona, and Andreas of Bistue (*Bestae ecclesia*), which is probably Bistue Nova (Vitez or Zenica), since the early church of this congregation has been discovered by excavation at Zenica. Other members were Victor, bishop of the unidentified *ecclesia Martaritana*, and among the lesser clergy one from the *ecclesia Sarsenterensis*, which has been identified with Aržana near Duvno. The first item of business was a complaint by the Bistue bishop about the poverty and depopulation of his diocese;[4] in a later discussion a speech delivered by *monasterii presidentes* indicates that monasteries were established in the interior.

The reasons for the second council three years later were the complaints about misconduct, and a general demand that the excessively large Salona diocese should be subdivided. Three new bishops are listed, of Sarsenterum, Muccur (Makarska), and Ludrum (probably Biskupjia near Knin),[5] and all those in the

---

[1] Jaffé-Ewald, RPR, 625, 626, 686, 738.

[2] Dyggve, *Byzantion*, 19 (1949), 73 ff., and *HSC*, 49 ff.

[3] Printed in Rački, *Monumenta spect. hist. Slav. merid.*, 3 (1894).

[4] The church of Bistue was at Zenica on the river Bosna, Truhelka, *WMBH*, 1 (1892), 273 ff., and *GZMBH*, 26 (1914), 222 f.

[5] *BD*, 37 (1914), 114 ff.

earlier council are represented apart from Victor of Martaritana. The three new bishops seem to be the result of subdivision of the more outlying areas of the Salona diocese, and they appear among the signitaries to the *Acta* of the council.

From the interior there is good evidence for the spread of Christianity. A basilica at Turbe near Travnik in the territory of Bistue Nova with a mausoleum has many features in common with the Marusinac basilica at Salona, while, apart from the church already mentioned at Zenica, early basilicas are known at Bréza and at Salvium (Glamoč).[1] At Milan a tombstone records the death in 475 of Aurelius the bishop of *civitatis Riditionis*, the city Rider (Danilo Kraljice near Šibenik).[2] The size of the Salona diocese led to the institution of a new country bishop (*chorepiscopus*), to act as assistant in the more remote areas. The sarcophagus of the *chorepiscopus* Eugrafus was placed at Manastirine and dates to) about 600, when the Salona bishop had received his archbishop's cloak (*pallium* from Pope Gregory in Rome.[3]

During the sixth century the Salona diocese was involved in the bitter struggle between Rome and Constantinople, which for a long period centred around the position of the Thessalonica patriarch. In the fifth century Salona had naturally looked towards the east, and the bishop was clearly taken aback when ordered rather peremptorily by Pope Gelasius to take measures against Pelagianism within his diocese. One of the later bishops, Stephanus, appears as *archiepiscopus Salonitanus*, a title he may have received from Rome rather than from Constantinople.[4] Competition for the allegiance of the bishops in Illyricum was constant in the fifth and sixth centuries, and it has been suggested that an independent Salona bishop was intended by Pope Zosimus in 418 to be a deputy (*vicarius*) for him in the area, as was the bishop of Thessalonica for the eastern half of Illyricum and Greece.[5] The domineering attitude of Justinian towards the church met with resistance in Italy and also from Salona. In the dispute over the Three Chapters (546) Justinian antagonized the western church in his attempt to reconcile monophysites to orthodoxy and the Salona church opposed the emperor along with the rest of the western clergy under Pope Vigilus. The creation of the new Metropolitan at Justiniania Prima affected Salona's position in Illyricum, since the new prelate was bound to be a loyal adherent of the emperor. In spite of this, relations between Rome and Salona still remained far from cordial, while

---

[1] Turbe: *GZMS*, 6 (1951), 135 ff., Zenica: n. 4 on p. 432, Bréza: Mazalić, *GZMBH*, 54 (1942), 259 ff.; Salvium: Sergejevski, *GZMBH*, 54 (1942), 131.

[2] *CIL*, V, p. 620, n. 7 and 6183a: *Aurelius civitatis Riditionis episcopus.*

[3] Egger, *FS*, 2, 108, n. 286.

[4] Migne *PL*, 67, p. 139 (Dionysius Exiguus); cf. Duchesne, *Liber Pontificalis*, 1, p. cxxx.

[5] J. Zeiller, *Origines*, etc., 134 f.

the rupture with the emperor steadily became more serious until eventually Bishop Honorius II's successor Frontonianus was removed from Salona to exile in Egypt (554) where he remained for eight years.[1]

During the last decades of the sixth century the Salona church declined rapidly not the least of the causes being the personal incompetence and unworthiness of the bishops. Under Natalis (580–92) the management of the church was scandalous. He was a stupid man who spent most of his life feasting and drinking. Much more serious was his tendency to grant valuable church assets to his friends and relations on such a scale that Pope Gregory eventually deprived him of office and excommunicated him, largely through the efforts of Natalis' bitter enemy at Salona, the Archdeacon Honoratus.[2] At the same time Gregory requested the prefect of Illyricum Jovinus to attempt a restoration of some order in the area.[3] He was instructed to appoint a new administrator for the patrimony of St. Peter (the first reference to such property) in Dalmatia, since the earlier administrator, Bishop Malchus of Delminium, was in league with Natalis. Malchus was summoned to Rome to give an account of his activities, and he remained there until his death.[4] Natalis was more cautious and by his discreet behaviour managed something of a reconciliation with Gregory. The latter was willing to allow a thorough investigation into the whole business by his representative in Dalmatia the subdeacon Antoninus and Bishop Florentius of Epidaurum; this was in 591, but Natalis died early in the following year.[5]

The election of a new bishop at Salona caused more trouble. Gregory demanded an election according to the western canonical rules and was delighted when his own man Antoninus was chosen.[6] However, the imperial party in the province, the other bishops and the mass of the population, were strongly opposed to him. The Pope then agreed to a second election, but ruled out the choice of a certain Maximus, about whom he had received many unfavourable reports.[7] This man was the leader of the imperial party and his enthusiastic election as bishop was supported by the emperor. Gregory bitterly attacked Maximus, but was powerless to remove him.[8] Within Dalmatia Gregory was supported by Sabinianus of Iader and his clergy, but eventually Maximus won acceptance after doing penance for his misdeeds (whatever these were) in 599 at 'the body of the blessed Apollinaris' in Ravenna, and was granted the *pallium*.[9] Thus

---

[1] Jaffé-Ewald, 927 (in 550), complaining about Honorius. Exile of Frontonianus: Victor Tonn. *ad ann.* 554 (*Chron. Min.*, 2, 203). The followers of this bishop are referred to by Pope Gregory in a later letter (ed. Hartmann-Ewald, *MGH, Epp.*, 1–2) as *Frontinianistae*.
[2] Gregory, *Epp.*, ii, 21; 22.   [3] *Epp.*, ii, 23.   [4] *Epp.*, v, 6.   [5] *Epp.*, iii, 8 ; 9.
[6] *Epp.*, iii, 32; 46.   [7] *Epp.*, iv, 16.   [8] *Epp.*, iv, 20; 38; v, 6; 39; vi, 3; 25; 46.
[9] *Epp.*, vi, 26; vii, 17; viii, 11; 24. Mansi, 10, 82 (in August 599).

ended nearly a decade of strife at Salona, all of which had taken place in the shadow of the Slav invasions and their occupation of much of the interior. Gregory's death in 604 terminated his correspondence and deprives us of this valuable source for the affairs of the Salona church.

Maximus was now well established and appears as *archiepiscopus* on a door lintel inscription; he is the last bishop of Salona about whom any details are recorded.[1] After his death two names appear in the list before Salona was overwhelmed by the Slavs in 614, and the last bishop is recorded fleeing to Italy.[2] The final episode in the history of the Salona church was the recovery from the Slavs of the relics of the Salona martyrs, arranged in 641 by the Dalmatian Pope John IV (640–2). These were brought to Rome and the portraits of the martyrs displayed on the wall mosaic in the oratory of St. Venantius in the Lateran palace, the actual images being copied carefully from the original wall-paintings in the shrines at Salona.[3]

IV *The Slav Conquest*

The province had barely been recovered from the Goths and restored to the proper control of the eastern Empire when a much more serious threat appeared, the invading Slavs and Avars advancing south and westward into Illyricum. In 547 they began to range through the Danubian provinces. In the next year they reached Dyrrhachium and with each invasion more and more places within the Empire fell permanently under their control. The imperial forces did not challenge their advance, but in one instance followed at a respectful distance with an army of 15,000 men.[4] In 550 Germanus at Serdica was preparing an advance into Dalmatia but he was forced to deal with a major invasion directed at Thessalonica.[5] In the next year the invaders again appeared in great strength and laid waste more areas. Thus the problem of Slav invasions became more threatening year by year, and a vast programme of fortifications was instituted by Justinian, for the most part in the Lower Danube area.[6]

In 567 another enemy appeared when the Avars drove the Gepidae from the Sirmium region. In the next year, along with a band of Hunnic Cotruriges, a force of 10,000 of them moved towards Dalmatia.[7] In 583 Sirmium was cap-

---

[1] III, 13131=*FS*, 2, 90, fig. 50.   [2] Bulić, *Kronotaksa*, 97 ff.
[3] *Liber Pontificalis* lxxiii (p. 330, ed. Duchesne). The portraits of the martyrs in the Lateran were copied directly from the wall-paintings in the oratories of the Salona amphitheatre, Dyggve *HSC*, 86 and pl. IV, 49.
[4] Procop., *BG*, iii, 29, 1 ff.   [5] Procop., *BG*, iii, 40, 1–7.
[6] Procop., *BG*, iv, 25, 1 ff.; also *de Aedif.*, iv, 7, 13, 17.
[7] Menander Protector, frg. 27 (*FHG*, IV, 233).

tured by the Avars under Baian and totally destroyed.[1] In order to prevent aid reaching the city a force was sent southwestwards into Dalmatia, and may have reached the Narona area, where a hoard of gold coins was concealed at this time, probably in 582.[2] During the following years most of the Slav raids were directed southeastwards against Constantinople, until a great victory over the Avars at Singidunum in the summer of 597 sent the whole mass of the Avar and Slav peoples moving southwestwards towards the Adriatic.[3] At this time the interior of the province was finally lost to Roman control, although the imperial commander based at Ravenna was still operating with forces in Istria two years later.[4] Until 600 the invaders never reached the coastal cities, and the great Christian cemeteries were still in use. In that year Bishop Maximus wrote about the increasing danger from the Slavs to Pope Gregory, who could offer little comfort to him.[5] In the early seventh century a disaster overwhelmed the cemeteries and the basilica at Manastirine,[6] although the city itself still remained safe behind its walls and the Romans controlled the great stronghold at Clusium (Klis), where the road from the interior descended from the mountains.[7] A letter from Gregory in November 602 reveals the Salona church in a sorry state, made worse by the unworthy behaviour of a recent bishop and by internal dissension, a situation also depicted in the history of the Salona church by the thirteenth-century Thomas the Archdeacon.[8] Probably during the years 612–14, under the administration of the proconsul Marcellinus,[9] Salona was destroyed by the Slavs and ceased to exist as a city. The latest dated record is the tombstone of the Abbess Johanna who had fled to Salona after the fall of Sirmium and died on 12 May 612.[10]

There is little evidence how the remainder of the coastal cities passed under

[1] Menander Protector, frgs. 64–6 (*FHG*, IV, 265 f., 268 f.), John of Antioch, vi, 33 f. A famous tile inscribed during the siege of Sirmium is now in the Zagreb Museum, Brunšmid, *Eranos Vindobonensis*, 1893, 331 ff.

[2] Bulić, *BD*, 25 (1902), 197 ff.; cf. Patsch, *Narona*, 104.

[3] In 587 a Slav army numbering 100,000 overran Illyricum; Menander Protector, frg. 47 (*FHG*, iv, 252). In 597 they were defeated near Singidunum and then began to move towards Dalmatia, where they captured a city *Vonkeis*; Theophyl. Simocatta, vii, 121 (ed. de Boor, p. 265 ff.), or *Valkeis*, Theophanes 1, 277. which lay somewhere in the interior, as well as forty strongholds.

[4] Paulus Diaconus, I, 4, 24.

[5] *Epp.*, x, 14: 'de Sclavorum gente, quae vobis valde imminet, affligor et conturbor'.

[6] Egger, *FS*, 2, 24 ff.

[7] G. Marini, *I Papiri diplomatici*, p. 121, n. lxxviii, mentioning 'castella, quae sunt super civitatem Salonitanam', and also referring to money 'pro redemptio captivorum'.

[8] Thomas the Archdeacon, c. 7–11.   [9] III, 9527.

[10] Egger, *FS*, 2, 109. The site of the convents and monasteries has been identified and planned at Rižinice and Crkvina near Salona, Dyggve, *HSC*, 61 ff., and pl. III, 19–20.

Slav control. The latest coin from Epidaurum is dated to the reign of Phocas (602–10). The flight of the Romans from there to Ragusa (Dubrovnik) a few miles to the north is recorded by the tenth-century Constantine VII Porphyrogenitus.[1] Most of the citizens from these places fled to safety on the islands, where the Empire still retained control of most strongholds. Many were taken prisoner. Some of the Salona population who had been captured were ransomed by the Dalmatian Pope John IV in 641 when he retrieved the sacred relics from the Salona shrines by means of an embassy to the Slavs. On the mainland the chief places which remained under Roman control were Iader (later Zara-Zadar), and the palace of Diocletian (Spalatum-Split) which was granted to the Salona refugees by Heraclius, although it had already been occupied for some time by civilians, possibly the workers in the state factories.[2] All the islands remained in Roman hands, from Cres in the Quarnerno to Melita (Mljet) near Dubrovnik. These isolated Adriatic communities were carefully fostered by the empire, and organized into the Theme of Dalmatia with a governor resident in Iader, under the general supervision of the Exarch at Ravenna. Nothing is known about the fate of the provincials who were overrun by the invaders. The few traditions of Roman life which had grown up in the interior soon passed away, although in some parts of the coastal hinterland sub-Roman communities maintained their individual character until the Middle Ages. Roman law survived in certain elements of Dalmatian law, but all city life disappeared as the major settlements were gradually abandoned by the few who had survived the initial disasters of the Slav Conquest.[3]

[1] Evans, *Archaeologia*, 48 (1884), 27; Const. Porph. *DAI*, c. 29.

[2] F. Šišić, *Provijest Hrvata*, I, 282, 35, and on the later occupation of the Palace, Lj. Karaman, *SH*, 419 ff.

[3] Const. Porph., *DAI*, c. 29 (trans. Jenkins, p. 125): 'The remnant of the Romans escaped to the cities of the coast and possess them still, namely Decatera (Acruvium-Kotor), Ragusa, Spalato, Tetrangourin (Tragurium), Diadora (Iader), Arbe, Vekla (Curicta-Veglia/Krk), Opsara (Apsorus), the inhabitants of which are called Romani to this day'; cf. *Comm. DAI*, 93 ff., and Jireček, *Die Romanen in den Städten Dalmatiens während Mittelalters (Denkschr. Akad. Wien.*, xlviii/3, xlix/1, 2.).

Appendices

APPENDIX I *Grants of* Imperium *involving Illyria from* 168 *to* 60 B.C.

	praetor	consul	date	status	triumph
L. Anicius Gallus	168	160	168–7	praetor, propraetor	*de rege Gentio et et Illurie[is]*, 167
C. Marcius Figulus	169	I 162 II 156	156	consul	(none)
P. Cornelius Scipio Nasica	by 165	I 162 II 155	155	consul	*d]e De[lmateis,* 155
Ser. Fulvius Flaccus	by 137	135	135	consul	none?
C. Sempronius Tuditanus	132	129	129	consul	*de Iapudibus,* 129
Ti. Latinius Pandusa			129	? propraetor	
L. Caecilius Metellus (Delmaticus)	by 122	119	119–7	119 consul 118–7 proconsul	*de De[lma]teis* 117
C. Cosconius	? 89	——	? 78–6	proconsul	none?
L. Culleolus (Cic., *Ep. ad fam.*, xiii, 41–2)	? 60	——	? 59	proconsul	
P. Licinius (Front., *Strat.*, ii, 5, 28)				?proconsul	

The Fasti of Dalmatia have been compiled recently by A. Jagenteufel, *Statt-halter*, etc., supplemented by R. Syme, *Gnomon*, 31 (1959), 510–18. Since these studies only one new item of evidence (n. 13 below) has been added. In the following list annotation has been kept to the minimum, with references only to the sources for the governorships and their chronology, plus the subject matter mentioned in the text of chapter 6, section II (p. 80 ff).

1. C. Vibius Postumus C. f. *cos. suff.* 5   9–?12
    'vir consularis, praepositus Delmatiae', Vell. Pat., ii, 116, 1; cf. Florus, ii, 25; Dio, lvi, 15, 3.

2. L. Aelius Lamia L. f.   ?   *cos.* 3   ?12–14
    'Aelius Lamia … in Germania Illyricoque et mox in Africa splendidissimis functus ministeriis', Vell. Pat. ii, 116, 3.

    It is not certain whether he commanded the army in Pannonia or that in Dalmatia. On his later career, *PIR*² A 200.

3. P. Cornelius Dolabella P. f. *cos.* 10   by 14–20.
    'leg pro pr. divi Augusti et Ti. Caesaris Augusti' honoured by the 'civitatis superioris provinciae Hillyrici', III, 1741 (Epidaurum). 'cuius (of Q. Iunius Blaesus in Pannonia) curam ac fidem Dolabella, vir simplicitatis generosissimae, in maritima parte Illyrici per omnia imitatus est', Vell. Pat., ii, 125, 5. 'legatus pro praetore', III, 2908; cf. p. 2273 (dedication in 18–19 by Legions VII and XI at Iader); III, 3199, 3201; cf. *VAHD*, 49 (1936–7), 151, pl. II (road building, before 18, 19–20, Salona, see Appendix IV below, p. 452); III, 9973; cf. *JÖAI*, 12 (1909), Bb. 32 (boundary settlement, Corinium), *JÖAI*, 12 (1909), Bb. 32, n. 3 (boundary settlement, Popović near Corinium), *VAHD* 54 (1952), 41 ff., pl. II (building of *campus* at Issa in 20), 'praefectus quinquennalis Dolabellae', III, 14712 (Salona), 'leg. pr. pr. Aug. [..', *RAD* 339 (1965), p. 134 (boundary settlement, Jablanac).

    The Epidaurum dedication establishes his presence before the death of Augustus (August 14), while he was back in Rome during 21, Tac., *Ann.*, iii, 47.

4. L. Volusius Saturninus L. f. *cos.* 3   before 29 to *c.* 40.
    'legatus Ti. C[aesaris divi Aug]usti f. patronus', III, 2975 (Aenona); 'legatus pro praetore Ti. C[aesaris Augusti], III, 2974 (Aenona); '[Legatus pro praetore Ti. Caesaris Aug. et C.] Caesaris Au[g. Germanici] praefectus urbi (*c.* 40–56), patronus', III, 2976 (Aenona); 'legatus C. Caesaris Augusti Germanici', III, 2882 (boundary settlement, Corinium); III, 8472 (boundary

settlement, Jesenice in Poljica), III, 9832; cf. p. 2328/11 (boundary settlement, Razvadje), III, 9833 (boundary settlement?, Oklaj); 'legatus pro praetore', III, 9972 (dedication to (Livia) Iulia Augusta (d. 29), Argyruntum), III, 14322 (dedication to Tiberius 34/5, Argyruntum); '(legatus pro pr.)', III, 12794 (Krć near Dubrava in Poljica).

The dedication to Iulia Augusta was probably set up before her death in 29, and he may have replaced Dolabella in 21. His patronage was honoured at Aenona after he had returned to Rome about 40 and was appointed to Prefecture of the City. On his long career as the adviser of emperors, see Tac., *Ann.*, xiii, 30.

5. L. Arruntius M. Camillus Scribonianus *cos.* 32   *c.* 40–42.

'Delmatiae legatus', Suet., *Claud.*, 13, 2; Orosius, vii, 6, 6; cf. Dio, lx, 15, 1, 2. (under year 42), Tac., *Ann.*, xii, 52. 'le[g.] pro pr. C. [C]ae[s]aris Aug. Germanici', III, 9864a (boundary settlement, Vaganj in the upper Vrbas valley). Felicius, his slave, *BD*, 28 (1905), 20 (Salona).

He was the son of M. Furius Camillus (*cos.* 8) and adopted by L. Arruntius (*cos.* 6); on his family in general, *PIR²*, A, 1140. After five days of rebellion he was deserted by the army, Suet., *Claud.*, 13; cf. Tac., *Hist.*, 1, 89, when he proclaimed the Restored Republic, Dio, lx, 15, 3; lv, 23, 4, and fled to Issa where he was killed by a common soldier Volaginius, Tac., *Hist.*, ii, 75; cf. Plin., *Ep.*, iii, 16, 7.

6. L. Salvius Otho M. f.   *cos.* 33   42–3
Suet., *Otho*, i, 2–3.

He replaced Scribonianus and dealt with troops who had killed their own officers, in spite of Claudius' having pardoned them. In 43 he was back in Rome, Dio, lx, 18, 4. Otho was less a regular governor than a special emissary of Claudius (Suetonius, *Otho*, i, mentions 'extraordinaria imperia') to clear up the aftermath of the rebellion.

7. (L. Calpurnius) Piso Cn. f.   *cos.* 27   after 43
'. . . . .P]isone leg. pro pretore (sic) [Ti] Claudi Caesaris [Aug. G]ermanici', III, 12794 (boundary settlement, Krć near Dubrava in Poljica).

Before the condemnation of his father he bore the praenomen Cn. It is not certain that the consul of 27 is the Piso in Dalmatia. He had been Prefect of the City at the accession of Gaius, and it was unusual to proceed to a provincial command after this office. On the other hand, he was younger than most in this office and lived on into Vespasian's reign, *PIR²*, C, 293; cf. *RE*, 3 (1899), 1884, while Claudius needed support from illustrious families.

8. C. Ummidius Durmius Quadratus C. f. *cos. c.* 40   *c.* 46–50
'legatus divi Claudi in Illyrico,' X, 5182; cf. 5180 (career record at Casinum).

Either Dalmatia or Pannonia, although the latter is called Illyricum on the diploma of 60, XVI, 4. On the Ummidii see now R. Syme, *Historia*, 17 (1968), 72 ff.

9. P. Anteius Rufus   *cos.* ?   50–?54

'legatus pro praetore', III, 14987/1, *SB*, 222, fig. 2 (rebuilding of *principia* at Burnum, 50, 51/2), *BD*, 31 (1908), 3, pl. II, fig. 1 (dedication to Claudius, 51/2, Oneum), III, 1977 (dedication to Claudius, 51/2, Salona).

He perished in 66, ordered to commit suicide by Nero. He was a wealthy man and this was a temptation to his enemies, Tac., *Ann.*, xiv, 14. His name was erased from the Burnum inscriptions, but restored after the death and condemnation of Nero. A freedman is recorded belonging to one of Anteius' freedmen, 'P. Anteius P. Antei Syri l. Herma' at Salona, III, 1947.

10. C. Calpetanus Rantius Sedatus Metronius? *cos.* ?   Nero

'[legatus C]aesaris', *BD*, 29 (1906), 208, n. 3485a; cf. *VAHD*, 47–8 (1924–5), 20 (Salona, fragment).

Attested with full names at Rome, VI, 916 = 31201.

11. A. Ducenius Geminus   *cos. c.* 56/7   *c.* 63–7

'leg. Caesarum [pro pr. prov. . . . . . . item prov. D]almatiae et exercitus[. . ., III, 7267; cf. *JÖAI*, 19/20 (1919), Bb. 323 ff. (dedication to Asclepius, Epidauros in Argolid), 'legatus Augusti pro praetore', *JÖAI*, 12 (1909), Bb. 30 (boundary settlement near Ivanova glavica), III, 9973 (boundary settlement, Corinium), 'legatus', III, 2883, cf. 15045/2 (boundary settlement, Corinium), 'legatus pro praetore, patronus', *JAK*, 2 (1908), 96 (dedication to Ducenius, Narona).

He was prefect of the city in 69, probably appointed by Galba, Tac., *Hist.*, i, 14, after having been probably proconsul of Asia in 67/8, *PIR*², D, 201.

12. M. Pompeius Silvanus   *cos.* 45   67–70

'legatus Augusti pro praetore', III, 9938 (boundary settlement, Dobropoljici near Asseria); cf. Tac., *Hist.*, ii, 86, 3; iii, 50, 2.

The boundary settlement has civilian *iudices* and was probably made when Legion XI Claudia was in Italy. In 70 Pompeius was back in Rome, Tac., *Hist.*, iv, 47, and was later *curator aquarum*, Front., *de aq.*, 102.

13. [. . . . . . .]tius Pegasus   *cos.* early under Vespasian   ?*c.* 71–4

l[egatus pr. praetore imp.] Vespasian[i Aug.], *ES*, 4 (1967), 119 ff. (boundary settlement, Southern Liburnia).

Pegasus was an eminent lawyer and had been appointed Prefect of the City before the death of Vespasian after a number of provincial governorships, *PIR*¹, P, 164; cf. W. Kunkel (1952), 133 f.

14. L. Funisulanus Vettonianus L. f. *cos.* ? 78   *c.* 80–3

  'legatus Augusti pro praetore provinciae Delmatiae', III, 4013 (career dedication, patron at Andautonia, Pannonia Superior); cf. XI, 571, *AE*, 1946, 205 (Forum Popili), 'legatus pro praetore', *AI*, 5 (1964), 13 ff. (boundary settlement, Kosijerevo on left bank of river Trebišnjica).

  He had been legate of IV Scythica in 62, Tac., *Ann.*, xv, 25. He is attested in Pannonia, which he held after Dalmatia, on 3 September 85, XVI, 30 (diploma), and 5 September 85, XVI, 31, and as legate of Moesia Superior *c.* 86 received decorations in Domitian's Dacian Wars, *PIR²*, F, 570.

15. Q. Pomponius Rufus *cos. suff.* Sept.–Dec. 95   *c.* 92–4

  'legatus Augusti pro praetore provinc. [M]oesiae Dalmat(iae) Hisp(aniae) etc.', VIII, 13; cf. p. 979, *AE*, 1948, 3 (Lepcis Magna), 'in Delmatia sub Q. Pomponio Rufo', XVI, 38 (diploma 13 July 94, Salona).

  The order of his career is confused. He is attested as consular governor of Moesia Inferior in 99, XVI, 44 f., and governed Dalmatia as a praetorian. For the reasons behind the appointment of a praetorian, shortage of suitable consulars and the political situation at Rome about 93, see R. Syme, *Gnomon*, 31 (1959), 512.

16. C. Cilnius Proculus C. f. *cos.* 87   95–8

  '[legatus pro praetore imp. Caesaris Nervae Traiani Aug. provinciae D]almatiae', *AE*, 1926, 123; cf. XI, 1833 (career dedication at Arretium).

  A diploma, XVI, 46, records him governor of Moesia Superior in 100, which he held after Dalmatia, and later he may have received decorations in Trajan's Dacian War in this post or as an independent army commander, *PIR²*, C, 732. Proculus' successor in Dalmatia (see below) arrived in 98, and therefore he held Dalmatia as a consular in succession to the praetorian Pomponius Rufus (n. 15 above), dispelling the notion that Domitian reduced the province to praetorian status after the departure of the Legion IIII Flavia. Proculus belonged to an ancient noble family of Etruscan Arretium, Stein, *Ritterstand*, 196 f. n. 3.

17. (. . . . .) Macer *cos.* ?   98–?

  Addressed on his arrival in Dalmatia in 98 by Martial in a poem and styled 'rector', x, 78. As successor to Cilnius Proculus, he will have been a consular, rather than praetorian, as suggested by A. Degrassi *FC*, 29. He cannot be identified readily with any known Macer of the period, R. Syme, *Gnomon*, 31 (1959), 515.

18. C. Minicius Fundanus L. f. *cos.* 107   ?108 ff.

  Honoured with statue and career inscription (fragmentary) at Šipovo in the Pliva valley, *GZMBH*, 38 (1926), 155, presumably as *patronus*, although no governorship is recorded, but the *cursus* survives only up to the legionary command. Friend of the Younger Pliny, *Ep.*, v, 16; cf. i, 9, iv, 15, and of Plutarch where he features in the dialogue on Peace of Mind, c. 1, and others, *PIR²*, M, 433.

19. [. . . . .]   under Trajan before 114

'[le]ga[tus imp. Cae]saris Nervae Traia[ni] Aug. Germ. Dacici pro pr[aetore] provinciae Delmatiae', XI, 4646 (dedication as *patronus*, Tuder).

The governorship is the last post on the fragmentary stone, and is preceded only by *curator operum publicorum*, Groag, *RE*, 10 (1919), 785, identifies him with C. Iulius Proculus M. f. (*cos.* 109) whose *cursus* in ascending order at Antium, X, 6658, ends with the latter appointment. The identification is not noted by *PIR²*, I, 497.

20. L. Vitrasius Flamininus L. f. *cos. suff.* 122   122 ff. (?Marcus)

'legatus ppr pr. Italiae Transpadanae et provinciae Moesiae Superioris et exercitus provinciae Dalmatiae', X, 3870 (career at Capua, preserved in probably inaccurate MS copy).

He is probably the Hadrianic suffect consul with the same names (XVI, 69), and a command in Transpadana, either praetorian or consular, is possible for Trajan and Hadrian, as for instance with C. Iulius Proculus (n. 19 above), X, 6658. An alternative date for the anomalous command involving the 'army of Dalmatia' is during the Marcomannic Wars, suggested by Zwikker, 163 ff., but he is mistaken in proposing a single command extending from Northern Italy to Serbia, although there were certainly disturbances within the province and extra troops in the interior at that time (p. 117) under Marcus. The Vitrasii were Campanian, of equestrian rank in the early Principate, R. Syme, *Gnomon*, 31 (1959), 514.

21. P. Coelius Balbinus Vibullius Pius,   *cos. ord.* 137   ?138 ff.

Honoured with a career inscription at Rome by the decurions of an unnamed city, VI, 1383. He was made a Patrician by Hadrian and elected *flamen Ulpialis*, signs of high social distinction. Dessau believed that he was related to Trajan (*PIR¹* C, 1241), while his tribe Sergia was that of Italica in Baetica. On the other hand, there is little particular significance in his ordinary consulship as colleague of L. Aelius Caesar in 137, R. Syme, *Gnomon*, 31 (1959), 513. Members of his household attested at Salona, III, 2294, 2295, 2561, 9009, 13925, suggest that he may have been a governor of the province in the years after 137. Sergia is one of the Salona tribes, and he could conceivably be a native of the province.

22. M. (Cutius Priscus Messius Rusticus) Aemilius Papus (Arrius Proculus Iulius Celsus)   *cos. suff.* before 138   attested in 147

'legatus eius (Pius imp.) pro praetore provinciae Delmatiae' on dedication to Pius in 147 at his native city Salpensa in Spain, II, 1282; also recorded as legate on his own career inscription, II, 1283, Salpensa. Attested as curator operum publicorum about 138–140, *AE*, 1934, 146; he was probably in Dalmatia *c.* 140 to 147.

23. Sex. Aemilius Equester   *cos.* ?   under Pius

'legatus Augusti pro praetore', *VAHD*, 51 (1930–4), 225 (building record by Cohort VIII Vol. c. R., Tilurium, some date under Antoninus Pius).

24. (?   ) Scapula Tertullus   *cos.* ?   161–9?

'legatus Augustorum p[rov. Dalmatiae]', III, 2809 (rebuilding of governor's residence (*praetorium*) by Liburnian communities, Scardona).

A Scapula Tertullus was the recipient of a rescript from Marcus and Commodus (176–80), *Dig.*, L, 18, 4, and these could be the two Augusti recorded on the Scardona text. On the other hand he could have been proconsul of Asia or Africa at the time, while the congested fasti of Dalmatia make it better to place Tertullus in the joint reign of Marcus and Verus (161–9), which is a blank otherwise. A consulship in the one-sixties followed by the Dalmatian governorship fits better with the father of the *consul ordinarius* in 195, R. Syme, *Gnomon*, 31 (1959), 514 f.

25. M. Didius Iulianus   *cos. suff.* ?175   176 f.

'legatus Augusti [pro praetore prov. P]onti et Bithyniae [item German]iae Dalmatiae Belgica[e]', VI, 1401 (career record at Rome, *patronus* of Bisica in Africa), 'inde Dalmatiam regendam accepit (Didius Iulianus) eamque a confinibus hostibus vindicavit', *Vita Did. Iul.*, i, 8 f.

On the disturbances in the province, see p. 117, and on his career, *PIR*², D, 77, and now H–G. Pflaum, *Sodales Antoniniani*, 60 ff.

26. C. Vettius Sabinianus Iulius Hospes C. f.   *cos. suff.* 175–6   ?178–9

'leg. Augusti pr. pr. provinciarum III Daciarum et Delmatiae....', *AE*, 1920, 45 (career as *patronus*, Thurburbo Maius in Africa).

On the chronology of his long career, A. Betz, *RE*, 8A (1958), 1861 ff.

27. L. Aurelius Gallus?   *cos. ord.* 174   in 179

'Her[c]. Aug. [s]ac. Val. Valen. v[et] ex 7 limite[m] pub. praeclus. ob dec(essum) Aur. Gall. leg. suo inp. aperuit im. Com(m)o[do II] et Mar[tio] Vero [II] cos. VI [kal.] Ma[ias], III, 3157–8663; cf. 14239/4, also drawing in Jagenteufel, 79, in 179 (Salona).

The reading of the name is uncertain, either AVR(elius) or AVF(idius). In *PIR*², A, 1387, Groag included a separate entry for this Aufidius Gallus, rather than identifying him with Aurelius Gallus, the *consul ordinarius* of 174, *PIR*², A, 1516, for whom there is a possible record in Rome in 179, VI,

36873. The Salona text refers to the dec(essum), departure rather than death, of the legate, and concerns an increase of the Salona territory into the Poljica area, see above, p. 228.

28. L. Iunius Rufinus Proculeianus   *cos* ?   early in 184

'legatus pro praetore', III, 3201 (building of new bridge in 184 over the river Hippius at Tilurium, by Novae, Delminium, and Rider).

He was earlier tribune of Legion XIII Gemina, III, 7770 (Apulum).

29. M. Cassius Apronianus   *cos. suff. c.* 183   185 ff.

Father of historian Cassius Dio (n. 33 below), and successor of n. 28, probably in 185 and after, Dio, xlix, 36, 4. On his career, *PIR*², C, 485.

30. Pollienus Auspex   *cos.* ? *c.* 208   ? Severus–Caracalla

IGR, III, 618 = *ILS*, 8841; cf. Stein *Moesien*, 83. The problem is complicated, involving the chronology of three generations, including two homonyms. Jagenteufel, 69 ff., follows the chronology of R. Egger, *JÖAI*, 19/20 (1919), Bb. 311 f., and dates the elder Pollienus Auspex in Dalmatia to 174/5, but see now A. R. Birley, *ES*, 4 (1967), 80 f., arguing for *c.* 193.

31. Fulvius Maximus   *cos. suff.* ?   ? 208 ff.

'.....Ma]ximus [v. c. leg.] Aug. pr. pr. [prov. Dalm.]', *VAHD*, 44 (1921) 30 (?dedication at Salona), '...Venetos Dalmata[s Libur]na regna post feros Iapudas Germaniarum consularis ....', XIII, 8007 (metric dedication, Bonna).

Attested in Pannonia Superior in 210, *AE*, 1944, 103 (Kornyë near Brigetio). If the Iapudae of the Bonn text refer to this office (an inaccuracy), then Dalmatia was held in the years immediately preceding, although the Salona fragment seems to record only one Augustus, when there were two from 198 to 211. The article *PIR*², F, 550 appeared before the Brigetio inscription.

In a forthcoming study (BJ 1968) G. Alföldy proposes the following chronology: *cos. suff. c.* 203. Dalmatia 203–6, Germania Inf. *c.* 206–9, Pannonia Sup. 209–12.

32. C. Iulius Avitus Alexianus   ? *cos. suff.* 217   217 ff.

'praeses [clementissimus?]', *JÖAI*, 19/20 (1919), Bb. 293 ff. (career dedication at Salona (fragmentary), by an auxiliary unit commander); cf. A. Radnóti, *Germania*, 39 (1961), 383 ff., also H–G. Pflaum, *BV–B*, 27 (1962), 82 ff., correctly rejecting Radnóti's compressed chronology of the career.

33. Cassius Dio Cocceianus   ? *cos. suff.* I, 205 or 206; II, *ord*, 229.   *c.* 224–6

Dio, xlix, 36, 1 and (Xiphilinus) lxxxi, 1, 2 f. On his official career, *PIR*², C, 492, and more fully, F. Millar, *Cassius Dio*, 5 ff.

34. L. Domitius Gallicanus Papinianus *cos. suff.* 238   ? 239 ff.
    'legatus pro praetore Dalmatiae', II, 4115 (career dedication to him as *patronus*, Tarraco in Spain); cf. also fragmentary record of his name at Senia, III, 10054; cf. Patsch, *Lika*, 100 (rebuilding city bath *balneum*).

35. Iulius Honoratus   *cos* ?   *c.* 241
    'leg. Aug. pr. pr.', on two milestones, III, 13327 (near Salvium), 13328 (between Panković and Skakavac), both under Gordian III (238–44), dated about 241.

36. Claudius Herennianus   *cos.* ?   in 247
    'vir clarissimus legatus Augustorum pr. pr.', III, 10174 (milestone, dated first half of 247, Siculi (Biač) on Salona territory). The two Augusti are Philipp and his son (*nobilissimus Caesar*), both mentioned on the milestone.

37. Aelius Florianus   *cos.* ?   *c.* 251–3
    'legatus Augusti pr. pr.', *BD*, 30 (1907), 111, n. 3616A and 3723A (milestone, Klis near Salona) under Trebonianus Gallus 251–3.

38. ?Ragonius Clarus
    'prefect of Illyricum and the Gallic provinces', under Valerianus (253–8), *SHA, tyr.trig.*, 18, 4 f.; almost certainly fictitious.

39. Septimius   in 271
    A usurper in Dalmatia (apud Dalmatas) under Aurelian, probably a governor, but killed soon afterwards by his own supporters, *Epit. de Caes.*, 35, 3, Zosimus, i, 49, 2.

Senatorial legates of uncertain date.

40. [..........] Bassus   first century
    '....]s Bassus [leg. Aug. pro pr.]', *VAHD*, 55 (1953), 104, fig. 1 (boundary settlement, Šušnjar between Vrlika and Koljane in upper Cetina valley). No ready identification. L. Annius Bassus was legate of XI Claudia in 69, Tac., *Hist.*, iii, 50, but all known boundary settlements were made in the name of the provincial governor, including the one in 69 (n. 12 above).

41. [..........] Blaesus   first century
    '......]Bleso (sic) leg. pro pr.', III 6407 (Promona architrave frag.). No ready identification; for possibilities see Jagenteufel, 110 ff.

42. [..........]   first century
    '....leg.] Aug. pro p[r....', Betz 34, n. 11 (boundary settlement, find-spot not recorded). A reference on the stone to the general Dolabella (n. 3 above) settlement (*forma Dolabelliana*) suggests a Julio–Claudian date, as also the form pro rather than pr.

43. [· · · · · · · · · · ·] ? first century
    '. . . .leg. Ca]es. Aug. Da[l]ma[tiae. . .', III, 6997 (dedication, Trocimia in Phrygia). A legate who became later proconsul of Asia.

44. [· · · · · · · · · ·] ? first century
    '. . . .l]eg. pro [pr. . . . .', III, 1807 (rebuilding of bath (*balneum*) at Narona).

45. [· · · · · · · · · ·] Second or early third century
    'leg. pr. p[r. pro]vinciae Dalmat[iae . . . .', VI, 1545; cf. 31677 (dedication with career at Rome).

46. [· · · · · · · · · ·] late second–early third century
    'leg. Augustorum pro pr. Moesiae item Dalmatiae. .', *AE*, 1955, 123 (career at Carthage); cf. *Karthago*, 4 (1953), 132 ff.

47. [· · · · · · · · · ·]
    '. . . . . .leg. A]ug. pr. pr. [. . . .', III, 1990 = 8573 (Salona).

48. [· · · · · · · · · ·] early third century
    'praeses prov. Pan[noniae Inferioris? Ma]c[edo]niae Dalmatiae agens vice prae[. . . . . .', *AE*, 1949, 61 (dedication by *Universus populus* at Sufetula in Africa); cf. H. Lieb in Reidinger, *Pannonien*, 250 f.

49. [· · · · · · · · · ·] Hadrianic
    Fragmentary *cursus*, found in Salona amphitheatre, records posts from military tribunate to legionary legate, with signs of special imperial favour; nominated (*candidatus*) for plebeian tribunate and praetorship by Hadrian. Possibly a governor, *BD*, 37 (1914), 33, 4303A = *AE*, 1922, 36; but see Alföldy, *ES*, 3 (1967), 30, who assumes him a native, possibly a relative of the Aequum *Iulii*.

APPENDIX III *The Legionary Titles* Claudia pia fidelis

Throughout the period from 42 until their departure from Dalmatia the Legions VII and XI bore the honorific titles conferred on them by Claudius after the failure of the rebellion of L. Arruntius Scribonianus (p. 83). During these years the titles are normally abbreviated to *C.p.f.*, but after the departure of Legion XI from Dalmatia in 69 the form *Cl.* becomes the rule; cf. Ritterling, *legio*, 1628 (Legion VII), 1705 (Legion XI). The presence or absence of these titles on tombstones and other inscriptions has been assumed to be firm dating evidence, but this has been questioned on the evidence of two Neronian boundary settlement inscriptions which record Legion XI, but without its proper titles (III, 15045/2; cf. *JÖAI*, 8 (1905), Bb. 53, fragmentary but recording a Neronian *iudex* Q. Aebutius Liberalis, a contemporary of A. Resius Maximus). One mentions A. Resius Maximus as centurion of Legion XI (with no titles), although the same officer appears on another settlement with the proper legionary titles (III, 9973). The problem here is to what extent boundary settlements can be regarded as 'official inscriptions', and whether irregularity in military titles generally throws doubt on the value of these titles to give a firm date before or after 42. These records of boundary settlements were not apparently (to judge from the poor quality of their lettering) set up by the government but by the communities involved. They marked the places where the boundary had been fixed, and would have to be recut or replaced as the lettering weathered, when errors and omissions in official titles could be expected. They must not be allowed to impugn the dating value of these titles on the tombstones of serving legionaries or veterans: such people would always be most careful in seeing that their tombstones bore the full titles of the unit – especially those which had been conferred for loyalty to the emperor. The point arises with a veteran of Legion VII buried at Siculi (Biač), where Claudius settled some veterans (III, 9712). Some scholars (Betz, p. 32 f., Pavan, *Dalmazia*, 208, n. 1) have assumed that this must be part of the Claudian settlement and, therefore, the tombstone must be dated after 42 in spite of the absence of the legionary titles *C.p.f.* On the other hand, it is possible that Claudius, who became emperor in January 41, could have made the settlement at Siculi before 42.

In normal times the maintenance of roads and bridges was a duty (*munus*) which fell on the local cities, and particularly on the larger landowners. Most of the milestones found in Dalmatia bear the names of second, third, and early fourth-century rulers, and were set up by the local communities at their own expense. In the case of more expensive projects, roads over mountain passes or larger river crossings, the government required the co-operation of groups of cities. The rebuilding of the important bridge across the river Hippius at Tilurium (*pons Tiluri*) was the work of Rider, Delminium, and Novae, all cities of the Delmatae in the area, and their efforts were co-ordinated by the governor L. Iunius Rufinus Proculeianus early in 184, III, 3201.

In quite a different category was the massive programme of strategic roads under Tiberius, built partly by the provincial Legions VII and XI controlling native labour, presumably mostly prisoners from the war of 6–9. The construction was begun soon after 9 and its completion was recorded on a series of stone plaques set up at Salona during the latter part of Cornelius Dolabella's governorship (14–20). The object of these roads was to link the main military centres near the Adriatic, including Salona, to the bases in the Save valley, especially at Siscia, Servitium, and Sirmium. This would ensure that any future rebellion in Dalmatia could be contained much more effectively than was possible in 6.

The construction of at least six separate major routes was recorded on three separate plaques. In the case of one (III, 3199; cf. 10157, dated before 18), only a fragment of the imperial titles is preserved, along with the name of Dolabella. The building of the other five was commemorated on two large stone plaques, both of which were later broken up and used in buildings. The reading of the destinations of some of the routes is far from certain, although there is no doubt that all the distances recorded were taken from Salona. Some were built by Legions VII and XI.

The first of these two plaques dates to 17 and originally recorded two routes (III, 3198a = 10156 and III, 3200):

1.   'viam] a colonia Salonitan(a)
                        ad f]in[e]s provinciae Illyrici
                        [......................]
                        cuius viai millia passus sunt
                        CLXVII munit per vexillarios
                        leg. VII et XI'

This was a road of 167 miles to the boundaries of the province, the longest distance recorded among the routes. The three long routes recorded below (nos. 3–6) went to the Strmica Pass, Central Bosnia, and the Sarajevo area. This could be the major route to Siscia, through the Lika polje and the Iapodes. The reference to the boundaries of 'Illyricum' suggest, on the other hand, not the Pannonian–Dalmatian frontier but the frontier with Italy. This is the only route in which Legion XI at Burnum was involved, and may be the coastal route to Liburnia. It may be the military road to the south: that from Tilurium to Bigeste and Narona was being built under Tiberius, III, 8512 (Lokvičić, 26/7).

2.   'item viam Gabinianam
                      ab Salonis Andetrium aperuit
                      at munit per leg. VII'

The Legion VII at Tilurium was reponsible on its own for the short stretch (*c.* 15 m.p.) from Salona to the old fortress Andetrium (gornje Muč). The road branched from the Salona–Tilurium road a little beyond Klis to Andetrium where it joined the main military route from Tilurium to Burnum. It is the only named road known in the province, and commemorates the campaigns of Caesar's proconsul A. Gabinius in 48–7 B.C., see above, p. 41.

The second plaque (III, 3201 = 10159 and III, 3198b = 10156b; cf. new readings by G. Alföldy, *AArch*, 16 (1964), 247 ff.) records three routes completed in 20, the year of Dolabella's departure. All three led towards the interior, and the mileage is recorded in each case, although no legions are recorded as having been involved in the construction:

3.   'viam a Salonis ad Hedum castel(lum)
                      Daesitiatium per mill[i]a passuum
                      CLVI munit'

This was a route 156 miles long to the Daesitiates who dwelt around Sarajevo (above, p. 170). The centre Hedum may be Bréza, where a *princeps* of that people is recorded. To reach the area from Salona in 156 miles only one line is really feasible: Salona–Tilurium–Aržano–Delminium–Bistue Vetus (Varvara)–Konjic–across the Ivan Pass–Stanecli (Kiseljak)–Bréza, approximately 156 m.p. (233 km). In military terms it is an obvious part of the pacification of this area begun seriously only in 9.

4.   'et idem viam at Batinum flumen
                      quod dividit Breuc[o]s Osseriatibus
                      a Salonis munit per mi[lli]a passuum
                      CLVIII'

A vital new reading by Alföldy (op. cit., 249). A route of 158 m.p. to the river Bathinus (Bosna) did not head for the Sarajevo area but for a point lower down along its course, and must be the route through Delminium and across to the

Upper Vrbas valley south of Bugojno (the line of the modern road from Split to the interior), then to Bistue Nova (Vitez) in the Lašva valley. From there it went northwards to some point on the Bosna, not along the winding and difficult valley, but on the higher ground to terminate at Maglaj, south of the frontier post at Doboj, as Alföldy suggests.

5. 'et idem viam [...........]
    munit ad imum montem Ditionum
    Ulcirum per millia passuum
    a Salonis LXXVIID
    P. Dolabella leg. pro
    pr.'

The route led for 77½ miles to the mons Ulcirus in the territory of the Ditiones. It lead north from Salona to the area of Knin and Burnum on the Titius and from there across the Strmica Pass to some point near the head of the river Una. Later under Claudius the road was extended through to Bosnian Novi on the Una, and into the Upper Sana valley around Ključ, where large numbers of milestones dated 47 have been located still *in situ*, III, 13329 ff., and on as far as Petrovac.

These routes laid the basis for the later road system of Dalmatia. Soon many diversions, short cuts, and loop roads were added to the system, especially among the high poljes of the northern Delmatae and the deep valleys of Bosnia. Obviously the evidence which has survived for the Tiberian road programme is not complete. The road leading inland from Epidaurum to Trebinje was built as early as Claudius, and may have been part of the original scheme under Dolabella, III, 10175 (Lučin Do near Mokropolje, 47–8). Elsewhere there are large numbers of milestones, most dated to the third and early fourth centuries, which attest roads built or maintained in an increasingly complex pattern. The last stage of the military roads in the hinterland may be that to Scodra. At Prud Orepak near Narona a milestone set up under Titus (79–81) marks the distance of 68 m.p. from Tilurium along the road to Scodra, *JAK*, 2 (1908), 101, n. 1. Road building and maintenance is attested as late as Valentinian I (364–7), *JÖAI*, 18 (1915), Bb. 188 (Ervenik gornje between Burnum and Smokovac gradina: marked X m.p. from Burnum). Once the major communication needs of the army were satisfied, the roads developed largely for local convenience. It is striking that the Claudian road north of the Strmica, a long winding journey through trackless forests, appears to have fallen out of use, and the Claudian milestones remain along the road, with no signs of later rebuilding. The situation was quite different in the poljes of the northern Delmatae, especially around Delminium, where recent research has revealed an intricate complex of different routes (E. Pašalić, *Naselja* map), although many of them were only open at different seasons of the year according to the extent of polje flooding. The road patterns on the later Peutinger Map and the Antonine Itinerary reflect the situation in the second century and later, and show the original strategic roads completely absorbed in the road-pattern of the province.

The best documented sphere of administration concerning the cities and other provincial communities is the settlement of boundary disputes. One cannot be certain that the demand for fixing precisely the boundaries between different communities arose in the first place from the communities themselves. It may be that the provincial government sought to break up the cohesion of the larger political units and ethnic groups, especially among the Delmatae and other peoples in the interior. In the case of the cities in the Ravni kotari, however, where most of the boundary settlements have been discovered, it was clearly the communities themselves which disputed possession of lands and caused the intervention of the provincial government to settle the disputes. All the settlements were made in the name of the provincial governor: his decision (*sententia*) appears to have been final, and no other authority is known to have been involved.

Many of the known settlements appear to have involved the revision or the more precise interpretation of the original settlement of the province (*forma provinciae*), much of which was completed under the governor Cornelius Dolabella. When a dispute arose the matter was normally brought before the governor sitting with his council of advisers (*assessores*), many of whom would be chosen from cities in the province. Usually a decision could not be made without some on-the-spot inspection of the land in question, and it was the normal practice to appoint an arbitrator (*iudex datus*), usually a senior centurion from one of the provincial legions, who would submit his proposed settlement to be confirmed (*determinare*) by the governor when expressing his judgement (*sententia*). Variations in the wording of boundary settlements reveal that different types of procedure existed for boundary disputes, depending on the legal status of the communities involved and the nature of the dispute. Almost all the settlements which survive were recorded on stone columns set up either at the point where the new boundary was established, or in the political centre of the communities involved. The majority were made during the Julio–Claudian period, especially under the governors L. Volusius Saturninus and A. Ducenius Geminus, but an isolated instance belongs to the last years of the third century.

III, 9973; cf. *JÖAI*, 12 (1909), Bb. 32 (improved reading), Corinium:
[e]dictu (sic) P. Corneli Dolabele (sic) leg. pro praetore determinav[it] S. Titius Geminus pr(inceps) posterior leg. VII inter Neditas et Corinienses restituti iussu A. Duceni Gemini leg. Aug. pro p[r.] per. A. Resium [M]aximum 7 leg. XI C.p.f. pr. posterior. et Q. Aebutium Liberalem (h)astat(um) posterior. leg. eiusdem.

The original settlement was laid down by judicial ruling (*edictum*) of Dolabella and fixed on the ground by Salvius Titius Geminus, senior centurion of Legion VII, between Corinium and Nedinum. It was apparently this same boundary which was re-established by two senior centurions of XI C.p.f. under the Neronian governor A. Ducenius Geminus. Dolabella's settlements are attested on fragmentary records elsewhere. One at Popović near Corinium, *JÖAI* 12 (1909), Bb. 32, n. 3, probably involved the boundary between the same two cities, while another, Betz, 34, n. 11 (findspot unknown), mentions a restoration of the original Dolabellan settlement (*forma Dolabelliana*) by a later governor. Disputes could arise even among the small Liburnian communities along the Velebit coastline. A dispute over access to fresh water between the Ortoplini (Stinica) and the Parentini was settled satisfactorily after a meeting (*ex conventione*) III, 15053; cf. Patsch, *Lika*, 22, but another dispute which broke out between the former people and the Beci (Jablanac) required the intervention of Dolabella who gave his decision (*ex dec(reto)*), *RAD*, 339 (1965), p. 134 (Jablanac near Stinica).

Under L. Volusius Saturninus four settlements are preserved. Under Gaius (37–41) a centurion Laco from Legion VII was assigned as *iudex* between the Neditae and the Corinienses, III, 2882 (Corinium), while three others concern small communities of the Delmatae. Two dealt with the three small peoples of the Poljica area near Salona, the Onastini, Pituntini, and Nerastini. L. Trebius Secundus the camp prefect (*praefectus castrorum*), probably of Legion VII at nearby Tilurium, 'settled the boundaries' (*terminos pos(u)it*) between the Onastini (Oneum) and the Nerastini (Neraste–Jesenice), III, 8472 (Jesenice). Here apparently there was no question of a *iudex*: the matter was simply decided by order of the governor after hearing evidence (*consilio athibito*) on which his judgement (*sententia*) was based. Volusius' settlement between the other two communities, Nerastini and Pituntini, is mentioned when the matter was finally decided under a Claudian legate (L. Calpurnius) Piso, III, 12794 (Krć near Dubrava in Poljica). Between these two the boundaries (*termini*) were resurveyed (*recogniti*) and fixed by Piso through C. Marius Maternus, centurion of Legion VII C.p.f. a process which Saturninus had set in motion some years earlier (*quos L. Volusius Saturninus statuendos curaverat*). Elsewhere, boundaries were settled by centurions of Legion XI and a tribune of Legion VII in the Promona region under Gaius: here the settlement arose from a meeting (*conventio*), after which the arbitrators were appointed, III, 9832 (Razvadje near Promona); cf. III, 9833 (?boundary settlement, Oklaj).

Hitherto all the settlements have concerned communities close to the coast. Under the ill-fated L. Arruntius Camillus Scribonianus a settlement was made between two minor peoples in the interior, communities of the Ditiones or of the Maezaei. A settlement at Vaganj near the Upper Vrbas valley records M' Coelius centurion of Legion VII as *iudex*, 'that he should decide (*regeret*) and fix (*poneret*) the boundaries between the Sapuates and the [La?]matini', III, 9864a. Under the Neronian governor A. Ducenius Geminus disputes broke out once more among the Liburnians in the Ravni kotari. He restored the old settlement between the Neditae and the Corinienses, made by Cornelius Dolabella more than forty years earlier, through two centurions; and it was also necessary for the same two officers to fix the boundary at another point by a survey on the ground for all to see (*fin[i]s inter N. et C. derectus mensuris actis*), III, 2883; cf. 15044/2 and *JÖAI*, 5 (1902), Bb. 5. On the east the Corinium boundary had to be fixed by another survey on the ground after a second meeting, in this case with the Ans[ienses], '[finis] inter A. et C. secundum [c]onventionem utriusque partis derectus mensu[ris] actis', *JÖAI*, 12 (1909), Bb. 30 (Ivanova glavica, 4 miles east of Corinium (Karin)). One of the centurions who settled this dispute was involved in another Liburnian settlement, between the Sidrini and the people of Asseria (Podgradje near Benkovac), *JÖAI*, 8 (1905), Bb. 53, fig. 12 (Bruška between Asseria and Medvidje). The last Julio–Claudian settlement in Liburnia was made between Alveria and Asseria under Pompeius Silvanus, III, 9938 (between Medvidje and Asseria). In this case the *iudices* were not the usual legionary centurions, but leading citizens from provincial cities which were not parties to the dispute. No boundaries are mentioned but the 'in re praesente' which the *iudices* 'dealt with by their judgement' (*per suam sententiam determin-averunt*) was presumably a settlement involving boundaries. In this case it was the *iudices* who made the decision: the governor had merely nominated them and apparently took no further part in the case. This may be due to their civilian status, and some of them may have been judges and *assessores* serving in his court. The occasion for their appointment was doubtless the absence of Legion XI C.p.f. in Italy during the civil wars.

Early under Vespasian the governor was still continuing with boundary prob-lems, but in one instance there is a sign of imperial interference. A tribune of Legion IIII Flavia felix, stationed at Burnum, was appointed *iudex* for some dis-pute, of which details have not survived, through the influence (*auctoritas*) of Vespasian himself by the governor Pegasus, an eminent lawyer of the period. There may have been some special aspects in the problem before the governor to cause this solitary instance of imperial interference, *ES*, 4 (1967), 119 f. At about the same time a settlement was made among the small and isolated communities of the Delmatae in the upper Hippius (Cetina) valley. At Šušnjar between Vrlika and Koljane C. Plotius Maximus was ordered to arrange the final settlement concerning the fixing of boundaries between the Lizaviates and the Barizani(ates), *VAHD*, 55 (1953), 104, fig. 1. He may have been a legionary centurion; the governor who appointed him is known only from his *cognomen* Bassus (n. 40 above, p. 449). The adjusting of the boundaries between the Burnum military territory (*prata legionis*) and the forest (*fines roboreti*) of Flavius Marcus, presumably a leading member of the Delmatae, by the procurator Ti. Claudius Augustanus (Alpinus L. Bellicius Sollers); cf. H–G. Pflaum, *Carrières*, 160, n. 68, early under Trajan was merely the decision of the imperial officer responsible and not subject to arbitration, III, 13250; cf. p. 2328/13 (Vedropolje near Uzdolje, east of Promona). The latest known settlement in the province was made between the cities of Salvium and Stridon (see above, p. 271) under the *praeses* Flavius Valerius Constantius (*c.* 281–4), the later emperor Constantius I. If the badly mutilated text is genuine it is a remarkable instance of continuity in provincial administration, with the same problems of boundary dispute being settled by a *iudex datus* (identity has been lost) in the last decades of the third century, III, 9860 (between Grahovo and Glamoč).

i Before A.D. 42

Origo	Legion XX	Legion VII	Legion XI	VII or XI
ITALY				
Regio II Apulia		Beneventum III, 14932 (*miles*)		
Regio VI Umbria		Aesis III, 9742 (*miles*) Pisaurum III, 2014 (*veteranus*)		
Regio VII Etruria	Luca III, 2911 (*veteranus*)	Arretium III, 2071 (*miles*) III, 8764 (*veteranus*) Florentia III, 1814 (*eques veteranus*) III, 8723 (*miles*) III, 9712 (*veteranus*)	Arretium III, 2840 (*veteranus*) III, 6418 (9896) (*veteranus*) Florentia Betz, 118 (*miles cornicen*)	
Regio VIII Aemilia		Bononia III, 14244/1 (*veteranus*) Forum Corneli III, 2716 (signifer) III, 14931 (*miles*)	Brixellum III, 14321/13 (= 15000) (*miles*) Parma *AE*, 1920, 63 (*veteranus missicius*) Regium Lepidi III, 9885 (*eques veteranus*)	Bononia III, 14239/5 (8761 = 12832) (*miles*)

Origo	Legion XX	Legion VII	Legion XI	VII or XI
Regio X Venetia–Histria	Brixia V, 4365 (*signifer*?)	Brixia III, 14946 (*veteranus*) Verona III, 2040 (*signifer*) III, 2041 (*veteranus*) III, 9939 (*veteranus*) III, 13976 (*miles*)?	Altinum III, 2062 and V, 2164 (*miles* or *veteranus*) Ateste III, 2835 (*miles*) Brixia III, 14997/2 (*miles*) Cremona III, 6416 (*eques*) III, 14997/1 (*miles*) III, 15001 (*miles*) Patavium? III, 9892 (2832); cf. *GZMBH*, 1899 487 (*miles* or *veteranus*) Parentium *Inscr. It.*, X, 2, 204 (*veteranus*) *Inscr. It.*, X, 2, 252 (*miles*)	
Regio XI Transpadana		Augusta Praetoria III, 9738 and *BD*, 26, p. 134, n. 3244 (*miles*) Ticinum III, 2913 (*veteranus*)	Eporedia III, 6413 (*miles*)	
Italy by tribe	Pollia III, 2030 (*veteranus*)	Stellatina V, 7161 (*veteranus*)	Stellatina III, 8758 (*veteranus*)	Camilia III, 13977 (*veteranus*)

Origo	Legion XX	Legion VII	Legion XI	VII or XI
Italy by tribe cont.		Scaptia *BD*, 26, p. 193, n. 3150 (*miles*)	Fabia? III, 14993 (*miles*) Velina III, 9709 (*veteranus*) Falerna III, 9710 (*veteranus*)	
Italy?		Clistinna III, 9736 (2714) (*miles*)		

Origo	Legion VII	Legion XI	VII or XI
Macedonia	Alorus *WMBH*, 12, 132, n. 1 (*veteranus*) Dyrrhachium III, 9741 (*miles*) Heraclea III, 9734; cf. p. 2269 (*miles*) Philippi III, 2717 (*miles*) III, 14933 (?)	Pelagonia III, 2017 (*veteranus*) Philippi III, 2031 (*miles*)	
Asia	Augusta Troas III, 2019 (*veteranus*) Sebaste (possibly Cilicia) III, 2048 (*veteranus*)		
Bithynia	Sinope Betz, 58 (*veteranus*)		

Origo	Legion VII	Legion XI	VII or XI
Galatia, Lycaonia, Paphlagonia	Amblada III, 9737 (*miles*) Laranda III, 2709 (*miles*) Pessinus III, 1818 (2 *veterani*) III, 2710 (9726) (*veteranus*) *JAK*, 2, 110, n. 1 (*veteranus*)	Laranda III, 2818; cf. p. 1626 (*veteranus*)	
Pamphylia–Pisidia	Conana III, 9733 (*miles*) Betz, 63 (*veteranus*) *BD*, 26, p. 130, n. 3321 (?) Isinda *BD*, 36, p. 14, n. 4407A (*eques*) Mylias III, 6364 = 8488 (*veteranus*) III, 8487 (*veteranus*) (*miles*)		
Pontus, Cappadocia	Pasimo *BD* 37, 66, n. 4657A (*veteranus*) Sebastopolis (possibly Asia), III, 8493 (?)		
Cilicia	Ninica *BD* 31, 79, n. 3959A (*miles*)		

ii After A.D. 42

Origo	Legion VII C.p.f.	Legion XI C.p.f.	VII or XI	Legion IIII F.f.
ITALY				
Regio VII Etruria		Florentia III, 1915, add. 8507; cf. p. 2328/121 (*veteranus*) III, 2837 (?) III, 9909 = 14321/6 (*miles?*) III, 14991 (?)		
Regio VIII Aemilia	Placentia *Sp.*, 71, p. 203, n. 534 (*veteranus*) III, 8769? (?)	Bononia SB, 216, n. 9 (*miles*) Placentia III, 14997 (*miles*) Ravenna *WS.*, 24, p. 382 (*miles*)		
Regio IX Liguria		Aquae Statiellae III, 2833; cf. 2328/161 (*miles*) III, 9904 = 14321/3 (?) Pollentia *SB*, 216, n. 10 (*miles*)		
Regio X Venetia-Histria		Cremona XIII, 7232 (*miles*) Betz 144 (*miles*) Feltria III, 15005 (*miles*)	Cremona III, 8434 (?)	

Origo	Legion VII C.p.f.	Legion XI C.p.f.	VII or XI	Leg. IIII F.f.
Regio X Venetia-Histria cont.		Tarvisium III, 9903; cf. p. 2328/12 (*miles*) Verona III, 15005/1 (*miles*) V, 3375 (*aquilifer*) [Brixia] *BD*, 35, 22, n. 684B (*speculator*)		
Regio XI Transpadana		Augusta Praetoria III, 2062 and 8747; cf. *JÖAI*, 6 Bb. 82 (*centurio*?) Comum III, 14998 (*miles*) Novaria III, 9906 = 14321/4 (*miles*)		
Italy by tribe	Scaptia III, 8199 (*veteranus*) III, 8200 (*veteranus*)	Stellatina III, 2054 = 8758 (*veteranus*)		Aniensis III, p. 43* 394/8*; cf. Betz, 218 (*miles*) or Gaul?
Macedonia	Heraclea *Sp.*, 47, p. 121, n. 33 (*veteranus*) *Sp.*, 77, p. 31, n. 3 (*veteranus*)	Heraclea III, p. 43* 394/4* (*miles*) III, 14999 (*miles*)	Heraclea III, 12903 (*veteranus*)	
Thrace	Philippopolis III, 6120 (*veteranus*)			

Origo	Legion VII C.p.f.	Legion XI C.p.f.	VII or XI	Leg. IIII F.f.
Asia	Augusta Troas *BD*, 37, p. 65, 4656A (?)			
Galatia	Pessinus III, 12498 (*imaginifer*)			
Pontus	*cognomen* Ponticus *Sp.*, 47, p. 147 (*veteranus*)	Amasia III, 13263 (*miles*)		
Syria	Berytus *Sp.*, 71, p. 210, n. 560 (*veteranus*)			
Hispania Tarraconensis		Caesaraugusta III, 6417 (*miles*)		
Baetica		Segovia (or Segontia, Tarrac.) III, 6419=9897 (*miles*)	Italica III, 8436 (*signifer*)	
Lugdunensis				Lugdunum III, 14995 (*aquilifer*)
Narbonensis	Vienna III, 14992 (*miles?*)	Vienna III, 8740 (*miles*) Forum Iulii III, 2839 (*veteranus*) Lucus Augusti III, 13251; cf. Betz, n. 25 (*miles*)		
Noricum		Iuvavum III, 14994 (*miles*)		

Origo	Legion VII C.p.f.	Legion XI C.p.f.	VII or XI
Dalmatia	Salona III, 8735 (*imaginifer?*) III, 8760 (*miles*) Sp., 71, p. 243 n. 650 (*veteranus*) Corinium III, 2885 (*miles?*)	Aequum III, 15004 (*miles*)	
Unidentifiable	Trernahensis III, 2715 (*miles*)		

CENTURIONS

	Arretium III, 2678; cf. 9699 Altinum III, 2914 Before 42	Verona III, 2834 = 9893; cf. p. 2328/12 Ariminum III, 14996 (*primipilaris?*) (*princeps?*) Before 42 Bovianum Vetus IX, 2564 Aquae Sextiae III, 2035 Aquae Statiellae III, 9905 Altinum *SB.*, 217 f., n. 13 (*praefectus castrorum*)		

APPENDIX VII   *Veteran Settlement in the First Century from the Legionary Garrison*

i Before A.D. 42

Place of settlement	Legion VII	Legion XI	Legion XX
Tilurium	III, 9726 (2710)		
Roški-Slap *deductio*		III, 2817 (7 Leg. IV Mac.) III, 9885 III, 2818 III, 6418 = 9896 (Mratovo)	
Asseria	III, 9939		
Narona (Pagus Scunasticus)	III, 8487 (2 ex.) III, 8488 *JAK*, 2, 110 III, 8493 Betz, 58 WMBH, 12, 132 Betz, 63 Betz, 66 = *GZMS*, 15–16 (1961), 324 III, 1813 (Narona) III, 1818 (Narona) III, 1815 Narona		
Salona	*BD*, 37, 66 III, 2033 *BD*, 27, 157 III, 2048 III, 9712 (Siculi)	III, p. 2328/121 (add. 1914; cf. 8506) III, 2017 III, 2056 III, 8579 (*missicius*)	III, 2030
Iader	III, 2913	III, 2918	III, 2911

ii After A.D. 42

Place of settlement	Legion VII C.p.f.	Legion XI C.p.f.	Legion III F.f.
Burnum		III, 2839 III, 15004/1 (2 *veterani*)	
Aequum	III, 9761 III, 14946	*VAHD*, 55, 185	
Salona	III, 8732 III, 2014 III, 2019 III, 14244/1 III, 2022 III, 2041 *RS*, I, 158 III, 8764 III, 9711 III, 12903 (Tragurium)	III, 9709 (Siculi) III, 9710 (Siculi) *VAHD*, 47–8, p. 40 III, 8758 *BD*, 37, 34	III, 2004
Narona	III, 1814	*GZMBH*, 35, 83 = *GZMS*, 15–16 (1961), 325 (Bigeste) III, 1811	
Imotski		III, 1915 = 8507; cf. p. 2328/121	

APPENDIX VIII *The Deployment of* Auxilia *in Dalmatia*

The coastal coloniae

Iader: Cohort II Cyrrhestarum (Augustus–Claudius).

Salona: Ala Pannoniorum (until 15), Cohorts II Cyrrhestarum (Augustus–Claudius), I Campana (Augustus–*c*. 86), Aquitanorum (*c*. 70–86), I Flavia Brittonum (*c*. 80–90), III Alpinorum (Augustus–185), VIII Voluntariorum (Augustus–Aurelian), I Belgarum (*c*. 100–), I and II milliaria Delmatarum (*c*. 170–early third century).

Narona: Cohorts XI Gallorum (*c*. 6–9), I Campana (early first century).

Epidaurum: Cohorts VI Voluntariorum (in 14–21), VIII Voluntariorum (early first century).

The coastal hinterland

Burnum: Cohorts Montanorum, II Cyrrhestarum (to *c*. 50), I Belgarum (third century).

Promona: Cohorts I Lucensium (early first), I milliaria Delmatarum (Severan).

Kadina Glavica: Ala Claudia nova (mid first century), Cohorts III Alpinorum (second century), I Belgarum (third century).

Magnum: Ala Claudia nova (mid first century). ·

Andetrium: Cohorts VIII Voluntariorum (garrison first century), III Alpinorum (garrison second century), I Belgarum (third century).

Tilurium: Cohort II Cyrrhestarum (early first century), Alae Claudia nova (mid first century), (Tungrorum) Frontoniana (70–80), Cohorts Aquitanorum (Flavian), I Belgarum (*c*. 100), III Alpinorum (second century), VIII Voluntariorum (garrison from end of first to third century).

Tihaljina: Cohort I Belgarum (third century).

Bigeste: Cohorts III Alpinorum, I Bracaraugustanorum, I Lucensium (garrison units in first century), possibly also I Campana, I Belgarum (garrison second–third century), VIII Voluntariorum (second century).

Northern Dalmatia

Raetinium: Ala Claudia nova (*c*. 70).

Doboj: Cohorts I Flavia Hispanorum (Flavian), I milliaria Delmatarum, I Belgarum (third century).

Užice: Cohorts I milliaria Delmatarum (probably garrison under Commodus).

Čačak: Cohorts VIII Voluntariorum (end of second century), I and II milliaria Delmatarum (third century).

APPENDIX IX *Auxiliary Units attested in Dalmatia*

For the movements of the individual units outside the province see Wagner, *Dislokation*, etc.

Ala Claudia nova miscellanea

c. 45–69 stationed at Magnum: III, 9816 (3164) Kadina Glavica (*eques*); *VAHD*, 56–59/2 (1954–7), II, 82 ff., n. 1 Drniš (*eques, duplicarius, decurio*); III, 9797; cf. *VAHD*, loc. cit., 83, n. 3 Drniš (*decurio*); III, 9796 (*eques*). Other records: *BD*, 38 (1915), 154 ff. Aequum (*veteranus*); III, 10033 Raetinium (*decurio*); III, 9327 (2712) Tilurium (*eques*); III, 2065 Salona (*missicius*). It was in Germania Superior by 74 (XVI, 20), and may have left Dalmatia with Legion XI C.p.f. in 69 to join Otho.

Ala (Gallorum) Picentiana

Possibly connected with L. Rustius Picens, *tr. mil.* and *praef. eq.*, III, 10094 Pharia; cf. Stein, *Beamte u. Truppenkörper*; 147 f., but against, Alföldy, *AArch.*, 14 (1962), 260.

Possibly stationed in Dalmatia in the early first century.

Ala (I) Pannoniorum; cf. Kraft, *Rekrutierung*, 156.

In Dalmatia under Augustus: III, 2016 Salona (*duplicarius*), but in Pannonia under Tiberius, Alföldy, *AArch.*, 14 (1962), 262.

Ala Parthorum

Under Augustus in Dalmatia, III, 8746; cf. *AArch.*, 14, (1962), 290 and *Situla*, 8, 96 f, n. 7. A unit composed of Parthian refugees, Tac., *Ann.*, vi, 37.

Ala I (Tungrorum) Frontoniana

In Dalmatia *c.* 70–80, III, 9735 Tilurium (*eques*). In Germany until rebellion of Civilis, and in Pannonia by 80 (XVI, 26).

Cohort I Alpinorum Equitata

Possibly in Dalmatia in the late first and early second century, III, 8762; cf. p. 2657 Salona (*eques coh. I Alp., vexillarius equitum coh. I Belgarum*). On the other hand he may have been transferred to Cohort I Belgarum in Dalmatia from the unit in Pannonia or Moesia. III, 14693; cf. p. 2657 Salona (?*[eques] coh. I A[....] singularis cos.*) is third century, Alföldy, *AArch.*, 14 (1962), 260.

Cohort III Alpinorum equitata

Augustus–*c.* 184–5

Stationed first at Bigeste: *JAK*, 2 (1908), 113 f. (*eques*); III, 14632 (*eques*) *JÖAI*, 36 (1946), Bb. 67 ff. (*miles, signifer*); III, 8491 (6366) cf. *GZMBH*, 26 (1914), 163 (*miles, optio, veteranus*); III, 8495, *JAK*, 2 (1908), 114, *JÖAI*, 36 (1946), Bb. 67 ff. (*eques*); cf. III, 1810 Narona (*centurio*).

Detachment at Burnum: III, 14321⁵ (9907) (*miles*); in service of legate's *officium* at Salona: III, 13906 (8725 and 8755) (*eques ex singularis*), *VAHD*, 53 (1950–1), 226, n. 35 (*miles, centurio, equites ex numero singularium*); cf. 8739 Salona (*decurio p[raepositus?]*); XVI, 38 (d. 13 Iul. 94) (*pedes*); IX, 2564 Bovianum vetus (*praefectus* in Julio–Claudian period).

Transferred about end of first century and probably stationed at Andetrium (Muč), III, 2746 (*centurio*); III, 14950 (*tesserarius, centurio*); III, 9886 Gradac near Scardona; III, 2759 Kadina Glavica (*decurio*); III, 2794 Matkovine (*miles*); III, 14935 Tilurium (*bucinator, signifer, centurio*); III, 2012 Salona (*miles, vexillarius equitum*); III, 14698 Salona (? *miles*), *BD* 37 (1914), 93 Salona (*miles honesta missione*); III, 12905 Salona (*milites*); III, 2058 Klis (*eques*); III, 2003 Klis (*veteranus*).

Transferred to Pannonia Inferior *c.* 184–5; cf. Alföldy, *AArch*, 14 (1962), 263 f. *Cohort*

Aquitanorum

mid–late first century

III, 2053 Salona (*miles*); III, 9760 Tilurium (*miles*).

The unit cannot be identified with the other numbered units of this series; cf. Alföldy, *AArch.*, 14 (1962), 265–6.

Cohort [?] *Asturum*

Possibly in Dalmatia at some period, III, 14705 Salona (*miles*), also XIII, 6538, a Dalmatian serving in Cohort I Asturum in Germania Superior.

Cohort I Belgarum equitata

For most of the first century probably in Germania Superior; cf. Tac. *Hist.*, iv 7. Not mentioned in the diploma of 94 (XVI, 38), but soon afterwards stationed in Dalmatia.

Its station was probably Bigeste (Humac): III, 14630 (dedication to *Fortuna Aug.*); III, 8484 (1790, 6362) reconstruction of temple to *Liber pater et Libera* in 173), *WMBH*, 12 (1912), 133 f. (*miles, signifer, centurio*); III, 8494 (*eques, decurio*), *GZMBH*, 22 (1910), 181 ff., *WMBH*, 12 (1912), 136 (*decurio*), *JAK*, 2 (1908), 113 ff. (*centurio*), Patsch, *Narona*, 69 ff., n. 2 (*eques*); cf. III, 1918 Vrgorac (*centurio praepositus*), III, 8437 Narona (*miles, tubicen*), III, 12810 Tihaljina Valley (*miles, immunis*).

Serving in the *officium* at Salona, *RS*, I, 160, n. 14; cf. *VAHD*, 50 (1928–9), 14 (*miles ex stratore*); III, 8756 (*centurio*); III, 2067 (*miles ex stratore duplicarius*); III, 3162b Salona? (*quaestuarius*); cf. III, 8762, p. 2657 (*vexillarius equitum* then *decurio*), *VAHD*, 55 (1953), 260, n. 4 (*miles*), *RS*, I, 158, n. 7; cf. *VAHD*, 50 (1928–9), 13 f. (*miles*); III, 3096; cf. *VAHD*, 53 (1950–1), 160 ff. Brattia (*centurio curagens theatri*).

Detachment at Tilurium: III, 9739 (*vexillarius, decurio*), *BD*, 26 (1903), 134 (*miles*).

Other records in Dalmatia: III, 14980 Burnum (*decurio*); III, 13229 Kadina Glavica (*centurio*); III, 2744; cf. p. 282 Andetrium (*vexillarius*); III, 8736b; cf. *GZMBH*, 26 (1914), 168 Doboj (*veteranus*).

Cohort I Bracaraugustanorum

First half of first century, transferred to Moesia perhaps *c.* 86–7.

Stationed at Bigeste: III, 1773; cf. Patsch, *Narona*, 90 (*praefectus*), Patsch, *Narona*, 74 f., n. 6 (*miles*), Patsch, *Narona*, 75 f., n. 7 (*miles*).

Cohort I Flavia Brittonum

Late first century, in Noricum under Trajan: III, 2024 Salona (*miles*).

Cohort I Campana (*Campanorum*) *voluntariorum c. R.*

First half of first century, later in Pannonia Inferior (Banoštor).

Perhaps stationed at Bigeste: III, 14623[3]; cf. *BD*, 25 (1902), 163 Narona; III, 8438 Narona (*miles leg.* XIII then *centurio ch.*). Other records: III, 8693 Salona (*miles custos Traguri*); III, 14246[1] Salona (*miles*); III, 10052 Lopsica (? *tribunus*).

Cohort II Cyrrhestarum

First half of first century.

Perhaps stationed at Burnum: *SB*, 217, n. 12 (*miles*); cf. *VAHD*, 56–9 (1954–7), II, 84 f., n. 2 (*miles*).

Other records: III, 14934 Tilurium (*miles*); III, 8734 Salona (*sagittarius*).

Cohort I milliaria Delmatarum

From under Marcus, when it was raised *c.* 170.

III, 1979 rebuilding city walls at Salona 170 (*tribunus*) cf. *JÖAI*, 19/20 (1919), Bb. 293 ff., 318, *c.* 217 (*tribunus*)?; III, 2006 (*centurio*); III, 8731 (*veteranus*); III, 14700 Klis (*miles*).

Possibly first stationed at Promona: III, 9829 (*centurio*) later in Northern Dalmatia, perhaps at Doboj; III, 14618 (12758) (? building record); cf. III, 8353 Užice (*miles*); III, 8335 (6230) Čačak (*decurio equitum*). Note also V, 707, *Inscr. It.*, x, 4,326, near Tergeste (*tribunus*).

Cohort II milliaria Delmatarum

From under Marcus, when it was raised *c.* 170.

III, 8655 (6374), rebuilding city walls at Salona 170.

Perhaps later at Čačak: *Sp.*, 98 (1941–8), 251, n. 494 (*tribunus*), *Sp.*, 77 (1934), 23, n. 35 Dubrava (*veteranus ex centurione*).

Cohort XI Gallorum

under Augustus?   III, 8439; cf. p. 1476 Narona (*decurio*?).

Cohort I Flavia Hispanorum (*veterana quingenaria equitata*)

Flavian period, stationed at Doboj: III, 14619 (12759) (*praefectus*).
In Moesia Inferior by 99.

Cohort I Liburnorum

? under Augustus: *JÖAI*, 36 (1946), Bb, 75 ff. Nedinum (*centurio*).
There is no other record of this unit; cf. Betz, *JÖAI*, loc. cit.

Cohort I Lucensium equitata

First half of first century, stationed at Bigeste: III, 8486 (*eques*); III, 8492 (*miles*); cf. III, 9834 Promona (*miles*); III, 8736 Salona (*praefectus*); VI, 31863 (*praefectus*). Later in Pannonia.

Cohort I Montanorum

Early first century: III, 15003 Burnum (*miles*); cf. Kraft, *Rekruterung*, 181.
Later in Moesia, probably by Claudius.

Cohort VI Voluntariorum civium Romanorum

Attested under the legate P. Cornelius Dolabella (14–21) with a *tribunus* L. Purtisius Atinas at Epidaurum, Novak, *Rad*, 339 (1965), 129; cf. D. Rendić-Miočević, *Akte IV Kongr. Epigr. Wien* (1963), 341, n. 11.

Possibly the same unit as Cohort VI Ingenuorum c.R. attested in Germania Inferior later in the first century, XIII, 8314–5 ; cf. E. Stein, *Beamte u. Truppenkörper*, 199.

Cohort VIII Voluntariorum civium Romanorum

From Augustan period: *NS*, 1912, 379 Rome ,Via Nomentana (*praefectus coh. quae est in Dalmatia* under Tiberius); cf. XI, 4749 Ariminum (*miles*).

Appendix IX

First stationed at Andetrium: III, 10182a–c stamped tiles COH VIII VOL (first century); cf. III, 9782 (*miles*); III, 2745 (*miles, vexillarius*). Recorded in diploma of 94 (XVI, 38).

Detachment at Epidaurum: III, 1742 (*centurio*); III, 1743; cf. p. 1028 (*miles*).

By the second century stationed at Tilurium: III, 13975 (*miles, centurio*); cf. *VAHD*, 51 (1930–4), 225 ff. (building of *turris ad aquam tollendam* under Pius), *BD*, 26 (1903), 129 altar to Minerva (*actarius coh., ex adiutore cornicularorium cos.*); III, 143367[1] (10182) tile stamp CHOR VIII vo[L]. In third century III, 13187 (*bucinator*, with title *Antoniniana*); III, 9732 (*miles*, with title *Antoniniana*); cf. III, 9724 (2706) (*centurio*, with title *Philippiana*); III, 14930 (*miles beneficiarius praefecti*).

Many records from Salona and its area, probably of men born there, III, 2045 (*miles*); III, 8757 (*miles*); III, 2052 (*miles, adiutor cornic. cos.*); III, 8765 (*eques*)?, *BD*, 34 (1911), 31 (*miles*); III, 2039 (*miles*); III, 12902; III, 2002 (*miles*); III, 8728 (*miles*); III, 8729 (*miles*); III, 14660[1] (8755) (*miles*), *BD*, 30 (1907), 116 Klis (*miles duplicarius*); III, 8672 Klis (*veteranus*); III, 8522 Pituntium (*miles, bucinator*); III, 14629[1] Tučepi (*veteranus*); III, 9708 Siculi (Biač) (*veteranus*); III, 12904 (*veteranus*), *BD*, 26 (1903), 199, ebd. 28 (1905), 159, stamped tiles, perhaps of the Marcomannic period, COH VIII VOL.

Detachment at Bigeste: III, 13875 Proboj (*centurio*); III, 8490 (6365) (*miles, centuriones*); cf. III, 1808 Narona *beneficiarius*). Also at Čačak: III, 8336 (6321) in 197 (*centurio*). As *bf. cos*: III, 12679 Doclea (*adiutor principis, beneficiarius cos.*).

Detachment at Halapić: *GZMBH* 40 (1928), 82 f. (*miles*).

474

Unit	Julio-Claudian	Flavian-Trajan	Antonine	After Marcus
Ala Cl. nova *c.* 45–70.	Westerner *VAHD*, 56– 59/2 (1954–7) II, 82 ff., n. 1 (*decurio*) CRD, (*eques,* *duplicarius*) Westerners (2) *BD*, 38, (1915), 154 ff. (*veteranus*) CRD, (?*eques*) CR Westerner III, 9727 (2712) (?*eques*) CRD, Tribocus Westerner III, 9816 (3614) (*eques*) P (*sesquiplicarius*) P Cugernus III, 9727 (2712) (*eques*) P Biturix III, 2065 (*missicius*) P Varcianus III, 9796 (*eques*) P Westerner III, 9796 (*eques* ?) P	Westerner? III, 10033 (*decurio*) CRD Raetinium XIII, 7023 (*eques*) P		
Ala (Tungr.) Frontoniana *c.* 70–80	Nemis III, 9735 (*eques*) P			
Ala Pann. until 15	Curunda (Spain) III, 2016 (*duplicarius*) P			

Unit	Julio-Claudian	Flavian-Trajan	Antonine	After Marcus
Ala Parth. *c.* 6–9	Parthian (*origo* Rome) III, 8746 (*decurio*) CRD Italia III, 8746; cf. AArch., 14 (1962), 290 (?) CR			
Coh. III Alpinorum until 185	Salinis (Alp. Marit.) III, 14632 (*eques*) CRD Bodiontius III, 14321/5 (9907) (*miles*) P Bodiontius III, 8495 (*eques*) P Caturix III, 8491 (6366) cf. *GZMBH*, 26 (1914), 163 (*miles*) P Eguius *JÖAI*, 36, (1946) 67 ff. (*miles*) P Eloci *JAK*, 2, (1908), 114 (?) P Velaunus *JAK*, 21, (1908), 113 f. (*eques*) P Westerners (2) III, 8491 (6366) (*optio* and *veteranus*) P	Westerner III, 13906 (8725 = 8755) (*eques ex sing.*) CR Native (2) *VAHD*, 53, (1950–1), 226, n. 35 (*miles, eques ex numero sing.*) P Celeia III, 2746 (*centurio*)	Westerner? III, 2759 (*decurio*) CR Noricum III, 14935 (*signifer*) CR, Westerner? III, 2003 (*veteranus*) CR, Dalmatian (3) III, 2012 (*miles, vexillarius equitum*) III, 14698 (*miles?*) CR III, 2058 (*eques*) CR Native (3) III, 2749? (*miles*) CRD III, 12905? (*miles*) CR III, 14950 (*tesserarius*) P Thracian III, 14950 (*centurio*) CR?	

Unit	Julio-Claudian	Flavian-Trajan	Antonine	After Marcus
Coh. III Alpinorum until 185 cont.	Vercianus *JÖAI*, 36, (1946), 67 f. (*eques*) P Daverzus XVI, 38 (dip. 13 Iul. 94) (*pedes*) P			
Coh. Aquitan. 70–*c.* 100	Camulodunum III, 2053 (*miles*) P Trebocus III, 9760 (*miles*) P			
Coh. I Belg. 100–third cent.		Daesitias III, 9739 (*vexillarius equitum*) P	Azina III, 8762; cf. p. 2657 (*vexillarius, equit. dec. equit.*) CR, Native *VAHD*, 55, (1953), 260, n. 4 (*miles*) P Maezaeus *WMBH*, 12, (1912), 133 f. (*miles*) P Delmata III, 8494 (*eques*) CR Native (3) III, 8437 (*equites* 1 (?)) P	Western III, 14980 (*decurio*) CR Pannonia *WMBH*, 11 (1912), 136 (*decurio*) CR Dalmatian III, 2744 (*vexillar.*) CR *RS*, I, 160, n. 4; cf. *VAHD*, 50 (1928–9), n. 14 (*miles* ex *stratorib.*) CR *RS*, I, 160, n. 7; cf. *VAHD*, 50, (1928–9), 13 f. (*miles*) CR III, 2067 (*mil. ex. strat. cos.*) CR Dalmatian Patsch,

Unit	Julio-Claudian	Flavian-Trajan	Antonine	After Marcus
Coh. I Belg. 100–third per cent. cont.				*Narona*, 69, n.2 (*eques*) CR III, 8376b; cf. *GZMBH*, 26 (1914), 168 (*veteranus*) CR Native III, 12810 (*miles immunis*) CR III, 3162b (*quaestuarius*) CR
Coh. I Bracar. until *c.* 86	Spaniard (2) Patsch, *Narona*, 74, n. 6 (*miles*) P Patsch, *Narona*, 74, n. 7 (*miles*)			
Coh. I Fl. Brittonum *c.* 80–100		Briton III, 2024 (*miles*) P		
Coh. I Camp.	Suessa III, 14246¹ (*miles*) CR Campania (2) III, 8693 (*miles, custos Traguri*) CR III, 14623³ (?) CR Ariminum III, 8438 (*centurio*) *ex* (*mil. leg.*)			
Coh. II Cyrrhest. until *c.* 45	Beroea (4) III, 14934 (*miles*) P			

Unit	Julio-Claudia	Flavian-Trajan	Antonine	After Marcus
Col. II Cyrrhest. until *c.* 45 cont.	*SB*, 217 (*miles*) P *VAHD*, 56–59/2 (1954–7) II, 84 f., n. 2 (*miles*) P III, 8734 (*sagittarius*) P			
Coh. I mil. Delmatarum *c.* 170–third century				Dalmatian (3) III, 8731 (*veteranus*) CR Native (2) III, 8335 (6320) (*decurio equitum*) CR III, 14700 (*miles*) P
Coh. II mil. Delmatarum *c.* 170–third century				Dalmatian *Sp.*, 77, 35 (*veteranus ex centurione*) CR
Coh. XI Gall. *c.* 6–9	Patavium III, 8439; cf. 1476 (*decurio* ?) CR			
Coh. I Lucens. until *c.* 80	Lucus Augusti III, 9834 (*miles*) P Spaniard (2) III, 8486 (*eques*) P			
Coh. Montan. until *c.* 45	Montanus III, 15003 (*miles*)			
Coh. VIII Voluntariorum Augustus–mid-third cent.	Ariminum XI, 4749 (*miles*) CR	Cemenelum III, 9782 (*miles*) CR Italy III, 2745	Italy or West *BD*, 26, (1903), 129 (*actarius, ex adiut. cornic. cos.*) CR	Dalmatian III, 13187 (*bucinator*) CR III, 2002 (*miles*) CR

Unit	Julio-Claudian	Flavian-Trajan	Antonine	After Marcus
Coh. VIII Voluntariorum Augustus-mid-third cent. cont.		(*miles?*) CR Celeia III, 2745 (*miles vexillarius*) CR Virunum III, 13975 (*miles*) CR Noricum III, 13975 (*miles?*) CR Dalmatian III, 8522 (*bucinator*) CRD	Dalmatian (10) III, 2045 (*miles*) CR III, 8757 (*miles*) CR III, 2052 (*miles adiut., corn. cos.*) CR III, 8765 (*eques*) CR BD, 34, (1911), (*miles*) CR III, 14629 (*veteranus*) CR III, 8490 (6365) (*miles*) CR III, 1743; cf. p. 1028 (*miles*) CR III, 12679 (*miles, adiut. princ. bf. cos.*) CR GZMBH, 40 (1928), 82 f. (*miles*) CR Native III, 2039 (*miles*) P	III, 8728 (*miles*) CR III, 8729 (*miles*) CR III, 14660 (8775) (*miles*) CR BD, 30, (1907), 116 (*miles, duplic.*) CR III, 8672 (*veteranus?*) CR III, 9732 (*miles*) CR III, 14930 (*milites*, one *benef, praef.*) CR III, 8672? (*veteranus?*) CR Beneventum III, 2706 (*centurio*)

Abbreviations

   P = Non-Roman(*peregrinus*)

  CR = Roman Citizen (*civis Romanus*)

CRD = Enfranchised Roman Citizen (*civitate Romana donatus*)

APPENDIX XI   *Sources for the Peoples of Dalmatia*

It will be most convenient to examine the main writers on Dalmatia in a roughly chronological order, beginning with the sixth-century B.C. Hecataeus of Miletus, whose observations were based on the Phocaean voyages in the seventh century, and ending with the last coherent picture from an ancient source, in the Geography of Claudius Ptolemaeus composed in the second century A.D. Later sources, for instance the Antonine Itinerary, the Peutinger Map, and the Ravenna Cosmography, the last composed in the seventh century, add little or nothing on the peoples of the province, recording road routes and places along them, rather than tribal areas. Within this body of material the clearest division is between the earlier Greek writers who give a picture of the ethnic geography of the Dalmatian coast in the fourth century B.C., and those of the second century B.C. and later, when the Celtic migrations and the rise and fall of the Illyrian Kingdom had brought about great changes. This separation is so complete that the three principal sources in the first category, Hecataeus, Pseudo–Scylax, and Pseudo–Scymnus, have been discussed in an earlier section along with the Greek exploration and settlement in the Adriatic (p. 3 ff. above).

The evidence of two major writers, both historians, stands between the early Greek writers and the more detailed monographs dealing with the Roman Wars of conquest. Polybius was the son of a leading politician in the Achaean League and, although he had a good knowledge of Illyria and its peoples, he does not conceal his hatred of them. His writings record events in Illyria from immediately prior to the first Roman intervention (229–228 B.C.) to the middle of the second century and the Roman war against the Delmatae in 156–155 B.C. On the Dalmatian coast he gives the first record of the *Delmateis*, ii, 15, 2, and records also the *Ardiaioi*, ii, 11, 12; 12, 2 (both in 229–228 B.C.), *Daorsoi*, xxxii, 9, 1 ff., and the *Labeates* by the area they inhabited, xxix, 3, 5. In a fragment there is the earliest record of the *Pannonioi*, frg. 64 (B–W 4, p. 523), cf. Mócsy, *RE*, supp. 9 (1962), 528, either those who bordered on Northeast Italy or the people in the interior of Dalmatia beyond the Delmatae. The *Encheleis*, v, 108, 8, placed by Pseudo–Scylax around the Gulf of Kotor, are placed by Polybius much further inland around Lake Lychnidus (Ohrid), later part of Roman Macedonia. More names of peoples appear from the writing of Livy, the Augustan historian, who drew extensively on the narrative of Polybius for the second century B.C. He records the *(V)ardaei*, xxvii, 30, 13; cf. *Per.* lvi, *Daorsi*, xlvi, 26, *Delmatae*, *Per.*, xlvii, lii cxxxi f., *Iapydes*, xliii, 31 f., *Labeates*, xliii, 19, xliv, 31 f., *Liburnii*, x, 2, *Pannonii*, *Per.*, cxxxi ff., *Pirustae*, xlv, 26, *Taulantii*, xlv, 26.

The first detailed picture of the population away from the Adriatic coast appears in the two major sources for the Augustan wars of conquest, the *Illyrike* of Appian, and Cassius Dio. Supplementing these is the Geography of Strabo, who was still incorporating new material in the last years of Augustus. The most valuable section in Appian's monograph on Roman wars in Illyria is the detailed account of Octavianus' campaigns in 35–33 B.C., based entirely on the emperor's memoirs; cf. J. Dobiaš, 241 ff. Where Appian is producing a single source his account is clear, but on some points he displays considerable ignorance of the geography, only to be expected in an author writing as far away as Alexandria. In his introduction to the *Illyrike* he records the *Encheleis* and the *Daorsoi*, ch. 2, followed with a long excursus on the adventures of the *Autariatai*, which confuses events of the early fourth century B.C. with those in the early third. Then there are sections on the early history of the *Ardaioi*, 3; cf. Dobiaš, 243 ff., on the date, while the *Taulantioi*, 2, are also mentioned in the introduction as well as later in connection with the campaigns of Octavianus, 16. Other peoples mentioned before the detailed narrative of the wars in 35–33 B.C. are the *Dalmatai*, 11 f., 17; *Iapodes*, 10, 14; *Liburnoi*, 3, 12; *Palarioi*, 10; *Pannonioi* under the name *Paiones* (they are called Paiones by the Greeks, but Pannonioi by the Romans), 14, those who dwell in the northern part of the later province Dalmatia. A number of minor peoples are listed in the section taken directly from, the memoirs of Augustus, 16: *Bathiatai, Docleatai, Glintidiones, Interphrourinoi Hippasinoi, Kambaioi, Kinambroi, Merromenoi, Naresioi, Oxyaioi, Perthoenotai, Pyrissaioi* [*Daisitiatai* see above, p. 50], also the *Posenoi*, 21, and the *Derbanoi*, 28. Also mentioned as separate peoples are the communities of the Iapodes attacked by Octavinus in 35 B.C., the *Moentinoi* (Monetium), *Avendeatai* (Avendo) and *Arupinoi* (Arupium), all in the Lika polje among the Cisalpine Iapodes, 16. Beyond the Velika Kapela mountains in the land of the Transalpine Iapodes were the *Metuloi* (Metulum), 19 ff., and the *Posenoi*, 21, with a centre probably somewhere east of Metulum. The third century historian Cassius Dio drew on many earlier sources for his narrative, although he uses the terms Pannonia and Dalmatia in the sense of the later imperial provinces, both of which he governed under Severus Alexander (p. 448 above). Thus the *Maezaeoi*, lv, 32, 4, are a people of Dalmatia, whereas for Strabo they are Pannonians. Elsewhere Dio records the *Ardiaioi*, xii, 49, 2 (Zon, viii, 19, 3; 20, 11: *Sardiaioi*); *Daisitiates*, lv, 29, 2; *Delmatai*, Zon, ix, 25, 9; Dio, xlix, 38, 2 f., lv, 28, 7 ff.; *Iapudes*, xlix, 35, 1 ff., and *Liburnoi*, xlix, 34, 2.

The geographer Strabo lived long enough to incorporate in his work information from the earliest years of the principate of Tiberius (14-37). Although he does not always mention them by name much of his information about Dalmatia derives from earlier Greek writers, Polybius, vii, 5, 1; Eratosthenes, vii, 5, 9, and Theopompus, vii, 5, 9; occasionally he offers criticism and even expresses frank disbelief in what he retails. Like Appian he read and used the memoirs of Augustus, iv, 6, 10, vii, 5, 4, and took from there much of his more recent information about the peoples in the interior. He names a number of peoples, *Ardaioi–Vardaioi*, vii, 5, 6; *Dalmateis*, vii, 5, 4; *Daorizoi*, vii, 5, 5; *Iapodes*, iv, 6, 1; vii, 5, 2. 4. 5; *Liburnoi*, vi, 2, 4; vii, 5, 9, and the *Pannonioi*, vii, 5, 3. This last name is the general description for a group of large peoples, the *Breukoi* and *Andizetoi*, both later included in Roman Pannonia, and the *Ditiones, Pirustai, Mazaioi, Daisitiatai*, who had Bato as their ruler, as well as a number of smaller peoples who dwelt in the direction of the Ardiaei, but not mentioned individually by Strabo. The passage is vital for the interpretation of Roman campaigns in Dalmatia and shows that before the provincial boundaries were settled, the peoples included later in Northern Dalmatia were correctly included among the Pannonians, a description found also in Appian's *Illyrike*. Also recorded by Strabo are the *Pleraioi*, vii, 5, 5. 7, and the *Autariatai*, vii, 5, 1. 6. 7. 11. He speaks of the great power once held by the latter people but records that in his own day they had become insignificant, who had suffered much at the hands of the *Skordiskoi*. Finally the *Taulantioi*, and the *Enchelees*, vii, 7, 8, are listed among the peoples of Macedonia. Little information is furnished about the peoples of Dalmatia in the Roman History Compendium of C. Velleius Paterculus. Although he had served on the staff of Tiberius during 6–8 (p. 71 above) he gives few details about the background of the campaigns, since he promised his readers a separate monograph on the war with full details of all the peoples involved, ii, 114. Using Dalmatia and Pannonia in the sense of the later provinces he records the fierce resistance of two Dalmatian peoples, *Desidiates* and *Perustae*, ii, 115, in the last year of the war.

All the above writers mention Dalmatian peoples as they figure in the narrative of Roman wars leading up to the conquest and organization of the province in 9. For the period immediately after this date two authors provide detailed pictures of the organization and location of the peoples included within Roman Dalmatia. The most valuable is the first century *Historia Naturalis* of the Elder Pliny, a distinguished scholar and administrator in the period from Claudius to Vespasian, cf. H–G. Pflaum, *Carrières*, 106 ff., n. 45, who died in 79 when his scientific curiosity encouraged him to remain near Pompeii too long during the eruption of Vesuvius, Plin., *Ep.*, vi, 16 to Cornelius Tacitus. The other source for the imperial province is the geographer Claudius Ptolemaeus. He was less interested in the details of peoples and places than in fixing correctly his system of longitude and latitude; cf. E. Polaschek, *RE*, supp. 10 (1965), 680 ff. Both Pliny and Ptolemy make use of earlier sources, as far back as the Greek writers of the fourth century B.C.

Pliny used the official description of the province (*formula provinciae*) compiled by the Roman government soon after the years of conquest, Detlefson, *Plinius* (1909), 26 ff., A. H. M. Jones, *CERP*, 491 ff. For distances and other measurements the works of M. Agrippa were used, *GLM*, 1 ff., but most of the section dealing with Dalmatia comprises the official inventory of the native peoples and their organization, iii, 139–44. The peoples listed are divided for judicial and administrative purposes into *conventus*, or assize groups, based on three centres in Southern Dalmatia, Scardona, Salona, and Narona. Within these three geographical groups are listed the names of native peoples as *civitates*:

Conventus Scardonitanus. The *Liburni* are placed between the rivers Arsia (Raša) and Titius. Once, notes Pliny, peoples in this area were known by a number of separate names and he reproduces the fourth century Greek list of the *Mentores, Himani, Encheleae, Buni,* and 'those whom Callimachus calls *Peucetii*'. Long before the Romans were involved in this part of the coast all these small communities had been either displaced or absorbed by the Liburnians. Introducing the official list of the Scardona *conventus* he records that it included the *Iapodes*, and the fourteen *civitates* of the *Liburni*, of whom he names the *Lacinienses, Stulpini, Burnistae,* and *Olbonenses*. This section on Liburnia was compiled after the organization of the province: in an earlier list, where the communities of Southern Liburnia are recorded under Regio X of Italy (p. 487 below), the *Liburni* and *Iapodes* are also recorded, iii, 130.

Conventus Salonitanus. Only a few peoples of the interior are included in this *conventus* but these were some of the most powerful in the province. Each is named with their number of *decuriae*, a pre-Roman social grouping which was incorporated into the organisation of the *civitates* to indicate the relative numerical strength of the different peoples (p. 185). In this *conventus* were the *Delmatae* (342 *decuriae*), *Deuri* (22), *Ditiones* (239), *Maezaei* (269), and the *Sardiates* (52). It is possible that the Deuri were the Derbanoi mentioned by Appian, *Ill.*, 28; certainly both were neighbours of the Delmatae.

Conventus Naronitanus. This is by far the largest of the three groups in Pliny's list, although most of the peoples named are reckoned much smaller in numbers of *decuriae* than those in the Salona *conventus*. The aggregate of *decuriae* for the Narona peoples is little more than half (539) of the total for those in the Salona *conventus* (924). Pliny records how Terentius Varro, the great scholar and antiquary who lived at the end of the Republic, spoke of as many as eighty-nine *civitates* attending regularly at Narona, presumably in an earlier *conventus* organized by the Republican proconsuls when it was the main Roman centre for all Illyricum. By the time the official list had been drawn up only the following *civitates* were included: *Cerauni* (24 *decuriae*), *Duersi* (17) clearly the *Daversi*, *Daesitiates* (103), *Docleatae* (33), *Deretini* (14), *Deraemestae* (*Deramistae*) (30), *Dindari* (33), *Glinditiones* (44), *Melcumani* (24), *Naresii* (102), *Scirtari* (72), *Siculotae* (24), and the *Ardiaei*, once the ravagers of Italy but now with no more than 20 *decuriae*. Other peoples listed by Pliny as inhabiting the area of the Narona *conventus*, but not constituted as *civitates* in the Roman scheme of organization, were the *Ozuaei, Partheni, Hemasini, Arthitae, Armistae* (emended by Detlefson, ed. p. 42, to *Partheni, Cavi, Hemasini, Masthitae, Arinistae*). Others who once inhabited the region in the southeast of the *conventus* between Epidaurum and Lissus were the *Labeatae, Endirudini* (Detlefson emends to *Enedi Rudini*), *Sasaei, Grabaei*, the *Illyrii* 'properly so-called', (*proprii dicti*), *Taulantii*, and *Pyraei*.

In Pliny's description of peoples in Dalmatia scholars have recognized three separate sources; cf. Alföldy, *Epigraphica*, 23 (1961), 53 ff. In date the latest is the official inventory of the *conventus*, with the officially constituted *civitates* listed in alphabetical order together with a number of *decuriae* as an indication of their size (viribus descriptis). It was compiled after the final conquest in 9, probably during the governorship of Cornelius Dolabella (14–20), who also organized the first system of boundary settlements in the cities of Liburnia (p. 456). The two earlier lists were in existence before the conquest and deal only with peoples in the coastal hinterland, a very small area of the province compared with that covered by the later *conventus* lists. Varro's eighty-nine *civitates* probably reflect the provincial organization set up in the early first century B.C., possibly after the activities of C. Cosconius in 78–76 B.C. (above, p. 35). These earlier *civitates* will have included many small coastal communities such as those mentioned in the settlement imposed after the removal of Gentius in 167 B.C., the *Rhizonitae* (Rhizon–Risinium), *Agravonitae* (Acruvium), and *Olciniatae* (Olcinium), small harbours along the coast north of Lissus, Liv., xlv, 26. The two lists of peoples which Pliny adds to the official *conventus* lists were probably derived from Augustus' account of the wars in 35–33 B.C. Most had been absorbed into new *civitates* in the reconstituted Narona *conventus* and although there are differences in the form of the names there is little doubt that Pliny and Appian are recording the same peoples. Thus the Endirudini are the Interphrourinoi, Grabaei–Kambaioi, Melcumani–Merromenoi, Ozuaei–Oxyaioi, Partheni–Pertheenetai, Pyraei–Palarioi (called Pleraioi by Strabo), Hemasini–Hippasinoi. None of these peoples existed as a separate *civitas* in Roman Dalmatia. With the notable exception of the Pirustae (see p. 173), all the *civitates* attested by later inscriptions from Dalmatia and elsewhere appear in the *conventus* lists of Pliny.

Most of the information about Dalmatia in the Geography of Ptolemy, ii, 16, 1–9, dates to the period of the imperial province, although some earlier material is included, in one instance from the earliest Greek sources. Along the coast south of Istria he lists the *Iapudes*, *Hyllaioi*, and *Boulimeis*. Then 'farther inland are the *Maizaioi*, *Derriopes*, and *Derrioi*; beyond the first two are the *Dindaroi*, beyond whom are the *Ditiones*, and beyond the *Derrioi* are the *Keraunioi*. Within Dalmatia are the *Daoursoi*, above whom are the *Melcomenioi* and the *Vardaioi*. Below these are the *Naresioi* and *Sardiotai*, and yet again below these are the *Sikulotai* and *Dokleatai*, also the *Piroustai* and *Skirtones* close to Macedonia.' The first list, naming the Hyllaioi and the Boulimeis, follows an early Greek source and preserves the earlier tradition which locates the Iapodes on the coast between Istria and the river Tedanius, a description which was probably accurate until the first century B.C. (p. 158). The other peoples listed in the interior are taken from a *conventus* list, although not all the major peoples such as the Delmatae in the Salona *conventus* and the Daesitiates in the Narona *conventus* are included. Ptolemy's location of the individual peoples is very brief and leads to almost complete confusion, being demonstrably wrong in almost every instance. The Derriopes named by him are otherwise unknown, but they may be the Deretini (14 *decuriae*) listed by Pliny in the Narona *conventus*.

The foundation and early status of the Liburnian communities under the Julio–Claudians is a complicated problem which arises from the three different descriptions included by the Elder Pliny in his *Historia Naturalis* (see table), composed under Nero and Vespasian; cf. Alföldy, *Epigraphica*, 23 (1961), 53 ff. In the description of communities in the tenth region of Italy, a subdivision organized early under Augustus, Pliny names some of Liburnia:

'Then there are those communities which it is not relevant to describe in a more detailed fashion: the *Alutrenses, Asseriates, Flamonienses Vanienses*, and others by the name of *Culici* (Detlefson emends to *Carici*), the *Transpadani* called *Foroiulienses, Foretani, Nedinates, Quarqueni, Tarvisani, Togienses*, and *Varvari*' (*HN*, iii, 130).

Apart from the Italian Foroiulienses, Degrassi, *Confine*, etc. 26 ff., Quarqueni, not identified, Tarvisani, *RE*, 4A, 2453, and Togienses, connected with river Togisonus in Northeast Italy, Plin., *HN*, iii, 121, all the communities mentioned are Liburnian. The Nedinates, inhabitants of the city Nedinum in Southern Liburnia, are omitted from the other passages on Liburnia. These come a few paragraphs later, one of communities named in the ethnic form which were included in the Liburnian judicial circuit based on Scardona (*conventus Scardonitanus*):

'In that circuit the following possess Italian status (*ius Italicum*): the *Alutae, Flanates* after whom the gulf (*sinus Flanaticus* – Quarnerno) is named, the *Lopsi*, and the *Varvarini*; then the *Asseriates* free of tribute and among the islands *Fertinates* and *Curictae*' (*HN*, iii, 139).

The third is a list of cities (*oppida*) in Liburnia:

'Then along the coast from *Nesactium* are the following: *Alvona, Flanona, Tarsatica, Senia, Lopsica, Ortoplinia, Vegium, Argyruntum, Corinium, Aenona*, the city of *Pasinum*; then the river *Tedanius* (Žrmanja) where *Iapydia* finishes. Islands in the bay with cities, apart from those mentioned above, are *Absortium, Arba, Crexi, Gissa, Portunata*. Returning to the mainland is the colony of *Iader*, 160 miles from *Pola*, then after 30 miles comes the island *Colentum*, after 43 miles the mouth of the river *Titius*' (*HN*, iii, 140).

Of the Liburnian communities mentioned the absence of the Nedinates from the second list (but not the third: see below) and that of the Lopsi from the first are probably errors. The other Liburnian peoples named in the first and second lists are the same. The different forms in which the names appear show that Pliny drew on different sources for each of the lists of peoples. They are the following: Alutrenses–Alutae ius Italicum, Asseriates–Asseriates immunes, Flamonienses Vanienses–Flanates ius Italicum (Flanona), Flamonienses Culici–Curictae immunes, Foretani–Fertinates immunes, (Lopsi)–Lopsi ius Italicum (Lopsica), Nedinates–(Nedinates ius Italicum or immunes) (Nedinum), Varvari–

Varvarini ius Italicum. Excluded from the first and second lists are more than half of the cities of Liburnia: the colony Iader, Senia, Ortoplinia, Tarsatica, Vegium, Corinium, Aenona, and Arba. With the exception of Ortoplinia, for which there is no evidence, all these cities are known to have been enrolled in the voting tribe Sergia, a definite indication that they were founded under Augustus. Absortium (Apsorus) was enrolled in Claudia, as was probably the other city on the same island, Crexi. The city of Pasinum cannot be located, and there is no evidence for the voting tribe of Argyruntum. Among the cities in the first and second lists, only the tribes of Lopsica and Fertinates (Fulfinium) are unrecorded: all the rest were in Claudia. The status of the islands Gissa (Časka on Pag) and Portunata (?Kornat) is unknown. Apart from those mentioned by Pliny only four other cities are known in Liburnia: Alveria, mentioned on a boundary settlement under the governor M. Pompeius Silvanus (69–70) and described as *Respublica*, III, 9938; Scardona at the mouth of the river Titius (Krka) was a Flavian foundation (*municipium Flavium*). Later cities at Sidrona (Cvijina Gradina near Medvidje) and the old legionary fortress of Burnum (Šuplja Crkva) on the Titius were probably founded in the early second century, the latter definitely by 118, III, 14321/24 and p. 217 f.

The foundation date of some of the cities can be fixed by inscriptions. Three, Apsorus, Crexi, and Argyruntum, probably became *municipia* under Tiberius. At Crexi an inscription set up by the two annual magistrates (*IIviri*) records the building of the senate house (*curia*) and portico (*porticus*) under Tiberius, III, 3148. Apsorus on the same island was probably founded at the same time. Three inscriptions set up under Tiberius suggest a similar date for Argyruntum (Starigrad Paklenica): one records the building of the city walls and towers (*murum et turres*) in 34–35 *JÖAI*, 12 (1909), Bb 49: a second was set up to the empress Livia (Iulia Augusta, mother of Tiberius) before her death in 29 by a councillor to celebrate his becoming a member of the city council (*ob dec.*, III, 9972): the third records unspecified building work carried out under the governor L. Volusius Saturninus in the period 34–37, III, 14322. The second establishes the existence of the city under Tiberius, while the first suggests that it was founded about the middle of his reign.

There remains the problem of the foundation date for the cities whose peoples are named in Pliny's first and second list: Alvona, Asseria, Flanona, Curictae, Fulfinium, Lopsica, Nedinum, and Varvaria, among which only Alvona, Flanona, and Lopsica appear among the cities of Pliny's third list. The enrolment of all these cities in Claudia is not evidence that they were established at the same time: in fact it can be demonstrated that two of the cities were established under different emperors. An early legionary tombstone from Alvona attests that the city was enrolled in Claudia, III, 3052, and in existence before A.D. 42 and therefore was probably established under Tiberius. On the other hand the presence of a priest of the deceased emperor Claudius (*flamen divi Claudii*) at Asseria points to that ruler as the founder, *JÖAI*, 11 (1908), Bb. 69, fig. 47. Apart from the tribe Claudia there is no precise evidence when the other cities in this group were established.

The Roman tribe Claudia was one of the oldest rural tribes, in which Roman citizens would be registered according to the area in which they lived and owned their property. Its name was derived from the great Claudian family (*gens Claudia*) which traced its origin to a Sabine chief who migrated to Rome in the sixth century B.C. With the enfranchisement of all Italy in the first century B.C. and the allocation of communities to the various tribes Claudia became concentrated in Central and Southern Italy, L. R. Taylor, *Voting Districts*, 35 f. With the much wider extension of the citizenship under Caesar and Augustus it was still necessary for every citizen to be registered in one of the tribes. There were no rules to decide the allocation of the newly-enfranchised, and very often they would take the tribe of the person to whom they owed their citizenship. Thus Fabia is associated with Caesar, while Sergia is the hallmark of Augustus, Taylor, op. cit., 221 f. Claudia suggests Tiberius and Claudius. The tribe was common around the northern Adriatic; apart from those in Liburnia, Emona (Ljubljana) in Pannonia, *CQ*, 56 (1963), 268 ff, Concordia and Novaria, V, 6514, in Italy were founded in Tiberius' reign. They have the title *Iulia* which could point to Caesar, but none of his known foundations were enrolled in Claudia.

Since the first list of Pliny was based on the official list of peoples in the *XI Regiones* of Italy drawn up early under Augustus, W. Kubitschek, *SB* 209 ff., argued that before the eastern boundary of Italy was fixed on the river Arsia some parts of Liburnia belonged to Italy. Therefore the most likely date for the foundation of the communities in the tenth region list is under Caesar or, at latest, early under Augustus. However, there is no evidence that the boundaries of Italy were ever extended thus far around the Adriatic, R. Thomsen, *Italic Regions*, 25–31, while the omission of the Augustan cities enrolled in Sergia (including the colony Iader) is quite inexplicable on this theory. The tribe Claudia, on the other hand, makes it far more likely that these Liburnian cities were established under Tiberius or Claudius. In the view of A. v. Premerstein, *SB*, 203 ff., their inclusion in the *regio* X list was due to their being granted Italian status (*ius Italicum*) or exemption from tribute (*immunitas*) under the census, and they are mentioned because they belonged to a district so close to Italy although, as Pliny notes, they are not strictly relevant. The Liburnians of the first list appear under Liburnia in the second, their names in the same official ethnic form (Roman authorities dealt with the people of a place, not the physical settlement itself), and with the two privileges mentioned above. There is an important distinction between these for the legal status of the community. Italian status could only be held by Roman *coloniae* and *municipia*, and conferred not only complete exemption from provincial tribute but the complete assimilation of the land to the status enjoyed by Italy. Unlike the conferring of titles such as *colonia* and *municipium*, this grant meant loss of revenue to Rome and was consequently a rare privilege indeed. The grants of *Ius Italicum* to Liburnian communities can only be explained by their physical nearness to Italy.

Exemption from tribute was quite different and in most of the cases where the privilege is attested it survived from early treaties and favours given during the Republic, mostly in settlements organized after major wars of conquest. It did not imply Roman city status, and could be granted to foreign communities (*civitates peregrinae*). The privilege of tribute-exemption only applied to land owned by citizens of the city in question: with Italian status the lands of the city were held in full Quiritarian (Roman) ownership; cf. A. H. M. Jones, *GC*, 131–4.

Pliny's third list names independent cities in Liburnia. In addition to the Augustan cities in Sergia, not mentioned in the first and second lists, it includes all those communities with Italian status (the omission of Varvaria from the third list is presumed an error) but not those which were merely exempt from tribute. These last cities were not then constituted as *municipia* when the third list was drawn up, and since the communities with Italian status, enrolled in the tribe Claudia, will have been *municipia*, both the second and third of Pliny's lists must date after the death of Augustus in 14. From the above evidence the different stages in the foundation and legal status of Liburnian cities can be identified.

The first stage was the grant of tribute-exemption to communities of Liburnia (*civitates peregrinae*) made before the first list was compiled. Later some of the communities attained Roman city status and at the same time Italian status because of their closeness to Italy. This is the stage when the second and third lists were compiled. The last stage was after the second and third lists when the few remaining *civitates peregrinae* became *municipia* and probably gained Italian status also. The dating of these different stages is supplied by evidence from the individual cities.

The first is Augustan, taken from the *Descriptio totius Italiae*, and the grants of tribute-exemption will have been made either early under Augustus or even under Caesar. The second and third lists are earlier than Claudius. Pliny does not record the Claudian colony at Aequum. Since the communities which were not Roman cities under Augustus appear in the third list along with Augustan cities and include the Tiberian *municipia* at Argyruntum and Crexi (see above),

Julio–Claudian Cities of Liburnia

Pliny, HN, III, 130 (Regio X)	HN, III, 139 (Liburnia)	HN, III, 140 (oppida)	Ptolemy, II, 16	Voting Tribe
....	....	Absortium	Ἀψόρος	Claudia
		Aenona	Αἰνῶνα	Sergia
Alutrenses	Alutae ius Italicum	Alvona	Ἀλουῶνα	Claudia
		Arba	Ἄρβα	Sergia
....	....	Argyruntum	Ἀργυροῦντον	Claudia?
Asseriates	Asseriates immunes	....	Ἀσσεσία	Claudia
		Colentum	Κόλλευνον	?
		Corinium	Κορίνον	Sergia
		Crexi	Κρέψα	Claudia?
Flamonienses Culici	Curictae immunes	....	Κούρικον	Claudia
Flamonienses Vanienses	Flanates ius Italicum	Flanona	Φλανῶνα	Claudia
Foretani	Fertinates immunes	....	Φουλφίνον	Claudia?
....	....	Gissa	....	?
		Iader colonia	Ἰαδερ κολωνία	Sergia
Nedinates	Lopsi ius Italicum	Lopsica	Λόψικα	?
		....	Νήδινον	Claudia
		Ortoplinia	Ὄρτοπλα	Sergia?
		civitas Pasini	....	?
		Portunata	....	?
		Senia	Σένια	Sergia
Varvari	Varvarini ius Italicum	Tarsatica	Ταρσατικά	Sergia
		....	Οὐαρουαρία	Claudia
....	....	Vegium	Οὐεγία	Sergia

the reign of Tiberius seems the most probable date for the second and third lists. In addition to Alvona, attested before 42, and almost certainly a Tiberian *municipium*, Flanona, Lopsica, and Varvaria became *municipia* under Tiberius. The last group, exempt from tribute in the second list and omitted from the third, Asseriates, Curictae, and Fertinates, did not become *municipia* until after the second and third lists had been drawn up: the most likely time is the reign of Claudius, who was honoured in one of this group by a personal cult after his death (at Asseria, see above). Nedinum cannot be dated in the scheme: since it appears in the first list among the *civitates peregrinae* and was enrolled in Claudia, its foundation took place after Augustus, probably under Tiberius or Claudius.

The chronology of city foundations in Liburnia may be summarised thus (cf. Alföldy, *Epigraphica*, 53 ff.):

Augustus: Iader *colonia*, Aenona, Arba, Corinium, Ortoplinia (?), Tarsatica, Vegium, Senia.

Tiberius: Apsorus, Argyruntum, Alvona, Crexi, Flanona, Lopsica, Varvaria.

Claudius: Asseria, Curicum, Fertinium.

Tiberius or *Claudius*: Nedinum.

Julio–Claudian: Alveria.

APPENDIX XIII *Imperial Nomenclature in the Interior*

Avendo

IULIUS   III, 10051; cf. p. 2328/175

AELIUS   III, 10051; cf. p. 2328/175

Arupium

IULIUS   III, 3011 (Doljane)

CLAUDIUS   III, 15084/1

FLAVIUS   III, 15088

P. AELIUS   III, 15089

Lika polje

IULIUS   III, 3005 frg. (Gornje Kosinj)?

     III, 10025 (3002); cf. p. 2328/171 (Široka Kula)?

FLAVIUS   III, 2993; cf. p. 2328/170 (Počitelj); III, 15054 (Komić).

P. AELIUS   III, 2999; cf. 1022 (Vrebac).

AELIUS   III, 2992; cf. p. 2328/170 (Lovinac); III, 2997 cf. Patsch, *Lika*, 97 (Udbina).

T. AURELIUS   III, 3005 (Kosinj)?

AURELIUS   III, 15054 (Komić); III, 2993; cf. p. 2328/170 (Počitelj), Patsch, *Lika*, 67 frg. (Vrebac).

Metulum

M. AURELIUS   III, 10057 (3020).

AURELIUS   III, 3023 (Primišlje), Brunšmid, *k. sp.*, n. 204.

Raetinium (Bihać).

IULIUS   III, 10038; III, 10039; III, 10040; III, 10041 (Golubić), III, 13272 (10336/a) (Brekovica), *Sp.*, 77 (1934), n. 2 (Pritoka).

FLAVIUS   III, 14324; III, 10033 (Golubić).

ULPIUS   III, 15077 (Čavkići).

AELIUS   *GZMS*, 12 (1957), 163, n. 1 (Golubić).

T. AURELIUS   Sp. 77 (1934), n. 25 (Prekaja).

AURELIUS   III, 14014 (Smoljani); III, 10034; III, 10036; III, 10037 (Golubić); III, 14015 (Doljani).

Sana Valley (Briševo–Ljubija).

IULIUS   *GZMBH*, 51 (1939), 12 (Blagaj).

ULPIUS   III, 14973, III, 14974 (Krnjeuša), *GZMBH*, 51 (1939), 12, *GZMS*, 12 (1957) 119, fig. 3 (Čikote).

P. AELIUS   III, 13236 (Mrkonjić Grad).

AELIUS   *GZMS*, 12 (1957), 119, fig. 3 (Čikote).

AURELIUS   *GZMS*, 12 (1957), 116 f., n. 8 (Čikote).

Pelva

FLAVIUS	III, 9857 (Prolog).
ULPIUS	III, 14319 frg. (Otinovci).
P. AELIUS	*WMBH* 11 (1909), 138, fig. 33 (Bos. Grahovo), ibid., 120, fig. 10 (Grkovci), ibid., 123, fig. 12 = III, 9848 (Gubin).
AELIUS	*GZMBH*, 42 (1930), 160 (Livno); *WMBH*, 11 (1909), 127, fig. 18 (Baštasi); ibid., 134, fig. 26 (Livno); ibid., 134, fig. 29 (Livno); III, 9850 (Suhača), Sp. 88 (1938), n. 29 (Suhača), Sp. 77 (1934), 30 frg. (Baštasi), III, 14971 frg. (Bos. Grahovo).
L. AURELIUS	*GZMBH*, 40 (1928), 91 (Vašarovin).
AURELIUS	III, 14317 (2763, 13230–13234) (Otinovci), III, 9851 (Suhača), *WMBH* 11 (1909), 129, fig. 21 (Vašarovin), ibid., 125, fig. 15 (Lištani).

Salvium

P. AELIUS	*GZMBH*, 40 (1928), 87 (Podgradina), III, 13236 (Halapić), *GZMBH*, 39 (1927), 263, n. 12 (Halapić).
AELIUS	III, 9864 (Jakir), III, 14249/2 (Salona), *GZMBH*, 39 (1927), 261, n. 10 (Glamoč), ibid., 40 (1928), 79 (Glamoč), III, 9861 (2760/a) (Glamoč), *GZMBH* 39 (1927), 263, n. 13. 13 (Halapić), *Sp.* 88 (1938), 23, ibid., 25 (Vrbica).
AURELIUS	*Sp.*, 88 (1938), 21 (Podgradina).

Delminium

IULIUS	*WMBH*, 9 (1904), 175.
FLAVIUS	*WMBH*, 9 (1904), 174, III, 14320/4.
P. AELIUS	III, 14976/7 (Borčani), *WMBH*, 11 (1909), 227 (Šuijica).
AELIUS	III, 14320/3.

Šipovo and *Jajce*

IULIUS	*WMBH*, 12 (1912), 141, fig. 65 (Šipovo).
FLAVIUS	III, 13237 (Šipovo).
AELIUS	III, 13984 = *GZMS*, 6 (1951), 310 = Šašel, 154 (D. Pecka).
AURELIUS	*GZMS*, 6 (1951), 305, n. 7 (Jajce).

Doboj   – – – – – –

Bistue Nova

IULIUS	*GZMS*, 13 (1958), 155, fig. 3 (Dolac); cf. Šašel 100.
FLAVIUS	*WMBH*, 12 (1912), 166, fig. 109; III, 12765; III, 12763; III, 12771; III, 13865 (Mali Mošunj), Sp. 88 (1938), n. 10 (Turbe).
ULPIUS	*GZMBH*, 44 (1933), 37 f. (III, 12762 + 12766); III, 14220 (8382, 13857) frg; III, 12788; cf. p. 2256 (Mali Mošunj).
P. AELIUS	III, 12761 (Fazlići).
AURELIUS	III, 12764–5; III, 12768-9-70; III, 13865 (Mali Mošunj).

Aquae S.

IULIUS	*GZMBH*, 48 (1936), 19, fig. 3 (Višnjica).
FLAVIUS	*Sp.*, 93 (1940), 10 (Bréza); III, 12755 (Blazuj).
P. AELIUS	*Sp.*, 93 (1940), 10 (Bréza).
AELIUS	*GZMBH*, 25 (1923), 414 frg. (Bréza).
T. AURELIUS	III, 8374 (2766/a); III, 13863 (Pazarić).
AURELIUS	III, 13863 (Pazarić); III, 12749 (8375) (Pazarić); *GZMBH*, 25 (1923), 413 frg. (Bréza); *GZMBH*, 48 (1936), 20, n. 2, ibid., 21, n. 4 (Višnjica); *Sp.*, 88 (1938), 15 (Fojnica).

Konjic

P. AELIUS	III, 14617/2 (Bjelemić); III, 14617/3 (Ostrožac).
AELIUS	*GZMS*, 9 (1954), 219, pl. VI 1–3 (Lisičići); *WMBH*, 9 (1904), 251, fig. 126 frg. (Lisičići); III, 12799 (8489) (Glavatičevo).
T. AURELIUS	III, 13860 (Lisičići); Sp. 88 (1938), 20 (Donje Selo).
AURELIUS	III, 13861 (Lisičići); III, 13862 (Radešine).

Bisute Vetus

FLAVIUS	*WMBH*, 11 (1909), 107, fig. 2, fig. 3; 108, fig. 4 frg.; 109 fig. 5.
ULPIUS	III, 13232 (Proslap).
AELIUS	*WMBH*, 11 (1909) 108, fig. 4; 109 fig. 5.
AURELIUS	*GZMS* 15–16 (1961), 233, fig. 4 (Gornje Vakuf).

Domavia

IULIUS	III, 12722 (8362).
CLAUDIUS	III, 12743 (Poznanovići).
ULPIUS	Sp. 75 (1931), 159 (Gornje Bukovica).
AELIUS	Šašel, 83 = *GZMBH*, 52 (1940), 23 ff. (12739–40) frg. (Tegare).
M. AURELIUS	III, 8297 (Sočanica).
AURELIUS	III, 12733; III, 12744 frg. (Bjelovac); *GZMBH*, 44 (1932), 4 (Bukovica near Ljubovija).

Skelani

CLAUDIUS	*WMBH*, 11 (1909), 158, fig. 69; ibid., 148 fig. 52.
FLAVIUS	III, 14219/10/12/13; *WMBH*, 11 (1909), 160, fig. 73; Sp. 88 (1938), 113 (Miljevina near Foča).
COCCEIUS	*GZMBH*, 42 (1940), 164.
ULPIUS	III, 14219/18 (Crvica).
P. AELIUS	*WMBH*, 11 (1909), 156, fig. 66.
AELIUS	III, 14219/18 (Crvica).
L. AURELIUS	III, 14219/6.
T. AURELIUS	*GZMBH*, 42 (1940), 164 (Crvica).
AURELIUS	*WMBH*, 11 (1909), 155, fig. 64; ibid., 157, fig. 68; ibid., 161, fig. 75 frg.
SEPTIMIUS	III, 14219/20 (Osatica).

Appendix XIII

Rogatica

FLAVIUS   III, 12747 (8368) (Rogatica); Sp. 77 (1934), p. 16, n. 20 (Stari Brod), 19 (Rudo).

ULPIUS   III, 14616 (Živaljević); *WMBH*, 12 (1912), 160, fig. 150 frg.

P. AELIUS   III, 8366–7; Sp. 71 (1931), 105 = Šašel, 68 (Radoinja).

AURELIUS   Sp. 77 (1934), 15 (Štitarevo); III, 12751 (8376/c) (Višegrad).

Municipium S.

P. AELIUS   III, 8310 (6344); III, 8308 (Kolovrat).

T. AELIUS   III, 8313 (6346); *Starinar*, 1950, 183 (Džurovo); Sp. 71 (1931), n. 289.

AELIUS   Sp. 98 (1948), 131 frg. (Komino); Sp. 71 (1931), 11 (Bijelopolje); III, 8312; *VHAD*, 15 (1928), 39, fig. 4; III, 8323 (6356; cf. p. 2255); III, 14604 frg., Sp. 71 (1931), 286; *GZMBH*, 53 (1941), 9 = Šašel 74.

SEX AURELIUS   III, 14604.

T. AURELIUS   *WMBH*, 12 (1912), 123, fig. 48; III, 8317 (6349; cf. p. 2255); III, 14605; III, 8309 (1708 = 6343); Sp. 77 (1934), n. 21 (Rošulja); III, 8298 (Čadinje).

AURELIUS   III, 8314, 8315 (6348), 8319 (6350), 8320 (6351), 8317 (6349; cf. p. 2255), 8318; Sp. 98 (1948), 303, ibid., 305; III, 8326 (6534), 8321 (6532), 8310 (6344); Sp. 71 (1931), 284, ibid., 285, ibid., 287; *GZMBH*, 53 (1941) 8 frg. = Šašel, 72; III, 8316 (Radošavac); Sp. 98 (1948), 291 (Komino); Sp. 71 (1931), 331 (Prijepolje); Sp. 98 (1948), 331 (Džurovo); Sp. 71 (1931), 316, ibid., 317 (Priboj).

Maluesa

FLAVIUS   III, 8349 (1670) (Požega); III, 8350 (Karan); Sp. 71 (1931), 197 (Tubići).

ULPIUS   III, 6316 (Gorobilje).

P. AELIUS   III, 8342 (1672) (Požega); III, 8340 (Karan).

T. AELIUS   III, 8339 (Visibaba); III, 15611 (Ježevica).

AELIUS   III, 8346 (1669) (Gorobilje); III, 8343; Šašel, 68 (Radoinja).

P. AURELIUS   III, 14607/1 (6315, 8348, 12719).

T. AURELIUS   III, 14608–9 (Gorobilje); III, 8338 (6317) (Arilje); Sp. 98 (1948), 327 (Prilipac); III, 8344 (1671) (Vranjani); III, 8347 (Karan); Sp. 39 (1903), 88 (Tubići); Sp. 98 (1948), 248 (Mačkat); III, 8354 = Sp. 98 (1948) 248.

AURELIUS   III, 8351 (Gorobilje); III, 8346 (1669); III, 12717 (Gradina, Arilje); III, 8341 frg. (Požega); III, 8339 (Visibaba); III 8343 (Karan); *Sp.*, 47 (1909), 186 frg. (Karan); III, 14611 (Ježevica); *Sp.*, 47 (1909), 183 frg. (Ježevica); *Sp.*, 71 (1931), 84 (Tubići); *Sp.*, 98 (1948), 477 (Vrtući); III, 12718; cf. p. 2328/116 (Vrtuči); III, 14613 (Bioška).

TABLE OF IMPERIAL NOMINA IN THE INTERIOR

Cities	Iulius	Claudius	Flavius	Cocceius	Ulpius	P. Aelius	T. Aelius	Aelius	M. Aurelius	T. Aurelius	Aurelius
1. Avendo	1							1F			
2. Arupium	1	1	1								
3. Lika polje	2		1 1F			1		1 1F		1	3 1F
4. Metulum					2 2F	2 1F			1		2 1F
5. Raetinium	3 3F 1L		2		1			1F		1	10 2F 3L FL
6. Briševo-Ljubija	1F				2	1		1			
7. Pelva			1		1	3 1F		6 5F			4 2F
8. Salvium						3		11			1
9. Delminium	1F		1 1F			2		1			
10. Sipovo-Jajce	1		3 1F					2			
11. Doboj											1
12. Bistue Nova	1F		5 2F		1 2F	1 1F		1F			5 7F
13. Aquae S.	1F		1		1 2F	F		1F		2	13 5F
14. Konjic					1F	3 1F		3 2F		4 1F	4
15. Bistue Vetus			5 1F		1F			2F			1
16. Domavia	1	1F				1			1		3
17. Skelani		3 1F	7	1F	1	1				1	4 1FL
18. Rogatica			3		2	3 1F		1			3 1F
19. Municipium S.					1	5	4 1F	8 3F		9 2F	17 21F
20. Maluesa			2 3F		1	6 3F	4 3F	3 1F	8	12	6 9F
	9 7F 1L	4 2F	32 9F	1F	10 8F	31 9F	8 4F	37 17F	10	30 3F	77 49F 3L 2FL

Also Septimius: Skelani 1+(F)
L. Aurelius: Pelva 1, Skelani 1.
Sex Aurelius: Municipium S. 1.
P. Aurelius: Maluesa 1.

All persons holding official positions, procurators, *beneficiarii consulares*, and others who are demonstrably not of local origin, are excluded.
F female
L freedman or freedwoman (*libertus* or *liberta*)
Where one member of a family bears a *praenomen* the same is assumed for other male members of the family, although this is often omitted on tombstones of *Aelii* and *Aurelii*.

497

There is no evidence to support the view that Lissus must be located in the sands around the mouth of the Drin (cf. M. Fluss, *RE*, 13, 731 ff.). The hills of Lješ and Mali Šelbuemit are the only ones in the area which fit Polybius' description of the capture of the city and the Acrolissus by Philip. The identification is made certain by the evidence for the defences studied by Prschniker and Schober, 14 ff. The problem of Lissus has been examined more recently by J. M. F. May, *JRS*, 36 (1946), 54 ff. with map fig. 5. Since the sources refer to Lissus as a harbour in the time of Caesar (Caes., *BC*, iii, 29, 3; 40, 5) he concluded that there was a harbour separate from the city at Lješ nearer the mouth of the Drin, but quite separate from the harbour Nymphaeum (Shjen - Gjin) three miles north of the Drin mouth where ships were stationed during the Civil War (Caes., *BC*, iii, 26). He maintains that the city could not have been used as a harbour in the time of Philip, since at that time the main volume of the waters of the Drin flowed out past Scodra and reached the sea in the river Bojanna. This is supposition. Strabo (vii, 5, 7) states that the Drilo (Drin) was navigable inland as far as the territory of the Dardanians, and there is no evidence that in antiquity it was not the navigable river it remained until the abnormal floods of 1857 which sent the waters past Scodra and into the Adriatic along the river Bojanna. The plan of the Lissus defences leaves no doubt that the place had a harbour (see above, p. 359). See now N. G. L. Hammond, *JRS*, 58 (1968), 2.

The stamped tiles collected in Dalmatia up to 1902 are listed in *CIL*, III (p. 408, 1038, 1653, 2179, 2275, 2328/19, 2328/178). For the Narona area this is supplemented by the studies of C. Patsch, *Hercegovina*, 100 ff., while later stamps from Salona were catalogued at intervals by F. Bulić, *BD*, 26 (1903), and following volumes. Four factories dominated the market in the first century, PANSIANA, Q. CLODIUS AMBROSIUS, SOLONAS, and C. TITIUS HERMEROS. Apart from CIN-NIANA, which almost matches the distribution of these four in quantity, they are the only stamps which are distributed evenly in virtually all the cities along the Dalmatian coast. There is no doubt that their manufacture belongs to the same period: Patsch, *Hercegovina*, 112, figs. 46–8, has demonstrated that the letters used in the dies of these stamps were cast in the same mould. It is possible that many tiles were manufactured in the same workshop but stamped with the names of different factories, a practice not unknown even in modern competitive industry (V, 8110/1–28; cf. XI, 6685/1–20; IX, 6078/22–28; cf. Chilver, *CG*, 176). PANSIANA is the commonest, and it is clear that a considerable proportion of its output was exported to Dalmatia. The earliest examples are stamped PANSAE VIBI, suggesting a link with the consul of 43 B.C., or perhaps C. Vibius Pansa, who is attested as legate of Augustus in Raetia (V, 4910), although neither is known to have been specially connected with Northern Italy. The site of the factory has not been fixed, but was certainly in the area of Aquileia: Calderini (*Aquileia*, 317) locates it at Pansano near Montfalcone. Many examples are stamped PANSIANA only, often with intricate ligatures, but most have imperial titles, beginning with Tiberius (TI PANSIANA), a few for Gaius (C CAESAR PANSI-ANA), and many for Claudius and Nero (TI CLAUD or NERO CLAUD PANSIANA), when the output of the factory appears to have been at its greatest. The latest are a few made under Vespasian (VESP CAES PANSIANA). There is no obvious reason why the factory ceased production, and it is possible that the tiles were stamped with the imperial titles only, although none are known in Dalmatia. The large quantity of PANSIANA stamps in Dalmatia was probably due to its being an imperial property, although none were used by the Roman army, since both the legions and auxiliary units produced their own tiles. The largest number comes from Salona, including Pharia and Issa, while examples of all the imperial stamps, apart from the earliest, appear at Narona, Epidaurum, and Acruvium. They are less common in the north of the coastline: in the Ravni kotari a few are found at Asseria and Iader, while isolated examples appear at Vegium and on Curicum. Clearly apart from the towns in the province close to the centre of manufacture, such as Albona, exports to the province were shipped to Salona, where most were used, while a few were carried in coastal vessels to the cities in the south. The second group are the products of Q. CLODIUS AMBROSIUS. These are not dated like the Pansiana factory products but from their style and lettering are assignable to the same period. They also were made somewhere in the Aquileia–Tergeste region and their distribution in Italy and in Dalmatia matches the Pansiana tiles closely (V, 8110/70; cf. XI, 6689/79; IX, 6078/62). Most appear at Salona, including its territory, and Narona, but they are also known at Iader, Asseria, Argyruntum, and Clambetae. They were used in large quantities by the settlers in the Narona territory for their expensive country houses. Third in order of quantity was the SOLONAS factory. Although they are frequently found in the northeast the factory was not in the Aquileia area but much further south in Aemilia (*regio* VIII). They are particularly common along the coast around Ravenna, Pisaurum, and Ariminum (V, 8110/136; cf. XI, 6686/1–8; IX, 6078/152 from Brundisium). The name does not derive from a family but from a community, the Solonates who are listed by Pliny (*HN*, iii, 116) in his schedule of the cities in Aemilia. In most cases the products are stamped SOLONAS or SOLONATE (in some cases retrograde) but one example at Salona appears to name two factory proprietors: C CAMARI PRIS(CI) L PLAUTI SOL(ONATIUM) (III, p. 2328/178 add. 10183). In Dalmatia it is found almost exclusively in Salona, but a few examples are found at Tasovčići (possibly on the Papii estates) in the Narona territory, and at Epidaurum. It is more common in Liburnia, appearing at Iader, Asseria, Sidrona, and Argyruntum. Further north an isolated example is found at Monetium in the Lika polje, while it appears among the half-dozen imported Italian products used in the Jupiter temple near Vegium (p. 202 above). The products of L. TITIUS HERMEROS appear in most centres along the coast, although not in the quantity of the others. Apart from Salona, Iader, and Narona, they occur at Sidrona, Vegium, and on Apsorus. They were manufactured somewhere in the Aquileia area or Northeast Italy, judging from their distribution (V, 8110/144; XI, 6689/243; IX, 6078/160). The Dalmatian market was very important for these factories. Their distribution, apart from Pansiana, is restricted to the northeast of Italy and the Dalmatian seaboard. In Italy they are scattered down the east coast, with a concentration at Firmum in Picenum.

Of nearly one hundred different stamps recorded at Salona more than thirty derive from known factories in Italy, all in the Aquileia area. In some instances virtually all their production seems to have gone across the Adriatic. The factory of Q. GRANIUS PRISCUS was at Aquileia (V, 8110/90) and its products are not found elsewhere, but in Dalmatia they appear at Clambetae, Aenona, Corcyra Nigra, Iader, and Stolac, where they are found in one of the luxurious villas.

Products of the EPIDII factory, and those made under its later owners C. PETRO-
NIUS APER and VALERIA MAGNA are attested (cf. Patsch, *Hercegovina*, 118), as well
as those of M. ALBIUS RUFUS, C. IULIUS AFRICANUS, EVARISTUS, L. MINICIUS PUDENS,
and the FAESONIUS factory. In most instances the products of these factories did
not travel beyond the coastal cities. The small number of stamped tiles in the
interior appear to have been made either by local municipal factories or by local
private enterprise. SISC(IA) appears at Japra Blagaj in the Sana valley (*Sp.*, 77
(1931), n. 46) and BISTUE in the upper Vrbas valley (*GZMS*, 15–16 (1961), 230,
fig. 1). Other locally stamped products are known at Plevlje (a few examples of
P. A(ELIUS) S(....), *WMBH*, 12 (1912), 129, fig. 57 f.; cf. also Evans, *Archaeologia*,
49 (1885), 41), the Aquae S.. area (III, 14030, 14334/1, 14336/3), and Domavia
(SATUR[NINUS], III, 13340/12). The absence of imported tiles away from the coast
is an example of how great was the economic separation of the coast from the
interior. It is strange that the coastal cities were so willing to import the Italian
products. Presumably in the pioneer period it was a necessity, and once estab-
lished it proved very difficult for local enterprise to make inroads on the market.
Some cities are known to have made their own tile kilns, but apparently not
before the late first century A.D. Some Liburnian landowners made their own.
Products from the estates of Sex. Metillius Maximus (DE SALT(U) SEX M(E)TILLI
MAXI(MI)) are found at Senia and on Curicum, where the lands may have been
(III, 1334/10 at Saline and Omiri, Patsch, *Lika*, 98, fig. 41) also those of L.
TETTIUS DESEDES at Iader (*BD*, 26 (1903), 149, 3 ex.) and in the northern Ravni
kotari (*JÖAI*, 8 (1905), Bb. 47, n. 2 Clambetae; III, 10183 Aenona). Neither of
these stamps is known elsewhere, nor is TRAGULAE at Iader (III, 14033) and
Asseria (*JÖAI*, 11 (1908), Bb. 86), MUTTIENI at Iader (III, 6364), Clambetae
(*JÖAI*, 8 (1905), 47, n. 3 many ex.), Aenona (III, 14031), and Argyruntum
(*JÖAI*, 12 (1909), Bb. 61), where the distribution indicates a local factory run
probably by an Italian settler family.

The largest group of local tiles appears at Salona, some of which were being
made in the fourth century, for instance those bearing the Greek name GALAX-
[IDOROS] from the baptistery in the *basilica urbana* (III, 15113/1) and those
stamped DALMATIA used in the Palace of Diocletian (p. 388). Others may have
been manufactured on the estates of Italian families, since they are not found
outside the city, for instance M IPPOLITUS (*BD*, 27 (1904), n. 973; cf. 26 (1903),
198, n. 903) and M LUTASIUS (*BD*, 30 (1907), n. 1304; cf. 28 (1905), n. 1304). In
one case an interesting connection can be established between Salona and a particular city in Italy. The rare name Maltinius is found only in two places. In Italy
at Nursia in *regio* IV two persons, one of them a freedman, are attested on tombstones (XI, 4576, 4577). In the Salona territory two tombstones of the family are

known, at Sučurac (III, 2425) and Klis (III, 2264), the former being dated to the second century or later by reference to marriage to a P. Aelius. Tiles stamped L MALTINI ABASCANTI are known from Salona (III, 2328/19 add. 3214/9) and Iader (III, 3214), and they also appear in the Proboj villa (see above, p. 398) near Vitina and Ljubuški (III, 13340/14) in the Narona territory. It is possible that the family owned urban property in the two cities and that the Proboj estates may at some time have been owned by them. The Maltinii can be studied because of their uncommon name. In other cases many of the stamps are fragmentary and, lacking parallels in the accessible Italian collections, their origin is not certain. Although almost all are stamped with Italian *gentilicia*, systematic identification will only be possible when the Dalmatian and Italian stamps are studied side by side. Some are patently local: DALMATIA is clearly so, possibly from a government factory at Salona, although it is confined to that place (III, 10183/16) and the Palace of Diocletian. Most were the products of privately owned kilns, often by families of city-council status. For instance P. LURIUS FIRMUS, unknown in Italy, is found at Acruvium where the Lurii were an established family (see above, p. 303), and also at nearby Risinium (III, 3214/19; cf. 10183/31). A comparable example may be the Iunii who produced tiles stamped IUNI on their estates at Potoci and Bijelpolje in the territory of Narona (*WMBH*, 9 (1904), 265, fig. 136), and also the Servilii at Stolac (III, 15114/2; cf. *WMBH*, 9 (1904), 284, fig. 167: SERVILIA), where Italian imports were widely used. The import of building materials from Italy into Dalmatia is not a unique phenomenon of the early Roman period. In the Middle Ages Italian bricks were imported through Narona's successor Metković and through Split, and the products of the Società Veneta in Pardenone prov. di Udine Italia are common in the poljes of Duvno and Livno (Patsch, *Hercegovina*, 117).

Amphorae

Large quantities of amphorae, the ubiquitous storage vessel for wine and oil, have been found in the southern part of the province, but only those at Narona have been studied for their origins. Recently the task of studying this class of vessel has been made much easier by the publication of the reasearch of M. H. Callander (*Roman Amphorae*, Oxford, 1965). The majority of those with makers' stamps, set either on the lid or neck of the vessel, are of first-century date and can be paralleled at Pompeii and other dated contexts. Some are known at Brundisium, whence they may have begun their journey to Dalmatia. A small group appears to originate from that port or from the Calabrian hinterland: APOLLONIUS (*WMBH*, 9 (1904), 286, n. 1, fig. 169 = III, 15117; cf. IX, 6079, 5, 6

(Brundisium), *EE*, VII (supp. *CIL*, IX), 242, 6 (Tarentum), X, 8051, 7), ARCHELAUS (*JAK*, 2 (1908), n. 1, fig. 8, cf. IX, 6388, 2 (Brundisium), Pais, *supp.* V, 1077, 29 (Aquileia)), L SALVIUS (Patsch, *Narona*, 116 f., n. 1, fig. 65; cf. *EE*, VIII, 242, 50 (Tarentum), XI, 6695, 83 (Baggiovara), V, 8112, 75 (Ivrea)), SEXSTUS (*WMBH*, 9 (1904), 287, n. 2, fig. 170; cf. IX, 6079, 50 (Brundisium)). Another stamp, NICEP(HORUS), appears in Salzburg (*JAK*, 2 (1908), 94, fig. 11; cf. III, 6010, 151, also in Tarentum: *EE*, VII, 242, 41–2), while of those named above the third is only attested elsewhere at Ivrea north of Turin. ALEXANDER, which is attested at Bononia and Mutina (XI, 6695, 9; cf. Pais, supp. V, 1077, 24) as well as at Narona (*BD*, 33 (1910), 135), probably originated from Northern Italy, as did also DION C[... (*JAK*, 2 (1908), 93, n. 2, fig. 9), which is also found at Aquileia and Ateste (Pais, *supp.*, V, 1077 57a–b). A more common north Italian product was VARIUS PACCI[ANUS] (Patsch, *Narona*, 117 f., n. 2, fig. 66), which is attested at Modena (XI, 6695, 94), Mantua (V, 8112, 85) and further afield at Virunum in Noricum (III, 12010, 33). A number of the other Narona stamps cannot be paralleled: AVID(IUS) (*WMBH*, 12 (1912), 82, fig. 15), M(ARCUS) AUR(ELIUS) A(....) (*WMBH*, 9 (1904), 287, n. 4, fig. 172), P(..) A(..) T(..) (*BD* 33 (1910), 135), SABDUS (*JAK*, 2 (1908), 94, n. 2, fig. 12), and [...]ANEPTES (*WMBH*, 9 (1904), 287, n. 3, fig. 171). Some of these products, possibly the two which bear the imperial names Aurelius and Aelius, were manufactured in the province, but the others may originate from small factories in Southeastern Italy. The problem of how these Italian amphorae reached Dalmatia has been discussed above (p. 411). Although the stamps noted here must represent only a fraction of those which reached the province, a pattern does emerge. The traffic was localized especially at Brundisium and its Calabrian hinterland. The vessels were not used for long land journeys, and with one or two exceptions all are close to the sea or navigable rivers. Once the ship in which they were conveyed had reached its main destination, the cargo of wine and oil would be emptied from these ungainly vessels, which were then stored near the quayside for the return voyage, in the manner of those which Patsch discovered *in situ* at Narona (*JAK*, 2 (1908), 91, fig. 5). The imports removed from the amphorae, which weighed empty between 40 and 60 pounds, would then be placed in more manageable containers for whatever land transport was necessary.

Arretine Sigillata

Italian factories dominated the market for good-quality household pottery in Dalmatia as much as in other European provinces in the first centuries B.C. and A.D. A group of Arretine potters have been studied at Narona (Patsch, *Herce-*

govina, 123 ff.). Particularly common are the products of L AN(NI) IN(GENUI), HELENUS, IUENES, LEUCI, and the most common RASI(NI). This potter appears frequently with various stamps from his full names L. Rasinius Pisanus. His wares were exported as far afield as the northern frontiers and the eastern Mediterranean. Vessels stamped SOLIMARUS indicate one of the fewer imports from the rapidly expanding south Gaulish factories, which began to win the markets from Arretium about the middle of the first century A.D.

Abbreviations

Roman numerals without prefix refer to volumes of *CIL*.

A Ant. Hung.	*Acta Antiqua Academiae Scientiarum Hungaricae*, Budapest.
A Arch. Hung.	*Acta Archaeologica Academiae Scientiarum Hungaricae*, Budapest.
ABSA	*Annual of the British School at Athens.*
AE	*L'Année Épigraphique*, Paris.
AEM	*Archaeologisch-epigraphische Mitteilungen aus Oesterreich-Ungarn*, Vienna.
AI	*Archaeologia Iugoslavica*, Belgrade.
Albania	*Albania: Revue d'archéologie, d'histoire, d'art et des sciences appliquées en Albanie et dans les Balkans*, Milan.
AMSI	*Atti e Memorie della Società Istriana di Archeologia e Storia patria*, Trieste.
Antiquity	*Antiquity*, a quarterly review of Archaeology, Cambridge.
Arch. Ért.	*Archaeologiai Értesitö*, Budapest.
Archaeologia	*Archaeologia*, or Miscellaneous Tracts relating to Antiquity, London.
Argo	*Argo: Informativno Glasilo za archeologijo Zgodovino umetnosti in Muzeologijo.* Narodni Muzej, Ljubljana.
Arheološki Vestnik	*Arheološki Vestnik (Acta Archaeologia)*, Slovenska Akad. znanosti in umetnosti, Ljubljana.
ARR	*Arheološki Radovi i Razprave (Acta et Diss. Archaeologicae)*, Zagreb.
Athenaeum	*Athenaeum*, Studi periodici di letteratura e storia dell' Antichità, Pavia.
BCH	*Bulletin de correspondence hellénique*, Paris.
BD	*Bullettino di archeologia e storia dalmata* (after 1927 continued as *VAHD*, see below), Split.
BerRGK	*Berichte der Römisch-Germanischen Kommission.* Frankfurt/Berlin.
BIAB	*Bulletin de l'Institut archéologique Bulgare*, Sofia.
Bibl. Class. Orient.	*Bibliographia classica orientalis*, Berlin.
BJ	*Bonner Jahrbücher*, Bonn.
BV-B	*Bayerische Vorgeschichtsblätter*, Munich.
Byzantion	*Byzantion: Revue internationale des Études Byzantines*, Brussels.

BzN	*Beiträge zur Namenforschung*, Heidelberg.
CAH	*Cambridge Ancient History*, Cambridge.
Carnuntina (1956)	Vorträge beim internationalen Kongress der Altertumsforscher Carnuntum *Romische Forschungen in Niederösterreich Bd. III*, Graz-Köln, 1956.
Chron. Min.	*Chronica Minora saec. IV. V. VI. VII.* ed. Th. Mommsen (*MGH Auct. Antiquiss.*, IX, XI, XIII), Berlin, 1892, 1894, 1898.
CIG	*Corpus Inscriptionum Graecarum*, ed. A. Boeckh and J. Franz, Berlin, 1825–77.
CIL	*Corpus Inscriptionum Latinarum*, Berlin, 1866–.
Članci	*Članci i Grada za kulturnu istoriju istočne Bosne*, Tuzla.
CQ	*Classical Quarterly*, London.
CW²	*Transactions of the Cumberland and Westmorland Antiquarian and Archaeological Society*, New Series, Kendal.
ČZN	*Časopis za Zgodovino in Narodopisije*, Maribor.
Dacia	*Dacia: Revue d'Archéologie et d'Histoire ancienne*, Bucharest.
Diadora	*Diadora: Glasilo arheološkog muzeja u Zadru*, Zadar.
EE	*Ephemeris Epigraphica*, Berlin.
Eirene	*Eirene: Studia Graeca et Latina*, Prague.
Epigraphica	*Rivista italiana di Epigraphia*, Milan.
ES	*Epigraphische Studien* (*Beihefte* of *BJ*), Köln-Graz.
FGrHist	*Fragmente der griechischen Historiker*, ed. F. Jacoby.
FHG	*Fragmenta Historicorum Graecorum*, ed. C. Muller, Paris.
FS, I, II, III	*Forschungen in Salona* (ed. R. Egger, W. Gerber, etc.) I (1917), II (1926), III (1939), Vienna.
Germania	*Anzeiger der Römisch-Germanischen Kommission des Deutschen Archaeologischen Instituts*, Berlin.
GGM	*Geographi Graeci Minores*, ed. C. Muller, Paris, 1855–61.
GIDBH	*Godišnjak istoriskog društva Bosne i Hercegovini*, Sarajevo.
GLM	*Geographi Latini Minores*, ed. A. Riese, Heilbronn, 1878.
GMKM	*Glasnik muzeja Kosova i Metohija*, Priština.
Gnomon	*Gnomon: Kritische Zeitschrift für die gesamte klassische Altertumswissenschaft*, Munich.
Godišnjak	*Godišnjak* publ. by *Centar za Balkanološka Ispitivanja* (Akad. nauk i umjetnosti B. i H.) Sarajevo.
GZMBH	*Glasnik Zemaljskog muzeja u Bosni i Hercegovini*, Sarajevo.
GZMS	*Glasnik Zemalskog muzeja u Sarajevo*, Sarajevo. (New Series of *GZMBH* beginning 1945).
Hermes	*Hermes: Zeitschrift für klassische Philologie*, Wiesbaden.
Historia	*Historia: Zeitschrift für alte Geschichte*, Wiesbaden.
HN²	B. V. Head, *Historia Nummorum*, 2nd. ed 1911.
IGR	*Inscriptiones Graecae ad res Romanas pertinentes*, ed. R. Cagnat, Paris, 1901–21.
ILCV	*Inscriptiones Latinae Christianae veteres*, ed. H. Diehl, Berlin, 1925–31.
ILLRP	*Inscriptiones Latinae liberae rei publicae*, ed. A. Degrassi I–II (Bibl. di Studi superiori, vol. 23, 40), Florence, 1963–5.
ILM	*Inscriptions Latins du Maroc*, fasc. 1, ed. L. Chatelain, Paris, 1942.
ILS	*Inscriptiones Latinae Selectae*, ed. H. Dessau, Berlin, 1892–1916.

Inscr. It.	*Inscriptiones Italiae*, Rome, 1936–.
JAK	*Jahrbuch für Altertumskunde*, Vienna.
JDAI	*Jahrbuch des Deutschen Archaeologischen Instituts*, Berlin.
JHS	*Journal of Hellenic Studies*, London.
JÖAI	*Jahreshefte des Oesterreichischen Archaeologischen Instituts*, Vienna.
JRS	*Journal of Roman Studies*, London.
Karthago	*Revue trimestrielle d'Archaeologie Africaine*, Paris.
Klio	*Klio: Beiträge zur alten Geschichte*, Berlin.
LA	*Laureae Aquincenses (memoriae V. Kuzsinszky dicatae)* I–II (*Diss. Pann.* ser 2, 10–11), Budapest, 1938–41.
Latomus	*Latomus: Revue des études Latines*, Brussels.
LF	*Listy Filologické*, Prague.
Libyca	*Bulletin du service des Antiquités* (Arch-Epigr.), Algiers.
Mansi	*Sacrorum conciliorum nova et amplissima collectio*, ed. G. D. Mansi, 1758–98. (repr. Graz, 1960–2).
MGH	*Monumenta Germaniae Historica*, Berlin.
Migne PL	J. P. Migne, *Patrologia Latina*, Paris.
MRR	T. R. S. Broughton, *The Magistrates of the Roman Republic*, New York, 1952–5.
MZK	*Mitteilungen der k. u. k. Zentralkommission zur Erforschung und Erhaltung der Baudenkmäle*, Vienna.
NC	*Numismatic Chronicle, and Journal of the Numismatic Society*, London.
NS	*Notizie degli scavi di antichità*, Rome.
PBSR	*Papers of the British School at Rome*, London.
PIR¹, PIR²	*Prosopographia Imperii Romani*, 1st. ed. v. Rohden, Dessau, and Klebs, 1898; 2nd. ed. Stein, Groag, and Peterson, A–I, 1933–, Berlin.
PP	*Past and Present*, A Journal of Historical Studies, Kendal.
PPS	*Proceedings of the Prehistoric Society*, Cambridge.
Pr. Zeitschrift	*Prähistorische Zeitschrift*, Berlin.
Rev. Arch.	*Revue Archéologique*, Paris.
Rad	*Rad Jugoslavenske Akademije znanosti i umjetnosti*, Zagreb.
Radovi	*Radovi Jugoslavenske Akademije znanosti i umjetnosti u Zadru*, Zadar.
RE	*Realencyclopädie der classischen Altertumswissenschaft*, ed. Pauly, Wissowa, etc., Stuttgart.
RIB	*The Roman Inscriptions of Britain: I Inscriptions on Stone*, ed. R. G. Collingwood and R. P. Wright, Oxford, 1965.
RIC	*The Roman Imperial Coinage*, ed. H. Mattingly and E. A. Sydenham, London.
RIÉB	*Revue internationale des Études Balkaniques*, Thessalonika, Belgrade, etc.
RLiÖ	*Der römische Limes in Oesterreich*, Vienna.
RM	*Rheinisches Museum für Philologie*, Bonn.
Rom. Mitt.	*Mitteilungen des Deutschen Archaeologischen Instituts, Römische Abteilung*, Rome.
RPAA	*Rendiconti della Pontificia Accademia di Archaeologia*, Rome.
RS	*Recherches à Salone*, ed. E. Dyggve, etc., I (1928); II (1933), Copenhagen.
RSA	*Rivista di storia antica e scienze affini*, Messina.
SA	*Studi Aquileiesi (in hon. G. Brusin)*, Aquileia, 1953.

Abbreviations

Šašel	A. Šašel-J. Šašel, *Inscriptiones Latinae quae in Iugoslavia inter annos MCMXL et MCMLX repertae et editae sunt*, Ljubljana, 1963.
SB	*Strena Buliciana-Bulićev Zbornik*, Split/Zagreb, 1924.
SH	*Serta Hoffilleriana (comm. et grat. V. Hoffiller)*, Zagreb, 1940 (= *VHAD* 18–21, 1937–40).
SIG³	*Sylloge Inscriptionum Graecarum*, ed. 3, W. Dittenberger, Leipzig, 1915–20.
Situla	*Situla*, published by Narodni Muzej, Ljubljana.
Sp.	*Srpska (Kraljevska) Akademija Spomenik*, Belgrade.
Die Sprache	*Die Sprache: Zeitschrift für Sprachwissenschaft*, Wiesbaden/Vienna.
Starinar	*Starinar: Organ arheološkog instituta Serb. Akad. Nauk.*, New Series, Belgrade, 1950–.
St. Cl.	*Studii Clasice*, Bucharest.
Syria	*Syria, Revue d'art orientale et d'archéologie*, Paris.
UBHJ	*University of Birmingham Historical Journal*, Birmingham.
Urbs	*Urbs*, publ. by Urbanistički Biro, Split.
VAHD	*Vjesnik za Arheologiju i Historiju Dalmatinsku* (continuation of *BD* after 1927), Split.
VHAD	*Vjesnik Hrvatskog Arheološkog Društva*, Zagreb.
WMBH	*Wissenschaftliche Mitteilungen aus Bosnien und der Hercegovina*, Vienna, 1893–1913.
WS	*Wiener Studien: Zeitschrift für classische Philologie*, Vienna.
WZ	*Westdeutsche Zeitschrift für Geschichte und kunst*, Trier.
ŽA	*Živa Antika*, Skopje.
Zbornik	*Zbornik Instituta za Historijske Nauke u Zadru*, Zadar.
ZfN	*Zeitschrift für Numismatik*, Berlin.
ZRNM	*Zbornik Radova Narodnog Muzeja u Beogradu*, Belgrade.

Bibliography: List of articles and other works cited

ABRAMIĆ, M., with COLNAGO, A., 'Untersuchungen in Norddalmatien', *JÖAI*, 12 (1909), Bb. 13–112.

ABRAMIĆ, M., *S. Donato, Führer durch das k. u. k. Staatsmuseum in S. Donato in Zara*, Vienna, 1912.

'Militaria Burnensia', *SB*, 221–8.

'Grčki natpisi iz Solina', *VAHD*, 47–8 (1924–5), 3–11.

'Speculatores i beneficiarii', *Starinar*, 3 (1933), 57–64.

'O novim miljokasima i rimskim cestama Dalmacije', *VAHD*, 49 (1926–7), 139–55.

'Der Sonnenschirm auf dalmatinischen und norischen Grabreliefs', *JÖAI*, 25 (1929), Bb. 53–62.

'Eines neues Kairos Relief', *JÖAI*, 26 (1930), 1–8.

'Opaske o nekim spomenicima staroga Poetovija', *ČZN*, 28 (1933), 129–44.

'Novi relijef bošantva Kairos', *VAHD*, 50 (1928–9), 1–12.

'Historijiski natpis iz Garduna', *VAHD*, 51 (1930–4), 225–9.

'Novi vojnički spomenici iz Andetriuma', *VAHD*, 51 (1930–4), 230–5.

'Über Darstellungen der Illyrier auf antiken Denkmälern', *ČZN*, 33 (1937), 7–19.

'Zapadna nekropola antikne Salone', *VAHD*, 52 (1935–49), 1–18.

'Tyche (Fortuna) Salonitana', *VAHD*, 52 (1935–49), 279–89.

'Novi votivni relijefi okonjenih božantva iz Dalmacije', *SH*, 297–307.

'Dva historijska natpisa iz antikne Dalmacije', *BIAB*, 16 (1950), 235–40 (*Zbornik Kazarow* I).

'Antike Kopien griechischer Skulpturen in Dalmatien', *Festschrift f. R. Egger*, I (1952), 303–26.

'Felix Aquileia', *SA*, 83–92.

ADCOCK, F. E., 'Caesar's Dictatorship', *CAH* 9 (1932), 691–740.

ALEXANDER, J., 'The Pins of the Jugoslav Early Iron Age', *PPS* 30 (1964), 159–85.

ALFÖLDY, G., 'Die Truppenverteilung der Donaulegionen am Ende des I. Jahrhunderts', *AArch. Hung.*, 11 (1959), 113–41.

'Die Sklaverei in Dalmatien zur Zeit des Prinzipats', *AAnt. Hung.*, 9 (1961), 121–50.

'Die Stellung der Frau in der Gesellschaft der Liburner', *AAnt. Hung.*, 9 (1961), 307–19.

509

'Municipes Tibériens et Claudiens en Liburnie', *Epigraphica*, 23 (1961, publ. 1962), 53–65.

'Σπλαῦνον—Splonum', *AAnt. Hung.*, 10 (1962), 3–12.

'Caesarische und augusteische Kolonien in der Provinz Dalmatien', *AAnt. Hung.* 10 (1962), 357–66.

'Die Gesellschaft der Urbevölkerung Dalmatiens zur Zeit der römischen Eroberung', *Annales Univ. Sc. Budapest, sect. hist.*, 4 (1962), 17–26.

'Die Auxiliartruppen der römischen Provinz Dalmatien', *AArch. Hung.*, 14 (1962), 259–96.

'Das Leben der dalmatinischen Städte in der Zeit des Prinzipates', *ŽA*, 12 (1963), 323–37.

'Cognatio Nantania. Zur Struktur der Sippengesellschaft der Liburner', *AAnt. Hung.*, 11 (1963), 81–7.

'Einheimische Stämme und civitates in Dalmatien unter Augustus', *Klio*, 41 (1963), 187–95.

'Die Namengebung der Urbevölkerung in der römischen Provinz Dalmatia', *BzN*, 15 (1964), 55–104.

'Eine römische Strassenbauinschrift aus Salona', *AArch. Hung.*, 16 (1964), 247–56.

'Des Territoires occupés par les Scordisques', *AAnt. Hung.*, 12 (1964), 107–27.

'Veteranendeduktionen in der Provinz Dalmatien', *Historia*, 13 (1964), 167–79.

Bevölkerung und Gesellschaft der römischen Provinz Dalmatien, Budapest, 1965 (cited as Alföldy, *Bevölkerung*).

'Caetennii', *Eirene*, 4 (1965), 43–53.

'Epigraphica', *Situla*, 8 (1965), 93–112.

'Tilurium, ein römisches Legionslager in Dalmatien', *BJ*, 165 (1965), 105–7.

'Epigraphisches aus Flanona (Plomin)', *Arheološki Vestnik*, 17 (1966), 503–5.

'Zur Italischen Gentilnamenforschung: Obultronii', *BzN*, NF, 1 (1966), 145–52.

'Taurisci und Norici', *Historia*, 15 (1966), 224–41.

Die Legionslegaten der römischen Rheinarmeen (*ES*, 3, *Beiheft 22* of BJ), Köln, 1967.

Die Personennamen im römischen Dalmatien (Beiheft 1 of *BzN*), in the press (cited as Alföldy, *PN*).

'Die Verbreitung militärischer Ziegelstempel in Dalmatien', *ES* 4 (1967), 44–51.

'Senatoren in der römischen Provinz Dalmatia', *ES* in the press.

ARNTZ, H., and ZEISS, H., *Die einheimischen Runendenkmäler des Festlands* (*Gesamtausgabe der Runendenkmäler* I), Leipzig, 1939.

BADIAN, E., 'Notes on Roman policy in Illyria (230–201 B.C.)', *PBSR*, 20 (1952), 72–93 (*SGRH*, 1–33).

BADIAN, E., *FC, Foreign Clientelae*, Oxford, 1958.

BADIAN, E., 'Waiting for Sulla', *JRS*, 52 (1962), 58 ff. (*SGRH*, 206–34).

BADIAN, E., *SGRH, Studies in Greek and Roman History*, Oxford, 1964.

BALLIF, PH., and PATSCH, C., *Strassen, Römische Strassen in Bosnien und der Hercegovina* I, Vienna, 1893.

BALSDON, J. P. V. D., 'Some questions about historical writing in the second century B.C.', *CQ*, 47 (NS 3) (1953), 158 ff.

'Rome and Macedon 205–200 B.C.', *JRS*, 44 (1954), 30 ff.

Review of Badian, *SGRH*, *JRS*, 55 (1965), 229–32.

BARB, A. A., *Burgenländische Heimatsblätter* (1951), 13, p. 216 ff.

BARBIERI, G., *L'Albo senatorio da Settimio Severo a Carino* (193–285)', Rome 1952.

BATOVIĆ, Š., 'Die Eisenzeit auf dem Gebiet des illyrischen Stammes der Liburnen', *AI*, 6 (1965), 55–70.

BAUER, A., 'Zum dalmatisch-pannonischen Krieg 6–9', (1894), 135–48.

'Die Anfänge oesterreichischer Geschichte: griechische Colonien in Dalmatien—Roms erster illyrischer Krieg', *AEM*, 18 (1895), 128–50.

BAUM, M. and SRJEVIĆ, D., 'Prvi rezultati ispitivanja rimske nekropole u Sasama', *Članci*, 3 (1959), 23–54.

'Novi resultati ispitivanja rimske nekropole u Sasama', *Članci*, 4 (1960), 3–31.

BEAUMONT, R. L., 'Greek influence in the Adriatic before the fourth century B.C.', *JHS*, 61 (1936), 159–204.

BENAC, A. (ed.), *Simpozijum o teritorijalnom i hronološkom razgravi-čenju ilira u praistorijsko doba*, (*Centar za Balkanološka Ispitvanja* 1), Sarajevo, 1964.

Simpozijum o ilirima u antičko doba (ibid., 2), Sarajevo, 1967.

BENNDORF, O., 'Ausgrabungen in Ossero', *AEM*, 4 (1886), 73–82.

BERSA, J. V., 'Dalmatinischer Alterthümer', *JÖAI*, 3 (1900), Bb 211–18.

BERSA, J. V., and SMIRIĆ, J., Note on excavations at Zara (Iader), *JÖAI*, 11 (1908), Bb. 6.

BERSA, J. V., 'Ausgrabungen auf dem campo colonna zu Zara', *JAK*, 4 (1910), 194–213.

BERSANETTI, G., 'Gli Auxilia di stanza nella Dalmazia nei secoli I–III', *Bull. dell. mus. dell. imp. Rom.*, 12 (1941), 47–59.

BETZ, A., *Untersuchungen zur Militärgeschichte der römischen Provinz Dalmatien* (*Abhandl. des arch-epigr. Seminares der Univ. Wien*. N.F. heft 3), Vienna, 1938.

'Die Leuchtturm und Flottenstation Salonae', *JÖAI* (*Wiener Jahresh.*), 35 (1943), Bb. 127–38.

'Neues zu den Auxilien in der römischen Provinz Dalmatien', *JÖAI*, 36 (1946), Bb. 67–78.

article 'C. Vettius Sabinianus Iulius Hospes', *RE*, 8A (1958), 1861–7, n. 43.

'Neue Inschriften aus dem römischen Dalmatien', *VAHD*, 56–59/2 (1954–7), II, 82–7.

BIRLEY, A. R., 'The duration of provincial commands under Antoninus Pius', *Coroll. Mem. E. Swoboda* (Graz, 1966), 43–53.

BIRLEY, E., 'A Note on the title Gemina', *JRS*, 18 (1928), 56 ff.

Roman Britain and the Roman Army, Kendal, 1953 (cited *RBRA*).

BOLKAY, ST. J., 'The Purple fish in the old Roman settlements of Hercegovina', *GZMBH*, 39 (1927), 1–2.

BOUSQUET, J., 'Inscription hellénistique de Dalmatie', *BCH* 85 (1961), 589–600.

BRADFORD, J. P., 'A technique for the study of centuriation', *Antiquity*, 21 (1947), 197–204.

Ancient Landscapes, London, 1957 (cited *AL*).

BRANCATI, A., *Augusto e la guerra di Spagna*, Urbino, 1963.

BRUNELLI, V., *Storia della citta di Zara I: dalle origini al MCCCCIX*, I., Venice, 1913.

BRUNŠMID, J., 'Eine griechische Ziegelinschrift aus Sirmium', *Eranos Vindobonensis* 331–3, Vienna, 1893.

Die Inschriften und Münzen der griechischen Städte Dalmatiens (*Abhandl. d. arch-epigr. Seminar Univ. Wien heft* 13 1898), Vienna, 1898 (cited as Brunšmid).

'Stari natpisi iz okoline Pozareveca u Srbiji', *VHAD*, 5 (1901), 1–18.

Kamen spomenici Hrvatskog narodnoga muzeja u Zagrebu, Zagreb, 1904–11 (cited as *K. Sp.*).

BRUNT, P. A., 'The Roman Mob', *PP*, 35 (1966), 3–27.

BUDROVICH, A., 'Per la lettura di alcune importanti inscrizioni Salonitane', *VAHD*, 56–59/2 (1954–7), II, 91–3.

BULIĆ, FR., *Inscriptiones quae in c.r. Museo Archaeologico Salonitano Spalati*, Split, 1886.

'Pagjine (municipium Pazinatium)', *BD*, 14 (1891), 163.

'Salvia in Dalmatia', *JÖAI*, 2 (1899), Bb. 109–12.

'Nomi e marche di fabbrica su tegoli e mattoni acquistati dall' c.r. museo in Spalato', *BD*, 26 (1903), 198–9; 27 (1904), 26, 155–6; 28 (1905), 159–60.

'Escavi nella necropoli antica pagana di Salona della Hortus Metrodori negli anni 1909 e 1910', *BD*, 33 (1910), 3–66, 130–5.

Kronotaksa solinskih biskupa, supplement to *BD*, 35 (1912).

Povodom Pedesetgodišnjice Jubileja, Split, 1931.

'Solentia (Solta, Šolta)—trovamenti antichi ed inscrizioni inedite', *VAHD*, 43 (1920), 105–16.

For the numerous articles of Bulić in *BD*, mostly publishing new inscriptions from Salona and its vicinity, see *Bibliografija Rasprava i Članaka*, IV, Historia 1, 64–83, with 547 entries, Zagreb, 1965.

BURY, J. B., *History of the Later Roman Empire from the death of Theodosius I to the death of Justinian*, vols. 1–2, London, 1923 (cited Bury *LRE*).

BÜTTLER, W., 'Ausgrabung eines prähistorischen Grabhügels bei Ervenik bei Kistanje', *VAHD*, 50 (1928–9), 354–64.

'Burgwalle in Norddalmatien', 21 *BerRGK* (1931), 183–98.

CAGIANO DE AZEVEDO, M., 'Aenona e il suo *Capitolium*', *RPAA*, 22 (1948), 193–226.

CALDERINI, A., *Aquileia Romana, ricerche di storia e di epigrafia*, Milan, 1930.

CALLANDER, M. H., *Roman Amphorae*, Oxford, 1965.

CARDIASCIA, G., 'L'apparition dans le droit des classes d' "honestiores" et d' "humiliores" ', *Rev. hist. de droit français et étranger*, 28 (1950), 305 ff. and 461 ff.

CARY, M., 'The Greeks and ancient trade with the Atlantic', *JHS*, 44 (1924), 166–79.

CASSON, S., *Macedonia, Thrace and Illyria*, Oxford, 1926.

CECI, E., formerly CEČIĆ, M.,
   I Monumenti pagani di Salona, Milan, 1962.
   I Monumenti christiani di Salona, Milan, 1963.

CEKA, H., 'L'activité monetaire dans l'Illyrie meridionale', *Bulletin i Universität Shtetëror i Tiranës—seria Shkencat Shoqerore*, 1 (1957), 17–34 (summ. in *Bibl. Class. Orient.* 6 (1961), 4 ff.).

ČERŠKOV, E., and POPOVIĆ, LJ., 'Arheološko konservatorski radovi', *GMKM* 1 (1956), 319–27.

ČERŠKOV, E., 'Oko problema komunicacija i polozaja naselja na Kosovu i Metohiji u rimskom periodu', *GMKM*, 2 (1957), 65–86.

CHARLESWORTH, M. P., 'Some fragments of the propaganda of Mark Antony', *CQ*, 27 (1933), 173–7.

CHEESMAN, G. L., *The Auxilia of the Roman imperial Army*, Oxford, 1914.

CHILVER, G. E. F., *CG, Cisalpine Gaul: Social and Economic History from 49 B.C. to the death of Trajan*, Oxford, 1941.

CICHORIUS, C., *Die Reliefs der Traianssäule*, vols 1–2, Berlin, 1896–1900.

CICHORIUS, C., *Römische Studien*, Leipzig, 1922 (cited *RSt*).

COLLART, P., 'Inscriptions de Philippes', *BCH*, 56 (1932), 192–231.

COLNAGO, A., and KEIL, J., 'Archaeologische Untersuchungen in Norddalmatien', *JÖAI*, 8 (1905), Bb 31–60.

COLNAGO, A., 'Obrovazzo', *JÖAI*, 11 (1908), Bb. 6–7.

'Untersuchungen in Norddalmatien', *JÖAI*, 18 (1915), Bb. 175–88.

CONS, H., *La province romaine de Dalmatie*, Paris, 1882.

ČOVIĆ, B., 'Ilirska nekropola u Čarakovu (Prijedor)', *GZMS*, 11 (1956), 187–204.

ČREMOŠNIK, G., and SERGEJEVSKI, D., 'Gotisches und Römisches aus Bréza bei Sarajevo,' *Novitates musei Sarajevoensis*, (1930).

ČREMOŠNIK, I., 'Nesto o antičkim naseljima u okolini Konjica', *GZMS*, 9 (1954), 179–88.

'Izvjestaj o iskopavanjima na Crkvini u Lisičićima kod Konjica', *GZMS*, 9 (1954), 211–26.

'Reljef Silvana i Nimfa iz Založja (Bihać)', *GZMS*, 11 (1956), 111–26.

'Crkvina u Golubiću', *GZMS*, 11 (1956), 127–36.

'Rimski ostači na gradini Zečovi', *GZMS*, 11 (1956), 137–46.

'Arheološka istrazivanja u Brodcu', *Članci*, 1 (1957), 127–49.

'Dalja istrazivanja na rimskom naselju u Lisičićima', *GZMS*, 12 (1957), 143–62.

'Rimski spomenici iz okoline Bihaća', *GZMS*, 12 (1957), 163–72.

'Narodna simbolika na rimskim spomenicima u našim krajevima', *GZMS*, 12 (1957), 217–34.

'Rimska vila sa slavenskim naseljem u Tutnjevcu', *Članci*, 2 (1958), 37–53.

'Arheološka istrazivanja u okolici Bihaća', *GZMS*, 13 (1958), 117–36.

'Panonska nošnja na rimskim spomenicima u Bosni i u drugim našim krajevima', *GZMS*, 13 (1958), 147–51.

'A la frontière des civilisation romaines et grecques', *Tkalčićev Zbornik*, 2 (1958), 7 ff.

'Spomenik sa japodskim konjanicima iz Zalažja kod Bihaća', *GZMS*, 14 (1959), 103–11.

'Iskopavanje u Ljušini 1957 godine', *GZMS*, 14 (1959), 137–47.

'Totenmahldarstellungen auf römischen Denkmälern in Jugoslawien', *JÖAI*, 44 (1959), 207–30.

'Nalazi bojene keramike u BiH u rimsko doba', *GZMS*, 15–16 (1961), 189–202.

'Nalaz terre sigillate iz Višica (Čapljina)', *GZMS*, 17 (1962), 115–40.

'Nošna na rimskim spomenicima u Bosni i Hercegovini,' *GZMS*, 18 (1963), 103–25.

'Die einheimische Tracht Norikums, Pannoniens und Illyricums und Ihre Vorbilder,' *Latomus*, 23 (1964), 760–74.

CUNTZ, O., 'Legionäre des Antonius und Augustus aus dem Orient', *JÖAI*, 25 (1929), 70 ff.

ČURČIĆ, V., 'Ein Flachgräberfeld der Iapoden in Ribić bei Bihać', *WMBH*, 7 (1900), 1–32.

'Reisenotizen aus dem Bezirke Petrovac', *WMBH*, 10 (1907), 368–75.

'Der Heraklesknoten (zur Chronologie des praehistorischen Silberfundes aus Gorica, Bez. Ljubuški)', *WMBH*, 11 (1909), 75–81.

DAICOVICIU, C., 'Gli Italici nella provincia Dalmazia', *Ephemeris Dacoromana*, 5 (1932), 57 ff.

'Les "castella Dalmatarum" de Dacie', *Dacia*, 2 (1958), 259–66.

DAVIES, O., *RME, Roman Mines in Europe*, Oxford, 1935.

DEGMEDŽIĆ, I., 'Arheološka istrazivanja u Senju', *VAHD*, 53 (1950–1), 251–62.

DEGRASSI, A., 'Minerva Flanatica', *Riv. di fil. e d'istruz. class.*, NS, 10 (1932), 87–91; *SVA*, 875–9.

'Fianona—il sito della citta antica e recenti scoperte', *NS*, 1934 3–9; *SVA*, 895–901.

'Albona—inscrizioni romane', *NS*, 1934, 113–6; *SVA* 907–9.

'I *Magistri Mercuriales* di Lucca e la *Dea Anzotica* di Aenona', *Athenaeum*, 15 (1937), 284–8; *SVA*, 495–9.

'Il monumento riminese di Q. Ovius Fregellanus', *Athenaeum*, 19 (1941), 133–40; *SVA*, 527–34.

Bibliography

'Le inscrizione di Tarsatica, origine e sito del municipio romano', *Epigraphica*, 4 (1942), 191–203; *SVA*, 931–42.

'Quattuorviri in colonie romane e in municipi retti da duoviri', *Memorie dell'Accademie nazionale dei Lincei, class. di scienze morali e storiche*, ser viii, vol. 2, 1949 (publ. 1950), 281–344; *SVA*, 99–177 (cited as Degrassi, *Quattuorviri*).

I Fasti consolari dell'Impero romano, Rome, 1952 (cited as Degrassi *FC*).

Il confine nord-orientale dell'Italia romana (Diss. Bernenses, 1, 6), Berne, 1954.

'I porti romani dell'Istria', *AMSI*, 5 (1957), 24–81; *SVA*, 821–70.

DEGRASSI, A., *SVA, Scritti vari di Antichità*, vols 1–2, Rome, 1962.

DELL, H. J., 'The origin and nature of Illyrian piracy', *Historia*, 16 (1967), 344–58.

DETLEFSON, D., *Die Anordnung der geographischen Bücher des Plinius und ihre Quellen (Quellen u. Forschungen zur alten Geschichte und Geographie, Heft 18)*, Berlin, 1909.

DEVOKO, A., and ZDRAVKOVIĆ, I., 'A propos d'une pierre avec inscription dans les ruines d'une église à Drenova', *Starinar*, NS, 1 (1950), 183–4.

DOBIÁŠ, J., *Studie k Appianově knize Illyrské*, Prague, 1930.

DOBÓ, A., *Publicum Portorium Illyrici* (Diss. Pann., 2, 16), Budapest, 1940.

DOMASZEWSKI, A. V., 'Die Inschrift eines stationarius', *Röm. Mitt.*, 17 (1902), 330–5.

'Die Beneficiarierposten und die römischen Strassennetze', *WZ*, 21 (1902), 158–211.

DOMASZEWSKI, A. V., and DOBSON, B., *Die Rangordnung des römischen Heeres* (BJ, 118 (1908), 1–270), 2nd ed. with additional notes and commentary, BJ, Beiheft, Köln, 1967.

DRAGEVIĆ, T., 'Römische Hausruine in Novi Seher, Bez. Žepče', *WMBH*, 6 (1899), 531.

DUDLEY, D. R., and WEBSTER, G., *The Rebellion of Boudicca*, London, 1962.

DUJMOVIĆ, F., 'Neokolico novih rimski natpisa iz okolice Šibenika', *VAHD*, 56–59/2 (1954–7), II, 123–6.

DUVAL, P. M., *Paris antique des origines au troisième siècle*, Paris, 1961.

DYGGVE, E., 'Forum de Salone', *Rev. Arch.*, ser. 6, vol. 1 (1933), 41–57.

'Ein Mausoleum des frühen IV. Jahrhunderts in Salona', *SH*, 257–61.

'L'influence des Goths à Salone', *Byzantion*, 19 (1949), 73–7.

DYGGVE, E., *HSC, History of Salonitan Christianity*, Oslo, 1951.

'Mogorilo', *Akte IX int. Byzant. Kong.* (1958), 131–7, Munich.

EGGER, R., 'Ein neuer Statthalter der Provinz Dalmatia', *JÖAI*, 19/20 (1919), Bb. 293–322.

EICHLER, F., 'Ein griechischer Marmorkopf aus Arbe', *JÖAI*, 25 (1929), 109–17.

ENSSLIN, W., article 'Marcellinus', *RE*, 14 (1928), 1446–8, n. 25.

EVANS, A., 'On some recent discoveries of Illyrian coins', *NC*, 20 (1880), 269–302.

'Antiquarian Researches in Illyricum', I–II *Archaeologia*, 48 (1884), 1–105; III–IV *Archaeologia*, 49 (1885), 1–167.

FALCON-BARKER, E., *1600 Years under The Sea*, London, 1961.

FARLATI, D., *IS, Illyricum Sacrum*, Venice, 1751.

FERLUGA, J., 'L'Administration Byzantine en Dalmatie', *Mem. Acad. Serb. Inst. Ét. Byz.*, 6, Belgrade, 1957.

FIALA, F., 'Die Ergebnisse der Untersuchung prähistorischer Grabhügel auf dem Glasinac im Jahre 1893', *WMBH*, 3 (1895), 1–38.

'Untersuchungen römischer Fundorte in der Hercegovina', *WMBH*, 3 (1895), 257 ff.

'Archaeologische Notizen: 1 Ein prähistorisches Kupfergerät, 2 Römische Funde aus Trnovo, 3 Römische Grablampen aus Sovići, 4 Römischer Grabfund aus Ljubuški,

5 Rotimlja, 6 Eine neue römische Wegroute, 7 Befestigtes römisches Lager in Struge', *WMBH* 3 (1895), 518–22.

'Kleine Mitteilungen: I Funde aus Dolnji-Unac, Römische Gräber in Dolnji-Vrtoče, II, 3 Römerbad bei Laktaši; III, Römische Funde: 1 Kupres, 2 Busovača', *WMBH*, 4 (1896), 170 ff.

'Ausgrabungen auf dem Debelo brdo bei Sarajevo im J. 1894', *WMBH*, 5 (1897), 124–30.

'Beiträge zur römischen Archaeologie der Hercegovina', *WMBH*, 5 (1897), 163–72.

'Römische Brandgräber bei Rogatica', *WMBH*, 5 (1897), 259–62.

FINE, J. V. A., 'Macedon, Illyria, and Rome 220–19', *JRS*, 26 (1936), 24 ff.

FISKOVIĆ, C., 'Arheološke biljeske s Pelješća', *VAHD*, 55 (1953), 217–37.

FLUSS, M., article 'Lissos', *RE*, 13 (1926), 731–36.

article 'Taulantioi', *RE*, 4A (1932), 2529.

FORNI, G., *Il Reclutamento delle legioni da Augusto a Diocleziano*, Milan-Rome, 1953.

FORTIS, A., *Viaggio in Dalmatia*, Venice, 1774.

FRÉZOULS, E., 'Inscription de Cyrrhus relative à Q. Marcius Turbo', *Syria*, 30 (1953), 247–78.

FRIEDLÄNDER, L., *Roman Life and Manners under the Early Empire*, English trans., London, 1907, repr. 1965.

GABRIČEVIĆ, B., 'Dva priloga poznavanju urbaništickog rozvoja antikne Salone', *VAHD*, 53 (1950–1), 155–62.

'Onekim mitričkim natpisma Sarajevskog muzeja', *GZMS*, 8 (1953), 141–4.

'Dvije ilirske opčine s područja Vrlike', *VAHD*, 55 (1953), 103–19.

'Iconographie de Mithra tauroctone dans la province romaine de Dalmatie', *AI*, 1 (1954), 37–52.

'Sarajevski medaljion s prikazom tračkog konjanika', *GZMS*, 9 (1954), 41–6.

'Une inscription inédite provenant de Senia', *AI*, 2 (1956), 53–6.

'Antička Issa—contribution historico-archaeologique au plan de regulation urbanistiques de la ville de Vis', *Urbs*, 2 (1958), 105–26.

'Problem severozahodnega područja Ilirov', A. Benac (ed.), *Simpozijum*, 215–29 (German, 230–52).

GABROVEC, S., 'Das Problem des nordwestillyrischen Gebietes', *Simpozijum*, 1 (ed. Benac), 215–52.

GAEBLER, H., 'Zur Münzkunde Makedoniens III: Makedonien im Aufstand unter Andriskos, Makedonien als römische Provinz', *ZfN*, 23 (1901), 141–89.

GILLAM, J. P., 'Also, along the line of the Wall', *CW*², 49 (1949), 38–58.

GNIRS, A., 'Grabungen und antike Denkmäler in Pola', *JÖAI*, 15 (1912), Bb. 239–72.

GRAF, A., *Übersicht der antiken Geographie von Pannonien* (*Diss. Pann.*, ser 1, fasc. 5), Budapest, 1936.

GRBIĆ, M., *Arheološki spomenici i nalazista u Srbiji* I: *Serbia occidentalis* (*Mon. et Stat. Rom. en Serb.*), Belgrade, 1952.

GRGIN, A., 'Tri nadgrobna spomenika iz Potravlaja u Dalmaciju', *SB*, 233–5.

'Novi rimski milijokaz iz donjokastelanskog polja', *VAHD*, 50 (1928–9), 22–5.

GROAG, E., 'Prospographische Beiträge: IV A. Ducenius Geminus', *JÖAI*, 19/20 (1919), Bb. 323–8.

article 'L. Iulius Ursus Servianus', *RE*, 10 (1919), 882–91, n. 538.

article 'Cn. Sertorius Brocchus etc.', *RE*, 2A (1923), 1753, n. 4.

article 'P. Sulpicius Quirinius', *RE*, 4A (1931), 827 ff.

article 'L. Tarius Rufus', *RE*, 4A (1932), 2320–3, n. 3.

GROSSE, R., article 'lembos', *RE*, 12 (1925), 1895.

article 'liburna', *RE*, 13 (1927), 143–5.

GUNJAČA, S., 'Nov privos ubikacije Tiluriuma', *VAHD*, 52 (1935–49), 50–2.

HAMMOND, N. G. L., 'The Kingdoms in Illyria *circa* 400–167 B.C.', *ABSA*, 61 (1966), 239–53.

HIRSCHFELD, O., and SCHNEIDER, R., 'Berichte über eine Reise in Dalmatien', *AEM*, 9 (1885), 1–84.

HIRSCHFELD, O., *Die kaiserlichen Verwaltungsbeamten bis auf Diocletian*, Berlin, 1905.

Kleine Schriften, Berlin, 1913.

HÖRMANN, C., 'Eine römische Siegelringplatte aus Bergold', *WMBH*, 1 (1892), 330.

'Inschrift aus Brekavica', *WMBH*, 1 (1893), 332.

'Erwebung einer numismatischen Sammlung für das Bosn-Herzeg. Landesmuseum', *WMBH*, 1 (1893), 338–40.

HÖRMANN, C., and RADIMSKY, W., 'Die Alterthümer von Osanić bei Stolac', *WMBH*, 2 (1894), 35–44.

HOERNES, M., 'Vorrömischer Grabstein von Jezerine', *WMBH*, 3 (1895), 516.

'Bruchstück eines zweiten vorrömischen Grabsteine aus der Gegend von Bihać', *WMBH*, 5 (1897), 337.

HOFFER, A., 'Fundorte römischer Alterthümer in Bezirke Travnik', *WMBH*, 5 (1897), 242–58.

HOFMANN, H., *Römische Militärgrabsteine der Donauländer (Sonderschr. d. Oest. Arch. Inst. 5)*, Vienna, 1905.

HOLDER, A., *Alt-celtischer Sprachschatz*, vols. 1–3, Leipzig, 1896–1914.

HOLLEAUX, M., *Rome, la Grèce et les monarchies hellénistiques au IIIe siècle avant J C (273–205)'*, Paris, 1921.

'The Romans in Illyria', *CAH*, 7 (1928), 822–57.

ILAKOVAC, B., 'Rimska metalna svjetiljka', *Diadora*, 1 (1959), 141–6.

'Ostaci antičke zgrade u Zadru', *VAHD*, 60 (1958), 43–58.

'Prehistorijski nalazi u Zadru', *Zbornik*, 2 (1958), 1–11.

'Novi nalaz ostalaka rimskih zgrada u Zadru 1960 god.', *Diadora*, 2 (1960–1) 271–82.

'Rimska zgrada u Krmčini kod Zadra', *Diadora*, 3 (1965), 213–17.

IPPEN, TH., 'Prähistorische und römische Fundstätten in der Umgebung von Scutari', *WMBH*, 8 (1902), 207–11.

Skutari und die nordalbanische Küstebene (Zur Kunde der Balkan-halbinsel I, Reise und Beobachtungen heft 5), Sarajevo, 1907.

IVOVIĆ, J., 'Nalazi starog rimskog novca u okolini Nikšica i na teritoriji Nikšičkog sreza', *GZMS*, 10 (1955), 199–209.

JADRIJEVIĆ, O., 'Novi rimski natpis s grada Sinja', *VAHD*, 51 (1930–4), 157–9.

JAFFÉ, PH., and POTTHAST, A., *Regesta Pontificum Romanorum* (2nd ed. cur. Loewenfeld, Kaltenbrunner), Leipzig, 1881.

JAGENTEUFEL, A., *Die Statthalter der römischen Provinz Dalmatia von Augustus bis Diocletian (Schriften der Balkankommission, Antiquar. Abt. 12)*, Vienna, 1958.

JARRETT, M. G., 'The African contribution to the Imperial Equestrian Service', *Historia*, 12 (1963), 209–26.

JELIĆ, L., 'Das älteste kartographische Denkmal über die römische Provinz Dalmatien', *WMBH*, 7 (1900), 167–214.

'Die Halbinsel Pelješac', *JAK*, 6 (1913–18), 227–35.

JIREČEK, C., *Die Romanen in den Städten Dalmatiens während des Mittelalters (Denkschr. Akad. Wien* 48/3, 49/1. 2.), Vienna, 1901–4.

JONES, A. H. M., *CERP, Cities of the Eastern Roman Provinces*, Oxford, 1937.

JONES, A. H. M., *GC, The Greek City*, Oxford, 1940.

'The Roman Civil Service (clerical and sub-clerical grades)', *JRS*, 39 (1949), 38–55; *SRGL*, 153–75.

'The Date and Value of the Verona List', *JRS*, 44 (1954), 21–9.

JONES, A. H. M., *SRGL, Studies in Roman Government and Law*, Oxford, 1960.

JONES, A. H. M., *LRE, The Later Roman Empire* (284–602), Oxford, 1964.

JOSIFOVIĆ, S., 'Der illyrische Feldzug Octavians', *ŽA*, 6 (1956), 138–62.

KÄHLER, H., 'Die *porta Caesarea* in Salona', *VAHD*, 51 (1930–4), 1–51.

KAHRSTEDT, U., 'Studien zur politischen und Wirtschaftsgeschichte der Ost- und Zentralalpen vor Augustus', *Nachrichten von der Gesellschaft der Wissenschaften Göttingen, phil.-hist. Klasse*, 1927, 1 ff.

'Zwei Erdlager in Jugoslawien', *SH*, 183–8.

KARAMAN, LJ., 'O počecima srednjevjekovnog Splita do godine 800', *SH*, 419–36.

KATAČIĆ, R., 'Die illyrischen Personennamen in ihrem sudöstlichen Verbreitungsgebiet', *ŽA*, 12 (1962), 95–120.

'Das mitteldalmatinische Namengebiete', *ŽA*, 12 (1963), 255–92.

'Ilyrii proprii dicti', *ŽA*, 13 (1963), 87–97.

'Namengebiete im römischen Dalmatien', *Die Sprache*, 10 (1964), 23–33.

'Die neuesten Forschungen über die einheimische Sprachschicht in den illyrischen Provinzen', *Simpozijum*, 1 (ed. Benac), 9–58.

'Zur Frage der keltischen und pannonischen Namengebiete im römischen Dalmatien', *Godišnjak*, 1 (Sarajevo), 1965, 53–76.

KELLNER, J., 'Römische Ruine bei Laktaši', *WMBH*, 1 (1893), 254–61.

'Römische Baureste in Ilidže bei Sarajevo', *WMBH* 5 (1897), 131–62.

KENT, J. P. C., 'Julius Nepos and the fall of the Western Empire', *Coroll. Mem. E. Swoboda*, 146–50.

KENYON, K., 'The Roman Theatre at Verulamium', *Archaeologia*, 84 (1935), 213–61.

KOERSTERMANN, E., 'Der pannonisch-dalmatische Krieg 6–9 n. Chr.', *Hermes*, 81 (1953), 345–78.

KOVAČEVIĆ, C., and MIRKOVIĆ, P., 'Die Ausgrabung auf dem Jezerinafelde unterhalb Pritoka bei Bihać', *WMBH*, 1 (1893), 189–94.

KRAFT, K., *Rekrutierung, Zur Rekrutierung der Alen und Kohorten an Rhein und Donau (Diss. Bernenses ser.* 1, fasc. 3), Berne, 1951.

KRAHE, H., *Lexicon altillyrischer Personennamen*, Heidelberg, 1929.

Die Sprache der alten Illyrier I: Die Quellen, Wiesbaden, 1955.

KROMAYER, J., 'Kleine Forschungen zur Geschichte des zweiten Triumvirats. V Die illyrischen Feldzüge Octavians', *Hermes*, 33 (1898), 1 ff.

KUBITSCHEK, W., *De Romanorum tribuum origine ac propagatione*, Vienna, 1882.

KUBITSCHEK, W., *IRTD, Imperium Romanum tributim descriptione*, Vienna, 1889.

'Salonitanische Inschriften', *JÖAI*, 6 (1903), Bb. 81–4.

'Gott Medauros', *MZK*, 1903, 170–3.

'Eine Sarkophag aus Doclea', *JÖAI*, 9 (1906), Bb. 87.

'Eine Inschrift aus Salona', *JAK*, 1 (1907), 78–84.

'Dalmatinische Notizen', *SB*, 209–19.

KUNKEL, W., *Herkunft und soziale Stellung der römischen Juristen*, 1952.

KURZ, K., 'Ministri ad Tritones', *St. Cl.*, 4 (1962), 301–13.

de LAET, S. J., *Portorium. Etude sur l'organisation douanière chez les Romains*, Bruges, 1949.

LAMBRECHTS, P., 'Over de Onslerfelijhkeigedachte bij de Romeinen: het Grafmonument van Q. Aeronius le Split', *Gents Bijdragen tot de Kuntsgeschiednis en de Oudheidkunde*, 17 (1957–8), 33–55.

LENSCHAU, T., article 'Pleuratos', *RE*, 21 (1951), 237 ff.

LESCHI, L., 'Autour de l'amphitheatre de Lambèse', *Libyca*, 2 (1954), 171–86.

LIEB, H., 'Der Praeses aus Sbeitla', in W. Reidinger, *Die Statthalter des ungeteilten Pannonien und Oberpannonien von Augustus bis Diokletian*, 239–47, Bonn, 1956.

LIEBL, H., 'Epigraphisches aus Dalmatien', *JÖAI*, 5 (1902), Bb. 1–8.

'Zum Sanitätswesen im römischen Heere', *Wiener Studien*, 24 (1902), 381–5.

'Inschriften aus Dalmatien', *JÖAI*, 6 (1903), Bb. 85–6.

LIEBL, H., and WILBERG, W., 'Ausgrabung in Asseria', *JÖAI*, 11 (1908), Bb. 17–88.

LISIČAR, P., 'Bilješke o rimskim natpisima s otoka Korčule', *VAHD*, 60 (1958), 125–9.

'Rimski strijili iz ninskih i zadarskih grobova', *Diadora*, 2 (1960–1), 215–22.

MADVIG, J. N., *Emendationes Livianae*, Hauniae, 1860.

MANDIĆ, M., 'Gradine, gromile i druge starine u okolici Livna', *GZMBH*, 47 (1935), 7–16.

MANN, J. C., 'The raising of new legions during the Principate', *Hermes*, 91 (1963), 483–9.

'The role of the frontier zones in Army recruitment', *Quint. Cong. Int. Limitis Rom. Stud.* (*ARR*, 3, 1963, 145–50), Zagreb, 1963.

MARCHESETTI, C., *I castellieri preistorici di Trieste e della regione Giulia*, Trieste, 1903.

MARASOVIĆ, T., (ed.) and others, *Istrazivanje i uredjenje Diokletijanove palače* (*Urbs*, 4 (1961–2)).

MARIĆ, R., 'Municeps municipii', *ŽA*, 8 (1958), 332.

MARIĆ, Z., 'Donja Dolina', *GZMS*, 19 (1964), 5–128.

'Problem sjevernog graničkog područja Ilira', A. Benac (ed.), *Simposijum*, 177–92 (french summ., 192–213).

MARINI, G., *I papiri diplomatici*, Rome, 1805.

MAROVIĆ, I., 'Novi i neobjavljeni nalazi iz Narone', *VAHD*, 54 (1952), 153–73.

MAY, J. M. F., 'Macedonia and Illyria (217–167 B.C.)', *JRS*, 36 (1946), 48 ff.

MAYER, A., 'Novonadjeni natpisi u Doklji i okonje', *VAHD*, 50 (1928–9), 65–72.

'Studije iz toponomastike rimske provincije Dalmacije', *VAHD*, 50 (1928–9), 85–119.

'Doprinosi poznavanju rimskih cesta u Dalmaciji', *VAHD*, 51 (1930–4), 125–50.

'De Iapodibus, populo illyrico Celtis commixto', *SH*, 189–99.

MAYER, A., *Sprache.*, *Die Sprache der alten Illyrier* (Oesterr. *Akad. Schriften der Balkankommission, phil. hist. Klasse*, lingu. Abt. 15) I: Einleitung. Wörterbuch der illyrischen Sprachreste, Vienna, 1957.

MEIGGS, R., *Roman Ostia*, Oxford, 1960.

MILLAR, F., *A Study of Cassius Dio*, Oxford, 1964.

MILTNER, F., 'Augustus' Kampf um der Donaugrenze', *Klio*, 30 (1937), 200–26.

MIROSAVLJEVIĆ, V., 'Central and Peripheral Finding-sites of Material Culture on the territory, of the Iapodians', *AI*, 3 (1959), 47–53.

MISILO, K., 'Rimski spomenici iz Bosne', *GZMBH*, 48 (1936), 15–26.

MIŠURA, A. P., *Colonia Romana Aequum Claudium*, Graz-Vienna, 1921.

MÓCSY, A., 'Die Territorium legionis und die Canabae in Pannonien', *AAnt. Hung.*, 5 (1953), 179–200.

'Zur Geschichte der peregrinen Gemeinden in Pannonien', *Historia*, 6 (1957), 488–98.

Die Bevölkerung von Pannonien bis zu den Markomannenkriegen, Budapest, 1939.

article 'Pannonia', *RE*, supp. 9 (1962), 515–776.

MOHOROVIČIĆ, A., 'Apsyrtides-Apsoros', *Carnuntina*, 3 (1956), 95–9.

MOMMSEN, TH., *Römisches Strafrecht*, Leipzig, 1899.

MORRIS, J., 'Changing fashions in Roman nomenclature in the Early Empire', *LF*, 86 (1963), 34–46.

MÜLLER, C., (ed.) *Claudii Ptolemaei Geographia*, Paris, 1883.

NESSELHAUF, H., 'Publicum portorii Illyrici utriusque et ripae Thraciae', *Epigraphica*, 1 (1939), 331–8.

'Die Legionen Moesiens unter Claudius und Nero', *LA*, 2 (1941), 40–6.

NIKOLANCI, M., 'Pharos—rimljani i Polibije', *VAHD*, 56–59/2 (1954–7), 2, 52–9.

'Contacts gréco-illyriens sur la cote est de l'Adriatique', *AI*, 5 (1964), 49–60.

NOLL, R., *Griechischer und lateinische Inschriften der Wiener Antikensammlung*, Vienna, 1962.

NOVAK, G., *Topografia i ethnografia rimskih provincije Dalmacije*, supp. 2 *BD*, 38 (1915), publ. 1918, Zagreb.

'Dimos i Herakleia', *SB*, 655–8.

'Die kolonisatorische Tätigkeit Dionysios des Älteren in der Adria', *SH*, 111–28.

'Isejska i rimska Salona', *Rad*, 270 (1949), 67–92.

'Das griechische Element in Dalmatiens Städten', *Carnuntina*, 3 (1956), 117 ff.

Vis, vol. I, Zagreb, 1961.

'Quaestiones Epidauritanae', *Rad*, 339 (1965), 97–121 (serb.), 123–40 (German).

NOWOTNY, E., 'Ein römisches Mysterienrelief im bosnisch-hercegovinischen Landesmuseum', *WMBH*, 4 (1896), 296–302.

OELMANN, F., 'Ein gallorömischer Bauernhof bei Mayen', *BJ*, 133 (1928), 51–152.

'Zum Verständnis des sogennanten liburnischen Grabcippus,' *VAHD*, 56–59/2 (1954–7), II, 48–57.

OOST, S. I., *Roman policy in Epirus and Acarnania in the age of the Roman conquest of Greece* (Arnold Foundation Studies, 4, *NS*), Dallas, 1954.

PAIS, H., *supp.*, *supplementum ad CIL V fasc.* 1, Rome, 1884.

PANCIERA, S., 'Liburna–Rassegna delle fonti, caratteristiche della nave, accezioni del termine', *Epigraphica*, 18 (1956), 130–56.

Vita economica di Aquileia in età romana, Aquileia, 1957.

PAPAZOGLU, F., 'Le municipium Maluesatium et son territoire', *ŽA*, 7 (1957), 114–22.

'Sur le territoire des Ardiéens', *Receuils de travaux de la Faculté de philosophie Beograd* t. 7, 1 (1963), 71–86.

'Les origines et la destinée de l'Etat Illyrien: Illyrii poprii dicti', *Historia*, 14 (1965), 143–79.

PARKER, H. M. D., *RL*, *The Roman Legions*, Oxford, 1928.

PAROVIĆ-PEŠIKAN, M., 'Les Illyriens au contact des Grecs', *AI*, 5 (1964), 61–81.

PAŠALIĆ, E., 'Novi prilozi poznavanju rimski cesta u Bosni i Hercegovini', *GZMS*, 8 (1953), 277–87.

'O antičkom rudarstvu u Bosni i Hercegovini', *GZMS*, 9 (1954), 47–75.

'Tragom rimske ceste od Mliništa preko Podrašnice do Banjaluke', *GZMS*, 9 (1954), 307–16.

'Quaestiones de bello Delmatico Pannonicoque 6–9', *GIDBH*, 8 (1956), 245–300.

'O hodološkim pitanjima u izucavanju antičke istorije', *GIDBH*, 9 (1957), 139–75.

'Römische Strassen in Bosnien und der Hercegovina', *AI*, 3 (1959), 61–73.

'Rimsko naselje u Ilidže kod Sarajevo', *GZMS*, 14 (1959), 113–36.

'Pogljedi na ekonomiky i initraznjosti rimske provincie Dalmacije', *GIDBH*, 10 (1959), 297–331.

PAŠALIĆ, E., *Naselja Antička naselja i komunikacije u Bosni i Hercegovini*, Sarajevo, 1960.

'Production of Roman mines and iron works in West Bosnia', *AI*, 6 (1965), 81–8.

PAŠKVALIN, V., 'Nalaz sa gradine Hrvačani kod Banjaluke', *GZMS*, 12 (1957), 259–62.

'Tri rimski natpisa sa područja Bosni i Hercegovini', *GZMS*, 13 (1958), 153–57.

'Bronzana votivna ruka iz Sasa', *GZMS*, 15–16 (1961), 203–9.

'Kultovi u antičko doba na području Bosne i Hercegovini', *GZMS*, 18 (1963), 127–53.

PASSERINI, A., *Le coorti praetorie*, Rome, 1939.

PATSCH, C., 'Eine revidierte Inschrift aus Humac', *WMBH*, 1 (1893), 330–2.

'Zwei römische Ziegelbruchstücke: IIII F.f. aus Ljubuški, XIV G.M.V. aus Velika Kladuša', *WMBH*, 3 (1894), 526.

'Die griechischen Münzen des bosnisches-hercegovinisches Landesmuseums', *WMBH*, 5 (1896), 113–28.

Arch.-epigr. Untersuchungen zur Geschichte der römischen Provinz Dalmatien I: '1. Römische Alterthümer aus Goražde', '2. Römisches aus dem Ramathale', '3 Neue und revidierte Inschriften', '4. Zwei Inschriften aus Pecka', '5 Lisičići und Umgebung (Narentathal)', '6. Zur Geschichte von Novae (Runović)', '7. Der Sandžak Novibazar in römischer Zeit,' *WMBH*, 4 (1896), 243 ff.

'Die griechisch-römische Privatsammlung Bosniens und der Hercegovina', *WMBH*, 5 (1897), 173–6

Arch.-epigr. Untersuchungen zur Geschichte der römischen Provinz Dalmatien II: '1. Die römischen Steindenkmäler des Museums zu Knin', '2. epigraphische Nachlese', '3. Weitere epigraphische Funde des J. 1895', *WMBH*, 5 (1897), 177–241.

'Die legio VIII Augusta in Dalmatien', *WMBH*, 5 (1897), 338–40.

PATSCH, C., and KOVAČEVIĆ, K., 'Die Ruine im Dorfe Doljani und die dort aufgefundenen römischen Inschriften', *WMBH*, 5 (1897), 340–3.

Arch.-epigr. Untersuchungen zur Geschichte der römischen Provinz Dalmatien III: '1. Die Iapoden', '2. Das Mithraeum von Konjica', '3. Münzen von Apollonia und Dyrrachium', '4. Eine Apollostatuette aus Vrzani bei Prnjavor', '5. Neue Denkmäler aus Županac-Delminium', '6. Zwei Ziegelstempel aus Ljubuški', '7. Kleine römische Funde und Beobachtungen', '8. Dalmatien und Dacien', '9. Notizen zur Geschichte der Donauprovinzen,' *WMBH*, 6 (1899), 154 ff.

Arch.-epigr. Untersuchungen zur Geschichte der römischen Provinz Dalmatien IV: '1. Die Iapoden', '2. Römische Fundstätten in Bezirke Bosnisch-Novi', '3. Neue Erwerbungen des Museums in Knin', '4. Das obere Cetinathal in römischer Zeit', '5. Eine Grabinschrift aus Aequum',

'6. Zwei Mithrasreliefs', '7. Die römische Ansiedlung in Grahovo', *WMBH*, 7 (1900), 33–166.

Arch.-epigr. Untersuchungen zur Geschichte der römischen Provinz Dalmatien V: '1. Die römische Ortschaften des Beckens von Imotski', '2. Epigraphische Einzelfunde', '3. Eine Inschrift aus dem Timokthale', '4. Die Flottenstation von Salona', '5. Keltische Flussgottheiten', *WMBH*, 8 (1902), 61–130.

PATSCH, C., *Arch.-epigr. Untersuchungen zur Geschichte der römischen Provinz Dalmatien* VI: '1. Zur Topographie und Geschichte von Županac-Delminium','2. Die römischen Ortschaften bei Šuica', '3. Zur Geschichte des Passes Velika vrata bei Kupres', '4. Ein Mysterienrelief aus Han compagnie-Vitez', '5. Aus Zenica-Bistua', '6. Eine römische Fundstelle bei Visoko', '7. Drei römischen Ruinenstätten in Bezirk Sarajevo', '8. Die römischen Ortschaften des Bezirkes Konjica', '9. Der römische Vorort des Bijelo polje bei Mostar', '10. Urnenfunde', '11. Eine römische Villa in Dretelj', '12. Die Kultur des Brotnjo', '13. Eine Ziegelplatte aus Stolac', '14. Zur Handelsgeschichte von Narona', '15. Zur Geschichte der römischen Stadt in Gradac bei Pošusje', '16. Eine abrozzierte Statue aus Lončari', '17. Ziegelstempel aus Flanona', '18. Eine römische Ortschaft in Podcrkvina Bezirke Vlasenica', '19. Fibelfunde', '20. Dalmatia und Nordwestafrika', *WMBH*, 9 (1904), 171 ff.

Arch.-epigr. Untersuchungen zur Geschichte der römischen Provinz Dalmatien VII: '1. Bistue Vetus', 2. 'Silvanusrelief aus Županac-Dleminium', '3. Municipium Salvium', '4. Neue Funde aus Grahavo', '5. Liber ara aus Brekovica', '6. Urnenfunde in Bugojno', '7. Aus der römischen Stadt in Skelani', '8. Die römischen Ansiedlungen in Sopotnica und Rogatica', *WMBH*, 11 (1909), 104–83.

Arch.-epigr. Untersuchungen zur Geschichte der römischen Provinz Dalmatien VIII: '1. Der Narentasee des Pesudo-Scylax', '2. Aus dem Sandschak Plevlje', '3. Grabmonumente aus Humac', '4 Šipovo in Plivathal, Mujdžići, Jajce', '5. Funde beim Baue der Strasse Han Bjelovac-Gradina', '6. Zwei Silberfunde, Bare-Tribovo, Mahovljani', '7. Vier Bronzen', '8. Notizen: Rogatica, Cadovina, Podpece-Drijenke, Ustikolina, Rama, Ankula, Drežnica, Travnik, Trstionicathal', *WMBH*, 12 (1912), 68–167.

'Piombo der legio XI Claudia P.f. aus Gardun', *JÖAI*, 1 (1898), Bb. 121 f.

article 'Brattia', *RE*, 3 (1899), 821.

PATSCH, C., *Lika, Die Lika in Römerzeit (Schriften der Balkankommission, Antiquar. Abt.* 1), Vienna, 1900.

'Die Städte Mal ... und Cap ... in Ostdalmatien', *JÖAI*, 5 (1902), Bb. 41–2.

'Miscellen: Heiligott Medaurus, Strassenstation Sturum, Fluss Katarbates (Liburnia)', *JÖAI*, 6 (1903), 71–6.

Das Sandschak Berat in Albanien (Schriften der Balkankommission, Antiquar. Abt. heft. 3.), Vienna, 1904.

'Sidrona', *JÖAI*, 8 (1905), 119–22.

PATSCH, C., *Narona, Zur Geschichte und Topographie von Narona (Schriften der Balkankommission, Antiquar. Abt.* heft. 5), Vienna, 1907.

'Thrakische Spuren an der Adria', *JÖAI*, 10 (1907), 169–74.

'Aus Albanien', *JÖAI*, 10 (1907), Bb. 101–2.

'Kleinere Untersuchungen in und um Narona', *JAK*, 2 (1908), 87–117.

'Aus Doclea', *JÖAI*, 11 (1908), Bb. 103–4.

*Bosnien und Hercegovina in römischer Zeit (Zur Kunde der Balkanhalbinsel, vol 15), Vienna, 1911.

Bibliography

PATSCH, C., 'Aus Narona', *JÖAI*, 15 (1912), Bb. 75–82.

PATSCH, C., *Hercegovina, Die Hercegovina einst und jetzt* (*Historische Wanderungen im Karst und an der Adria*: 1 teil: *Osten und Orient* 2 reihe N.F. 1), Vienna, 1922.

'Zur Geschichte von Sirmium', *SB*, 229–32.

PATSCH, C., *Beiträge V/1, Beiträge zur Völkerkunde von Südosteuropa: V Aus 500 Jahren vorrömischer und römischer Geschichte Südosteuropas*, 1 teil: *Bis zur Festsetzung der Römer in Transdanuvien* (*Sitz. Ber. Akad. Wien, phil-hist. Klasse* 214, 1), Vienna, 1932.

PATSCH, C., *Beiträge VI, VI Die einstige Siedlungsdichte des illyrischen Karstes* (*Sitz. Ber. Akad. Wien, phil-hist. Klasse*, 215. 3), Vienna, 1933.

PATSCH, C., *Beiträge V/2, V. 2 teil: Der Kampf um den Donauraum unter Domitian und Trajan* (*Sitz. Ber. Akad. Wien, phil.-hist. Klasse*, 217, 1), Vienna, 1937.

'Der Jupiter Parthinus', *Klio*, 31 (1938), 439–43

PAVAN, M. *Richerche sulla provincia romana di Dalmazia*, Venice, 1958.

PETROVIĆ, J., 'Rimski novac iz Obudova', *GZMS*, 10 (1955), 181–97.

'Arheološki referati iz Bugojna i Ljubije Japra', *GZMS*, 13 (1958), 267–71.

'Novi arheološki nalazi iz doline Gornjeg Vrbasa', *GZMS*, 15–16 (1961), 229–34.

PFLAUM, H-G., 'Deux carrières équestres de Lambèse et de Zana (Diana Veteranorum)', *Libyca*, 3 (1955), 123–54.

article 'Procurator' (Nachträge), *RE*, 23 (1957), 1240–1279.

Les carrières procuratoriennes équestres sous le Haut-empire romain (*Instit. franc. d'archéologie de Beyrouth, Bibl. Arch. et Hist.* t. lvii), Paris, 1960–1.

'Un nouveau gouverneur de la province de Rhétie etc.', *BV–B*, 27 (1962), 82–99.

'Du nouveau sur les *agri decumates* à la lumière d'un fragment de Capoue, *CIL* X 3872', *BJ*, 163 (1963), 224–37.

PICARD, G-CH., 'Deux senateurs romains inconnus', *Karthago*, 4 (1953), 121–35.

PINK, K., 'Lokale Prägungen aus dem Sinus Rhizonicus', *SH*, 527–35.

POGATSCHNIG, L., 'Alter Bergbau in Bosnien', *WMBH*, 2 (1894), 152–7.

POLASCHEK, E., article 'Pharos', *RE*, 19 (1938), 1866.

article 'Ptolemaios als Geograph', *RE*, supp. 10 (1965), 680–833.

POSEDEL, J., 'Kostane pločiće za igru u zadarskom arheološkom muzeju', *VAHD*, 52 (1935–49), 59–62.

'Zadarski zrtvenik carice Faustine', *VAHD*, 53 (1950–1), 163–5.

PRASCHNIKER, C., and SCHOBER, A., *Archaeologische Forschungen in Albanien und Montenegro* (*Schriften der Balkankommission, Antiqu. Abt.* 8), Vienna, 1919.

PREMERSTEIN, A. V., and VULIĆ, N., 'Antike Denkmäler in Serbien', *JÖAI*, 3 (1900), Bb. 105–78.

PREMERSTEIN, A. V., VULIĆ, N., and LADEK, F., 'Antike Denkmäler in Serbien', *JÖAI*, 4 (1901), Bb. 73–162.

PREMERSTEIN, A. V., and VULIĆ, N., 'Antike Denkmäler in Serbien und Macedonien', *JÖAI*, 6 (1903), Bb. 1–60.

PREMERSTEIN, A. V., 'Bevorrechtete Gemeinden Liburniens in den Stadtlisten des Plinius', *SB*, 203–8.

'Der Daker- und Germanensieger M. Vinicius (*cos.* 19 v. Chr.) und sein Enkel (*cos.* 30 und 45 n. Chr.)', *JÖAI*, 28 (1933), 140–63, 29 (1935), 60–81.

PRIJATELJ, K., 'Neokolico rimskih nadgrobnih portreta u arheološkom muzeja u Splitu', *VAHD*, 53 (1950–1), 135–53.

'Einige hellenistische Elemente in der Skulptur des antiken Salona', *AI*, 1 (1954), 29–35.

RADIMSKY, W., 'Die Alterthümer der Hocheben Rakitno in der Hercegowina', *WMBH*, 1 (1893), 169–79.

'Die Gradina von Majdan, ein neuer Fundort von La Tène Bronzen in Bosnien', *WMBH*, 1 (1893), 180–3.

'Vorläufiger Bericht über die Ausgrabungen in der Nekropole von Jezerine bei Bihać', *WMBH*, 1 (1893), 195–202.

'Prähistorische und römische Ruinen und Bauwerke im Flussgebiet der Sana', *WMBH*, 1 (1893), 203–17.

'Generalbericht über die bisherigen Ausgrabungen der römischen Stadt in Gradina bei Srebrenica', *WMBH*, 1 (1893), 218–53.

'Die römische Befestigung auf Crkvenica und das *castrum* bei Doboj', *WMBH*, 1 (1893), 262–72.

'Römische Gräber bei Han Potoci nächst Mostar', *WMBH*, 1 (1892), 303–7,

'Zwei römische Reliefsteine aus der Umgebung von Srebrenica (Lošnica und Ljubovija)' *WMBH*, 1 (1893), 328–30.

'Das Bišćepolje bei Mostar', *WMBH*, 2 (1894), 1–34.

'Reste römischer Ansiedlung in Šipraga und Podbrgje', *WMBH*, 2 (1894), 36–49.

'Die römische Ansiedlung und Befestigung von Čitluk im Brotnjopolje',

'Die römische Ansiedlung und Befestigung von Krehin Gradac', *Archaeologische Tagebuchblätter*, *WMBH*, 2 (1894), 57–61.

RADIMSKY, W., 'Römische Grabsteine aus Fatnica', 'Die römische Ansiedlung und das angebliche *castrum* von Trn bei Banjaluka', 'Das römische-mittelalterliche Grabfeld von Ložnica im Bezirke Srbrenica', 'Die Burgruine von Stržanj bei Šujica', 'Die Burgruinen auf dem Berg Kamešnica bei Livno', 'Die Gradina von Mošunj Mali bei Travnik', 'Die Kirchenruine von Pistauna bei Čazin und die römische Ansiedlung von Ljušina bei Otoka', 'Bužaningrad bei Livno', *Archaeologische Tagebuchblätter*, *WMBH*, 2 (1894), 61–70.

'Die Nekropole von Jezerine in Pritoka bei Bihać', *WMBH*, 3 (1895), 39–218.

'Die römische Ansiedlung von Majdan bei Varcar Vakuf', *WMBH*, 3 (1895), 248–56.

'Zwei Bronzen aus Čapljina', 'Die Gradina von Turbe bei Travnik', 'Zwei Bronzen aus dem Plivagebiet bei Jajce', 'Die prähistorisch-römische Befestigung von Kalesia in bzw. Zvornik', 'Einige Alterthümer von Gačko in der Hercegovina', 'Über einige prähistorische und römische Baureste bei Grahovo in bzw. Livno', 'Ein Legionsziegel aus Kladuša velika in Bosnien', 'Drei Funde aus dem Bezirke Ljubuški', 'Kolossale Fibel aus Ivanjska bei Banjaluka', 'Zwei Funde aus der Gegend von Bilek', *Archaeologische Tagebuchblätter*, *WMBH*, 3 (1895), 284–97.

'Die Gradina Čungar bei Čazin', *WMBH*, 4 (1896), 135–69

'Prähistorische Wallbauten im Bezirke Bihać', *WMBH*, 4 (1896), 101–12

'Der Narenta-See des Scylax', *WMBH*, 4 (1896), 129–34.

'Die vorgeschichtlichen und römischen Alterthümer des Bezirkes Županac in Bosnien', *WMBH*, 4 (1896), 135–69.

'Funde aus der Gegend von Grahovo', 'Die römische Burgruine von Biogradci am Mostarsko blato', *Archaeologische Tagebuchblätter*, *WMBH*, 4 (1896), 185–201.

'Berichte über die Ausgrabungen von Domavia bei Srebrenica in 1892 und 1893', *WMBH*, 4 (1896), 202–42.

Bibliography

'Die romische Ziegelei von Pijavice bei Jajce', 'Der Wallbau Ilijina greda im Bezirke Trebinje', 'Die Gradina Kosovaca bei Kosanje in Bz. Zvornik', 'Der römische Meilenstein bei Trnovo im Bezirke Jajce', 'Die Wallbauten Orlovac und Služanjska gromila im Bezirke Mostar', 'Die römische Ruine Gradina Mihaljević im Bezirke Srebrenica', 'Der Wallbau Glavica bei Radić veliki im Bezirke Krupa', *Archaeologische Tagebuchblätter*, WMBH, 5 (1897), 263–75.

'Reste einer römischen Ziegelei und eines Brennofens in Sarajevo', WMBH, 6 (1899), 527.

RADNÓTI, A., 'C. Iulius Avitus Alexianus', *Germania*, 39 (1961), 383–412.

RAKNIĆ, Ž., 'Dvojni epigrafički spomenik iz Burnuma', *Diadora*, 3 (1965), 71–84.

'Kultna slika Silvana s područja Liburna', *Diadora*, 3 (1965), 85–90.

RATKOVIĆ, A., 'Relief Epone iz Koprna u Dalmacije', *Diadora*, 1 (1959), 133–9.

'Neokolico novih ilirskih epigrafičkih spomenika iz Ridera', *Diadora*, 2 (1960–1), 225–34.

REISCH, E., 'Die Statuenbasis des C. Sempronius Tuditanus', *JÖAI*, 11 (1908), 276–97.

'Das Standlager von Burnum', *JÖAI*, 16 (1913), Bb. 112–35.

RENDIĆ-MIOČEVIĆ, D., 'Prilozi etnografiji i topografiji naše obale u staro doba—Iadastini', *VAHD*, 52 (1935–49), 19–34.

'Dva skupna nalaza rimskog carskog novca kod Dugopolja u Dalmacije', *VAHD*, 52 (1935–49), 239–78.

Ilirska onomastika na latinskim natpisima Dalmacije (Supp. III to *VAHD*, 52), Split, 1948.

'Iliri u natpisima grčkih kolonija u Dalmaciji', *VAHD*, 53 (1950–1), 25–55.

'Tri povijesna natpisa iz Dalmacije', *VAHD*, 53 (1950–1), 167–79.

'Novi i neobjelodanjeni natpisi iz Dalmacije', *VAHD*, 53 (1950–1), 211–32.

'Onomastička pitanja sa territorija ilirskih Dalmata', *GZMS*, 6 (1951), 33–47.

'Novi iliroki epigrafički spomenici iz Ridera (Municipium Riditarum)', *GZMS*, 6 (1951), 49–64.

'Druzov boravak u Dalmaciji u svijetlu novog viskog natpisa', *VAHD*, 54 (1952), 41–50.

'Novi epigrafički prilozi Ilirskoj onomastici sa territorije Dalmata', *VAHD*, 55 (1953), 245–55.

'Quelques remarques sur les monnaies de Dalmatie', *1st. Congr. Numism.* (1953 publ. 1957), 2, 83–7 (Paris).

'Da li je spelaeum u Močičima sluzio samo mitrijačkom kultu?', *GZMS*, 8 (1953), 271–6.

'Neue Funde in der altchristlichen Nekropole Manastirine in Salona', *AI*, 1 (1954), 53–70.

'Ilirske pretstave Silvana na kultnim slikama s područja Dalmata', *GZMS*, 10 (1955), 5–40.

'Onomastičke studije sa territorije Liburna—prilozi ilirskoj onomastici', *Zbornik*, 1 (1955), 125–44.

'Ricordi aquileiesi nelle epigrafi di Salona', *SA*, 67–81.

'Illyrica- Zum Problem der illyrischen onomastichen Formel in römischer Zeit', *AI*, 2 (1956), 39–51.

'Neue epigraphische Belege für den Namen Germanus im illyrischen Namengut Dalmatiens', *Germania*, 34 (1956), 237–43.

'Zlatni nakit iz helenističko-ilirske nekropole u Budvi', *Opuscula Archaeologica*, 4 (Zagreb, 1959).

'Neokolico monumentalnih nadgrobnih stela s portretima iz sjeverne Dalmacije', *Diadora*, 1 (1959), 107–30.

'Coh. VI Voluntariorum: nota epigraphica', *VAHD*, 61 (1959), 156–8.

'Ilirske onomastičke studije (I)', *ŽA*, 10 (1960), 163–71.

'Onomastique illyrienne de la Dalmatie ancienne', *Atti e Mem. VII cong. internaz. di scienze onomastiche vol. 3 (Firenze-Paris 1963)*, 273–7 (1961).

'Princeps municipi Riditarum (Uz novi epigrafički nalaz u Danilu)', *ARR* 2 (1962) 315–334.

'P. Cornelius Dolabella: problèmes de chronologie', *Akte IV int. kong. gr. u. lat. Epigr. (Wien 1962)*, 1964, 338–45.

'Ilirske onomastičke studije II', *ŽA* 13–14 (1964) 101–110.

'Ballaios et Pharos. Contributions à la typologie et à l'iconographie des monnaies gréco-illyriennes', *AI* 5 (1964) 83–92.

'Zur Frage der Datierung des Psephisma aus Lumbarda (Sill.³ 141)', *AI* 6 (1965) 77–80.

RICE HOLMES, T., *The Architect of the Roman Empire*, 1 (1928), 2 (1931), Oxford.

RICHARDSON, K. M., and WHEELER, R. E. M., *Hill Forts of Northern France (Soc. Ant. Lond. Research Rep, 19)*, Oxford, 1957.

RITTERLING, E., *legio* article 'Legio', *RE*, 12 (1924–5), 1211–1829.

RITTERLING, E., 'Zur salonitaner Inschrift, *BD*, 29, 3485A', *VAHD*, 47–8 (1924–5), 20–1.

ROBERT, L., 'Inscriptions hellénistiques de Dalmatie', *Hellenica*, 11–12 (1966), 505–41

RODENWALDT, G., 'Ein attischer Jagdsarkophag in Budapest', *JDAI*, 67 (1952), 31–42.

ROSTOVTZEFF, M., *SEHRE², Social and Economic History of the Roman Empire* (2nd ed. rev. P. M. Fraser), Oxford, 1957.

SALANKI, J., 'Figulus oder Scipio', *Arch. Ért.*, 1940, 258–60.

de SANCTIS, G., *Storia di romani*, Turin, 1907.

SARIA, B., 'Bathinus flumen', *Klio*, 23 (1930), 92–7.

'Bathinus-Bosna', *Klio*, 26 (1933), 279–82.

'Emona als Standlager der legio XV Apollinaris', *LA*, 1 (1938), 245–55.

article 'Dalmatia (als spätantike Provinz)', *RE*, supp. 8 (1956), 21–59.

ŠAŠEL, J., 'Rimski natpisi u Đerdapu', in *Limes u Jugoslavije* I (Belgrade, 1961), 155–64.

'Calpurnia L. Pisonis auguris filia', *ŽA*, 12 (1963), 387–90.

'Probleme und Möglichkeiten onomastischer Forschung', *Akte des int. Kong. für gr. u. lat. Epigr. (Wien, 1962)*, Vienna, 1964, 352–68.

SASSE, CH., *Die Constitutio Antoniniana*, Wiesbaden, 1958.

SCHMITTHENNER, W., 'Octavians militärische Unternehmungen in den Jahren 35–33 v. Chr.', *Historia*, 7 (1958), 189 ff.

SCHLOSSER, J. von, *Beschreibung der altgriechischen Münzen*, I, Vienna, 1893.

SCHULZE, F., 'Roman Registers of Births and Birth-certificates', *JRS*, 32 (1942), 78–91; 33 (1943), 55 ff.

SCHULZE, W., *LE, Zur Geschichte lateinischer Eigennamen*, Berlin, 1904.

SEECK, O., 'Zusammensetzung der Kaiserlegionen', *RM*, 48 (1893), 602 ff.

SELEM, P., 'Egipatska božantva u arheološkom muzeju u Splitu', *VAHD*, 61 (1959), 94–110.

SERGEJEVSKI, D., 'Epigrafska nalazak u Šipovu', *GZMBH*, 38 (1926), 155–8.

'Rimski kamenci spomenici sa Glamočkog polja', *GZMBH*, 39 (1927), 255–67.

'Rimski kamenci spomenici sa Glamočkog i Livanjskog polja i Ribnika', *GZMBH*, 40 (1928), 79–97.

'Rimski spomenici iz Livna i Prekaje', *GZMBH*, 43 (1931), 19–23.

'Numismatičke Belezke', *GZMBH*, 44 (1932), 23–30.

Bibliography

'Kasno-antički spomenici iz Zenice', *GZMBH*, 44 (1932), 35–56.

'Novi nalazi na Glamočkom polju', *GZMBH*, 45 (1933), 7–14.

'Rimska grobnja na Drini', *GZMBH*, 46 (1934), 11–41.

'Rimski spomenici iz Bosne', *Sp.* 77 (1934), 1–28.

'Iz rimske arheologije', *GZMBH*, 47 (1935), 17–22.

'Novi kameni spomenici iz Ustikoline i Rogatice', *GZMBH*, 48 (1936), 3–14.

'Neue Aschenkiste aus Ribić', *Pr. Zeitschr.*, 27 (1936), 211–26.

'Das Mithraeum von Jajce', *GZMBH*, 49 (1937), 11–18.

'Kasno-antičke spomenici iz okolice Jajca', *GZMBH*, 50 (1938), 49–63.

'Rimski spomenici iz Bosne, Rimski natpisi iz Bosne', *Sp.* 88 (1938), 95–130.

'Rimski natpisi iz Bosne, Užičkog Kraja i Sandjaka', *Sp.* 93 (1940), 133–60.

'Arheoločki nalazi u Sarajevu i okolici', *GZMS*, 2 (1947), 13–50.

'Rimska cesta na Nevesinjskom polju', *GZMS*, 3 (1948), 43–62.

'Nove akvizicije odjeljenja klasične arheologije Zemaljskog muzeja u Sarajevu', *GZMS*, 3 (1948), 167–87.

'Japodske urne', *GZMS*, 4–5 (1950), 45–92.

'Kasno-antičke mauzolej u Turbetu', *GZMS*, 6 (1951), 135–44.

'Novi i revidirani rimski natpisi', *GZMS*, 6 (1951), 301–10.

'Kasno-antički spomenici iz Šipova', *GZMS*, 7 (1952), 41–57.

'Rimski miljokaz sa ceste Narona-Salona', *GZMS*, 10 (1955), 149–50.

'Epigrafski nalazi iz Bosne', *GZMS*, 12 (1957), 109–25.

'Pluteji iz bazilike u Žalozju', *GZMS*, 13 (1958), 137–45.

'Rimska cesta od Epidauruma do Anderbe', *GZMS*, 17 (1962), 73–109.

'Rimska cesta Narona-Leusinium', *GZMS*, 17 (1962), 110–13.

'Rimski rudnici željeza u sjeverozapadnoj Bosni', *GZMS*, 18 (1963), 85–102.

'Borne frontière romaine de Kosijerevo', *AI*, 5 (1964), 93 ff.

'Iz problematike ilirske umjetnosti', *Godišnjak* (Sarajevo), 1 (1965), 119–42.

SHERWIN-WHITE, A. N., *Roman Society and Roman Law in the New Testament*, Oxford, 1963.

ŠIŠIĆ, F., *Povijest Hrvata*, Zagreb, 1925.

SMITH, R. E., *Service in the Post-Marian Roman Army*, Manchester, 1958.

ŠONJE, A., 'Nalaz rimskog natpisa na Časki kod novalje na otoku Pagu', *ŽA*, 8 (1958), 311–22.

SREJOVIĆ, D., 'Ispitivanje ninske nekropole u Sasama 1961–2', *Članci*, 6 (1965), 7–48

STARR, CH. G., *The Roman Imperial Navy*, Cornell, 1941 (repr. 1960).

STEIN, A., *Der römische Ritterstand*, Munich, 1927.

Die Legaten von Moesien (Diss. Pann. ser. 1, fasc. 11), Budapest, 1940.

STEIN, E., *Geschichte des spätrömischen Reiches* 1 (Vienna, 1928), continued as *Histoire du Bas-Empire*, 2 (1949), Paris–Brussells–Amsterdam.

Die kaiserlichen Beamten und Truppenkörper im römischen Deutschland unter dem Prinzipat, Vienna, 1932.

STIPČEVIĆ, A., *Bibliographia Illyrica*, Sarajevo, 1967.

STICOTTI, P., *Doclea, Die römische Stadt Doclea in Montenegro* (*Schriften der Balkankommission, Antiqu. Abt.* 6) Vienna, 1913.

'Pago', *SH,* 179–81.

ŠTUK, N., 'Insula Tauris—Šćedro ili Šipan?' *SB*, 275–8.

SUIĆ, M., 'De situ magni lacus Naroniani in Anonymi (Scylacis) Periplo', *GZMS*, 8 (1953), 111–29.

'Novi antikni epigrapfički spomenik iz Nina', *VAHD*, 52 (1935–49), 53–8.

'Liburnski nadgrobni spomenik (Liburnski *cippus*)', *VAHD*, 53 (1950–1), 59–95.

'Novi natpisi iz sjeverne Dalmacije', *VAHD*, 53 (1950–1), 233–48.

'Prilog poznavanju odnosa Liburnije i Picenuma u strije Željezno doba', *VAHD*, 55 (1953), 71–101.

'Istočna Jadranska obala u Pseudo Skilakova Periplu', *Rad*, 306 (1955), 121–81.

'Limitacija agera rimskih kolonija na istočnog jadranskoj obali', *Zbornik*, 1 (1955), 1–36.

'O municipalitetu antičke Salone', *VAHD*, 60 (1958), 11–42.

'Novija arheološko-topografska istrazivanja antičkog Iadera', *Zbornik*, 2 (1958), 13–51.

'Kasnoantička enofora iz Burnuma', *Diadora*, 1 (1959), 95–106.

'Pravni polozaj grčkih gradova u Manijskom zalivu za rimski Vladavine', *Diadora*, 1 (1959), 147–73.

'Municipium Varvariae', *Diadora*, 2 (1960–1), 179–96.

'Orientalni kultovi u antičkom Zadru', *Diadora*, 3 (1965), 91–128.

'Autohtoni elementi u urbanizmu antičkih gradova našeg Primorja', *Godišnjak* (Savajevo), 1 (1965), 163–78.

SYME, R., 'M. Vinicius (*cos.* 19 B.C.)', *CQ*, 27 (1933), 142–8.

'Some Notes on the Legions under Augustus', *JRS*, 23 (1933), 14–33.

Review of Swoboda, *Octavian und Illyricum*, *JRS*, 23 (1933), 63–6.

'The Northern Frontiers under Augustus', *CAH*, 10 (1934), 340–81.

'Lentulus and the Origin of Moesia', *JRS*, 24 (1934), 113–37.

'Galatia and Pamphylia under Augustus: the governorships of Piso, Quirinius, and Silvanus', *Klio*, 27 (1934), 122–48.

'Pollio, Saloninus and Salonae', *CQ*, 31 (1937), 39–48.

'Augustus and the South Slav Lands', *RIEB*, 4 (1937), 33–46.

SYME, R., RR, *The Roman Revolution*, Oxford, 1939.

'Roman Senators from Dalmatia', *SH*, 225–32.

'Personal Names in Tacitus *Annals* i–vi', *JRS*, 39 (1949), 13 ff.

SYME, R., *Tacitus*, Oxford, 1958.

SYME, R., CE, *Colonial Élites*, Oxford, 1958.

Review of Jagenteufel, *Statthalter*, *Gnomon*, 31 (1959), 510–18.

'The Wrong Marcius Turbo', *JRS*, 52 (1962), 87–96.

SWOBODA, E., *Octavian und Illyricum*, Vienna, 1932.

SZILAGYI, J., *Aquincum*, Budapest, 1956.

TAYLOR, L. R., *The Voting Districts of the Roman Republic*, Rome, 1960.

THALLÓCZY, L., 'Über die Bedeutung des Namens Bosna', *WMBH*, 1 (1892), 333–6.

THOMSEN, R., *The Italic Regions*, Copenhagen, 1947.

TRUHELKA, C., 'Depotfund afrikanischer und anderer Bronzemünzen von Vrankamen bei Krupa', *WMBH*, 1 (1893), 184–8.

'Ein römisches Gebäude in Zenica, Die römischen Ruinenfelder von Stolac und Umgebung', *WMBH*, 1 (1893), 273–302

'Die römische Drinathalstrasse in Bezirke Srebrenica', *WMBH*, 1 (1893), 308–14.

Bibliography

'Archaeologische Forschungen auf der Burg von Jajce und in ihrer nächsten Umgebung', *WMBH*, 2 (1894), 87–93.

TRUHELKA, C., and PATSCH, C., 'Römische Funde in Lašvathale–1893', *WMBH*, 3 (1895), 227–47.

TRUHELKA, C., 'Aufdeckung einer römischen Ruine bei Vitina', *WMBH*, 3 (1894), 522–6.

'Eine Abrasaxgemme aus Sarajevo', *WMBH*, 5 (1897), 344–5.

UNTERMANN, J., *Die venetischen Personennamen*, Wiesbaden, 1961.

VEITH, G., *Feldzüge, Die Feldzüge des C. Iulius Caesar Octavianus in Illyrien in den J. 35–33 v. Chr.* (*Schriften der Balkankommission, Antiquar. Abt.* 8), Vienna, 1914.

'Zu den Kämpfen der Caesarianer in Illyrien', *SB*, 267–74.

VELIČKOVIĆ, M., 'Prilog provčavanji rimskog rudarskog basena na Kosmaju', *ZRNM*, 1 (1958), 95–118.

VERMASEREN, M. J., *CIMRM, Corpus Inscriptionum et Monumentorum religionis Mithriacae*, 1 (1956); 2 (1960), The Hague.

VITTINGHOFF, F., *Kolonisation, Römische Kolonisation und Bürgerrechtspolitik unter Caesar und Augustus* (*Abh. Akad. Wiss. u. Lit. Mainz*, 1951, n. 14) Wiesbaden, 1952.

VORLIČEK, E., 'Römische Alterthümer in Branjevo, Bezirk Zvornik', *WMBH*, 6 (1899), 529.

VOUKSAN, D., 'Les mosaiques romains de Risan', *Albania*, 4 (1932), 77–86.

VULETIĆ-VUKASOVIĆ, V., 'Ein römischer Adler von der Insel Curzola in Dalmatien', *WMBH*, 5 (1897), 343–4.

VULIĆ, N., 'Contributi alla storia della guerra di Ottaviano in Illiria nel 35–33 della campagna di Tiberio 15 a.C.', *RSA*, NS 7 (1903), 487 ff.

'Antike Denkmäler in Serbien', *JÖAI*, 7 (1904), Bb. 1–12; 8 (1905), Bb. 1–24; 12 (1909), Bb. 147–204 13; (1910), Bb. 197–228; 15 (1912), 213–8.

VULIĆ, N., and PREMERSTEIN, A. v., 'Antički spomeniki i Srbiji I', *Sp.*, 38 (1900).

VULIĆ, N., LADEK, F., PREMERSTEIN, A. v., 'Antički spomeniki i Srbiji II' *Sp.*, 39 (1903).

VULIĆ, N., 'Antički spomenici i Srbiji III, IV', *Sp.*, 42 (1905), 47 (1909).

'Antički spomenici naše zemlje', *Sp.*, 71 (1931); 75 (1933); 77 (1934), 31–54; 98 (1941–8) 1–343.

'*Nekolico pitanja iz antičke istorije naše zemlje i rimske starine* (Mon. Serb. Acad., Sect. Soc. Sciences 39, ed. Ostrogorsky), Belgrade, 1961.

VULPE, R., 'Gli illiri dell'Italia romana', *Ephemeris Dacoromana*, 3 (1925), 129–258.

WALBANK, F. W., *Philip V of Macedon*, Cambridge, 1940.

Commentary on Polybius, vol 1, Oxford, 1957.

WALTZING, J-P., *Études historiques sur les corporations professionelles chez les romains* 1–4, Louvain, 1895–1900.

WEIGAND, E., 'Die Stellung Dalmatiens in der römischen Reichkunst', *SB*, 77–105.

WHEELER, R. E. M., and T. v., 'The Roman Amphitheatre at Caerleon, Monmouthshire', *Archaeologia*, 78 (1928), 111–218.

WILKES, J. J., 'A Note on the mutiny of the Pannonian Legions in A.D. 14', *CQ*, 56 (1963), 268–71.

'Σπλαῦνον—Splonum again', *A Ant. Hung.*, 13 (1965), 111–25.

'The military achievement of Augustus in Europe; with special reference to Illyricum', *UBHJ*, 10 (1965), 1–27.

'Fourth century Rebuilding in Hadrian's Wall Forts', *Britain and Rome* (Essays presented to Eric Birley), ed. B. Dobson and M. G. Jarrett, Kendal, 1966.

Review of G. Alföldy, *Bevölkerung und Gesellschaft der römischen Provinz Dalmatien*, BJ, 166 (1966), 646–54.

'A new Governor of Dalmatia', *ES*, 4 (1967), 119–21.

ZANINOVIĆ, M., 'Ilirsko pleme Delmati', *Godišnjak* (Centar za Balkanološka ispitivanja, vol. 2), 4, 27–92, Sarajevo, 1966.

ZEILLER, J., *'Les origines chrétiennes dans la province romaine de Dalmatie*, Paris, 1906.

ZGANJER, B., 'Kelti i Iliriku', *VAHD*, 53 (1950–1), 13–23.

ZIPPEL, G., *Die römische Herrschaft in Illyrien bis auf Augustus*, Leipzig, 1877.

ZWIKKER, W., *Studien zur Markussäule I*, Amsterdam, 1941.

Indexes

1 Index of Peoples and Persons

Melia Anniana, 314
Meliteni (Melite is.), 49 f.
Melius, 314 n.
Melus, 166 n.
Memmius Regulus, P., *cos. suff.*, 31, legate in Moesia, 114
Menodorus (Menas), admiral, 53
Mentores, 3, 7
Mercury (Mercurious, Mircurius), 237 n., 287 n., 413
Meromeni, 49
Mescenii, 232 n.
Messa, 232 n.
Messala, (. . . . .), *cos. ord.* 280, 335 n.
Messalla Corvinus; *see* M. Valerius Messalla Corvinus
Messila, 163
Messor, 163 n., 232 n.
Metellus Celer, Q.; *see* Q. Caecilius Metellus Celer
Metillius Maximus, Sex., tile stamp, 501
Metinii, 203
Metrodorus, funeral-garden (*hortus*) of, 360
Metulenses (Metulum), 282 n.
Mevia Felicula, 307, 311
Mevius T.f. Celsus, T., 307
Minerva, 195
Minerva Flanatica, 195
Minicius Faustinus, Cn., *cos. suff.* 116, 321
Minicius Faustinus Sex. Iulius Severus, Cn.; *see* Iulius Severus
Minicius L.f. Fundanus, C., *cos. suff.* 107, governor, 85, 273, 334, 445
Minicius Natalis, L., *cos. suff.* 106, 328
Minicius Pudens, L., tile stamp, 501
Minidii, 255 n.
Minotaur, 399
Minucius Basilus, L., praetor 45 B.C., Caesarian commander in Illyricum, 40, 87
Mithras, cult in D., 428; dedications to, 199, 201, 233, 241 n., 251 n., 252 n., 274 n.; Mithraic cave, 254, 265 f.; Konjic Mithraeum, 276, 400, 402
Mithridates VI Eupator, king of Pontus, 229, 285
Modestus, 334 n.
Modii, 209
Moentini (Monetium), 50, 159, 265
Moesians, 168
Moici, 213 n.
Molossians, Epirote, 9
Mucatra, 119 n.
Mucius Dasius, 249 n.
Mun (. . . . .), Illyrian ruler, 29
Mundus, Byzantine general, 425 f.
Münzer, F., 32
Muttienus, tile stamp, 501
Mutilii, 213 n., 219 n.
Mutilius P.f. Crispinus, P., 85, 332

Naevienus Seneca, T., 306
Naevii, 306

Naevius Firmus, M. 306
Naevius Simplex, Q., 306
Nantania, *cognatio*, 187 n.
Narcissus, cognomen of Iulii, 232 n.
Narensii (Naresii), 49 f, 155 f., 164, 166, 171, 249, 277, 287, 400
Narses, Byzantine general, 427
Nasidius Secundus, M., 270 n.
Nassii, 304
Nassius Q.f. Certus Draco, Q., 305
Nassius Iulianus, 305
Nassius Phoebus (Salonitanus), M., 305
Nassius Sotericus, M., 305
Natalis, bishop of Salona, 434
Nedetai (Nedinum), 4
Nepotianus, father of Iulius Nepos, 421
Nerastini, 228
Nero, son of Germanicus Caesar, 218, 288
Nero, emperor 54–68, 83, 95 n., 106, 109, 114, 145, 205, 212, 272, 280, 289, 295
Nerva, M. Cocceius, emperor 96–98, 250, 265, 295; Divus Nerva, 213 n., 234 n., 305
Nestaioi, 5
Nestoi, 3, 5, 8 n.
Nicephorus, amphora stamp, 503
Nicolaus of Damascus, historian, 187
Niemann, G., 387
Nindia, 171 n.
Noema, 232 n.
Norbanus Flaccus, C., *cos.* 38 B.C., 57
Noricans (Norici), 59, 146, 167; Roman allies, 53
Notarius Secundus, C., 310
Novak, G., 223
Novenses, 125 f., 245, 395
Novii, 300
Numerius Rufus, Q., tribune of plebs 57 B.C., legate of Caesar, 39, 229, 319
Nymph, on coins of Issa, 11
Nymphs, cult of, 199

Obultronii, 232 n.
Octavia, sister of Augustus, 55 f.
Octavia, Rufina, 312
Octavianus Caesar, *see* Augustus
Octavii, 85, 116, 134, 199, 213 f., 232 n., 266 n., 310, 312, 314, 332
Octavius, Q., 332 n.
Octavius, Cn., *cos.* 165 B.C., 55 n.
Octavius [.] f. Certus, P., 312
Octavius Sex. f. Constans, Sex., 312
Octavius C.f. Macer, C., 214 n.
Octavius, M., Pompeian commander, 40 ff.
Octavius Macer, C., 312
Odovacar, King of Italy, 473–493, 421, 424
Offonii, 232 n.
Olbonenses, 218
Olciniatae (Olcinium), 27, 256
Olsoi, 4
Onastini (Oneum), 228
Opia, 197

2 Index of Places

Roman names are indicated in small capitals

3　Index of Subjects

abbess, 436
actarius, 121
actus, in centuriation, 208, 226
adiutores, 422; *principis praetorii*, 123; in *officium* of
　legate, 121
adlectio, to senate, 332 n.
administration, Roman under Republic, 247;
　Caesarian, 39; Ostrogothic, 424
aerarium militare, 108, 137
aerarium Saturni, 322
ager centurionatus, see centuriation
agnati, 187
agriculture, 180, 182, 194, 197, 396, 405, 414
alae, cavalry, 137, 144 n.; prefects of, 151
Alae, at Siscia in 7, 72
　Claudia nova miscellanea, 141; decurions, 145,
　　267 n.; equites, 148, 242, 267; *missicius*,
　　150; recruits, 144 f.; veteran, 150
　Pannoniorum, 140 f.
　I Parthorum, 140
　(Tungrorum) Frontoniana, 141; recruit, 145
alliances, Rome and Issa, 30; Roman in Illyria,
　17 f., 20; Rome with Scordisci, 65;
　Scerdilaidas and Philip V, 21 f.; Gentius
　and Perseus, 24 f.
allies, Roman in Illyria, 22, 26, 40, 135 f.
alumnus, 236
ambassadors, Roman, 26
amber (*electron*), 4, 353, 411 f.
ambush of A. Gabinius, 48 B.C., 41, 54, 91, 240
amicitia, Issa and Caesar, 229
amphitheatre, Salona, 383 ff., 85, 225, 323, 377
amphora, 344, 410; Greek, 7; lids, 343; stamps,
　411; trade, 411
apodyterium, 379
aqueducts, 373; Salona, 372 f.; capacity, 225
ara Augusti, Liburniae, 218
arcarius fisci, Dalmatiae, 284
arces (native strongholds), 184

archaeological evidence, lack of for native
　peoples, 178
archaeologists, Yugoslav, 178
archbishop (*archiepiscopus*), Salona, 430, 433,
　435
Arians, in D., 425, 432
aristocracy, tribal, 189; under Romans, 287
armour, of Iapodes, 159
arrow-heads, 413
Arval Brethren, 333
aspalathos, shrub, 227, 388
ἄστυ, used for native stronghold, 183
atrium, 375, 405; *Atrium Libertatis* (Hall of
　Liberty), 45
augurs, 234 n., 303, 308
augustales, see seviri
Augustan Shore (*litus Augustum*), 419
auxilia, institution of, 137; Gallic, 89; role in D.,
　105, 135–52, 168, 239 f.; forts, 395; com-
　manders, 150 ff.; native, 201; recruitment,
　196; centurions, 152; veterans, 231; social
　background, 147 ff.; distinction from
　legions, 136 f.; at Bigeste, 164, 176, 247;
　at Doboj, 171; Epidaurum, 252 f.;
　Tilurium, 24 f.

balneum, 378
banquets, 308; civic, 335, 367; native, 187; ritual,
　402
barrack-room (*contubernium*), 138 f., 148
barrels, timber, 408
basilicas, civic, 260, 279, 368 f., 371; cruciform
　at Salona, 425, 431; urbana at Salona,
　101 n., 430
baths (*thermae*), civic, 378 ff., 201, 279 f., 285;
　imperial, 229; winter (*hiemales*), 251, 335,
　378; military, 152; private houses, 375 f.;
　villas, 399, 403
beads, glass, 353

PLATE 1 Coast south of Salona behind Makarska

PLATE 2 Sinjskopolje from northwest

PLATE 3 Village alongside flooded Popovopolje, Hercegovina

PLATE 4 Entrance to Neretva gorge from south

PLATE 5 (opposite) Aerial view of Tragurium (Trogir) from west

PLATE 6 Second-century B.C. Greek family tombstone from Issa (Vis)
Brunšmid, 25 n. 14

PLATE 7 View of Lissus town and citadel from Acrolissus (p. 338)

PLATE 8 Lissus and acropolis from west with Acrolissus in background
(p. 362 f.)

PLATE 9 Tower of Lissus (p. 363)

PLATE 10 First-century Roman triumphal monument from Tilurium, showing tropaeum of arms and native prisoners bound at its foot. M. Abramić, ČZN 33 (1937) 7 ff.

PLATE 11 Dedication to Augustus' empress and Tiberius' mother Iulia Augusta (Livia) set up under the governor L. Volusius Saturninus before 29 by C. Iulius Sulla at Argyruntum in Liburnia to celebrate his admission to the city council, although the letters OB DEC were added after an erasure (p. 203), CIL III 9972

PLATE 12 Tombstone relief from Salona showing Augustan legionary veteran T. Fuficius and members of his household, his wife, son and daughter, and three ex-slaves (p. 111) CIL III 2030

PLATE 13 Early first-century tombstone from Tilurium of legionary L. Fabius who came from the colony Conana in Pisidia BD 26 (1903) 130 n. 3321

PLATE 14 First-century tombstone from Andetrium of Ser. Ennius Fuscus soldier in Cohort VIII Voluntariorum originating from Cemenelum in Southern Gaul. It was set up by his wife Fulvia Vitalis who appears alongside him on the stone, CIL III 9872

PLATE 15 Pons Tiluri (Gardun) from south. In the middle can be seen
the river crossing where the Cetina leaves Sinjskopolje. The photograph
is taken from near the site of the legionary fortress Tilurium (p. 97)

PLATE 16a, b, c Front and sides of tombstone (in the form of an altar) set up at Salona for Q. Aemilius Rufus, a *beneficiarius consularis*. On the left side is a lance and on the right a writing-tablet and stylus-box, the insignia of his office (p. 124)

CIL III 12895

PLATE 17 Fertile land of Pagus Scunasticus (Humac) awarded to
legionary veterans at the beginning of Tiberius' reign (p. 112 f.)

PLATE 18 Two early first-century military tombstones from Pagus Scunasticus (Humac) in the territory of Narona (p. 112 f.). On the left is the legionary veteran C. Licinius from Sinope on the Black Sea, on the right is Betulo, son of Karno, from the Alpine Eguii, a serving soldier in Cohort III Alpinorum Betz 58 (otherwise unpublished), Sašel n. 115

PLATE 19 First-century tombstone of legionary veteran L. Barbius [......] and his wife Quintia set up at Salona by their daughter Barbia Paulla. In the second part she tells that she set it up also to Silvia Delicata, who died aged 18, whom Paulla had hoped would one day set up a tombstone for her
VAHD 47/48 (1924–5) 40 n. 5205 A

PLATE 20 Early third-century tombstone of Thracian Aurelius Mucatra, who died while serving in a detachment of Legion I Italica based at Salona (p. 119)

CIL III 2009

PLATE 21 Grave monument from Bol on the south side of Brattia (Brač), with relief of marine deity CIL III 6247; cf. R. Egger, VAHD 54/59 (1954-7) II, pl. XI fig. 7 and p. 133 f.

PLATE 22 Tombstone of Rubria Maximilla (in Split museum). An example of the round 'Liburnian tombstone' crowned with a pine-cone (p. 412)

PLATE 23 Aerial view of Aenona (Nin) from south (p. 203 f.)

PLATE 24 Dedication to Augustus from Iader as 'founder of the colony' (*parens coloniae*), recording the rebuilding of walls and towers by Ti. Iulius Optatus (p. 207)

CIL III 2907 (now in Verona)

PLATE 25 Site of Narona (Vid) from southeast (p. 245 f.)

PLATE 26 Fragments of Augustan building record on marble, from
Narona and dating to after 12 B.C.
VAHD 54 (1952) 164 f.

PLATE 27 Site of Doclea from northwest. On the right is the river
Morača, on the left the Širalja torrent-bed (p. 363 ff.)

PLATE 28 Building of defence towers in the first century B.C. by officers of the *conventus* at Narona (p. 247)
CIL III 1820

PLATE 29 Plaque recording the rebuilding of the city-wall at Salona in 170 by Cohort II Delmatarum milliaria
CIL III 6374 (8655)

PLATE 30 Centuriation (indicated by black and white arrows) south
of Salona (p. 225 f.). Part of modern Split appears on the left

PLATE 31 Second-century tombstone of slave Victor set up at Narona by his parents Eutyches and Ursula
CIL III 8467

PLATE 32 First-century plaque of freedmen *seviri* at Salona
CIL III 2097a

PLATE 33 Early tombstone of freedman at Narona

PLATE 34 Group of late milestones at Kiridžinski dol on the road
between Sarajevo and the Drina valley

PLATE 35 Sarcophagus of Pomponia Vera at Salona
CIL III 14827/2

PLATE 36 Late third or early fourth-century sarcophagus of younger members of Salona upper classes. It records Valerius Dinens, an equestrian (*vir egregius*), and his wife Attia Valeria and was set up by the latter's mother Octavia Quieta

CIL III 13044

PLATE 37 Porta Suburbia at Salona from the east

PLATE 38 City wall at Aenona in west sector

PLATE 39 Narona city wall in northwest sector

PLATE 40 Arches supporting road across river and marshy ground in southern part of *urbs nova* at Salona

PLATE 41 Foundations of colonnade in Iader *capitolium* from northwest
(p. 368)

PLATE 42 Basilica of Doclea forum from northwest (p. 371)

PLATE 43 Aerial view of Salona amphitheatre from southwest (p. 383 ff.)

PLATE 44 Clay lamp in the form of a gladiator swordsman from Salona

PLATE 45 Salona theatre from northeast (p. 386)

PLATE 46 South front of Diocletian's Palace, Split, in the late nineteenth century from southwest (p. 387 ff.)

PLATE 47 North gate of Diocletian's Palace, Split

PLATE 48 Robert Adam's drawing of Diocletian's Mausoleum in Split,
from the west

PLATE 49 Aerial view of Diocletian's Palace from north

PLATE 50 Fifth-century Palace at Polača on the north side of the island Mljet (Melite)

PLATE 51 Mogorjelo villa: southwest range

PLATE 52 Tombstone at Salona of merchant C. Utius, commemorating
also his brother and his concubine Clodia
VAHD 50 (1928–9) pl. V and p. 56 f.

PLATE 53 Late third-century sarcophagus made from imported marble
found at the Manastirine shrine Salona. It depicts the legend of Phaedra
and Hippolytus
R. Egger, *FS*, 2, 33 ff.

PLATE 54 Aerial view of Manastirine shrine from northwest (p. 431)

PLATE 55 Manastirine shrine from east

PLATE 56 Sixth-century capital from entrance to Salona baptistery

PLATE 57 Sixth-century capital with bulls' heads relief from Salona

PLATE 58 Fragment of plaque recording martyrdom of Domnius in 304 from Manastirine shrine, Salona (p. 429)
Egger, *FS*, 2, 75 n. 81 fig. 44

PLATE 59 'Good Shepherd' sarcophagus of early fourth century from Manastirine shrine Salona
Egger, *FS*, 2, 29 ff.